Praise for *When Presidents Lie*

"Provocative, intriguing and insightful . . . I admire Alterman for doing about the only thing one can to further the cause of truth in a world riven with deceit: explain the failings of the past to the powers of the present in the hope that example will do more good than exhortation. Stories are almost always more effective than sermons, and the stories Alterman tells in *When Presidents Lie* are important reading for the men and women making the life-and-death decisions of our own time." —*Newsweek* managing editor Jon Meacham, *Los Angeles Times Book Review*

"This book is essential reading not only for insiders but for outsiders as well because it makes a strong case that the end result of major deceptions is almost always negative and always unpredictable. In addition, this is an astute study of presidential decision-making—if lying instead of telling the truth can be so dignified—along with critical examination of the news media's unfortunate but recurring role in facilitating presidential lying. . . . I've never read a better explanation of why presidents lie."

—former White House aide John W. Dean, *The Washington Monthly*

"Alterman has made a powerful and compelling argument in support of the proposition that presidential deception in matters of state having to do with war and peace seriously undermines public confidence in government."

— former Senator Gary Hart, *The New York Times Book Review*

"Alterman documents the growing contempt by administration officials for the press and congressional oversight. . . . *When Presidents Lie* is a history lesson in four parts." —Ken Bode, *The Boston Globe*

"Invoking pragmatism rather than principle, Alterman sets out to prove that under no circumstances is the 'necessary lie' permissible. It not only erodes public trust in government, he argues, but also, by giving a lie's victims and its perpetrators a skewed view of reality, leads to foreign policy disasters that otherwise could have been avoided." —Daniel Kurtz-Phelan, *San Francisco Chronicle*

"Full of moral complexity and challenge, this book ought to be considered one of the most important works the left has produced in recent years."

—Dan Kennedy, *The Boston Phoenix*

"Illuminating insights and persuasive documentation. . . . Provocative . . . this is a valuable work indeed." —Myron A. Marty, *St. Louis Post-Dispatch*

"Alterman makes clear, lies have consequences, often in blood . . . an apt assessment of where we have come to."

—Paul Waldman, *The American Prospect*

"A carefully documented account . . . [a] sobering, thoughtful historical perspective." —*Ruminator*

"Crack political journalist examines the culture of deceit that has marred the American presidency, footnoting every word. . . . Throws bones worth chewing long and hard." —*Kirkus Reviews* (starred)

"A timely and insightful book." —*Booklist*

PENGUIN BOOKS

WHEN PRESIDENTS LIE

Termed "the most honest and incisive media critic writing today" in the *National Catholic Reporter* and author of "the smartest and funniest political journal out there" in the *San Francisco Chronicle,* Eric Alterman is Professor of English at Brooklyn College of the City University of New York, "The Liberal Media" columnist for *The Nation,* the "Altercation" weblogger for MSNBC.com (www.altercation.msnbc.com), and Senior Fellow at the Center for American Progress, where he writes and edits the "Think Again" column. Alterman is also the author of the national bestsellers *What Liberal Media? The Truth About Bias and the News* (2003, 2004) and *The Book on Bush: How George W. (Mis)leads America* (with Mark Green, 2004). His *Sound & Fury: The Making of the Punditocracy* (1992, 2000) won the 1992 George Orwell Award and his *It Ain't No Sin to Be Glad You're Alive: The Promise of Bruce Springsteen* (1999, 2001) won the 1999 Stephen Crane Literary Award. Alterman is also the author of *Who Speaks for America? Why Democracy Matters in Foreign Policy* (1998). A frequent lecturer and contributor to virtually every significant national publication in the U.S. and many in Europe, he has, in recent years, been a regular columnist for *Worth, Rolling Stone, Mother Jones,* and *The Sunday Express* (London). A longtime Senior Fellow of the World Policy Institute at New School University and former Adjunct Professor of journalism at NYU and Columbia, Alterman received his B.A. in history and government from Cornell, his M.A. in international relations from Yale, and his Ph.D. in U.S. history from Stanford. He lives with his family in Manhattan, where he is at work on a history of postwar liberalism.

WHEN PRESIDENTS LIE

A History of Official Deception and Its Consequences

ERIC ALTERMAN

Penguin Books

Once again, to my girls: Diana Roberta Silver and Eve Rose Alterman.
"Searching for a little bit of God's mercy / I found living proof."

PENGUIN BOOKS
Published by the Penguin Group
Penguin Group (USA) Inc., 375 Hudson Street, New York, New York 10014, U.S.A.
Penguin Group (Canada), 90 Eglinton Avenue East, Suite 700, Toronto, Ontario, Canada M4P 2Y3 (a division of Pearson Penguin Canada Inc.)
Penguin Books Ltd, 80 Strand, London WC2R 0RL, England
Penguin Ireland, 25 St Stephen's Green, Dublin 2, Ireland (a division of Penguin Books Ltd)
Penguin Group (Australia), 250 Camberwell Road, Camberwell, Victoria 3124, Australia (a division of Pearson Australia Group Pty Ltd)
Penguin Books India Pvt Ltd, 11 Community Centre, Panchsheel Park, New Delhi – 110 017, India
Penguin Group (NZ), cnr Airborne and Rosedale Roads, Albany, Auckland 1310, New Zealand (a division of Pearson New Zealand Ltd)
Penguin Books (South Africa) (Pty) Ltd, 24 Sturdee Avenue, Rosebank, Johannesburg 2196, South Africa

Penguin Books Ltd, Registered Offices:
80 Strand, London WC2R 0RL, England

First published in the United States of America by Viking Penguin, a member of Penguin Group (USA) Inc. 2004
Published in Penguin Books 2005

10 9 8 7 6 5 4 3 2

THE LIBRARY OF CONGRESS HAS CATALOGED THE HARDCOVER EDITION AS FOLLOWS:
Alterman, Eric.
When Presidents lie : a history of official deception and its consequences / Eric Alterman.
p. cm.
Includes index.
ISBN 0-670-03209-3 (hc.)
ISBN 0 14 30.3604 1 (pbk.)
1. Political ethics—United States. 2. Presidents—United States.
3. United States—Foreign relations. 4. Deception. I. Title.
JK468.E7A63 2004
327.73'009'045—dc22 2004053580

Printed in the United States of America
Set in Bembo with Serlio • Designed by Daniel Lagin

ACKNOWLEDGMENTS

I began this book in the winter of 1993, shortly after passing my oral examinations in U.S. history at Stanford University. During its eleven-year gestation period, I authored thousands of magazine and Internet columns and articles, four additional books, a second edition of my first book, and a doctoral dissertation from which the sections on Yalta and the Cuban Missile Crisis of this book are drawn. Even so, I never put this book down. I have lived with the historical problems and issues it raised for me for eleven years now. I like to think I have finally got a grip on them, but of course, that will be for the reader to decide.

The decision to undertake the work derived from my frustration with the ahistoricism of American political discourse coupled with my love of well-written historical scholarship. I first developed this love, I believe, in my eleventh-grade American history class, thanks to my teacher, the late Werner Feig. It was further inspired by the friendship, guidance, and exemplary scholarly standards of my undergraduate honors thesis adviser, Cornell diplomatic historian Walter LaFeber. At Yale, where I did my master's degree in international relations, I had the opportunity to refine my abilities as a writer and scholar while trying to write papers that lived up to the expectation of Professor Paul Kennedy, whose life and work I continue to hold in the highest esteem. At Stanford, I was professionally trained by a host of fine scholars, but I was particularly fortunate to choose, as my thesis adviser, Barton J. Bernstein, whose knowledge of the topic of postwar U.S. history I believe to be unparalleled, and whose generosity as an adviser and whose unstinting critical standards as a scholar have influenced virtually every page of this book. In fact, the original idea for the study derived from a speculative footnote in one of Bart's essays, which raised the question of whether Lyndon Johnson might not have felt quite so powerfully compelled, both politically and psychologically, to press on hopelessly in Vietnam if his predecessor had been brave enough to tell the world of the compromise that ended the Cuban Missile Crisis.

I also received thoughtful readings of the material that would eventually comprise much of the Yalta and Cuba sections of this book from the other members of my dissertation committee, professors Gordon Chang and David Holloway, as well as a detailed, erudite reading of the Cuba section from

Sheldon Stern, the former chief archivist and historian at the John F. Kennedy library and the author of the superlative study of the missile crisis, *Averting "The Final Failure": John F. Kennedy and the Secret Cuban Missile Crisis Meetings.* My thanks to them for their improvements on what they originally read. Naturally, this book rests on the work of countless professional historians and journalists working on the issues I have covered, and I can only hope that both the text and the source notes reflect my many intellectual debts.

Speaking of presidential libraries, my research on the first three sections of the book was aided enormously by the archival staffs of the Franklin D. Roosevelt Presidential Library in Hyde Park, the Harry S. Truman Presidential Library in Independence, the John F. Kennedy Presidential Library in Boston, and the Lyndon B. Johnson Library in Austin. I also received travel grants for my research from the Truman, Kennedy, and Johnson libraries. The documents made available through the National Security Archive and the Cold War International History Project, both in Washington, have also proven invaluable to my research.

Unfortunately, the Ronald W. Reagan Library in Simi Valley has not seen fit to open most of its vast archives to scholars, and President Bush has overturned, by presidential fiat under Executive Order 1392, the law that would have ensured the timely opening of these papers apparently indefinitely. I fear that the Central American section of the book reflects this lack of access to the Reagan administration's records. I regret this, but I don't see how it could be otherwise. Given that the law already protects any information related to present national security issues, the only reason for this refusal to open the taxpayer-supported archives is to spare its alumni what personal and political embarrassment that might result from its disclosure. This kind of protection from the scrutiny of professional historians and historically minded journalists may be the norm in dictatorships across the world, but we Americans deserve better and should demand more. I urge everyone who reads this book to join in the campaign to see the law of the land returned to its original intent, so that future scholars will not encounter the difficulties in this that I did. Check the website *http://openthegovernment.org* for details.

I have been blessed with many close friends with a scholarly bent in my life, and I'm afraid I have not been shy in imposing upon them for thoughtful readings of my work. This is my sixth book, and if I am not mistaken, the distinguished authors and historians Todd Gitlin, Michael Kazin, Michael Waldman, and Kai Bird have read all or part of just about all of them, offering me the kind of honest criticism and encouragement that only decades of friendship can ensure. My debt to each of these scholars is beyond words, but I should like at least to acknowledge it here.

Because I began this work more than a decade ago, I've literally received help from more people than I can remember, so I will have to thank some people anonymously. My friend Andy Jordan donated his skills as a librarian to help me track down key documents, and Karen Abrams donated her copy-editing talents. Thanks to both of them. A number of able graduate students and former *Nation* interns also spent time in archives, libraries, and scouring the Internet to clean up mistakes I had made and ensure that the book would be as accurate as possible. For their diligent archival fact-checking, I'd like to thank Sarah Snyder and Christopher Morrison of Georgetown University, Kevin McCarthy and Justin Vogt, formerly of *The Nation*, and especially Landon Hall of Columbia University.

This book, like many of my past works and, to the degree it is under my control, my future ones, was edited by Rick Kot. As editors go, Rick's personal loyalty, attention to detail, and unerring ear for felicitous expression make him the tops, the Mona Lisa, the Tower of Pisa, etc., and I never forget how lucky I am to have him on my side. Thanks also to Rick's able assistant, Alessandra Lusardi, for her meticulous work and to Ellen Ellender and Bruce Sylvester, my copy editors. Thanks to my agent, Tina Bennett, for being a constant source of advice and encouragement. It is a great privilege to be able to make a decent living as a serious nonfiction writer in America. In addition, I'd like to thank all my collegues at *The Nation*, MSNBC.com, and the Center for American Progress for their support and indulgence of my work.

Finally, I need to thank my girls, Diana Silver and Eve Rose Alterman, for all the sacrifices involved in allowing me to finish, and for all the fun (and some of the tsoris) as I did it. Thanks, too, to my parents, Carl and Ruth Alterman. After all, I couldn't have written the book if I hadn't been born.

I have several times had occasion to say that it never pays for our government to give false impressions to the American public with the view to enlisting its support for short-term purposes, because this always revenges itself later when it becomes necessary to overcome the wrong impressions one has created.

—George F. Kennan to John Lukacs, 1994, in Kennan and Lukacs, *George F. Kennan and the Origins of Containment*

Always tell the truth. It's the easiest thing to remember.

—David Mamet, *Glengarry Glen Ross* (1992)

CONTENTS

WHEN PRESIDENTS LIE

I. INTRODUCTION: ON LIES, PERSONAL AND PRESIDENTIAL

Report: Presidents Washington Through Bush May Have Lied About Key Matters
—*The Onion* (2002)

During the final days of the Clinton presidency, Tracfone, a prepaid cellular phone service, began running a TV ad with some familiar footage of recent American presidents. First up was Richard Nixon insisting that he was not a crook. Next came former president Bush asking his fellow Republicans to read his lips, and promising "No new taxes." Finally, the screen cut to Bill Clinton waving his finger at a television camera and sternly proclaiming that he "did not have sexual relations with that woman, Ms. Lewinsky." The spot ended with the advertiser claiming, "Talk is cheap." Almost immediately Tracfone received what it termed a "cease-and-desist letter" from the White House. The problem was not that President Clinton took offense at the claim that he was—like all modern presidents—not to be trusted to tell the truth. Rather, the White House lawyers explained that the presidency had a long-standing policy "prohibiting the use of the president's name, likeness, words or activities in any advertising or commercial promotion." The accusation of presidential lying, well, no one could really argue with that.

In American politics today, the ability to lie convincingly has come to be considered an almost prima facie qualification for holding high office. Many of the lies that officials tell are obviously harmless. Audiences demand to be flattered and politicians feel compelled to oblige. The denizens of every locality expect a visiting politician to sing the praises of the "beauty" and "energy" of their fair city. The members of every interest group count on being told that their issue is "vital" and that the senator, congressman, or president who is making an appearance could not be more "delighted to be here among such good friends." With a few exceptions, when any American politician publishes a campaign autobiography, he is accepted as its author merely for the sake of convenience. When *New York Times* columnist Maureen Dowd wished to mock George W. Bush's policies toward China, she noted, "W. devoted only one paragraph of his autobiography to his six-week trip to China after college to visit his parents when his father was envoy to Beijing. He wrote nothing about Chinese culture. He merely noted that the Chinese dressed alike—'drab'—and rode bikes that looked alike."[1] But Dowd knew as well as anyone in Washington that the president did not "write" his autobiography, a job that was delegated to adviser Karen Hughes, and it is far from clear that he even read it. Yet the lie is passed over for the sake of the larger point she seeks to make, and no one even thinks to raise this issue.[2] In this regard, the campaign autobiography is similar to the ritual that takes place whenever a U.S. politician sees his name floated as a potential president or even vice president. The candidate is expected to respond that he has no interest in leaving his current position, for admitting the truth of his ambition would mark him as woefully inexperienced and probably disqualify him for the office. So the candidate lies, the media dutifully report his position, everyone even remotely connected to the story understands the fiction, and we all get on with our lives. The editors of the satirical newspaper *The Onion* take the media's "shock" at the revelations of presidential deception to its logical conclusion with a breathless report of George Washington's cherry tree fable: "Evidence suggests, however, that the entire tale may have been bogus from the start. This is doubly damning to the presidency's reputation, for it is not merely a lie, but a lie about *not* telling lies."[3]

This is not to argue that all lies are equal. Of course some lies retain the power to shock. But as we will see in the forthcoming pages, this is less and less true of those told by any president. As *The Washington Post* ombudsman Michael Getler noted with euphemistic delicacy in May 2004, regarding President Bush's case for war, "Almost everything we were told before the war, other than that Saddam Hussein is bad, has turned out, so far, not to be the case: the weapons of mass destruction, the imagery of nuclear mushroom clouds, the links between al Qaeda and Hussein, the welcome, the resistance, the costs, the numbers of troops needed. All of these factors were presented by the administration with what now seems, at best, to have been a false sense of certainty."[4] And yet, when the media discovered they had been actively and repeatedly misled by members of the Bush administration on the crucial matter of whether to take the nation into its first "preemptive" war, the reaction was one of combined almost blasé denial and excuse. Whatever one thinks of the coverage of the overall argument for war, it is curious in the extreme to note that virtually every major news media outlet devoted more attention to the lies and dissimulations of one *New York Times* reporter, Jayson Blair, than to those of the president and vice president of the United States regarding Iraq.[5] The enormous reaction to the Blair story, which included lengthy soul-searching articles based on massive internal investigations and resulted in the forced resignations of the top two editors at the *Times*, dwarfed any discussion of whether the president and his advisers had been honest in their arguments for war. Given that these two deceptions took place virtually simultaneously, they demonstrate that while some forms of deliberate deception remain intolerable in public life, those of the U.S. commander in chief are not among them.

Given that we have become accustomed to a culture in which everyday political lies are taken for granted, it is nevertheless remarkable to what degree presidential lies have shaped our postwar history. Yet the consequences of these lies have received precious little attention. True, the Washington establishment became unmoored over Bill Clinton's dishonesty about his adulterous relationship with Monica Lewinsky, but nearly all felt compelled to justify this position with the qualification that his statements had been made "under oath," to distinguish them from garden-variety presidential lies.[6]

The question of presidential dishonesty was also addressed with surprising vigor during the 2000 election. Vice President Gore's campaign was consistently challenged by the media for his alleged inability to control his falsehoods. Most of these controversies centered on claims by Gore that reporters deemed to be exaggerations of his political accomplishments; stories in which he slightly embellished or misremembered a few details. In contrast, George W. Bush, who was widely understood to have trumped Gore on the "character" issue—according to both polls and media coverage—was caught in a falsehood about his arrest record, as well as any number of deliberately misleading statements about his record in Texas as well as his previous experiences in private business and in the Texas National Guard. Yet George Bush's dishonesty never rose to the level of a major issue in the election, due to the fact that it did not comport with the larger story that the media had chosen to tell about each candidate. In this version, Gore's "lies" were emblematic of his alleged discomfort with his own persona; of his inability to relate to people as a "real person" rather than a constantly calculating politician. George W. Bush's falsehoods, however, were understood to be unrelated to any particular election narrative, and hence were ignored or excused regardless of their potential significance for his presidency. As ABC News's Cokie Roberts explained, in defense of herself and her colleagues, Bush's deceptions were not part of "the storyline . . . in Bush's case, you know he's just misstating as opposed to it playing into a story line about him being a serial exaggerator."[7]

In other words, lies were only important insofar as they signaled "character" problems with a candidate. If the candidate did not have a recognized "character issue," he was, according to these odd rules of the game, free to lie.[8] Bush would take considerable advantage of this paradox once president, as well, as will be discussed in the conclusion of this book. For now, our point of departure must be to recognize that we presently operate under an unstated assumption that a certain amount of lying to the public by our presidents and other politicians has become a given in U.S. politics. In this context, the substantive issue becomes which kinds of lies are forgivable—or even admirable—and which lies are not.

In *When Presidents Lie,* I propose to reopen this debate by examining the lasting consequences of presidential lies. I do not do so from the perspective of a moralist. While the moral consequences of lying are certainly a worthy subject for a book, they are not the subject of this one. Parents have been warning children against lying for millennia, with merely mixed success at best. Most people, like most presidents, know that lying is "wrong," but most people do it anyway. The argument has certainly failed to convince most postwar U.S. presidents. My hope is that the consequential arguments in this book will prove more convincing than the morality-based ones have been in the past.

This book is a detailed examination of four key presidential lies: Franklin Roosevelt and the Yalta accords, John Kennedy and the Cuban Missile Crisis, Lyndon Johnson and the second Gulf of Tonkin incident, and Ronald Reagan and Central America in the 1980s. In each case, the president told a clear and unambiguous falsehood to the country and to Congress regarding a crucial question of war and peace. This is not to say that the presidents in question told only lies. In some cases they may have repeated facts that they mistakenly believed to be true, but continued to repeat them even as they later learned of their falsity. For instance, Lyndon Johnson clearly became convinced that U.S. forces had been attacked in the Gulf of Tonkin on August 4, 1964. In his case, the lying did not really begin in earnest until he and his advisers were informed of the truth a few days later. Ronald Reagan and Franklin Roosevelt no doubt believed some of the false assurances they offered up in defense of their respective policies, but not the ones upon which this book focuses.

We are all aware that, as Michel de Montaigne stated, "The opposite of truth has a hundred thousand shapes and a limitless field."[9] Meanwhile, the theories of Ludwig Wittgenstein, William James, John Dewey, Jacques Derrida, Michel Foucault—to say nothing of those of Sigmund Freud—have done much to call into question our ability to know the "truth" of any situation at any time, much less to accurately describe it.[10] As Friedrich Nietzsche asks, "Do the designations and the things coincide? Is language the adequate expression of all realities?"[11] But the fundamental question of the usefulness of language itself in replicating the truth remains outside the scope of this study and could not possibly be done justice in the context of the issues I seek to address.[12] It is my intention in this study to deal with lies, knowingly told. I have chosen lies relating to matters of war and peace in part because I consider that to be the arena for the most sacred and demanding of presidential duties, as military matters are where presidential words carry the greatest power, being largely hidden from citizens to a degree that, say, economic or environmental conditions cannot be. Presidential speechwriter Theodore Sorensen has observed, for instance, "The final difference in [President] Kennedy's treatment of foreign and domestic affairs was the relative influence of congressional and public opinion. His foreign policy actions were still constrained within bounds set by those forces, but they operated more indirectly than directly and his own powers of initiative and decision were much wider."[13]

In none of these cases do I take the president or his advisers to task for the morality or even the hypocrisy of their lies. I take hypocrisy to be a given in the practice of politics, rather like money, ego, avarice, and the occasional sex scandal or act of public-minded self-sacrifice. And while some of these lies may have been more or less "immoral" than others, such distinctions in this case miss the point, as I focus exclusively on the real-life consequences of the lies, in terms of both the policies the presidents pursued and the debased discourse they inspired. Hence, I have not gone back to any of the living principals and invited them to offer retroactive excuses, apologies, or defenses. Motives and mea culpas are not at issue here, as my proof can be found exclusively in the historical record: in this case, in the public discourse of the nation and in its government's actions at home and abroad. By investigating the long-term effects of the lies in question to determine their practical consequences for the president himself, his party, and the country at large, I argue that in each case, these lies returned to haunt their tellers (or in the cases of FDR and JFK, whose presidencies were cut short by death, their successors), destroying the very policy that the lie had originally been told to support. Without exception, each of the presidents (or his successor) paid an extremely high price for his lies. So, too, did the nation to whose leadership he was entrusted.

On Lying

In an essay written in 2000 for a small Jewish magazine called *OLAM,* Seymour Hersh, the great investigative reporter, attempts to draw a connection between lying to one's family and lying to one's nation:

> I grew up with the notion of presidential good—in the belief that the men running our nation were honorable and trustworthy. FDR was a god and

Harry Truman became one. The authority of the president and my father were commingled in my mind. I still remember with reddening shame the white lie I told my father as a teenager about a small dent I'd put in his car. I was caught, of course, and lied as long as I could. It was more than just being caught—there was a sense that I'd failed a crucial test of citizenship or manhood. Lying to Dad today can lead to betrayal of state tomorrow.[14]

Hersh laments the fact that "The children, and parents, of today have a different view of their leaders, and they're not wrong. Presidents don't tell the truth, and their national security advisers can no longer distinguish their propaganda from their reality." But instead of distinguishing between these lies, or drawing on the lessons of his own brilliant career in exposing different types of government deception, Hersh falls back on the same lessons he learned as a child, when he believed that FDR and Harry Truman were divinely inspired truth tellers:

> We, as parents and children, still understand—as my father did—that our personal and family life must revolve around integrity and trust. We don't lie to our children and they are expected to tell us the truth—when it matters. So here's the idea. We have these men—these presidents and national security advisers, these Nixons and Kissingers and Clintons—who have the right to take our children and train them in the art of killing and being killed, in the name of America, and we don't hold them to the same standards we insist upon in our family life. We don't accept that they stop the lies and propaganda. We accept without complaint the fact that our leaders tell lies and put personal needs above those of the citizenry. It's a necessary cost of the commonweal, we say. We shrug our shoulders, or make feeble jokes about a president who fabricates an enemy attack, as in the Gulf of Tonkin, or undermines the sanctity of the electoral process as in Watergate, or wags his finger in our face as he misrepresents his abusive relationship with an intern.[15]

In the course of this book, I hope to demonstrate that such views, even when expressed by so famously a tough-minded individual as Seymour Hersh, are simultaneously naive and ahistorical with regard to America's past presidents and their unwillingness to lie. Lying is actually a far more complicated business than most of us, Mr. Hersh included, appear willing to admit.

Both the Hebrew Bible and the New Testament demonstrate considerable ambivalence when it comes to lying, offering evidence that its consequences, both moral and temporal, are entirely situational. While the Israelites are commanded not to bear "false witness," any number of cases can be found in the

Five Books of Moses in which the authors appear to genuinely approve of lying, so long as it helps to ensure the survival of the Israelites. The best known of these takes place in Genesis (27:12), when Jacob deliberately deceives his father into giving him his blessing (and inheritance) rather than his brother Esau. Jacob appropriates his father's blessing and is the better for it, but other examples abound.[16] In Exodus (1:20), the Egyptian midwives ordered to kill the Israelites' first-born sons explain that they cannot do so because the Israelite women are "livelier" than their Egyptian counterparts and deliver their babies before the midwives arrive. This deception is also explicitly approved. "Therefore God dealt well with the midwives; and the people multiplied, and waxed very mightily." In Judges (4:23), the wife of Heber the Kenite deceives the captain of the army of Jabin, king of Canaan, for the purpose of killing him, much to the apparent delight of the story's author.

The New Testament judges lying more harshly, but again with important exceptions. John (8:44) identifies Satan as the father of all lies. In Acts (5:5), Ananias is struck dead for allegedly lying to the Holy Ghost about his willingness to lay all his possessions at the feet of Peter and John. But in what is perhaps the best-known deception of all the Gospels, when Peter, in order to protect his life, denies three times before the cock crows that he is one of Jesus' disciples, he is left by God to punish himself.[17]

Early Christian writers betray similar ambivalence. In "Against Lying," Augustine categorizes eight different kinds of lies according to their respective degrees of sinfulness. All are to be avoided if possible, but given the hierarchy he creates, it is clear that some of them are less likely to be avoided than others.[18] Similarly, Aquinas distinguishes between categories, with some lies leading only to venial sin and others to mortal sin. The former are told "for the sake of our neighbor's good" or "where some little pleasure is intended," while the latter are told to injure others. Moreover, Aquinas continues, while lying is not allowed even in the case of preventing someone from harm, "to conceal the truth prudently by means of an evasion" is, on occasion, permitted.[19]

Though we may try to teach our children that lying is always wrong, few of us actually believe this to be the case ourselves. Lying, with "all things being equal," is probably wrong, we can agree, but "all things" are never equal. Much of our social life is lubricated by a host of apparently (and often genuinely) harmless lies, whether for reasons of tact or manners. Any number of daily occurrences inspire the telling of inconsequential lies in which the act of dishonesty is not merely morally justifiable, but close to a moral imperative.[20] Who among us would wish to condemn Tom Sawyer for lying when he takes responsibility for Becky Thatcher's accidental tearing of a special page from her teacher's book, and accepts the whipping in her stead? Her father, a judge, terms this to be "a noble, a generous, and magnanimous lie . . . a lie that was worthy to hold up its head and march down through history breast to breast with George Washington's lauded Truth about the hatchet!" On a more elevated plane, consider the case of Huck Finn on his raft, going down the Mississippi accompanied by his friend, the escaped Negro slave Jim. Jim tells young Huck that he plans to steal his family from the woman who owns them. Huck is conflicted: slaves are property, and the woman who owns Jim's family "never did [Huck] no harm." And just as Huck is wrestling with this dilemma, two slave-catchers, looking for Jim, call out to him from shore, demanding to know if anyone is on the raft with Huck, and if so, is it a black or white person? "White," Huck heroically lies. Who would dare advise the hero to betray his friend by replying "black," thereby ensuring a life of misery and human degradation for him and his family?

In his short treatise "On a Supposed Right to Lie from Altruistic Motives," Immanuel Kant takes the rather extreme position that "Truthfulness in statements that one cannot avoid is a human being's duty to everyone, however great the disadvantage to him or another that may result from it." Kant holds this duty to be unconditional, a "sacred command of reason," and "not to be restricted by any conveniences." His French contemporary Benjamin Constant argued that Kant's principle, "if taken unconditionally and singly, [would] make any society impossible." He pursues Kant's own example of "whether it is a crime to lie to a murderer who asked us whether a friend of ours whom he is pursuing has taken refuge in our house." Constant takes the answer to be self-evident. To tell the truth in such a case is to aid in the commission of an evil deed and to put one's friend's life at risk. The relative injustice of telling a potential murderer a deliberate untruth obviously pales in comparison. But Kant refuses to grant Constant's point. He insists that "if you have, by a lie, prevented someone just now bent on murder from committing the deed, then you are legally accountable for all the consequences that might arise from it. But if you had kept strictly to your word, the public justice could hold nothing against you, whatever the unforeseen consequences might be." For Kant, truth telling is ultimately "a rule that by its essence does not admit of exceptions."[21]

It is unlikely that anyone, Kant himself included, would actually go as far as he advises to avoid telling a deliberate untruth. But in practice, most of us do not go far at all to avoid falsehoods. Hannah Arendt notes that while factual accounts are rarely compellingly true on their perceived merits, owing to the contingency and unpredictability of real life, lies often are. They are frequently more appealing—and even more plausible-sounding—than reality to the teller, because the liar has the crucial advantage of knowing in advance his perceptions and desires of his audience.[22]

Personal relations are characterized by far more lying than many of us are aware of or even recognize as such, as data from such diverse fields as sociology, linguistics, and social psychology have demonstrated. Deborah A. Kashy and Bella M. DePaulo observe, "Lying is a fact of social life rather than an extraordinary or unusual event. People tell lies to accomplish the most basic social interaction goals, such as influencing others, managing impressions and providing reassurance and support."[23] According to one study, most people tell between one and two lies each day, with subjects admitting to lying to between 30 and 38 percent of the people in their lives. (And, of course, they lie to pollsters, too, so these figures themselves may be questionable.) Obviously, different people tell different kinds of lies in different situations. Researchers find that "lies are less often told in the pursuit of such goals as financial gain and material advantage and instead are much more often told in the pursuit of psychic rewards such as esteem, affection and respect." Men often lie for self-aggrandizement purposes, while women frequently lie to avoid tension and conflict, and to minimize hurt feelings and ill will.[24]

Lying is likewise considered a normal part of doing business in America in many industries today. In a lengthy examination of the role of truth and lies in the entertainment industry, *Los Angeles Times* writer David Shaw reported in 2001, "In Hollywood, deception is, for reporters and those who depend on them, a frustrating fact of everyday life. It appears to involve everything from negotiations and job changes to casting, financing and scores from test screenings." *Premiere* editor Anne Thompson explains that opening gross figures for a new film are routinely "made up—fabricated—every week." Movie producers ask reporters to lie for them without shame or compunction. According to Patrick Goldstein, a movie reporter and columnist for the *Los Angeles Times,* "truth" in the movie business "is what makes a good story, period. They spend their days making it up as they go along; I'd have to be a wacko idealist to expect them to be truthful with me."[25] In June 2001, a *Newsweek* reporter discovered that a number of Sony Pictures Entertainment productions were receiving consistently enthusiastic blurbs from a nonexistent film critic named "David Manning," alleged to work for the *Ridgefield Press,* a small Connecticut weekly.[26]

Lying also scarcely even raises an eyebrow in the journalistic world of women's magazines—at least as it pertains to sex. According to the testimony of a group of editors who appeared at a New York City forum on the topic, lying about sex in their magazines' pages is more common than telling the truth. In one apparently typical tale, a writer named Laurie Abraham, at work on a story for *Glamour* on "reviving your sex life," quoted a friend of many years, who told her "that she and her husband—they had been married, like, eight years—had sex five times a week. And so it was edited out and it was actually changed to three times a week!" Why? "Because the editor couldn't believe that a couple, married for eight years, was having sex five times a week."[27]

The difference is really one of degree between these writers and editors and some of the top CEOs of major U.S. corporations when it comes time to report their earnings. Enron and the accounting firm Arthur Andersen became symbols in 2002 for dishonest reporting of sales and profits, but once the great economy boom of the 1990s ended in bust, these practices were revealed to have been extremely widespread among large corporations, their accounting firms, and the analysts upon whom investors relied to assess them. In just one week in the summer of 2002, we saw the results of years of willful media blindness: Arthur Andersen LLP found itself convicted of obstructing justice. Tyco International Ltd.'s chief executive, L. Dennis Kozlowski, was charged with massive tax evasion and accused of making secret pay deals with underlings. Cable giant Adelphia Communications Corp. admitted falsifying numbers and making surreptitious loans to shareholders. Xerox Corp. was forced to pay a $10 million fine for purposely overstating revenues. Merrill Lynch & Co. paid $100 million to settle New York State charges that analysts misled investors. Wal-Mart workers in twenty-eight states joined together to sue the company for demanding that they file false time-clock reports to avoid overtime payments. Three Rite Aid corporation executives were charged with a securities and accounting fraud that led to the largest restatement of earnings ever—or until WorldCom Inc. announced that same week that it was restating earnings by nearly four billion dollars over a period of five quarters, following the discovery of "massive fraud" in its earlier statements. This figure soon grew to more than nine billion.[28] Here again, while "creative accounting" or openly practicing massive fraud can lead to jail sentences in a few instances, lying, by itself, appeared to carry little if any professional social stigma in the business world. Jeffrey Pfeffer, a professor at Stanford Business School, explains, "Straight-talk is not sought, it is not rewarded, it is not valued" in corporate America. The stock market, and, hence, most corporate executives, preferred "beguiling lies to inconvenient truths."[29]

Dishonesty has become so pervasive a part of our public discourse that in some cases, the very same people who pose as defenders of absolute truth feel no compunction about relying on deception to do so. Take the case of ex-Watergate felon Charles Colson, who, following a prison conversion, founded a national prison ministry, authored thirty-eight books—selling over five million copies—along with daily radio commentaries and a regular column in *Christianity Today,* the nation's most important evangelical magazine. In the winter of 2002, Colson discussed the case of the popular historian

Steven Ambrose, who had been accused of plagiarizing portions of his work. Colson's column condemned what he termed America's "post-truth society" in which "even the man on the street sees little wrong with lying." How ironic, therefore, that although the column appeared beneath Colson's byline and alongside his photo, the words he claimed as his own were actually the work of one Anne Morse, one of two full-time writers Colson employs, along with various "contract" writers, to churn out his column.[30]

Colson's own lack of self-awareness notwithstanding, he makes a valid point. When people talk about lies in American society today, they tend to do so—at least in public—with a degree of naiveté that becomes its own sort of dishonesty. As Louis Menand has observed, "The dissembler is always part of a universe of dissemblers." And though many of us may hide this awareness even from ourselves, "all adult interactions take for granted a certain degree of insincerity and indirection. There is always a literal meaning, which no one takes completely seriously, and an implied meaning, which is what we respond to even when we pretend to be responding to the literal meaning, [and] a great deal of literature (also a great deal of situation comedy) is built around imaginary cases in which one character misreads another character's code, or in which someone suffers by insisting on making explicit what the rest of the world knows is better left concealed by euphemism or denial."[31]

Menand's is a relatively straightforward observation, but it has nevertheless gotten lost in the context of contemporary American political debate. During the impeachment crisis of 1998–99, much of official and semiofficial Washington professed to be exercised about the fact of Bill Clinton's lying to the nation about his extramarital sex life. While many pundits insisted that the relevant issues were constitutional—regarding the president's ability to carry out the laws of the land and the sanctity of the grand jury process, etc.—a number of highly regarded commentators chose to interpret the issue starkly in terms of lies and lying. "I'd like to be able to tell my children, 'You should tell the truth,'" Stuart Taylor of the *National Journal* said on NBC's *Meet the Press.* "I'd like to be able to tell them, 'You should respect the president.' And I'd like to be able to tell them both things at the same time." "We have our own set of village rules," complained David Gergen, editor at large of *U.S. News & World Report,* who had worked for both Ronald Reagan and Richard Nixon, as well as Clinton, and therefore could not claim to be a stranger to official mendacity. "The deep and searing violation took place when he not only lied to the country, but co-opted his friends and lied to them."[32] Cable talk-show host and former Democratic congressional aide Chris Matthews explained, "Clinton lies knowing that you know he's lying. It's brutal and it subjugates the person who's being lied to. I resent deeply being constantly lied to."[33] Pundit George Will, a frequent apologist for President Reagan's deceptions, went so far as to insist that the president's "calculated, sustained lying has involved an extraordinarily corrupting assault on language, which is the uniquely human capacity that makes persuasion, and hence popular government, possible. Hence the obtuseness of those who say Clinton's behavior is compatible with constitutional principles, presidential duties and republican ethics."[34]

Different Presidents, Different Lies

The case of Bill Clinton, while perhaps the best publicized of presidential lying in recent times, is also not included here, because it is not relevant to my investigation. In contrast to the tenor of the opinions quoted above, I share with the philosopher Thomas Nagel the belief that lies told in the private realm, by a president or any other public figure, are no one's business but that of the liar and his intimates. Without such a distinction, Nagel persuasively argues, civilization becomes impossible. "Just as social life would be impossible if we expressed all our lustful, aggressive, greedy, anxious, or self-obsessed feelings in ordinary public encounters," Nagel argues, "so would inner life be impossible if we tried to become wholly persons whose thoughts, feelings, and private behavior could be safely exposed to public view."[35] To the degree that Clinton lied publicly, in this view, he did so only because he was being pursued by a fanatical group of politicians and ideologues who sought—with the unlimited resources of the Independent Counsel's office—to make his private life public, something that had happened to no previous president during the nearly 220-year course of the American republic. Clinton lied about his adulterous behavior to spare himself and his family further public humiliation. However objectionable it may be and whatever misjudgments Clinton may have made to land him in so unhappy a quandary, it is hardly comparable to lying about peace treaties or the causes of war. (Richard Nixon and Watergate were also eliminated as a choice for this book in part because those lies and their consequences have already been so thoroughly documented and discussed. Moreover, I attribute Nixon's lies to his own personal neurosis and criminal character, and hence consider the case to be less instructive than those I've included.)

The issue that does concern this book is presidential lying about matters of state that is alleged to be undertaken for the public good. This sort of manipulation of the truth derives from an old and venerable tradition in statecraft, one that can be said to trace its lineage to ancient Athens. Plato defended a false story that he imagined might be told to people in order to persuade the poor to accept less, and hence safeguard social harmony. According to this story, God had mingled gold, silver, iron, and brass in fashioning rulers, auxiliaries, farmers, and craftsmen, intending these groups for separate tasks in a harmonious hierarchy. The lesson for the poor was to accept their lot in life without too much complaint, lest they upset the divine order. Centuries later, Niccolò Machiavelli explained to his would-be princes that lying is necessary in a wise ruler simply because men inevitably lie, and it is better to do the lying than to be the one lied to. "Because men would not observe their faith with you," you in turn are not bound to "keep faith with them."[36]

The right of members of Congress to lie is actually enshrined in the U.S. Constitution. Article I, Section 6, states that, with regard to senators and representatives speaking on the floors of their respective bodies, "for Speech or Debate in either House, they shall not be questioned in any other Place." The document's framers wrote this law to encourage free and open debate among representatives, uninhibited by the threat of lawsuits. Yet the result, as in the case of Senator McCarthy, has been the assertion of the right to lie with impunity.

Even without resort to constitutional complexities, any number of everyday factors tend to interfere with a contemporary American president telling his constituents what he knows to be the unvarnished truth about almost any topic. Among the most prominent is the argument that average citizens are simply too ignorant, busy, or emotionally immature to appreciate the difficult reality that is political decision making. The pundit/public philosopher Walter Lippmann, writing in 1924, famously likened the average citizen in a democracy to a deaf spectator sitting in the back row of a sporting event. "He does not know what is happening, why it is happening, what ought to happen; he lives in a world which he cannot see, does not understand and is unable to direct."[37] Echoing these musings in his 1969 memoir, *Present at the Creation,* former secretary of state Dean Acheson wrote:

> The task of a public officer seeking to explain and gain support for a major policy is not that of the writer of a doctoral thesis. Qualification must give way to simplicity of statement, nicety and nuance to bluntness, almost brutality, in carrying home a point. . . . In the State Department, we used to discuss how much time that mythical "average American citizen" put in each day listening, reading, and arguing about the world outside his country. Assuming a man or woman with a fair education, a family, and a job in or out of the house, it seemed to us that ten minutes a day would be a high average. If this were anywhere near right, points to be understandable had to be clear. If we did make our points clearer than truth, we did not differ from most other educators and could hardly do otherwise.[38]

Acheson's view of the attention span of the average citizen appears optimistic today, given what appears to be a steady decline of Americans' interest in politics and public policy, coupled with the news media's increasing focus on tabloid fare and "soft" features.[39] Political scientists estimate the percentage of the public that is both interested and knowledgeable about even major foreign policy issues to be in the area of 8 to 20 percent.[40] Yet "clearer than truth," in Acheson's formulation, is a tricky term. Acheson means it to imply that a president was able to reach a higher level of truth in his public statements by not making a fetish of adhering to what he knew to be accurate—which is another way of excusing a lie. So, too, is the argument, frequently heard in modern times, that the government's need to act swiftly and in secrecy on matters of diplomacy and national security makes such democratic consultation impossible, even were it feasible given the relative ignorance of the populace.

These questions are significant ones, however, as the foundation of democracy is public trust. "How," John Stuart Mill quite rightly asks, can citizens either "check or encourage what they were not permitted to see?"[41] Without public honesty, the process of voting becomes an exercise in manipulation rather than the expression of the consent of the governed. Many a scholar has persuasively argued that official deception may be convenient, but over time, it undermines the bond of trust between the government and the people that is essential to the functioning of a democracy.

Presidents, too, know that lying to their constituents is "wrong," both in the strictly moral and philosophical sense and in the damage it causes to the democratic foundation of our political system. Yet they continue because they believe the lies they tell serve their narrow political interest on the matter in question. When, in early 2002, the Pentagon was forced to retract a plan to create an Office of Strategic Influence for the purposes of distributing deliberate misinformation to foreign media, President George W. Bush tried to undo the damage by promising, "We'll tell the American people the truth." At the very same moment the controversy was taking place, however, Bush's solicitor general, Theodore Olson, was filing a friend of the court brief in a lawsuit against former Clinton administration officials whom Jennifer Harbury—a young woman whose husband had been killed in Guatemala by a CIA asset—accused of illegally misleading her about the knowledge they possessed regarding her husband's killers. Olson's brief argued, "There are lots of different situations when the government has legitimate reasons to give out false information," as well as "incomplete information and even misinformation." (The Supreme Court dismissed the suit and refused to rule on the legality of official lies.)[42]

Of course, presidential lying is hardly a new concern in American history, particularly where matters of war and peace are concerned. Excessive secrecy, a close cousin of lying and frequently its handmaiden and inspiration, has been a key facet of American governance since literally before the nation's founding. Reporters were barred from the Constitutional Convention in 1789, and delegates were forbidden to reveal their deliberations. The ultimate success of the endeavor does not obviate the larger problem to which it points. "Concealment," notes the philosopher Sissela Bok, insulates bureaucracies from "criticism and interference; it allows them to correct mistakes and to reverse direction without costly, often without embarrassing explanation and it permits them to cut corners with no questions being asked."[43]

Rare is the leader who does not argue for the necessity of secrecy while conducting sensitive negotiations with either friend or foe. From the earliest days of the republic, the president, under authority of Article II, Section 2, of the U.S. Constitution as commander in chief, has restricted the dissemination of information relating to defense and foreign policy. Presidents have passionately argued that they could not preserve the peace nor protect the nation without keeping large portions of the actions of their government secret. This was true in Philadelphia in 1789, and it remains true today. The judiciary branch generally endorses this view, and hence key sections of the very same Constitution that give Americans a right to examine the actions of their leaders have been declared functionally null and void as a result. The need for secrecy in certain situations is a real one, and citizens instinctively understand that no modern state can reveal everything to everyone, lest the safety of those same citizens be compromised. But there is a line between refusing to divulge information and deliberate deception. Politicians cross this line at their own peril.

Keeping a secret is not the same as telling a lie, just as refusing a comment is not the same as intentionally misleading. But it takes a brave politician to risk attack for honestly doing the former, when he can just as easily dispose of the problem with an easy resort to the latter. America in its infancy was blessed with the leadership of many such brave leaders whose sense of personal honor and destiny overrode their narrow political self-interest. For instance, in 1795, President Washington refused to supply the House with details of the treaty that his emissary John Jay had negotiated with Great Britain. He demanded that the legislature appropriate funds to carry out its terms, but refused to enumerate them, insisting that his "duty to [his] office forbade it."[44] This was antidemocratic behavior on the part of Washington, but it was admirably honest. If the Congress did not want to appropriate funds for purposes it did not understand, it was free to refuse. Within a generation, however, this dedication to secrecy in the conduct of diplomacy had degenerated into a policy of deliberate dishonesty. During President Monroe's administration, Secretary of State John Quincy Adams intentionally sent the Senate incomplete sets of documents relating to a set of Central American treaties in order to receive, by subterfuge, its advice and consent. When challenged, he published a series of letters under the pseudonym "Phocion," to mislead unsuspecting readers regarding the nature of South America's revolutions.[45]

These deliberate evasions and dishonest occasions frequently accompanied the conduct of American diplomacy during the nation's first century, particularly when that diplomacy threatened to spill into war. For instance, the name of Abraham Lincoln first came to public recognition when, as a nearly anonymous congressman in 1848, he rose on the floor of the House to respond to that body's decision to "recognize" the existence of war with Mexico. In fact, no war with Mexico had existed until President James K. Polk falsely insisted that the southern nation had attacked an American army detachment on American soil. Lincoln demanded to know the precise "spot" upon which this alleged attack had taken place. Polk did not respond.[46]

The stakes of presidential lies grew immeasurably as the United States began its march toward superpower status. While lying to lure the United States into a war of conquest with Mexico was hardly a trivial presidential action, nor were President McKinley's exaggerations and misinformation with regard to Spain's conduct in Cuba that led America to war there a half-century afterward, it was not until after America entered World War II that the nation moved into an era of permanent wartime footing and lying, and its attendant dangers became a continuous feature of the nation's political and cultural life.

The president present at the creation of this new nation was Franklin Delano Roosevelt, who successfully led America into war to a considerable degree by stealth and deception. The president liked to call himself a "juggler," who "never let my right hand know what my left hand does." He was perfectly willing, in his own words, to "mislead and tell untruths if it will help win the war."[47] Against the background of the 1937 Neutrality Act, Roosevelt added a "cash and carry" provision to permit England and France to buy American weapons. The president made his case to Congress and the nation in deliberately disingenuous terms, presenting what was really a step toward belligerency as a measure to avoid war. The measure, he assured the country, "offers far greater safeguards than we now possess or have ever possessed to protect American lives and property." Roosevelt also deployed warships in the Atlantic and the Azores, and landed U.S. troops in Iceland, all the while insisting his primary intention was to keep the nation out of war. Roosevelt, moreover, frequently exaggerated the country's vulnerability to the American people. He vastly exaggerated the number of aircraft possessed by the Axis powers, as well as their rate of production. In April 1939, he warned the newspaper editors that "the totalitarian nations . . . have 1,500 planes today. They cannot hop directly across our 3,000 miles but they can do it in three hops . . . It would take planes based at Yucatan, modern bombing planes about an hour and fifty minutes to smash up New Orleans." A year later, before the same audience, Roosevelt repeated the point using similar language, though now he claimed that "the European unmentioned country" in question "could put 5,000 bombing planes into Brazil."[48]

During the 1940 election campaign, as Lyndon Johnson would do twenty-four years later, Roosevelt repeatedly assured Americans that their sons would not be sent to fight in "foreign wars." On November 2 he stated flatly, "Your president says this country is not going to war."[49] In early September 1941, however, a U.S. destroyer, the *Greer,* tracked a German U-boat for three hours and signaled its location to British forces before the sub turned and attacked. It had been issued secret orders to escort British convoys and aid in the effort to sink German submarines. In an eerie foreshadowing of the second Gulf of Tonkin incident, the *Greer* escaped unharmed, but FDR used the incident to denounce Germany. "I tell you the blunt fact," Roosevelt explained, "that this German submarine fired first . . . without warning and with deliberate desire to sink her." Without informing Americans how the ship had provoked the submarine, FDR used the alleged incident to step up U.S. participation in the undeclared war against Germany in the North Atlantic. One month later, three U.S. warships were torpedoed and one sunk while on convoy duty in the North Atlantic; 172 men were lost. This enabled FDR to persuade Congress to repeal what remained of the Neutrality Act's restraint upon his power. In the case of easing America's reluctant entry into the European war, the president's guile-filled gamble was rewarded when, following the Japanese attack, Germany declared war on the United States, thereby proffering an engraved invitation into the European conflict. Employing this analogy, Senator J. William Fulbright would later remark that "FDR's deviousness in a good cause made it much easier for [LBJ] to practice the same kind of deviousness in a bad cause."[50]

During the Cold War, presidential deception for security purposes became routinized, defended in elite circles as a distasteful but necessary matter of realpolitik and, frequently, national survival. This was true not only for the men responsible for lying but also for those independent intellectuals and scholars who might be expected to object most vociferously. Thomas A. Bailey, dean of diplomatic historians, argued in 1948, "Because the masses are notoriously short-sighted, and generally cannot see danger until it is at their throats, our statesmen are forced to deceive them into an awareness of their own long-term interests . . . Deception of the people may in fact become necessary [as] . . . the price we have to pay for greater physical security."[51] The combined threats of Soviet expansionism and potential nuclear attack, and the requirements for secrecy and vigilance they created, were deemed to be so compelling that Americans simply could no longer enjoy the luxury of leaders telling them the truth, lest this truth be exploited by a perfidious adversary. This principle, late enshrined into law by a series of Supreme Court cases, would be neatly enunciated during the Cuban Missile Crisis by Assistant Secretary of Defense for Public Affairs Arthur Sylvester, who informed Americans, "It's inherent in [the] government's right, if necessary, to lie to save itself."[52]

The era's Magna Carta would prove to be an April 1950 internal bureaucratic report to President Truman entitled "NSC-68." Though the document remained classified until 1975, it functioned within the government as the operational blueprint for the policy of containment, inspired by George Kennan's theological treatise known as the "Long Telegram," and published as "The Sources of Soviet Conduct," in *Foreign Affairs,* under the pseudonym "X." As the end product of extensive interagency negotiation, NSC-68 lacked Kennan's poetic flair. But its prescriptive elements were clear, present, and dangerous to the norms of constitutional democracy. Believing that the Kremlin leaders were possessed of a "new fanatic faith," seeking "absolute authority over the rest of the world," the authors argued that "the integrity of our system will not be jeopardized by any measures, covert or overt, violent or non-violent, which serve the purposes of frustrating the Kremlin design."[53] In 1795, James Madison had warned that "No nation could preserve its freedom in the midst of continual warfare." But in 1962, John Kennedy found himself leading a nation in which "no war has been declared, [but] the danger has never been more clear and its presence has never been more imminent." As in all wars, truth would necessarily be among the first casualties. The necessity of the noble lie thus became almost an a priori assumption within the American elite during the Cold War, so deeply and widely held was the consensus regarding the threat posed to the United States by global Communism.

Even so, the idea that a president might tell the nation an outright lie remained a shocking one to many Americans, as President Eisenhower would learn to his considerable chagrin. When, on May 1, 1960, Soviet premier Nikita S. Khrushchev initially disclosed that an American plane had been shot down inside Soviet territory, Eisenhower's minions were quick to issue denials. The White House stuck to its story that a NASA "weather research plane" on a mission inside Turkey might have accidentally drifted into Soviet territory, and identified the pilot as Francis Gary Powers, a civilian employee of Lockheed. The White House fiction turned out to be Nikita Khrushchev's cue to disclose to the Supreme Soviet, "Comrades, I must let you in on a secret. When I made my report two days ago, I deliberately refrained from mentioning that we have the remains of the plane—and we also have the pilot, who is quite alive and kicking." Howls of laughter followed as the premier added that the Soviets had also recovered "a tape recording of the signals of a number of our ground radar stations—incontestable evidence of spying." Eisenhower admitted to his secretary, "I would like to resign."[54]

The president's staff scrambled to distance him from what was clearly an embarrassing lie. They put out the false cover story that the president had been unaware of the flights—though in fact he had been deeply involved in their planning, including even the targets upon which Powers had been assigned to eavesdrop. Yet Chief of Staff Andrew Goodpaster apparently instructed Secretary of State Christian Herter, the "president wants no specific tie to him of this particular event."[55] While the president professed to "heartily approve" of a proposed congressional investigation of the incident, he privately instructed the CIA and the Joint Chiefs of Staff to do whatever necessary to try to thwart it and went so far as to order his Cabinet officers to hide his own involvement even if called upon to testify under oath.

Author James Bamford argues that Christian Herter did lie to the committee, misinforming it that the U-2 flight program had "never come up to the president." Eisenhower, argues Bamford, was therefore guilty of the subornation of perjury, and Herter of perjury.[56] (In 1977, former CIA director Richard Helms would be sentenced to two years in prison for a similar offense.) What's more, they were committing these crimes not to protect "our intelligence systems," as the president had instructed the National Security Council, but to protect Eisenhower's own political standing. Powers had already signed a confession and all of the eavesdropping equipment from the plane was already on display to the public in Moscow's Gorky Park.[57] But an election year was coming up, and the president did not want to take any chances with exposure of the unflattering truth. Though his role in the planning of the flight and the deception that ensued was not revealed until decades after his death, Eisenhower never fully recovered from the humiliation. Two years after he left office, Eisenhower was asked by reporter David Kraslov about his "greatest regret." The ex-general replied, "The lie we told [about the U-2]. I didn't realize how high a price we were going to have to pay for that lie."[58]

Forty years later, Eisenhower's concern about his own honor and credibility in the face of having been revealed to be a liar seemed a quaint relic of a bygone era. Americans have since learned of so many lies told to them by their leaders that most have adapted to official falsehood as a way of life.

According to a major 1996 survey by *The Washington Post,* Harvard University, and the Kaiser Family Foundation, in 1964 three in four Americans trusted the federal government all or most of the time, a view shared by barely one-third that number in the later poll. While Americans are often found to be shockingly ignorant regarding the affairs of their government, it is a remarkable discovery of recent research that the more Americans know about their government, the less they trust it. Among those with high levels of knowledge about current issues or politics, 77 percent expressed only some confidence in the federal government, a view shared by 67 percent less-informed respondents.[59] And while these numbers briefly improved following the September 11, 2001, attacks on the nation, President Bush's dissembling with regard to the threat posed to the United States by Iraq during 2002 and early 2003 sent those numbers tumbling down to their preattack levels, and lower.[60]

The Problem of Feedback

As noted earlier, these conditions constitute a decidedly unhealthy situation for any democratic system. But the quality of the nation's democracy, like the issue of the morality of lying in general, carries precious little weight when a president or one of his advisers is trying to decide how to avoid telling his constituents an uncomfortable truth. Or, more precisely, whatever weight it does carry derives exclusively from the perception that the president is revealing to the nation a difficult truth as an uncommonly brave and statesmanlike act. In fact, presidents often offer such revelations as substitutes for admitting the more compromising facts that lie buried beneath them.

The pragmatic problem with official lies is their amoeba-like penchant for self-replication. The more a leader lies to his people, the more he *must* lie to his people. Eventually the lies take on a life of their own and tend to overpower the liar. Lying may appear to work for a president in the short term and, in many cases, it does. But a president ignores the consequences of his deception at his own political peril.

Albert Hirschman has observed that the notion of unintended consequences is as old as the Greek hubris-nemesis sequence. Moreover, he notes, the "reconnaissance and systematic description of . . . unintended consequences have [ever since the eighteenth century] been a major assignment, if not raison d'être of social science."[61] What social scientists term the "system effects" or "feedback effects"—which are intimately related to what political scientists and, in another context, economists term "path dependency"—of official lying in politics are both enormous and enormously understudied. Robert Jervis writes, "In a system, the chains of consequence extend over time and many areas. The effects of action are always multiple. Doctors call the undesired impact of medications 'side effects.' Although the language is misleading, there is no criterion other than our desires, coupled with our expectations, that determines which effects are 'main' and which are 'side'—the point reminds us that disturbing a system will produce several changes." Jervis deploys a variety of examples from environmental policy to demonstrate an obvious but frequently ignored argument. "Wishing to kill insects, we may put an end to the singing of birds. Wishing to 'get there' faster, we insult our lungs with smog. Seeking to protect the environment by developing non-polluting sources of electric power, we build windmills that kill hawks and eagles that fly into the blades; cleaning the water in our harbors allows the growth of mollusks and crustaceans that destroy wooden piers and bulkheads; adding redundant safety equipment makes some accidents less likely but increases the chances of others due to the operators' greater confidence and the interaction effects among the devices; placing a spy in the adversary's camp not only gains valuable information but also leaves the actor vulnerable to deception if the spy is discovered; eliminating rinderpest in East Africa paves the way for canine distemper in lions because it permitted the accumulation of cattle, which required dogs to herd them, dogs which provided a steady source for the virus that could spread to lions."[62]

In society, as in nature, the failure to appreciate the fact that the behavior of the actors is in part responsible for the environment that will later impinge on them leads observers—and actors as well—to underestimate actors' influence.[63] In terms of the literature of path dependency, we see in a presidential lie the kind of "causal mechanism" that inspires the "inherent logic of events" through which "the impact of decisions [in this case, lies] persists into the present and defines alternatives for the future."[64] In the cases I examine here, the paths set forth by a presidential lie relating to an important matter of state, while inherently unpredictable, are nevertheless predictably uncontrollable and almost always negative.

In the pages that follow, I plan to elucidate a political dynamic that mimics the natural world described above. A president may create problems that go unremarked upon at the time of the initial lie. Presidents, like the rest of us, almost never consider the system effects of their lies, particularly the "feedback loop" these lies create. But these consequences are considerable, unavoidable, and, in the four case studies I examine, politically fatal. The reasons are simple. In almost all cases, the problem or issue that gives rise to the lie refuses to go away, even while the lie complicates the president's ability to address it. He must now address not only the problem itself, but also the ancillary problem his lie has created. Karl Kraus once mused, with only slight exaggeration, that many a war has been caused by a diplomat who lied to a journalist and then believed what he read in the newspapers. The tendency for leaders to believe their own propaganda over time is one form of what first CIA agents and, later, political scientists have come to call "blowback." One feature of blowback is that its effects are almost always portrayed as unprovoked, often inexplicable actions, when in fact they are typically caused by actions initially taken by the government itself.[65] The point here is that in telling the truth to the nation, presidents may often have to deal with complex, difficult, and frequently dangerous problems they would no doubt prefer to avoid. But at least these are genuine problems that would have arisen irrespective of the leader's actions. This is, after all, inherent in the job description. But once a president takes it upon himself to lie to the country about important matters, he necessarily creates an independent dynamic that would not otherwise have come about, and we are all the worse for it.

As I have already stated, this book purposely avoids the two best-known recent cases of presidential lying—those that resulted in the resignation of one president and the impeachment of another—and focuses instead on much more popular presidents. Furthermore, I was far more interested in examining the lies of presidents that I admire (Roosevelt, Kennedy, and, to a lesser degree, Johnson) as well as those who are perceived as heroic figures by so many Americans (Roosevelt, Kennedy, Reagan) and whose lies, moreover, were, like Lyndon Johnson's, inextricably tied to what were popularly viewed at the time as their moments of unsurpassed personal popularity and political triumph. In doing so, I hope to demonstrate that presidential deception—and the practical and political misfortunes that inevitably accompany it—are the presidential rule rather than the exception. All the presidents discussed in this book believed themselves to be acting on the basis of patriotic necessity when deceiving the nation. Roosevelt believed himself to be preserving the postwar peace. Kennedy understood his deception as necessary to protect a politically unpopular compromise that had been necessary to prevent a potential superpower war. Lyndon Johnson felt it necessary to deceive in order to prevent the spread of Communism in Southeast Asia, just as Reagan believed he was doing two decades later in Central America. Even George W. Bush doubtless believed that the false stories he told the nation with regard to Iraq were offered in the service of national survival. It is my contention that these presidents succeeded not only in fooling the nation but also in fooling themselves. And in each case, the president or his party was made to pay for his deceptions along with the country they so cavalierly misled. As we shall see in the coming chapters, presidential dishonesty about key matters of state—whether moral or immoral—is ultimately and invariably self-destructive. It should be avoided at all costs. Period.

II. FRANKLIN D. ROOSEVELT, HARRY S. TRUMAN, AND THE YALTA CONFERENCE

And, of course, I learned all about Yalta, and there's very little in our history that's been lied about as much. They said Roosevelt sold out the United States, which was a damn lie, of course; if the Russians'd lived up to their agreements that they made at Yalta, there wouldn't have been any trouble at all, but they didn't; they never lived up to an agreement they made ever, and that's what caused the trouble, and we all know what happened as a result.

—Harry S. Truman, quoted by Merle Miller, in *Plain Speaking: An Oral Biography of Harry S. Truman*

Yalta. Few words have entered the popular political lexicon with such destructive force. Yalta itself is an imposing Crimean resort town, but it was there in early February 1945 that Joseph Stalin, perhaps the most effective mass murderer in human history, met with Franklin Roosevelt and Winston Churchill, perhaps the twentieth century's two greatest champions of freedom and democracy, to plan the final phase of World War II and map out the contours of the postwar world. When it was over, Stalin, history's villain, went home and kept his word about their agreement, while Roosevelt and Churchill lied about theirs. Therein lies one of the great and, for American democracy, most painful ironies of the beginning of the Cold War. The vicious killer atop the Soviet evil empire honored the deal; the Americans and their British allies reneged. And that's how the Cold War began.

Politically and metaphorically, the term "Yalta" would become a shorthand term for diplomatic distrust, malfeasance, treachery, and, to some, even treason. More than a half-century later, and a decade after the Soviet Union collapsed, pundits and politicians continued to employ it as a signal of political disgrace. Following his first meeting with Russian leader Vladimir Putin in 2001, President George W. Bush proclaimed to a cheering throng in Warsaw, "No more

Munichs, no more Yaltas," and was lauded for having done so by William Safire of *The New York Times* and James Hoagland of *The Washington Post*.[1, 2]

"No More Let Us Falter"

The Yalta conference took place on the cusp of what Philip Roth's fictional alter-ego Nathan Zuckerman termed "the greatest moment of collective inebriation in American history." On the threshold of a great military victory conducted almost entirely abroad, the United States was entering the world stage in its premier performance as the globe's unchallenged military, economic, and moral exemplar. It had just rescued humanity from the scourge of a criminally murderous regime led by a demonic dictator bent on world domination. It was, President Truman would later claim, "the greatest nation on earth . . . the greatest nation in History . . . the greatest that the sun has ever shone upon." Joined by Winston Churchill, the personification of Old World stoicism, and Joseph Stalin, America's new avatar of emerging Slavic democracy, the country's inspirational wartime leader, President Roosevelt, traveled six thousand miles under great personal hardship to ensure that the mistakes that had undermined Woodrow Wilson's attempts to build a stable postwar peace a generation earlier would not be repeated. This time the world would not be divided up in secret, hidden from the notice of the world's populations. The United States, having fought long and hard to prevent Europe from falling victim to the nightmare of Fascism, would now ensure that the European peace was constructed on the twin pillars of democracy and prosperity, which together would guarantee that no such tragedy would ever arise again.

The president's polio-induced paralysis and extremely poor health—the seriousness of which was kept secret from the public—lent his dramatic trip an air of uncompromising commitment and perseverance. In December of 1944, Dr. Robert Duncan had conducted a thorough examination of the president and had given him only a few months to live, owing to, as Lord Charles Moran described it, "hardening of the arteries of the brain in an advanced stage."[3] Roosevelt would, in fact, be dead within ten weeks of his return from Crimea.

To make the arduous journey, FDR not only had to travel a great distance under wartime peril, but also had to endure less than ideal conditions upon his arrival. Nazi soldiers had thoroughly despoiled the once idyllic, rustic village, and Churchill complained that if the Allies had looked for ten years they could not have found a worse meeting place. The prime minister initially resisted the choice, but once Roosevelt accepted Stalin's invitation, Churchill had no alternative but to stifle his complaints and stock up on libations, as only an adequate supply of whiskey—which the prime minister claimed was good for typhus and deadly for lice—would make a stay there bearable.[4] The telegraph from 10 Downing Street to 1600 Pennsylvania Avenue read: "No more let us falter! From Malta to Yalta! Let Nobody Alter!"[5]

Complications arose almost immediately when the conference host, Marshal Stalin, offered his guests generous hospitality but precious few concessions. To secure the Soviet dictator's support for the creation of a powerful United Nations—which, unlike Wilson's impotent League of Nations, would be underwritten by the military muscle and political will of the Great Powers—Roosevelt was forced to agree to a plan lending U.S. legitimacy to Soviet predominance in Poland and elsewhere in Eastern Europe. Internal State Department documents reveal that the Americans had feared that such concessions might be necessary, though they hoped to avoid them.[6] In fact, though this was never revealed to the country at large, the president never really had any choice in the matter. The Red Army's occupation of these countries would ultimately determine the shape of their political futures, regardless of Churchill's or Roosevelt's opinion.

In the final moments of the talks, the president also offered Stalin extensive territorial concessions in East Asia in exchange for a Soviet promise to invade Japan. These, too, were hard bargains to accept, but FDR and his military advisers considered them essential to winning the war and creating a durable peace. The U.S. Joint Chiefs of Staff, in particular, were adamant about the need to bring the Soviets into the war in the Pacific in order to reduce the likely number of American casualties there during the still-expected invasion. The highly secret Manhattan Project, designed to build the atom bomb, remained mired in uncertainty at the time, and hence could not serve as a basis of wartime planning.[7] (FDR's chief of staff, Admiral William Leahy, worried almost to the moment it was dropped that the bomb would likely be a failure.)[8] Even without an accord at Yalta, the Red Army was free to invade Manchuria, but the United States would then have had no means of negotiating its demands. Indeed, President Truman's advisers would later conclude that they could not prevent the Soviets from coming into the war as they saw fit should the United States try to withdraw from its Yalta commitments.[9] Given the historic political power of isolationism in America, FDR was understandably reluctant to commit the country to arrangements requiring a long-term U.S. military presence abroad in the future. However, he had little room to maneuver. Between the Soviets' demands, backed up by the victories of the Red Army, on the one hand, and the difficulties of trying to explicate complex diplomatic trade-offs to a nation that had no experience in making them in its short history as a world power, on the other, the president felt himself caught in a bind that limited his ability both to get what he wanted and to explain what he had gotten. So he decided to do what he had done so often while leading the nation throughout the war: he kept the details of his deals to himself, figuring he would work out a way to explain them when the time was right.

Roosevelt had already shown himself to be a leader who was deeply untroubled by his own deceptions and frequently appeared to prefer them to the truth, almost as a matter of personal aesthetics. Covering FDR in 1936, then-*New York Times* White House correspondent Turner Catledge remarked, "Roosevelt's first instinct was always to lie, but halfway through an answer, the president realized he could tell the truth and get away with it, so he would shift gears and something true would trickle out."[10] Throughout his life, observes his biographer Geoffrey Ward, "FDR was his own least reliable witness, unable or unwilling to tell the truth" about his own history. "There were always wiser men and women than Franklin Roosevelt in American public life, people who were better informed, more consistent, less devious," Ward continues. "But there were none whose power to inspire both love and loathing was so great, none whose political success or apparent self-assurance exceeded his."[11] Roosevelt may not have been a genius in the conventional sense, as Ward notes, but he understood his limitations and enjoyed an admirable ability to exploit his strengths. Roosevelt was possessed of great common sense and the gift of inspiring the belief in others that he was acting on their behalf, whether or not that was the case. "A second-class intellect," as Justice Oliver Wendell Holmes had famously appraised him shortly after his first inauguration, "but a first-class temperament."[12]

FDR's trade-offs at Yalta were those of a shrewd nineteenth-century European realist, but he was president of a country that lacked a comparable political tradition and he had no inclination to learn its fundamental principles. At sixty-three years old and in failing health, Roosevelt had no desire to try to undertake its education. The war had been publicly fought under the flag of American idealism, on behalf of the spread of freedom and democracy, and with a purposely myopic view of Stalin and the Soviet Union. Roosevelt decided that the postwar peace must be constructed under the same flag. The perceived gulf between the rosy rhetoric of President Wilson and the secret deals of Versailles had destroyed his vision of a League of Nations. This was a vision to which FDR himself felt considerable attachment, and he was therefore not about to allow a few "inconvenient" facts about the Soviet Union or its likely behavior in Eastern Europe following the war to interfere with his grand plans to lay the foundation of a new structure for world peace. During the war, Roosevelt had predicted the emergence of a "clean, shining America," wealthier and more productive than any nation in the world.[13] That cynosure could hardly be party to a secret accord that appeared to abandon entire nations of Poles, Czechs, Slovaks, and others to the iron hand of Communist dictatorship—particularly when these nations furnished so many new Americans and Democratic voters.

Rather than try to elide the truth, in the hope that in the fluidity of the situation he might later improve on his bargain, FDR decided instead simply to lie to the country, to the Congress, and even to his closest advisers about the nature of the deal he had struck. The president no doubt expected that he could prevail upon the Soviets to lighten up a bit in Eastern Europe over time, and he placed great faith in his ability to solve any problems that arose in the new United Nations. In the meantime he would juggle his various constituencies as best he could, keeping his eye on the big picture, as they battled one another on this or that devilish detail.

Unfortunately, Roosevelt did not live long enough to work his magic on the various parties involved and convince them to trust to his good judgment. Instead, within just ten weeks of his return from Crimea, he left the remains of his bargaining in the hands of his inexperienced vice president—a man who knew less about Roosevelt's thinking about the shape of the Yalta agreements than even Joseph Stalin did.

The Cold War Commences: An Alternative Explanation

Though it shaped our national life and political imagination for nearly half a century, Americans still lack a convincing explanation for the cause of the Cold War. Historians have complex analyses of the situation, which defy easy labels, but for many years the historiography of the period has tended to fall into one of three categories. Those labeled "orthodox" can generally be depended upon to focus on Soviet perfidy and American innocence.[14] Many (but not all) "revisionist" historians, in contrast, tend to emphasize U.S. responsibility and Soviet reaction.[15] So-called post-revisionists rarely confront the issue of "guilt" explicitly, but nevertheless typically view the Soviets as implacable under Stalin and the Americans as occasionally misguided, but generally prudent and high-minded, given the weakness of Western Europe's position following the war.[16] In this latter interpretation, the Cold War was simply fated by the geopolitical and ideological differences between the two superpowers and the power vacuum that lay between them. A more recent variation, advanced by leading post-revisionist John Lewis Gaddis, pins responsibility for the Cold War almost entirely on Stalin's personality. "Stalin waged Cold Wars everywhere," according to this interpretation: "within the international system, within his alliances within his country, even within his family." The chain of causality that led the United States and the USSR to 1945 had many links,

Gaddis admits. But "it took one man," he writes, "responding predictably to his own authoritarian, paranoid, and narcissistic predisposition to lock [the Cold War] into place."[17]

Ultimately, such interpretations are matters of faith, reflective more of the psychological and ideological assumptions that underlie them than of a convincing marshaling of the evidence. As Melvyn Leffler has pointed out, Gaddis's most recent interpretation, which quickly achieved something akin to consensus status as the accepted interpretation of the Cold War in the U.S. mass media, "resonates with the triumphalism that runs through our contemporary culture."[18] In fact, whatever its long-term causes—and there were many—and whatever its ultimate moral and political justification, the immediate impetus for the Cold War, as this book will argue, was just this: the United States reneged on the deal FDR had signed at Yalta. Because so few Americans were aware of what the accord actually entailed, and because some who were aware were dishonest about its clear implications, the U.S. government only further poisoned relations with the Russians by accusing them of being the party to refuse to honor the agreement. The problem was soon compounded by the propaganda offensive the Americans launched to defend their actions at home—lest they be accused in a rapidly transformed political culture of selling out the country's interests to the Communists. These reactions and counterreactions, coupled with unconscionable genuine shock at the brutality of Soviet actions in Poland and across Eastern Europe, intersected with an outbreak of mass paranoia in American politics, which soon crippled the government's own ability to deal with the realities of Soviet power and the construction of a peaceful postwar world. Once Americans had convinced themselves of a Soviet betrayal at Yalta, they no longer trusted diplomacy or negotiation with Moscow on any issue. "The Russians understand only one thing," as General Lucius Clay reportedly told his staff in Berlin. "That's force."[19]

None of this seemed inevitable, or even possible, to the men gathered in the Lividia Palace at the beginning of 1945. The historic high point of East-West relations came on the last night of the conference, as the three leaders toasted one another and what they believed to be their epochal achievement in laying the foundation for the postwar peace during the previous week. The evening's feast also represented perhaps the final moment when sober-minded men and women might have been able to entertain hopes for the creation of a world system based on cooperation and mutual respect. Over generous provisions of vodka and caviar, Roosevelt compared the feeling inside the Lividia Palace to "that of a family." Stalin hoped that "relations in peacetime . . . [would be] as strong as they had been in war." Churchill felt "we are all standing on the crest of a hill with the glories of future possibilities before us."[20] Harry Hopkins, Roosevelt's closest adviser, said to Robert E. Sherwood, his future biographer, "We really believed in our hearts that this was the dawn of the new day we had all been praying for and talking about for so many years. . . . We had won the first great victory of the peace."[21]

"A Great Hope to the World"

Back home, the anticipation leading up to the unveiling of the Yalta agreement had been immense, as virtually no one in the United States even knew where the president had gone. When the mystery was finally revealed and the accord announced with the president still abroad, it inspired nearly universal acclaim in the United States, even from the president's sworn political opponents. Republican former president Herbert Hoover announced to a Lincoln Day dinner of the National Republican Club in New York that the accord would "offer a great hope to the world," and called it "fitting that it should have been issued to the world on the birthday of Abraham Lincoln."[22] New York governor Thomas Dewey, readying his 1948 Republican presidential bid, praised the pact for making "a real contribution to a future peace." Prewar isolationist leader and Republican senator Arthur Vandenberg called the announced agreement "by far the best that has issued from any major conference." Senate majority leader Alben Barkley (D-KY) sent a cable to the president, congratulating him for "one of the most important steps ever taken to promote peace and happiness in the world."[23]

Mainstream media reaction was hardly more restrained. Key newspaper editorials rejoiced that the meeting had "justified and surpassed" all hopes, "removed a lot of bogeys," and provided a "firm foundation upon which all can advance."[24] As the editors of the mass-circulation *Life* magazine would write with typical Henry Luce-ian avuncularity, "when an international conference is acclaimed by such diverse voices as the Moscow press, the *New York Times,* the New Deal Columnists and Herbert Hoover, there must be something to it."[25] Luce's *Time,* perhaps the nation's most influential publication regarding foreign affairs, called the Yalta deal "the most important conference of the century," and added that "all doubts about the Big Three's ability to cooperate in peace as well as in war now seem to have been swept away."[26] The oracular pundit Walter Lippmann, the country's leading individual voice on foreign affairs, informed his readers that "The military alliance is proving itself to be no transitory thing, good only in the presence of a common enemy, but in truth the nucleus and core of a new international order."[27]

During the war, Americans had been fed a steady diet of pro-Soviet propaganda, about both the nation and its allegedly admirable leader, "Uncle Joe"

Stalin. Not even the horrific slaughter of Polish officers, soldiers, and civilians captured by the Red Army at Katyn in the autumn of 1939, and discovered by FDR in 1944, dissuaded Roosevelt from his conviction of the necessity of making a friend of Russia.[28] The president's desire that the successful wartime partnership might be continued in peacetime was naturally an extremely popular notion.[29] A State Department survey of three hundred newspapers and sixty periodicals found a strong majority of editorial comment in favor of the Yalta accord, though it noted that the future of "free elections" in Poland would prove extremely important to maintaining that support.[30] The same *Life* article that lauded the agreement—which, like all the media comment, was based on a false understanding of its Polish provisions—also warned that unless U.S. Soviet ambassador W. Averell Harriman and his British counterpart, Archibald Clark-Kerr, "prove loyal to the trust given them at Yalta," and ensured that Poland would become "genuinely democratic and independent, as Stalin has so often promised it would be," the likely result of Yalta "will be merely that America has had a hand in killing Poland." *Life* instructed the ambassadors not to be "so fearful of offending Russia" that they "muff their assignment." Allowing for the difference in the meaning of the words "self-determination" and "democracy" between the United States and the USSR, *Life* counseled calm. "We need not be too afraid of the difference over the meaning of these words," its editors noted, "the danger is in the chance that Russia's policy . . . may change and become as totalitarian abroad as it is at home."[31]

The few dissenting voices to the initial chorus of approval began and ended in the shadows of American politics. They could be found almost exclusively within the political and cultural ghettos of East European immigrants, especially Polish Americans, and among the sorry lot of "never-say-die" isolationists.[32] The latter group, however, had lost its most eloquent champion, Senator Vandenberg, to the other side and so lacked a credible national spokesperson; the former group never had one in the first place. The Polish government-in-exile denounced the deal from London as a bitter sellout, as did the Polish American Congress, to no great effect. Members of Congress of Polish descent also wrote angry letters.[33] The response to these muffled protests was one of indifference, even from the president's opponents. The Republican *New York Herald Tribune* published a cartoon portraying a frumpy old man going over the accords with a magnifying glass. Its caption: "Just as I suspected! A misspelled word!" Its title: "The 100% or Nothing Critics." Uncle Sam looked on from above with tolerant amusement.[34]

Unfortunately, the accolades were published before anyone had the opportunity to examine seriously much of the accord, much less see its (secret) fine print. Roosevelt had carefully laid the groundwork for his propaganda campaign by inviting conservative South Carolina ex-senator James F. "Jimmy" Byrnes to the conference. Shuffled from meaningless meeting to meaningless meeting and then sent home early, before the final deals were negotiated, the garrulous, deeply vain Byrnes was deliberately kept unaware of the true nature of the tough bargains Roosevelt was making behind closed doors. Even so, Byrnes, who would soon become Harry Truman's secretary of state, was intent on trumpeting his own influence at the conference and the president's willingness to act on his advice. He made the nearly seven-thousand-mile trip back to America in just thirty-eight hours and called a press conference, attended by "every newspaper man who could crawl, walk or run," according to *Time,* "without wasting a minute." With Roosevelt's blessing, *Time* noted, Byrnes set himself up as "the official interpreter of the Crimean Charter to the U.S. people and Congress."[35] After the press conference, Byrnes had lunch and a two-hour discussion with fifteen senators, and then met with the Senate Foreign Relations Committee at the home of its chairman, Tom Connally of Texas. Byrnes also lunched with all of the Republican congressional leaders before undertaking a steady stream of briefings with individual senators, newspaper columnists, and interested parties.

In every one of these meetings, he portrayed the deal as an unambiguous victory for Roosevelt and the United States. He credited FDR with being the "chairman of the conference," who "displayed real skill, great tact, great patience and good humor" to achieve his goals. While many commentators had worried that Stalin might be likely to dominate the proceedings held on his home turf, Byrnes assured them that "the decisions reached did not reflect any domination of the meeting by the Soviet Premier. . . . And if any of the Big Three might be said to have made more impression on the results than the other two, that man was the president," a view that is not exactly borne out by the minutes he took of the meetings.[36]

Like Vice President Truman, Byrnes had almost no experience in international diplomacy. He misrepresented the nature of the accord on Poland and falsely applied this mistaken interpretation to the rest of Eastern Europe as well, telling the assemblage, "The three great powers have announced that they will act jointly to provide a provisional government" for Poland. He also repeatedly referred to a "new Polish provisional government of national unity" that would be made up of "not either the London government or the Lublin government, but a provisional government which will have representations from both of those factions and from Poles in Poland." Byrnes was assiduously questioned on this point, and his answers repeatedly relied more on hope than on the experience of the negotiations that had just taken place. For instance, according to Byrnes's own minutes, Stalin proved extremely pessimistic about any significant role for the London Poles in any future Polish government, insisting, "The main personalities of the Warsaw government don't want to have anything to do with the Polish government in London." But his meaning apparently eluded Byrnes.[37]

As Byrnes's was the only account available on the day the accord was announced, a gullible press corps gave it almost complete credence, despite its obvious inconsistencies.[38] (How could Byrnes have known what had taken place after he left? How could he be sure he had heard and seen everything of consequence at the meetings?)[39] One reason Roosevelt felt he needed to put up with the annoyance of the preening Byrnes at Yalta was the haunting precedent of Woodrow Wilson's unhappy trip to Versailles two and a half decades earlier. FDR, while sharing many of Wilson's goals for the creation of a worldwide organization to maintain world peace, viewed with contempt the haughty and ultimately counterproductive manner in which Wilson had tried to sell the concept to the public. Americans now had a fear of being "hornswaggled" at yet another international conference, as *The New York Times*'s James Reston put it, and FDR needed to lay this concern to rest.[40] As they likewise wished to avoid a repeat of the disastrous Versailles experience, many in the media and in Congress had warned Roosevelt to be forthright and honest in explaining exactly what had taken place in Crimea. The *Times* editors called for "a break from the past" and "real explanations from American sources," while Arthur Vandenberg, the Republicans' most influential voice in foreign policy, had given a publicly acclaimed speech on "the need for honest candor" from the president.[41] This was good advice, but Roosevelt had no intention of taking it.

Ask Me No More Questions

Ironically, it would be James Reston himself who, almost alone among his colleagues, managed momentarily to pierce the universal euphoria. James Barrett "Scotty" Reston was just beginning a half-century career with the *Times,* during which he would repeatedly demonstrate an uncanny ability to speak to, and for, the psyche of official Washington and its incipient political Establishment. If a president had a problem with "Scotty" Reston, he had a very large problem indeed.[42] Just after the report's initial release, Reston carefully assessed the deal's intentional ambiguities, noting, "what really interested the Capital were the things that the Big Three statement did not even mention." The most prominent of these was Japan, which, Reston pointed out, appeared nowhere in the document. The reporter also observed that the Crimean communiqué made no reference to the Polish government-in-exile in London, while it did describe the Lublin government as the "present Government" of Poland. Nevertheless, Reston explained, "the general reaction here to the section on the Big Three's communiqué dealing with Poland was one of relief that President Roosevelt had made the United States position clear."[43] Of course, it did nothing of the kind.

Reston's ability to pinpoint the agreement's chief weaknesses in one breath and ignore them in the next perfectly reflected the collective cognitive dissonance that the Yalta agreement seemed to inspire in Washington. Reston's mentor, Walter Lippmann, advised, "There can be little doubt that [the president's men] have not come back holding any important secrets that embarrass them."[44] Led by Lippmann and Reston, much of Washington embraced the accord on the basis of a hopeful ignorance, as if a peaceful future depended on a willingness to avoid asking too many uncomfortable questions.[45] *Life's* editors went so far as to predict that "former premier [Stanislaw] Mikolajczyk [leader of the Polish government-in-exile] will be invited to head the new [Polish] government. He and his peasant party are friendly to Russia. . . ."[46]

Although allowing key questions to remain both unasked and unanswered would ultimately prove fateful to Roosevelt's ambitions, and doom his hopes for the construction of a peaceful world, FDR's deceptions were remarkably effective, in a manner that would be impossible for any national politician to emulate today. The most notable of them were his evasions regarding his rapidly deteriorating health. While his inability to focus on matters of state for more than two to four hours a day had come to limit his effectiveness, the president proved so adept at masking his infirmities during the 1944 election campaign that his personal physician, Dr. Ross McIntire, confided in his diary, "It made me doubt my accuracy as a diagnostician."[47] By the time of his trip to Yalta, Roosevelt suffered from cardiological and pulmonary inconsistencies, high blood pressure, sinusitis, anemia, and bleeding hemorrhoids. The president's ashen complexion shocked and surprised many of the people he met during his arduous trip.[48] During the Yalta talks, he was threatened by an attack of *pulsus alternans,* in which strong heartbeats alternate with weak ones. The president's doctor immediately put a stop to his scheduled activities, and Roosevelt recovered.[49] While there is no evidence to indicate—or any medical reason to suspect—that FDR's sickness affected the quality of his thinking or decision making, he clearly conspired with his aides and doctors to construct an image of a man of far greater physical capacities than he, in fact, possessed.[50]

Samuel Rosenman, FDR's speechwriter, claims in his memoir *Working with Roosevelt,* published in 1952, that the president worked "extensively" on the second and third drafts of the crucial speech he would deliver to both houses of Congress during the voyage back from Yalta and later reviewed drafts with his son-in-law John Boettiger. But in an oral history interview conducted in 1968 and 1969, Rosenman told a different version of the events, expressing his frustration that, despite having made a long voyage to Algiers to meet the presidential party on its way home, he found "the President was so worn out that contrary to his usual custom he just wouldn't go to work." Moreover, even in his memoir he admits to finding FDR's speech betraying his deteriorating condition. In Rosenman's words, "It was quite obvious that the great fighting eloquence and oratory that had distinguished him in his campaign only four months before were lacking. The crushing effect of twelve years of the Presidency was beginning to be more and more evident."[51] Had he been healthy, he might have offered a more honest accounting of the Yalta agreement in his speech. But given how consistently FDR had lied in the past without any particular compunction, such speculation seems based more on hope than history.

"The Best I Can Do"

In retrospect, Roosevelt's decision to follow the path of deception has the flavor of Greek tragedy. Providence offered the president an historic opportunity to teach his fellow citizens some hard lessons about the realities of international politics. As the victorious leader of a magnificently successful wartime alliance, America's only four-term president, and a nationally beloved figure near the height of his popularity, Roosevelt was uniquely placed to disabuse Americans of some of their more romantic beliefs about the world. The ailing president chose, instead, to flatter their ignorance. Despite their long history of involvement in the global marketplace as buyers and sellers, the American people were new to the concept of diplomatic give-and-take. The country's history until then had involved a counterproductive swing between viewing foreign policy as akin to commercially profitable missionary work, and the equally implausible desire simply to withdraw from world affairs whenever the natives failed to appreciate America's plans to improve them. The buffer of two oceans, a vast expanse of land, and a dearth of powerful neighbors had combined to create habits of mind that led Americans to believe that they could construct a world system based on what they considered their own universally applicable principles, rather than on more traditional considerations of balances of power.

While Roosevelt knew that he could not escape typical diplomatic calculations in negotiations at Yalta, he was unwilling to spend the political capital necessary to explain why Americans had to accept them as well. Instead he went before a joint session of Congress after his return from Crimea and told Americans what they, in their innocence and ignorance, expected to hear. Yalta, he promised, spelled "the end of the system of unilateral action and exclusive alliances and spheres of influence and balances of power."[52] While this description fit comfortably into Americans' self-images, it had nothing to do with the hard bargaining FDR had just completed in Yalta.

Roosevelt was well aware of the weaknesses of the deal he had just signed. He knew, for instance, that he had failed to secure Poland's freedom at Yalta. But "freedom" as such was hardly Roosevelt's primary concern, nor Churchill's, for that matter. When Averell Harriman pointed out to Roosevelt that a sphere-of-influence arrangement appeared to be in the offing for the Balkans, FDR explained that his aim was "to insure against the Balkans getting us into a future international war." Harriman had noted in October 1944 that FDR had demonstrated "very little interest in eastern European matters except as they affect sentiment in America."[53] After difficult and occasionally acrimonious haggling, the final language on the arrangements for Poland's future contained no assurances for replacing Moscow's Lublin-based regime with members of the London-based Polish government-in-exile. The accord did speak of including "Poles from abroad," but given the lack of specificity, those could just as easily have implied Communist union leaders in Cleveland or Milwaukee as members of the government-in-exile. (This fact did not elude the London Poles, who bitterly denounced the accord when it became public.)[54] While the accord called for elections, it contained no means to assure their fairness, nor even any firm date by which they might be held.

Stalin did agree to sign the American "Joint Declaration for a Liberated Europe," in which the three powers announced their "determination to build in cooperation with other peace-loving nations a world order under law, dedicated to peace, security, freedom and general well-being of all mankind."[55] Practically, however, the document was almost meaningless, as, once again, it defined none of its terms. An early American draft providing for "free and unfettered elections," jointly administered, was watered down at the Soviets' request to require only "consultation" between the three powers, "looking toward" free elections at some unspecified date.[56] Instead of pledging to "immediately establish appropriate machinery for the carrying out of the joint responsibilities set forth in this declaration," the Soviets won a concession that merely obliged them to "immediately take measures for the carrying out of mutual consultation."[57] The conference record demonstrates, however, that the changes made in the American draft provoked little discussion, as it was never intended as much more than a sop to American public opinion, particularly Polish American opinion.[58] When Molotov worried that the statement was "too much," Stalin is recorded to have replied, "Never mind . . . we'll work on it . . . do it our own way later."[59] In a near mirror image of this conversation, Admiral Leahy, the president's chief of staff, apparently had complained to Roosevelt upon departing from Yalta that the agreement's language on Poland was "so elastic that the Russians can stretch it all the way from Yalta to Washington without ever technically breaking it." "I know, Bill," Roosevelt responded. "I know it. But it is the best I can do for Poland at this time."[60]

Roosevelt's willingness to make concessions to Stalin did reflect some inescapable realities. In the first place, the Red Army had liberated Poland and Eastern Europe in perhaps the most costly military victory in all human history, leaving as many as twenty-seven million dead.[61] Already tending toward paranoia on security matters on the basis of both ideology and experience—together with Stalin's own neurotic tendencies—the Soviet leaders' one nonnegotiable condition was that they be allowed to install friendly governments in the nations that stood between the USSR and Germany, with Poland being the most crucial. As they already occupied those nations anyway, little short of war—and certainly not any sentimental attachment to what they regarded as a bourgeois conception of democracy—was going to stop them.

Stalin's own view of the determining factors can be seen in a joke he told after the war: Churchill, Roosevelt, and Stalin went hunting and finally killed their bear. Churchill said, "I'll take the bearskin. Let Roosevelt and Stalin divide the meat." Roosevelt said, "No, I'll take the skin. Let Churchill and Stalin divide the meat." Stalin remained silent so Churchill and Roosevelt asked him, "Mr. Stalin, what do you say?" Stalin simply replied, "The bear belongs to me—after all, I killed it." The bear, as Simon Sebag Montefiore aptly notes, was Hitler and the bearskin was the whole of Eastern Europe.[62]

Before going to Yalta, the president had informed congressional leaders that "the Russians had the power in eastern Europe, that it was obviously impossible to have a break with them and that, therefore, the only practical course was to use what influence we had to ameliorate the situation."[63] Churchill, the U.S. State Department, and the U.S. War Department were, if anything, even more pessimistic. The British prime minister complained to his personal secretary, upon departing for Crimea, "Make no mistake, all the Balkans, except Greece, are going to be Bolshevised, and there is nothing I can do to prevent it. There is nothing I can do for poor Poland, either."[64] Perhaps a concerted plan of opposition to Soviet expansion undertaken during the war could have changed the political facts on the ground once it ended. But by now it was already too late. In a post-Yalta, off-the-record interview with American journalist Edgar Snow in the spring of 1945, Soviet foreign commissar Maxim Litvinov asked, "Why did you Americans wait till right now to begin opposing us in the Balkans and Eastern Europe? You should have done this three years ago. Now it's too late, and your complaints only arouse suspicion here."[65]

Likewise, given that the United States and Britain had not consulted Stalin during the negotiations for the Italian armistice of 1943, they could hardly have expected to be considered full partners in governing those nations that surrendered to the USSR.

In a remarkably cynical rendering of their conversation in Moscow in October 1944, Winston Churchill and Joseph Stalin, according to the former, secretly divided up Europe between them. As Churchill records in his memoirs, the two men dealt each other control of the fates of great nations according to the following formulas, which the prime minister jotted down on a piece of paper: Rumania, Russia 90%, the others 10%; Greece, Great Britain 90%, Russia 10%; Yugoslavia 50% each; Hungary 50% each; Bulgaria, Russia 75%, the others 25%. According to Churchill's recollection, which was later found to be unsupported by either the British or Soviet records, "Stalin studied the sheet for a moment and then silently penciled a large check by the figures. After a long pause, I had a second thought. 'Might not it be thought rather cynical if it seemed we had disposed of these issues, so fateful to millions of people, in such an offhand manner? Let us burn the paper.'" "No, you keep it," Stalin allegedly replied. Churchill says he added, "It was better to express these things in diplomatic terms and not to use the phrase 'dividing into spheres' because the Americans might be shocked."[66] While Churchill's recollection may not have been accurate—or even represented an honest attempt to be accurate—it is at least indicative of how little faith he placed in the grand schemes proposed by FDR, whom, on Averell Harriman's advice, he did not even bother to inform about his discussions with Stalin.[67] Churchill also proved quite pessimistic about the ability of a future United Nations Organization to keep the peace in Europe, and was well aware that he could not count on the Americans to do so, either (even though they eventually did in the context of NATO and the Cold War). Shortly after the Tehran conference in the winter of 1943, Roosevelt had insisted in a letter, "Do please don't ask me to keep any American forces in France. I just cannot do it! I would have to bring them all back home."[68]

Had Roosevelt been sincerely committed to trying to prepare his nation for the harsh realities of the postwar world, he would have taken a page from the young diplomat and Soviet scholar George Kennan. Writing from the U.S. embassy in Moscow, Kennan advised his president simply to acknowledge publicly that the Red Army had conquered half of Europe and was not about to give it up. He recommended the United States "should drop all thoughts of free elections in Poland and Eastern Europe because it would be impossible to achieve this when the Russian armies entered the area, and it would only irritate Moscow unnecessarily."[69] Indeed, the Soviets were no more likely to risk the creation of a democratic pro-American government in Poland on the basis of free elections than the United States would have been to allow a Communist, pro-Soviet one in Mexico. And given the bloody history of Central Europe, their paranoia derived from rather compelling circumstances. State Department briefing materials prepared for Roosevelt's trip to Yalta advised him to plan for a "predominant" Soviet influence in Poland and Eastern Europe.[70] This was just fine with FDR, who gave no indication of caring at all what kind of governments came into being in Eastern Europe, so long as they did not interfere with his larger plans.[71] The president clearly communicated to Stalin at their meeting in November-December 1943 that he understood Soviet security concerns as they applied throughout Eastern Europe, the Baltics, and the Balkans.[72] This suggested that whatever concern Roosevelt might be forced to demonstrate on behalf of the Polish government-in-exile would be strictly for domestic—read "Polish American"—consumption, and that Stalin need not concern himself with it.[73]

When going before Congress to deliver his speech about the accord, FDR chose to credit Stalin with concessions at Yalta that the murderous dictator had plainly never made. Expanding on the false statements and exaggerations that Byrnes had offered when he initially outlined the deal on Poland, Roosevelt explained instead that postwar "political and economic problems" would be "a joint responsibility of all three governments," who would "join together during the temporary period of instability after hostilities, to help the people . . . solve their own problems through firmly established democratic processes."[74] The president also promised that appointed interim governments in formerly Fascist nations "will be as representative as possible of all democratic elements in the population and that free elections are held as soon as possible thereafter." Turning to Poland specifically, he asserted that the goal of all three great powers had been nothing more than to create in "Poland, a strong, independent and prosperous nation with a government ultimately to be selected by the Polish people themselves."[75]

The Polish portions of his speech were hardly the only examples of FDR's deliberate mendacity. He lied outright when he insisted "this conference concerned itself only with the European war and with political problems of Europe, and not the Pacific war." In fact, FDR had negotiated a secret agreement with Stalin whereby, in exchange for a Soviet promise to invade Japan soon after the defeat of Germany, Roosevelt agreed to a return to Russia's position in the Far East prior to her defeat by Japan in 1905, including an endorsement of Soviet claims to the return of South Sakhalin (ceded by Japan to Russia in 1875 by voluntary treaty but retaken by Japan in the Russo-Japanese war); to recognition of existing Soviet hegemony in Outer Mongolia; to the lease of Port Arthur as a naval base; to the preeminence of Soviet commercial interests in Dairen, which was to be made a free port; and to joint Sino-Soviet operations of the Manchurian railways, which connect Russia with Dairen. (In addition to the reinstatement of the pre-1905 status quo, FDR agreed to support Soviet claims to the Kurile Islands, which connect northern Japan with the Soviet peninsula of Kamchatka and which, initially penetrated by both countries, had been Japanese since 1875).[76]

In his Yalta speech Roosevelt did not even bother to mention the unresolved Anglo-U.S.-Soviet dispute over the amount of Germany's reparations; or the vexing problem of just how many votes the Soviets could claim in the UN General Assembly. (The Soviets, citing the precedent of the British commonwealth, originally demanded sixteen, but settled for three.) Instead the president focused on the value of the Big Three's cooperation per se, rather than its substance. He admitted quite early to "special problems created by a few instances, such as Poland and Yugoslavia," which led each side to "argue freely and frankly across the table." Nevertheless, FDR assured his audience that "on every point, unanimous agreement was reached. And more important than agreement of words, I may say we achieved a unity of thought and a way of getting along together."

In a few of these instances, Roosevelt had perfectly defensible reasons to say less than he knew to be true. Lying about peaceful negotiations during wartime is a categorically different act than lying about warlike acts in peacetime, and far less troubling. Successful military operations often require secrecy and sometimes even deception. In the case of Yalta, the Nazis had not yet surrendered in Europe, and Japan continued to fight furiously in Asia. At the time of the accord, the USSR was still party to a treaty with Japan while its military strength was wholly concentrated in Europe. Public discussion of an agreement to invade Japan after the German surrender might have risked a Japanese preemptory first strike inside Soviet borders. Stalin had agreed to the deal, moreover, only under conditions of secrecy, which would enable him to send divisions across Siberia without alerting the enemy to his plans. "At both Yalta and Potsdam," Edward Stettinius later recalled, "the military staffs were particularly concerned with the Japanese troops in Manchuria. Described as the cream of the Japanese Army, this self-contained force, with its own autonomous command and industrial base, was believed capable of prolonging the war even after the islands of Japan had been subdued, unless Russia should enter the war and engage this army."[77] While military imperatives therefore dictated secrecy for a time vis-à-vis the Far East, they do not justify the outright lie, which was gratuitous. (Ten years later, when the Yalta papers were finally released, Senate minority leader William Knowland [R-CA] would denounce FDR for this "false official report to the legislative branch of government.")[78]

Regarding the United Nations agreement, the president's case is considerably more problematic. He did not admit that he had agreed to give Stalin extra votes in the General Assembly, perhaps because he expected to be able to convince the dictator to forgo them later, or because he planned to secure additional votes for the United States.[79] (Truman would be "completely flabbergasted" when he learned of this concession.)[80] Roosevelt and his advisers could not bring themselves to believe that Stalin would stick to so transparently foolish an arrangement in a body that was designed to be little more than a global debating society. The Americans likewise did not wish to address Stalin's argument regarding the unfairness of the six votes held by the British Commonwealth, but controlled exclusively by England, since Britain would naturally object as well.[81] And with respect to Poland and Eastern Europe, FDR's dishonesty was merely an act of political cowardice.

Roosevelt's cause in winning the appreciation of his countrymen and -women on the Yalta pact was no doubt helped by the tremendous human drama that quite obviously underlay it. The president, as was evident to anyone who saw him at close quarters, was not a well man. The demanding trip had appeared to add years to Roosevelt's sickly complexion. In his address to Congress, FDR broke with his own precedent and allowed himself to be wheeled down the aisle to reach the lectern, rather than leaning on a friend or crutches, as he made the difficult "walk" to the well of the rotunda. "I hope you will pardon me for the unusual posture of sitting down during the presentation of what I want to say," he entreated his grateful audience. "But I know that you will realize that it makes it a lot easier for me in not having legs; and also because I have just completed a fourteen-thousand-mile trip."

This confession inspired an emotional outpouring of cheers and applause from those present. As Secretary of Labor Frances Perkins, herself close to tears, recalled it, this was "the first reference he had ever made to his incapacity, to his impediment, and he did it in the most charming way. I remember choking up to realize that he was actually saying, 'You see, I'm a crippled man.' He had never said it before and it was one of the things that nobody ever said to him or even mentioned in his presence. . . . He had to bring himself to full humility to say it before Congress."[82] Until this moment, the public had had no idea that the president of the United States could stand only briefly, and walk only when helped by another person. The newsreels never captured the degree of his infirmity; the White House press corps never mentioned it. Photographers assigned to the president would go so far as to block the vision of anyone who tried to violate the unspoken rule of not portraying his condition. Even the opposition Republicans never exploited it. This was FDR's "splendid deception." And here was Roosevelt, after all this effort to conceal his disability, in effect saying to the country, "I am an old leader, tired and sick, and I have nothing left to hide from you." Given how little the speech really did reveal to the country about what had taken place at the Lividia summer palace, however, one can hardly help but marvel at FDR's near superhuman political will, doing whatever was necessary to win the confidence of his intended audience. Unfortunately the Yalta address was one deception that would not turn out to be quite so "splendid."

A Brutal Dictator Who Kept His Word

Just how did Franklin Roosevelt expect to bridge the distance between what he announced to America and what he had accepted in Crimea? History offers few clues. We know he had no illusions about how misleading his representation of the agreement he had signed had been. Defending the deal to Adolf Berle, who was about to become his ambassador to Brazil, he admitted, "I didn't say the result was good. I said it was the best I could do."[83] The president died barely six weeks after his March 1 address to Congress and he did not feel well enough to work much during the interim. The historical record, moreover, was clouded by the deliberately false impression of FDR's final days created by Winston Churchill. (Here we have an example of a deception about a deception.) In his attempts to portray Roosevelt as wishing to pursue a "get tough" policy with Stalin in the aftermath of the conference, Churchill excised those comments from their correspondence—the two corresponded repeatedly in the weeks after returning from Yalta—in which FDR advised Churchill to "minimize" any disagreements with the Soviet Union over Poland. The president also insisted, against Churchill's wishes, that the Russians not be excluded from an economic mission, as he did not want to give the impression that "we were disregarding the Yalta decision for tripartite action in liberated areas. [This] might easily be interpreted as indicating that we consider the Yalta decisions as no longer valid."[84] Churchill also contradicted himself, however, by blaming FDR's refusal to join him in an adversary stance on the president's failing health: "We can see now the deadly hiatus which existed between the failing of President Roosevelt's strength and the growth of President Truman's grip of the vast world problem. In this melancholy void, one President could not act and the other could not know."[85]

FDR also did not share Churchill's alarm with regard to the Soviet interpretation of the Crimea agreements, and he repeatedly attempted to calm the increasingly agitated prime minister. With each telegram, Churchill urged Roosevelt to assist him in influencing Moscow regarding Poland, even going so far as to pass along reports from London Poles alleging political repression under the new government.[86] According to Churchill's interpretation, the Soviets were not adhering to the agreed-upon composition of the Polish government.[87] Churchill telegrammed Roosevelt with a proposed letter for Stalin voicing their disapproval of the developments in Poland.[88] But the president refused to join in the protest.[89] As he wrote to Churchill, "I can assure you that our objectives are identical . . . The only difference is one of tactics."[90] Despite his repeated assurances that the American interpretation of the Yalta accords was in sync with Britain's, in a letter written thirteen days before his death, FDR cautioned Churchill against any "attempt to evade the fact that we placed, as clearly shown in the agreement, somewhat more emphasis on the Lublin Poles than on the other two groups from which the new government is to be drawn," lest the two leaders "expose [them]selves to the charge that we are attempting to go back on the Crimea decision." This would be his final communication on the subject.[91]

Churchill himself had returned from Yalta spouting promises of a new era of the brotherhood of man. As he told the House of Commons, "The impression I brought back from the Crimea, and from all my other contacts, is that Marshal Stalin and the Soviet leaders wish to live in honourable friendship and equality with the Western democracies." He was equally optimistic in private. "Poor Neville Chamberlain believed he could trust Hitler," he mused. "He was wrong. But I don't think I'm wrong about Stalin."[92]

As the situation in Eastern Europe began to sour, however, Churchill changed his opinion, adopting for public consumption the position that he had been deceived at Yalta. Still, he did nothing to endanger the trade-offs he had negotiated on Britain's behalf that were the quid pro quo of the Polish deal. For instance, he instructed Anthony Eden on March 5 not to challenge Russian actions in Romania lest it have the effect of "compromising our position in Poland and jarring Russian acquiescence in our long fight in Athens." On the 12th he ordered Eden to hold back again "for considerations well known to you [i.e., Greece], accepted in a special degree the predominance of Russia in this theater [Romania]."[93] Relations were further strained by Stalin's anger over the Anglo-American decision to exclude the Soviets from the surrender negotiations regarding German forces in northern Italy, then under way in Berne, Switzerland, which he deemed to be contrary to the principles of unconditional surrender.[94]

During the same period, Roosevelt intimates had grown accustomed to outbursts by the dying president expressing private frustration with Stalin's post-Yalta behavior, including one accusing Stalin of breaking "every one of the promises he made at Yalta."[95] This gave Averell Harriman and others fuel to argue that FDR was preparing to enlist in the Cold War struggle that such observers generally regarded as imminent.[96] Perhaps it was, but in terms of the policy decisions Roosevelt actually reached, along with any explicit entreaties to his most important ally, Winston Churchill, there is precious little hard evidence to support this claim. The point is crucial, for while there were many good reasons for the existence of the Cold War—including the incompatibility of American and Soviet social and economic systems, Stalin's paranoia and the murderous policies it spawned, Russia's historically expansionist tendencies coupled with those same tendencies in the brutal Soviet form of Marxism-Leninism, America's new global definition of its national security needs, and both sides' missionary ideologies—it did not have an infinite number of specific causes. The most convincing explanation for why a wartime alliance turned ugly in the immediate postwar period was the American decision to walk away from the Yalta accords, even as it blamed the Soviets for doing the same. Despite the failure of the West to secure better terms for the Poles at Yalta, both the American representative in Moscow, Averell Harriman, and Britain's Archibald Clark-Kerr did try repeatedly in the aftermath of the meeting to pressure Stalin to agree to the creation of a new Polish government that included the leadership in London.[97] Since Yalta called only for the "Provisional Government which is now functioning in Poland [to] be reorganized on a broader democratic basis with the inclusion of democratic leaders from Poland itself and from Poles abroad"—and made no mention either of a reconstituted government or of the London Poles—Stalin correctly charged that the American position was "tantamount to direct violation of the Crimean Conference decisions."[98] The dictator certainly had little reason to offer the very concession to the two ambassadors that he had been unwilling to grant to Churchill and Roosevelt, at a time when he could have demanded something in return. An unbreakable deadlock immediately ensued; Poland's fate was sealed, and East-West relations began their half-century spiral downward.

To argue that it was the United States (and Britain), rather than the USSR, that betrayed its signature on the Yalta accords is not to excuse Soviet policies in Eastern Europe, for Stalin consolidated the gains he had won in Poland with savage efficiency. Nor is it to suggest that resistance to Stalinist tyranny was unnecessary or undeserved. By the time FDR returned to address Congress about the future of peace and freedom, the Lublin Poles were already at work arresting or liquidating their opponents, assisted by the Soviet NKVD.[99] Some form of struggle—whether physical, political, cultural, or psychological—was called for to defend what democracy remained in Europe and to prevent totalitarianism from gaining the upper hand. One can convincingly make the case that had the Cold War not been catalyzed by American dishonesty and forgetfulness about Yalta, it would almost certainly have happened anyway. That is a counterfactual argument that extends well beyond the scope of this study. For purposes of the discussion, the Cold War took place when it did and the way it did at least partially in response to America's refusal to keep its word given at Yalta.

But while Stalin may be history's most bloodthirsty mass murderer, we cannot make the logical leap that he therefore also had no intention of honoring the Yalta accords or remaining on reasonably amicable terms with the United States, if only for purely pragmatic reasons. Paradoxical though it may appear, Stalin could have (for "bizarre, Byzantine" reasons, as Isaac Deutscher puts it) remained "legalistically scrupulous . . . in his bargains with his bourgeois allies."[100] As Arnold Offner writes in his magisterial history of the era, "To be sure, Stalin was a brutal dictator who directed a murderous regime. But there is no evidence that he intended to march his Red Army westward beyond its agreed-upon European occupation zones, and he put Soviet state interests ahead of desire to spread Communist ideology. He was also prepared to deal practically with the U.S., whose military and economic power he respected."[101] While the Western leaders operated on a far higher moral plane in their deeds than the Soviet dictator, they proved considerably less meticulous in keeping their word as given at Yalta, and considerably less savvy about the motivations and machinations of their adversary. Once President Truman got it into his mind that the Soviets were bent on "world conquest," for instance, virtually every action taken by the Russians was attributed to this desire and this desire alone.[102]

Death Intervenes

Franklin Roosevelt may well have believed that he could navigate these jagged shores, prevailing upon Stalin to loosen his grip a bit on Poland while gradually swaying U.S. domestic opinion into accepting de facto Soviet political control in much of Eastern Europe. FDR was hardly naive about Stalin's intentions for Poland and Eastern Europe, but like most of his advisers, he believed that peace in the postwar world depended on the ability of the four great powers—the United States, the USSR, Great Britain, and China—to work together under the umbrella of the United Nations to keep order within their respective spheres of influence. In fact, Roosevelt's concept of a postwar world governed by a condominium of four policemen, restraining not only German and Japanese militarism but Soviet expansionism and British and French imperialism, was never well defined, much less pragmatically scrutinized. As Warren F. Kimball has observed, "His concept was vague, ill defined, and full of distinctions so subtle (or ignored) that even his closest advisers were uncertain about how it would work."[103] Eleanor Roosevelt thought the idea to be "fraught with danger," and here, she proved prophetic.[104]

History does not provide answers to hypothetical questions, but new evidence from the bowels of the Kremlin indicates that Stalin, for all his homicidal cruelty and demented paranoia, was primarily, in the words of Russian historians Vladislav Zubok and Constantine Pleshakov, "a hard-nosed realist" when it came to diplomacy.[105] He was certainly not averse to expanding his rule and that of the Soviet system as far and wide as prudence would allow. "Notwithstanding his reputation as a ruthless tyrant," they write, Stalin "was not prepared to take a course of unbridled unilateral expansionism after World War II. He wanted to avoid confrontation with the West. He was even ready to see cooperation with the Western powers as a preferable way of building his influence and solving continuous international issues. Thus, the Cold War was not his choice or his brain-child."[106] These two historians see Stalin's postwar foreign policy as more defensive, reactive, and prudent than it was the fulfillment of a master plan.[107] While Soviet influence resulted in the destruction of traditional societies and the imposition of the Soviet police-state model on those nations against the wills of their respective populaces, Norman Naimark argues on the basis of the East German experience that Stalin and the Russians "Bolshevised the zone not because there was a plan to do so, but because that was the only way they knew how to organize society."[108]

This putative desire for a moderated, relatively peaceful competition with the West does in fact hold up to scrutiny in virtually every area of the world beyond those nations imprisoned inside the Soviet empire. Stalin's reply to Churchill, Albert Resis notes, during their so-called percentage discussions in Moscow in October 1944, provides "astounding evidence of how far Stalin was willing to go, verbally, at least, in sacrificing the interests of revolutionary Communist parties abroad for the sake of Big Three unity," though he complained of his inability to influence the Italian Communists who were prepared "to tell Stalin to go to the Devil" and "to mind his own business."[109] In November of that year, Stalin gave voice to the belief that the bases of the Alliance were not "accidental or transitory motives, but vitally important and long-lasting interests," above all, "preventing new aggression or a new war, if not forever, then at least for an extended period of time."[110]

In 1945, the Russian historian Leonid Gibiansky has shown, Stalin was still extremely keen on retaining the benefits of a U.S.-Soviet power condominium and consolidating the Soviet Union's military and diplomatic gains. The post–Cold War opening of Soviet archives has revealed memoranda prepared for Stalin during the war by his key foreign policy advisers that appear to presuppose continued cooperation with the West on matters related to Germany and Japan and the maintenance of informal spheres of influence.[111] Indeed, even Norman Naimark, whose research into the brutal Soviet treatment of the German population has influenced so many historians of the Cold War, nevertheless concludes that despite all the Soviets' contradictory impulses there, their main goals prior to 1947 were "geostrategic and economic." They desired "a German government that would not threaten Soviet Security. To these ends, the Soviets were willing to sacrifice the interests of the German communists and promote those of the 'bourgeois' parties."[112] David Holloway, in his much-admired history of the Soviet atomic bomb project, defined Stalin's aims in this period as the need "to consolidate Soviet territorial gains, establish a Soviet sphere of influence in Eastern Europe, and have a voice in the political fate of Germany—and if possible—of Japan."[113] In Asia, according to the documents unearthed by scholars Goncharov, Lewis, and Xue, Stalin's aim was to form "an alliance with China to curb Japan," though newly discovered evidence suggests that Stalin may have taken a larger role in providing military aid to Mao and the Chinese Communists than was previously understood.[114] Kathryn Weathersby makes a similar case based on new evidence for Stalin's ambitions regarding Korea.[115]

The Soviets, Molotov once explained, had "full confidence" in Roosevelt's sincerity and commitment to cooperation in working out differences.[116] But they jettisoned the notion of cooperation once they came to believe that the Americans were no longer interested.[117] Perhaps Stalin and Roosevelt's working relationship might have resulted in a stable, if competitive, world system divided between the free and unfree. Such a world might have avoided the murderous proxy wars between the two sides in Asia, Africa, and Latin America, which killed millions of people; the costly and dangerous nuclear arms race; and all the abuses of civil liberties and political paranoia in U.S. domestic politics that the Cold War inspired. Truman himself later speculated, "If Roosevelt had been in a position of good health, he probably could have gone further than anyone else. . . . He had this appeal to world opinion that no one else had." But Truman also concluded that he did not "think anyone could have got the Russians to stand by their agreements" because, in his view, "it was the domestic proposition in Russia that [Stalin] had to get on top of to keep the military from taking over. . . . Everything in Russia is a conspiracy."[118] As some have suggested, however, without the Cold War we might have experienced a far less safe and stable world, with problems like those of Bosnia, Serbia, and Croatia metastasizing and spreading over a fifty-year period.[119] Domestically, FDR's combination of luck and political skill had proven so effective during the previous twelve years that he might well have succeeded in deflecting the revelations that he deliberately misled the nation about Yalta. But in dying at such a critical moment after the conference, the wily Roosevelt finally outsmarted himself. Failing to prepare either his appointed successor or the nation he led for what followed is among the blackest marks on a great man's legacy.[120]

In Harry S. Truman, Roosevelt could hardly have chosen a successor less adept at managing the conflicting currents and diplomatic ambiguity with Stalin and the Soviet Union. To most who knew him, Truman was a plain-speaking, uncomplicated man who believed first and foremost in clarity. Temperamentally, he was FDR's polar opposite and preferred making one decision and then moving on to the next problem, often regardless of whether he had sufficient information to make an informed judgment or even if the decision in question might more profitably have been postponed. In as near an un-Rooseveltian manner as can be imagined, following a full two days' negotiating at Potsdam, Truman grumbled, "I was beginning to grow impatient for more action and fewer words."[121] This decisiveness initially thrilled some of FDR's old advisers, who had grown frustrated with the late president's desire to retain all available options at all times. "A complete and definite contrast to FDR," the former U.S. ambassador to the Soviet Union, Joseph Davies, observed. Undersecretary of State Joseph Grew wrote to a friend in early May, "When I saw him today I had fourteen problems to take up with him and I got through them in less than fifteen minutes with a clear directive on every one of them. You can imagine what a joy it is. . . ."[122] Davies, who argued consistently and unsuccessfully for a policy of cooperation with the USSR, would eventually discover the advantages of Roosevelt's more considered manner once the Cold War began in earnest.[123]

A failure in business, Truman owed his political career to the fact that, as a forty-year-old army captain in World War I, he had impressed his fellow soldiers, one of whom happened to be the son of Kansas City political boss Tom Pendergast. The machine ran Truman for the county board, where he demonstrated an impressive flair for successful administration and road building, which eventually landed him in the U.S. Senate. When the party elders objected to FDR's renaming the philo-Soviet Henry Wallace to another term as vice president, the still unknown Truman was named as a compromise candidate who offended none and inspired few. His best-known statement on the crisis in Europe upon receiving the nomination, prior to American entry into the war, was "If we see that Germany is winning we ought to help Russia and if Russia is winning we ought to help Germany and that way kill as many as possible."[124]

The former haberdasher tended to view world politics through the lens of his own small-town machine experience. "If you understand Jackson County," he once explained, "you understand the world."[125] The Soviets, according to Truman, were "like people from across the tracks whose manners were very bad."[126] And Joseph Stalin was "as near Tom Pendergast as any man [Truman] knew."[127] During the constant conflict over Poland, Truman vacillated between viewing Stalin as "a fine man who wanted to do the right thing" and as a minor-league politician who did not understand the basic rules about buying off one's opposition. Why didn't "Uncle Joe" make "some sort of gesture—whether he means or not to keep it?" Truman once asked his diary. "Any smart political boss will do that."[128]

Not surprisingly, Harry Truman was completely at sea in attempting to understand what FDR thought he had achieved at Yalta. He had not been informed of FDR's whereabouts while the conference was taking place. At this point in time, Truman barely knew the president and had only been introduced to the secretary of state. Neither FDR nor any of his top advisers had made the slightest effort to keep Truman up-to-date about the status of the secret talks and the strategy that underlay them. Shortly after becoming president, Truman admitted to being unclear about the provisions of Yalta, especially those regarding Poland, finding new meanings in it every time he read the accord.[129] "They didn't tell me anything about what was going on," he complained to Henry Wallace. And he lamented to Treasury Secretary Henry Morgenthau Jr., "Everyone around here that should know something about foreign affairs is out."[130] Truman was therefore wholly dependent on his staff to explain the text's confusing implications. Yet because of Roosevelt's obsessive secrecy and his willingness to allow advisers and the public alike to believe what they wished about his policies, however contradictory their own interpretations, no one could clear up Truman's confusion. In fact, none of FDR's advisers knew very much, and most of what they thought they did know was wrong.

The Envoy

FDR's top advisers were already divided about the Soviets when the deeply unprepared and impressionable new president assumed office in mid-April 1945. Soviet ambassador W. Averell Harriman was fighting a furious battle to head off what he termed a "20th century barbarian invasion of Europe."[131] The son of legendary robber baron Edward H. Harriman, he had inherited Union Pacific from his father and was unaccustomed to any treatment that did not accord him what he considered his proper worth. During his time in Moscow as ambassador, he had grown virulently anti-Soviet, in part over his frustrations in dealing with Stalin and in part over the injuries done to his own considerable ego. Harriman's pride in his own judgment often tended toward the excessive. John J. McCloy later commented that "Most of the people who worked with Averell on Wall Street felt he did not pull his weight."[132]

Between 1943 and 1944, Harriman had labored to placate the Soviets by trying to convince the London Poles to concede to the Russians on essential questions of political organization and security. He considered the Polish government-in-exile to be "predominantly a group of aristocrats, looking to the American and the British to restore their position and landed properties and the feudalistic system," and made it clear to American reporters in Moscow that any solution to the problem of Poland must be judged first by the standards of "vital United States interests" and only secondarily as to what might be "fair and equitable to the Polish people." He added that he made a distinction "between the Government in London and the Polish people as such."[133] In March 1944 he also repeatedly reassured Stalin that the United States "did not want to interfere in the internal affairs of the Polish people but believe[d] that they could be brought around to take the proper action." Poland, he insisted, was a problem from the American perspective, owing largely to "public opinion in the United States on the Polish question."[134] It was a tribute to Harriman's ability to argue contradictory points simultaneously to different audiences that Stalin, Molotov, and Khrushchev considered him to be an advocate of friendly relations between the United States and the USSR, long after he had done his utmost to poison them.[135]

This myopia would continue to be a consistent theme of U.S. relations with the Soviet Union during the entire period in which Harriman sought to help guide their ultimate direction. To offer just one instance, Stalin received Harriman at his Black Sea vacation home in Gagra in the autumn of 1945 during a particularly tense period of negotiation regarding the Far East, and announced that the Soviets would simply step aside and let the United States have its way in Japan. The Soviet Union "would not interfere," he told Harriman. While the isolationists had long been in power in the United States, Stalin himself had never followed a policy of isolation but "perhaps now the Soviet Union would adopt such a policy. Perhaps, in fact, there was nothing wrong with it." Harriman wrote in his memoir that he understood Stalin to be considering not "isolation in the classical American" pattern, but instead "a policy of unilateral action" in Eastern Europe toward those nations on or near its borders.[136] Yet as Walter LaFeber and many historians have conclusively demonstrated, America's "isolationist" policies were themselves extremely "unilateralist" when it came to enforcing a policy of friendly borders, regardless of any alleged concerns regarding democracy or human rights.[137]

That even so sophisticated an observer as Harriman was unable to grasp this elementary principle would bode extremely ill for the hopes of any post-Roosevelt U.S.-Soviet understanding.

Harriman would later rewrite his own personal history, iincluding gliding over some incidents and recasting others to give the impression that he had always been the hard-liner on Poland that he later became. He also sought to bring the dying FDR's views into line with his own. By the time of the president's fatal embolism, according to Harriman, FDR had reversed himself almost 180 degrees. FDR had become convinced that "the Russians needed us more than we needed them," and hence would back down on all substantial matters if only the United States refused to compromise.[138] As we have seen, this was largely, if not entirely, wishful thinking on Harriman's part. In fact, the ambassador had worked furiously in Moscow during the final moments of FDR's life to try to rewrite FDR's communications to Stalin, because he feared they were overly conciliatory as offered.[139] While Roosevelt was a stubborn man and a wartime leader who did not much care what the wealthy aristocrat Harriman thought about anything—a product of the American aristocracy himself, FDR was unlikely to be awed by another man's wealth or personal power—in Harry Truman, the ambassador found a far more willing pupil.

The crucial meeting of the opening of the Cold War may have come during the new president's second week in office. Among the attendees were War Secretary Henry Stimson, General George Marshall, and Admiral Leahy, who all agreed that the Soviets had done next to nothing to justify a break with the Yalta accords. The opinions of Stimson—a crusty old World War I veteran, former secretary of war under William Howard Taft, secretary of state under Herbert Hoover, secretary of war again under FDR, and founder, by acclimation, of the U.S. foreign policy establishment—carried perhaps as much credibility on matters of war and peace as those of any American alive. In a postpresidential interview, Truman later called him "the best man in the Cabinet."[140] The "Colonel" was privately offended by those Americans whom he found "anxious to hang on to exaggerated views of the Monroe Doctrine and at the same time bite into every question that comes up in Central Europe."[141] He blamed the nation's emphasis on what he termed "idealism" and "altruism" rather than on the "stark realities" of the postwar world for the new tension in U.S.-Soviet relations. Overall, he thought the Soviets "had often been better than their promise" on military matters, and considered Poland an extremely unwise test case, warning the president against "heading into very dangerous water . . . without understanding how seriously the Russians took this Polish question." He added that "the Russians perhaps were being more realistic than we were in regard to their own security."[142] Despite his best efforts to make the case, he observed to his diary, he found the president to be "evidently disappointed at [his] caution."[143] Leahy, a staunch anti-Communist who considered the Yalta accords to be a disaster that failed to secure a free government in Poland, nevertheless tried to explain to Truman that they were "susceptible to two interpretations" and, though unfamiliar with the Polish situation, he concurred with Stimson.[144]

These were military men, and as such they were primarily concerned about continued Soviet participation in the war against Germany and what looked to be the forthcoming invasion of Japan. Leahy recorded, however, that while the group did not reach any "consensus of opinion," it was shifting toward confrontation. It was the civilians at the meeting, including Secretary of State Edward R. Stettinius, Navy Secretary James Forrestal, and Harriman, who had flown in from Moscow to try to influence Truman, who were all proponents of a fight, even, as Leahy noted, "if Russia should slow down or stop its war effort in Europe and Asia."[145]

Harriman's role in the secret talks at Yalta, including even the Far Eastern agreements, gave his personal interpretation of events particular force, for no one was better placed to clear up Truman's confusion about what had actually happened there. Instead, Harriman worked to confuse the neophyte leader even further. He explained to the president, "Frankly, one of the reasons that made me rush back to Washington was the fear that you did not understand, as I had seen Roosevelt understand, that Stalin is breaking his agreements."[146] In fact, Harriman had seen no such thing, which explains why he had begun planning his trip even before FDR died. The telegram traffic between Churchill and FDR shows Churchill consistently trying to convince FDR to join him in protests, including a possible all-out breach with Stalin over the issue of Poland, and the American president counseling in return, right up until the day before he died, to try to "minimize the general Soviet problem as much as possible because these problems, in one form or another, seem to arise every day and most of them straighten out." He also asked Churchill to clear all public statements with him beforehand so as not to cause a misunderstanding.[147] These telegrams were later collected for Truman, who became curious about the conflicting advice he was receiving, but this did not take place until the end of May.[148] During the meeting in question, he returned angrily and repeatedly to the issue of Yalta, insisting, "Our agreements with the Soviet Union so far had been a one-way street. If the Russians did not wish to join us they could go to hell."[149]

Whether it was this meeting that convinced him or, as some suggest, he had already made up his mind, when Soviet foreign minister Molotov arrived at the White House later the same day, Truman greeted him like a man trying to pick a fight in a bar—or at least he said he did.[150] His actual behavior that day is shrouded in braggadocio and is described differently in the several versions of the story told later. Truman probably warned Molotov that the United States would demand that "the Soviet government carry out the Crimea decision on Poland." He also handed him a memorandum that equated fulfillment of the Yalta decisions with establishment of a "new" government in Poland.[151] In Truman's ghosted recollection, a shocked Molotov responded, "I have never been talked to like that in my life." The president then has himself retorting, "Carry out your agreements, and you won't get talked to like that."[152] But according to both Charles Bohlen and Andrei Gromyko, who were also present, Truman merely ended the meeting by announcing, "That will be all, Mr. Molotov. I would appreciate it if you would transmit my views to Marshal Stalin."[153] The president later bragged, "I let him have it. It was the straight one-two to the jaw."[154] But the same night, Stimson confided to his diary that he felt "very sorry for the President because he is new on his job and he has been brought into a situation which ought not to have been allowed to come this way. I think the meeting at Yalta was primarily responsible for it."[155]

The intellectually acrobatic Averell Harriman later criticized Truman for overreacting to the very advice that he himself had proffered, identifying this meeting as the precise moment the Cold War began.[156] If that was so, responsibility belongs clearly on American shoulders, with Harriman himself carrying the heaviest load of all.[157] Acting on Harriman's false rendering of the Yalta negotiations given by the ambassador at a meeting on April 20, in which he explained that "Stalin had discovered that an honest execution of the Crimean decision would mean the end of the Soviet-backed Lublin control over Poland," the nervous and inexperienced Truman deliberately threatened and insulted the Soviet foreign minister, and accused his government of acting in bad faith.[158] No doubt Truman, ignorant of what had really taken place, believed Harriman's account to be true. (Molotov, aware of Stalin's likely reaction to the insult, transmitted only Truman's message, faithfully and without theatrics. But many years later, he offered his opinion that Truman was "a bit half-witted. . . . Far behind Roosevelt in intellect.")[159] The president's mid-1950s desire to sensationalize his rudeness to Molotov provides a prototype for the macho swagger that would come to characterize official American pronouncements on the Cold War. One 1995 Truman biographer conflated those sharing Truman's questionable memory to "Everyone there."[160] That so many historians have eagerly repeated Truman's version without any caveats is also quite revealing and disturbing.[161]

Harriman, meanwhile, decided to put off returning to Moscow in order to do what he could to further sabotage U.S.-Soviet relations at home. Immediately after the Truman-Molotov meeting, he flew to San Francisco, where the UN negotiations were taking place. There, he informed the U.S. delegation that the Russians were working by "chisel, by bluff, pressure and other unscrupulous methods" to subvert the Yalta accords, and pronounced the two sides' differences irreconcilable.[162] Walter Lippmann walked out of a Harriman briefing, so horrified was he by its belligerent tone. I. F. Stone, writing in *The Nation,* wondered "if the main business of the United Nations conference on International Organization is not to condition the American people psychologically for war with the Soviet Union."[163] Nevertheless, most journalists were happy to swallow the Harriman line, together with its proverbial hook and sinker. *Newsweek*'s Ernest K. Lindley wrote that Moscow was "treading on the waters of bad faith. . . . The Yalta agreements had hardly been proclaimed," Lindley insisted, "before the Russians began to back away from them," and added that this had been "entirely plain to Roosevelt before he died." Harriman's memoir, coauthored with Elie Abel, would brag with some justice of having convinced various scribes to publish "Harriman's warnings under their own signatures."[164]

Poland Is Lost, Again

After Harriman finally returned to Moscow, Truman came to rely most heavily on James Byrnes to explain Yalta to him, a move that caused considerable consternation within the government. "Mr. Byrnes," Dean Acheson observed, "is not sensitive or lacking in confidence."[165] But he soon installed himself—with the nervous new president's blessings—as a kind of "assistant president," an older brother figure more schooled in the ways of high politics than Truman, and more confident in his own knowledge than he had any right to be.[166]

As Truman told John Olin, a former Senate colleague from South Carolina, he intended to choose Byrnes to be secretary of state because "it's the only way I can be sure of knowing what went on at Yalta."[167] But as we have seen, Byrnes, while relatively more honest than Harriman, knew far less about what had really taken place in Crimea than he pretended. In his innocent ignorance, he misled his close friend Truman just as he had misled Congress and the press upon his return from Crimea.[168] Curiously, Byrnes seemed, at least at one level, to be fully cognizant of some of the problems raised by even his rose-colored view of the proceedings he had witnessed at Yalta, but he acted on none of those concerns. When he sent his "minutes" of the conference to Truman shortly after FDR's death, Byrnes felt compelled to add a warning: "When you read this you will immediately see reasons why it should be kept under lock and key. Should it fall into the hands of anyone close to the columnists, it could start a war on several fronts."[169] Even so, Byrnes's notes could only explain the extremely limited number of discussions he both attended and understood. The strange confluence of events that led Byrnes to assume the role of secretary of state proved to be yet more bitter fruit of FDR's deception.

A graph of the history of U.S.-Soviet relations would look like a steep mountain, with its summit representing the February 10 formal dinner at Yalta. Between February and April, the mountain would lose a bit in altitude, but remain high. Following the April 23 Truman-Molotov meeting, the graph would chart a sharp slope downward, which would continue to decline with only the slightest interruption until the Cold War became the only way to imagine superpower relations.

Even allowing for some misunderstanding and ambiguity on the American side regarding Poland, it was the United States who undertook the first indisputable repudiation of the Yalta agreement. FDR and Stalin had agreed there that only countries that had declared war on Nazi Germany by March 1 would be admitted to the General Assembly. But once the UN talks got under way in San Francisco, the United States went back on its word and voted to seat Argentina, which had failed to meet that rather generous deadline.[170]

Next, on May 3, the pro-Soviet Polish government arrested sixteen prominent anti-Communist Poles under trumped-up charges. As the efforts against Germany and Japan became increasingly successful, American leaders grew less interested in compromise and the Soviets angrier and more defensive about what they perceived to be the Americans' refusal to honor what for them was the most crucial aspect of the postwar arrangements.[171] The administration then somehow lost the Soviet request for $6 billion in reconstruction credits. Whether its claim was true or not, the Russians could hardly be expected to believe it. Immediately following Germany's May 5 surrender, Truman abruptly canceled the British and Soviet lend-lease policy, turning boats around in the water. The president claimed to be complying with the letter of congressional law, but to the starving Soviets it proved a "brutal" signal ending wartime cooperation.[172] Four days later, Harriman sent a memo to the president suggesting that "the Yalta agreements be re-examined in light of Soviet violations."[173] In preparation for the July meeting at Potsdam, a follow-up to Yalta, Truman's official State Department briefing suggested that the president ignore the "normal construction" of the Far Eastern protocol. Instead, it advised, "either singly or in conjunction with Great Britain," U.S. negotiators should attempt to rewrite the accord in its favor. It also urged Truman to obtain Soviet commitments on a number of issues of U.S. concern before the United States agreed to fulfill the promises that Roosevelt had made at Yalta.[174] When the Soviets surprised the Americans by agreeing to scale back the gains that had been offered to them in the deal, Truman and Byrnes responded by attempting to overturn the protocol entirely.[175] American attitudes at Potsdam were undoubtedly affected by the news of a successful test of the atom bomb in the New Mexico desert just days earlier. With the American team wearing the weapon "rather ostentatiously on our hip," in Stimson's words, Truman was now working to forestall the Soviet invasion of Japan, which Roosevelt and Harriman had conceded so much to guarantee.[176] Harriman, no doubt encouraged by his success thus far, even suggested to Truman that the United States use alleged Soviet violations of Yalta to scrap the deal entirely.[177] Byrnes had come to the view that "somebody made an awful mistake in bringing about a situation where Russia was permitted to come out of a war with the power she will have."[178] (That fall, Stimson found Byrnes "very much against any attempt to cooperate with Russia" and looking "to having the presence of the bomb in his pocket, so to speak, as a great weapon to get through.")[179]

Truman concurred entirely. Fortified by the Bomb and urged on by Harriman and Byrnes, he set about to reverse the "awful situation,"[180] unconcerned with the ramifications for the future of the U.S.-Soviet relationship. As he explained to the officers' mess aboard the USS *Augusta* on his way home from Potsdam, "the United States had now developed an entirely new weapon of such force and nature that we did not need the Russians—or any other nation."[181]

At Potsdam, which took place from July 17 to August 2, 1945, Truman, Stalin, and Clement Atlee, whose Labour Party had defeated Churchill's Tories, followed up on the issues left unfinished at Yalta, including the governance of Germany and the settlement of territorial disputes in Eastern Europe (particularly Poland) and they issued their ultimatum to Japan. Among the most controversial decisions, taken over Truman's objections, was to transfer former German territory east of the Oder and Neisse rivers to Polish and Soviet administration, coupled with the expulsion of the German populations of these areas, pending a final peace treaty. Stalin's demand for reparations, meanwhile, was finessed into permission to strip the Russian zone of Germany of all of its useful capital equipment and other resources.

Stalin Is Confused

The Soviets had initially hewed quite closely to the letter—if not necessarily the spirit—of Yalta. Despite the clear American violations, Stalin kept his own word as it was recorded on the agreements he had signed. He also stuck meticulously to the cynical October 1944 deal he had made with Churchill, as the Soviets did not interfere with Churchill's repression of the Greek Communists, nor push their military advantage when confronted in Iran. They stayed out of Finland entirely and even withdrew Bulgarian troops from Thrace and Macedonia. Soviet-sponsored elections in Hungary impressed one U.S. reporter as fairer than those in New York City, even though the Communists performed pitifully. But when the Soviets forced the Romanian government to remake itself and enter into a bilateral trade agreement, the Americans could not abide it. Nor would Truman recognize the Kremlin's provisional government in Bulgaria. Regarding Poland, the Soviets had offered FDR a deal in early April in which approximately 80 percent of the cabinet posts of a newly formed Polish government would go to members of the Lublin Committee, with the rest being distributed to the London Poles, an offer that went beyond what was demanded by the terms of the Yalta accord. The United States, meanwhile, backed off from its provisional agreement on German reparations to the USSR. Although he admitted "morally [Germany] should have been made to pay," Truman decided that "America was not interested in reparations for anybody." The president had therefore refused Soviet requests to hold a meeting of the Reparations Commission agreed upon at Yalta, until the United States was finally able to alter the agreements at Potsdam. The Soviets accepted even this. Nevertheless, the Americans were soon violating even the new agreement. By now the terms of the ultimate deal had become so confused that neither side really understood them, and, hence, each felt free to violate them at will as it simultaneously accused the other side of doing so.[182]

The Soviets never understood why the Americans were so eager to throw away the entire Yalta framework upon which Roosevelt, Stalin, and Churchill had worked so laboriously on, all over a disagreement about the fate of Poland. "Why can't the president leave Poland to us?" Stalin asked Harriman. "Doesn't he realize that this is the invasion route through which Western Europe has always invaded Russia? Why doesn't he realize that we must have a friendly neighbor?" Harriman explained that, "with all the Polish votes there were in the United States, no American president could ever survive."[183] Even this reasonable-sounding excuse was entirely false. True, the president of the Polish-American Congress, Charles Rozmarek, had declared himself a Republican, but took few of his compatriots with him. And the dependably right-wing *Chicago Tribune* insisted during the 1946 elections that to vote for the party of FDR and Truman would only be "an encouragement to continue the policies of loot, starvation, and exile" toward "the people of Poland, Hungary, Czechoslovakia, Yugoslavia and the Baltic States."[184] But precious few U.S.

elections, even in such heavily ethnic districts, turn on foreign policy issues. In fact, Polish Americans were still among the most loyal members of FDR's New Deal coalition. Perhaps as many as three Midwestern Democratic congressmen lost elections in 1946 for reasons that might be attributable to Yalta, although in at least two of these cases, internal party divisions offer a more convincing explanation.[185] Moreover, while the Poles were undoubtedly unhappy about the turn of events in their nation following Yalta, and did truly yearn for a democratic alternative, Western support for the government-in-exile may also have been misplaced. In May of 1945, Acting Secretary of State Joseph E. Grew informed President Truman that based on "many first hand reports . . . there is not much enthusiasm for the present London Government."[186]

Privately, U.S. leaders ceased even to pretend to live up to Yalta. When Truman sent Harry Hopkins to Moscow at the end of May to talk to Stalin, the Soviet leader complained that the U.S. attitude toward the Russians had "perceptibly cooled once it became obvious that Germany was defeated." The Americans seemed to be behaving as if the Soviets were "no longer needed."[187] The old Roosevelt hand did not try to justify his government's Polish position on its merits, but instead pleaded indulgence based on the need to appease American public opinion.[188] Stalin would not allow himself, he said, to "use Soviet public opinion as a screen," but spoke only of the anger and confusion "in Soviet government circles as a result of recent moves on the part of the United States government."[189]

While Stalin was obviously operating on the basis of a false equation between the relative influence of public opinion in a democracy and a brutal dictatorship, the distinction between Soviet dictatorship and U.S. democracy has been used as a false crutch by those who seek to exonerate the Americans for their role in the eventual collapse of the Yalta understandings. In his extremely influential 1972 history of the Cold War, John Lewis Gaddis chose as the primary cause of the breakdown Stalin's unwillingness to employ the diplomatic flexibility that is the prerogative of antidemocratic regimes. His argument rested on the fact that while democratic politicians must pay a price for defying public opinion, dictators do not and are therefore freer to make difficult concessions.[190] In fact, President Truman defied public opinion frequently at crucial junctures in the early Cold War, at no apparent cost whatever in political support. Most Americans were hardly even aware of what actions he was taking, so uninterested were they in foreign affairs.[191] But Gaddis's argument is further weakened by its refusal to focus on the myriad American reversals of FDR's positions in the post-Yalta era.

Those who examined the agreements carefully, even within the Truman administration itself, often came to see that their president's positions were based on a misreading of what had taken place in Crimea. Walter Lippmann explained that the British ambassador to Moscow, Archibald Clark-Kerr, had admitted that he, too, interpreted the Yalta accord on Poland much as the Soviets did. He was stymied, however, by the fact that Winston Churchill shared the American desire to rewrite the accords.[192] James Byrnes would also come to recognize the truth. At a June 6, 1945, dinner with Davies, he admitted, "There was no justification under the spirit or letter of the agreement for insistence by Harriman and the British Ambassador that an entirely new Government should be created and that members of the London Émigré Polish Government should be included."[193] Byrnes tried, as secretary of state in September 1945, to work out a deal on Poland that conformed to the actual accords, rather than the American misinterpretation of them, and asked the Soviets for only cosmetic concessions to justify it. But this effort ran smack into the political fallout from FDR's decision to mislead the nation about the nature of the accords in the first place. John Foster Dulles, the Republicans' foreign affairs spokesperson and a member of Byrnes's delegation, threatened a massive political attack upon hearing of the deal. Because neither Byrnes nor Truman were willing to admit to the fact of the initial deception, Byrnes had no choice but to bow to Dulles's demands. All of the internal American bickering about its negotiating position confused the Soviets. As one official asked Charles Bohlen of Byrnes, "When is he going to start trading?" But he wasn't because, politically, he couldn't.[194] The Americans were hoist on their own proverbial petard.

By the summer of 1945, Truman realized that he, too, had been misled about the nature of the deals reached between Stalin and FDR at Yalta. He chose to downgrade their importance and continue down the same contentious path—declaring the accords reached there to be just an "interim agreement," subject to reassessment in light of changed circumstances.[195] Byrnes reinforced Truman's decision by advising his boss not to blame himself for Roosevelt's "duplicity and hypocrisy."[196] Politically speaking, it was a rock and a hard place. If the president admitted that FDR had deceived the country, the Democrats—and Truman—would pay the price. Roosevelt's dishonesty had created a Frankenstein, and the monster was driving U.S. foreign policy.

Harry Truman never comprehended the effect of his actions in refusing to abide by FDR's Yalta understanding with the Soviets. He sincerely wanted good relations with Moscow, but only under the conditions that the United States was able to achieve at least 85 percent of "what we wanted on important matters."[197] Truman did make a number of efforts to try to find some kind of accommodation with the Soviets as relations seemed to go sour. He sent sick old Harry Hopkins, trusted by Stalin as FDR's closest adviser, and a onetime secret emissary between the two leaders, to fly all the way to Moscow in the spring to see if he and the dictator might not find a way to iron things out. In October 1945, Byrnes announced that the United States would not intervene in any country bordering on Russia and would "never join in any groups in those countries in hostile intrigue against the Soviet Union."[198] In another effort, Truman wrote to Stalin after Churchill's Iron Curtain speech, offering to send the *Missouri* to bring him to the United States so that he, too, could make his case to the American people.[199] But these gestures could not overcome the increasing atmosphere of hostility and suspicion between the two nations. Harriman visited Stalin in the Crimea in October, and came away worried that the Soviet leader had grown "inordinately suspicious of our every move."[200] Indeed, as the new year began, Truman found himself privately threatening war unless the Soviets were made to shape up and accept U.S. demands.[201]

Yalta and the Establishment

In 1945 and 1946 the American people were in no mood to question the foreign policy judgments of their leaders. Most had little interest in or knowledge of foreign affairs generally, except as they specifically related to the war. Nine days after FDR's address to Congress, only 9 percent of those questioned told pollsters that they disapproved of the Yalta accords, though few could explain their provisions with any accuracy. "Public ignorance concerning the actual decisions of the Crimea declaration is colossal," complained a State Department report. Nevertheless the nation's citizens remained extremely optimistic about the prospect of future U.S.-Soviet cooperation.[202] This hopeful moment, however, did not last, and through the remainder of 1945 the American public began losing faith in the Soviet Union much as its leadership did.[203] But excluding a few Midwestern congressional districts with heavy East European immigrant populations, foreign relations were hardly a priority for the nation, which by now was primarily concerned more with absorbing the effects of demobilization and extremely anxious about jobs and the transition to a peacetime economy.[204]

The attentive audience for the Yalta accords, once the initial excitement of their announcement had passed, was therefore minimal. On the outer edges of respectability were the East European nationals, who hated everything about the agreements. They were joined by the ragged remnants of the prewar isolationist forces. On the left, devotees of the Popular Front—which included groups associated with *The Nation* magazine, *The New Republic,* and former vice president Henry Wallace—applauded any and all forms of U.S.-Soviet cooperation, virtually regardless of its substance. Most Americans who were aware of the relevant issues were somewhere in between.

The opinions that mattered most were those of the members of the insider Establishment. By virtue of their positions in the government, media, top law firms, and other related areas, these men determined the shape of the larger debate.[205] Though it would guide the direction of U.S. foreign policy for the coming four decades, the American Establishment was still in the earliest stages of its development. In 1945 its members' primary concern was America's ambition to create a world system that would allow for both a stable peace and free trade between like-minded nation-states, while simultaneously blunting the country's periodic attempts to try to withdraw from the world stage. Shaken by the U.S. nonresponse to Hitler and the power of the isolationists to stymie the president while Britain fought alone, they were willing to apply just about any possible means to prevent a return to the prewar political status quo.

At this point in time the Establishment was anti-Communist, but had not yet made a fetish of its opposition. Its fixed principles were few and eminently malleable: maintain U.S. world leadership; support free markets; punish aggression; support England; and oppose violent revolution everywhere. This minimalist consensus allowed the inclusion of Stimson and Acheson's cosmopolitan Anglophilia as well as the rigid, main-street moralism of Republican John Foster Dulles without stretching its fundamental ideology beyond its breaking point.

The Establishment generally embraced Yalta, though its members did so with a deeper understanding of the concessions FDR had felt compelled to make than most Americans—or even Truman himself. *U.S. News & World Report* editor David Lawrence complained after the accords were released that "Poland has been lynched and . . . American opinion in large part agrees that the lynching was all right."[206] The editors of *Time* professed to see "a big black hearse . . . waiting to carry the Polish Government in Exile into the Potter's Field of history" even before Roosevelt had returned from Crimea.[207] Yet like Lippmann and Reston, they had resigned themselves to the agreement's many imperfections.[208]

Yalta did not begin to inspire controversy within the Establishment until Roosevelt's deceptions about it became unavoidable. The first unpleasant surprise occurred during the UN negotiations in San Francisco, when *Newsweek* reported the existence of the secret agreement through which the Soviet Union would get its extra votes in the General Assembly.[209] Senator Arthur Vandenberg (R-MI), who headed the congressional delegation to the conference and whose support was so crucial to the emerging internationalist consensus, complained, "If I had known this I would never have accepted to be a delegate." Pundits Walter Lippmann and Marquis Childs recommended that the talks immediately be suspended.[210]

The UN crisis failed to seriously sully Yalta's good name only because the unease it caused was quickly subsumed by the larger Polish crisis. Five weeks after *Time*'s editors spied a hearse driving Polish freedom to Potter's Field, they were up in arms over the Soviet failure to keep its promises to "replace Russia's Lublin lackeys with a [Polish] government which would be fairly representative and suit the U.S. and Britain as well as the USSR."[211] By June, the magazine was already seeing "the possibility of World War III . . . in the horrified world public's eye."[212]

The Truman administration only contributed to the increasingly sinister speculation about what had really taken place at Yalta by failing to reveal the existence of FDR's secret Far Eastern accord with Stalin once the war had ended, and by perpetuating the lie that no more secrets about the agreement remained to be revealed. As had James Reston in his initial report, many members of the Establishment remained remarkably uncurious about just what concessions FDR had made to secure Soviet cooperation against Japan. *New York Times* military specialist Hanson Baldwin, writing in October 1945 in the Establishment flagship, *Foreign Affairs,* published by the Council on Foreign Relations, reported only that "Stalin had agreed (though probably not in writing) to enter the Pacific War either 'within' or 'about' (the exact phrasing is not known publicly) three months after V-E day."[213] Nowhere, however, did he even broach the subject of just what concessions Roosevelt might have offered Stalin in return. Six months earlier, Henry Luce had worried in *Fortune,* "If our hardboiled school of liberals acquiesces in the destruction of Poland for the sake of big three unity, will it also acquiesce in the partition of China?"[214] It did not occur to Luce that it may have already done so.

This public ignorance would prove costly both to the accord as well as to the Establishment's ability to resist charges of a purposeful sellout once its terms were finally revealed. Then-Secretary of State Edward Stettinius compounded the problem when he falsely insisted that the UN voting formula was absolutely the only secret agreement remaining undisclosed to the American people, except for "the military plans agreed to at Yalta and related matters connected with the defeat of the enemy."[215] Truman soon replaced Stettinius, whom he considered "as dumb as they come,"[216] with Byrnes, who could not make up his mind whether to lie about the accords or just to fudge his answers. At a September 3 press conference, the hapless Byrnes announced he "remembered well discussions" of the Far East at Yalta—something FDR had explicitly refuted—but denied that they gave the Soviets the Kuriles and

South Sakhalin. He voiced support for the Soviet position but avoided answering numerous specific questions about whether these matters had been secretly settled, or even discussed, at Yalta.[217] Later, in December, when asked point-blank by Republican Senator Styles Bridges whether the administration was holding any details about Yalta and the Far East, Byrnes responded with a prevaricating "I do not recall the various agreements. It is entirely possible that some of the agreements at Yalta affected China in some way or another."[218] In fact, he had furiously been trying to alter them at Potsdam the previous July.

Finally, at a January 22, 1946, press conference, Acting Secretary of State Dean Acheson admitted the existence of the Far East deal, but he, too, denied that it included the Kuriles. Byrnes followed up a week later, but said that he personally had had no idea of the deal because he had left Yalta the day before FDR made it, and there were no copies of it anywhere in the State Department. He did not know, moreover, where Roosevelt had kept his copy at the White House. All he knew was "it was in the hands of the President and I can not say where the President had it." He had only learned of it recently, though he was not sure exactly when. Rather amazingly, he did not take the opportunity to defend the agreement on the basis of military necessity, which had been FDR's most important motivation and that of the Joint Chiefs who lobbied for it. The secretary said only that he "did not know why there would have to be an agreement because I was not there. I don't know of any reason why there should have to be. I only know from the facts there was."[219]

President Truman took an even stranger tack. Asked about the accord at a January 31 press conference, Truman said he learned of the Far East deal while reviewing the agreement's text in preparation for the Potsdam Conference in July. The Soviets, who must have been watching the Americans squirm with a mixture of both glee and alarm, soon made liars of all of them by publishing the relevant portions of the secret protocol, and occupying their new possessions.

In refusing to reveal the truth about the accords, the administration only aided and abetted the Yalta conspiracy-mongers, who with time would become more and more influential. Stettinius clearly knew about the accords, at least by May, and Byrnes was aware of them at Potsdam in July, since he had tried to revise them there.[220] Byrnes, moreover, had mentioned the deal back in September and while trying to evade Senator Bridges's pointed questioning.[221] Truman himself had been fully briefed by Stettinius and Bohlen immediately after he became president in mid-April, and by Harriman, once he returned from Moscow roughly ten days later. According to Charles Bohlen, when, in late April, Soviet foreign minister Molotov asked Truman whether "the agreements in regard to the Far Eastern situation made at Yalta still stood," Truman replied that they did, and proposed a toast to Marshal Stalin.[222] Later, in June, my research has discovered he requested and received a secret memo from George Elsey that described all of the agreements reached at Yalta, explicitly detailing the secret Far East accord.[223]

But Truman would never admit to this even after the fighting in Asia ended in mid-August. Perhaps because U.S. officials no longer wanted or needed a Soviet invasion of Japan, and lacked the courage to admit this publicly, they had no choice but to misrepresent the initial commitments. Truman even lied to his own cabinet, denying that the Russians had any rights in Manchuria at all.[224] He also issued orders to the U.S. military to try to prevent the Soviet military from seizing the gains FDR had promised them, and to Harriman to do what he might to undermine negotiations between Russia and China to fulfill the Yalta deal.[225] A harbinger of the price to be paid for these tactics could be found in the *Chicago Tribune,* which vociferously denounced "Roosevelt's secret agreement" and reported the existence of more such secret Yalta deals, including imaginary ones that turned Korea over to the Russians and promised them delivery of huge numbers of U.S. ships after the war.[226]

At the time these events took place, however, they had little discernible impact on Establishment debate, or the larger political culture. When the terms of the Far Eastern agreement were finally published on February 11, 1946, exactly a year after the original deal had been signed, most Establishment critics and the larger American public remained deferential to presidential policy.[227] Some newspapers criticized the excessive secrecy, but almost none the decisions themselves, and even fewer the lies.[228] Writing in *The New York Times,* Arthur Krock defended the original decision to keep the agreement quiet on the grounds of military necessity, even through the "first risky months of the occupation" of Japan, but added "fair criticism may be lodged after that."[229] Still, Krock's column was hardly harshly phrased, and the focus of his discussion remained on finding ways to convince the Soviets to live up to their imaginary Yalta commitments.[230] The *Times*'s editors were similarly unalarmed, noting that the "sorry bargain" of the "sell-out of China" had been mandated by the need "to have Russia enter the war against Japan to bring that conflict to a quicker end."[231]

Only the isolationist/ethnic critics focused their fire on the "deceit and duplicity" of President Roosevelt. Clare Boothe Luce, wife of Henry and an influential Republican politician in her own right, insisted that the New Dealers "will not, or dare not, tell us the commitments that were overtly or secretly made in moments of war's extermination by a mortally ill President, and perhaps mortally scared State Department advisers."[232] The *Chicago Tribune* returned to reporting imaginary agreements, this time fixing German and Italian reparations and authorizing Stalin to create a two-million-strong German slave-labor force for the next twenty years. *U.S. News & World Report* reported another accord in which each military commander was given full control over anything and everything in his occupation zone, thereby allowing the Soviets to strip Manchuria clean. (In fact, as Ambassador Edwin Pauley would inform Truman in November, the Soviets were turning over all Japanese munitions and ammunition to the Chinese Communists, preparing them to win the civil war.)[233] While these fantastic arguments remained out of the political mainstream when initially offered, they would be resurrected in tenser times with explosive results.

The Making of Consensus

February of 1946 would prove the cruelest month yet for U.S.-Soviet relations. Stalin's deeply ideological "election" speech came on the ninth. The next day Winston Churchill visited the White House, where he previewed the "Iron Curtain" address he was to deliver shortly in Fulton, Missouri.[234] On the sixteenth, Canadian authorities announced the arrest of twenty-two alleged atomic spies. George Kennan's famous "Long Telegram" from Moscow appeared six days later, crowning and summing up a series of extremely pessimistic reports he had been sending steadily. ("I think there can be no more dangerous tendency in American public opinion than one which places on our government an obligation to accomplish the impossible by gestures of good will and conciliation toward a political entity constitutionally incapable of being conciliated," he wrote in one.)[235] The twenty-seventh found Arthur Vandenberg, whose Michigan district contained a considerable East European ethnic population, demanding to know, "What is Russia up to now?" *The New York Times* warned that America might be losing the peace and argued, "The West did not fight one totalitarianism . . . to yield to another." The following day, responding to the political pressure implied by Vandenberg and fearing for his job, Byrnes addressed the Overseas Press Club and promised to resist "aggression," in a tough speech that *The New York Times* correctly interpreted as "a warning to Russia" and a significant "reorientation of America's international relations."[236]

Byrnes's attempts to salvage something of Yalta, however, were roundly denounced as appeasement. Admiral Leahy compared Byrnes's policies to those of Neville Chamberlain at Munich, and blamed his conversion on the "communistically-inclined" State Department.[237] Byrnes would resign by April, falsely citing health concerns, to be replaced by General Marshall.[238]

By summer, Truman declared himself tired of being pushed around by the Soviets, who were "chiseling" on all of their agreements.[239] He ordered Clark Clifford, who in turn delegated the assignment to George Elsey, to draw up a formal indictment outlining all Soviet violations of Yalta and its successor agreements. The assignment was taken extremely seriously, as letters were sent out to all relevant cabinet secretaries and top military officials asking for arguments and evidence.[240] The so-called Clifford-Elsey Report of September 1946—the first such comprehensive document since the end of the war—was supposed to cite all the various means by which the Russians were "chiseling," but its authors had had a hard time coming up with specific instances. The Soviets, they complained, were projecting "the effective range of Soviet military power well into areas which the United States regards as vital to its security." Their ultimate aim was "to weaken the position and destroy the prestige of the United States in Europe, Asia and South America." Nevertheless, when it came to actual violations of signed agreements, the prosecutors failed to produce evidence. The Joint Chiefs of Staff noted that the USSR had adhered to its wartime accords, while General Lucius Clay, the U.S. commander in occupied Germany, acknowledged the same. Dean Acheson, speaking for the State Department, was likewise unwilling to accuse the Soviets of violating the letter of any agreements. Clifford and Elsey were therefore forced to admit that it remained "difficult to adduce direct evidence of literal violations." Regarding Poland, the best the authors could come up with was the fact that the Soviets had resorted to "numerous technicalities" to "act unilaterally" with regard to the Lublin—later Warsaw—government.[241]

Moreover, as Arnold Offner notes, the report made no effort whatever to achieve balance or objectivity:

> Despite Truman's being vague on every conference but Potsdam the report provided no sketch of the complex diplomacy from 1942 through Yalta that might have provided some basis to attribute current conflicts to causes other than just Soviet aggression. There was no mention of Byrnes's contentious diplomacy at the Potsdam Conference that led the Soviets to charge that the U.S. had reneged on its Yalta commitment to $10 billion in reparations. Nor was there reference to Clay's belief that the Russians had honored their agreements in Germany and could be negotiated with, or that the Russians had allowed free elections in Hungary and Czechoslovakia and withdrawn their troops from northern Norway and Bornholm Island. There was no indication that Moscow had reason to fear a revived Germany or a Japan and perhaps reasons to seek assurances about control of the Straits to protect their vital regions, much as Britain held sway at Suez and the U.S. at Panama, and

that they now intended to patrol the Mediterranean. Moreover, Moscow had allowed U.S. forces into Korea, hardly protested U.S. predominance in China and acceded to it in Japan.[242]

Excluding Henry Wallace, who would soon be forced out of the administration and, eventually, out of polite society entirely, this hard-line consensus now reigned unchallenged within the Establishment. When Moscow offered cooperation, the Americans suspected a trap; when it behaved aggressively, it simply confirmed what they already knew. The Americans had come to regard their security and way of life to be remarkably fragile and beleaguered in the face of the Communist challenge, despite clear superiority in every measurable category of power and influence. In the 1940s the Soviets had no long-range air force, no atomic bomb, no surface fleet, no capacity to attack America, and no ability to inflict damage on the American economy.

Even so, relations continued to deteriorate. When England withdrew its support for anti-Communist forces in Greece and Turkey, Truman and Acheson found they needed to invoke almost apocalyptic rhetoric to convince Congress to appropriate the funds to replace them. On the advice of Senator Vandenberg, Truman decided to "scare the hell out of [American people and Congress]" in order to secure the initial $400 million in aid.[243] By the time of the administration's propaganda offensive on behalf of the Marshall Plan in June, it had become a commonplace to warn that the Soviets were bent on world domination, while attributing nothing but altruistic motives to the United States. The brutality of the February 1948 Communist coup in Czechoslovakia, following the blockade of Berlin in June, only provided further confirmation of these views.

Bullitt's Bullet

The question of Yalta itself lay fallow in American politics during this period, and played little role in the 1946 or 1948 elections. Republicans would occasionally cite the conference for having created various world problems—one Republican tried to cut the State Department budget for wine, blaming the Yalta accords on alleged drunkenness in the American delegation—but the issue generally failed to excite.[244] By continuing to charge the Russians with having failed to live up to their commitments, the Truman administration managed to contain the damage that the revelations of the truth might otherwise have caused. In April of the 1946 election year, Truman praised Yalta as a worthwhile effort to test Stalin and the Soviet Union on the seriousness of their dedication to peace, but given the actual Soviet performance, the

United States would simply have to rely on force in the future.[245] In response to a concerned note from Eleanor Roosevelt in March, he explained that with regard to the Yalta accords, "we carried them out to the letter. . . . Russia has not kept faith with us."[246] George Marshall and Dean Acheson would visit Vandenberg at home for the purpose of flattering his considerable ego,[247] an effort that paid off in his ability to define the border of respectable opinion on the Right, where he merely urged the administration to "use every influence at our command, including our fiscal resources, in insisting upon the faithful execution" of Yalta.[248] Privately, he called the Far Eastern agreement a "mistake . . . at China's expense, for Russia's belated and unnecessary entry into the Jap war."[249] But he did not level charges of treason. Neither Vandenberg, nor Dulles, nor presidential candidate Thomas E. Dewey made an issue of Yalta during the 1948 campaign.

The calm, however, was deceptive, for 1946 also saw a young Army veteran named Joseph McCarthy elected to the Senate from Wisconsin. The corrupt Chinese Nationalists were failing to hold their own in their civil war with Mao's far more disciplined Communist forces. In August 1948, apostate Communist spy Whittaker Chambers named the former State Department official and Yalta delegate, Alger Hiss, as a fellow Communist before the House Un-American Affairs Committee. That same month, *Life* magazine published the first of a two-part article by William C. Bullitt, FDR's first ambassador to the USSR, in which he viewed the Soviets with the blind hatred of a scorned lover. *Life*'s editors felt compelled to explain that they were publishing the article because, "like most Americans," they had been "worried by signs that our victory in World War II only marked an interlude before World War III."[250] The reason: Yalta.

The situation, as Bullitt described it, was this: "Three years ago . . . we stood on a summit of power rarely scaled by any nation. . . . Today, only three years later, our insecurity is such that we may be forced into war this year." The fault lay with Soviet "partisans" and "sympathizers" working in the State Department, the Treasury Department, and Army wartime agencies. President Roosevelt, moreover, was inclined to give Stalin "everything he wanted" and "ask nothing in return" at Yalta. "Swept away by the waves of pro-Soviet propaganda which they had launched to win support of the American people for the appeasement line," Roosevelt and his advisers traveled to Yalta to "pave the way for the final triumphs of Soviet diplomacy at U.S. expense."

Bullitt and *Life*'s editors were not yet ready, however, to lay the blame for this catastrophe on Roosevelt's own treachery. Rather, in their view, his ill health left him vulnerable to the Soviet dupes and agents in his administration. "President Roosevelt was more than tired," Bullitt explained, though he offered no sources to support that contention and had been nowhere near the president at the time. He "had difficulty in formulating his thoughts and greater difficulties in expressing them consecutively." Nevertheless, he conspired "secretly, behind the back of China [to] sign with Churchill and Stalin an agreement by which vital rights of China in Manchuria were sacrificed to Soviet imperialism." This agreement "gave Stalin a deadly instrument for the domination of China and the eventual mobilization of her manpower and resources for war against us." Bullitt's plot thickened when Harry Truman, too, appeared to fall victim to this same pro-Soviet virus when he chose to rely on General George C. Marshall for advice about China. Marshall listened to the "Communists and fellow travelers in the Department of State . . . who were devotees and expounders of the evil nonsense that the Soviet Union was a 'peace-loving democracy' and the Chinese Communists mere 'agrarian reformers who had no connection to Moscow.'"[251]

If McCarthy had lost his Senate race, if Dewey really had defeated Truman, if Chiang's troops had pulled together sufficiently to stave off the Chinese revolution, if the Soviets had not exploded an atom bomb, if Whittaker Chambers had never met Alger Hiss . . . then Bullitt's arguments might never have migrated into the mainstream of American politics. Somehow, though, he managed to articulate virtually all of the themes that would dominate the nation's political dialogue within eighteen months. Turning the Democrats' false Yalta narrative on its ideological head, Bullitt did not blame the failure of the postwar regime on either Soviet mendacity or America's misguided generosity. Instead, he charged treason, based on a never fully explicated combination of FDR's deviousness, foolishness, and mental incapacity, and Communist subversion—a subversion so deeply embedded in the government that it outlasted Roosevelt and continued to manipulate Harry Truman years later.

Despite its prominent appearance in the most visible and highly circulated periodical in Henry Luce's empire, Bullitt's diatribe failed to gain a foothold in the public discourse. President Truman had worked hard to armor himself against just such attacks during that year's presidential campaign by running against Stalin and the Soviets as ardently as Dewey and the Republicans. With his political fortunes flagging and his reelection prospects looking dim by late in 1947, President Truman seized on a strategic memo by Clark Clifford and adviser James Rowe, advising him to turn leftward on domestic issues while veering rightward on foreign policy. "The worse matters get, up to a fairly certain point—real danger of imminent war," the memo advised, "the more is there a sense of crisis. In times of crisis the American citizen tends to back up his president."[252]

The country's subsequent sense of crisis during this period—the so-called War Scare of 1948—was therefore wholly government-manufactured. Despite the fact that, as State Department counselor Charles Bohlen explained in a confidential January 1948 memo, the government considered its position "vis-à-vis the Soviets better now than at any time since the end of the war,"[253] the tactic of alarming the public worked. Truman began giving speeches on "the critical nature of the situation in Europe," the necessity for "speedy action," and the "great urgency" of the Soviet threat.[254] Together with his escalation of Franklin Roosevelt's wartime loyalty program, now covering more than two million government employees and more than seventy allegedly subversive groups, Truman's frightening rhetoric successfully disarmed his Republican opponent. But it also contributed to the creation of a noxious atmosphere of fear and insecurity during his second term.[255] More than three thousand government officials would lose their jobs in the Truman administration, owing to "loyalty" concerns, as the country descended into what Supreme Court justice William O. Douglas would call a "Black Silence of Fear."[256] It was into this cauldron that Whittaker Chambers threw "Alger Hiss, secret Soviet spy at Yalta."

"Lucifer Himself"

Republicans were profoundly embittered by their surprising presidential defeat in 1948, which discredited their moderate wing. The terminal illness of Arthur Vandenberg and the surprising defeat of John Foster Dulles in a special New York Senate election helped to push the party even further into the arms of the militants. As the China situation continued to worsen, Republicans redoubled their efforts to discover villains to blame and conspiracies to unmask. In this ideological quest, all roads led to Yalta. Yalta was the common denominator in America's sellout of Poland, its impotence vis-à-vis China, and the impressive (though still largely imaginary) buildup of Soviet military power, now threatening to engulf America and its allies. "The Yalta agreement," thundered Minnesota Republican Walter Judd, "surrendered the freedoms of three-fourths of the people of the world" and provided "the blueprint which has been followed by the Communists in the conquest of China."[257] No longer merely a term for "something historically measurable," Raymond Swing would comment in *The New York Times Magazine* in February 1949, Yalta "has become a byword for failure, folly and treason."[258] Bullitt had sketched the plot, but it remained to Whittaker Chambers, former Marxist empiricist and furtive spy turned right-wing Spenglerian and Christian exhortationist, to write the screenplay.

Chambers had spied for Stalin during the 1930s, before converting to religious anti-Communism. He then became a book reviewer and briefly foreign editor of *Time,* where he wrote about the Yalta conference from New York. (Henry Luce later paid his legal fees.) Chambers had privately accused State Department functionary Alger Hiss of participating in a Communist cell to Assistant Secretary of State Adolf A. Berle Jr., immediately following the 1939 Nazi-Soviet nonaggression pact. But Supreme Court justice Felix Frankfurter, a Hiss mentor, and others assured Berle that the charge was false, and Chambers, merely an imaginative paranoid. Right-wing journalist Isaac Don Levine kept the accusation alive in ensuing years, focusing on its alleged implications for Yalta.

At a meeting between Hiss and Assistant FBI Director D. M. Ladd, Ladd raised Levine's charges, published in a 1945 issue of *Reader's Digest,* "claiming that at the Yalta Conference, Hiss had persuaded the late President Roosevelt to agree to the admission of the Ukraine and Byelorussia to the UN [as independent voting members] at a meeting where Roosevelt, Hiss and Stalin were present." In Ladd's words, "Hiss said that this was a fabrication because he had never met with Roosevelt and Stalin alone, and besides, he does not speak the Russian language." (In fact, the Yalta papers later demonstrated that Hiss had opposed this concession.)[259] Two years later, in the fanatical anti-Communist monthly *Plain Talk,* Levine charged that "Certain high and trusted officials in the State Department, including one who had played a leading role at Yalta and in organizing the UN, delivered confidential papers to Communist agents who microfilmed them for dispatch to Moscow."[260] Chambers himself had published a quirky, quite brilliant, historical fantasy in *Time* immediately after Yalta. Entitled "Ghosts on the Roof," it charged the president with a betrayal of world historical proportions by positing a celebration on the roof of the Lividia Palace at Yalta, where the ghosts of Tsar Nicholas and the Tsarina celebrated Stalin's achievement of Russia's historic imperial ambitions. Chambers believed he was communicating what he called "the hard facts about Soviet foreign aggression" at the time. By linking his belief that at Yalta, Franklin Roosevelt had knowingly given the U.S. seal of approval to the realization of Soviet imperial ambitions in Europe and Asia, to his tale of Soviet espionage, Chambers recast the tale of the failure of U.S. foreign policy in the postwar era as one of perfidious betrayal and deliberate subversion, with Alger Hiss taking a place at the center of world history. Chambers's story would transport the accusations of democratic treason from the swamps and lowlands of American political debate directly into its vital center.

Jay Vivian "Whittaker" Chambers was a remarkably melodramatic man with a profoundly conspiratorial view of history. Secretive and paranoid, he became a self-created hero in his own private Dostoyevsky novel, doing ideological battle with the anti-Christ on behalf of what he believed to be a doomed and impotent God.[261] Chambers was convinced that the fate of human history had been determined at Yalta, first by FDR's concessions to Soviet "foreign aggression" and second by America's willingness to concede China to the Communists by way of FDR's secret Far East agreement. "It is certain," he later explained, "that between the years 1930 and 1948, a group of almost unknown men and women, Communists or close fellow travelers, or their dupes, working in the United States government . . . affected the future of every American now alive. . . . If mankind is about to suffer one of its decisive transformations, if it is about to close its 2000-year-old experience of Christian civilization, and enter upon another wholly new and diametrically different, then that group may claim a part in history."[262]

Chambers's historical analysis was virtually identical to Bullitt's: naive in the best of times, but near death's door and easily manipulated by wily Communists at Yalta, FDR had unknowingly conspired with Stalin to Bolshevize the world. But while Bullitt could not place a name to or a face on the conspirators, Chambers pointed his finger at the man his lawyer called "Lucifer himself": Alger Hiss.

If Chambers was a character out of a Dostoyevsky novel, then Hiss emerged fresh from an F. Scott Fitzgerald story. Raised fatherless in genteel poverty, he had managed, through luck, diligence, great intelligence, and good manners, to secure his own adoption by the best and brightest of the New Deal. He participated in the drafting of the Declaration on Liberated Europe before the conference began, and accompanied Secretary Stettinius and a small group of advisers to Marrakech, Morocco, for a briefing concerning American proposals and strategy for the upcoming meeting. At the conference itself, according to Hiss historian Allen Weinstein, "The American delegation was an imposing one, and Hiss was far from being the most prominent or most influential member." His duties involved assembling and preparing briefing papers for the secretary on various issues, and organizing the American position on the future of the United Nations.[263] In his capacity as an adviser on matters related to the United Nations, Hiss objected to a draft proposal allowing the Soviets two additional votes in the UN General Assembly, unaware that Roosevelt had already conceded the point.[264] After the conference ended, the Soviets suggested, and the Americans agreed, that Hiss be named to head the San Francisco working group charged with the creation of the new world organization.

Hiss's accusers on the House Un-American Activities Committee (HUAC) concocted a much more interesting role for Hiss at Yalta. In the HUAC version, Hiss conspired with the Soviets to sell out Poland and Eastern Europe by passing along secret information about U.S. military and diplomatic positions to the Russians—thereby alerting them to easily exploitable divisions and weaknesses in the Anglo-American negotiating stance. He then prevailed upon the ailing Roosevelt to offer major concessions to the Soviets in China, thereby intentionally paving the way for the victory of Mao and the Chinese Communists.[265] While the evidence of Chambers's accusations against Hiss has grown stronger with post–Cold War revelations, none has ever emerged to support the claim that Hiss did any Soviet spying at Yalta.

The trial of Alger Hiss proved the first great political media trial of the American Century. Chambers had initially been reluctant to accuse Hiss of being a spy and was almost comically miscast in the role of indicter, given his own history of espionage, treason, perjury, and furtive homosexuality. He consistently enraged HUAC investigators by changing his testimony and withholding crucial evidence—for fear, he said, of his life, and out of charity toward Hiss. During his first HUAC appearance in August 1948, Chambers had charged Hiss with Communist Party membership but denied the espionage charge. Not until December, and then again in March 1949, did Chambers accuse Hiss of being one of the "most zealous" Russian spies in Washington. Hiss, who was then secretary of the Carnegie Endowment for International Peace and a prospective secretary of state in a future Democratic administration, demanded the opportunity to confront his accuser. The resulting trial transformed American politics. Nearly four decades later, the reporter David Remnick would observe of the case that it became "the *Rashomon* drama of the Cold War," in which "one's interpretation of the evidence and characters involved became a litmus test of one's politics, character, and loyalties. Sympathy with either Hiss or Chambers was more an article of faith than a determination of fact."[266]

The members of HUAC were particularly interested in exploiting Chambers's testimony to blame Roosevelt and Truman for selling out the nation's honor and security. The committee's acting chair, Karl Mundt of South Dakota, focused on China, where the administration was still in the process of trying to write off the Chiang regime at minimum political cost. Mundt used Chambers's account to announce that he, personally, had discovered that, "there is reason to believe that he [Hiss] organized within the [State] department one of the Communist cells which endeavored to influence our Chinese policy and bring about the condemnation of Chiang Kai-shek." He demanded to know whether Hiss had "drafted or participated in drafting parts of the Yalta Agreement." When Hiss replied, "To some extent, yes," Yalta once again became front-page news.[267]

The Democrats, however, were slow to gauge the shifting political winds around them. Speaking just after Chambers's initial appearance, Truman mocked the committee, accusing it of contravening the Bill of Rights, of "slandering a lot of people who don't deserve it," and of creating a "red herring." Following Hiss's rebuttal, the president went even further. By giving voice to its "wild and false accusation," HUAC, along with the Republican Party, had become the "unwitting ally of the Communists in this country."[268] Indeed, within the administration, almost no one credited Chambers's fantastic tale. Alger Hiss had been a protégé of the sainted Oliver Wendell Holmes, of Felix Frankfurter, and of Dean Acheson. He had been recommended for his current job by John Foster Dulles, and had recently been named to head a commission by George Marshall. Four years earlier, "young, handsome Alger Hiss" had been singled out for praise in *Time,* no less, on Luce's explicit orders, for being in a "class by himself" during his skillful handling of the UN conference in San Francisco. The author of these words had been none other than Whittaker Chambers.[269]

But much had changed since 1945. The relentless campaign conducted by the Truman administration to convince Americans that it was the Soviets who had walked away from their word at Yalta had borne fruit in the form of a political discourse in which accusations of deliberate betrayal had gained increasing credence. FDR's promises about the postwar world upon his return from Yalta had begun to look like a grim ruse. The New Dealers who returned from Crimea speaking of "the dawn of a new day" were now viewed as foolish idealists at best, possible traitors at worst. Truman and company had argued that FDR and company had simply been overly trusting of Stalin and the Russians. But the East European ethnics, the isolationists, and even *Time*—and its foreign editor, Whittaker Chambers—were well aware shortly after the announcement of the Yalta accords that Poland indeed had been abandoned. The victory of the Communists in China following on FDR's concessions to the Soviets there made the entire project seem a cruel exercise in deception—perhaps self-deception, perhaps something worse. The combination of official dishonesty and a world appearing to spin out of control and into Communist hands created in the United States a political dynamic bent on discovering conspiracies and unmasking traitors at the heart of the American system. When President Truman tried to appease these forces with alarmist rhetoric and tougher internal security measures, he succeeded only in lending them encouragement. Clifford complained to Truman in April 1949 of an "ominous trend in the United States toward the increasing curtailment of freedom of expression" and worried that it "played into Soviet and Communist hands."[270] While Truman, Clifford, and Acheson and company found this dynamic dangerous and difficult to manage, they nevertheless vastly preferred it to the truth—which would involve somehow explaining that, yes, the charges of perfidy were true, but that all the actions in question had been undertaken on purpose. Even the normally loyal *Washington Post* rebuked Truman for his "desire to suppress the whole business."[271] A grand jury eventually indicted Hiss for perjury, a charge that everyone understood was merely a stand-in for espionage, with Hiss himself a symbol of a much larger conspiracy. His trial began on June 1, 1949, and it was covered by an extraordinary group of celebrity reporters. CBS sent Edward R. Murrow; *The New Yorker,* A. J. Liebling; and the *New York Post,* its colorful sportswriter, Jimmy Cannon, whose coverage ran on the front page. Four journalists present would publish books on the case. Henry Luce sent a private stenographer. *The Nation*'s Robert Bendiner did not exaggerate when he wrote:

> Acquittal should prove the undoing of the House Committee on Un-American Activities: That body would stand revealed as a collection of gulls who for two years had followed the lead of a man regarded by a jury of average Americans as a monumental liar or a mental case. Conviction, on the other hand, would show that Communist conspiracy had gone much farther in the United States than the run of liberals have thought possible, and that it has agents more devious, more highly placed, and more successful than any yet brought back.[272]

While the trial's evidence barely even touched on Yalta, the issue remained preeminent in the public debate and the defense strategy. James Reston worried that Hiss was being portrayed as "the man who sat at Franklin Roosevelt's right hand at Yalta, a great power in the direction of the nation's policy." "He did not make policy at Yalta," Reston assured his readers. "He was one of the many technicians who did small jobs when he was told."[273]

When the first trial ended in a hung jury on July 8, 1949, some frustrated Red-hunters concluded that civil liberties were a luxury America could no longer afford. Appearing on a radio program immediately after the non-verdict was announced, young Richard Nixon, Hiss's primary nemesis on HUAC, publicly demanded an inquiry into Judge Kaufman's "fitness" for his position. The junior Republican representative and erstwhile member of the bar admitted that, while Justice Kaufman might have had legal grounds for his decision to exclude certain testimonies, "the average American wanted all the technicalities waived in this case."[274]

A second trial began on November 17, and, by January 21, Hiss was pronounced guilty on two counts of perjury. Four days later, he was sentenced to five years in the federal penitentiary—a term he began serving at a medium-security facility in Lewisburg, Pennsylvania, upon the exhaustion of his appeals process in March 1951.

Failing to read the tea leaves, Secretary of State Acheson responded to Hiss's January guilty verdict and the anti-Communist hysteria that accompanied it by quoting the Sermon on the Mount, promising not to turn his back on a friend. This was exactly the wrong moment to demonstrate his high-minded sense of noblesse oblige, for the Republicans erupted with fury. Karl Mundt offered up a frenetic speech in which he dwelled on "the formation of our policy toward China, which has resulted in the disastrous collapse of autonomous China and the complete domination of that once-great ally of ours by the Moscow-supported armies of Communism." Mundt went on to list the "considerable coterie of Communist sympathizers in the Far Eastern Division of the State Department," who owed their allegiance not to America but to Alger Hiss.[275] Mundt was interrupted, however, by a still-unknown junior senator from Wisconsin named Joseph McCarthy, who wondered if Acheson's "most fantastic statement" meant he would also not "turn his back on other Communists who were associated with Hiss?" Styles Bridges followed by asking "just how deep Mr. Hiss's influence ran" in the State Department. Senator William Jenner observed that the "Alger Hiss group . . . engineered the Yalta sellout and had turned Communism loose around one-half of the world."[276] Indiana Republican Homer Capehart told a lurid tale on the Senate floor in which Hiss, alone in a room with Roosevelt, Stalin, and an interpreter, with the doors closed, somehow forced the American leader to cave in to Communist demands. "How much are we going to take?" he demanded. "Fuchs and Acheson and Hiss and hydrogen bombs threatening outside and New Dealism eating away the vitals of the nation. Is this the best America can do?"[277]

Richard Nixon capped the congressional reaction on January 26, 1950, with a virtuoso four-hour performance he called, "The Hiss Case: A Lesson for the American People." In what might be termed Nixon's own political Magna Carta, the young congressman drew the following lesson: "Five years ago, when Alger Hiss was arranging postwar conferences," the Soviet orbit drew in only 180 million people and "the odds were nine to one in our favor." Now 800 million souls lived "under the domination of Soviet totalitarianism" and "the odds are five to three against us." Closing with a dramatic flourish, he urged, "We owe a solemn duty to expose this sinister conspiracy for what it is." The ambitious representative left the House floor to a standing ovation, and a political star was born. That year, Nixon defeated Helen Gahagan Douglas in the race for a California Senate seat. Virtually alone in mainstream American politics, she had blamed the failure of Yalta not on Soviet faithlessness, but on the death of Franklin Roosevelt and the repudiation of his policies by his successor, President Truman.[278] Such views gave Nixon ample opportunity to paint his opponent as an infamous "pink lady," not to be trusted with the security of her country. Within two years, he would be vice president.

Just two weeks after Nixon's floor speech, Joe McCarthy was scheduled to speak to the Ohio County Republican Women's Club of Wheeling, West Virginia. Originally, he had planned to focus on questions related to aid to the elderly or housing issues. Inspired by the Hiss verdict, however, McCarthy decided to borrow material from Nixon's speech. "Alger Hiss," he told the club, "is important not as an individual any more, but rather because he is so representative of a group in the State Department."[279] There were now eight hundred million people living "under the absolute domination of Soviet Russia," while "on our side, the figure has shrunk to about 500,000." He then held aloft his famous "list" of 205 Communists "still working and shaping policy in the State Department." (A day later, the figure had dropped to only fifty-seven. The precise numbers turned out not to matter much.) By the end of February, McCarthy had become a national leader and one of the more influential men in the Republican Party.

Though it sprang from many political, cultural, and psychological sources, McCarthyism drew considerable power from the Democrats' dishonesty about Yalta. Americans felt cheated by the unfulfilled promises FDR had made regarding Poland, Eastern Europe, and the postwar world. They were frightened and unnerved by the Russian bomb and the Chinese revolution, and psychologically unprepared for the concept of any nation's unwillingness to follow America's example or appreciate its benevolence. The Truman administration had blamed the Soviets for failing to live up to their commitments, but never made a convincing argument as to why the Americans were so easily taken in. Alger Hiss provided an answer.

Like William Bullitt, McCarthy and his supporters dwelled repeatedly on Hiss's supposed dominion over a "physically tired and mentally sick Roosevelt."[280] McCarthy insisted that the accord had been drafted by "Hiss and Gromyko, and an Englishman whose name I do not recall at the moment," and spoke repeatedly of Hiss's "Svengali-like influence over Secretary of State Stettinius."[281] FDR's former ambassador to China during the Yalta talks, General Patrick J. Hurley, soon amplified McCarthy's tale by suddenly remembering that State Department Communists had been passing secret information to the "Chinese armed Communists," who had information about Yalta that had been denied to Hurley. The general said he tried to raise this issue with President Roosevelt in March of 1945, but found him to be "just a loose bag of bones."[282] Hurley, who had reversed his position on the agreement by 180 degrees, provided no evidence to support this contention, but evidence was hardly the point. He insisted that Stalin had not actually broken any agreements because "We cowardly surrendered to him everything that he had signed and we did it in secret." Yalta, he argued, proved to be "the State Department's blueprint for the Communist conquest of China."[283] The problem was not the false placement of trust at Yalta, as Truman and his advisers would argue: it was, in Joe McCarthy's words, those who had engaged in "twenty-years of treason." "We know that since Yalta the leaders of this Government by design or ignorance have continued to betray us," thundered McCarthy. "We also know that the same men who betrayed America are still leading America. The traitors must no longer lead the betrayed."[284]

The Nixon-McCarthy interpretation of Yalta soon became Republican Party boilerplate. No longer confined to the ghettos of American political culture, the cult of the Yalta "sellout" became part of mainstream Republicanism, providing explanations for everything from the rise of Soviet power to the outbreak of the war in Korea.[285] Owing to the conventions of objective journalism, newspapers reported McCarthy's wildest accusations with the same degree of seriousness and sobriety they accorded to respectable political figures. When McCarthy charged, for instance, that General George Marshall and Secretary of State Dean Acheson were part of a pro-Communist conspiracy that relied, in part, on their role of creating "enticements" to the Soviets to enter the Far Eastern war, *The New York Times* printed this nonsensical accusation without context or rebuttal.[286] Other newspapers followed suit, and McCarthy's influence was magnified throughout both the Establishment and the country at large.

The Hiss case also provided Republicans with their key arguments for conducting a government-wide witch hunt to root out more Hiss-like spies and still-unrevealed secret agreements. Dean Acheson, George Marshall, and the late Harry Hopkins, among others, were all considered suspect.[287] In his *Foreign Policy for Americans,* Republican leader and heir apparent Robert Taft insisted Roosevelt's policies "were supplemented by something perhaps more sinister in the indirect influence of communism and Communists on American statesmen. . . . It is significant that Alger Hiss was also at the [Yalta] conference and evidently made his influence felt. . . ."[288] What the country needed, therefore, was not more "secret agreements of Yalta," which have "placed Russia in a position where it is a threat to the world," but the replacement of State Department "Communists" by a president and a secretary who had no sympathy for them.[289] In September of that campaign year, American Veterans of Foreign Wars (VFW) demanded that "all Government officials, high or low, responsible for the United States being 'sold out at Yalta' be driven from office and punished to the full extent of the law," along with "those responsible for putting radicals and homosexuals into Government departments."[290]

Hiss's conviction in his second trial not only discredited the liberals who had supported him in the larger political arena but also weakened potential opposition to McCarthyism by dividing the forces that might have opposed it. Anti-Communist liberals split along pro- and anti-Hiss demarcations, weakening both sides. *The New Leader* described the division within liberal anti-Communism as falling between "Soft" pro-Hiss liberals who were either "blind to the political realities exposed by the case" or "emotional . . . innocents," who could not "look the Cold War in the face"; and "Hard" unemotional sophisticates, up to the task of Cold War ideological combat.[291] While few self-proclaimed liberals went so far as *Commentary* managing editor Irving Kristol, who offered a few kind words for McCarthy himself, the Hards' willingness to grant the legitimacy of the Red-hunting project left liberals in no position to mount a united defense against its assault on free speech, civil liberties, and the free exchange of ideas. Arthur Schlesinger, for instance, freely granted that the American reaction to the threat of Communist subversion was "largely hysterical and contemptible," but was nevertheless unwilling to condemn it as altogether unnecessary.[292] Since American political culture has never been good at making the careful distinctions to which liberal intellectuals cling, both McCarthy's wild charges and Chambers's paranoid imaginings became treated as matters of fact. Hiss was no longer just the low-level spy that Chambers convinced the jury he had been, but had become a satanic mastermind who single-handedly manipulated FDR to sell out Poland and China at Yalta. Not only Communists were to blame, so were liberal New Dealers. Sociologist David Riesman pointed out that in appearing to lend credence to these extreme views, a guilty Hiss had done the country "a far more serious disservice than in his earlier, very likely inconsequential espionage and other efforts to influence foreign policy."[293]

The 1952 election-year publication of Chambers's memoir, *Witness,* further implanted this interpretation in the heart of American political culture. With an initial printing of 100,000 copies, serialization and promotion in a special edition of *The Saturday Evening Post,* four full pages in *Time,* and all of the attendant publicity, Chambers's morality tale of betrayal and redemption dominated the top spot of *The New York Times* best seller list for nearly four months.[294] Despite its equation of liberals with Communists, and Communists with spies, Leftist luminaries (including Sidney Hook in *The New York Times Book Review* and Philip Rahv in *Partisan Review*) celebrated the book in the media.[295] Robert Bendiner's earlier prediction in the pages of *The Nation* now appeared unassailable: HUAC's prestige had soared; Red-hunting had grown respectable; civil liberties became suspect, and Yalta, a curse.

FDR: Patsy or Proxy?

By the early 1950s Roosevelt's "Spirit of Yalta" had virtually no defenders of any consequence in the American Establishment. Nearly every politician remotely connected to the conference became forced to account for his role in it. Following on a hypothesis once proffered by Harry Hopkins, former secretary of state Stettinius had tried to offer an original excuse in 1949, with his account of the Yalta conference, entitled *Roosevelt and the Russians.* Stettinius proposed that a benevolent Stalin had been overturned by his hard-line Politburo after Yalta, for "having been too friendly and having made too many concessions to the capitalist nations."[296] Although his arguments were quickly ridiculed in the media,[297] in a May 15, 1945, memo, Soviet expert and assistant secretary of state Charles E. Bohlen had written, "Even at Yalta, we all felt that the Soviet failure to carry out the agreement reached there had been due in large part to opposition inside the Soviet Government which Stalin had encountered on his return."[298] Averell Harriman, soon to run for governor of New York, and harboring his own presidential ambitions, came before the Senate Foreign Relations Committee in late 1950 and offered an extensive history of his own participation in the conference, which featured a role for Stalin comparable to that portrayed by Stettinius and Bohlen. He insisted that "the postwar problems have resulted not from the understandings reached at Yalta but from the fact that Stalin failed to carry out those understandings and from aggressive actions by the Kremlin." If Yalta had actually been a "sell-out," he asked, perfectly encapsulating the Democratic position, then why had the Soviets "gone to such lengths to violate the Yalta understandings?" This "fact," he insisted, "has provided the rallying point for the free world in their collective effort to build their defenses and to unite against aggression."[299]

Given the emotionalism of the discourse, the Establishment found itself with no choice but to co-opt the McCarthyites by adopting limited aspects of their arguments and throwing up the occasional sacrificial lamb—often with far-reaching and wholly unpredictable results. With the Left successfully decimated by McCarthyite attacks, liberals became the targets of McCarthyite harassment as well. Universities dismissed faculty members if they would not cooperate with federal investigative authorities, who demanded that they finger their colleagues. The leaders of the labor movement expelled those with alleged ties to the Communist menace who did not hew to the anti-Communist line. Hollywood moguls, public school principals, law partners, and research laboratory heads all felt compelled to submit to the McCarthyite monster. The cost to the progressive cause in politics and culture—in discoveries never made, movies never filmed, novels never published, unions never organized, movements never inspired, political alliances never formed, civil rights never demanded, and ideas never imagined—is literally incalculable.[300] The net result was a kind of homogenization of American culture in all areas that had once fostered creativity. As one network television executive complained as late as March 1956, "The trouble with people who've never joined anything and therefore are 'safe' for us to use is that they aren't usually very good writers, or actors or producers or hell, human beings."[301]

Within the State Department, Dean Acheson found himself compelled to "clean out" virtually every adviser who had been associated in any way with U.S.-China policy during Yalta and immediately afterward, leading to a near complete lack of Asian expertise in U.S. foreign policy, just when it became most needed vis-à-vis the crisis on the Korean peninsula. Almost every issue became perceived in the context of undoing the alleged done at Yalta.

Representative Paul Shafer (R-MI) wondered in June 1950: "If China is not worth defending, why get excited about South Korea?" The answer, he explained on the floor of the House, could be found in "the text of the secret deal at Yalta" that "revealed how China and Korea had been flung into the Soviet orbit . . . through secret deals, deceit, and double dealing. Alger Hiss was Roosevelt's adviser at Yalta."[302] The Truman administration recognized the danger inherent in this charge, and together with a host of other no less symbolic motivations, undertook to fight in Korea, despite Secretary Acheson's apparent decision to rule out just such a move in a well-reported speech to the National Press Club just before the North Korean attack.[303] Acheson privately explained to a friend that in Korea, the United States was "fighting the second team, whereas the real enemy is the Soviet Union." President Truman also noted to columnist Arthur Krock that "if any fire breaks out elsewhere . . . we will abandon Korea. . . . We want any showdown to come in Western Europe, where we can use the bomb."[304]

The only remaining question regarding the Yalta agreement after 1950 was whether FDR's alleged sellout had been an honest but naive gesture or a purposefully traitorous scheme. In the interest of promoting the former interpretation, the Truman administration needed to distinguish itself from its predecessor's mistake by toughening up its attitude toward potential security risks at home, and by taking care not to give its political adversaries the slightest excuse to charge it with softness abroad. Truman consistently expanded internal government loyalty investigations between 1947 and 1952. Negotiations with the Russians were ruled out as a matter of principle, for even an implicit acknowledgment that the Soviets might approach such talks with the serious intent of reducing tension would have been taken as an admission that the Republican charge on Yalta had merit. This argument met with virtually no opposition among liberals and former New Dealers, save perhaps the lonely Popular Front supporters associated with *The Nation* magazine and a few small but independent leftist publications. Indeed, *The New York Times*'s editorial page criticized the very idea of summit diplomacy, which it insisted would only benefit the Soviet Union and might even lead to a "Super Yalta," something it insisted would turn out even worse than the "much criticized original."[305]

Despite the evidence of the administration's anti-Communist zeal, association with Yalta continued to plague the Truman-Acheson foreign policy. In August 1951, former president Hoover, whose initial enthusiasm for the accord had been so important, made front-page news by condemning the agreement for "selling the freedom of half a billion people down the river." Yalta, argued Hoover, was "where we lost the peace and wandered into this land of hot and cold wars."[306] Later in the year, when in order to complete negotiations on a U.S.-Japan peace treaty, Truman felt compelled to appoint the Republican Foster Dulles to represent him—the very same Foster Dulles who had undermined James Byrnes's post-Yalta negotiations in Moscow—Dulles promised the Senate that the new treaty represented "the first formal act which the United States will have taken which involves a clear abandonment of Yalta," along with "total [U.S.] freedom from any obligations" deriving from the Crimean pact.[307] Hostile witnesses to the treaty argued that it only confirmed Yalta, something the Senate was loath to do. The Foreign Relations Committee debated whether it was necessary to amend the treaty to ensure that it not be understood to imply a confirmation of Yalta. While the explicit language was ultimately rejected, pundits observed that the debate marked the first steps toward Yalta's official repudiation.[308]

Yet, however many accommodations were made to contain it, the controversy over Yalta simply would not die. When Truman dismissed Douglas MacArthur in April 1951, Yalta became front-page news once again. Conservatives furiously argued that the dismissal represented "as great a military victory for Soviet Russia as Stalingrad, and as great a diplomatic victory as Yalta."[309] MacArthur's false insistence that he had originally opposed the treaty led to spirited attacks on Yalta in the mainstream media among many publications that had initially supported it with great enthusiasm. Columnist Raymond Moley and the editors of *Time* were particularly harsh. Moley blamed Yalta for the Soviet "Manchurian" threat and complained, in McCarthyite language, of the "Acheson-type" thinking that had influenced a "sick and weary" president there.[310] *Time* blamed Yalta for Chiang's defeat in China and reported the existence of General Hurley's apocryphal 1945 report by a "high-powered team of fifty experts" warning General Marshall of the dangers of allowing the Soviets into Asia.[311]

Yalta continued to plague Democrats through the 1952 elections, and by now some of the party's own candidates had begun exploiting its bad name. A young Massachusetts representative and Senate contender by the name of John Fitzgerald Kennedy even inserted angry assessments by former Polish diplomats and generals into the *Congressional Record*.[312] In the contest for the Republican nomination, Robert Taft hammered away at Yalta and the "indirect influence of Communists" that gave rise to it as a means of firing up the faithful and distinguishing himself from General Eisenhower.[313] The former allied commander, however, criticized only the "political decisions" that had been reached there.[314] These differences were largely stylistic, as neither Republican took public issue with the rampaging Senator McCarthy, though Taft's embrace was certainly less equivocal. (The general decided to skip a planned defense of George Marshall to be given in McCarthy's home state at the senator's request.)[315] The party platform, nonetheless, promised to "repudiate all commitments contained in secret understandings, such as those of Yalta, which aid Communist enslavements."[316] *The New York Times, Time, The Saturday Evening Post,* and many other publications endorsed the Republican stance.[317] Those Democrats who did not join in did their best merely to avoid the issue. The party did issue a fact sheet designed to defend President Roosevelt, countering, for instance, the accusation that the accords had explicitly ceded China to the Communists, in measured language that urged voters to read the original document. The Democratic platform restated the familiar line, condemning the "violation of the Soviet Union's most solemn pledges" made to Roosevelt.[318]

Both the Republican presidential candidate, General Eisenhower, and the Democrat, Governor Adlai Stevenson, were reluctant to pick up the Yalta cudgels themselves during the fall campaign. Eisenhower did allow himself a promise of its repudiation in a statement issued on Pulaski Day, while his vice-presidential candidate, Richard Nixon, in New York, called for a rejection of those parts of the accord "which abet the communist slavery of free nations."[319] Nixon's role in the Hiss case, his bulldog campaign tactics, and the background noise provided by McCarthy's lurid accusations out on the stump allowed the Republicans to exploit the emotional power of the country's anti-Yalta fervor without committing Eisenhower to too forceful a position.

The Eisenhower Solution

Once Eisenhower took office in 1953, however, he immediately attempted to defang the issue.[320] The president asked Congress to adopt a functionally meaningless resolution that accused the Soviets of having "perverted" wartime agreements, without specifying which perversions he had in mind.[321] His own party, having offered nine separate resolutions calling on the government to renounce the deal, refused this offering. Soon Eisenhower was experiencing the same spirited denunciations from Senator McCarthy and his allies—the still-isolationist *Chicago Tribune, U.S. News & World Report,* the upstart conservative newsweekly for businessmen; right-wing pundits George Sokolsky and Westbrook Pegler; and ethnic organizations like the Polish American Congress and the Assembly of Captive European Nations—that Truman had endured.[322] *The New York Times*'s editors heartily endorsed the proposal, calling it "one of the most potentially important declarations made by President Eisenhower," and likely "to free us from past commitments . . . [r]estoring the moral position of the nation." To the editors of the *Times,* it represented "the fulfillment of a campaign pledge,"[323] even though it was designed to take the place of a specific campaign pledge requiring the agreement's explicit repudiation. This inconvenient fact interested virtually no one in the Establishment or the mainstream media debate.

International relations professor Samuel L. Sharp, writing in *The New Republic,* blamed much of the subsequent reaction against the accord on the "irritating righteousness in the way some Democratic spokesmen explained and justified Yalta" at the time of its announcement. But it was easier, Sharp noted, "to capture the imagination" of the American public than "to recapture China and Poland."[324] Lyndon Johnson's indefatigable biographer Robert A. Caro argues that by supporting Eisenhower against the Taft Republicans—who were hoping to use their new control of both ends of the legislative process to reject Yalta once and for all—the newly elected Senate minority leader helped to deal a devastating blow to the Republican Old Guard and the vestiges of Midwestern isolationism. The Taft wing of the party, as Caro correctly notes, "believed as an article of faith that other, secret agreements had been made at Yalta," and Taft intended to use the power of the majority in the Senate to obtain those alleged texts in the hopes of demonstrating the truth of the now seven-year-old charge of "sellout." His ultimate goal was the circumscription of presidential treaty-making powers to prevent any such secret accords in the future.[325] *Newsweek*'s chief congressional correspondent, Sam Shaffer, notes the almost hysterical enthusiasm Republicans had been building against Yalta, should they ever control both the Congress and the presidency:

> It should have been so easy for Republicans . . . to translate the dream into reality. . . . All that was needed to make the dream come true was a sweep in which a Republican Congress and a Republican President could join hands in repudiating the Yalta Agreements as soon as possible after taking the oath of office on inaugural day. It is difficult to comprehend today how intensely the Republican politicians clung to this article of faith.[326]

Adding irony upon irony, it was Johnson, the Democratic minority leader, who saved Eisenhower on this issue, and helped lay the groundwork for the imperial presidency he would so unhappily misuse in Vietnam a decade later. But the short-term result—reinforced when Stalin died on March 4 while the resolution was being considered—was the enshrinement of the original Democratic doctrine of Soviet perfidy as the official American interpretation for the failure of Yalta. With a Republican war hero/president, the Eastern wing of its own party, and the Johnson-led Democrats all lined up in favor of blaming the Soviets for violating the agreements, without examining what those agreements said overly closely, Taft and his allies had nowhere to turn to give voice to their pent-up frustrations on the issue. The watered-down Senate resolution, in Johnson's words, would serve only "to notify mankind that Americans are united against Soviet tyranny."[327]

Taft, McCarthy, and their Republican allies did manage to extract a measure of revenge when Eisenhower and Dulles nominated Charles Bohlen, Roosevelt's Yalta interpreter, to be ambassador to Moscow in March 1953. Bohlen's confirmation hearings were extremely contentious, as the senators returned yet again to the Yalta role of Alger Hiss. McCarthy's forces held up the nomination and suggested that Bohlen was a security risk and a questionable "family man"—in other words, a homosexual. Many conservatives helped out. Everett Dirksen (R-IL) , later the party's floor leader, shouted, "Chip Bohlen was at Yalta . . . I reject Yalta. So I reject Yalta men."[328] Eisenhower eventually had to intervene personally, assuring supporters at a press conference that no "left-wing holdovers" had "slipped Bohlen over on him."[329] Together with the Republicans' strong tradition of party discipline, Eisenhower's assurances were enough to silence most of the critics and ensure Bohlen's confirmation. A year later, a similar dynamic occurred when the Senate voted on the Bricker Amendment, which would have limited the president's abilities to forge executive agreements without explicit congressional approval. A version of the amendment, whose support derived in part from the desire of the Republican senators to restrict future presidents from signing agreements like "the outrageous Yalta accords," came within a single vote of the necessary two-thirds majority, with liberals alone daring to oppose it openly. It was defeated only by Eisenhower and Dulles's panicked lobbying effort, operating in tandem with Lyndon Johnson's sophisticated manipulation of his Senate colleagues' interests and demands. The vast majority of Republicans, still hoping to prevent "more Yaltas," voted against their own president.[330]

Even with the country enjoying relative peace and prosperity under the popular President Eisenhower, the ghost of Yalta simply would not go quietly into the night. It returned to haunt political discourse yet again, in 1955, when Secretary of State Dulles decided, over the vociferous objections of Winston Churchill and the British government, to publish the secret papers from the conference. While the disclosure undercut what remained of the treason charge, it generated its own series of problems. The manner of the papers' exposure was peculiar and revealing. Four days after promising the British government to continue to keep them secret, in order to protect the historical reputations of Churchill and Roosevelt as well as to prevent new protests from both the French and the East Europeans, Dulles leaked the documents to *The New York Times.* In keeping with presidential tradition Dwight Eisenhower insisted that he had never read the Yalta papers and knew nothing about the decision to release them.[331] His administration's position on the accord was that while they continued to bind the Soviets, they no longer obligated the United States, owing to previous Soviet violations.[332] Also in keeping with tradition, James Reston, who played a key role in convincing Secretary Dulles to release the papers, published a front-page analysis in which he spoke of the "tragedy of Yalta," which he defined as a conflict between British "pragmatism and cynicism" and American "idealism and optimism" in the face of Soviet perfidy.[333]

This interpretation was immediately condemned as inaccurate by Churchill, the only survivor among the three major figures at Yalta. Churchill claimed that Britain's role in the Far Eastern agreements had been "remote and secondary," as "neither I nor [Foreign Secretary Anthony] Eden took any part in making it." Churchill's point may have been technically correct, but it was, as Warren F. Kimball points out, deliberately misleading, for Churchill had outlined to Stalin virtually the same concessions Roosevelt was forced to make at Yalta, during his October 1944 meeting with Stalin in Moscow. Moreover, he mischievously told his countrymen upon the agreement's release that, while there had been many reproaches in the United States about the concessions made to Soviet Russia, the responsibility rested with the Americans' own representatives. To the British the problem was indeed "remote and secondary."[334, 335] France and Canada denounced the publication, as did various unnamed diplomats from unnamed countries, who regarded it as a violation of all known diplomatic protocol.[336] Democrats, including Senate Foreign Relations Committee chair Walter George and Majority Leader Lyndon Johnson, condemned the manner in which the documents were leaked, accusing Dulles of trying to score political points against the opposition by reopening a controversal issue and "putting a strain on the unity of America and the unity of the Free World." The Senate would be "well-advised," Johnson averred, "to leave history to the professional historians."[337] New York Democrat Herbert Lehman went even further, calling the papers' publication "a perversion of history . . . published completely out of context." Like all Democrats, he, too, wished "Russia had not cruelly and cynically violated both the spirit and the letter of that [Polish] phase of the Yalta agreement." He blamed the "shameful act" on Dulles and Eisenhower's "cynical and devious motive" of not only scoring partisan points.[338]

No one in the media or in either political party seemed to notice that the U.S. government had been misleading its people about the nature of the accords for the previous decade. Likewise, none of the secret agreements imagined by opponents ever materialized, nor did any evidence for the alleged Svengali-like role played at the conference by Alger Hiss. The strongest reaction mustered was that of Senate Minority Leader William Knowland (R-CA), who compared Alger Hiss's presence in the American delegation "to a man playing poker with a mirror at his back, in which his opponent could see his hand before the play began."[339] Hiss, who had been released from Lewisburg Penitentiary after serving forty-four months, in November 1954, confirmed his signature on an argument that disputed FDR's decision to grant the Soviets three votes in the UN General Assembly, thereby completely confusing his accusers.[340] Knowland also vociferously denounced Roosevelt for lying to Congress about the fact of the Far Eastern deal during his March 1, 1945, address. Senator McCarthy insisted that a cover-up remained in place.[341] But McCarthy and his "ism" were weakening, and few in the Establishment believed it necessary to placate him as generously as in the immediate past. The domestication of former McCarthyite Richard Nixon through his ascension to the vice presidency was not irrelevant to this calculation. The first of the many "new" Nixons to grace American political history now informed the Executive Club of Chicago that he did not believe "there actually was any deliberate attempt to sell us out to the Communists" at Yalta.[342]

A second contretemps arose when General MacArthur attempted to discredit those documents demonstrating that he, too, had emphasized the need to do whatever necessary to bring the Soviets into the war in the Far East.[343] The MacArthur position was actually a curious one, since it maintained that he had informed Roosevelt, in the form of a forty-page memo given to the president before the conference, that an invasion of Japan was no longer necessary, because Japanese peace overtures indicated that unconditional surrender was imminent. In fact, a MacArthur spokesman had informed journalists just before Yalta that "we must not invade Japan proper unless the Russian army is previously committed to action."[344] James Forrestal's contemporaneous diary entry has MacArthur calling for the intervention of sixty Red Army divisions in Manchuria.[345, 346]

The Republican National Committee also published a report entitled "Highlights of the Yalta Papers and Related Data," which rehearsed all the traditional themes, and highlighted FDR's unkind remarks about Poles, Jews, and other minorities, in time for the 1956 elections. But without a Democratic president to oppose, its charges enjoyed minimal impact. The party did seek to tar Averell Harriman, now governor of New York, in a paper called "New Dealers Deny and Decry Importance of Yalta Papers After Ten Years of Secrecy." When asking "who engineered the fateful deals" at Yalta, Republicans insisted that the evidence "points the finger squarely at one Averell Harriman." Three years later, the future vice president, Republican Nelson Rockefeller, defeated the incumbent governor, after attacking the deal before East European New York ethnic groups as "one of the great betrayals of history."[347] Just how much influence these attacks may have carried, however, is impossible to say. Even in New York, the governor's election could hardly be said to turn on a thirteen-year-old foreign policy issue.

The Democrats did not bother to defend Yalta itself in either 1956 or 1958 but simply rebutted the now outlandish-sounding Republican charges—charges that appeared all the more ridiculous since it was a Republican president who was implicitly being charged with the cover-up.[348] Even the Establishment began endorsing the Truman-Eisenhower interpretation of the conference. "Seldom in history," wrote Raymond Sontag in *Foreign Affairs* in July 1955, "has deception been so successful and so decisive as that perpetrated at Yalta by the Soviet leaders at the expense of Britain and the United States."[349] The Republican platform, meanwhile, no longer thought fit to mention it. While the usual suspects charged what was now considered an Eisenhower "sellout," the general public remained unimpressed and unconcerned. With a Republican president and even Richard Nixon on board, mainstream opinion soon reverted to the original Truman interpretation of Yalta, ignoring the now impotent Taft-Nixon-McCarthy version of Yalta.

The reversion to the pre-McCarthyite interpretation led once again to the entirety of the blame for the collapse of Yalta being placed on the Soviets' shoulders. The key political question for the Establishment, therefore, was whether to personalize this to the perfidious Joseph Stalin himself, or to generalize the charge to apply to all Communists and hence the USSR's post-Stalin leadership. With Stalin dead, the former interpretation would open the door to improved U.S.-Soviet relations, while the latter would ensure a permanent frost between the two superpowers. Why, after all, bother to negotiate with a nation that reserves the right to lie? What politician would be fool enough to risk it?

The country faced just this question in 1955 when the Eisenhower administration commenced nuclear weapons negotiations with the Soviets in Geneva. Senator McCarthy predictably charged that the talks themselves represented a "thumping Communist victory," likely to result in "another giveaway . . . another Yalta."[350] Senator Knowland entered into the *Congressional Record* a full nine pages of "some treaties and agreements broken by Soviet Russia," including most prominently the East European portions of Yalta.[351] The lesson of that conference, as General Hurley had stated to the Senate Armed Services Committee four years earlier, was that "America was in a position at Yalta to speak the only language the Communists understand, the language of power."[352] In an article in *Foreign Affairs,* the efficacy of negotiations with the Soviets was also weighed in light of the "grinning spectre of Yalta," a figure its author compared to the smile of the Cheshire cat.[353] Even the editors of *The New York Times* echoed this view, arguing that, "The Yalta record must raise new doubts as to the value of any agreement with the Communists."[354] In other words, not even a Republican president and former Allied commander could be trusted at the bargaining table. Here was yet another legacy of Roosevelt's post-Yalta deception.[355] Given the post-Yalta experience, however, the concern of an overeager American administration rushing to make any kind of deal with the Soviets was hardly a significant one. At a 1954 conference, Secretary of State John Foster Dulles asked one of his aides if he would be satisfied if the Soviet foreign secretary would accept free elections and the reunification of Germany. "Why, yes," his aide responded. "Well, that's where you and I part company," Dulles retorted. "[Be]cause I wouldn't. There'd be a catch in it."[356]

In other words, no American president could or should trust any Communist leader to keep his word on any matter of mutual interest. When problems arose, they would be settled exclusively by the threat of force. If the U.S. threat in any way lacked credibility, the Soviets would take that as a signal to walk all over us, as they had done after Yalta, when we failed to go to war to defend Eastern Europe. Yalta, like "Munich," therefore became a permanently operating metaphor governing U.S. foreign relations, one that required our leaders to talk tough to the Russians and to be ready to back up their tough talk with force, regardless of what any given situation might have best called for. If they failed to do so, they risked "another Yalta," with all the connotations that word now implied. It was in these lessons that politicians like John F. Kennedy were schooled, these lessons that prepared him for making decisions about Soviet missiles in Cuba or Chinese troops in Vietnam. It would take the threat of nuclear holocaust in 1962 before an American president could risk "another Yalta" vis-à-vis nuclear weapons negotiations. Almost a decade of warfare in Vietnam, as well as more than 58,000 American lives, would be dedicated to protecting against the same danger in Southeast Asia. Even in the 1980s, President Ronald Reagan knew better than to trust the Communists to negotiate in good faith in either El Salvador or Nicaragua. Germany remained unnecessarily divided for more than forty years. Even more bizarrely, the Hiss case never achieved closure. As late as 1996, the case was still reverberating in odd ways in American politics, as potential CIA director Anthony Lake found himself on the defensive, and his nomination eventually torpedoed, in part because he voiced equivocation when asked on national television about the now fifty-year-old question of Hiss's guilt.[357] If Yalta had finally died as a poisonous political issue in American politics, it continued to rule as a misguided metaphor.

In the end, Yalta's impact on American political life and the contours of history is regrettable not only because of the undeniable damage it inflicted on the nation's political discourse, but also because it served to corrupt what was truly a noble cause: the American-led resistance to the spread of Soviet tyranny and the revival and protection of European civilization. Had FDR and, later, Harry Truman been willing to entrust their public with the truth about Yalta, U.S. leaders could have chosen to rally the nation and its allies in opposition to the humanitarian horrors of Stalinism without resorting to dishonest claims and demonstrably false accusations. We can imagine an alternative history in which America was spared the evils of McCarthyism, one in which liberals and Democrats fought to create a postwar order based on the courage of their convictions rather than the constant capitulation to conservative critics in defense of their somehow suspect patriotic credentials. The Cold War was, in some form, almost certainly unavoidable. But perhaps America might have fought it more honorably, honestly, and, not least of all, prudently had its leaders the courage to level with its people about how this might be accomplished. Who can truly say what was lost in the bargain?

III. JOHN F. KENNEDY AND THE CUBAN MISSILE CRISIS

Has any president ever enjoyed the degree of public veneration extended to John Kennedy following the Cuban Missile Crisis? Writing in *The New Yorker,* the normally quite reserved Richard Rovere observed, "No one who watched developments here failed to be impressed by the forethought, precision, subtlety, and steady nerves of the President and those around him in preparing our bold and ultimately successful initiatives."[1] Employing a locution that would be much quoted in the coming decades, Kennedy aide and historian Arthur Schlesinger Jr. called Kennedy's performance a "combination of toughness and restraint, of will, nerve and wisdom, so brilliantly controlled, so matchlessly calibrated, that it dazzled the world."[2] Roger Hilsman, another former Kennedy aide, credited the president with "a foreign policy victory of historical proportions."[3] Brother Robert Kennedy emotionally evoked a nation filled "with a sense of pride in the strength, the purposefulness and the courage of the President of the United States."[4]

Given the narrative of the events that the public was being told at the time, these accolades were hardly exaggerations. The Cuban Missile Crisis *was* a heroic tale in which the cool-headed president played the dashing, romantic lead. National news coverage quickly assumed the tone of movie-star publicity sheets. Speaking of the president's post-crisis press conference, *Time* correspondent Hugh Sidey reported that "Kennedy thrust his hand deep into his coat pockets, a familiar tic that signaled he was back in high fettle."[5] *The New Republic*'s Richard Strout was even more attuned to the cinematic potential of the occasion, as he wrote, "The crowd of 381 reporters stood respectfully and then breathlessly watched the tall, slim, auburn-haired young man, with the handkerchief protruding just the right distance, stride quickly to the podium and begin talking."[6]

However romanticized by the media, the Cuban Missile Crisis remains a remarkable story. The Soviets, secretly and deceptively, placed nuclear missiles in Cuba just before an American midterm election in which the issue of the alleged threat from Communist Cuba was shaping up to be a major point of weakness for the Democrats. Pressured by his advisers to attack immediately, either through bombing or a full scale invasion, Kennedy rejected this counsel as too risky for two adversaries armed with nuclear weapons. Instead he embarked on a complicated mix of diplomacy backed up by the threat of force. He issued his Soviet counterpart, Nikita Khrushchev, a public ultimatum, but also offered him an escape route that would minimize his public embarrassment. By choosing the option of a "quarantine" of Cuba, rather than the more belligerent suggestions of his advisers, Kennedy saved the world from a potentially catastrophic nuclear war. By offering up a public pledge not to invade Cuba—when the United States never had any intention of doing so, anyway—Kennedy gave away nothing of real substance but allowed his adversary to claim a partial, if extremely hollow, victory and thereby avoid complete and total humiliation.

The Official Story

This account—the "official story" of the Cuban Missile Crisis—is of a piece with the heroic qualities that so many journalists have attributed to this most complicated and perplexing of our presidents. The man who inspired so many to reach for greatness had little time for idealism himself. Kennedy's contradictions are so large that, even four decades after his murder, his presidency evades any kind of tidy summation. He took inexcusable liberties with countless women's affections, and since some of them turned out to be spies and/or Mafia moles, he may have endangered the nation's security—and certainly his own career—as a result. He pursued a policy of attempted assassination toward Fidel Castro in Cuba, again using the Mafia as his go-between. And he was willing to allow a group of South Vietnamese generals to overthrow (and without Kennedy's foreknowledge, murder) U.S. ally Ngo Dinh Diem, lying about the American role in the decision. But Kennedy's ability to motivate, charm, and impress those around him with his cool, dispassionate intellect; his endless energy; and his ability to inspire others to sacrifice continue to trump his flaws in the public imagination today no less than they did at the time of the missile crisis. Indeed if only the official account had been true, former Kennedy National Security Adviser McGeorge Bundy would have no need today to reconsider his statement published in 1964 in *Foreign Affairs* magazine, praising JFK for his "strength, restraint, and respect for the opinions of mankind" in the handling of the crisis.[7] Bundy concluded, as would many later commentators, that the solution to the crisis demonstrated that "the armed strength of the United States, if handled with firmness and prudence, is a great force for peace."[8]

But for those who attempt to examine the foundation beneath the sturdily constructed Kennedy myths, there are always complications, and perhaps no incident is more central to the myth—and more complicated beneath its surface—than the missile crisis. It was the missile crisis that inspired a top U.S. official to assert, for the first time, the principle of the government's "right to lie" to the American people. When asked at a press conference whether U.S. intelligence had detected the presence of Soviet missiles in Cuba on October 19, 1962, assistant secretary of defense for public affairs Arthur Sylvester promised, "The Pentagon has no information indicating the presence of offensive weapons in Cuba."[9] But of course, on that very same day top U.S. military officials were urging the president to order a full-scale invasion of Cuba to address the problem of the offensive Soviet missiles there. Sylvester later explained his decision: "It's inherent in [the] government's right, if necessary, to lie to save itself," he insisted. "News generated by the actions of the government . . . [are] part of the arsenal of weaponry that a President has," he concluded. "The results, in my opinion, justify the methods we used."[10] In the euphoria of the moment, few people at the time questioned this logic. Given the long-term impact of the lying that the Kennedy administration casually undertook in telling the story of the missile crisis, Sylvester's calculation might not be quite so simple today.

Although John Kennedy cautioned others to avoid the appearance of gloating over the perceived shaming of Nikita Khrushchev in the aftermath of the missile crisis, he could not help himself from later bragging among intimate friends, "I cut his balls off."[11] Many pundits and politicians were no less reticent in their own public statements. "For the first time in twenty years," wrote Walter Trohan, Washington bureau chief for the deeply conservative, anti-Roosevelt *Chicago Tribune,* "Americans can carry their heads high because the President of the United States has stood up to the premier of Russia and made him back down. . . . Mr. Kennedy ended a course of appeasement [that included the] shameful surrender at Yalta of the peoples of Eastern Europe and Asia. . . . Americans were proud when youthful Mr. Kennedy thrust his jaw in a fighting attitude and faced up to the bully in the Kremlin."[12] "Faced with a showdown," Zbigniew Brzezinski would later write in the *Department of State Bulletin,* "the Soviet Union didn't dare to respond."[13]

The actual events of October 1962 were so gripping that journalists hardly needed to add their own melodramatic flashes, but they could not pass up the opportunity to do so anyway. *Newsweek* began its coverage: "Everything that happened on the surface took place in seven short days—seven days in which the world had to face up to the true terrors of its existence as it has never done before . . . By the way it handled the situation, the United States has . . . gained a new sense of confidence in charting the perilous course through the cold war. The Soviet Union on the other hand, stands a liar before the world, a reckless adventurer for trying to upset the balance of power."[14] *Time*'s contribution read: "Generations to come may well count John Kennedy's resolve as one of the decisive moments of the 20th century. For Kennedy was determined to move forward at whatever risk. And when faced by that determination, the bellicose Premier of the Soviet Union first wavered, then weaseled, and finally backed down."[15] In an editorial oddly titled "Ten Days That Shook the World," *The New York Times*'s editors observed, "Confronted with American military might and firmness of purpose, Mr. Khrushchev abandoned his illusion that we might be 'too liberal to fight' and is staging a military retreat from the Western hemisphere."[16] Its star reporter, James Reston, added, "In his [Kennedy's] dealings with the Russians, he has probably removed the Soviet illusion that America would not fight and thus reduced the chances of miscalculation in Moscow."[17]

But as with all "great" events, the truth about the Cuban Missile Crisis only trickled out in stages. The earliest accounts of the affair depended almost entirely on the recollections of the president and his men, most of who formed the "ExComm"—technically the Executive Committee of the National Security Council, but in reality a group of largely like-minded, mostly conservative members of Kennedy's cabinet, sprinkled with former top government officials who were gathered together to help the president solve the crisis. Without exception, all concerned performed their grim duty with stoic heroism, according to the press reports of the time.

Perhaps the most overwrought, and certainly the most influential, of the early retrospectives appeared in *The Saturday Evening Post* in December of 1962. This account was given particular currency because one of its coauthors, Charles Bartlett, was known to be a close confidant of the president and had even spent a post-crisis weekend at his Virginia estate. His coauthor, Stewart Alsop, was also a social acquaintance of the president's. (Kennedy had graced Stewart's brother, pundit Joseph Alsop, with a visit to his dinner party on the very night of his inauguration.)[18] The magazine billed it as an "exclusive, behind-the-scenes report" and an "authoritative account of top-secret sessions of the National Security Council's Executive Committee," even though its language was sometimes closer to that found in a Superman comic than in serious journalism.[19]

The Bartlett-Alsop story established the narrative framework. It opened with Dean Rusk's now famous quote: "We were eyeball to eyeball and the other guy just blinked." By the authors' estimation, these words "deserve to rank with such immortal phrases as 'Don't shoot until you see the whites of their eyes,' for they epitomize a great moment in American history." The story's heroes, not surprisingly, were John and Robert Kennedy, with the latter being described as "the leading dove" in the ExComm's deliberations because of his opposition to an air strike that might be portrayed as "a Pearl Harbor in reverse."[20]

The *Saturday Evening Post* account was untouched by ambiguity, nuance, or contradiction, regardless of uncooperative fact. For instance, Secretary of Defense Robert McNamara initially dismissed the missiles in Cuba as merely "a domestic political problem." Owing to Kennedy's previous tough talk, that did not pose a new strategic threat to U.S. security.[21] His view was initially endorsed by both Roswell Gilpatric and Llewellyn Thompson, and to a considerable degree by Assistant for National Security McGeorge Bundy.[22] The analysts were inclined to take this position not only because it was in accordance with McNamara's existential argument but because they were also well aware that, at the moment of the crisis, the United States possessed 3,000 nuclear weapons deliverable anywhere in the world on 172 ICBM launchers and 1,450 long-range bombers. The Soviets, on the other hand, possessed approximately 25 to 44 ICBM launchers, perhaps 200 bombers, and a total of no more than 250 nuclear weapons.[23] (The actual numbers remain classified.) But Bartlett and Alsop only report: "On one point all present agreed, the Soviet missiles had to be removed or destroyed before they were operational," even if this meant nuclear war. As the authors quoted Robert Kennedy, "We all agreed in the end that if the Russians were ready to go to nuclear war over Cuba, they were ready to go to war, and that was that. So we might as well have the showdown then as six months later." This risk, however, was wholly justified. "If they'd got away with this one," explained one "member of ExComm" quoted by the authors, "we'd have been a paper tiger, a second class power."[24]

While the *Post* account featured a generous assortment of heroes, it did not shy away from including a cast of necessary villains, as well. This story had two black hats. The first was Nikita Khrushchev, obviously, merely because he was a Communist, and a scheming one at that. The second was the U.S. representative to the United Nations and former governor of Illinois, Adlai Stevenson, who had been John Kennedy's liberal opponent for the 1960 Democratic presidential nomination and the darling of liberal intellectuals. The Kennedys and their allies hated Stevenson passionately.[25] He was the only member of the ExComm who had spoken ardently and openly for a missile trade with the Soviets. " 'Adlai wanted a Munich' says a non-admiring official who learned of his proposal. 'He wanted to trade the Turkish, Italian and British missile bases for the Cuban bases.' "[26]

In the official version of the Cuban Missile Crisis, reflected in the story above as well as all the early accounts of the affair, the story of the proposed missile trade reads as follows: During the tensest moments of the crisis, as Ex-Comm members were deciding between various proposed military actions to remove the missiles and were trying to judge the likelihood of conventional or nuclear war in each scenario, Kennedy received a lengthy, confused letter from Khrushchev in which the Soviet premier basically offered to settle the crisis on American terms, asking only a noninvasion pledge in return. The Americans were elated at the news, but their joy was short-lived. Within twenty-four hours, as *Time* would report, "Khrushchev suddenly proposed his cynical swap; he would pull his missiles out of Cuba if Kennedy pulled his out of Turkey. His long, rambling memorandum was remarkable for its wheedling tone—that of a cornered bully. . . . Kennedy bluntly rejected the missile swap and increased the speed of the U.S. military buildup."[27] The White House issued a statement upon receiving the second letter, complaining that the Soviet proposal "involves the security of nations outside the Western Hemisphere. But it is the Western Hemisphere countries and they alone that are subject to the threat that has produced the current crisis," and insisting it would discuss the matter no further.

Kennedy, wrote Arthur Schlesinger Jr. in *A Thousand Days: John F. Kennedy in the White House,* published in 1965, was "perplexed" by Khrushchev's offer to trade, and "regarded the idea as unacceptable and the swap was promptly rejected."[28] Theodore Sorensen, in *Kennedy,* published the same year, recalled that the "President had no intention of destroying the alliance by backing down."[29] But the angry Americans remained divided as to how to proceed. They worried that any serious discussion of the Turkish missiles would rattle a fragile ally and shake the confidence of the entire NATO alliance in American leadership. But they also knew that the U.S. Jupiter missiles that were placed in Turkey under NATO authority were, as a practical matter, in McGeorge Bundy's formulation, "worse than useless," and in Robert McNamara's, "a pile of junk."[30] They were, Roger Hilsman reported, "obsolete, unreliable, inaccurate, and very vulnerable—they could be knocked out by a sniper with a rifle and telescopic sights." In the event of war, they would need to be either fired immediately or dismantled to protect against a likely accident. According to political scientist Graham Allison and others, Kennedy had, in fact, ordered them removed months before the crisis. But bureaucratic inertia had thwarted the president's plan, and hence Kennedy found himself stuck in a damned-if-you-do, damned-if-you-don't situation.[31] With the pressure building from Congress and the military to begin bombing Cuba, Robert Kennedy, Ex-Comm's "leading dove," came up with the idea of a "Trollope ploy," based on a commonplace plot device of the nineteenth-century British novelist. Instead of replying to Khrushchev's second letter, the president would pretend never to have received it. He would instead reply only to the first and accept its terms. Amazingly, the ploy worked, and Kennedy was therefore never forced to choose between going to war to retain weapons he considered "more or less useless" and, in Sorensen's words, "destroying the alliance by backing down."[32] While a few critics on the left and the right attacked Kennedy for being either too forceful or too weak, such criticism only made his actions seem more sensible to the vast majority of Americans, and to the elite Establishment commentators who set the tone for the larger public discussion of the traumatic event. Immediately following the end of the crisis, Kennedy's approval ratings shot up to 77 percent and those who had questioned the wisdom of his course were forced to confess their errors. Walter Lippmann, who, virtually alone among respectable Establishment voices, had publicly advocated a missile trade, offered up a mea culpa column in which he praised the young president for showing "not only the courage of a warrior, which is to take the risks that are necessary, but also . . . the wisdom of the statesman, which is to use power with restraint."[33]

In the jubilation that followed the ostensible Soviet capitulation, the U.S. news media applauded the Kennedy administration's resolve with regard to the Jupiter missiles. A *New York Times* headline on October 29 read, "Turkey Relieved at U.S. Firmness: Gratified That Bases Were Not Bargained Away." The only evidence that the Istanbul-based (anonymous) *Times* reporter offered his readers was a single quote from an anonymous Turkish editor: "I feel as though we had won. This is the payoff for our policy of strength and reliance on the United States."[34] A *U.S. News & World Report* writer in Ankara found "relief that the U.S. President had rejected Khrushchev's proposal that U.S. missiles in Turkey be withdrawn in exchange for the withdrawal of Soviet missiles in Cuba."[35] The Turkish media reinforced this interpretation with expressions of gratitude and renewed confidence in U.S. firmness as an ally.[36] *Time* provided its readers with a special report explaining why U.S. missiles in Turkey were in no way comparable to those the Soviets had placed in Cuba. "Khrushchev's offer to remove his missile bases from Cuba if the U.S. would dismantle its missiles in Turkey was a cynical piece of statesmanship," the magazine explained. "It took shrewd advantage of the frets and feelings expressed by many peace-loving non-Communist handwringers in the U.S. and other countries." While the comparison did inspire what *Time* called "superficially plausible slogans," in fact, "the Russian bases were intended to further conquest and domination, while U.S. bases were erected to preserve freedom. The difference should be obvious to all."[37]

In the immediate aftermath of the crisis, U.S. officials, perhaps mindful of the damage that Yalta had done to the fabric of political debate, went to great lengths to deny any possibility of the existence of secret agreements. Days after the announcement of the victory, however, Secretary McNamara ordered the Turkish missiles destroyed and photographs taken of the missiles (once dismantled) cut up and destroyed.[38] The process took six months and involved only the most pro forma consultation with Turkey and the NATO allies. Once this delicate operation was complete, a handful of Republicans and conservatives in the media, in both the United States and Europe, grumbled about the appearance of a covert deal.[39] To assuage their concerns, administration officials went before Congress and the media to mock the very idea of a deal. Kennedy himself informed *The New York Times*'s C. L. Sulzberger that the Soviet premier "could not have thought of really getting us to dismantle Turkey" and pretended that he "simply could not understand" what Walter Lippmann had in mind in his now famous column on the topic.[40] In testimony to the Senate Foreign Relations Committee, Secretary of State Rusk was asked by Bourke Hickenlooper (R-IA) to affirm that a "deal" or "trade" had in "no way, shape or form, directly or indirectly been connected with the settlement . . . or had been agreed to." He replied, "That is correct, sir." Faced with similar questions from the committee about the possibility that the administration had made a deal involving the Jupiters, Secretary of Defense McNamara responded, "Absolutely not . . . the Soviet Government did raise the issue . . . [but the] President absolutely refused even to discuss it. He wouldn't even reply other than that he would not discuss the issue at all."[41]

Outside the halls of congressional hearing rooms, administration officials steadfastly maintained their denials. In a number of press conferences following the crisis, State Department spokesman Lincoln White continued to reinforce the administration's public narrative when he consistently stated that there was no relationship in "any way, shape, or form" between the Cuban missiles and the Jupiters in Turkey.[42] National Security Adviser McGeorge Bundy, appearing on *Meet the Press* in December 1962, stated unequivocally that the U.S. public knew "the whole deal" and that nothing secret had taken place.[43] Bundy also wrote to French political philosopher Raymond Aron that those "who would spread rumors" about a Jupiter trade "of course, must be pretty far gone in their mistrust of the United States to start with." Concerned about the potential for such mistrust, Dean Rusk instructed the U.S. embassy in Ankara to reiterate to Turkish officials that Kennedy had not dealt away the Jupiters to resolve the confrontation, while he took it upon himself to reassure the Western Hemisphere allies.[44] In a 1964 NBC *White Paper* on the missile crisis, Bundy explained that a missile trade would have brought "the gravest kind of political danger" for the United States, because if such a deal had been undertaken "at the point of a gun, the Atlantic Alliance might well have come unstuck."[45] Had Bundy chosen his words more carefully, he might have added "public" as a qualifier to "missile trade" when speaking of the perceived dangers to the alliance. In fact, a private missile trade *had* taken place. But Americans were still years away from learning any of the facts about it.

Another Hero?

The first book-length consideration of the crisis continued the practice of taking the great men at their own words. Henry M. Pachter's *Collision Course: The Cuban Missile Crisis and Coexistence* (1963) recounted the settlement in language that appeared to preclude any contrary possibilities. Merely "to ask the question means to answer in the negative," he concluded:

> Kennedy's aim was precisely to end these swashbuckling attacks on peace and security. He had started an action to show once and for all that the Soviet wave can be stopped. The style of this action demanded that it be carried through as it had been started. Khrushchev would have to withdraw his missiles unconditionally. . . . To abandon the bases in Turkey under pressure meant to endanger an allied government and to precipitate a not-too-prosperous country into a new crisis. No matter how obsolete the bases might be, they could not be traded now. At stake were Turkey's friendship and the stability of the entire NATO and CENTO system of alliances of which Turkey is a keystone. Khrushchev might think of Castro as a pawn and of Cuba as an object of barter, but the United States could not treat an ally in such a way. . . . For the stability of peace and for the preservation of the balance of power, it was necessary for America to stand by all her promises.[46]

In the summer of 1964, however, Roger Hilsman, who had been Kennedy's assistant secretary of state for intelligence, revealed in *Look* magazine (and in his 1967 book, *To Move a Nation*) that the story was not quite as straightforward as first told. Hilsman revealed a tantalizing account of secret negotiations being undertaken during the crises. These talks, Hilsman believed, helped bring the two parties together and hence saved the world from nuclear war. Employing many of the same dime-store thriller narrative devices favored by Bartlett and Alsop, Hilsman, too, spoke of the moment when Khrushchev offered to trade the Cuban missiles for those in Turkey as "the blackest hour of the crisis." He noted speculation among the president's men that "hard-liners in the Kremlin, possibly backed by the military, might be taking over. . . ."[47]

Hilsman's primary revelation dealt with discussions during the crisis between ABC News correspondent John Scali and a Soviet embassy official who used the name "Fomin." According to Scali's report to Hilsman, Fomin suggested that the Soviet UN representative would be receptive if Adlai Stevenson proposed to resolve the crisis by linking the removal of Soviet missiles with a U.S. pledge to never invade Cuba.[48] Since Scali was acting as an informal agent of Hilsman himself, under the watchful eye of Secretary of State Rusk, the story puts its author at the center of the eventual settlement.

Hilsman argues that Khrushchev's initial peace overture "must have been drafted just about the same time as the instructions to Fomin. For the two communications were clearly related: the cable indicated a willingness to negotiate, and the unofficial approach through Scali suggested a formula for the negotiations." Hilsman also speculates that the premier's second, more demanding letter was "encouraged" by Walter Lippmann's column advocating a trade. Whatever the origin of the idea, the very suggestion of a trade gave rise to some impressive, if decidedly misguided, theatrics on the part of Scali to his Soviet counterpart. An exchange of Soviet missile bases "was completely, totally and perpetually unacceptable," Scali apparently told Fomin. "It had been unacceptable in the past, it was unacceptable today, and it would be unacceptable tomorrow and *ad infinitum*."[49]

The next important early history of the crisis came with the 1966 publication of *The Missile Crisis,* Elie Abel's book-length journalistic investigation, a work that would prove authoritative for at least three years.[50] An experienced and respected Washington journalist who had been John Kennedy's and Robert McNamara's first choice for Defense spokesperson, and who had been asked again to take the job in early 1962, Abel told a fuller version of the same story that Pachter had. Briefed extensively by George Ball, Robert McNamara, Llewellyn Thompson, and Roswell Gilpatric, and given access to the notes taken by Robert Kennedy that later formed the basis of Kennedy's own book on the crisis, *Thirteen Days,* Abel fleshed out much of the material reported by Bartlett and Alsop, adding considerable nuance and explication, including some debate between ExComm members over the wisdom of making some sort of trade with Moscow.[51] Abel's interpretation of Stevenson's intervention was also much less brutal than that channeled through *The Saturday Evening Post*'s writers by President Kennedy. Abel explained that Stevenson had included the idea of a trade in the context of a proposed overall settlement designed to "demilitarize, neutralize and guarantee the territorial integrity of Cuba." He did so in the belief that "people would certainly ask why it was right for the U.S. to have bases in Turkey, but wrong for the USSR to have bases in Cuba." Stevenson was also convinced that "the U.S. ought to be willing to pay some price for the neutralization of Cuba if that meant getting the Russians out, along with their missiles."[52] Nevertheless, he infuriated the more conservative members of ExComm, who shared the president's public contempt for the "soft" path the UN representative advocated.

According to Abel, Kennedy, too, rejected Stevenson's suggestion out of hand. While "the President had his own doubts about their [the Turkish Jupiters'] continued value and was willing to consider removing them in the right circumstances," Kennedy insisted that "this was not the right time for concessions that could wreck the Western Alliance; seeming to confirm the suspicion Charles DeGaulle had planted that the U.S. would sacrifice the interests of its allies to protect its own security." Abel notes some discussion among ExComm members of trying to find a way to remove the missiles without appearing to have done so at the Russians' behest, perhaps by urging Turkey to petition the United States for their replacement by a Polaris submarine. "Although Stevenson has been identified as the chief advocate, men with established reputations for cold-war toughness" were also heard to give voice to such speculation. But these options were all rejected. "It was one thing," Abel notes, "to discuss the liquidation of overseas bases around the conference table, in the framework of a general disarmament conference; quite another thing to sacrifice the Turkish bases under threat from Soviet missiles in Cuba trained on the U.S."[53]

Abel reported that Kennedy "sensed at once that the Turkish missiles were a side issue. In the end, if he had to order an armed attack on Cuba, leading perhaps to general war, it would not be because the U.S. five years before had stationed Jupiter missiles in Turkey. It would be because the Russians had tried by stealth to alter the balance of forces between East and West in the year 1962."[54] Stevenson's suggestion led Robert Kennedy to decide that he "lacked the toughness to deal effectively with the Russians at the UN in liquidating the missile crisis," and Kennedy then urged bringing in the conservative Republican John J. McCloy to shore up the UN representative in New York. According to Abel, the "bitter aftertaste" of the scorn Stevenson endured as a result of this decision stayed with him until his death.[55]

In the mid-1960s most Americans were not yet accustomed to questioning the honor and veracity of their leaders, and so even the most vociferous critics of Kennedy's behavior during this period accepted the official and quasi-official versions of the Cuban missile story. Nevertheless these sanctioned accounts did inspire a number of revisionist books and articles that questioned not the facts of the case, as they had been presented, but the wisdom and prudence of the president's actions. Early revisionists argued that Kennedy recklessly risked war, perhaps even nuclear war, to protect his political interests.[56] Conservatives expressed anger at the degree of the public compromise Kennedy offered Khrushchev, and would have preferred an invasion of Cuba to a peaceful settlement of the crisis that left Castro's regime standing.[57] Since, except in periods of extended crisis, American political culture tends to marginalize those critics perceived to be at either end of the political extreme, both sides' criticism probably had the effect of reinforcing the mainstream belief that Kennedy had indeed performed heroically. The slain president's deification in the aftermath of his assassination, moreover, made it extremely difficult for most Americans to countenance any objective assessment of his presidency, much less of a policy that appeared to result in so glorious a victory.

The incident therefore lay unexamined until 1969, when Theodore Sorensen edited Robert Kennedy's crisis diary for publication under the title *Thirteen Days: A Memoir of the Cuban Missile Crisis.* Kennedy's memoir advanced the true story to a significant extent, revealing for the first time the late-night Saturday meeting with Anatoly Dobrynin in which Robert Kennedy warned that war was just days away unless the Soviets relented. Second, the book explained that "there could be no quid pro quo or any arrangement made under this kind of threat or pressure, and that in the last analysis this was a decision that would have to be made by NATO. However, [Kennedy] said, President Kennedy had been anxious to remove those missiles from Italy and Turkey for a long time before the crisis began. He had ordered their removal some time ago, and it was our judgment that, within a short time after this crisis was over, those missiles would be gone."[58]

This dramatic admission confirmed what many secretly believed, but few had openly said aloud: that the removal of the Turkish missiles and the removal of the Cuban missiles were inextricably linked—not only in the minds of both parties, but also in the settlement of the crisis itself. Kennedy's memoir soon became the Bible of the still remarkably lively missile crisis debate.[59] Because of its posthumous publication, as well as Robert Kennedy's burgeoning reputation for giving voice to difficult truths, people were even less eager to question his version of events than they had been that of his deified brother. As Kennedy presented it, there had been no deal: he had merely informed the Soviets of what the president had been planning to do in the future, and had indeed tried to do in the past—namely, to get rid of the missiles. Those who suspected that something had been afoot had their suspicions confirmed, but the most controversial speculation—that there was an explicit secret deal like that made by Roosevelt at Yalta—was laid to rest. This version of the story, moreover, was consistent with the spirit of the times. In 1962, the United States was still very much in the deep-frozen mind-set of the Cold War. Yalta had demonstrated the futility of negotiating with Communists, and nothing had taken place during the ensuing seventeen years to give the mainstream a reason to reconsider. By 1969, however, Vietnam had destroyed the Cold War consensus, and hard-line anti-Communism had fallen out of favor in both intellectual and academic circles. The deal described in *Thirteen Days* painted the Kennedys as softer and more supple negotiators than had previously been the case, and placed them in implied contrast to the Vietnam villains Lyndon Johnson and Richard Nixon. The "no compromise" position that Kennedy's men had so carefully constructed in the aftermath of the crisis now proved a liability to the two slain leaders' reputations for heroism. The new story, while more complex, was far more appropriate to a moment in American history when compromise and conciliation had become the watchwords of political culture.

More Than Met the Eye

The first historian to begin to correct the official record turned out to be none other than Arthur Schlesinger Jr. Given special access by the family to the Kennedy archives for his 1978 biography, *Robert Kennedy and His Times,* Schlesinger filled out much of the story at which *Thirteen Days* had only hinted. Schlesinger based his own description of the late-night meeting with Dobrynin upon a memo that Robert Kennedy had written to Dean Rusk about it, but apparently had never sent.[60] Kennedy explained that he told Dobrynin:

> That there could be no quid pro quo—no deal of this kind could be made. This was a matter that had to be considered by NATO and that it was up to NATO to make the decision. I said it was completely impossible for NATO to take such a step under the present threatening position of the Soviet Union.[61]

Additionally, Schlesinger noted that Kennedy stressed to Dobrynin that this understanding would be canceled at once if the Soviet government tried to claim public credit for it.[62] At some subsequent point, Kennedy (or perhaps Sorensen, who says he cannot remember) crossed out part of the letter, so that it read: "~~If some time elapsed—and per your instructions, I mentioned four or five months.—I said I was sure that these matters could be resolved satisfactorily.~~[63] Whoever did it, the decision recalls Joseph Kennedy's advice to his sons: "Never write it down."

Schlesinger's account brings us much closer to the truth because it illuminates the Kennedys' desire to deceive not only America's NATO allies, Congress, and the American people, but also some of their close advisers in the ExComm, in order to conclude a secret deal with the Soviets that they consistently denied ever took place. "Probably no one except the Kennedys, McNamara, Rusk, Ball and Bundy knew what RFK had told Dobrynin," Schlesinger writes. "The American people certainly did not know until Robert Kennedy himself described the meeting in *Thirteen Days,* a half-dozen years later—and then his account was so muted that Harold Macmillan believed to the end of the day that no such bargain was ever struck." Schlesinger also includes information regarding the deal's aftermath, during which Khrushchev and Dobrynin attempted to codify the bargain through an exchange of letters. Bobby Kennedy, however, refused to accept them, lest one day they turn up as evidence at a politically inconvenient moment.[64]

There the story stood until 1982 when, on the twentieth anniversary of the crisis, six Kennedy advisers joined together to issue a statement on the incident to be published in *Time.* In it, Dean Rusk, Robert McNamara, George Ball, Roswell Gilpatric, Ted Sorensen, and McGeorge Bundy, drawing on Schlesinger and *Thirteen Days,* admitted the fact of the deal, but then argued that it "could not be a 'deal'—our missiles in Turkey for theirs in Cuba—as the Soviet government had just proposed." The reason for this, they explain, was "the matter involved the concerns of our allies, and we could not put ourselves in the position of appearing to trade their protection for our own." What happened instead, they argue, was that as "Secretary Rusk had begun the necessary discussions with high Turkish officials . . . it was entirely right that the Soviet government should understand the reality," and, hence, Bobby Kennedy merely explained it to them. The Kennedy aides also insisted that the discussion of the nondeal needed to be kept secret because "any other course would have had explosive and destructive effects on the security of the U.S. and its allies. If made public in the context of the Soviet proposal to make a 'deal,' the unilateral decision reached by the President would have been misread as an unwilling concession granted in fear at the expense of an ally." The Kennedy men concluded with praise for "our own President, whose cautious determination, steady composure, deep-seated compassion, and above all, continuously attentive control of our options and actions brilliantly served our country."[65]

Six years later, McGeorge Bundy told essentially the same story in his 1988 memoir/meditation on the nuclear age, *Danger and Survival: Choices About the Bomb in the First Fifty Years,* adding the detail that it had been Dean Rusk who had proposed the Robert Kennedy mission to Dobrynin. The nine men present (including President Kennedy, McNamara, RFK, George Ball, Roswell Gilpatric, Llewellyn Thompson, and Theodore Sorensen) were all concerned "by the cost of a public bargain struck under pressure at the apparent expense of the Turks, and aware as we were from the day's discussion that for some, even in our own closest councils, even this unilateral private assurance might appear to betray an ally, we agreed without hesitation that no one not in the room was to be informed of this additional message."[66]

In fact, even these attempts at a full and honest explanation of the deal turned out to be based on an account that was incomplete and ultimately misleading. At the end of the 1980s, new archival sources, glasnost, perestroika, the resulting implosion of the Soviet Union, and some candid discussions about the crisis between U.S. and USSR officials brought to light crucial new details about the deal, though in some respects, they also added to the confusion.[67]

The most dramatic piece of new information came at a January 1989 conference in Moscow, when Anatoly Dobrynin rose to challenge Robert Kennedy's posthumous statement in *Thirteen Days* that he had given a virtual ultimatum to the Soviet ambassador in their Saturday-evening meeting. Dobrynin asked the Americans, twenty-seven years after the fact, to finally own up to the truth. Theodore Sorensen apparently decided at this point that the American version of the events was no longer tenable. He stood up and announced that he had what he called "a confession to make to my colleagues on the American side, as well as to others who are present. . . . I was the editor of Robert Kennedy's book. It was, in fact, a diary of those thirteen days. And his diary was very explicit that this was part of the deal; but at that time it was still a secret even on the American side, except for the six of us who had been present at that meeting. So I took it upon myself to edit that out of his diaries, and that is why the Ambassador is somewhat justified in saying that the diaries are not as explicit as his conversation."[68]

Yet the revelations had only just begun. *Thirteen Days,* as well as all of the other published accounts, gave students of the crisis every reason to believe that had Khrushchev not caved in on Sunday, a missile strike against Cuba—and hence possible steps up the ladder of military escalation toward general war—was imminent. Most held it to be no more than twenty-four to thirty-six hours away. However, at a 1987 conference and in his subsequent memoirs, Dean Rusk revealed that following the Saturday-evening mini-ExComm meeting, the two brothers convened yet another secret gathering, this one including only Secretary of State Dean Rusk and Llewellyn Thompson. Here Robert Kennedy was given further instructions about what he might be allowed to say to Dobrynin. Thompson then left the room, and Secretary Rusk, alone with the president and vice president, received permission to put into motion a new plan in the event the Robert Kennedy–Dobrynin meeting failed to settle the crisis. Should all else fail, Rusk arranged with Columbia University president Andrew Cordier to have Cordier telephone his close friend, UN secretary general U Thant. Cordier would then instruct him as to the exact language through which the United States would be willing to accept a missile trade if publicly requested by the UN chief. Had Khrushchev refused Kennedy's offer of a private deal, it appears likely that the "Cordier ploy" would have gone into effect and President Kennedy would have acceded to a public deal with the previously authorized language that he, together with Rusk and Bobby Kennedy, had themselves scripted.[69]

When Anatoly Dobrynin published his memoirs in 1995, he added many tantalizing details to the story, but not all of them can be corroborated. Dobrynin seemed to think that the deal was negotiated during two separate meetings with Robert Kennedy: one on Friday night, and another on Saturday. At the first, Kennedy apparently left the room to call his brother during their talks, and returned to inform Dobrynin that the United States would remove the missiles from Turkey once the overall situation had been normalized. Dobrynin's memory on this point has been challenged, however, and it may be that he was describing just the Saturday-night meeting, while confusing it with earlier meetings during the crisis, though White House phone logs do appear to offer at least circumstantial support for his version.[70] Whether on Friday or Saturday night, however, Bobby Kennedy was extremely agitated and concerned, according to Dobrynin, that the U.S. military could not be contained much longer. Dobrynin's contemporaneous notes on file in the Moscow archives quote Robert Kennedy as follows: "If the missiles in Turkey represented the only obstacle to a settlement on the terms that had just been outlined, the president saw no insurmountable difficulties. His main problem was a public announcement . . . [which] would damage the structure of NATO and the position of the United States as its leader."[71] Dobrynin replied that this was "a very important piece of information," and promised to pass it along to Moscow as quickly as possible. The discovery in Moscow's archives of the memo that Dobrynin sent to Gromyko immediately after this meeting confirms this recollection.[72]

In his memoirs, Nikita Khrushchev calls this offer, received during a Politburo meeting at his dacha, the culmination of the crisis. At that point, Khrushchev decided to accept President Kennedy's proposals, "all the more since his consent to remove American missiles gradually from Turkey made it possible to justify our retreat."[73] The next day, Dobrynin called Kennedy to consent to the deal, and the two men met again. Dobrynin notes that Kennedy "once again asked me to maintain strict secrecy about the accord on

Turkey."[74] Radio Moscow then broadcast Khrushchev's favorable reply in English, making no mention of Turkey or Italy. That was the first time Soviet citizens had heard anything about Cuban missiles.

The Khrushchev-Dobrynin account has been supplemented by details provided by historians Alexandr Fursenko and Timothy Naftali. Citing notes taken during the October 28 meeting of the Soviet Presidium, they argue that Khrushchev had opened this meeting with the declaration to his colleagues that, "In order to save the world, we must retreat." He was preparing to ask his colleagues to support him in accepting the terms of Kennedy's letter, though he was concerned that he would be forced to do so without any movement from the president on the issue of the Jupiters. At this point, in dramatic fashion, an assistant to Khrushchev named Oleg Troyanovsky accepted the call from the Foreign Ministry containing the news of Dobrynin's urgently decoded cable. Interrupting the meeting, Troyanovsky read his notes on the cable, and Khrushchev quickly made up his mind.[75] Troyanovsky later told producers of a CNN documentary that it was Kennedy's final concession that solved the crisis.[76]

On Monday October 29, Dobrynin handed Robert Kennedy a letter from Khrushchev to President Kennedy, which promised not to disclose the matter of the Turkish missiles, but also "highlighted the idea that the Soviet leadership was accepting the terms of the accord on Cuba after the president's agreement to decide the question of American missile bases in Turkey."[77] A day later, Tuesday, October 30, Robert Kennedy returned the letter, explaining that the president "was not prepared to formalize the accord, even by means of strictly confidential letters, and that the American side preferred not to engage in any correspondence on so sensitive an issue." Very privately, Robert Kennedy added that "some day—who knows?—He might run for president, and his prospects could be damaged if this secret deal about the missiles in Turkey were to come out."[78] Sergei Khrushchev says his father was not offended by this. "He understood: President Kennedy didn't want to leave any traces to go down in history and he was afraid of being accused of catering to the communists. Nothing could be done about that . . . the important thing was that they, the president and Father, understood each other's aspirations and could trust each other."[79]

Unanswered Questions

Dobrynin's account, coupled with Rusk's and Sorensen's respective admissions and along with the careful historical excavation of many historians and professional researchers who have investigated the crisis, plugged many of the holes in the narrative of the incident that had appeared during the previous three decades. Nevertheless, many important questions remain unanswered. Clearly, for instance, the Kennedys made some version of the deal they continually denied, but where did its terms originate? The idea may have been inspired by Walter Lippmann's October 25 column advocating a trade. The Soviets were well aware of Lippmann's influence in official circles and may have concluded that the column was officially blessed if not officially inspired. (Indeed, Lippmann had originally helped convince Stevenson to accept his post in the administration when it was offered, and had been invited to comment on a draft of Kennedy's famous inaugural address. He contributed by toning down the references to the Soviet "enemy" to "adversary.")[80] Later archival research revealed that Khrushchev had, in fact, read Lippmann's column, and the pundit told Anatoly Dobrynin that while the president himself had not suggested the piece, he had consulted with members of the Arms Control and Disarmament agency, "possibly with John McCloy."[81] Meanwhile, *The New York Times* also carried an article by Max Frankel the previous day, in which administration officials were said to acknowledge the "appeal of the [trade] argument." One noted, "It was conceivable that the United States might be willing to dismantle one of the obsolescent American bases near Soviet territory." The following day Frankel reported "unofficial" interest in such a trade.[82] The Soviets, no doubt, read the *Times,* as well, and this may have been another source for their terms for the deal.

In January 1989, however, Dobrynin made the surprising claim that the issue of a Turkey-Cuba missile trade first came up in his conversation with Robert Kennedy at the Soviet embassy.[83] Georgi Shaknazarov, an aide to Mikhail Gorbachev, who attended one of the U.S.-Soviet discussions, corroborated the view that the idea of the missile trade "was born here in the Soviet Embassy, in a conversation, maybe with Robert Kennedy. . . . Dobrynin got the impression from this conversation that this could serve as the basis for agreement."[84] In addition, researchers have discovered that Georgi Bolshakov, a KGB officer and one of Robert Kennedy's closest contacts in the Soviet embassy, wrote to his superiors that "Robert Kennedy and his circle consider it possible to discuss the following trade: The U.S. would liquidate its missile bases in Turkey and Italy and the USSR would do the same in Cuba."[85] Sergei N. Khrushchev's study of his father's foreign policy also attributes the idea to a late-night meeting on October 26 between Kennedy and Dobrynin, during which Robert Kennedy left the room briefly, made a call from the next room, and returned to say, "The president said that we are prepared to examine the question of Turkey. Favorably." The author notes, "The ambassador had not dreamed of such a reply." Again, he presents no documentary evidence, but appears to be relying on his father's and Dobrynin's memoirs.[86]

Nevertheless, such accounts offer strong if circumstantial evidence that Robert Kennedy was originally responsible for the terms of the trade.

Did the deal include the Italian Jupiters as well as the Turkish ones? This answer, too, remains unclear. Robert McNamara gave orders to dismantle both sets of missiles immediately after the crisis ended. Many historians believe that the Italian missiles must have been included in the RFK-Dobrynin deal, but no one has been able to pin down any of the participants as to whether they were formally or informally part of the agreement.[87] Robert Kennedy never mentioned anything in his memo to the president about the Italian Jupiters, but he does quote himself in *Thirteen Days* saying, "President Kennedy had been anxious to remove those missiles from Italy and Turkey for a long period of time."[88] Fidel Castro told a Havana conference on the crisis that he had once asked Soviet foreign minister Gromyko exactly this question, but came away with the confusing reply: " 'Turkey, yes, but not Italy.' But in that message that Nikita was reading and the translator translating, it said, 'We have withdrawn, will withdraw, are withdrawing' that is, it referred to the withdrawal of the missiles from Turkey and Italy."[89] In his unverifiable memoirs, Khrushchev explains, "I didn't tell Castro that Kennedy promised to remove the missiles from Turkey and Italy, since that agreement was just between the two of us."[90]

Fallen Myths

These issues aside, the new information also reversed the conventional wisdom on other matters of confusion that had hitherto been accepted as crisis gospel. Declassified tapes of the ExComm discussions, for instance, demonstrate that it was not Robert Kennedy who suggested ignoring Khrushchev's second letter and responding only to the first—the so-called Trollope ploy—as Kennedy's memoir and many other accounts proposed.[91] Inside the ExComm, Gilpatric, Bundy, Sorensen, and Stevenson had all proposed the idea at various points in the crisis.[92] Roger Hilsman's account of the secret discussions between John Scali and Alexander Fomin—whose real name was Feklisov—also turns out to be a blind alley. The talks were never officially sanctioned on the Soviet side, and Feklisov did not report his contacts with Scali to KGB headquarters until after their second meeting. The news of that meeting did not, therefore, arrive until Saturday, October 27, Moscow time, and it was another four hours before the KGB sent the message to Foreign Minister Gromyko. Khrushchev, hence, would have known nothing about these contacts until after he composed both of his letters to Kennedy. Khrushchev's first letter and Feklisov's communication therefore could not have been "clearly related," much less "drafted at the same time," as Hilsman claimed. Feklisov even disputes Hilsman's account that he approached Scali rather than the other way around.[93] Their talks no doubt did influence the American team, but only on the basis of a false understanding of the origin of Feklisov's instructions.

Another crisis myth to fall victim to evidence was the universally held belief that Robert Kennedy acted as the ExComm's "leading dove." While the president's brother did voice discomfort early in the crisis about the possibility that his brother might be compared to Tojo, should the U.S. launch a surprise (i.e., Pearl Harbor–type) attack on Cuba, minutes of the October 27 ExComm meeting record the attorney general saying that he would prefer an air attack on the missile sites to a confrontation with Soviet ships on the quarantine. Recalling how the explosion of the battleship *Maine* in Havana harbor in 1898 had helped precipitate U.S. entry into the Spanish-American War, Robert Kennedy wondered aloud ". . . whether there is some other way we can get involved in this through, uh, Guantanamo Bay, or something, er, or whether there's some ship that, you know, sink the *Maine* again or something."[94] At various points during the early part of the crisis, Kennedy mused aloud on various forms of military attack, such as on Thursday, October 25, when he suggested that the United States "knock out their missile base as the first step," adding that a ten-minute warning would reduce accusations of an American Pearl Harbor.[95] He received no support for this proposal. Robert Kennedy was also among those who most vociferously and angrily sought to discredit Adlai Stevenson's dovish proposals. Perhaps alone in the presence of just his brother, his personal staff, or even with Georgi Bolshakov, Bobby Kennedy was a dove. And he certainly deserves a lion's share of the credit for the ultimately peaceful settlement of the crisis. But many of his ExComm-related statements and actions were hawkish in the extreme and had they been accepted, they would certainly have led to war, possibly nuclear war. In reality, the only consistent dove in the ExComm, save Stevenson, was John Fitzgerald Kennedy.

Much the same can be said about Secretary of Defense Robert McNamara, who, after decades of public silence on Vietnam-related matters, began a campaign in the mid-1990s to recast himelf in the role of insider war opponent, an effort that included countless interviews, a misleading memoir, and cooperation with Errol Morris's fascinating but highly problematic documentary, *The Fog of War,* released at the end of 2003. In that film, an eighty-six-year-old Robert McNamara claims, with regard to the missile crisis, "Kennedy was trying to keep us out of war. I was trying to help him keep us out of war." As journalist Fred Kaplan noted in his review of the film, "The first part of that statement is true. The second part is also true, at least for the first two of the crisis's 13 days." In fact, although he had identified the missiles as a mere "domestic political problem," on October 18, McNamara endorsed the Joint Chiefs of Staff's invasion proposal. "In other words," he is heard to say on Kennedy's secret taping system, "we consider nothing short of a full invasion as practicable military action, and this only on the assumption that we're operating against a force that does not possess operational nuclear weapons." A week later, during the crucial discussions of the final endgame, McNamara was arguing against the blockade and in favor of a military solution, insisting, "I don't see any way to get those weapons out of Cuba—never have thought we would get them out of Cuba—without the application of substantial force . . . economic force and military force." Two days later, on October 27, McNamara tried to convince Kennedy to refuse any offer of a missile trade and instead to prepare for a series of actions necessary "before we attack Cuba." His plan called for the launching of five hundred sorties a day for seven days, together with a land and sea invasion.[96]

Yet another example of reputation inflation can be seen in the hagiographic accounts of the ExComm itself. The great political scientist Hans Morgenthau argued, "The Cuban crisis of 1962 . . . was the distillation of a collective intellectual effort of a high order, the likes of which is rare in history."[97] Organizations expert Thomas Halper added, "The Executive Committee was important in helping plumb the reality of the situation. . . . The men chosen were calm, rational and frank . . . the Committee was the scene of intellectual conflict . . . and not emotional quarreling arising from interpersonal friction." It therefore "permitted . . . the freedom essential for effective discussion" and "made the best use of available time"[98] Bartlett and Alsop even counted among the crises' great benefits "the inner sense of confidence among the handful of men with the next-to-ultimate responsibility."[99]

But as the ExComm conversations became declassified and its tapes available and properly transcribed, they revealed a quite different decision-making dynamic. Indeed, excluding the magnificently calm and collected JFK himself, whose mastery of the situation becomes all the more impressive when one considers both the stakes and the combined array of experience and political status of those who sought to follow a more militaristic path, much about the ExComm loses its luster at close range. James Nathan argues that the transcripts of the October 16 and 27 meetings "hardly show a cool delineation of alternatives or a deliberate dissection of well-gamed actions. The voices are halting. The sentences are incomplete. Thoughts ramble. Memories slip and options ooze into the ether."[100] The atmosphere, as Robert Kennedy did report, also seemed to build into a kind of political pressure cooker. We hear of its members' near breakdowns and long, unexplained absences. We hear of one assistant secretary so frightened and distracted that he drove into a tree at 4:00 A.M.[101] Other members spoke of feeling themselves and their colleagues to be under "intense strain," often in a "state of anxiety and emotional exhaustion."[102] Given the treatment he received at its hands, Adlai Stevenson might be forgiven for considering the ExComm "the damnedest bunch of boy commandos running around . . . you ever saw."[103]

Some scholars have even questioned whether the ExComm itself was, at least in part, a kind of political charade. The fact that the president, his brother, and a few others secretly decided to offer a deal on the Jupiters before meeting with the full committee on Saturday night leads Barton Bernstein to suggest that the ExComm may have been considerably less influential than commentators generally portray it. According to Bernstein, "what is unclear, still, is how important the ExComm deliberations were in helping [the president] decide. Did the group, or particular members, substantially influence him? Or were the sessions, whatever his early intentions, soon part of a larger, unstated presidential strategy to build a consensus for his policies?"[104] ExComm's relative lack of liberal representation save the much-maligned Stevenson would also suggest that its purpose included political cover as much as wide-ranging debate. The incredibly cool and calculating president, as the transcripts repeatedly demonstrate, always expected that a trade of sorts would be necessary, and repeatedly indulged his own close advisers' hawkish musings, particularly those of Bundy, who seemed not to understand what was in the cards. (Only the Kennedys were aware of the taping system, which John Kennedy may have been planning to use for his future memoirs. The other participants believed themselves to be acting in confidence.) Kennedy, too, appeared alone in grasping how much of the rest of the world would perceive the actions that the others proposed undertaking. As he explained to his more hawkish defense secretary, most of America's allies viewed Cuba "as a fixation of the United States and not a serious military threat," adding, "They think that we're slightly demented on the subject. . . . A lot of people would regard this [proposed attack] as a mad act by the United States which is due to a loss of nerve because they will argue that taken at its worst the presence of these missiles really doesn't change" the nuclear balance of power at all.[105] As JFK was undoubtedly the most perspicacious strategic analyst in his administration, who is to say he was no less savvy in dealing with the potential threats and drawn daggers of those closest to him?

In order to keep potentially influential conservative opponents "inside the tent," JFK may have conceived of the ExComm discussions as a means of implicating potential adversaries in the conception and execution of any plan for dealing with the situation. This would explain, historian Mark White notes, why men like Richard Goodwin, Chester Bowles, and Arthur Schlesinger were excluded from the group, why Stevenson was so isolated, and why a wider-ranging debate—in which "softer" solutions had greater legitimacy—was never allowed to take hold inside the group.[106] Kennedy was confident that the liberals were going to support a deal, no matter what. If White is correct, the president's ploy worked brilliantly. His thesis is given added support by Kennedy's well-known hatred of meetings of any kind. "Not one staff meeting was ever held with or without the president," under John Kennedy, according to Theodore Sorensen. "The few meetings that were held," adds Garry Wills, "were shams."[107] And in the final Cuba discussions, where the real decisions were reached, John Kennedy, as Bernstein points out, "called the meeting, selected the participants and excluded about eight men." Here, Kennedy "pushed for making the Jupiter deal and everyone there loyally accepted it, though some had earlier expressed serious opposition to it." The central fact in this decision-making process, Bernstein notes, was that "the president made clear that he cared deeply about this issue; he chose the policy and nobody would resist him. They were the president's men, and he was the president."[108]

Yet another false assumption to be disproved by new evidence was the belief that the Soviets and Cubans were either paranoid or disingenuous to justify the missile placement—at least in part—on the basis of fear of a potential U.S. invasion of Cuba.[109] In fact, both the Russians and the Cubans were justified in their concerns. There was, of course, the Bay of Pigs, and when that conspiracy failed, Robert Kennedy told CIA director John McCone that disrupting Castro's regime was "the top priority in the U.S. Government—all else is secondary—no time, no money, effort or manpower is to be spared."[110] Bernstein notes that, under Robert Kennedy's direction in February 1962, Brigadier General Edward Lansdale was putting together a plan for a "revolt which can take place in Cuba by October 1962." Three weeks later, General Maxwell Taylor concluded, "Final success will require decisive U.S. military intervention."[111]

Historian James Hershberg has discovered that "throughout the first ten months of 1962, Operation Mongoose, the Kennedy administration's secret program of covert operations against Cuba, was closely coordinated with enhanced Pentagon contingency planning for possible U.S. military intervention to bring about Castro's downfall. During this period, U.S. officials actively considered the option of sparking an internal revolt in Cuba that would serve as a pretext for open, direct military action."[112] In March the U.S. Joint Chiefs of Staff proposed an absolutely incredible series of actions, including acts of terrorism against U.S. citizens, the U.S. space program, and internationally bound air travel—including students—for the purposes of surreptitiously provoking a global reaction that would justify a U.S. invasion and occupation of the island.[113] This operation continued right up until the crisis, and there is some evidence that top officials were looking for ways to ratchet it up, potentially as far as war, just as the crisis was dawning. On October 4, Robert Kennedy expressed to the National Security Council members working on Mongoose the president's dissatisfaction with the operation's lack of progress and the need for "more dynamic action," including sabotage.[114] According to authors Ernest May and Philip Zelikow, Robert McNamara met with the Joint Chiefs of Staff, McGeorge Bundy, and other officials on October 15 to review "contingency plans for a massive air strike on Cuba and for an invasion."[115] Even after discussing the evidence of Soviet missiles in Cuba on October 16, Robert Kennedy held a Mongoose meeting later that same day in which he pushed for more aggressive action and pleaded for new ideas of actions that could be taken against Cuba.[116]

The Cubans and Soviets were aware of much of this plotting, though certainly not all of it.[117] They definitely knew more than the American public, and it would certainly have influenced their behavior. Robert McNamara has since admitted, "If I was a Cuban and read the evidence of covert American action against their government, I would be quite ready to believe that the U.S. intended to mount an invasion. . . . I can very easily imagine estimating that an invasion was imminent."[118] Yet during the entire crisis, the American people were led to believe that Khrushchev's decision to place the missiles in Cuba—and Castro's willingness to accept them—constituted a wholly unprovoked attempt to threaten the United States and upset the global balance of power. Had they known that the Cuban regime had good reason to wish to defend itself against U.S.-supported subversion and potential aggression, Kennedy's public hard line might have been viewed with considerably less sympathy, both in the United States and abroad.

Foreign policy experts and U.S. intelligence sources, moreover, were aware of the Soviets' and Cuban's well-founded fear of invasion, though this did little to affect their thinking about the crisis, either before or during. In September 1962 CIA analysts concluded that "the main purpose of the present military buildup in Cuba is to strengthen the Communist regime there against what the Cubans and the Soviets conceive to be a danger that the U.S. may attempt by one means or another to overthrow it." A State Department study prepared after the crisis also concluded, "We have no doubt that Castro, and probably the Soviets too, were increasingly worried in the winter and spring of 1962 about the possibility of a new U.S. invasion attempt."[119] Coupled with the perceived provocation of the U.S. deployment of nuclear missiles, which were useful only in a first-strike situation, directly on the Soviet border in Turkey, Khrushchev's decision to place the missiles in Cuba was hardly irrational, and, to a considerable degree, predictable.[120]

The most significant falsehood of the crisis, however, involved the account of the missile trade itself. Not only did the Kennedys lie to the country, to Congress, to America's NATO allies, to their own advisers, to their friends, and to former presidents Truman and Eisenhower, they also went to considerable lengths to destroy the reputation of a loyal public servant, Adlai Stevenson, who had the courage to suggest inside the ExComm a similar solution to that pursued surreptitiously. How and why they did so is both instructive and important.

First, John Kennedy appears to have shown confusion at times about his decisions relating to the Turkish Jupiters before the crisis began. Musing on the Soviets' Cuban deployment on Tuesday, October 16, Kennedy complained, "It's just as if we suddenly began to put a major number of MRBMs in Turkey. Now that'd be goddam dangerous, I would think." When McGeorge Bundy explained, "Well, we did, Mr. President," Kennedy answered, "Yeah, but that was five years ago."[121] In fact, the Jupiters became operational, according to Bernstein, in April 1962, just six months earlier. The missiles—but not the warheads, which American forces retained—were then apparently turned over to the Turkish government on October 22.[122]

Yet many early accounts of the crisis suggested that the president was well aware of the presence and significance of the U.S. missiles based in Turkey, and that he had long been exploring ways to remove them. The typical story, as told by Elie Abel, involves the president's instructing Dean Rusk to raise the issue with the Turks, who then objected to their dismantling. Undersecretary George Ball was then ordered to raise it again, and according to Abel, the idea was again rebuffed. "It was, therefore, with a doubled sense of shock that Kennedy heard the news that Saturday morning [October 27]. Not only were the missiles still in Turkey but they had just become pawns in a deadly chess game. Kennedy reflected sadly on the built-in futilities of big government." The president, according to Abel, "became so irritated at this turn of events that he stalked from the room where ExComm was meeting." When Kenneth O'Donnell, special assistant to the president, followed, Kennedy allegedly instructed him to check the history of presidential orders for the removal of the Turkish missiles. O'Donnell supposedly reported back that the most recent order had been a National Security Council action memorandum issued in the third week of August 1962—only two full months before the Cuban crisis.[123]

Abel's primary source for this story was Robert Kennedy, who tells the same tale in *Thirteen Days.* The president "wanted the missiles removed even if it would cause political problems for our government. . . . The President believed that he was President and that, his wishes having been made clear, they would be followed and the missiles removed. He therefore dismissed the matter from his mind. Now [Saturday, October 27] he learned that the failure to follow up on this matter had permitted the same obsolete Turkish missiles to become hostages of the Soviet Union. He was angry."[124] This description of the Turkish situation was used as a source by nearly everyone who wrote at length about the crisis.[125]

In fact, the initial decision to place the missiles in Turkey was a hurried and generally ill-considered response to the domestic political hysteria occasioned by the 1957 Soviet Sputnik launch into space. The decision never enjoyed terribly firm support inside the military, however, owing to the many obvious problems with the quality of the missiles and the strategic conundrum that they created.[126] After a Joint Congressional Committee on Atomic Energy recommended against deployment in February 1961, the National Security Council took up the issue, but failed to come up with any concrete measures to reverse or even address it.[127] In late April 1961, Secretary of State Rusk floated the notion of withdrawing the missiles at a Central Treaty Organization (CENTO) meeting in Ankara, but the Turkish representatives objected, noting that the Turkish parliament had only recently appropriated the funds to pay for them, and hence the government would suffer considerable humiliation at their removal. Rusk accepted this reasoning and returned home to inform the president that a delay in the removal of the missiles was probably the best course. Kennedy concurred.[128]

Whatever action Kennedy may have intended, the Kennedy/Khrushchev Vienna summit of June 4, 1961, appears to have intervened and undermined further plans to remove the Jupiters. On June 22, George McGhee of the State Department reported to McGeorge Bundy that "action should not be taken to cancel projected deployment of IRBM's [*sic*] to Turkey . . . on the view that, in the aftermath of Khrushchev's hard posture in Vienna, cancellation . . . might seem a weakness." McGhee's sentiment evidently carried the day.[129] Finally, in August 1962, Kennedy did issue a National Security action memorandum relative to the removal of the missiles. This memo, however, did not contain an *order* to dismantle the Jupiters, but instead asked the much more preliminary question, "What action can be taken to get Jupiter missiles out of Turkey?"[130] Thus, the oft-told story of President Kennedy's preemptive efforts at removal and his subsequent frustration with bureaucratic obstacles rested on, at best, substantial misconceptions or, at worst, serious distortions of the truth.

Kennedy appears to have been aware that the missiles were a source of serious concern to the Soviets in the autumn of 1962, thus making the confusion that he initially evinced in the October 16 discussion with Bundy somewhat mysterious. Otherwise, why would he have instructed aides George

Ball and Paul Nitze to meet again with the Turkish ambassador in June to try to work out a solution? Why would he have issued the NSC action memorandum during the third week of August 1962, addressing the problem? Moreover, *The New York Times* published a Soviet complaint about the deployment in September, and the transcript of the president's September 13 press conference indicates some familiarity with it.[131] In fact, by early October the Kennedy administration was already consolidating arguments to be used in response to claims that equated the Jupiter missile deployment to Soviet actions in Cuba.[132] So to the degree Kennedy appears confused at the outset of the missile crisis, that confusion must have been temporary at best.

"The Coward in the Room"

With respect to Adlai Stevenson's suggestion in ExComm meetings that the United States consider trading the Jupiters in Italy and Turkey, as well as demilitarizing Guantánamo, both Kennedys played a nasty double game. As we have seen, a careful reading of the transcripts of the men's discussion throughout the crisis period indicates that John Kennedy was consistently preparing for a trade, even while his aides believed that they were getting ready for war. The president set the wheels of a deal in motion on Saturday, October 20, when he asked ExComm member Paul Nitze to study the potential problems for NATO that might arise from withdrawing the Jupiters from Italy and Turkey. On the following Monday, the president ordered Maxwell Taylor to instruct NATO's Supreme Allied Commander in Europe, General Norstad, to destroy the Jupiters if any attempt were made to fire them.[133] Kennedy also asked George Ball for a report from Turkish Ambassador Raymond Hare, outlining likely Turkish reaction to the deal he was clearly considering.[134]

Throughout the second week of the crisis, Kennedy's conversations with his advisers featured scattered comments and asides proclaiming the virtues of a Turkey-for-Cuba trade. Soon after receiving Khrushchev's second letter, the president told the British ambassador, David Ormsby-Gore, "From many points of view the removal of missiles from Turkey and Cuba to the accompaniment of guarantees of the integrity of the two countries had considerable merit."[135] Later he said to the ExComm, "In the first place, we last year tried to get the missiles out of there, because they're not militarily useful, number 1. Number 2, it's going to—to any man at the United Nations or any other rational man—it will look like a very fair trade." And here is JFK describing his own thought process: ". . . thinking about what—what we're going to have to do in a day or so, which is . . . sorties . . . and possibly an invasion all because we wouldn't take missiles out of Turkey, and we all know how quickly everybody's courage goes up when the blood starts to flow and that's what's going to happen in NATO, when they—we start these things and they grab Berlin, and everybody's going to say, 'Well that was a pretty good proposition.' . . . Let's not kid ourselves . . . today it sounds great to reject it [the trade] but it's not going to, after we do something. . . . We can't very well invade Cuba with all its toil, when we could have gotten them out by making a deal on the missiles in Turkey. If that's part of the record, I don't see how we'll have a very good war."[136] In yet another ExComm discussion, Kennedy explained, "Well this is most unsettling now, George [Ball], because he's [Khrushchev] got us in a pretty good spot here. Because most people would regard this as not an unreasonable proposal. I'll just tell you that . . . I think you're going to find it very difficult to explain why we are going to take hostile military action in Cuba, against these sites that we've been thinking about . . . [while] he's saying: 'If you'll get yours out of Turkey, we'll get ours out of Cuba.' I think we've got a very touchy point here. . . . You're going to find a lot of people think this [trade] is a rather reasonable position." Later on, the president adds, "Let's not kid ourselves. They've got a very good proposal. . . ."[137]

Kennedy appears to have received little encouragement for his dovish musings from the members of the ExComm, whether for reasons of the threat itself, the Soviet relationship, or alliance management. Mac Bundy responded at one point, his voice filled with emotion, "I think we should tell you . . . the universal assessment of everyone in the government who's connected with alliance problems—if we appear to be trading the defense of Turkey for the threat in Cuba, we will face a radical decline." So, too, believed Robert McNamara, as we have already seen.[138]

Virtually alone, mocked and misinterpreted, Adlai Stevenson argued vigorously in support of the president's ideas in the ExComm, and for this, the Kennedys set out to destroy him. Stevenson's position in the crisis has been as carefully and thoroughly distorted as Kennedy's, proving once again that the victors write history.

When Stevenson put forth his plan for the missile trade to the ExComm, including the evacuation of Guantánamo, he did not reject the possibility that U.S. military action might still be required. Stating his position in a letter to the president, Stevenson emphasized that "the national security must come first." However, the military *"means adopted have such incalculable consequences that I feel you should have made it clear that the existence of nuclear missile bases anywhere is* NEGOTIABLE *before we start anything . . ."* (italics in original). Despite his hope for a diplomatic solution, Stevenson also acknowledged that "we can't negotiate with a gun at our head" and "if they won't remove the missiles [from Cuba] and restore the *status quo ante* we will have to do it ourselves."[139] According to Stevenson's biographer, the ambassador defended his approach to the situation to Kenneth O'Donnell at a party during the crisis: "I know that most of those fellows will probably consider me a coward for the rest of my life for what I said today. But perhaps we need a coward in the room when we are talking about nuclear war."[140]

Inside the ExComm, the president angrily rejected Stevenson's suggestion, a reaction that was welcomed by the ExComm's conservative Republicans, Douglas Dillon and John McCone, as well as by Robert Lovett, a former secretary of defense in the Truman administration, who had once admitted to JFK that he had voted for Nixon. McCloy, moreover, lectured Stevenson that, so long as the Soviet missiles in Cuba were "pointed, for all you know, right now at our heart . . . It puts us under a very great handicap in carrying out our obligations, not only to our Western European allies, but to the hemisphere."[141] Although Stevenson's position was hardly different from that contained in Averell Harriman's October 22 letter to the president, or from the ambitious and potentially quite useful peace plan put forth by Brazil,[142] Robert Kennedy nevertheless sent Arthur Schlesinger to the UN with Stevenson, instructing him, "We're counting on you to watch things in New York. That fellow is ready to give everything away."[143]

Immediately after the crisis Kennedy set about to ruin Stevenson's reputation. When Charles Bartlett asked the president for his cooperation in writing the inside story of the crisis for *The Saturday Evening Post,* Kennedy sent Michael Forrestal to slander Stevenson. Forrestal told Bartlett on background that the reason why people suspected that a missile trade might be taking place "was all Adlai's fault." Forrestal explained, "The president opposed the idea and later prevented Khrushchev from getting it."[144] Kennedy had also asked to see a prepublication copy of the article in order to make whatever changes he felt to be necessary. When Bartlett provided the president with the draft, the one-time journalist "marked it up" considerably before returning it. According to Alsop, Kennedy "cut out two or three sentences which reflected [Stevenson spokesman] Clayton [Fritchey]'s explication and justification for Stevenson's position on the bases."[145] According to Bartlett, who later admitted to an interviewer that he thought Kennedy needed to rid himself of Stevenson altogether, Kennedy's military aide, Ted Clifton, played the role of emissary and the article returned with "Kennedy's prints all over it." Alsop wished to hold onto the manuscript as a souvenir, but Bartlett "threw it in the fire at Stewart's house to protect Kennedy."[146] Stevenson's argument was thus presented as seeming less rational than it actually was. A photo caption in the article read "Stevenson was strong during the UN debate, but inside the White House, hardliners thought he was soft."[147] What makes this incident appear even odder, and Kennedy's actions even more egregious, is that on some level, he professed to admire Stevenson's reckless courage in proposing the trade to the ExComm. "I wouldn't think a guy who's as smart a politician would expose himself. There are a lot of bastards in there who hate his guts and think he's an appeaser. To set yourself up to those guys is a pretty risky operation."[148]

The "non-admiring official" who accused Stevenson of wanting "a Munich" was, in fact, John Kennedy, the son of one of the Munich pact's most vociferous supporters. Alsop also informed his informal editor about the "Adlai wanted a Munich" line before the article went to press. Upon having it rechecked for publication, the president is said to have responded, "I want it in."[149]

John Kennedy had two reasons for wishing to destroy Adlai Stevenson politically. First, he and his brother passionately hated the man. They thought him haughty, effeminate, overly intellectual, and possibly homosexual, if J. Edgar Hoover was to be believed. The Kennedys also resented how slowly Stevenson had come to support John Kennedy's bid for the presidency in 1960, as he continued to hope that lightning might strike and the nomination would fall his way for the third time in a row. Kennedy had offered him the post of secretary of state in return for the former Illinois governor's endorsement in the 1960 race, but Stevenson proudly refused and told reporters that Kennedy was "too young" to be president and "not up to the job." (After the 1960 Oregon primary, JFK warned Stevenson, "Look, I have the votes for the nomination and if you don't give me your support, I'll have to shit all over you.")[150] Moreover, the president and the attorney general may have feared that their own power base was threatened by Stevenson's perceived heroic status in the eyes of the most liberal elements of the party, whom they also detested. Stevenson had seen his political stock rise after his virtuoso "hell freezes over" speech, in which he confronted the Soviet ambassador to the UN about the missiles in Cuba, and he could have emerged in a position to cause real trouble in the future over, say, Vietnam. But far more critical than even these blood feuds was the Kennedys' need to destroy the integrity and perceived respectability of the suggestion of a Cuba-for-Turkey missile trade. Without this anti-Adlai campaign, some enterprising journalist or Republican congressman might stumble across the notion that Kennedy, while publicly claiming total victory, had secretly made a deal not unlike the one Stevenson had proposed.

Stevenson quickly found himself held up to public ridicule and worse. For the rest of his life he was never able to escape from the opprobrium the "Munich" imputation had earned him. The *New York Daily News* ran a headline reading "Adlai on Skids Over Pacifist Stand on Cuba." Kennedy's potential presidential opponent, Barry Goldwater, called on his rival to fire

Stevenson, "because Adlai just doesn't understand Communism and the modern world." The president, he insisted, should "rid his Administration of those who have consistently urged a soft policy toward Communism, both in Cuba and elsewhere in the world."[151] Kennedy's support for his beleaguered appointee in the face of such calls proved a model of understatement.

Stevenson was not the only top official who saw his role purposely distorted in the aftermath of the crisis. Robert Kennedy, as evidenced by his oral history of the crisis, was also quite harsh on both Lyndon Johnson and Dean Rusk. In it, RFK explained, "Johnson was against our policy on Cuba in October of '62. . . . After the meetings were finished," Johnson "would circulate and whine and complain about our being weak." Kennedy further added that Johnson appeared to collapse after the final ExComm meeting, which had dwelled on invasion plans, though he omitted any such discussion from *Thirteen Days.* Kennedy also mocked Johnson's frequent contention that he had been at Kennedy's side during the crisis, insisting, "He was there for the first meeting, I think. Then he went to Hawaii because he didn't want to . . . indicate that there was a crisis at hand. He wasn't there at all when the decisions were being made."[152] In fact, the vice president, after returning on October 20 from a speaking tour, had attended 42 of 47 such meetings from October 22, 1962, to March 29, 1963, with his five absences occurring in November and December.[153] Regarding Dean Rusk, who contributed as much to solving the crisis peacefully as anyone, save perhaps Khrushchev and the Kennedys, Robert Kennedy later claimed that the secretary of state "frequently could not attend our meetings" and that "he had a virtually complete breakdown mentally and physically."[154]

Not all of the Kennedys' targets were among their own aides and potential political rivals. Before and during the crisis, Robert Kennedy and Georgi Bolshakov, a KGB official working under journalistic cover, had enjoyed a mutually beneficial relationship. On October 23, according to Fursenko and Naftali, Bolshakov met with *New York Daily News* writer Frank Holeman, who informed him that someone in the attorney general's office, possibly Kennedy himself, "considered it possible to discuss the following trade: The U.S. would liquidate its missile bases in Turkey and Italy and the USSR would do the same." Bolshakov's notes, the authors write, say that "the conditions of such a trade can be discussed only in a time of quiet, and not when there is the threat of war."[155] Charles Bartlett also passed word to Bolshakov of the possibility of a trade. These contacts may have helped give Khrushchev the assurances he needed that the crisis could be solved peacefully. (They may also have inspired his second letter to Kennedy.)

In the immediate aftermath of the crisis, however, the Kennedys decided to blow Bolshakov's journalistic cover and destroy his usefulness as a go-between. Bartlett, the Kennedys' unofficial mouthpiece, mentioned Khrushchev's use of a Soviet journalist in October to lie about the building of missile sites in Cuba. The president's friend, pundit Joe Alsop, included an even less oblique reference to Bolshakov in a post-crisis *Washington Post* article entitled "The Soviet Plan for Deception," thereby dooming his usefulness in the United States forever.[156] Ambassador Dobrynin informed Moscow that the article contained facts that only the Kennedys could have provided, and this quite understandably angered Khrushchev.[157] He wrote to Kennedy after the crisis, "We read now various articles by your columnists and correspondents . . . who as it would seem have no relation to confidential channels set up between us. Judging by the contents of these articles it is clear that their authors are well informed and we get the impression that this is not a result of an accidental leak of the confidential information. . . . This is evidently done for the purpose of informing the public in a one-sided way." Adding that "a minimum of personal trust is necessary for leading statesmen of both countries," the Soviet premier promised that "these channels will cease to be of use and may even cause harm," if the leaks continued.[158] Kennedy replied, hypocritically, "I am sorry that he is returning to Moscow . . . we shall miss him very much."[159] Bolshakov ended his days in Moscow an underemployed alcoholic. His crime was that he possessed the knowledge of the Kennedys' lie regarding the missile trade.

The Cuban "Threat"

None of the men who perpetrated these deceptions has ever expressed any public remorse about the role he played in misleading the world about the settlement of the missile crisis—particularly with regard to the missile trade itself. McGeorge Bundy admits that the seven survivors "misled our colleagues, our countrymen, our successors, and our allies" by "allow[ing] them to believe that nothing responsive had been offered to the Soviets to end the crisis." He concurs that a misleading message of "unwavering firmness toward the Soviets was communicated to the American people," a decision he justifies by arguing, "for all its costs, secrecy prevented a serious political division both within the United States and in the Atlantic Alliance."[160] Theodore Sorensen explains that he was the most junior person aware of "RFK's oral message on JFK's behalf regarding the assured ultimate dismantling of the Jupiters in Turkey." Sorensen adds that as the Kennedy intimate who was "least 'officially' connected to national security matters," he "felt I had not authority to reveal this information on my own."[161] Arthur Schlesinger Jr., who did not know the truth of the matter until he discovered it in the

Kennedy archives, justifies the deception as follows: "The willingness to make this additional concession doubtless helped persuade the Russians that the American government was truly bent on peace (and accounts for the indulgent treatment the Kennedys later received in Soviet accounts of the crisis). Perhaps there may be a place for secret diplomacy, at least when nuclear war is involved and when no vital interests of a nation or ally are bartered away."[162] Pierre Salinger, like Arthur Sylvester before him, argued following the crisis that "lies and disinformation were the means by which democracy . . . defends itself in a cold-war situation against an enemy which can operate in secret."[163]

Putting aside their petty political intrigues, if one were constructing a high-minded justification for the Kennedys' deception, one would not have to tax one's mind terribly hard to come up with a powerful set of arguments in favor of withholding the truth. No one understood the delicacy of his position better than John Kennedy. As he told *Newsweek* editor Ben Bradlee in February 1963: "The presence of 17,000 Soviet troops in Cuba . . . was one thing viewed by itself, but it was something else again when you know there were 27,000 U.S. troops stationed in Turkey." He then added, "It isn't wise politically to understand Khrushchev's problems quite this way."[164]

Indeed, in the autumn of 1962, before any Soviet construction workers were even discovered in Cuba, Fidel Castro's government was already a contentious issue in John Kennedy's presidency. Die-hard Kennedy loyalist Roger Hilsman admitted that Kennedy's attempts to make Richard Nixon look weak on Cuba during the 1960 election campaign boomeranged once Kennedy took office. "The fact of the matter," Hilsman admits, "was that President Kennedy and his administration were peculiarly vulnerable on Cuba. He had used it in his own campaign against Nixon to great effect, asking over and over why a Communist regime had been permitted to come to power just ninety miles off our coast. Then came the Bay of Pigs, and now the Soviets were turning Cuba into an offensive military base. . . ."[165] Kennedy's envoy to India, economist John Kenneth Galbraith, seconded Hilsman's assessment. "Once they [the missiles] were there," he insists, "the political needs of the Kennedy administration urged it to take almost any risk to get them out."[166] On Wednesday morning, the day the quarantine went into effect, Robert Kennedy reportedly told his brother, "If you hadn't acted, you would have been impeached," a judgment with which the president concurred.[167]

Brother Bobby had a point. When Kennedy decided to abort the Bay of Pigs landing without air cover in April 1961, he not only doomed the tiny army of exiles there, he also contributed to the pressure he would soon face to overthrow Castro's dictatorship. In the period leading up to the 1962 midterm elections, the Republicans, aided by their allies in the media, did their best to turn up the heat on Kennedy vis-à-vis Cuba, intent on returning some of the fire that had scorched Nixon two years earlier.

At the time Republicans accused the administration of purposely hiding important facts about a Soviet military buildup in Cuba from the American people. Kennedy spoke of Soviet "technicians" there; the Republicans called them "troops." Kennedy called Soviet missiles "defensive"; Republicans, of course, preferred the description "offensive." Although former president Eisenhower had warned against making Cuba "an object of partisan fighting," many Republicans and conservative journalists considered the issue simply too inviting to pass up.[168] Some Democrats were hardly more sympathetic. On September 20 two major Senate committees, Armed Services and Foreign Relations, issued a joint statement in favor of the use of force against Cuba, should it prove necessary. The man behind the resolution was the enormously influential Richard B. Russell of Georgia, who hoped "to get the president off his dead ass" on the issue.[169]

A September 14 editorial in *Time* insisted, "The U.S. simply cannot afford to let Cuba survive indefinitely as a Soviet fortress just off its shores and a cancer throughout the hemisphere."[170] A week later, *Time* featured a lurid hammer and sickle on its cover for its story on the Monroe Doctrine, which quoted numerous prominent Republicans demanding a blockade or invasion. "Just Get It Over With," a subhead proclaimed. *Time*'s editors casually dismissed Soviet warnings that an invasion could lead to nuclear war as "nothing more than a bluff."[171]

"The Congressional head of steam on this is the most serious that we have had," National Security Affairs adviser McGeorge Bundy felt compelled to warn the president. Bundy feared that the administration "may appear to be weak and indecisive." The president had to speak out with "a very clear and aggressive explanation" of U.S. policy to establish that the Cuban problem was "within our control."[172] In fact the CIA was, at the time, undertaking all manner of bizarre secret attempts to unseat Castro and even to assassinate him. These included such schemes as hiring Mafia hit men and manufacturing exploding cigars or lacing them with LSD, among other plots. None of them worked, and the U.S. government has not honestly accounted for them to this day. Even the 1992 CIA publication on the history of the agency's role in the missile crisis contains no mention whatever of these shenanigans, and many Americans are still blissfully unaware of them.[173]

Back in the autumn of 1962, however, Kennedy felt highly confident that Cuba would not give him any trouble before the election. He had received a secret communication from Khrushchev, via Anatoly Dobrynin, promising, "nothing will be undertaken before the American Congressional elections that could complicate the international situation or aggravate the tension in the relations between our two countries."[174] This guarantee led Kennedy to believe that he was free to sound off as tough as he liked about Cuba without consequence. At his press conference on September 13, the president seized the initiative and opened with the following: "If at any time the Communist buildup in Cuba were to endanger or interfere with our security in any way . . . or if Cuba should . . . become an offensive military base of significant capacity for the Soviet Union, then this country will do whatever must be done to protect its own security and that of its allies." But he also decried the "rash" and "loose" urgings of those who wanted an invasion of Cuba. Such talk, he complained, gave "a thin color of legitimacy to the Communist pretense that such a threat exists."

What the president did not realize at the time, however, was that he was creating a situation whereby, if Khrushchev double-crossed him—as, of course, he did—the president's own words could be quoted back to him as justification for demanding military action. Had Kennedy simply dismissed the pathetic notion of a plausible military "threat" to the world's most powerful nation from tiny little Cuba, Castro and Khrushchev would have been all but powerless to hurt him.[175]

Most of the nation's editorial boards supported the president's position, but the *Chicago Tribune* blamed Kennedy's "hands-off" policy for the fact of Cuba's military buildup and demanded to know, "When is Mr. Kennedy going to face the facts?"[176] The *Tribune* reported, "Havana is ringed by military hardware, managed by Russians and Cubans." The next day, reprinting a story from the *New York Daily News,* it informed readers, "So many Russians are landing in Cuba that Premier Fidel Castro has been forced to launch a crash program to house them." The newspaper also explained that the overwhelming majority of the Cuban people were clamoring for the United States to liberate them, though, of course, it neglected to offer any evidence.[177] The *Tribune*'s hectoring coincided with a Republican drumbeat against Castro and the administration's Cuban policy. Many Democrats joined in as well. Both houses of Congress adopted resolutions advising the president to use arms to combat Cuban aggression or protect U.S. security. But Republican Kenneth Keating of New York, who would soon reveal the existence of the Soviet Cuban missile sites, called the resolution "worthless," and demanded a "more decisive policy."[178] And when Keating made his front-page announcement of the arrival of Soviet troops on the island, two Democratic senators, George Smathers and Strom Thurmond, called for a U.S. military attack.[179]

Kennedy had effectively created his own dilemma in Cuba. At the beginning of 1962, it was the sole foreign policy issue on which the administration's record was viewed by the public as more negative than positive. By September, more than 70 percent of those who told pollsters that they cared about the issue were supporting harsh measures, including some who believed the United States should "starve them out."[180] Because of his belligerent rhetoric on Cuba, coupled with the long, tangled history of the Monroe Doctrine, the president was in no political position to offer the Soviets a public compromise once the crisis began. While he could not live, politically, with the symbolically threatening—but strategically meaningless—missiles on the island, neither could he allow the equation between the Jupiters in Turkey and the Russian missiles in Cuba that Moscow could obviously be expected to make.

Publicly, the administration refused to countenance any comparison between U.S. missiles in Turkey and Soviet missiles in Cuba. A U.S. Information Agency Policy Guidance advised State Department officials to deny the analogy, but "only if hostile comment compares Cuban bases to U.S. bases in other countries."[181] Once the ExComm received Khrushchev's second letter offering a formal trade, the White House released a statement denouncing the idea, objecting to "inconsistent and conflicting proposals [involving] the security of nations outside the Western Hemisphere."[182] The Pentagon offered reporters a briefing, summarized in an October 24 *Chicago Tribune* editorial entitled "Why Cuba Isn't Like Turkey." Pentagon officials were reported to argue that "the aggressive designs of the Communists are well established by their words as well as their actions; while for 60 years the United States has shown that it has no desire to subvert the Cuban government."[183] On the same day, the State Department sent out guidelines containing similar language to U.S. embassies and consulates around the world.[184]

The Danger of "Retreat"

Despite his best efforts to protect his flanks by including so many conservatives on the ExComm, moreover, Kennedy left himself particularly vulnerable to conservative attack should the details of the deal ever become known.[185] His very willingness to negotiate with the Russians, rather than launch an immediate military action, had already left him open to right-wing complaints. The hawkish ExComm consultant and former secretary of state Dean Acheson later criticized him even without knowledge of the deal. Acheson complained, "I felt we were too eager to liquidate this thing. So long as we had the thumbscrew on Khrushchev, we should have given it another turn every day."[186] ExComm member Paul Nitze also believed, "We should have pushed our advantage with greater vigor. . . . We could have pushed the Kremlin in

1962 to give up its efforts to establish Soviet influence in this hemisphere."[187] The men whom historian Gaddis Smith called "the paladins of the Monroe Doctrine" also believed that Kennedy had betrayed the sacred text, for which they never forgave him. Veteran diplomat Robert Murphy denounced the president's "docile submission to a dangerous violation of the Monroe Doctrine." Spruille Braden, another old Latin American hand and fanatical anti-Communist, called Kennedy's promise not to invade an "all-out defeat for the Monroe Doctrine" and a violation of America's pledged word.[188]

Many conservatives in Congress and the media echoed this line of attack. Robert D. Crane, writing in the right-wing scholarly journal *Orbis,* complained that the Soviets had escaped the crisis "with no more appreciation of American resolve than when they entered it." In Crane's estimation, the United States had failed in furthering its goal of "reversing the entire course of the communists' global strategy and, ultimately, of forcing them to abandon their ideology."[189] Speaking of Kennedy's promise not to invade Cuba in William F. Buckley Jr.'s *National Review,* David Lowenthal observed, "Nothing closer to an explicit retraction of the Monroe Doctrine has ever been made by any President." Kennedy's failure would now "assist the growth of Communist military power and subversion in this hemisphere."[190] Kennedy nemesis Richard Nixon, writing in *Reader's Digest,* lamented that Kennedy's unwillingness to undertake an air strike or an invasion "enabled the U.S. to pull defeat out of the jaws of victory."[191]

A group of conservative activists soon organized the Committee for the Monroe Doctrine. Backed by some Republican congressmen, pundits like Buckley, and former military officers such as Admiral Arthur W. Radford, the committee accused Kennedy of guaranteeing a "Communist colony" in violation of the Monroe Doctrine's prohibition against the extension of a foreign "system" into the Western Hemisphere. Barry Goldwater joined Representative Bob Wilson, chairman of the House Republican campaign committee, to ask the president to abrogate the agreement with the Soviet Union. The no-invasion pledge, they complained, had "locked Castro and Communism into Latin America and thrown away the key to their removal."[192] Senator Homer Capehart of Indiana complained that Kennedy had given Communism a "deed to Cuba" forever.[193] One can only imagine the kind of political apoplexy these right-wingers would have exhibited if Kennedy had revealed the terms of his deal and let the world know that he had, in fact, negotiated a peaceful end to the crisis by means of mutual concession.

Some of Kennedy's most serious potential problems regarding the Cuba matter lay within the U.S. military. General Curtis LeMay put the case most graphically: "The Russian bear has always been eager to stick his paw in Latin

America. Now we've got him in a trap, let's take his leg off right up to his testicles. On second thought, let's take off his testicles, too."[194] Upon hearing of the crisis's peaceful solution, Admiral George W. Anderson declared, "We've been sold out." Even close Kennedy ally and Joint Chiefs chairman Maxwell Taylor would have trouble being convinced. Discussing the crisis years later, he exclaimed, "I was not aware of the fact [that] the President had discussed with State the desirability of getting the missiles out of Turkey until this time [the second Saturday of the crisis]. And I opposed it, obviously. When you've got the guy on the run, why say, 'Come back, we'll give you a piece of cake!' "[195] Even after Khrushchev appeared to back down—and while the missile trade remained secret—LeMay and the rest of the Joint Chiefs wanted to invade Cuba, anyway. In a memo to the president, forwarded but opposed by Taylor, the officers insisted that Khrushchev's apparent capitulation was merely a ruse, an effort "to delay direct action by the United States while preparing the ground for diplomatic blackmail." They recommended an immediate air strike and invasion, unless there was "irrefutable evidence" that dismantling of the missiles had already begun.[196]

Judged purely on the basis of how well he sheltered his decision-making process in the crisis from his personal political interests, Kennedy's performance is much better than many critics allege, though hardly as impressive as the many keepers of his flame would claim. His defenders are no doubt correct when they argue that, were the president to view the crisis strictly with an eye toward the forthcoming midterm elections, the path of least resistance would have been a military attack. Americans in the twentieth century unfailingly supported their president in the early stages of military conflict, and many of the most influential members of the ExComm, including its Republican and military components, were clearly chafing at the bit to end the suspense and begin the bombing. The leadership of Congress was also solidly behind an immediate attack.[197] But the argument often heard from Kennedy defenders—that no one in the ExComm was ever heard to bring up domestic political ramifications in trying to choose the correct course—is both false and disingenuous.[198] In the first place, Douglas Dillon did raise the matter when, on October 18, he passed a note to Theodore Sorensen. "Have you considered the very real possibility," Dillon asked, "that if we allow Cuba to complete installation and operation readiness of missile bases, the next House of Representatives is likely to have a Republican majority?"[199] Second, since the ExComm was made up of both Republicans and Democrats, it would have been highly inappropriate—as well as counterproductive—to speak of a national security crisis in terms of electoral politics, regardless of how large the topic may have loomed in the decision makers' minds. Third, and finally, we have already seen how willing the Kennedys were to ignore the ExComm when it came to making their final decision about how to proceed. The fact that they did not seek partisan strategic advice from its members, therefore, proves little, beyond their basic political good sense.

The new evidence also points to a relative vindication for the Kennedys with regard to those revisionist critics who, like I. F. Stone, argued that they were "unwilling to be put in the position of paying any but the most minimal [political] price for peace."[200] The Kennedys were clearly prepared to accept the cost of peace; they simply weren't willing to admit their acceptance. Had the brothers been forced to back down publicly, the top military brass would have been furious were they to learn of the secret agreement, as would much of the CIA, the Pentagon, and the once and future national security Establishment. But General Norstad and the good soldier Maxwell Taylor would probably have helped to try to keep everyone in line with policy. The Kennedys would also certainly have handed the Republicans a political issue for November, though it is impossible to know just how many votes, or seats in Congress, such a victory would have been worth. Americans do not generally vote on foreign policy issues and certainly not in elections for local and statewide representatives. Moreover, the Eisenhower alumni in the ExComm—Lovett, Dillon, and McCone—would have offered valuable political cover. Had Kennedy been faced with a hostile Congress, he certainly would have seen his legislative program curtailed and many of his foreign policy initiatives questioned. But because he lied, he was hailed as a bipartisan hero.

To a seasoned, decidedly unsentimental politician, this could hardly have seemed a difficult choice. It looked even better nearly thirty years later, when Soviet General of the Army Anatoli I. Gribkov, one of the planners of the Cuban operation, made the claim that thirty-six nuclear warheads and 158 tactical nuclear warheads were already in Cuba prior to the time that the blockade began. Gribkov also claimed that Soviet commanders in Cuba had been given "fire control" authority in the event of a U.S. invasion.[201] While the latter assertion has never been fully substantiated, recent scholarship based on Soviet documents suggests that, at least at certain points prior to October 22, local commanders did have the authority to use specific tactical nuclear weapons against U.S. invasion forces.[202] Kennedy's decision to offer the Soviets a deal on the Turkish missiles therefore looks a good deal more prescient than anyone could have known at the time.

The NATO alliance might likewise have experienced some unpleasant turmoil had the deal been revealed. Alexander Haig, later secretary of state, was then an action officer on a Pentagon team detailed to write an analytical study of the crisis from a military point of view. During the course of his research, he stumbled on the fact that the Jupiters were being dismantled in Turkey and Italy in secrecy, and immediately complained to his superiors. With his typical flair for melodramatic assertion, Haig would later argue:

> The loss of the Jupiters represented a significant reduction in Turkish national security—not only in terms of the missiles themselves, but because their disassembly symbolized a loss of American will to defend a NATO ally. The removal of the Jupiters was already sending a shudder through the whole Western alliance, particularly since the U.S. had agreed to take out its Jupiters without consulting its allies. If we would not defend Turkey, would we defend West Germany or France? The Europeans had always feared that the U.S. would abandon its allies if it came to a choice between the destruction of European or American cities. The removal of the Jupiters, which protected Europe, in return for the removal of the Soviet missiles in Cuba, which threatened the U.S., would certainly be seen as proof that Washington did, in fact, put the safety of its own people above that of its allies.[203]

Writing in *Foreign Affairs* in the crisis's immediate aftermath, Henry Kissinger gave public voice to some of Haig's fears, warning, "We must be careful in the coming months not to feed the suspicion that we have purchased the withdrawal of Soviet missiles from Cuba by concessions of European interests."[204] But of course the Kennedys had done precisely that.

The concerns of both Haig and Kissinger appear to have been based on considerable and perhaps intentional exaggeration. The Turkish government might have experienced some discomfort from public trade, but it could easily have been placated—as it eventually was—by the replacement of the Jupiters with less vulnerable and more accurate sea-based Polaris submarine missiles. The Italians would likely have been pleased, as their government was in the process of trying to improve relations with the Eastern Bloc.[205] The administration's willingness to trade European missiles to ameliorate a threat close to home would doubtless have been regarded as a worrisome precedent by many members of the alliance. But it is unlikely that any of the apocalyptic prophecies of ExComm members and Kennedy administration officials that were treated so respectfully in the official and semiofficial histories of the crisis would have come to pass.[206] McGeorge Bundy felt certain, years after the fact, that Harold Macmillan, "who supported Kennedy in his public rejection of the Turkish trade, would have backed him at least as strongly in accepting it."[207] Neither the British nor the Germans were in any position to take public issue with the U.S. government on a matter of central importance to the Atlantic alliance. Harold Macmillan was even willing, temporarily, to demobilize the Thor missiles in England during a proposed conference, to allow the Soviets to save face.[208] A public deal would ironically have likely pleased the French, since it would have confirmed what they suspected about U.S. nuclear commitments in the first place. The semiofficial *Revue Militaire d'Information* accused the United States of having made a missile deal with the Soviets and thus having demonstrated its willingness to sacrifice the security of its allies. The Gaullist press used this argument on behalf of France's independent Force de Frappe. When the French did leave NATO, their decision was based more on the belief that the United States was less and less interested in continental security and more likely to involve Europe in a war of little relevance to its interests. Upon announcing his nation's withdrawal from the alliance in February 1966, de Gaulle explained, "While the prospects of a world war breaking out on account of Europe are dissipating, conflicts in which America engages in other parts of the world—as the day before yesterday in Korea, yesterday in Cuba, today in Vietnam—risk, by virtue of that famous escalation, being extended so that the result would be a general conflagration. In that case Europe—whose strategy is, within NATO, that of America—would be automatically involved in the struggle even when it would not have so desired."[209]

Based on a close examination of the political composition of each relevant government and its relationship to the Kennedy administration, Barton J. Bernstein concludes that "a formal trade, especially a public one, would have unnerved some governments, particularly the German and British and probably the Dutch; it would have confirmed the analysis of President Charles de Gaulle of France, delighted Canada, and probably pleased the Italian, Belgian, Greek, Danish and Norwegian governments." Latin American countries, Bernstein notes, could not have welcomed the idea of a U.S. invasion, no matter what their public posture. Their aid depended on an affirmative vote in the OAS, but almost all were frightened by the potential Castroite radicalism in their own countries—something another "Yanqui" invasion would have been certain to inspire.[210]

In the end, the sensitivities of the other nations, NATO members or otherwise, probably counted for very little in the political calculus of the president. In 1961 Kennedy had told Secretary Rusk that the allies "must come along or stay behind. . . . [W]e cannot accept a veto from any other power."[211] And Theodore Sorensen has added that "in matters of primary importance," Kennedy did not feel "that approval of the Alliance was a condition that pressed on him."[212] Still, it was much preferred for all concerned not to have to face the issue officially. Thus, the administration denied the agreement to even the closest allies, as when Secretary of State Rusk informed British Ambassador to the U.S. David Ormsby-Gore that "there had been no 'cozy deals' in connection with the change in the Soviet position. The only thing that

Khrushchev was getting . . . was that the United States would not intervene militarily in Cuba" provided that removal of the offensive weapons could be verified.[213] After the crisis, in 1973, and still under the misperception that no deal had taken place, Harold Macmillan wrote, "All America's allies would feel that to avoid the Cuban threat the U.S. had bargained away their protection."[214]

A Price Paid in Moscow

Ironically, though it may have contributed to his downfall as Soviet premier and general secretary of the Communist Party, Nikita Khrushchev also had critical motivations to keep the deal a secret. Since the Soviet people had never been informed of the missile crisis before Khrushchev's Sunday, October 28, radio address announcing its solution, he did not operate under remotely similar domestic constraints. He did, however, have reason to fear the same accusation of selling out the security of a close ally to improve his own nation's security, just as Kennedy did with NATO. This charge would hurt the Soviets not only with Castro, but with other allies and potential allies, including Mao's China, where Khrushchev was already under fire for his unwillingness to risk nuclear war over the crisis. As it happened, not only did Mao attack Khrushchev anyway, but Soviet-Cuban relations suffered grievously as well.

Upon hearing of Khrushchev's apparent capitulation on the radio, Castro is reported to have reacted "volcanically," furiously storming out to visit his troops and refusing to meet with the Soviet ambassador for days.[215] On October 31, Castro expressed in a letter to Khrushchev some of his deep resentment over the Soviets' handling of the crisis resolution. "I do not see how," Castro wrote, "you can state that we were consulted in the decision you took. . . . There are not just a few Cubans, as has been reported to you, but in fact many Cubans who are expressing at this moment unspeakable bitterness and sadness."[216] Castro later explained at a conference on the crisis that Khrushchev's announcement "produced a great deal of indignation, because we felt that we had become some kind of bargaining chip. Not only was this a decision taken without consulting us . . . we were humiliated." He was particularly aggrieved, he later explained, because, "From the international political point of view—for the honest, peace-loving people in the world; people who supported socialism in Cuba, or independence, or anything—it made no sense to exchange missiles in Cuba for missiles in Turkey. If the cause was Cuba, what did Turkey have to do with the defense of Cuba? Nothing at all!"[217] Following the announcement of the deal, Castro made a top Soviet emissary, Anastas Mikoyan, wait for ten days before granting an audience to begin to try to work things out. Castro's emotional vituperation was particularly painful to the old men of the Kremlin because, as Mikoyan later explained to

Rusk, "old Bolsheviks," such as the two of them, had "been waiting all our lives for a country to go Communist without the Red Army. It happened in Cuba and it makes us feel like boys."[218]

Khrushchev honorably kept his word to the Kennedys. When the Presidium distributed the letters between the two leaders to the rest of the Central Committee, Khrushchev deliberately omitted those from October 28 that could have exonerated his position. In his speech at the session, the premier said only that peace was preserved because "mutual concessions were made to achieve a compromise," and only mentioned the Cuba noninvasion pledge.[219]

This willingness to keep the trade secret, long after Kennedy's assassination, "cost him dearly," in the words of Anatoly Dobrynin. In a 1998 interview with CNN, the former Soviet diplomat lamented, "The whole world was under the impression that Khrushchev lost because he had given in to the pressure of a strong president, that he had taken everything out of Cuba and gotten nothing in return. No one knew anything about the agreement regarding the missiles in Turkey."[220] Within two years, Khrushchev found himself out of power in what turned out to be a bloodless coup. While the records of the October 14, 1964, politburo meeting remain secret, a memo for the prosecution that is now available shows a vicious attack on the premier's perceived failure to have bargained a quid pro quo for his strategic retreat in Cuba. "Not having any other way out," the author, Dmitri Polyanski wrote, "we had to accept every demand and condition dictated by the U.S., going as far as permitting U.S. airplanes to inspect our ships. At the insistence of the U.S., the missiles, and also most of our forces there, had to be withdrawn from Cuba. . . . This incident damaged the international prestige of our government, our party, our armed forces, while at the same time helping to raise the authority of the United States."[221]

Nikita Khrushchev had apparently hoped to use the resolution of the crisis to embark on what Averell Harriman termed, in a secret memo to McGeorge Bundy, a "palpable relaxation of tensions, presumably of some duration" with the United States. In a series of conversations in Moscow after the crisis, the Soviet leader had implied to Harriman that he would have liked to negotiate a "limitation if not reduction in military spending" in order to free the funds to modernize Soviet agriculture. Khrushchev felt he had "quite enough missiles," but needed an American accord in order to "curb the appetite" of his generals.[222] But because of their need to demonstrate continued "toughness" based on the false rendering of the crisis, the Kennedys were not interested in any such stabilization of relations. The result was that, following the crisis, the Soviets embarked on a massive nuclear and conventional arms buildup in order to achieve parity with the United States. This, in turn, forced the United States to match and eventually exceed the Soviets by devoting an enormous percentage of its government research budget and an increasingly larger part of its industrial complex to the largely nonproductive area of weapons manufacturing. Here was yet another legacy of Kennedy's deception.

The president, meanwhile, acted as if the situation remained unchanged vis-à-vis Cuba. He continued to humor the Joint Chiefs about the possibility of an invasion in the aftermath of the crisis. He promised forty thousand cheering Cubans at Miami's Orange Bowl that the flag of Brigade 2506, humiliated during the Bay of Pigs invasion, would "be returned to this brigade in a free Havana."[223] (Privately, meanwhile, Kennedy terminated Operation Mongoose and instructed anti-Castro exiles to stop harassing Cuban ships. He also met with a French journalist named Jean Daniel in November 1963 and apparently acknowledged U.S. responsibility for the conditions that caused the revolution and expressed a desire to make some sort of deal with a Soviet-free, though still Communist, Cuba (though he also could not resist initiating new attacks against the regime).[224] Neither Soviet nor American negotiators raised the issue of the withdrawal of the Jupiters during the UN-based negotiations designed to settle the details of the crisis, under firm instructions from both Washington and Moscow.[225] U.S. government officials like McGeorge Bundy's aide Robert Komer, who remained ignorant of the deal, continued to argue in favor of retaining the weapons well into 1963.[226] And so the secret held for nearly three decades.

The Costs of a Thirty-Five-Year Secret

Even though the truth about his and his brother's deception has now been readily available since 1989, assessments of John Kennedy's handling of the Cuban Missile Crisis have only grown more favorable with time. In 1997, during the observation of the thirty-fifth anniversary of the crisis, any number of celebratory articles were published and speeches made lauding the cool, calculated manner in which the peace had been saved and America's honor redeemed. In their edited version of the ExComm transcripts published that same year, Ernest May and Philip Zelikow refer to Saturday, October 27—the day the Kennedys plotted their secret trade with Anatoly Dobrynin and then participated in an apparently phony ExComm meeting—as "the finest hours of John F. Kennedy's public life."[227]

But the Kennedys' decision to mislead the world about the nature of the deal they concluded to end the crisis gave rise to many unhappy subsequent phenomena. The U.S. government, the American people, and by extension, much of the world have paid a tremendous and multifaceted price for the lies that were told about the incident. These lies begat other lies, which in turn created an entire mythological apparatus surrounding the Kennedys and their administration that helped to imprison their successors in a labyrinth of false and dangerous assumptions about the world. In the endless celebrations of the Kennedys' role in solving the missile crisis, precious little attention has yet been paid to these considerable costs.

The first and most obvious of these costs was to the quality of American democracy. While a few members of Congress and of the larger public were convinced that Kennedy and company were dissembling, they lacked the means to compel the president and his aides to reveal the truth. Representative Kenneth Keating (R-NY) observed that the explanations the administration offered in early 1963 to defend its decision to replace the Jupiters with Polaris missiles based on offshore submarines "does not jibe with statements by the Defense Department officials before the Cuban Crisis was resolved." Referring to the attacks on Stevenson, he noted that during the crisis, talk of a trade inside the White House was criticized as "Munich-like."[228] Barry Goldwater suspected a deal at the time, but he lacked any proof and did not know how to go about finding it. On the floor of the Senate he angrily demanded, "Mr. President, what goes on?" Was the dismantling of the Turkish and Italian Jupiters, he asked, "some kind of deal involving Cuba and disarmament plans?"[229] Goldwater never discovered the truth, and most of his right-wing allies were compelled to settle for mere grumbling about their suspicions. In a speech later placed in the *Congressional Record,* former senator William F. Knowland observed, "Our government denied then and denies now any such deal, but without advance consultation and agreement with our Italian and Turkish Governments we have taken our missiles out of those two countries. Was it a historic coincidence or was it a deal with Khrushchev? I don't know. Senators of both parties with whom I discussed it in Washington don't know. Have we become so much a captive of the 'peace at any price' and 'better Red than dead' philosophy that we are prepared to surrender bit by bit and piece by piece under constant nibbling tactics of the Soviet Union?"[230] Many such speeches and articles were entered into the *Congressional Record* by conservative congressmen who also lacked the evidence to pursue the matter. Already tending toward paranoia as evinced by its lurch into McCarthyism and embrace of the John Birch Society, the American Right could not but have its concerns about—and its alienation from—the federal government raised by the suspected deception carried out by the Kennedy administration.

On the Left, however, many thoughtful historians and journalists accused the Kennedys of sins they had in fact only pretended to commit. That the

Kennedys appeared willing to place their own political interests before those of the nation in avoiding nuclear war provided a great shock to many liberals and New Leftists who did not wish to believe the president and his brother to be capable of such moral callousness. Sidney Lens complained in *The Progressive,* "The willingness to gamble with the idea of nuclear war, even when victory would simply mean ashes, indicates a loss of touch with reality, almost a suicidal impulse."[231] Thomas Paterson saw in the president a Cold War obsession with toughness, manliness, and revenge: "The President's desire to score a victory, to recapture previous losses, and to flex his muscles accentuated the crisis and obstructed diplomacy. Kennedy gave Khrushchev no chance to withdraw his mistake or save face. . . . He left little room for bargaining, but instead issued a public ultimatum and seemed willing to destroy, in Strangelovian fashion, millions in the process."[232] This legend still lives on nearly four decades later in the popular imagination. In his memoirs, published in 2000, the novelist Martin Amis quotes his friend Christopher Hitchens's quip, "Like everyone else, I remember exactly where I was standing and who I was with at the moment that President Kennedy nearly killed me."[233] Had the Kennedys told the truth about the Turkish trade, these suspicions could have been laid to rest before they were able to sow the seeds of further distrust—a distrust that would help lay the foundation for the angriest and most divisive elements of the 1960s antiwar movement. Together with the right-wing alienation described above, this distrust would help create a legacy of skepticism between the governing and the governed in America that endures today.

The "Duty" to Lie

The Kennedys' systematic deception of the news media during the crisis also had lasting, damaging effects. The missile crisis not only inaugurated what Assistant Secretary of Defense Arthur Sylvester called the U.S. government's "right to lie," as part of the president's "arsenal of weaponry."[234] Sylvester also explained that it was important for the United States to speak "with one voice to your adversary," thereby implicating the media in the fight. The management of news, moreover, he added, "is one of the power factors in our quiver. This precise handling of the release of news can influence developments in the kind of situation in which military, political and psychological factors are so closely interrelated." Indeed, to manage the flow of information during the crisis, the departments of Defense and State issued directives requiring their personnel to report all conversations with media representatives to departmental superiors.[235] When members of the media voiced concerns about this policy, administration officials defended it by arguing, "We are aiming at dangerous reporting assisted by irresponsible or careless officials. . . .

[T]his kind of reporting exists, and . . . there are such officials."[236] Moreover, "a point of important principle is involved. In the conduct of the public business for which he is responsible, the Secretary of course has a right to know what his policy officers are doing" with regard to the flow of information.[237] White House appointments secretary Kenneth O'Donnell put the case most plainly to a group of journalists: "You are either for us or against us."[238] There was no room for even the aspiration to objectivity in the Kennedy administration's Cold War worldview. Nor can it be said that the media were much in the mood to challenge this dualism. Unless a writer or editor enjoyed the cachet of a Walter Lippmann or the stubborn independence of an I. F. Stone, he could hardly be expected to challenge the ideological verities of the day. By 1962, these verities included the government's right to lie whenever its challenged definition of "national security" dictated the need.

Some of the administration's lies were trivial, and could hardly be expected to inspire protest among rational men and women. The question that inspired Sylvester's famous assertion actually concerned the president's alleged "cold," which kept him off of the campaign trail, when in fact he was attending meetings of the ExComm. Telling reporters that the president was ill when he was not does not fall under the category of imminent threats to the freedom and dignity of the Republic. But next came the false October 19 statement that the Pentagon had no information indicating that offensive weapons were present in Cuba. This was followed three days later, on October 22, by a memo issued by presidential press secretary Pierre Salinger that outlined twelve areas of national security that required "caution" before reporters and editors rushed to publish what they learned. No member of the media either complained about or refused to cooperate with Salinger's guidelines. When the Cubans shot down an American U-2 spy plane on October 27, this dramatic incident went entirely unreported in the American media, by gentlemen's agreement, lest it overly excite the population and lead to a demand for immediate war.[239]

The great powers of the media were surprisingly sanguine in the face not only of the suspected lies themselves, but also of the government's repeated assertion of its right to employ them. Not a single reporter seems to have pursued the story of a possible missile trade very energetically, to the degree that any pursued it at all. Because McNamara, Bundy, Rusk, et al. had assured them that no secret deals had been done, they simply accepted them at their word, and the removal of the Turkish and Italian Jupiters so quickly thereafter was therefore regarded as coincidence. In a November 1963 article entitled "Strange Aftermath of the Cuban Deal," a reporter for *U.S. News & World Report* disclosed that just ninety days after the crisis ended, the United States started withdrawing the Jupiters. This was done, the article reported, "without consulting European allies."[240] Perhaps because of the president's assassination, the story ended there and was never pursued again.

Reaction was also surprisingly muted to the administration's assertion of its right to lie. Representing the last gasp of anti-FDR isolationism, the deeply anti-Kennedy *Chicago Tribune* was one of the few papers to object vociferously. "The Kennedy administration has attacked the ancient right of the American people to know the truth about their government," its editors complained. The *Tribune*'s editorial noted that unlike Presidents Roosevelt, Truman, and Eisenhower, the administration did not even invoke the right of "executive privilege" but merely "asserted the right of government to let the people know only what the government wishes them to know." This was, in the view of the editors, "a long step toward the managed propaganda found within a Communist dictatorship."[241]

Media powers without such partisan leanings, however, were considerably less incensed. *U.S. News & World Report* carried a brief story entitled "How U.S. Newsmen Were Misled About Cuba," focusing on the October 15 Pentagon statement, "the threat in Cuba is not now a military threat," and the fact that the United States had ruled out either an invasion or a blockade.[242] The magazine merely noted that these statements had been false, but drew no conclusions and made no protests about them. *Newsweek* raised the question not of whether, but "How Much Censorship?" should be allowed in peacetime. The editors decided that if the administration did "mislead the public, it accomplished its tactical end—allowing U.S. strategists to work in secrecy. . . . The pragmatic argument for the news policy was compelling: It had worked. It was part of the grand strategy by which the U.S. had risked nuclear war—and won without one."[243] James Reston later observed, "As long as the officials merely didn't tell the whole truth, very few of us complained. But as soon as Sylvester told the truth, the editors fell on him like a fumble."[244]

The disinclination of the media to challenge the administration's "right to lie" in the case of Cuba would have deleterious effects on the media's ability to hold the government accountable in the future. While it is impossible for the media to compel government officials to tell the truth, had these officials been forced to worry about the likelihood of a press firestorm over the discovery of a lie—or at least about the possibility of public opprobrium—they might have been more reluctant to engage in the systematic deceit that took place routinely during the Johnson and Nixon administrations. The theoretical foundation of the First Amendment lies in the media's ability to hold public officials accountable. But if these officials feel free to lie to the press—and by extension, the nation—with impunity, then democracy becomes pseudo-democracy, as the illusion of accountability replaces the real thing. It would take a defeat in war and a presidential resignation to force the media to face up to this problem squarely and reassert its Constitutional role as the people's guardian of the government.

The Essence of Deception

No less significant than its effect on the political realm was the Kennedy misinformation's effect on American intellectual life. In its aftermath, the Cuban Missile Crisis proved almost custom-cut to fit the cloth of American political science. It was a contained event, seemingly encompassing only two weeks and a limited number of political actors, thereby making it both easily comprehensible and manageable as a research topic. Its inherent drama naturally piqued the curiosity of scholars, and the coterie of former Kennedy aides' obsession with their subsequent treatment in history—particularly those whose reputations had been destroyed by Vietnam—meant their private documents and self-serving memoirs would become readily available. That a number of the participants received prestigious academic appointments in Cambridge, New York, and elsewhere further contributed to the likelihood that the story of the crisis would have a resonance far greater than just an account of a brief period in the history of superpower relations.

The text through which much of the nation learned to understand the "meaning" of the Cuban Missile Crisis—by virtue of perhaps thousands of university-level political science and international relations courses—was a small book first published in 1971 by Harvard professor Graham Allison, entitled *Essence of Decision*.[245] In its explication of the missile crisis specifically and the American political process generally, *Essence of Decision* became what one analyst called "a near-sacred text."[246] The work was summarized in most American textbooks on international relations, and virtually all monographs on foreign policy analysis make some reference to it. Between 1971 and 1991, according to political scientist David A. Welch, Allison's book was cited in over eleven hundred articles in journals listed in the Social Sciences Citation Index, including every periodical touching political science, and in others as diverse as the *American Journal of Agricultural Economics* and the *Journal of Nursing Administration*.[247] Its methodology quickly became the subject of a special conference at the RAND Corporation and the primary theme of a new course at the Woodrow Wilson School at Princeton.

Allison's work did not spring directly from the perceived facts of the Cuban Missile Crisis. Rather, the crisis provided the normative foundation for the application of ideas that were already taking shape independently. Allison himself noted that his findings, first published in the *American Political Science*

Review in September 1969, might be viewed as "the most recent but still unfinished 'evolving paper'" of what was then the Research Seminar on Bureaucracy, Politics, and Policy at Harvard's Institute of Politics.[248] In addition to Allison, the seminar included Richard Neustadt, Morton Halperin, Warner Schilling, Thomas Schelling, Ernest May, Stanley Hoffmann, Fred Ikle, William Kauffman, Andrew Marshall, Don Price, Harry Rowen, James Q. Wilson, and Adam Yarmolinski. The reach of these members into the most prestigious and influential organs of elite political thought made them a kind of board of directors of American political science and international relations study.[249]

In the original article, Allison lamented that "the disgrace of political science is the infrequency with which propositions of any generality are formulated and tested."[250] The missile crisis provided an opportunity to test Allison's theory about the interactions of leaders and bureaucracies in a dramatic, real-life situation, one in which most of the participants were still alive to provide details, and in which virtually all of the necessary information—at least on the American side of the conflict—was being made available to scholars.

Allison's understanding of the terms of trade concerning the Turkish and Cuban missiles is absolutely central to his analysis. It emphasizes what he believes to be the bureaucracy's refusal to support Kennedy's desire to remove the Turkish missiles, rather than Kennedy's insistence on trying to overthrow Castro, as the origin of the crisis. Allison places enormous emphasis on the frustration John Kennedy allegedly experienced when he discovered that his pre-crisis command to remove the missiles from Turkey had been ignored. He reported that "the president had twice ordered their removal in the spring of 1962, at presidential insistence. Rusk had raised the issue with the Turkish foreign minister, heard loud objections, and allowed the matter to drop. For the secretary of state, removal of the obsolete missiles from Turkey did not justify a row with the Turkish government. The President had raised the matter a second time with the State Department and made it plain that he wanted the missiles removed, even at some political cost. But again, State Department representatives found the Turks intransigent and decided against allowing the issue to become a source of discontent in relations with Turkey and the NATO alliance."[251] Allison also makes much of Kennedy's inability to ensure that the blockade of Cuba be moved from eight hundred miles off the shore of the island to only five hundred, thereby giving the Soviet ships more time to consider their options before facing a potential conflict.[252] However, both of these assumptions, which are absolutely critical to Allison's analysis, have proven to be false.[253]

Allison's version of the Turkey-for-Cuba trade is drawn largely from *Thirteen Days.* He even says at one point, "Had RFK not written his memoirs, and indeed, quite probably, had he had the opportunity to edit his first draft," he would never have included so honest an account.[254] Like Robert Kennedy, Allison places considerably more emphasis on the implicit ultimatum of an imminent American attack in swaying the Soviets. Nevertheless he is puzzled by the fact of the ultimatum,

> given the President's unique perspective and his particular problem (removal of the Russian missiles from Cuba without war) . . . especially in light of his earlier preference for postponing forceful action. One can understand how representatives of the State Department who had failed to negotiate removal of the Turkish missiles, might be persuaded by the argument that a deal would split the NATO allies. But the President had already been willing to pay part of that price, since many Europeans would interpret the de-fusing of the Turkish missiles as the first step in a deal, whatever the United States said. Why should his concern for the problem that withdrawal would mean for the NATO allies now dominate his interest in giving Khrushchev an acceptable path away from war?[255]

Here Allison's view is clouded not only by his misperception of the Kennedys' earlier actions regarding the Turkish missiles, but also by the misleading account offered up in *Thirteen Days.* Kennedy had not yet done what Allison assumes he had with the Turks, and later did far more than he knew, with regard to the missiles' removal.

Allison questions whether the "private exchange" between Kennedy and Dobrynin can be "properly labeled a 'deal?'" His answer: "At the initial level, there could be no 'deal.' Let the issue be clear: the Russian missiles must be removed with no strings attached. But at a second level, let there be no misunderstanding. The President had intended that the Turkish missiles be removed more than a year ago. Nothing had changed."[256] Here, false information leads Allison to false conclusions.

The influence of Allison's analysis would go a long way toward enshrining the model of "Bureaucratic Politics" as the governing paradigm for much of American political science. Allison collaborated with Mortin Halperin to formalize this paradigm, and applied it in analyses of any number of topics, including the entry of the United States into Vietnam, U.S. China policy, the Marshall Plan, American-Turkish relations, the Antiballistic Missile (ABM) decision, and U.S. international economic policy. Harvard's Kennedy School made bureaucracy politics the centerpiece of its new public policy program, as Allison became its dean. By the 1980s, his framework was hailed as "one of the most widely disseminated concepts in all of social science."[257]

The bureaucratic politics paradigm was applied to Kennedy's decision-making process in the crisis and the manner through which it was communicated to support Allison's thesis that the organizational processes of a bureaucracy can nullify the decisions of leaders. The thesis further vindicated President Kennedy's actions during the crisis because it had the effect of releasing him from culpability for what might have been considered his own responsibility in helping to cause it, and attributing that responsibility instead to a nameless, faceless bureaucracy, unable to answer for itself. The Allison paradigm also enshrined crisis decision making as the most effective means of governance, since the bureaucracy it described was unlikely to respond to a chief executive's wishes in any other circumstances. We might safely speculate that presidents and so-called crisis managers working under its influence were less than reluctant to allow given problems to percolate to crisis proportions, because crises came to be seen as opportunities for effective governance, rather than the potential disasters they had once been.

Neither politics nor ideology played any role in Allison's bureaucratic model. Congress is not even present, and neither, really, is democracy. As political scientist Stephen D. Krassner has pointed out, Allison's analysis "obscures the power of the President [and] undermines the assumptions of democratic politics by relieving high officials of responsibility." Why bother to hold elections when success or failure was unrelated to the key decisions reached in any given policy area? "Elections," Krassner continued, "have some impact only if government, the most complex of modern organizations, can be controlled. If the bureaucratic machine escapes manipulation and direction even by the highest officials, then punishment is illogical. Elections are a farce not because people suffer from false consciousness, but because public officials are impotent, enmeshed in a bureaucracy so large that the actions of government are not responsive to their will."[258]

Needless to say, in the middle of the catastrophe of Vietnam, a political science doctrine that served to distance decision makers from the results of their decisions was not exactly a hard sell among those who had been making those decisions. It was also particularly welcome among the scholars and writers who wished to continue thinking well of the intentions of their friends and colleagues who had served in the administration during a time when the foreign policy establishment found itself under relentless attack on campus. (Allison made it clear that he shared Richard Neustadt's view that the memories of participants, drawn from his interviews, would take precedence over any documentary evidence, particularly when the latter contradicted the former—another potential evasion of responsibility for the men behind the war.)[259] Placed in the context of the Bureaucratic Politics paradigm, as Krassner further notes, Vietnam was a failure of the "machine"—a war, as Arthur Schlesinger Jr. argues, "which no President desired or intended." This "machine," which demanded a policy that could neither succeed nor be successfully terminated, was not a reflection of a misguided ideology or the hubris of U.S. government officials; rather, it was the inevitable product of the simple inner workings of bureaucratic cogs and wheels.[260] No one, not even the president, was ultimately responsible or could responsibly be held up to censure by his fellow citizens.

By adopting Allison's paradigm, political scientists not only confused millions of students about the facts of the missile crisis, it gave them a deeply flawed understanding of the nature of the American political process and its alleged imperviousness to rational leadership from the top. More recently, the "Tower Commission report exposed the flaws of instant bureaucratic analysis," notes author J. Gary Clifford, "when it simplistically blamed the Iran-Contra Affair on a loose cannon in the White House basement and exonerated a detached president who was allegedly cut out of the policy 'loop.'"[261] They did not examine the policy that lay beneath the scandal, much as Allison had ignored Kennedy's attempts to overthrow the Cuban government and his decision to allow the Turkish deployments to proceed despite his stated misgivings. But as Krassner rightly points out, "The ability of bureaucracies to independently establish policies is a function of presidential attention."[262] If John Kennedy had made the removal of the missiles from Turkey a priority, it would have happened. If Ronald Reagan had made it clear to the top members of his administration that he wanted all laws to be scrupulously followed with regard to the Contras, it is highly unlikely that Oliver North, William Casey, John Poindexter, and the rest of his staff would have embarked on the projects that eventually grew into the Iran-Contra scandal.

A Lie's Legacy

No doubt the most important and enduring legacy of the Kennedys' decision not to tell the truth about the missile crisis settlement was the political impact it had on the United States after the president's death. Consistent with the views held in the popular media, the legacy of the crisis itself is generally considered to be an extremely positive one by most historians and scholars of the crisis. The Harvard-based defense strategist Thomas Schelling said nothing terribly controversial when he insisted that "the Cuban missile crisis was the best thing to happen to us since the Second World War. It helped us avoid further confrontations with the Soviets; it resolved the Berlin issue; and it established new basic understandings about U.S.-Soviet interaction." McGeorge Bundy concurred, adding, "[I]t was a tremendously sobering event with a largely constructive long-term result . . . I really do think that the Cuban missile crisis was a massive risk reducer."[263] Analyst and diplomat Raymond L. Garthoff has speculated that "the crisis opened up a degree of greater belief in the possibility of mutual accommodation." And Theodore Sorensen says he believed that the effect of the crisis on the president's advisers "was to purge their minds, at least temporarily, of Cold War cliches."[264]

Certainly President Kennedy's June 10, 1963, American University speech, in which he announced, "If we cannot now end our differences, we can at least help make the world safe for diversity," was one positive legacy of the crisis, from the standpoint of achieving world peace and stability. The address was reprinted in the Soviet press, and the Soviets briefly stopped jamming Western radio stations. The Soviets immediately agreed to inspections of their nuclear power stations at the International Atomic Energy Agency in Vienna, and the Atmospheric Test Ban Treaty was signed within six weeks.[265] The crisis undoubtedly led both superpowers to take a step back from the brink of confrontation and attempt to find ways to contain the Cold War lest it lead to unintended catastrophe. It sobered the men in charge of maintaining the world's peace, at least insofar as it related to direct U.S.-Soviet conflict. Not until the 1980s and the election of Ronald Reagan would either side even consider the possibility of a military conflict between the two Cold War principals.

These are significant accomplishments, not to be dismissed. But most histories and virtually all popular media discussions of the crisis have focused exclusively on these legacies without much cognizance of what might be termed their underside. What Americans saw in the president's apparently spectacular victory was, quite naturally, an example for future diplomacy for himself and for his successors. Many members of the administration who remained in the dark about the deal, however, were also the primary architects of the Johnson administration foreign policies—including, most prominently, LBJ himself. Their judgment was therefore corrupted not only by their own ignorance of what had really taken place during the crisis, but also by the expectation raised in the public by its false understanding of it.

Discussing the phenomenon that Stephen Van Evera calls "blowback," political scientist Jack Snyder notes the various ways in which elites tend to become entrapped in their own myths. "Insofar as the elite's power and policies are based on society's acceptance of imperial myths, its rule would be jeopardized by renouncing the myths when their side-effects have become costly. To stay in power and to keep central policy objectives intact, elites may have to accept some unintended consequences of their imperial sales pitch."[266] Thus, with respect to the missile crisis, even the introduction of new information about it often had no impact on the Kennedy (and soon Johnson) men's understanding of what really happened.

In its broad outlines Kennedy's Cuban Missile Crisis deception is strangely similar to that fashioned by FDR more than seventeen years earlier upon returning from Yalta. In each case, a Democratic president cut a deal with his Soviet counterpart that recognized and respected his adversary's interests while simultaneously securing the United States' most important goals.[267] But in neither case was the president willing to confide even in some of his closest political advisers—much less the American people—about the traditional diplomatic give-and-take necessary to close the deal, so threatening did each leader find the notion of a publicly admitted political compromise. Roosevelt portrayed his negotiated settlement in the misleading language of Wilsonian idealism, thereby painting a false and ultimately unsustainable view of Soviet motives and likely behavior in the minds of his countrymen. Kennedy dressed up a partial compromise in the cloth of unmitigated victory—a kind of unconditional surrender on the part of his adversary without even a shot being fired. Both presidents imprisoned their successors and their nation's political culture in a self-reinforcing psychological labyrinth of dangerous delusion.

In the wake of the Cuban Missile Crisis, a belief in the beneficent power of strategically deployed military force became the sine qua non of the Kennedy-Johnson administration foreign policy team. Consider the intoxicated praise of the Kennedy men as they describe the import of the success that, in Arthur Schlesinger's words, "dazzled the world." The historian and former adviser argued that "the ultimate impact of the missile crisis was wider than Cuba, wider than even the Western Hemisphere. . . . Before the missile crisis people might have feared that we would use our power extravagantly or not even use it at all. But the thirteen days gave the world—even the Soviet Union—a sense of American determination and responsibility in the use of power which, if sustained, might indeed become a turning point in the history of the relations between East and West."[268] Robert Kennedy, with full knowledge of the secret deal that he himself had negotiated, nevertheless boasted at the 1964 Atlantic City Democratic convention: "[President Kennedy] realized also that in order for us to make progress here at home, that we had to be strong overseas—that our military . . . had to be strong. He said one time, 'Only when our arms are sufficient, without doubt, can we be certain, without doubt, that they will never have to be employed.' So when we had the crisis with the Soviet Union and the Communist Bloc in October of 1962, the Soviet Union withdrew their missiles . . . from Cuba."[269] Roger Hilsman agreed that "the Soviets backed down in the face of a threat that combined conventional and strategic power."[270] The only debate these advisers would entertain was on the question of whether it was America's nuclear or its conventional arsenal that had caused the Soviets to turn tail and run. ExComm member Paul Nitze would insist that America's "undoubted superior nuclear capability" proved the decisive factor.[271] Henry Kissinger concurred: "The crisis could not have ended so quickly and decisively," he wrote, "but for the fact that the United States can win a general war if it strikes first and can inflict intolerable damage . . . even if it is the victim of a surprise attack."[272] McGeorge Bundy was among those who argued that it was U.S. conventional superiority that ultimately solved the crisis—and local conventional superiority, at that—as the Soviets had no hope of matching the military power that Kennedy could bring to bear on Cuba. The U.S. nuclear advantage, therefore, never entered into either side's calculations.[273] Arthur Schlesinger has also attributed this view, posthumously, to President Kennedy.[274] All of these judgments were predicated on the false conviction that Kennedy had faced down the Soviets without resorting to the Turkish trade.

The missile crisis thus cemented in the minds of American policy makers the idea of force as a ladder whose individual rungs could be used as a means of communicating "will" and "toughness" to a recalcitrant adversary. In examining the impact of Kennedy's successful form of "coercive diplomacy," the political scientist Alexander George worried that "the failure to comprehend the special characteristics of the Cuban crisis may well have contributed to . . . the Johnson administration's decision to use air power as a coercive instrument against North Vietnam in 1965."[275] In fact, George could not have known just how badly the "special characteristics" of the Cuban situation had indeed been misunderstood, since he was unaware of the Turkish trade. It was such misunderstandings, Barton Bernstein notes, "created by the myth of the crisis settlement, that Kennedy's successor, Lyndon B. Johnson, would bear in future years."[276]

Bernstein wonders, "what influence, analysts may profitably speculate, did the widespread belief in Kennedy's great victory in the missile crisis play as President Johnson struggled on, even against the counsel of advisors, for his own triumph in Southeast Asia in 1966–1968? Might he have felt psychologically, and even politically, more free to change policy if he had known, along with his fellow Americans, the truth of the October 1962 secret settlement?"[277] The degree to which Americans' false understanding of the missile crisis helped to lead to catastrophe in Vietnam cannot be quantified, but it can be observed in action.

This influence took three forms. First were the unconscious assumptions that were the inevitable result of the crisis, which were never discussed or put on paper, but which nevertheless provided the intellectual foundations of U.S. thinking about Vietnam. Such assumptions are particularly significant vis-à-vis the conduct of the war because so much of the strategic plan was determined not by the local conditions in Vietnam, but by American theories derived independently, and then imperfectly applied to Vietnam. When one considers that the Vietnam War was largely viewed in Washington as a proxy contest with the Soviets—and sometimes the Chinese—the underlying presumptions about the nature of the Cold War take center stage.

As George would later observe, for many members of the Kennedy administration, the president's illusion of success in forcing the Russians to back down without a missile trade "demonstrated the potentialities of a coercive strategy that had been all too seldom employed in defense of American interests throughout the world. The major lesson, as they saw it, was that the Cuban case showed that success in such international crises was largely a matter of national guts; if the president could convey resolution firmly and clearly, the opponent would back down in the face of superior American military capabilities."[278] "The belief that force could be managed for discrete diplomatic ends was exhilarating to these men," James A. Nathan argues, "for it resolved a dilemma that had been building for nearly 200 years."[279] By 1962, force had long since trumped diplomacy as the means through which states settled their differences. But this development occurred just as the means by which states were able to inflict violence on one another had expanded beyond any rationally measurable gain in doing so.

Nowhere was this truer, and nowhere did it have greater consequences, than in the United States, whose nuclear arsenal at the time dwarfed that of the USSR or Britain, the other two nuclear powers. In American politics, by the time of the Kennedy administration, the failure of the Munich conference was viewed as a step in the process whereby the suggestion of diplomacy became an invitation to the accusation of the crime of appeasement. With the failure of Yalta—and its subsequent misinterpretation in American political culture—the suggestion of settling differences with the Communists through diplomacy had become the near–moral equivalent of treason. But if force could be used in a manner that was "proportionate and effective," if it could be made "a discrete instrument of bargaining," Nathan observes, then "the inner dynamic of Soviet expansionism could be tamed and defeated without incommensurate dangers."[280] To the alleged "lessons"of Munich and Yalta were now added those of the misreported missile crisis. Together they formed the intellectual DNA of U.S. foreign policy and the American people's understanding of the world.

From Cuba to Vietnam

All the lessons described above were applied, if only semiconsciously, to Vietnam. So, too, were a few the Kennedy men thought they learned consciously. The perceived success of the ExComm structure led to suggestions in early 1965 that Johnson convene a similar group to explore alternatives for dealing with Vietnam.[281] Moreover, many administration members, notes historian Brian VanDeMark, "readily assumed that 'controlled' escalation would dissuade Ho Chi Minh in 1965 as surely as Nikita Khrushchev had been in 1962."[282] Dean Rusk, in late 1965, anticipated "that the other side may look down the road ahead and decide that it is too costly or too dangerous for them to persist. This has happened with the Greek guerillas, the Berlin blockade, Korea and the Cuban missile crisis."[283] As Cyrus Vance, a high-ranking official in both Kennedy's and Johnson's Pentagon, later observed, "We had seen the gradual application of force applied in the Cuban Missile Crisis, and had seen a very successful result. We believed that if this same gradual and restrained application of force were applied in . . . Vietnam, that one could expect the same kind of result; that rational people on the other side would respond to increasing military pressure and would therefore try and seek a political solution."[284]

A further example of such thinking can be found in Robert McNamara's recommendations for escalating U.S. involvement in Vietnam, during the crucial debates of the summer of 1965. In order to successfully "create conditions for a favorable outcome by demonstrating to the VC/DRV that the odds are against their winning," McNamara proposed troop increases and continued bombing sorties against North Vietnam that "should increase slowly from 2,500 to 4,000 or more a month." After the troops were deployed and "some strong action had been taken in the program of bombing . . . we could, as part of a diplomatic initiative, consider introducing a 6–8 week pause." According to this conceptual framework, the Vietnamese Communists would then realize, as the Soviets supposedly had in 1962, that they would have to seek a political solution, because the United States possessed overwhelming force as well as the will to use it.[285] ExComm hawk Douglas Dillon specifically blamed the impact of the missile crisis on Robert McNamara's conduct of the war. Dillon had attended early cabinet meetings on the subject and became disgusted with Johnson's and McNamara's decision to move slowly "up the ladder" of military escalation in Vietnam, rather than simply fight the war to win it from the outset. Dillon agreed with his interviewer, James G. Blight, that these two men "overlearned the lesson of the missile crisis," believing that "the gradual approach always works."[286]

The Vietnam hawk W. W. Rostow, then head of the State Department's

Policy Planning Staff, wrote to Averell Harriman in early 1966 that he regarded "the analogy between the Cuban Missile crisis and the Viet Nam war as legitimate. Both are conscious and purposeful Communist efforts to shift the balance of power against us at a decisive point."[287] Senator Richard Russell, who by 1966 was urging negotiations for a cease-fire, still framed his stance in terms of the Cuban crisis. He believed that the United States needed to seek an honorable peace that did not involve "temporizing with the Russians," as had been the case when he and others "earnestly and vigorously fought to kick communism, Castro and the missiles out of Cuba."[288] Indeed, at a crucial meeting of President Johnson's advisers on November 24, 1964, during which the decision to send massive numbers of ground troops was being debated, Secretary Rusk compared the plan to Kennedy's choice to stand down the Russians during the Cuban Missile Crisis; it was, however, a "misleading argument," as the historian David Kaiser notes, based on Rusk's misreading of Kennedy's compromise.[289] Ironically, writing from the perspective of the revisionist Left, Leslie Dewart offers a correlative theory. Dewart wonders whether the fact that "the Soviet unwillingness to precipitate a nuclear exchange, even in defense of a socialist revolution, removed some uncertainties from U.S. policy planning," which "may have been an important factor in the decision to bomb North Vietnam early in August 1964 after the Gulf of Tonkin incident."[290]

Finally, it should be recalled that Vietnam arose out of a political context that was also heavily formed by the mislearned lessons of the missile crisis. Inexperienced and lacking confidence in his judgment in foreign affairs, President Johnson felt himself very much at the political mercy of the Kennedy men and the policies they prescribed. "Without them I would have lost my link to John Kennedy, and without that I would have had absolutely no chance of gaining the support of the media or the Easterners or the intellectuals. And without that support I would have had absolutely no chance of governing the country."[291]

"Toughness" had been at a premium in American politics before John Kennedy appeared to face down Nikita Khrushchev in Cuba, but following the young president's assassination, this particular brand of "strength" became the standard against which his successors were measured—and would measure themselves. Kennedy and Johnson biographer Robert Dallek has argued that "Kennedy had demonstrated his toughness in the Cuban missile crisis, and now Johnson would have to show the Chinese and the Russians that he was as ready to stand up to them."[292] Indeed, during the July 1965 deliberations over escalation, Johnson was concerned that the Communists were misinterpreting U.S. (and his) determination in Vietnam. Meeting with his advisers, Johnson stated,

"Kennedy called up reserves and put [the] nation on war footing after Vienna and Soviets understood that. In [the] missile crisis they understood that. For 20 months we have been restrained—and I don't want them to misunderstand me."[293] Moreover, Lyndon Johnson, we know from Doris Kearns's testimony, was deeply haunted by John Kennedy's political ghost and the fear that he would not measure up to its demanding terms. Johnson's psychological torment was not, as Garry Wills points out, "that the Kennedys considered him a usurper, but that they came, in time, to make him feel like one himself."[294]

Perhaps the most heartbreaking aspect of the war is that Johnson understood the extent of the quagmire in which he was becoming involved when he entered it. He had few illusions about Vietnam. Before the Gulf of Tonkin incidents, in May 1964, he complained to McGeorge Bundy, "I stayed awake last night thinking of this thing. . . . It looks to me like we're getting into another Korea. . . . I don't think that we can fight them 10,000 miles away from home. . . . I don't think it's worth fighting for and I don't think that we can get out. It's just the biggest damned mess that I ever saw."[295] But having come of political age in the poisonous aftermath of Yalta, Johnson feared the political impact of "losing" Indochina to the Communists as Harry Truman and Dean Acheson had "lost" China a decade earlier. He was, according to Kearns's account, "as sure as any man could be that once we showed how weak we were, Moscow and Peking would move in a flash to exploit our weakness. . . . And so would begin World War III. So you see, I was bound to be crucified either way I moved."[296]

Even more than a Far Right domestic reaction or a Communist mobilization abroad, however, Lyndon Johnson feared Robert Kennedy. For if he did not fight in Vietnam, Johnson complained to Kearns:

> There would be Robert Kennedy out in front leading the fight against me, telling everyone that I had betrayed John Kennedy's commitment to South Vietnam. That I had let a democracy fall into the hands of the Communists. That I was a coward. An unmanly man. A man without a spine. Oh, I could see it coming all right. Every night when I feel asleep I would see myself tied to the ground in the middle of a long, open space. In the distance I could hear the voices of thousands of people. They were all shouting at me and running toward me: "Coward! Traitor! Weakling!" They kept coming closer. They began throwing stones. . . .[297]

Hawkish pundits like the Kennedy ally Joseph Alsop were not above exploiting what they perceived to be LBJ's psychological vulnerability on this issue, comparing his own wavering conduct of the war in Vietnam with the tough-minded consistency that JFK had successfully conveyed during the missile crisis. In late 1965, Alsop, a JFK intimate, attacked Johnson for being too timid in pursuing the war. "For Lyndon B. Johnson," Alsop taunted, "Viet-nam is what the second Cuban crisis was for John F. Kennedy. If Mr. Johnson ducks the challenge, we shall learn by experience about what [it] would have been like if Kennedy had ducked the challenge in October, 1962."[298] In his taped conversations, McGeorge Bundy can be heard warning the president, "Joe Alsop is back breathing absolute fire and sulfur about the need for war in South Vietnam. I'm going to see him this afternoon and find out just how alarmed he is."[299]

As Alsop's machinations indicate, Johnson's political paranoia was not wholly unfounded. Robert Kennedy did despise him and was looking for any available means to humiliate him politically. And the political pressure on Johnson from other avenues was also quite strong. Much of this pressure, again, was a by-product of the missile crisis and its universally false interpretation. During the initial consultations about how to respond to the alleged attacks on U.S. forces at the Gulf of Tonkin, Johnson briefed the congressional leaders but revealed none of the doubts about the nature of those attacks that the military command had passed along. Senator Bourke Hickenlooper, quick to compare the situation to the missile crisis, stated, "Cuba was a bold and dangerous operation as far as Washington is concerned. No one knows what would have happened if we had not reacted. Is it possible this follows the same route? If we don't react, what kind of position does that put us in with the North Vietnamese?"[300] Hickenlooper and other members of Congress, including Senate Armed Services chair Richard Russell and House Speaker W. Everett Dirksen, firmly supported Johnson's desire to carry out reprisals with all due haste and force. Indeed, House minority leader Charles Halleck (R-IN) sought to ease the president's mind about the wording for the Tonkin Gulf resolution, declaring that he would not face partisan opposition, for "there was never any hesitation when we had the deal about Cuba. I was the first to speak up and say—Mr. President, count me in."[301]

Johnson did not make his own task any easier, moreover, by consistently referring to Kennedy's stand-down of the Soviets in Cuba out on the campaign trail and elsewhere as a means of establishing his bona fides as president and his legitimacy as a wartime leader. In Los Angeles in October 1964, the president proudly proclaimed, "I saw President Kennedy in the Cuban crisis in thirty-eight different meetings, and we got up to the last hours, Khrushchev had his missiles trained on this country that would completely wipe out San Francisco and Los Angeles. I saw the generals with their stars come into the room and the admirals with their braid and the Secretary of State with all his diplomatic experience. I listened to every word. I never left home in the morning a single morning that I knew I would get back that night to see Lady Bird and those daughters."[302]

Robert Kennedy, whose hatred for Johnson had only grown with time, laughed at Johnson's contention, insisting that Johnson had never been "in on any of the real meetings." But RFK employed rhetoric no less belligerent, and deliberately misleading, since he possessed firsthand knowledge of the trade that Johnson did not. In a February 17, 1966, statement, Bobby Kennedy said Hanoi "must be given to understand as well that their present public demands are in fact for us to surrender a vital national interest—but that, as a far larger and more powerful nation learned in October of 1962, surrender of a vital interest of the United States is an objective which cannot be achieved."[303] Given Kennedy's role in both making the deal with the Soviets and then covering it up later, the shamelessness of this claim is truly impressive.[304] Indeed, in 1969 Theodore Sorensen, in a book of praise for Jack and Robert Kennedy, wrote scathingly of what he termed the "'Cuban Missile Crisis Syndrome,' which calls for a repetition in some other conflict of Jack Kennedy's tough stand of October 1962 when he told the Russians with their missiles either to pull out or look out!"[305] In 1995 Robert McNamara argued that it was "highly probable" that John Kennedy would likely have reversed course in Vietnam and withdrawn U.S. troops before getting bogged down in a war there because he "appeared willing" to trade the Jupiters during the missile crisis—a contention that only adds further painful layers of irony.[306] If JFK had been willing to admit this at the time, perhaps Johnson would not have felt quite as trapped by the Kennedy machismo mythology.

The Power of Myth

One of the most curious aspects of the story of the settlement of the missile crisis has been the enduring power of the original myth of the Kennedys' refusal to bargain with Moscow, despite the repeated publication of incontrovertible evidence to the contrary. In the summer of 1989, after Sorensen had admitted the truth about the trade (and more than a decade after Arthur Schlesinger Jr. had revealed it in his biography of Robert Kennedy), the conservative polemicist Mark Falcoff argued that the "Establishment Consensus" forged in the wake of the crisis "has exercised a remarkable influence over the way successive American administrations have approached larger strategic issues ever since." This consensus, Peter Rodman, a George H. W. Bush administration national security official, has written, demonstrated the utility of "controlled, limited escalation of force as a way of conveying American determination by a combination of firmness and restraint." American policy makers thus arrived at the conviction that "we could achieve our objectives without actual resort to overwhelming violence." This, Rodman concludes, was for many of those who managed the crisis "the most important lesson . . . in the nuclear era."[307]

Falcoff remained convinced that Kennedy had previously made a decision to withdraw the missiles from Turkey, only to be frustrated by "administrative oversight and bureaucratic inertia." He is grateful for his belief that Kennedy "resisted an explicit trade, since it would have been seen as rewarding Soviet aggression and, of course, it would have put a very different 'spin' on the crisis. It presumably would have taught different lessons—both to the Soviets and to the United States." He therefore laments the fact that "the most dramatic and dangerous nuclear crisis in the postwar period . . . has rendered the notion of a ladder of escalation very nearly irrelevant for purposes of policy. This is so because at virtually every rung the same restricts hold. According to the Establishment Consensus, small conflicts run an unacceptable risk of becoming large; large, conventional conflicts run an even more unacceptable risk of becoming nuclear; nuclear conflict is unthinkable." Falcoff ends by "clinging to the hope that the Soviets have learned, or may yet learn the same lessons from the Cuban missile crisis that we have"[308]

In this case, the public "lesson" of the crisis is more important than the truth of the crisis itself. Because no one who knew the truth of the deal revealed it for more than a generation, the lessons imparted were based on the image that John Kennedy sought to project. Falcoff "clings" to the hope that the Soviets learned the same lesson, but if he had been paying closer attention to the historical record, he would have discovered that the Soviets would have been expected to learn something quite different. Falcoff was writing against a background of frustration with the unwillingness of many in Congress to take a more aggressive position in Central America against Soviet-aided regimes there. He complained that, given the U.S.-Soviet nuclear parity, "it seems disingenuous to claim that we could respond now as forcefully and credibly to the emplacement of Soviet strategic weaponry in Nicaragua as President Kennedy did in Cuba more than a quarter-century ago." Still, he mocks the U.S. Congress's hesitation to use greater force in Central America. "We are now so far from being able, politically, to sustain anything that resembles even the pre-1965 period of the Vietnam War that the U.S. Congress has fixed the U.S. military mission at 65 officers and men." As Falcoff's analysis inadvertently demonstrates, the false interpretation continued to bedevil American politics and relations with the rest of the world.

The Reagan administration, hoping to take advantage of false memories in 1984, sought to mobilize support for its attempts to overthrow Nicaragua's Sandinista government by publicly portraying the shipment of relatively unsophisticated Bulgarian L39 aircraft to the Nicaraguans as a threat akin to the deployment of nuclear weapons to Cuba in 1962.[309] These attempts failed miserably.

Future Clinton defense secretary Les Aspin argued with much greater success in 1991, when the opponent was Iraq, "The model is the Cuban missile crisis of 1962. In that crisis, as in this one, the United States sought to restore the status quo ante—no Soviet missiles capable of reaching the United States in Cuba. Then as now, there was no backing down on the basic demand. The missiles had to go then, and Iraq had to leave Kuwait now."[310] Had Aspen known the truth about Kennedy and Cuba, one wonders if he would have been so quick to hold his actions up as a model—or perhaps he might not have concluded that the threat of war was the only conceivable response to any form of international conflict.

This particular historical metaphorical battle came close to repeating itself—this time, as farce—in the autumn of 2002 when President George W. Bush attempted to convince the nation and the world that the time had come for the United States to launch a "preemptive" war against Iraq. The president likened the "threat" from Iraq to the missile crisis, which had taken place almost exactly forty years earlier: "As President Kennedy said in October of 1962: 'Neither the United States of America nor the world community of nations can tolerate deliberate deception and offensive threats on the part of any nation, large or small. We no longer live in a world,' he said, 'where only the actual firing of weapons represents a sufficient challenge to a nation's security to constitute maximum peril.'" The comparison, according to a *New York Times* reporter, "was intended, his aides acknowledged, to give the confrontation a sense of urgency and to explain why the United States could wait only weeks or months to disarm the Iraqi leader."[311] After Bush addressed the nation, the White House released spy satellite photographs of alleged Iraqi nuclear facilities, intended explicitly to recall Kennedy's decision to show photographs of Soviet missiles in Cuba, though Mr. Bush's pictures revealed only buildings, not weapons. Cuba was a faulty historical analogy, however, since the country was not facing an adversary of the power of the now-defunct Soviet Union, and Iraq had no missiles aimed at the United States or capable of reaching it. Moreover—as many ex-Kennedy aides hastened to explain—Bush was seeking to launch a preemptive attack in Iraq, while President Kennedy had personally ruled out just such a course of action against Cuba.[312]

But the metaphor, however incompletely understood and improperly applied, was a powerful one, and Bush's opponents rushed to invoke the same shining moment in American history to make a point opposite that of the president. Most effective of these, for reasons of emotional resonance as well as eloquence, was Senator Edward M. Kennedy. He argued in reply that his brother had purposely avoided a preemptive assault against Cuba, and had chosen a naval quarantine instead, and that his brother Robert had argued that a surprise first strike against Cuba would be a "Pearl Harbor in reverse." A "preventative military action," Senator Kennedy argued, was ill advised both then and now.[313] Few commentators, for or against the Iraq invasion, appeared to understand much about how the Cuban crisis was actually resolved. Writing in the online magazine *Slate,* Fred Kaplan pointed out that owing to the fact of the last-minute secret deal Kennedy offered Khrushchev, "if [George Bush] wants to emulate John Kennedy, shunning the possibility of a compromise that avoids war may not be the way to go."[314] While the true history of the crisis's resolution eluded most debaters, Bush and his advisers were not above exaggerating the level of threat facing the United States at the time, to give greater legitimacy to the analogy. *Washington Post* diplomatic correspondent Michael Dobbs wrote in January 2003, "In 1962, Kennedy decided that the presence of Soviet missiles in Cuba was an intolerable threat to the nation's security; Bush feels much the same about the spread of weapons of mass destruction."[315]

Still, the myths of national glory die hard, even among the very scholars responsible for the accuracy of the historical record. Kaplan argued in his essay on Cuba that while tapes and other evidence of the deal had, by this time, "been available for a few years from the John F. Kennedy Library, . . . almost no histories of the crisis have incorporated or properly interpreted them."[316] While his point may be overstated—many historians had in fact incorporated the new evidence into their work by 2002—Kaplan's charge was on the mark with regard to some of the best-known and most admired works on the crisis. In his prize-winning history of President Kennedy's life in the White House, published in 1993—four years after Theodore Sorensen's "confession"—Richard Reeves told the story of the missile crisis with no mention of the extensive Kennedy-Dobrynin negotiations save those falsely portrayed in *Thirteen Days.*[317] Writing on the op-ed page in *The New York Times* on the thirty-fifth anniversary of the crisis, Reeves added that Kennedy "was surprised at how little the Soviet leader settled for in exchange for withdrawing the missiles: an American pledge not to invade Cuba."[318]

Perhaps the most curious example of the power of the mythical missile crisis is the case of Roger Hilsman. In 1996 the former State Department intelligence chief published a second book on the crisis, dedicated to John and Robert Kennedy. He promises the reader that he has included information that he "was not at liberty to write before."[319] Yet Hilsman, whose post-crisis career has been spent in academia, then goes on to repeat the very same accounts he told twenty-five years earlier, which have since been discredited. He tells the story of John Scali and "Alexander Fomin" without any realization that their discussions had nothing to do the crisis's solution, and includes the canard that "Fomin's approach through Scali and the Khrushchev cable were really a single package." He complains that "the Moscow broadcast linking the Soviet missiles in Cuba to the American Jupiter missiles in Turkey had been inspired by a newspaper column published on Wednesday by Walter Lippmann proposing that missiles in Cuba be traded for missiles in Turkey. The hard-liners may have pushed the other members to equate the two, which would tend to justify the Soviet decision to deploy missiles to Cuba in the eyes of the rest of the world, who did not know that Kennedy had long before made a decision to remove the American missiles from Turkey."[320]

The author then proceeds to attack Lippmann for his "presumptuousness" in undertaking "to instruct the U.S. government when it had been working night and day on the crisis for 10 days. It was irresponsible of him to publish the piece in the midst of the crisis, when he did not know of JFK's effort to remove the Jupiters from Turkey and had made no attempt to check with the administration to find out its view of the missiles in Turkey, and whether or not it had been trying to do something about them. The incident is an illustration of self-important journalism—or at least self-important columnist journalism—at its worst."[321] In fact, Lippmann did consult with George Ball before he wrote the column, and no attempt was made to dissuade him from his conclusions. Second, JFK made no genuine efforts to remove the missiles from Turkey, and so Lippmann could not be faulted for not being aware of any. Third, if the Soviets *were* inspired by Lippmann's column to ask for a trade—and we have no evidence of this either way—then the world is in his debt, since it was this trade that eventually solved the crisis on a peaceful basis. Finally, in attacking Lippmann for putting forth a good-faith suggestion of how to end the crisis, Hilsman in effect attacks one of the primary functions of a free press. Yet through such efforts are the myths of the crisis perpetuated, and the false lessons they taught are reinforced for a new generation of leaders.

The mere fact that, nearly forty years later, Hollywood would invest upward of $100 million (including advertising) in *Thirteen Days,* a film that attempted to re-create the missile crisis, speaks to the continuing power the event holds over the nation's collective imagination. As the writer Bruce Handy noted before its release, the film's backers were "counting on a certain historic resonance if not quite unalloyed nostalgia, to sell their account of how the world almost ended." One of its marketers told Handy that people in their forties "want to share this with their children, this experience of . . . the most terrifying aspect of the cold war."[322]

Released in late 2000/early 2001, *Thirteen Days* does portray the American side of the deal relatively accurately. It seeks to create its own heroic Kennedy myth, however, by means of introducing a host of fictional characters into the drama. Kevin Costner was cast as Special Assistant Kenneth O'Donnell, who in real life was responsible primarily for presidential scheduling. Though he barely registers in the ExComm transcripts, in the film version he is seen taking an active role in helping the Kennedys save the world from imminent destruction. One minute O'Donnell is seen criticizing the president for going soft on the Commies, the next he is taking on Mac Bundy for suggesting the same. Portrayed as a cross between an über-aide barking orders at quivering politicos and a shaggy dog who follows his master around with Scotch-filled Waterford crystal, O'Donnell instructs Adlai Stevenson to stand up to the Soviets at the UN and tells a fighter pilot to pretend he was not shot at in Cuba. Cynics looking for an explanation of this rather odd historical fictionalization might consider the fact that the film was partially funded by O'Donnell's son, Earthlink cofounder Kevin O'Donnell.

Film critics typically described *Thirteen Days* as a "by-the-numbers recreation" and "close to perfect."[323] In fact the film took countless liberties with the documentary record:

- It conveniently skips Robert McNamara's initial arguments that the Russian placement of the missiles should be ignored because it made them strategically meaningless, lest they undercut the film's entire rationale.
- It ignores the record of U.S. efforts to destabilize the Castro regime, including possible invasion plans being readied at the time of the placement.
- It explicitly whitewashes the Kennedys' plot to discredit the dovish Adlai Stevenson, whose recommendations they largely—and secretly—ended up following.
- It credits Walter Lippmann's column with proposing the missile trade, without evidence.
- It places the Kennedys' meetings that decided in favor of a missile trade inside the ExComm, when in fact they deliberately kept these secret.

Interestingly, much of official Washington was outraged when Costner and Oliver Stone offered up their spurious version of the Kennedy assassination in Stone's 1991 film, *JFK*. No one wanted to see Stone's conspiratorial take on the assassination and the Vietnam War replace the official version. Yet when a film funded by O'Donnell's own family sought to rewrite the historical record in such a way as to flatter the original mythmakers, it was met with approval and appreciation. *Thirteen Days* was screened at the White House and largely praised by pundits and historians alike, albeit with reservations.[324]

A "Victory" Too Sweet?

Historians and participants are divided on the question of what John Kennedy would have done if Nikita Khrushchev had not accepted the bargain Robert Kennedy offered to Anatoly Dobrynin on the night of October 27, 1962. Certainly every public utterance of the president seemed predicated on the likelihood of war. The military was preparing to attack the missile sites, and Robert Kennedy told Dobrynin that he was unsure how long the president could hold out against the generals' pressure. But the secret history of the crisis has taught us how unwise it is to rely on John Kennedy's public record in making sense of the matter. Virtually every one of Kennedy's private comments to his aides, to his brother, and to David Ormsby-Gore, his close confidant, echoes the belief that the United States could not sustain a war that began over its refusal to make a deal that possessed "considerable merit."[325] Robert McNamara has concluded that Kennedy was "willing, if necessary, to trade the obsolete American Jupiter missiles in Turkey for the Soviet missiles in Cuba in order to avert this risk [of all-out war]. He knew such an action was strongly opposed by the Turks, by NATO, and by most senior U.S. State and Defense Department officials. But he was prepared to take that stand to keep us out of war."[326] This was why he gave Dean Rusk, whose role in the crisis has been done a disservice by Robert Kennedy, permission to put the so-called Cordier ploy into place, should the Russians refuse Robert Kennedy's Saturday-night offer. Rusk also opined, "I think it's very likely that the Andrew Cordier ploy would have been attempted on Monday if it had been necessary."[327] The trade would have come as a rude surprise to the ExComm members who thought they were the ones helping the president to make his decision. As Douglas Dillon told his interviewer, "The Rusk revelation . . . really shocked me. I had no idea that the President was considering such a thing."[328]

In a 1969 exchange with Roger Hilsman in *The New York Review of Books,* Ronald Steel suggested, "In retrospect it might have been better if the missile sites had been completed and then used as the basis for negotiations over broader issues. Not only would we have been spared the dangers of marching to the nuclear brink, but we would have been denied what Hilsman calls 'a foreign policy victory of historical proportions.' That 'victory' inspired the euphoria of power that led Lyndon Johnson to become obsessed by the imperial adventure launched so 'idealistically' by Kennedy and his advisers. . . .

Now that the empire has begun to crumble, some of its intellectual underpinnings are beginning to seem increasingly flimsy."[329]

Had Khrushchev held out a bit longer, and Kennedy been forced to make the public deal that McNamara and Rusk are convinced he would have accepted, the legacy of the missile crisis might have been a much happier one for the United States and the world. The Russians would not have been compelled to accept a public humiliation—unearned, at that, since they made a better bargain than they could admit—and Khrushchev would likely never have been removed from power. The United States would have had a much more energetic partner in the search for a peaceful modus vivendi in the Cold War, and the Soviets might have been less eager to build up their military machine and nuclear arsenal to guarantee they were never so embarrassed again.

An appreciation for the compromise at the heart of the settlement might have prevented the intoxicated orgy of self-congratulation the crisis inspired in America's political class, which helped lead us to Vietnam. The notion of "coercive diplomacy" would have lost some of its luster, and the aura of invincibility that appeared to glisten around the deployment of U.S. military threats anywhere and everywhere would likely have dimmed considerably. The government's "right to lie" would not have gone unchallenged by a quiescent news media, which went on to accept years of lies about Southeast Asia before allowing itself to trust its eyes and ears. A false rendering of the missile crisis would not have corrupted American political science and international relations study and given use to the defective theoretical propositions derived from it. Adlai Stevenson's reputation would not have been destroyed on fictitious grounds, as he would have been recognized as at least a partial author of the solution that eventually solved the crisis.

Finally, while Kennedy did have the courage to offer the Russians a genuine compromise in order to deflate the crisis and pursue a policy of nuclear limits, he lacked the courage to admit the deal to even his closest advisers. When Lyndon Johnson ascended to the office of president, therefore, he did so in much the same fashion that Truman succeeded Roosevelt. A power in the Senate and an expert on domestic policy and politics, he had no idea what his legendary predecessor had truly agreed to with the Soviets. Johnson spent his presidency trying to live up to a portrait of unbending strength and nonnegotiable demands that Kennedy's men, in their ignorance of the secret trade, had painted of his performance in the missile crisis.

The false rendering of the crisis taught President Johnson, his advisers, and the American people an updated version of the lesson that Harry Truman says he learned at Potsdam: "Force is the only thing the Russians understand."[330] But the president and his men now believed they could communicate their message in stages, through threats and bombing raids. This lesson was then applied to conflicts not only with the Russians and Cubans, but also with the Vietnamese, the Cambodians, the Nicaraguans, the Iraqis, and any other nation deemed to be in conflict with U.S. national interests. The Cuban Missile Crisis was undoubtedly the high moment of John Kennedy's presidency in public relations terms, and probably functions as the zenith of American power in the post–Yalta world. Never again would a victory appear quite so unambiguous as the moment when Nikita Khrushchev took to the airwaves to announce his nation's capitulation to American terms. Kennedy used this opportunity wisely, moving to ratchet down the arms race and conclude important arms control agreements with the Soviets in the aftermath of the crisis. But these came at a considerable cost to the nation and the world. No wonder Robert Kennedy would later ponder "if we did not pay a very great price for being more energetic than wise about a lot of things, especially Cuba."[331] Neither he nor his brother would live to see just how expensive a victory it would be.

IV. LYNDON B. JOHNSON AND THE GULF OF TONKIN INCIDENTS

The biggest lesson I learned from Vietnam is not to trust government statements. I had no idea until then. —J. William Fulbright

In April 1995, the U.S. Immigration and Naturalization Service (INS) rejected applications from fifty Vietnamese citizens who claimed to have been hired as secret commandos by the CIA more than twenty-five years earlier. They were captured by the North Vietnamese, they say, and imprisoned in forced-labor camps. The INS refused to comment on its decision, but in order to make it, they had to ignore a cable from former Defense Intelligence Agency analyst David F. Sedgwick that presented "specific and detailed information" backing the men's contention that they were "U.S. contract employees and that, prior to their capture, they were paid with appropriated U.S. Government funds." They were seized, according to one official, while engaging in U.S.-directed missions to "collect intelligence, conduct military and psychological operations" against the North Vietnamese. Former adviser for national security McGeorge Bundy recalled of the operation: "It didn't work. Nearly all the commandos were killed, captured or lost." "The majority were captured alive," notes John Mattes, a former investigative counsel for the Senate committee on prisoners of war, and tried as "war criminals." At that point, Mr. Mattes recalls, "we wrote them off. We went to their families and said, 'They're dead.' We did nothing to seek their return or release. We kept the operation secret."[1]

While the raids—which featured CIA-supplied time bombs and demolition charges placed inside cigarette cartons and the like—were judged to be "essentially worthless" by U.S. officials, they were hardly without historical significance. On August 2, 1964, a U.S. destroyer, the *Maddox,* was approached by a tiny fleet of Vietnamese PT boats in the Gulf of Tonkin, an arm of the South China Sea between Vietnam and China, with, according to the ship's captain, "the apparent intention of launching a torpedo attack."

Confusion remains about who fired first, but if the Vietnamese were indeed planning an attack, it proved to be wholly unsuccessful. All of the Vietnamese vessels were quickly driven home or sunk by the superior U.S. force. Both the naval officers and the civilian superiors in the government found the incident to be almost inexplicable and at the very least irrational.

In fact, one of the CIA-directed commando raids had taken place in the area only two days earlier. As then-U.S. defense secretary Robert McNamara noted in his memoir of the war, *In Retrospect: The Tragedy and Lessons of Vietnam* (1995), some believed that the commando operations "may have provoked a later and very significant North Vietnamese response in the Tonkin Gulf."[2] Meanwhile, on August 4, a far more confusing incident took place, and U.S. forces reported a second attack. The news was relayed to President Johnson, who shortly commenced America's first direct military attack on North Vietnam.

Made in secret and without explanation, the INS's 1995 decision to deny the Vietnamese commandos refuge in the United States was wholly of a piece with the manner of U.S. entry into the Vietnam conflict. It is also consistent with the decision of the U.S. Veterans Administration to refuse all claims for combat compensation in Vietnam to any American who sustained an injury before August 5, 1965, the day that Congress passed the Gulf of Tonkin Resolution and the United States officially went to war.

Confusion . . . and Deception

At 11:37 P.M. Eastern Standard Time, on the night of August 4, 1964, President Lyndon Johnson appeared on television to announce that he had just ordered U.S. forces to bomb North Vietnam. The "aggression by terror against the peaceful villagers of South Viet-Nam has now been joined by open aggression on the high seas against the United States of America," the president explained. "Repeated acts of violence against the armed forces of the United States must be met not only with alert defense, but with positive reply. That reply is being given to you as I speak tonight." Even so, the president promised, "we still seek no wider war."

Johnson, working through his old friend, the chairman of the Senate Foreign Relations Committee, J. William Fulbright (D-AR), prevailed upon Congress to pass a resolution conferring upon him the authority to take "all necessary measures to repel any armed attacks against forces of the United States and to prevent further aggression." This vague mandate, passed unanimously in the House and with only two dissents in the Senate, would effectively allow Johnson to wage an undeclared war in Vietnam. "Like Grandma's nightshirt," he liked to quip, "it covered everything."[3] When support for the war collapsed years later, some in Congress attempted to argue that the resolution had been unfairly exploited by the president and was never intended to give him the power he eventually assumed. Embittered by what he considered to be the duplicity of those who had once supported him, LBJ would later be heard to complain, "I don't even criticize them for taking that position, if that's what their conscience dictates. But I just wish their conscience had been operating when they were making all these other decisions. Because Congress gave us this authority. In August, 1964, to do 'whatever may be necessary.' That's pretty far-reaching. That's—the sky's the limit."[4]

While Johnson may have had a legitimate argument regarding the exact wording of the resolution itself, the precipitating events he described to Congress and the American people on August 4, 1964, almost certainly never took place. In fact the president was wrong—in virtually every detail of his presentation. In some matters he was being deliberately deceptive; in others, he was simply—and quite understandably—confused. The so-called second Gulf of Tonkin incident has indeed proved to be one of the most confusing events in postwar American history. But confusion alone cannot justify the liberties that Lyndon Johnson took with the trust of Congress and the nation regarding the event upon which he chose to base his decision to take the country to war.

In its dishonesty about the situation in Vietnam, the Johnson administration was not so different from its predecessors. Members of the Eisenhower administration had invented reasons to refuse to abide by the 1954 Geneva peace accords. During the late years of the Eisenhower administration and the early years of the Kennedy administration, the United States was moving from the position of financing the French fight against the insurgency led by Ho Chi Minh and the Communist Vietminh front he created in 1941 to taking over the fight itself. Following the collapse of French forces at Dien Bien Phu in 1954 and the (allegedly) temporary division of the nation into a Communist-led north and a non-Communist south at an international conference in Geneva that year, the United States began to assume responsibility for the war itself while trying to create a visible set of institutions in the new nation of "South Vietnam" it sought to foster. Because the northern side, led by Ho, never recognized the division of the country and neither did many of the people in South Vietnam, the Americans found themselves simultaneously trying to fight a war, create a nation, and defy international opinion, which supported the election scheme that had been agreed to in Geneva for both halves of the country. But given the demands of its Cold War mind-set, coupled with then-popular theories of falling dominoes, little internal dissent was voiced and few Americans outside of the Washington Establishment were even aware of the struggle being waged.

The government of South Vietnam represented army and oligarchic factions, rather than any genuine popular movement, and rather quickly, the demands of war overtook all others. The Americans were determined to avoid the mistakes of the French as they gradually raised the number of "advisers" in Vietnam, and soon loosened regulations that prevented them from participating in hostile engagements with the enemy, but they could not elude the essential contradiction of "saving" a people from Communism who did not give much indication of wishing to be saved. The Kennedy men always seemed to feel they could improve on the South Vietnamese leadership without ever knowing how or with whom. The Joint Chiefs of Staff admitted at the time that "free elections would be attended by the almost certain loss of [Indochina] to Communist control,"[5] and President Eisenhower himself put the likely number of voters for the Communist leader, Ho Chi Minh, at "possibly eighty percent."[6] Defense Secretary Robert McNamara later explained to President Johnson that it was "only the U.S. presence after 1954" in South Vietnam in the form of American advisers that "enabled [the U.S.-supported prime minister Ngo Dinh] Diem to refuse to go through with the 1954 provision calling for nationwide free elections in 1956."[7] And the authors of *The Pentagon Papers* admitted that virtually the entire U.S. policy was based on the false notion that South Vietnam was in any meaningful fashion a genuine nation. "South Vietnam," they wrote, "(unlike any of the other countries in Southeast Asia) was essentially the creation of the United States."[8] Spokesmen for the Kennedy administration likewise engaged in a deception when they denied any foreknowledge of or responsibility for the November 3 coup that resulted in the murder of the corrupt Diem. They knew in advance and approved of the coup—if not the murder itself.[9]

The fact that the Vietnam War was begun with a lie would end up tainting the entire conflict in the eyes of U.S. citizens once the falsehood was discovered. Sending young men off to die on the basis of an honest mistake is the risk any leader of a great power might undertake. But sending them to die in a war in which they are not trusted with the truth is, morally, a far more troubling act. As with Yalta and the Cuban Missile Crisis, the president deceived the nation not for reasons of national security but for reasons of political expediency. And just as before, the ultimate price paid by the country would far exceed any that could have been imagined.

Even leaving aside its horrific consequences for the people of Southeast Asia, the Vietnam War was a catastrophe for the United States by almost any conceivable measure. Nearly $200 billion was expended on the effort. Of the over three million Americans sent to Vietnam, more than 58,000 died, over 300,000 were wounded, and another 519,000 were injured. Nearly 2,500 soldiers were also classified as "missing in action" and are presumed dead.[10] Many soldiers who survived physically intact paid an enormous psychic and emotional cost. Five years after the war's end, Vietnam veterans were dying at a rate 45 percent higher than those who did not serve in the war, with a suicide rate that was 72 percent higher and a higher incidence of almost all forms of violent deaths.[11] Their own government exposed them to toxic chemicals later found to be connected to at least nine diseases including lung cancer, prostate cancer, adult diabetes, and both spina bifida and leukemia in their offspring.[12] Add to these costs the class and racial fissures Vietnam engendered. The sons of well-to-do Americans routinely avoided the draft through college deferments and other methods available to those with sophisticated doctors and lawyers at their disposal. Meanwhile, in Vietnam, nonofficers died at a rate almost eight times that of their commanders. Soldiers who had not finished high school were three times as likely to be killed as those who had. The same is true of those from poor and lower-middle-class families compared with those whose parents earned $17,000 a year or more.[13]

As an institution, the U.S. military was itself deeply wounded by Vietnam, as the morale and professionalism of its soldiers and officers all but disintegrated under the strain of the war. Massacres were covered up at the highest levels. "Body counts"—the number of enemy soldiers allegedly killed in battle—were routinely overstated. Some 550,000 soldiers, more than 10 percent of those sent to Vietnam between 1965 and 1972, deserted. At home, another 570,000 American men evaded the draft.[14] More than two thousand who served attempted to "frag"—to assault with the intent to kill, harm, or intimidate—their commanding officers.[15] In about a hundred of these incidents, the officer who was the target of the attack was murdered. Narcotics and other drugs were as plentiful and available to U.S. soldiers in Vietnam as cigarettes and candy. By the war's end, the Pentagon admitted that about a third of U.S. troops were using heroin, and roughly 20 percent had been addicted at one time.[16]

By 1967, the costs at home were evident every night on the evening news. In addition to the creation of an angry and vocal protest movement, the war inspired a degree of bad faith and mistrust in the nation's political leadership that continues to poison our political system to this day. A Gallup Survey reported in 1967 that almost 70 percent of the American population felt that the administration had deceived the public about Vietnam.[17] A Harris Survey of the same year concluded that Americans' most "serious criticism" of President Johnson was the fact that "he was not honest about sending troops to Vietnam."[18] Such figures—and feelings, given the numbers of people involved—were astonishing for a modern American president, particularly a war president still involved in the conflict in question. Domestically, Lyndon

Johnson's dreams of a Great Society were frustrated when political consensus collapsed as racial, regional, and class-based animosities increased. Cities burned in race riots. The dollar weakened as the war-burdened U.S. economy overheated. Across the world demonstrators burned American flags and declared their support for our enemies. The very people to whom we believed we were proving our "credibility" viewed the endeavor with a mixture of horror and disgust, while our adversaries found strength and opportunity in America's weakened, divided state. By the time it was over, the war ended up causing many of the unhappy events it was designed to prevent, and then some.

"Vietnam. Vietnam. Vietnam."

The great and painful irony of America's Vietnam misadventure is the fact that, although Lyndon Johnson was aware of its likely consequences before he entered into it, he felt trapped by historical and political circumstance. Johnson was, in many respects, as generous and beneficent a man as any who ever reached the Oval Office, and he wanted to use the enormous powers of that office to help the people who most needed it. When Johnson became a congressman in 1937, Robert Caro notes, there was no electricity in the Texas Hill country, and by the time he became a senator in 1948, he had brought power there. Johnson drove advisers crazy with requests for electrification projects, despite the fact that the counties were insufficiently populated to justify them according to the regulations. "He simply wore down the president and his men."[19] Like other New Dealers, Lloyd Gardner observes, "Johnson was enthusiastic (and probably a bit amazed) at the discovery that government really did have immense powers to change the life of the downtrodden." "The kid" was, as FDR adviser Tommy "the Cork" Corcoran admitted, "the best congressman for a district that ever was."[20]

As president, Johnson determined to do for nearly everyone on the planet what he, through FDR's programs, had been doing for the 200,000 poor people he served in South Texas. This need was deeply emotional. His wife, Lady Bird, recalls watching him view John Ford's 1940 film of John Steinbeck's novel *The Grapes of Wrath,* "crying quietly for about two hours at the helpless misery of the Okies."[21] Aside from his hero, FDR, Johnson was able to use the power of the presidency to bring these people—including particularly those Americans who had forever lived their lives in the shadow of official racism and discrimination—closer to a horizon of genuine social justice than any man before him. The Johnson presidency, as Caro, one of his most severe critics, admits, marked the "high-water mark of the tides of social justice" in the twentieth century.[22]

Lyndon Johnson was large; he contained multitudes. His intense and outsized emotions pulled him in many directions simultaneously. Dean Acheson noted that the president had "as many sides to him as a kaleidoscope."[23] His aide Joseph Califano added that Johnson was a man who could be "altruistic and petty, caring and crude, generous and petulant, bluntly honest and calculatingly devious—all within the same few minutes."[24] Many of his closest advisers could not help noticing that Johnson seemed, almost congenitally, to prefer deviousness to candor, trickery to truth. He demanded that people burn the extremely ordinary teacher-student letters he had written as a young high school teacher, checking with their recipients repeatedly to make certain they had done so. Even the copies of his college newspaper dealing with specific incidents involving his life there have been removed from the collections held in the college library.[25] According to Caro, it was there that Johnson also developed the nickname "Bull," which was short for "bullshit," owing to the fact, according to one classmate, he "just could not tell the truth."[26] "In dealing with people," Clark Clifford admitted, "I often had the feeling that, he would rather go through a side door even if the front door were open."[27] According to Robert Kennedy, admittedly a deeply biased source, in allegedly the very last conversation he had with his brother, on November 21, 1963, the president devoted himself to detailing many ways in which "Lyndon Johnson was incapable of telling the truth."[28] In addition, uncontrollable mood swings resulted in LBJ making overly emotional judgments, so that his own deep-seated beliefs and intellectual constructions competed with his outsized emotionalism to guide his reactions to world events.

Intellectually, historian Walter LaFeber notes, Johnson interpreted the civil war in Vietnam within two competing historical contexts. "The first was the 1930s, the years when as a young congressman he used the New Deal to help the poor of Texas, but also watched European powers 'appease' Hitler's territorial demands at the 1938 Munich conference. Johnson believed ever after that the New Deal could work anywhere, but only if appeasement was tolerated nowhere." The president had convinced himself, through what journalist Jonathan Schell termed a kind of "psychological domino theory," that any compromise in Vietnam would lead, as the Munich agreement had, directly to world war. Johnson shared the widely held belief that Russia and China remained allies long after the Sino-Soviet split took place, and he later explained to Doris Kearns:

> You see, I was as sure as any man could be that once we showed how weak we were, Moscow and Peking would move in a flash to exploit our weakness. They might move independently or they might move together. But move they would—whether through nuclear blackmail, subversion, with regular armed forces or in some other manner. As nearly as anyone can be certain of anything,

> I knew they couldn't resist the opportunity to expand their control over the vacuum of power we would leave behind us. And so would begin World War III.[29]

The Texan's determination to fight in Vietnam, LaFeber adds, also arose out of his view of the American frontier and of himself as an actor in that particular ongoing drama. Asia, he declared in 1967, was the "outer frontier of disorder." It had to be civilized, as the pioneers had civilized his home region of Texas: "with a rifle in one hand and an axe in the other." One of his close friends, Congressman Wright Patman of Texas, called Johnson "the last Frontiersman."[30] Johnson had visited South Vietnam as vice president and deployed extremely extravagant language in hailing the United States as its protector, the way an idealistic sheriff might were he coming to bring civilization to a remote outpost of the West. To go back on his word, he later observed, would be shameful and unmanly.[31]

The president understood the stakes of any involvement in Southeast Asia. He knew that the political and social achievements that he dreamed would mark his presidency would be jeopardized and quite possibly destroyed. He realized that his allies would soon become his adversaries. And he knew that he was handing his enemies a proverbial sword. But he felt helpless to avoid the commitment nonetheless. With deeply plaintive regret Johnson complained to his confessor, Kearns:

> All my programs. All my hopes to feed the hungry and shelter the homeless. All my dreams to provide education and medical care to the browns and the blacks and the lame the poor. . . . Oh I could see it coming all right. History provided too many cases where the sound of the bugle put an immediate end to the hopes and dreams of the best reformers: the Spanish-American War drowned the populist spirit; W.W.I. ended WW's New Freedom; WWII brought the New Deal to a close. Once the war began, then all those conservatives in Congress would use it as a weapon against the Great Society. You see, they never wanted to help the poor or the Negroes in the first place. But they were having a hard time figuring out how to make their opposition sound noble in a time of great prosperity. But the war. Oh, they'd use it to say that they were against my programs not because they were against the poor—why, they were as generous and as charitable as the best of Americans—but because we had to beat those Godless Communists and then we could worry about the homeless Americans.[32]

Johnson believed that he would be damned no matter which way he turned. He had convinced himself that his most deeply felt yearnings for the country and for his own Roosevelt-like role in the history books would be impossible to achieve if he showed weakness in Vietnam. "If I don't go in now," he admitted long before America's commitment to the war had become irreversible, "they won't be talking about my civil rights bill, or education or beautification. No sir, they'll push Vietnam right up my ass every time. Vietnam. Vietnam. Vietnam. Right up my ass."[33]

Transcripts of Johnson's secretly taped conversations reveal the pain the president experienced in trying to find a path out of the dilemma he saw before him. In late May 1964, more than sixty days before the Tonkin Gulf incident, Johnson complained to his adviser for national security affairs, McGeorge Bundy, of getting into the "biggest damned mess that I ever saw." When Bundy replied that he, too, thought it an "awful mess," Johnson volunteered that he had been observing his valet, Kenneth Gaddis, that day, a man with "six little old kids, and he's getting out my things. And I just thought about ordering his kids in there. And what in the hell am I ordering him out there for? What the hell is Vietnam worth to me? . . . What is it worth to this country?" Johnson knew full well, as he told Bundy, "it's damned easy to get in a war but it's gonna be awfully hard to ever extricate yourself if you get in."[34]

It was not, moreover, as if Johnson did not have powerful voices supporting him in his desire to steer clear of the impending catastrophe he sensed in the jungles of Southeast Asia. Earlier that same day Georgia senator Richard Russell, the influential, pro-military chair of the Senate Armed Services Committee—and an important mentor from LBJ's days as a young senator—advised him that a war in Vietnam would prove "the damnedest mess on earth." The United States, he said, would be "in quicksand up to its neck." In a follow-up conversation, Johnson queried Russell about the pro-war faction's arguments regarding the strategic importance of Vietnam. Russell told the president that he was unimpressed with the logic of Kennedy's "brain trusters who say that this thing has got tremendous strategic and economic value and that we'll lose everything in Southeast Asia if we lose Vietnam." In fact, according to the venerated senator's calculations, "It isn't important a damn bit, with all these new missile systems." Johnson admitted that he did not "think the people of the country know much about Vietnam and I think they care a hell of a lot less," but he worried, histrionically, that he might be impeached if he did not go to war. Russell, sympathetic, did not minimize "the difficulty of how you tell the American people you're coming out" of the conflict without their thinking "that you've just been whipped, you've been ruined, you're scared." But this did not mitigate the power of his dire predictions. "I tell you," the Armed Services Committee chairman promised the president, "it'll be the most expensive venture this country ever went into. . . . It'll take a half million men. They'd be bogged down in there for 10 years. . . . If it got down to . . . just pulling out, I'd get out."[35] Russell, recall, was among the most outspoken of Senate hawks when it came to Soviet encroachments into Cuba, demanding that the president "get off his dead ass" weeks before the missiles had been discovered.[36] His support for a ratcheting down of Kennedy's commitment to Vietnam, therefore, would have been all the more compelling. Significantly, however, Russell refused his friend's request that he state his position on the floor of the Senate to lay the groundwork for Johnson one day to follow suit.

"I Am Not Going to Lose Vietnam"

Both Fredrik Logevall and Kai Bird have marshaled considerable evidence to argue that if, in fact, Johnson had wished really to pursue Russell's advice—as well as his own sound instincts—he might have had a much clearer field of action than either man imagined. In 1964 the public remained almost entirely disengaged from the issue of Vietnam. At the end of that year, 25 percent of Americans surveyed by the Gallup organization were not even aware of any fighting going on there. Of those who were aware, a Council on Foreign Relations survey discovered that half favored withdrawal and just under a quarter "were definitely in favor" of using U.S. ground forces to win the war if necessary. These numbers were confirmed in a University of Michigan poll released in mid-December. In early 1965, a full 81 percent responded positively to the question of whether Lyndon Johnson should "arrange a conference with the leaders of Southeast Asia and China and see if a peace agreement can be worked out."[37] The mood of the nation could be characterized as most acquiescent to the idea of a greater involvement in the war, as James Reston pointed out in *The New York Times,* but hardly clamoring for one. And this was long before Americans had any idea how punishing and grueling such a war was likely to be or of the sorry quality of our allies in South Vietnam.[38] Had the public been made aware of even a fraction of the corruption, unpopularity, and antidemocratic character of the Saigon regime, along with the tenacity of its enemy, its inclination to take part in the conflict might have waned even further.

The lack of enthusiasm for a war in the country at large, in fact, was a matter of some concern inside the Johnson administration as early as the spring of 1964, according to *The Pentagon Papers,* particularly regarding the "portion of those 37 percent of Americans who desir[ed] our withdrawal from the region."[39] In the opinion of Assistant Secretary of State for Public Affairs Robert J. Manning, not much could be done "to make Americans feel happy or confident about the situation." The problems, he averred to the president, were plentiful, including bitter memories of Korea, the French experience in Indochina, and "the ugliness and frustration that seeps out of Saigon," all of which, Manning admitted, "were poor material upon which to build understanding and confidence. Too many available answers are unfavorable answers."[40]

Within the political Establishment, moreover, Richard Russell's concerns were hardly unique. Johnson received a memo almost the same day he spoke to Russell from Senate Majority Leader Mike Mansfield (D-MT) that stated, "I do not conclude that our national interests are served by deep military involvement in Southeast Asia."[41] The third leg of the Democrats' congressional leadership in foreign affairs, Foreign Relations Committee chair J. William Fulbright, also favored a negotiated settlement in lieu of a wider war.[42] Support for neutralization could also be found among the most respected names in academia. Hans Morgenthau, the influential father of the American "realist" school of foreign policy analysis, argued early in 1964 for the creation of a "Titoist" Vietnam. In June of 1964 his name appeared atop a petition of five thousand academics calling for just such a policy—a statement that *The New York Times*'s editors considered to be front-page news. Manning lied in reply, insisting that no thought was being given to expanding the war at the time.[43] Morgenthau's view would soon become conventional wisdom among academics who accepted the moderate—rather than radical—critique of America's involvement in the war. Johnson, however, would not even allow his administration to dignify Morgenthau's views with a response, and insisted that McGeorge Bundy cancel a planned debate with the respected University of Chicago political scientist.[44]

Diplomatically, among America's allies and certainly its adversaries, the war was considered a catastrophe waiting to happen. Most had watched in horror as France wasted her blood and treasure trying to hold on in Vietnam, and almost all observers expected the same results to await the United States if, in its hubris or naiveté, it believed itself above a similar fate. Despite enormous pressure by Johnson and the U.S. State Department, by the end of 1965 exactly one nation in the entire world—Australia—could be said to be unambiguously supportive of the American war in Vietnam. Thailand, the Philippines, and South Korea—all recipients of enormous amounts of American aid—were critically supportive.

In the media, a decision to negotiate a deal would likely have won plaudits from many powerful voices, including the editors of *The New York Times* and the nation's most influential pundit, Walter Lippmann. Both would become stern and consistent critics of the decision to escalate. (Manning noted in his memo to the president that both were "already lost.") Unlike virtually all the politicians whom Johnson consulted, moreover, Lippmann was able to face up to the full political and diplomatic implications of his argument for withdrawal. When McGeorge Bundy warned Lippmann that a neutralization agreement—like that being promoted by French president Charles de Gaulle—would result in a Communist takeover, Lippmann shot back, "Mac, please don't talk in such clichés" and celebrated the plan the following day in his column. Worried, the White House summoned Lippmann for a meeting with the president. Johnson, too, asked Lippmann how such an accord could guarantee that South Vietnam would remain non-Communist. Lippmann replied that it would not, but argued that Johnson had no sensible alternative. Any attempt to impose a military solution would fail for the United States as surely as it had failed for France.[45]

Though they could not ignore his political influence, Johnson and Bundy refused even to consider the substance of Lippmann's criticism, as they noted ruefully to each other, in a conversation taped by Johnson, "If they came across the line from the other side and fired at our compound, he would want us to say, 'Thank you.'" Bundy responded, "He hates force."[46] These comments were made on February 23, 1965. Just three days later, Johnson would admit to McNamara, "Now we're off to bombing these people. We're over that hurdle. I don't think anything is going to be as bad as losing, and I don't see any way of winning," thereby confirming Lippmann's view as his own.[47] And yet, not only did he lack the courage to act upon that view, he insisted on mocking—with the support of his top political aides—those like Lippmann, Fulbright, and others who gave voice to his own doubts.

While Lippmann and the *Times* were relatively lonely voices in early 1964, within a year they became leaders of a growing chorus. By January 1965, the newspapers that had called upon the Johnson administration to rule out further escalation included the *Times,* the *St. Louis Post-Dispatch, The Milwaukee Journal,* the *Minneapolis Star, The Des Moines Register,* the *New York Post,* the *Indianapolis Times,* the *San Francisco Examiner,* the *Chicago Daily News,* and *The Hartford Courant.* Even the right-wing (but still isolationist) *Chicago Tribune* warned that if the United States did not withdraw from Vietnam, it was likely to be forced out. "The irony of this impertinence," its editors complained, "has rarely been exceeded in the checkered history of American global meddling and foreign aid doles."[48]

But both the public and the press are quite fickle and can be easy to manipulate, at least in the short term, particularly in matters of war and peace. Uncharacteristically, Johnson, the great manipulator of all things political, doubted his own ability to carry public opinion on behalf of a peaceful settlement. To be fair, the opposition would have been quite strident. Influential Republicans Strom Thurmond, Richard Nixon, and of course Barry Goldwater had been arguing for victory at all costs. A typical Goldwater speech of the period railed against the "backdownmanship" of the Johnson administration, and warned: "Make no bones of this. Don't try to sweep this under the rug. We are at war in Vietnam. And yet the president, who is commander-in-chief of our forces, refuses to say—refuses to say, mind you—whether the objective there is victory."[49] The foreign policy Establishment, while flexible, was more hawkish than not. Its unofficial "chairman," former high commissioner of Germany John J. McCloy, who served as chair of both the Council on Foreign Relations and the Ford Foundation, believed that Vietnam was a "crucial" test in the Cold War. "You've got to do it. You've got to go in," he insisted, mustering all the gravitas that the wisest of Wise Men had to offer.[50] Hawkish newspapers like the *Los Angeles Times, The Boston Globe, The Seattle Times, The Dallas Morning News, The Kansas City Star,* and the *St. Louis Globe-Democrat* pressured in the language of post-Yalta "sellouts." On the op-ed pages, Joe Alsop beat his chest for war just as frequently as Lippmann counseled caution. Giving Johnson a taste of what lay in store for him if he chose the path of peace, Alsop insisted that a defeat in South Vietnam would mean the loss "of all that we fought for in the Second World War and the Korean War."[51]

A genuine debate on the merits of war was possible at this moment, but Johnson unaccountably seemed to fear open debate more than secret war. How such a debate would have concluded is, of course, impossible to predict, but one is hard-pressed to understand why Johnson would have felt himself at so untenable a disadvantage if he had chosen the alternative of withdrawal. Following his landslide victory in the 1964 elections, Vice President Hubert Humphrey advised the president that 1965 would be "a year of minimum political risk for the Johnson administration," and Johnson could pretty much do what he wanted.[52] McGeorge Bundy later admitted, if Johnson "had decided that the right thing to do was to cut our losses, he was quite sufficiently inventive to do that in a way that would not have destroyed the Great Society."[53] All the conflicting currents on the matter eventually led William Bundy, one of the war's key architects and most enthusiastic supporters, to conclude that Johnson could have carried public opinion with him "on whatever course he chose."[54]

But choosing peace would clearly have been the braver course, politically, for it would have invited the attacks of the hawks and required a spirited defense on the part of the president and his men. Choosing war, ironically, would defang his opponents and leave dovish opponents with nowhere else to turn. Moreover, war seemed to comport better with Johnson's own self-image, which he consistently confused with that of the United States. In his anguish over the dangers awaiting in Vietnam, Johnson taunted himself with the likely arguments his opponents would use against him should he choose peace over war. Given the hard-line anti-Communist consensus that ruled American politics in the early 1960s, any politician who publicly counseled restraint in any instance when a Communist challenge appeared at hand risked a great deal. As Senate majority leader, Johnson had witnessed, and participated in, the debates over Korea and the so-called Quemoy and Matsu crisis, and no doubt noted the vulnerabilities created for Vice President Nixon during the 1960 campaign when Democrat John F. Kennedy exploited the latter during a presidential debate—one in which Nixon was not free to respond in kind without revealing classified information.[55] Johnson's own psyche was a product of a volatile mixture of anti-Communist ideology and Texas machismo and he was by no means critical of the consensus of the time on foreign policy. Toughness vis-à-vis the Communists—or at least the perception thereof, as President Kennedy had demonstrated during the Cuban Missile Crisis—was just about the most uncontroversial position an American politician could take in 1964. And a willingness to go to war, particularly for a leader who could not separate his own manhood and perceived self-respect from that of the entire nation, was just about the only universally agreed-upon way to prove it.

When Senator Russell warned him of the quagmire that awaited the nation in Vietnam, Johnson replied, "All the senators are all saying, 'Let's move, let's go into the North.' They'd impeach a president that would run out, wouldn't they?"[56] He complained, "Run and let the dominoes start falling over—and God Almighty, what they said about us leaving China would just be warming up . . . I see [Richard] Nixon is raising hell about it today. [Barry] Goldwater too. . . ." This was certainly true. The domino theory was considered an unquestioned political reality in the spring of 1964, and Johnson would have been risking much in seeking to defy it. Goldwater, the likely Republican nominee, had criticized the president on national television in May, bitterly noting, "I think the first decision is that we are going to win," and he recommended the bombing of bridges, roads, and all other supply lines from the North to the South.[57] Johnson told Russell he had been speaking with his longtime friend, Texas wheeler-dealer A. W. Moursund, the night before, and Moursund had insisted, "Goddamn, there's not anything that'll destroy you as quick as pulling up stakes and running." When Johnson countered, "Yeah, but I don't want to kill these folks," Moursund advised the president, "I don't give a damn. I didn't want to kill 'em in Korea, but if you don't stand up for America . . ." There was "nothing that a fellow in Johnson City won't forgive," Moursund insisted, "except being weak."[58]

Despite all he knew about the dangers that lay in wait for his presidency and his country in Vietnam, the president could not escape the logic of his old friend's argument. Johnson would later complain to Kearns, "If I left that war and let the Communists take over South Vietnam, then I would be seen as a coward and my nation would be seen as an appeaser and we would both find it impossible to accomplish anything for anybody anywhere on the entire globe." The ugly debate he witnessed in Congress following the victory of the Communist revolution in China scarred his memory and provided a cautionary example of what happens to a Democratic president when Asian nations are permitted to "go Communist."

> Everything I knew about history told me that if I got out of Vietnam and let Ho Chi Minh run through the streets of Saigon, then I'd be doing what Chamberlain did in World War II. . . . There would follow in this country an endless national debate—a mean and destructive debate—that would shatter my Presidency, kill my administration, and damage our democracy. I knew that Harry Truman and Dean Acheson had lost their effectiveness from the day that the Communists took over China. I believed that the loss of China had played a large role in the rise of Joe McCarthy. And I knew that all these problems, taken together, were chickenshit compared with what might happen if we lost Vietnam.[59]

Johnson never let these concerns stray far from his mind when making decisions about Vietnam. When George Ball warned him in 1965 that America's campuses were beginning to heat up in opposition to the war, the president shot back, "George, don't pay any attention to what those little shits on the campuses do. The great beast is the reactionary elements in the country. Those are the people that we have to fear."[60]

Johnson's fear was partially due to his worries about the domestic repercussions of allowing a Communist military takeover in South Vietnam, in part because of the damage it would do to his own political reputation, and in part because he could not separate that reputation from the reputation of the United States itself. The former Senate majority leader who had watched Joe McCarthy's rise and fall from a front-row seat was not about to allow the fires that consumed Harry Truman's administration do the same to his.

Within hours of taking the oath of office, President Johnson pledged to carry out John Kennedy's policies "from Berlin to South Vietnam."[61] Within two days of Kennedy's assassination, Johnson made his first statement on the war, and left little room for ambiguity. "I am not going to lose Vietnam," he said. "I am not going to be the President who saw Southeast Asia go the way China went."[62]

As Johnson knew quite well, Kennedy had never wavered in public from the hawkish path on Vietnam. While the slain president did, on occasion, express his doubts privately to various insiders—and may even have initiated a process that would begin a withdrawal following the 1964 election—he never shared such plans with reporters or anyone likely to repeat them while he was still alive.[63] In the meantime, Kennedy had quite publicly and enormously expanded America's commitment to South Vietnam while in office and had sent Lyndon Johnson there to assure its leaders of his steadfast commitment. Typically, LBJ informed the media that Ngo Dinh Diem struck him as "the Winston Churchill of Southeast Asia" while privately admitting, "Shit, Diem's the only boy we got out there."[64] Just weeks before he traveled to Dallas, Kennedy told Chet Huntley and David Brinkley, "If South Vietnam went, the door would open for a guerrilla assault on Malaysia," which would "give the impression that the wave of the future in Southeast Asia was China and the Communists." Johnson was committed, he solemnly swore just hours after the assassination, to carrying on Kennedy's legacy, including "seeing things through in Vietnam."[65]

Yet another element of the fear that helped push Johnson toward war was his psychological obsession with the political threat posed to him by the ambitions of the slain president's brother, Attorney General Robert Kennedy. The president's anxiety, while not altogether misplaced—Kennedy did resent him and would happily have seen him resign—nevertheless betrays a degree of paranoia that profoundly corrupted his usually shrewd political instincts. Johnson worried that Robert Kennedy would cry "coward" and "betrayal" if he did not pursue the war, when in fact, he ended up doing just that because of Johnson's insistence on continuing it long after it had begun to tear the country apart at home.

Johnson's fears on this matter were also powerfully reinforced by the foreign policy advisers he inherited from President Kennedy: the so-called brain trusters who so little impressed Richard Russell. These men, whose perceived intellects, social ease, meritocratic achievements, and intimate connections to one another far exceeded those of the president, intimidated the hardscrabble alumnus of South West Texas State Teachers College, in San Marcos, Texas, a third-class school even by the standards of the time and place, which boasted exactly one faculty member with a doctorate during the time of Johnson's attendance, and fifty-six professors with no degree at all.[66] Moreover, Johnson's sensitivities to what he perceived to be anti-Southern prejudice among the Eastern Establishment intellectuals exceeded the level of merely obsessive. A confident maestro in the orchestration of complex political arrangements regarding extremely ambitious domestic legislation, Johnson felt himself to be a naïf in the world of foreign policy mandarins. Deeply insecure about his own lack of knowledge and (relatively) meager educational background, the president proved particularly pliable with regard to the suggestions of the highly credentialed men whom his Harvard-educated predecessor had chosen to guide America's relations with the world.

All the President's Men

Johnson's compulsion to please the men he thought were in some unattainable way "better" than he was may help to explain his committing to the war in so secretive and self-defeating a manner. Excluding George W. Ball, those friends and advisers who counseled restraint were Johnson's friends and Senate colleagues: men like J. William Fulbright, Mike Mansfield, and Richard Russell, Vice President Hubert Humphrey, longtime Democratic adviser Clark Clifford, and the young wunderkind, Bill Moyers. These were men who understood the importance of winning elections and the need to pursue policies that were understood and accepted by the people who would be doing the voting. They were hardly naive about Communism abroad or anti-Communism at home. But they feared the devil they did not know—the fighting of a land war in the jungles of Indochina—more than the political ones at home with whom they were familiar. Johnson felt he knew what these men knew; he had trained some of them, and been trained by others. He did not need their approval nor did he feel it necessary to question his own assumptions when their conclusions did not match his own. They were all in the same game, but only Lyndon Johnson had managed to make himself president.

But the Kennedy men were of a different breed entirely; these were cool, self-confident intellectuals who believed they could calmly and efficiently manage an Asian land war as they had done only recently with a nuclear crisis in Cuba. There were almost no devils in any details they did not know or could not eventually master. They welcomed crises, particularly foreign policy crises, because they believed in their clarifying powers, and because they understood that large bureaucracies needed great events to kick them in their proverbial pants and help to steer a more energetic course. Following Cuba, they had become almost intoxicated with their collective ability to manage events on the greatest scale imaginable. They had just won a nuclear showdown with the Communists—or so most of them believed—and they had done so in secret, without much help from Johnson the vice president. They were therefore not about to be pushed around by the leaders of some fifth-rate agrarian society whose soldiers ran around in black pajamas. Lyndon Johnson desperately wanted these men to respect him, even if it meant getting involved in a potentially disastrous war.

As bullying as he was to subordinates whose weaknesses he had discerned, Johnson could be equally obsequious to people who made him feel in some way inferior. On reputation alone, the Kennedy clique gave him plenty of reasons for concern. There was Kennedy's adviser for national security affairs McGeorge Bundy, a Phi Beta Kappa graduate of Yale and an extremely young dean of the College of Arts and Sciences at Harvard. Though he had some of his own doubts and occasionally expressed these in extremely oblique terms to Johnson, Bundy tended to support war not only on strategic grounds, but also on political ones. Early in 1964 he advised the president, "as an ex-historian . . . the political damage to Truman and Acheson from the fall of China arose because most Americans came to believe that we could and should have done more than we did to prevent it. This is exactly what would happen now if we should seem to be the first to quit in Saigon."[67] In addition to his sterling academic credentials, Bundy had written a book defending Acheson on this very point, thereby adding further to the credibility of his reading of history.

Joining Bundy in the war party was Secretary of State Dean Rusk, also a Phi Beta Kappa man, a Rhodes Scholar, and the former president of the Rockefeller Foundation. Rusk was a diplomat who, with the exception of his secret intervention during the Cuban Missile Crisis, rarely had much use for diplomacy. When Lyndon Johnson was deciding whether to escalate the war or accept one of George Ball's proposals to seek an exit strategy, in part because America's allies were so united in opposition to our war policies, Rusk replied that "it is more important to convince the Communist leadership than to worry about the opinion of non-communist countries"—a rather amazing statement for the most important foreign minister in the Western alliance.[68] A fanatical anti-Communist, Rusk once told a British journalist, "When the Russians come invade Sussex, don't expect us to come help you."[69] Given his prejudices and personal style, Rusk was happy to put himself and his department in a wholly subordinate position to the Department of Defense, thereby depriving Johnson of any valuable input regarding the diplomatic costs of the war in Europe and elsewhere.

No doubt the man who most impressed the president was Robert McNamara. A Harvard Business School graduate and the former president of

Ford Motor Company, McNamara was a figure, even in this impressive company, of unsurpassed self-possession and confidence. The ultimate "can-do" executive, he could reduce any problem presented to him to numerical inputs and outputs. McNamara displayed little patience for doubt, second guesses, or gray areas. There were problems and there were solutions, period. It was only a matter of putting all the information into the right places and ensuring that the answers flew freely to the men who required them.

Like Lyndon Johnson, McNamara was also a compulsive liar. He told one set of stories to one group of people and then turned around and explained behind closed doors that the opposite was true. On occasion he may have forgotten which version actually represented the truth, and so he found himself defending propositions that, however illogical, enabled him to appear to have been right all along.

Robert McNamara ran the Department of Defense as if it were the biggest private company on earth—which in fact it would have been, had it been private—and thereby ignored much about what was unique to its character and mission. Moreover, McNamara treated the American people with the same contempt a successful CEO enjoys demonstrating to pesky stockholders. They had, in his mind, the right to the information he chose to give them and nothing more. Unfortunately, he ignored the elementary rule that governs all informational systems: "Garbage in, garbage out." When it came time to evaluate the progress of the war he was planning and implementing, McNamara forgot that he had been fabricating, dissembling, and at times outright lying about the conflict almost from day one. He also neglected to factor in that the intense pressure he placed on the military to provide palpable signposts of progress led many of those who reported to him up and down the line to fabricate the information they were providing as well. As early as March 1962, for instance, British officials were shocked to hear U.S. ambassador to Vietnam Frederick Nolting tell them of the pressure he felt to demonstrate results.[70] But human nature being what it is, McNamara came to believe his own lies as well as those he inspired others to tell him. In his 1999 investigation of the war, *Argument Without End: In Search of Answers to the Vietnam Tragedy,* McNamara seems to imply that if he had known the truth about what took place in the Gulf of Tonkin, the United States might never have gone to war. But the Secretary of Defense could easily have discovered the truth within days of the crisis had he committed himself to doing so before advising Lyndon Johnson to embark on a series of rash military and political responses.[71] In fact, the great mathematical mind of the Vietnam War built an entire system on an edifice of information that would not survive even the most cursory of audits. The literally incalculable cost of this faulty application of systems analysis—and Johnson's unwitting reliance on it—would soon become evident for all to see.

To Lyndon Johnson, however, Robert McNamara was a kind of guru: the "smartest man" he had ever known, in whose presence you could "almost hear the computers clicking." Senator Russell spoke of McNamara's "hypnotic" influence over the president, and Johnson's aide Harry McPherson would remark, "Johnson promoted McNamara everywhere . . . No doubt he was trying to win over [the Kennedy people] as his personal friends and supporters."[72] Johnson even considered creating a prime-minister-like position for McNamara, so that his influence might be felt on all aspects of policy, foreign and domestic. When Senator Mansfield, concerned about the direction the war was taking, advised Johnson to ask "those who have pressured you in the past to embark on this course and continue to pressure you to stay on it" for an accounting, not only for "what immediate advantages it has in a narrow military sense, but [also] where does it lead in the end?" Johnson treated the majority leader's suggestion as near treason. "I consider Bob McNamara to be the best Secretary of Defense in the history of this country," was all he would say in reply.[73]

These men constituted what Rusk would call the "Inner War Cabinet," or the "Awesome Foursome" as one wag termed them. Johnson would look around him, as Tom Wicker reported, "and see in Bob McNamara that it was technologically feasible, in McGeorge Bundy that it was intellectually respectable, and in Dean Rusk that it was historically necessary."[74] That McNamara, Bundy, and Rusk also provided a nexus to the most influential centers of the elite liberal Establishment—the faculties of the top Ivy League schools, the top editors of *The New York Times,* and the chief officials at the Council on Foreign Relations—only added to their ability to undermine the president's self-confidence in the conduct of foreign affairs. Their hawkishness meant a great deal to Johnson in part because of the respect he held for many of them individually, but also for the permission it implicitly gave him to ignore the growing protests of so much of the intellectual community to his war policies.

Though he later tried to portray himself as a skeptic, and even had the temerity at one point, forty years after the events in question, to compare himself to a Quaker protestor who set himself on fire in front of the Pentagon to protest the war, Robert McNamara proved relentless in his pressure on Johnson for escalation. In June 1964, for instance, according to taped conversations, when Johnson noted that he was hearing advice that might justify a withdrawal, McNamara immediately countered—"pressing very hard" in the judgment of historian Michael Beschloss—"I just don't believe we *can* be pushed out of there, Mr. President. We just can't *allow* it to be done. You wouldn't want to go down in history as having . . ." The president interrupts, in accordance, "Not at all," apparently before McNamara can finish the phrase "lost Vietnam to Communism" or some similarly related warning.[75] McGeorge Bundy concurred, assuring the president the "Goldwater crowd," which was demanding war in Vietnam, was far "more numerous, more powerful and more dangerous than the flea bite professors" likely to object.[76] Longtime Johnson aide Bill Moyers later recalled that privately "Johnson would look at the Kennedy people around him like Robert McNamara and McGeorge Bundy and Dean Rusk," and "would later muse out loud as to what they would think if he had taken a position which in their mind would have seemed softer."[77]

Unfortunately for his ability to choose between competing alternatives, Johnson interpreted almost all dissent as disloyalty, and he was famously a politician to whom personal loyalty was all. "I don't want loyalty," he once told an aide. "I want *loyalty.* I want him to kiss my ass in Macy's window at high noon and tell me it smells like roses. I want his pecker in my pocket." The Kennedy men worked hard to prove themselves in this regard and they largely succeeded. "If you asked those boys in the cabinet to run through a buzz saw for their President, Bob McNamara would be the first to run through it," Johnson would muse. "And I don't have to worry about Rusk either. Rusk's all right."[78] (Of Bundy he was never quite so certain.) One unhappy result of Johnson's loyalty obsession was that it required his aides not merely to stifle their doubts about the wisdom of his policies, but to stifle their consciences about telling the truth. Vice President Humphrey wrote his boss a courageous memo on February 17, 1965, drafted with Thomas Hughes, who headed the State Department's Bureau of Intelligence and Research, in which he argued that a large attack on North Vietnam would undermine the administration's foreign policy across the map. He cited the political costs to Harry Truman of the Korean War and noted that "the chances of success are slimmer" in Vietnam. He advised the president to cut his losses and find a way out. Johnson's response was swift and furious: the vice president would be excluded from all meetings of the National Security Council for months.[79]

If Lyndon Johnson had decided to lie about the war—or anything else—his aides and allies had a choice: they could lie with him, or they could go back to private life. And if they did go back to private life, they had better go quietly, rather than with some dramatic flourish to publicize what might be a principled disagreement over policy. In a letter Robert McNamara sent to LBJ after the president decided he was unreliable on Vietnam policy and "promoted" him to the World Bank, McNamara is positively effusive: "No man could fail to be proud of service in an Administration which has recorded the progress yours has in the fields of civil rights, health, and education," he writes, making a list from which foreign policy is notably absent. In closing, McNamara adds, "I will not say goodbye—you know you have but to call and I will respond."[80] Resigning over principle is a rare occurrence in the history of the U.S. government, and the notion that a man could be loyal to an ideal rather than an individual did not exist in Johnson's universe. Lyndon Johnson took everything personally.

Finally, one can hardly discuss Lyndon Johnson's decision to go to war in Vietnam without acknowledging the unavoidable element of racially tinged machismo in Johnson's character that helped inspire it. Though such characteristics were hardly unusual in a man of his time and place, Johnson seemed to exhibit them in typically outsized proportions.[81] The carefully crafted Hollywood image of John Wayne loomed almost as large as that of John Kennedy in Lyndon Johnson's America, and the president manifested the myth Wayne embodied as much as any twentieth-century American politician. Johnson would occasionally construct a family legacy for himself in which his grandfather died at the Alamo, as if no one would ever dare go back to the record. (When one writer did so, Johnson countered with another lie, this time falsely placing his grandfather at the battle of San Jacinto.) He told his press secretary to "paint the portrait of a tall tough Texan in the saddle," even though he was not a good rider. During the Dominican crisis the president of the United States instructed an aide about to speak to a Dominican rebel leader, "Tell that son of a bitch that unlike the young man who came before me I am not afraid to use what's on my hips." When Senate majority leader Mike Mansfield suggested a plan for the neutralization of Vietnam, Johnson replied contemptuously, "He['s] got no spine at all."[82] And when one of the members of his administration started exhibiting dovish tendencies on the war, Johnson said contemptuously, "Hell, he has to squat to piss."[83] Regarding Vietnam, he would brag to reporters, "I didn't just screw Ho Chi Minh. I cut his pecker off."[84] In a story that is almost too horrific to be believed, according to biographer Robert Dallek, when a group of journalists once asked Johnson why he felt so strongly about the need to continue the fight in Vietnam, the president of the United States is reported to have "unzipped his fly, drew out his substantial organ, and declared, 'This is why!'"[85]

Racially, the "otherness" of the Southeast Asians made them indecipherable to Johnson, except as a potential threat to America's worldly good fortune, like the Indians John Wayne frequently fought on-screen or the Mexicans who populated the Southwest when Johnson was growing to manhood. "If you didn't watch," Johnson warned of the latter, "they'll come right into your yard and take it over if you let them. And the next day they'll be right there on your porch, barefoot and weighing 130 pounds, and they'll take that, too. But if you say to 'em right at the start, 'Hold on, just wait a minute,' they'll know they're dealing with someone who'll stand up. And after that you can get along just fine."[86]

Whatever the most direct cause, some combination of these factors acting on him, through him, and inside him made it impossible for Lyndon Johnson even to imagine telling the truth to the nation about what really happened in the Gulf of Tonkin on August 4, or how little he actually knew of the affair when he ordered American bombers to strike and then asked Congress for the power to begin a war.

Deciding for Deception

It can certainly not be argued that Lyndon Johnson's fears and insecurities alone caused America's entry into Vietnam. As with the Cold War itself, some measure of the U.S. involvement in the conflict can be cast in the hues of historic inevitability. While some Kennedy partisans insist that the slain president planned to withdraw soon after the 1964 election, the fact that so many of his advisers had reached a consensus taking the opposite course—and that so many Republicans were also clamoring for the most belligerent response possible—implies that any president who risked challenging them would have had to be willing to expend considerable capital in order to contain the potential political damage. While much of the public was wholly disengaged from the issue, the percentage of Americans who believed that the United States might possibly lose such a war during this period—or even withdraw from it at any time without winning—was approximately zero.[87] It would have taken an even braver John Kennedy to let South Vietnam fall to the North than the one who secretly negotiated an end to the Cuban Missile Crisis. After all, there would be no disguising such a "defeat" as he had disguised his compromise in Cuba. And Johnson, as evidenced on many occasions, could not help but associate Kennedy's perceived moment of glory in Cuba with his own struggle to win in Vietnam. When Robert Kennedy suggested that Johnson read a passage in a history about the Civil War, during an uncommonly generous exchange between the two men, Johnson replied in a heartfelt note that began not with a reference to Lincoln or Lee, but to Kennedy, and "the agony of the Cuba Missile crisis."[88]

Kennedy had a much deeper interest in the politics of foreign policy than Johnson ever developed and a much greater sophistication when it came to assessing America's role in trying to influence the outcome of—or staying clear of—the various conflicts that arose throughout the globe during his presidency. He was also much better than Johnson was at admitting his mistakes and attempting to learn from them, with the Bay of Pigs fiasco being the prime example. Finally, Kennedy, unlike Johnson, was able to listen to the opinions of those with whom he disagreed and adjust his own views accordingly. Sir Isaiah Berlin once commented of Kennedy: "I've never known a man who listened to every single word that one uttered more attentively. And he always replied very relevantly. He didn't obviously have ideas in his own mind which he wanted to expound, or for which he simply used one's own talk as an occasion, as a sort of launching pad. He really listened to what one said and answered that."[89]

Kennedy's handling of the Cuban Missile Crisis demonstrates, furthermore, that he was not likely to be as entranced by the tough-guy posturing of his aides when it came to the risky use of force. As James Reston had reported on the very day after the settlement was announced—October 29, 1962—Kennedy viewed the crisis "not as a great victory, but merely as an honorable accommodation in a single isolated area of the 'cold war,'" thereby "rejecting the conclusion of the traditional 'hard-liners' that the way to deal with Moscow everywhere in the world is to be 'tough' as in Cuba."[90] While Johnson was (like Dean Rusk) willing to support a missile deal in private, his public declarations of assertiveness knew few bounds.

Would President Kennedy have recognized the folly of trying to shape Indochina to our liking? Would he have leveled with the American people about the reasons for his decision? Of course we will never know, but the indications are that he would, at least, have avoided many of the fateful political mistakes that Lyndon Johnson made in Vietnam—the mistakes that forced him to pile one lie on top of another in order to cover up his initial deception.

The great flaw in Johnson's Vietnam policies and the one for which he stands most clearly guilty in history's judgment was his insistence that no open dialogue about the wisdom of going to war be allowed to take place. When Lyndon Johnson finally decided that he had no choice but to fight in Vietnam, he never found within himself the courage to be forthright with the country about his decision. For even more than the idea of the war itself, Johnson dreaded a democratic debate about it. On the one hand, as the president told Richard Russell, he was "fearful that if we move without any authority of the Congress that the resentment would be pretty widespread and it would involve a lot of people who normally would be with us." But "if we asked for the authority, on the other hand," Johnson complained of Russell's Senate colleagues, "I would shudder to think that if they debated it for a long period of time, and they're likely to do that. So I don't think the choice is very good."[91] Here, again, Johnson relied heavily on the advice of the Kennedy brain trust, particularly McNamara. The secretary of defense told the president in the spring of 1964 that that he thought "it would be wise for you to say as little as possible"[92] to the country about the war. Johnson's decision to try to take the world's oldest democracy to war in secret would ultimately doom not only his presidency and the dreams he held for using his power to improve people's lives, but also much of the historic trust Americans had once granted their elected leaders.

Johnson may not have been aware that he had decided to take the nation into war in secret, but without such a conscious decision, it becomes nearly impossible to explain his actions. In June 1964, Johnson was asked at a press conference whether the United States was preparing to "move the Vietnam war into the North." He flatly denied that any plans had been made, despite the fact that Representative Melvin Laird (R-WI) had publicly stated that McNamara had already briefed House committees on plans to do just this.[93] At a September 28 campaign stop in Manchester, New Hampshire, Johnson promised, "What I have been trying to do, with the situation I found, was to get the boys in Vietnam to do their own fighting with our advice and our equipment." He did not think, he said, "we were ready for American boys to do the fighting for Asian boys." The following month, in Akron, Ohio, LBJ was loudly cheered when he said repeatedly that he wasn't going to "send American boys nine or ten thousand miles away from home to do what Asian boys ought to be doing for themselves."[94] But Johnson had already committed himself, and though no one spoke of it publicly, all of the appropriate wheels inside the government were spinning in the same direction. In Johnson's own mind, too, he appears to have settled on engagement as the only course available to him. For when he heard the first murky reports of what took place in the Gulf of Tonkin that August night, he expended almost no effort to discover the truth behind them. Instead he decided to initiate a war.

Meanwhile, in the Gulf of Tonkin . . .

The so-called first incident took place on August 2, 1964, when a U.S. destroyer, the *Maddox,* was patrolling the Gulf of Tonkin off the coast of North Vietnam as part of a surveillance exercise, called a "DeSoto Patrol." Sailing originally from Taiwan, the *Maddox* entered the Tonkin Gulf on July 31 and began a sweep up the coast of North Vietnam. The ship had been ordered to stay at least eight miles from the coast and four miles from offshore islands. Unknown to the ship's commander, Commodore John Herrick, U.S.-armed, -trained, and -directed South Vietnamese commandos had attacked two North Vietnamese islands in the gulf, Hon Me and Hon Ngu, just one day earlier under a program called "Oplan 34-A." These had been among the most violent raids against North Vietnam proper undertaken so far. The commandos launched additional raids on both August 1 and August 2.[95]

Retaliation against the U.S. sponsors of the raid came on the afternoon of August 2 when three North Vietnamese PT boats suddenly shot out from behind Hon Me toward the *Maddox*. Herrick ordered his ship headed for the open sea, but the boats followed in hot pursuit. Herrick opened fire on the torpedo boats well before they were in range to fire back, and called for help from the local *Ticonderoga* aircraft carrier nearby, whose pilots sank one PT boat and disabled the remaining two, which sputtered harmlessly home.[96] Although Congress would later be told there was no connection between the *Maddox*'s patrol and the incident, this was false information. As with most of the DeSoto patrols, the *Maddox* was equipped for its mission with a mobile communications-interception facility known as a "communications van" or "comvan," whose receivers were designed to pick up North Vietnamese communications along the coastline. The commando raids were designed in part to stimulate these communications.[97] Indeed, in January 1964, General Westmoreland had asked that "the DeSoto Patrol scheduled for February be designed to provide the forthcoming 34A programs with critical intelligence." Missions were to be planned for the Gulf of Tonkin "no later than August 11, for the primary purpose of determining DRV coastal patrol activity."[98]

Despite some tough talk directed at subordinates, Johnson decided to hold off on a full-fledged retaliatory attack. Edwin Moïse, author of a detailed, and for now, definitive study of the Tonkin incidents, speculates, among others, that the NSA intelligence intercepts must have informed him that the approach had been ordered by a single commander, rather than a higher North Vietnamese authority. NSC staffer Michael Forrestal had informed McGeorge Bundy that "it seems likely that the North Vietnamese and perhaps the Chicoms [Chinese Communists] have assumed that the destroyer was part of this operation. . . . It is also possible that Hanoi deliberately ordered the attack in retaliation for the harassment of the islands."[99] In fact, Edwin Moïse was to be informed during his research in Vietnam twenty-five years later that a mix-up occurred on the part of the PT boat commanders, and a recall message was sent to them when superiors realized they were speeding toward the *Maddox*. Two contemporaneous DRV documents (Democratic Republic of Vietnam) support this account.[100] Meanwhile, Johnson was looking to convey an impression of firm resolution as a contrast to the perceived trigger-happiness of his expected opponent Barry Goldwater. Moïse believes that Johnson had intercepts of these communications, given to him by McNamara, demonstrating that the "attack" had been an error and had been called off. In any case, the president decided simply to lodge a formal protest with Hanoi. That very night Dean Rusk, speaking in New York, noted that many incidents since 1945 could have led to war "if sobriety had not exercised a restraining influence."[101]

Behind the scenes, however, Johnson was readying the Congress for a military response. He telephoned Robert McNamara to ask him to call together a group of fifteen or twenty top members of the congressional Foreign Affairs Committee to promise them that he was to go to war. "I want to leave an impression on background . . . that we're gonna be firm as hell," he explained. "The people that're calling me up want to be damned sure I don't pull 'em out and run . . . Goldwater is raising so much hell about how he's gonna blow 'em off the moon."[102] Indeed, Johnson made his first-ever use of the historic "hotline" to Soviet premier Nikita Khrushchev to let him know that he could not be expected to behave so patiently after the next such incident. More ominously, the very same day, administration officials approved additional Oplan commando operations for the next night.[103]

These new attacks took place on the evening of August 3, as South Vietnamese forces, directed by American advisers, orchestrated two more swift boat raids against the North Vietnamese coastline. Fearing more significant retaliation this time, Commodore Herrick—who had now been informed of the raids—decided that his mission represented an "unacceptable risk." He sent a coded message to headquarters asking that it be terminated immediately, but his request was rejected by his superiors in Honolulu, who insisted that such a move would fail to "adequately demonstrate United States' resolve to assert our legitimate rights in these international waters."[104] At the president's personal order, however, they agreed to strengthen the patrol by placing a second destroyer, the *C. Turner Joy,* under Herrick's command. Back in Washington—which was twelve hours behind Saigon time—an analyst at the National Security Agency received intercepts that indicated a North Vietnamese attack on the U.S. destroyers in the Tonkin Gulf was imminent.[105] NSA informed the Pentagon immediately, which, in turn, relayed the message to Captain Herrick, who received it early that evening in Vietnam. In Washington, meanwhile, Lyndon Johnson was instructing both Bundy and McNamara to have North Vietnamese targets ready in the event of another attack. Both men assured the president that they had already prepared them.[106]

On the moonless night of August 4, 1964, barely more than an hour after Herrick had received the Pentagon's warning, events finally appeared to be coming to a head. The *Maddox* began sending reports to headquarters in Honolulu that it had fallen under "continuous torpedo attack" by North Vietnamese boats. All of the twenty-one torpedo reports originated with a twenty-three-year-old sonarman named David E. Mallow, who had enlisted in the Navy two years earlier. Mallow was extremely inexperienced at his post and had never found himself in a situation comparable to this one, given the oddity of the weather patterns in the gulf and the complexities they created for discerning sonar signals when combined with the noises and interference the ship itself emitted. When Mallow thought he spotted a torpedo attack, he alerted the *Turner Joy,* whose guns then began firing for four straight hours. The *Maddox,* however, could find no targets at all for its own response. The soldiers posted to the *Turner Joy*'s sonar detected no torpedoes, and none of the U.S. pilots flying overhead launched from the aircraft carriers the *Ticonderoga* and *Constellation* nearby that night made any visual sightings of enemy ships at all.

Amid the chaos, one gunner on the *Maddox* came within milliseconds of following an order to squeeze the trigger of his five six-inch guns on a target that turned out to be the *Turner Joy.* "If I had fired," he later recounted, "it would have blown it clean out of the water."[107]

It was 9:00 A.M. in Washington when Defense Secretary Robert McNamara received the report of alleged attack. Twelve minutes later, he called Johnson, who was meeting with Democratic congressional leaders, planning for the upcoming civil rights bill. Now, it is a cardinal rule within the Pentagon—a rule that McNamara may or may not have known—to assume that all first reports from a war zone are inaccurate. The fog of battle—and even the anticipation of battle—often prevents anyone from seeing much of anything clearly. "They have?" Johnson thundered when he heard about the supposed attack, according to then-House majority leader Carl Albert, who had stayed on after the congressional breakfast. McGeorge Bundy suggested the president wait before acting precipitously, but Johnson would have none of it. "Now I'll tell you what I want," Johnson said to McNamara. "I not only want those patrol boats that attacked the *Maddox* destroyed, I want everything at that harbor destroyed; I want the whole works destroyed. I want to give them a real dose."[108]

Though Johnson did not give the final order for the attack until late that evening, Alexander Haig, who was working at the Pentagon, concluded, "There was never any realistic doubt that an air raid would take place." By 10:00 A.M. McNamara had an "action group" in his office going over selected targets.[109] McGeorge Bundy reported that the luncheon meeting at which the course of the attack was decided upon "was marked by thoroughness, clarity and an absence of significant disagreement."[110]

Immediately after making his decision, Johnson asked his congressional lobbyist, Lawrence O'Brien, "What effect [will] bombing the hell out of the Vietnamese tonight have on this [civil rights] bill? I'd think [Congress] would be a little more reluctant to vote against the president." O'Brien stated the obvious when he replied, "It certainly is not going to hurt us." Aide Kenneth O'Donnell also recalled that the president "was wondering aloud as to the political repercussions and questioned me rather closely as to my political reaction to his making a military retaliation. . . . His opponent was Barry Goldwater, and the attack on Lyndon Johnson was going to come from the right and the hawks, and he must not allow them to accuse him of vacillating or being an indecisive leader."[111]

To be fair to Johnson, he was dealing with another crisis that same day. James Chaney, Andrew Goodman, and Michael Schwerner, three young "freedom riders" who had disappeared in Mississippi, were discovered to have been murdered, sparking a political firestorm that would severely complicate Johnson's efforts to achieve peaceful integration in the South. But it was abundantly clear to the president's advisers that he was not terribly interested in hearing about any complications that might have arisen regarding the original reports of the night's confusing events. He melodramatically warned the congressional leaders to whom he reported the incident against any leaks to the media as "Some of our boys are floating around in the water." He described a more moderate response than the one he was actually planning as "We can tuck our tails and run, but if we do these countries will feel all they have to do to scare us is to shoot the American flag."[112]

The report that McNamara had given Johnson was quickly called into question. Almost immediately after issuing an alert about the alleged attack, Herrick sent in another report that read "Review of action makes many reported contacts and torpedoes fired appear doubtful. Freak weather effects on radar and overeager sonarmen may have accounted for many reports. No actual visual sightings by *Maddox*. Suggest complete evaluation before any further action taken."[113] This sent the Pentagon into a panic, with cable traffic flowing furiously back and forth. "Everybody and his dog" was addressing questions directly to Herrick, recalled one participant. The questions came faster than the ship could decode them. After a flurry of pointed inquiries from the highest levels of the Pentagon, Herrick sent a new message in which he reversed himself yet again. This missive read: "Further recap reveals *Turner Joy* fired upon by small-caliber guns and illuminated by searchlight. *Joy* tracked two sets of contacts. Fired on 13 contacts. Claim positive hits 1, 1 sunk, probable hits 3." But then Herrick continued, "*Joy* also reports no actual visual sightings or wake. Have no recap of aircraft sightings but seemed to be few. Entire action leaves many doubts except for apparent attempted ambush at beginning. Suggest thorough reconnaissance in daylight by aircraft."[114] James B. Stockdale, flying off the deck of the *Ticonderoga* "with the best seat in the house from which to detect boats," moving directly over the *Maddox* and the *Turner Joy* with no surface haze or ocean spray to cloud his vision, saw "nothing." "No boats, no boat wakes, no ricochets off boats, no boat gunfire, no torpedo wakes—nothing but the black sea and American firepower." Stockdale was initially relieved when he heard of Herrick's telegram calling the attack into question. He thought, "At least there's a commodore up there in the gulf who has the guts to blow the whistle on a screw up." Alas, the next morning someone woke him up with orders for reprisal strikes. "Reprisal for what?" Stockdale replied. "How do I get in touch with the president? He's going off half-cocked." The United States, he worried, was "about to launch a war under false pretenses."[115]

In between his second and third cables, Herrick had somehow become convinced that the attack was real. He cabled Admiral Ulysses S. Grant Sharp Jr., commander in chief of U.S. forces in the Pacific (CINPAC) in Honolulu, that he was now "certain that the original ambush was bona fide." "How do we reconcile all this?" McNamara wondered. "There isn't any possibility there was no attack, is there?" he asked Sharp. "Yes . . . there [was] a slight possibility," the admiral admitted. McNamara noted for the record that the administration "obviously" did not want to attack the North Vietnamese "until we are damned sure what happened." In that case, Sharp suggested, perhaps the United States might postpone its retaliation, "until we have a definite indication that this happened."[116]

Alas, neither man was willing to follow this sage advice. If they had, the course of the American war in Indochina would quite possibly have been altered, albeit in unpredictable ways. Instead, under heavy pressure from McNamara, who, in turn, was being pressured by his boss, the president, Sharp decided at 5:15 that despite the many contradictory signals and lack of hard data from the ship itself, the "weight of evidence supported" the notion that an attack had taken place. In fact, the balance of this "evidence" turned out to consist of the NSA radio intercepts of North Vietnamese communications. But if either man had looked carefully, he would have discovered that the crucial intercepts referred to the August *2* attacks, not to anything that allegedly took place on August 4. (McNamara quickly stamped these intercepts "Classified," and continued to wave them at doubters without revealing their contents.) Nevertheless, on August 4 they proved sufficient to convince the commander in chief of U.S. forces in the Pacific and the secretary of defense that the time had come for the United States to begin bombing.

In his forthcoming book, *Perils of Dominance: Imbalance of Power and the Road to War in Vietnam* (Berkeley: University of California Press), historian Gareth Porter details the evidence that McNamara kept Lyndon Johnson in the dark about the requests from both naval Task Force commander Herrick and CINCPAC Sharp for an investigation of the supposed August 4 attack before any retaliation was carried out. Porter asserts that McNamara effectively took the decision out of Johnson's hands by failing to inform him of the uncertainty of the two key military authorities in the theater of operations.

Herrick and CINPAC in Honolulu were being deluged with questions that, McNamara acknowledges, were being "asked on behalf of a president who had already committed himself . . . and had the air time." The president's top men, too, were committed in their own ways to the truth of the attack, regardless of what had really taken place. For many months, Johnson's advisers had been looking for a pretext for a full-scale attack of the North Vietnamese. They had convinced themselves that such a move would reinvigorate the collapsing Saigon regime and provide the foundation for a government and society that the CIA was terming "extremely fragile" and potentially "untenable" by the end of the year.[117] Dean Rusk speculated at the time that "a pervasive infusion of Americans" might be the only possible way to seize South Vietnamese leaders "by the scruff of the neck and insist they put aside all bickering."[118] Pentagon historians would later summarize the extant view for Robert McNamara: South Vietnamese leader General Khanh and his cronies "would not be able to feel that assurance of victory until the U.S. committed itself to full participation in the struggle, even to the extent of co-belligerency.

"If the U.S. could commit itself in this way," the logic went, "U.S. determination would somehow be transfused into the GVN." What was needed, therefore, was "to find some means of breakthrough into an irreversible commitment of the U.S."[119] This commitment, however, required the impetus of some act of overt belligerence by North Vietnam—or at least the appearance of one.

A War Waiting to Happen

Under Secretary McNamara's direction, the Pentagon had already drawn up extensive plans for full-scale U.S. entry into the war. McNamara had grown increasingly panicked about the sorry state of South Vietnamese forces following his March 1964 trip there. The government was almost unimaginably corrupt, and the army's will to fight for it all but nonexistent. He did not think either one would be able to hold out against the well-disciplined, highly motivated enemy much longer.[120]

The State Department, meanwhile, had been planning for a possible war resolution as early as January, under the direction of Walt W. Rostow, who headed its Policy Planning Council before it was taken over by assistant secretary of state for Far East Asian affairs William Bundy.[121] Contingency planning continued through the winter and spring, in various meetings in

State, Defense, and the NSC, but domestic events and electoral politics continued to take precedence in the minds of the president and his key advisers. Following a March 4 meeting at which the Joint Chiefs had urged the president to "get in or get out," Johnson carped that he did not have "any Congress that will go with us, and we haven't got any mothers that will go with us in a war. And [in] nine months I'm just an inherited—I'm a trustee. I've got to win an election."[122] A May 24 top-level meeting likewise failed to chart a clear course, despite McNamara's pungent observation that "the situation is still going to hell. We are continuing to lose. Nothing we are now doing will win." McGeorge Bundy added in a memo prepared for another high-level meeting, on June 10, that it would probably not be propitious to bring up the idea again "until Civil Rights is off the Senate calendar," as going forward "requires that the Administration [is] ready to give answers to a whole series of rather disagreeable questions," including the matter of a blank check for the president. The passage of a resolution, he noted, "would require major public campaign by the Administration" including "a Presidential message, which should itself be preceded by a clear indication of the increasing firmness of the Administration's position."[123] Two days later, his brother William urged the president to "urgently review with the Congressional leadership a resolution along the lines" of the one he had drawn up allowing for a vast expansion of the war. (It would soon be put to use.) But he stopped short of unequivocally endorsing its immediate introduction.[124]

The decision for war appears to have been made—or not made—over time and more on the basis of not wishing to upset prospects for the passage of Johnson's civil rights bill and the overall election planning strategy than as a result of any discomfort or dissension about the chosen course of engagement.

Robert Kennedy, always an important factor in Johnson's deliberations whether in person or spirit, also counseled patience. He, too, felt that the civil rights bill had to be a priority, and he advised Johnson that the country was just not ready for "a declaration of war," which was how he viewed a congressional resolution.[125] William Bundy later concluded that without a clearer sense of where the administration wanted to go with its resolution, "it would be a political football rather than a declaration of national will, as the cards then lay. I think that was what influenced the President to pull back from the idea."[126]

But the Vietnamese on both sides of the border refused to cooperate with Johnson's preferred schedule. On July 27, one week before the second incident, General Khanh had informed Ambassador Taylor that what the South Vietnamese forces needed to inspire them to fight was a demonstration of American seriousness. He specifically did not mention a large ground force, but appeared to be in the market for "reprisal tit-for-tat bombing" to motivate his own people and perhaps intimidate those in the North.[127] William Bundy headed an interagency team whose task was the creation of a scheme to save South Vietnam in spite of itself and to bring Congress and the country along. A detailed war plan was readied: Khanh would agree to begin "overt air attacks against targets in the North" with a guarantee that the United States would protect South Vietnam in the likely event of "North Vietnamese and/or Chinese retaliation." The U.S. Congress would pass a resolution in support of this war within about twenty days of the attacks. Under no circumstances were Congress or the country to be informed of the deliberate provocations necessary to begin the war, nor of the fact that U.S. direct attacks were to begin imminently once the resolution passed.[128] This plan was shelved for the same reasons earlier ones had been, though, according to William Bundy, the decision had been "very close indeed."[129]

The events of August 4, however, seemed to offer the administration exactly the opportunity McGeorge Bundy had described as necessary in his June memo. While the election was months away and the civil rights bill still on the table, the alleged attack would almost certainly ensure the "rapid passage by a very substantial majority" of any resolution the president presented.[130] Meanwhile, "everyone on duty," Alexander Haig later observed, "wanted to make it possible for the President to do what he wanted to do."[131]

In an emergency National Security Council meeting called that morning, CIA director John McCone offered one last opportunity for reconsideration, explaining that he thought the North Vietnamese were merely "reacting defensively to our attacks on their offshore islands." The director of the U.S. Information Agency, Carl Rowan, also counseled caution, asking, "Do we know for a fact that the North Vietnamese provocation took place? Can we nail down exactly what happened? We must be prepared to be accused of fabricating the incident!" McNamara replied that they would know for certain by the following morning.[132] But clearly that was too long to wait. Dean Rusk demanded "an immediate and direct retaliation by us." McGeorge Bundy's handwritten notes from the August 4 NSC meeting reveal someone present asking the question:

> What is 34-A [O-Plan] role in all This?
> Must be cause; no other is rational.[133]

While the president himself did wonder, "Do they want a war by attacking our ships in the middle of the Gulf of Tonkin?" he ultimately set aside this question. Later that evening (but before the president's address), having been informed of the incident by Johnson, Barry Goldwater confirmed the president's instincts with his own statement, telling the press, "I am sure that every American will subscribe to the actions outlined in the President's statement. I believe it is the only thing we can do under the circumstances. We cannot allow the American flag to be shot at anywhere on earth if we are to retain our respect and prestige."[134] At the meeting with congressional leaders earlier that day, McNamara assured Bourke Hickenlooper of Iowa that the evidence was absolutely clear on the attack. The hawkish Hickenlooper no doubt struck a sensitive chord with the president when he wondered aloud whether "there is a comparison between Cuba [and the missile crisis] and this? Cuba was a bold and dangerous operation as far as Washington was concerned. No one knows what would have happened had we not reacted."[135]

A second confusing melodrama arose when Johnson decided that he wanted to be able tell the nation about his bombing decision. The confusion over whether the attack had taken place at all—which continued until Herrick decided that it probably had—created a serious timing problem. Johnson had initially wanted to make the announcement so that it could be featured on the 7:00 P.M. newscasts, but this proved impossible, as McNamara could not confirm the attack in time, much less launch the bombers and await their safe return. It soon began to look, recalls Alexander Haig, then an aide to McNamara, "as though the president's announcement, having missed the seven o'clock news, might also miss the 11:00 P.M. program (as well as the final deadline for East Coast morning newspapers)." Johnson was phoning McNamara repeatedly, according to Haig, demanding to know when he could go on the air. "The television crew was standing by," Haig notes, "the networks were waiting; prime time was dwindling away." As McNamara later explained to Admiral Sharp, "Part of the problem here is just hanging on to this news, you see. The President has to make a statement to the people, and I am holding him back from making it, but we're forty minutes past the time I told him we would launch."[136]

Johnson wanted to wait long enough so as to ensure the safety of the crews, but as the minutes ticked away, he grew increasingly frantic. "Bob," he yelled, "I'm exposed here! I've got to make my speech right now." The final newscasts of the evening went on at eleven, and Johnson and McNamara worked furiously to try to meet this deadline. When Admiral Sharp told McNamara that it would be eleven on the East Coast by the time the planes reached their targets, McNamara retorted that the enemy would know as soon as the planes were launched. Sharp was unhappy with the secretary's response. After all, he knew, just because the planes were in the air, didn't mean the North Vietnamese could guess where they were headed.[137] In fact it took even longer than Sharp had estimated. At 11:20 P.M. EDT, Sharp telephoned McNamara again and told him the planes had launched at 10:43 and would not be in place to cover their targets for another hour and fifty minutes. At that point McNamara decided, "To hell with it. The president could make his announcement." "I'd sure as hell hate to have some mother say, 'You announced it and my boy got killed,'" Johnson worried aloud. "I don't think there's much danger of that, Mr. President," his trusted aide reassured him.[138]

The president finally went on the air at 11:36 P.M., EDT, to announce that U.S. air strikes had already taken place against "gunboats and certain supporting facilities in North Vietnam." This was untrue. No planes targeting naval vessels took off until more than an hour and a half after Johnson's speech. McNamara then gave further details to the media at 12:02 A.M., explaining exactly which targets had been hit, even though he had been specifically informed by Admiral Sharp that the planes were still on their way. His subsequent explanation that the president had waited until the planes were already within enemy radar range before going on the air was soon belied by Rear Admiral Moore aboard the *Ticonderoga,* who admitted, "I don't believe they were on radar when the President started speaking."[139]

In fact, the first round of planes did not reach their first target until 1:15 A.M. (EDT) and the second not until 2:30 A.M. McGeorge Bundy explained, "The timing of the President's address to the nation was complex. The address must be timed so as not to give any battle advantage to the North Vietnamese but at the same time must precede any announcement of the operation from the other side. The time, which was eventually agreed to, met this requirement."[140] According to Edwin Moïse, Johnson's broadcast was monitored in Hanoi by a radio listening unit in the Foreign Ministry, who warned the air defense forces to expect an impending American attack. Shortly afterward, a radar station detected the incoming planes and Hanoi managed to shoot down two of the attacking aircraft. Lieutenant Richard C. Sather was killed over North Vietnam. Lieutenant Everett Alvarez ejected from his aircraft and was captured near the North Vietnamese port of Hon Gay. He fractured his back in the fall, and was eventually moved to a prison camp in Hanoi, where he experienced eight and a half years of physical and mental abuse.[141] To Alexander Haig, this pilot "symbolizes all the American men who fell in battle in Indochina . . . because their government could not make up its mind to behave like a nation at war."[142] This criticism surely nagged at the president, for a month after the attack, McGeorge Bundy was still seeking to reassure him. "There is still no evidence whatever that the timing of your announcement adversely affected the success of the operation in any way. All the evidence, indeed, runs the other way," he promised Johnson.[143]

The loss of one pilot's life and the capture of another were just the first of a series of unhappy results of Johnson's decision to attack North Vietnam.

Next came the passage by Congress of the Southeast Asia Resolution, usually called the "Gulf of Tonkin Resolution," three days later. Though Johnson remained adamant about preventing any extended debate in Congress about his war plans, he insisted that the body put its institutional stamp on the war from its beginning. He told his advisers that President Truman had been foolish to fight the Korean War without explicit congressional sanction: only if Congress was involved on the "takeoff" would it accept responsibility for a "crash landing."[144] Johnson was deeply concerned about the political consequences of taking the country to war without proper preparation. "I'm fearful," he had told Robert Kennedy before the Tonkin events, "that if we move without any authority of the Congress that the resentment would be pretty widespread and it would involve a lot of people who normally would be with us."[145]

"Don't"

Three months earlier, a group of officials led by George Ball had already begun work on a draft resolution that would endorse "all measures, including the commitment of force" to defend South Vietnam or Laos. At a May 24 NSC meeting, McNamara insisted that the resolution be withheld from Congress unless Johnson decided to use U.S. combat—as opposed to training—forces in South Vietnam. Three weeks later Bundy wrote, "On balance, it appears that we need a Congressional resolution if and only if we decide that a substantial increase of national attention and international tension is a necessary part of the defense of Southeast Asia in the coming summer."[146]

When that "substantial increase" arrived on August 4, McGeorge Bundy's brother, William, now assistant secretary of state for East Asian and Pacific affairs, was vacationing on Martha's Vineyard, believing that no new steps on the war would be taken before the election. He received an urgent call from Rusk, instructing that he come back to work immediately. Bundy returned to Washington at 3:30 that afternoon, and soon joined Undersecretary of State George Ball and Abram Chayes, who had recently resigned as the State Department legal adviser, in drafting a congressional resolution. William Bundy remembers being told of a second attack, "and that the President was determined to retaliate and . . . to seek a Congressional resolution."[147] McGeorge Bundy's memory matches his brother's. "This, I remember quite specifically. He [Johnson] called me up and said we're going to go for a resolution and I said something skeptical [because] of a general feeling that if you want a durable Congressional resolution you don't go for it on the basis of some snap event and a surge of feeling around the snap event. And he makes it clear to me that the matter's decided and he's not calling for my advice—he's calling for my . . . action in carrying out a decision, which I then do."[148] The unthinking haste with which this decision was taken can be seen in the exchange that Bundy had with White House aide Douglass Cater, shortly after his conversation with the president. "Isn't this a little precipitous? Do we have all the information?" Cater asked. "The President has decided, and that's what we're doing," declared the adviser for national security affairs. "Gee Mac," Cater persisted, "I haven't really thought it through." Bundy then put an end to the discussion with a one-word reply: "Don't."[149]

Johnson was eager to avoid Truman's error in Korea, but not so eager that he would risk an honest debate in Congress—either about what had happened in the gulf or what to do about Vietnam. He was, moreover, particularly unwilling to share his plans when he still had an election to win and was preparing to portray himself as the "peace" candidate.

The administration's resolution alleged the attacks in the gulf to be "part of a deliberate and systematic campaign of aggression that the Communist regime in North Vietnam has been waging against its neighbors." It empowered the president to "take all necessary steps, including the use of force," allowing him to do pretty much whatever he wanted with the American military. J. William Fulbright (D-AR), whom the president prevailed upon to guide the measure through the Senate, explained the resolution to his colleagues before the vote took place. "[The resolution] would authorize whatever the commander in chief feels is 'necessary,' including the landing of large American armies in Vietnam or China." Undersecretary of State Nicholas Katzenbach would later tell the Senate Committee on Foreign Relations that the resolution constituted "the functional equivalent" of a declaration of war.[150]

Fulbright accepted the assignment because he had not yet become sufficiently suspicious or courageous to look too carefully into the resolution. The Arkansan did worry about its long-term implications, the vagueness of its language, and the possibility that he was not being fully informed by the president. Indeed, Johnson ensured that his old friend remained in the dark regarding the exchange of telegrams between Herrick and the Pentagon or the OPLAN attacks in the days preceding the incident. While Fulbright knew better than to trust the wily Johnson, in August of 1964 for a southern Democratic foreign policy leader, this particular president was the only one available. He did not "normally assume," he explained, "a President lies to you," but shared the prevalent view with Senator Charles Mathias (R-MD) that even if Congress agreed to sign "this blank check" it would never need to be cashed. "All you'll have to do is wave it in front of your creditors and they'll go away," Mathias predicted. As Fulbright saw it, the resolution was a means of preventing war, not entering into one: "These people would give up if we would just bomb them in a serious way, and they could see what we could do. Then they would stop."[151] The idea was simple and straightforward, and while attractive to Americans, had little relationship to what had actually taken place in the gulf, nor for that matter, with anything at all in Vietnam.

A "Blank Check"

Fulbright shared the widespread belief in the nation's need to demonstrate its resolve for the purpose of avoiding a larger fight. He also had no desire to upset Lyndon Johnson, who was not only his friend and the head of his party, but an extremely popular and famously vindictive politician. Though he may have suspected Johnson, Fulbright was unwilling, within the storm of an apparent Cold War crisis, to try to slow the process down enough to investigate what actually occurred in the Gulf of Tonkin. According to Arthur Schlesinger Jr., as vice president elect Johnson had lobbied John Kennedy energetically to name Fulbright to be secretary of state, but Fulbright's segregationist votes and harsh criticism of Israel finally made him unacceptable. (Johnson was also irked that Fulbright did not campaign more actively for the job).[152] And though Johnson had engineered the coup that led Fulbright to his chairmanship, the president told advisers that he considered the independent-minded senator to be an inveterate leaker, and therefore not to be trusted. Johnson would later tell Senate majority leader Mike Mansfield, "I'm afraid if I talk to Fulbright . . . he'll tell *The New York Times.* . . . You just can't talk to Fulbright."[153] He accordingly never informed him of the secret operations against North Vietnam, much less of the state of confusion in the White House. Hence Fulbright inadvertently misled his fellow senators whenever one of them tried to learn precisely how the incident had come about. Questioned by Allen Ellender (D-LA), a critic of U.S. Vietnam policy, Fulbright offered up the false assurances from McNamara and Rusk that there had been no connection whatever with any Vietnamese ships that might have been operating in the same area. When Ellender persisted, explaining that he was "trying to discover if our forces could have done anything which might have provoked these attacks," Fulbright insisted that "categorically" this had not been the case.[154]

At Johnson's insistence, the hapless Fulbright successfully fought off efforts by Senator Gaylord Nelson (D-WI) to tighten the amendment's language so as to limit its authority to cover only "the provision of aid, training assistance and military advice." Nelson's amendment also noted for the record that Congress "should continue to attempt to avoid a direct military involvement in the Southeast Asian conflict." Fulbright assured Nelson that such restrictive language was unnecessary. "Everyone I have heard has said that the last thing we want to do is become involved in a land war in Asia," he argued. U.S. power "is sea and air, and that is what we hope will deter the Chinese Communists and the North Vietnamese from spreading the war."

With impressive prescience, Ernest Gruening (D-AK), who had unsuccessfully pleaded with Fulbright to hold a full inquiry before passing any measure—or at least to scale back the language of the Johnson resolution—warned his colleagues that they were signing "a predated declaration of war."[155] Wayne Morse (D-OR) predicted that "history will record that we have made a great mistake in subverting and circumventing the Constitution of the United States" by giving the president "warmaking powers in the absence of a declaration of war. What is wrong with letting the Constitution operate as written by our constitutional fathers?" he asked. "Why should we give arbitrary discretion to mere men who happen to hold office at a given time, when the American people and their lives are at the mercy of those mere men?"[156]

The open-ended resolution ultimately passed without amendment, with only Gruening and Morse dissenting. Fulbright's arguments were augmented by typical wartime jingoism, spouted by the likes of Richard Russell. ("Our national honor is at stake," he insisted. "We cannot and we will not shrink from defending it.")[157] The debate took less than ten hours in the Senate and only forty minutes in the House, where the vote was unanimous. Rarely was either chamber even one-third full when the issue of going to war was being discussed. The FBI later collected the names of citizens who sent supportive telegrams to Senator Morse.[158] Both dissenters would be unseated in their next elections.

As author Paul Kattenberg correctly argues, "If Congress does not fulfill the role of loyal opposition in foreign policy, that role does not seem to get fulfilled at all."[159] Congress's unwillingness to look more deeply into the administration's allegations of what had and had not taken place in the Gulf of Tonkin constitutes a signal failure to uphold its constitutional war-making responsibilities. Decades later Robert McNamara would argue that "the fundamental issue of Tonkin Gulf involved not deception, but rather, misuses of power bestowed by the resolution." Congress, he insisted, "recognized the vast power the resolution granted to President Johnson, but it did not conceive of it as a declaration of war and did not intend it to be used, as it was, as authorization for an enormous expansion of U.S. forces in Vietnam—from 16,000 military advisers to 550,000 combat troops."[160] McNamara is quite wrong. Congress was voting to give the president these extraordinary powers solely on the basis of deception, though some of it was genuine self-deception on the part of the people doing the deceiving. Moreover, politically speaking, a Democratic Congress did not really have much choice but to give its support to the president in a matter of war and peace in 1964. As James Reston pointed out at the time, once put on the spot by Johnson and McNamara, "The Congress was free in theory only. In practice, despite the private reservations of many members it had to go along . . . it had the choice of helping [Johnson] or helping the enemy, which is no choice at all." The specter of potential warmonger Barry Goldwater waiting in the wings, moreover, was an even more powerful argument for not demanding too much in the way of evidence from the president.[161] Congress believed that an attack had taken place because McNamara and company offered no reason to doubt it. They knew that Johnson could, if he wished, use the resolution to begin a war, but they were given assurances it would not happen.

We now know almost certainly that no attack took place on that fateful night in the Gulf of Tonkin. Following an exhaustive examination of the evidence undertaken over a period of a decade, Edwin E. Moïse concluded that what the inexperienced sonarman on the *Maddox* thought were the signs of a torpedo attack were really a combination of a localized meteorological phenomenon usually termed "Tonkin Spook," coupled with the noise of the ship's own motor. Moïse explains:

> The only major category of evidence that seriously tended to support the idea of an attack was naked-eye sightings from the destroyers. The radar evidence was at best very ambiguous. The sonar evidence was negative. The evidence from aerial photography was negative. The reports of the pilots—both those who were over the destroyers during the night, and those who searched for wreckage and oil slicks on the following morning—were powerfully negative. The electronics intelligence evidence—the lack of detections of enemy radar use or convincing communications intercepts—was negative. The results of interrogations of DRV naval personnel captured during the next few years were very fully negative. . . . The reports of tired men under stress who, while looking out into a dark night that they were convinced hid PT boats . . . cannot begin to counterbalance the impossibility of this version of events.[162]

Johnson, McNamara, and company likely remained hazy on the details of the incident throughout the period leading up to the passage of the resolution and even for a few days beyond it. But the truth soon became clear. CIA deputy director Ray Cline had been reading the enemy intercepts from the gulf as they came in. He was, he later said, "trying to be upbeat, and say there was an attack . . . I wasn't out to up-end the President." But Cline did note that almost none of the signs that would normally have accompanied an attack was present. Those that did appear to corroborate an attack were dated not to the fourth of August but to the second, about which there was little controversy. Feeling an obligation to give the unhappy news to the President's Foreign Intelligence Advisory Board (PFIAB), Cline called Johnson adviser (and former Truman aide-de-camp) Clark Clifford, who chaired the board. Clifford, in turn, relayed Cline's conclusions to Johnson, probably on August 10, though both men apparently relayed them no further.[163]

Now that he had accomplished what he had set out to do, Johnson could afford to behave more prudently with his bombers. During the so-called "third" Gulf of Tonkin incident, which took place a few weeks later, on September 18, and proved just as factually inconclusive as the second, McNamara and Rusk both argued in the NSC for additional air strikes. Rusk insisted that it was important not to doubt the word of "our naval officers on the spot," while McNamara wanted "to show the flag and prove to Hanoi and the world that we are not intimidated." But this time George Ball countered, "Suppose one of those destroyers is sunk with several hundred men aboard. Inevitably there'll be a Congressional investigation. What would your defense be?" The intelligence mission of those destroyers that North Vietnam found so provocative, Ball asserted, was obviously achievable by other means. "The evidence will strongly suggest that you sent those ships up the Gulf only to provoke attack so we could retaliate." Johnson weighed Ball's comments and decided not to take any action, telling his defense secretary, "We won't go ahead with it, Bob. Let's put it on the shelf." No doubt concerned about how Ball's scenario might play out with relation to the fictional second incident, LBJ spoke of the precedent of the Pearl Harbor hearings and the accusations that the Roosevelt administration had deliberately provoked the attack to ensure U.S. entry into the war. The president advised McNamara and the rest of his hawkish advisers that he was "not interested in rapid escalation on so frail evidence and with a very fragile government in South Vietnam."[164] Johnson also confided to George Ball his opinion that "those dumb, stupid sailors were just shooting at flying fish."[165]

Yet the confusion continued, and in many cases increased. William Bundy, for example, has written that Johnson was referring to the third, not the second, incident with his "flying fish" comment, but he has told his account in so many different ways it has become impossible to tell exactly to which incident he is referring. At the time, however, Bundy and many others in the administration worked furiously to try to convince Congress, the media, and the nation that they were considerably more certain of the August 4 attack than any of them had any right to be. William Bundy also continues to insist that no one "had any doubt that day that the second attack had taken place. . . . There was definitely not any fabrication that day. What was said was what was believed."[166] Unfortunately, Bundy is being far too generous to himself and his colleagues. A great deal more was known about the situation than the White House ever acknowledged, and had it been known in Congress at the time, it is at least possible that the precipitous rush to war might have been averted.

The truth of the matter was settled to a considerable degree with the publication in 2001 of Johnson's secretly recorded private Oval Office tapes for this period. During one conversation, recorded on September 18, while Johnson was trying to decide how to respond to the still murky "third" incident, he admitted to McNamara that he doubted that the second incident ever took place. "Now, Bob," he explained:

> I have found over the years that we see and we hear and we imagine a lot of things in the form of stacks and shots and people running at us, and I think it would . . . make us very vulnerable if we conclude that these people were attacking us and we were merely responding and it develops that that just wasn't true at all. And I think we ought to check that very, very carefully. And I don't know why in the hell, some time or other, they can't be sure that they are being attacked. It looks like to me they would hear a shot or see a shot or do something before they just get worked up and start pulling a [General Curtis] LeMay on us. I think that if we have this kind of response and then it develops that we just started [it] with our own destroyers that people are going to conclude . . . that we're just playing cops, trying to get a lot of attention, and trying to show how tough we are. I want to be tough where we . . . are justified in being tough. . . . But I sure want more caution on the part of these admirals and these destroyer commanders . . . about whether they are being fired on or not.

When McNamara responded "Yeah," he elicited this priceless piece of vintage Johnsonianism:

> I don't want them just being some change o'life woman running up and saying that, by God, she was being raped just because a man walks in the room! And that looks to me like that's what happens in the thirty years that I've been watching them. A man gets enough braid on him, and he walks in a room and he just immediately concludes that he's being attacked.

Now, Johnson is being unfair here to the military, as it was clearly pressure from above—namely, from Johnson himself and from McNamara—that forced the naval chain of command to provide an assessment of the "attack" before it was comfortable doing so. In any case, the president wanted to make certain this time that an attack actually did take place, and instructed McNamara:

> Take the best military man you have, though, and just tell him that I have been watching and listening to these stories for thirty years before the Armed Services Commission and we are always sure we've been attacked. Then in a day or two, we are not so damned sure. And then in a day or two more, we're sure it didn't happen at all. . . . Just say that you want to be sure . . . that we were fired upon. Because you just came in . . . a few weeks ago [The second Tonkin incident had occurred fewer than six weeks earlier.] and said that "Damn, they are launching an attack on us—they are firing on us." When we got through with all the firing we concluded maybe they hadn't fired at all.

McNamara attempted to argue with the president, insisting that a "substantial engagement" had taken place (though it is not entirely clear from the context of the conversation whether he is referring to the second or the third incident). But Johnson appears convinced that no incident—at least none that would even remotely justify either the political or military response of the United States—had occurred. He asks McNamara, "Well, what is a 'substantial engagement?' Mean that we could have started it and they just responded?" When the secretary responds, "But they stayed there for an hour or so . . ." Johnson cuts him off. "They would be justified in staying, though, if we started shooting at them." [167]

Of course, none of these concerns was ever shared with Congress or the nation. Though never coordinated as a deliberate conspiracy, the Tonkin Gulf deception soon grew to epic proportions, generating its own momentum. For instance, Johnson implied to the nation that the North Vietnamese had no cause for concern regarding the presence of a U.S. destroyer off their shores. In fact, the U.S. government had secretly been conducting a series of operations against the North Vietnamese for nearly three years. Beginning in May of 1961, President Kennedy ordered the CIA to undertake a program of covert action against Hanoi, including the infiltration of agents into North Vietnam to gather intelligence and commit acts of sabotage. These attacks were expanded in December 1963 at Lyndon Johnson's request.

Op Plan 34-A

Dissatisfied with the progress of the war, Johnson had approved a covert action plan called "Operations Plan 34-A-64" or "Op Plan 34-A," which included guerrilla raids against the Ho Chi Minh Trail. The impetus to increase the size and severity of these attacks came in March 1964, after McNamara returned from a dispiriting trip to South Vietnam. The defense secretary disparagingly called the OPLAN attacks "pinpricks" that "were accomplishing nothing." William Bundy concurred, referring to them as "pretty small potatoes," and began thinking of ways to enhance them. But the program's effectiveness was marred by one unalterable weakness: despite enormous U.S. efforts, the South Vietnamese had, according to one State Department official, "no capability to strike against the North even in a subversive way like this." They failed to report for their missions; when they did report, they were frequently drunk, and should any of them ever make it into North Vietnam, they would "never show up again."[168] Stronger measures were therefore needed, and the Americans were getting ready to provide them.

Johnson's involvement in these operations helps explain why he was reluctant to make much of the first Gulf of Tonkin incident. Commodore John Herrick, commander of the *Maddox,* did not know of the raid that had taken place two days earlier, and was therefore unaware of the possibility that the North Vietnamese PT boats had been sent in retaliation. But U.S. officials in Washington had apparently made the connection, which explains Secretary of State Rusk's classified cable to General Maxwell D. Taylor, U.S. ambassador to Vietnam and the top U.S. official in charge of the war in that country, the following night: the "Maddox incident is directly related to [North Vietnam's] efforts to resist these activities."[169] On the night of August 3, the United States and their Vietnamese allies launched yet another commando raid. According to enemy communications intercepted by the *Maddox,* the North Vietnamese confused that mission with Herrick's patrol.

The second incident appeared to provide the administration with exactly the opportunity for which it had been hoping. A retaliation would shore up the South Vietnamese, teach the North Vietnamese and Chinese a lesson, and defang Barry Goldwater's hawkish attacks, thereby isolating the Republican and his supporters on the far fringes of mainstream opinion. As Michael Forrestal would later observe, "If you had decided, as some people wanted to decide, that we were going to embark on bombing anyway for tactical reasons, then you had to find a way to do it. And the Tonkin Gulf for those people was made to order."[170]

At the very least, as McGeorge Bundy later admitted, "The Gulf of

Tonkin incident was seized by the president as a time for him to take his resolution on Vietnam to the Congress. And he made that decision and arranged that broadcast before there was really absolutely clear-cut evidence as to what had happened out there. . . . [H]e made a quick decision on an incompletely unverified event."[171] But the truth is even more damning. Johnson, together with Robert McNamara, ensured that the administration would receive maximum political benefit from the incident by vastly simplifying what he knew and deliberately falsifying much of what he did not. Both men consistently misled all questioners—including members of the media, the Congress, and most of the rest of the government—with regard to virtually everything concerning the U.S. presence in the gulf as well as to the incident itself. They thereby deliberately prevented any understanding of just why the United States was going to war that might have been possible. Just how much of this misinformation was intentional and how much represented genuine confusion is impossible to know. But in every instance, the reports that were issued were intended to portray the Vietnamese as more aggressive than they had so far proven to be, the United States as more pacific, and the situation in North Vietnam as a great deal simpler than it really was.

When McNamara briefed the press about twelve hours after getting word about the August 4 incident, he explained that the *Turner Joy* had reported that "the destroyer had been fired upon by automatic weapons while being illuminated by searchlights."[172] He had already given this story to the NSC and he repeated it again when, accompanied by Secretary of State Rusk and General Wheeler, he testified before the Senate Foreign Relations Committee on August 6. When asked for specific details, he claimed they were three-inch guns. In fact no one had ever credited the entire North Vietnamese navy with possessing anything larger than 1.5-inch guns, with torpedo boats falsely believed to have one-inch guns. In fact, none were fired at all. McNamara also insisted that the ships were attacked while cruising at least thirty miles from the North Vietnamese coast. This figure is double the true distance of the vessels when the imaginary attack took place. Speaking of the U.S. retaliatory raids, the defense secretary also argued, "We think there were very few civilian casualties because these bases and the depot were in isolated portions of North Vietnam." In fact, the depot in question was in Vinh, the capital of Nghe An province. (Casualties were actually light, because the U.S. pilots did an exceptionally good job of hitting only their targets.)[173]

The day following the raids, Johnson made a long-planned speech at Syracuse University in which he once again condemned the "aggression, deliberate, willful and systematic" that had "unmasked its face to the entire world."[174] Two days later he repeated the claim of "complete and incontrovertible evidence" in response to an official protest from Nikita Khrushchev, who must have known of the falsehood and concluded accordingly. U.S. representative to the UN Adlai E. Stevenson made a similarly misleading statement before the Security Council on August 5.[175] On August 7, the State Department released an equally false and misleading account for dissemination.[176]

Called before Congress, Johnson's aides were compelled to answer specific questions about the incident. Testifying before the Senate Foreign Relations Committee, in response to a tough interrogation by Senator Wayne Morse, who had been tipped off by a source inside the Pentagon, McNamara lied outright. To Morse, the secretary repeatedly insisted, "Our Navy played absolutely no part in, was not associated with, was not aware of, any South Vietnamese actions, if there were any. I want to make that very clear to you. The *Maddox* was operating in international waters and was carrying out a routine patrol of the type we carry out all over the world at all times. . . . I say this flatly; this is a fact." As Morse persisted, McNamara repeated versions of this statement, each in the most categorical terms possible.[177] Years later, angry senators would confront McNamara with a leaked cable of instructions to the *Maddox,* telling the destroyer to draw North Vietnamese patrol boats "to northward away from the area 34A operations." The commander of the Pacific Fleet had ordered the patrol extended, instructing it to avoid "interference with 34-A ops."[178]

When asked by Senator Albert Gore how the *Maddox* officers could not have known about the South Vietnamese operations when Herrick had sent a cable days earlier complaining of the danger they presented to his mission, McNamara replied: "They were not aware of the *details* which, of course, is what I said."[179] McNamara would also continue to insist that while Commodore Herrick was indeed fully aware of the fact of the raids, the "U.S. Navy" somehow was not. Perhaps most egregious was McNamara's pretense that these attacks were South Vietnamese–owned and –operated. McNamara insisted that he "did not have any knowledge at the time of the attack on the island."[180]

In his 1995 memoir, *In Retrospect,* McNamara describes his testimony on this point as "honest but wrong." But in his memoir of Vietnam, *Secrets: A Memoir of Vietnam and the Pentagon Papers,* Daniel Ellsberg, who began work as an assistant to Assistant Secretary of Defense John McNaughton, notes that part of his job was to ensure that the operational details of these raids were disseminated throughout the Pentagon. Ellsberg inists that "*every particular detail* of these operations was known and approved by the highest authorities in Washington, both military and civilian"[181] (italics in original). In fact, U.S. naval officers had given the order for the very same raids about which he was being questioned, and both McGeorge Bundy and Cyrus Vance had explicitly approved them.[182] The Senate hearing lasted about one hundred minutes; its House counterpart, less than an hour.

The Elusive "Intercepts"

To those who remained at all skeptical about the attack, McNamara insisted that he had in his possession North Vietnamese intercepts proving the American case, but that these remained too sensitive to be released to the public. He also ordered the Joint Chiefs to send a "flash" message to the commanders of all U.S. units involved in the action, asking for evidence "of type, which will convince United Nations Organization that the attack did in fact occur." The commanders responded as best they could, but could not produce what did not exist. (Investigators would later claim to turn up a single bullet.) The official Navy history of the Vietnam War continues to this day to insist that the second incident took place.[183] On the wall of the Lyndon Johnson Library in Austin, Texas, the museum exhibition that deals with the incident explains that the two ships reported the attack, and what happened next led to "some debate" in later years.[184] Perhaps less forgivable is Dean Rusk's 1990 memoir, *As I Saw It,* written with his son Richard. In it, the authors attempt to prove that the incident took place, once again, by confusing the reader with the dates of the two incidents. As with McNamara's and Sharp's (perhaps deliberately sown) confusion over the dates of the North Vietnamese intercepts, Rusk notes, "The Republic of Vietnam today celebrates August 2—the day of the Tonkin Gulf attacks—as part of its national war effort against the Americans, so whatever happened that night in the Tonkin Gulf, evidently it takes credit for it now." Of course no one disputes the fact of an attack on August 2, and the former secretary of state's account must therefore be considered disingenuous. It is only the August 4 attack that matters, and Rusk adds nothing new to this argument. Instead he cites, once again, "our intercept of North Vietnamese radio transmissions."[185]

In the short run the administration's policy of deception worked brilliantly, and the media accepted its account with little dissent.[186] *Time* offered its readers a particularly lurid version of the imaginary attack, going so far as to endow the *Maddox*'s radar systems with the power to track torpedoes, something that was technically impossible at the time. "There were at least six of them," the magazine's correspondents wrote, "Russian-designed 'Swatow' gunboats armed with 37-mm and 28-mm guns, and P-4s. At 9:52 they opened fire on the destroyers with automatic weapons, this time from as close as 2,000 yards. The night glowed eerily with the nightmarish glare of airdropped flares and boats' searchlights. For 3½ hours, the small boats attacked in pass after pass.

Ten enemy torpedoes sizzled through the water. Each time the skippers, tracking the fish by radar, maneuvered to evade them."[187]

Other publications followed suit, though few could match *Time*'s flare for melodrama. *Newsweek* wrote, "A PT boat burst into flames and sank. . . . Another PT boat exploded and then the others scurried off into the darkness nursing their wounds."[188] No mainstream publication questioned even the smallest detail of the official U.S. government story. Thus *The Washington Post* opined:

> The United States turned loose its military might on North Vietnam last night to prevent the Communist leaders in Hanoi and Peking from making the mistaken decision that they could attack American ships with impunity. But the initial United States decision was for limited action, a sort of tit-for-tat retaliation, and not a decision to escalate the war in Southeast Asia . . . The great mystery here was whether the attacks by North Vietnamese PT boats on the American vessels were part of some larger scheme on the Communist side to escalate the war.[189]

Adding a gripping minute-by-minute description of the firefight, *The New York Times* reported that the U.S. destroyer "was on a routine patrol when an unprovoked attack took place" and that "there was no ready explanation why the PT boats would in effect attack the powerful Seventh Fleet." Its editorial page called the incident "the beginning of a mad adventure by the North Vietnamese Communists."[190] James Reston helpfully explained that the U.S. retaliatory bombing was "not an invitation to expand the war but to negotiate." He added that the attack was known to be "premeditated" and undertaken with the "acquiescence of the Communist Chinese."[191] *Times* military reporter Hanson W. Baldwin, a graduate of the Naval Academy at Annapolis, added that "the attack . . . may reflect a deliberate policy of attempting to goad the United States into retaliatory action."[192] Just why North Vietnam would want to purposely involve itself in a war with the United States, however, Baldwin did not say.

The network anchors were likewise enthusiastic supporters of Johnson's actions. Americans were fighting, Walter Cronkite explained to millions of television viewers watching *The CBS Evening News,* "to stop Communist aggression wherever it raises its head."[193]

Meanwhile virtually all the media praised America's "restrained" response to the nonexistent attack. Only *Time, The New York Times,* and *The Arizona Republic* allowed even the possibility that the North Vietnamese might have had reason to be concerned about the appearance of a U.S. destroyer off their coast, before rejecting the charge as Communist propaganda. None picked up on an August 7 front-page report in the Paris daily *Le Monde,* which reported in some detail a much larger role than had been admitted for U.S. forces in encouraging and supporting guerrilla operations against North Vietnam—a report that worried the State Department, but not the U.S. media.[194] Typically, the reporters simply chose to pass along whatever officialdom handed out. Tom Wicker informed *Times* readers, "The Chinese are believed here to be the instigators."[195] *New York Daily News* editors urged Johnson to launch immediate air strikes against China. If that caused war, well, "it may be our heaven-sent good fortune to liquidate not only Ho Chi Minh but Mao Tze-tung's Red mob at Peking as well." The *News* editorial also celebrated the "singe dealt to Ho's wispy whiskers."[196]

Media reaction could hardly have been more favorable. *The Washington Post* was so supportive that Johnson joked it had become his house organ. *Newsweek,* owned by the Washington Post Company, noted, "Mr. Johnson's calculatedly cool and restrained handling of the naval attacks seemed to bring him even more public confidence than he might have expected."[197] *The New York Times* and the newsweeklies were similarly admiring, as were the networks. Even Walter Lippmann approved of the president's moderate response to the crisis, though he never ceased warning about the dangers of a land war in Asia.[198] In September, following news of the so-called "third Gulf of Tonkin incident," the editors of *The New York Times* found it "disturbing" and "sobering" that "some people—presumably among [the president's] military and civilian advisers—had urged rapid retaliation and American bombing of North Vietnam." They were soothed, however, by the fact that, "As was to be expected, the President had a cooler head and correctly rejected that advice." Had he not done so, the editors explained, "The United States would have been in an indefensible position before world public opinion if it had bombed North Vietnam as 'retaliation' against bullets and torpedoes that—even accepting the official interpretation—were never fired."[199]

Still, even this level of support for his policies did not satisfy Johnson. In September 1964 he complained to the journalist William S. White about how "if you look at the Lippmanns and the Restons and the Alsops and the Rowland Evanses on Kennedy around here in 1960 and the Joe Krafts, and the rest of them, I think the Johnsons had a real minimum of personal treatment. Now when I get some of it, it's bad, but when other people get it, it's par for the course."[200] Yet it was precisely this falsely earned level of trust, respect, and admiration—coupled with the journalistic mores of the day—that prevented the press from looking more closely into the incident. Not until nearly four years later—after Fulbright had already begun to hammer away at the issue—would the *Times* return to what really had happened in the Gulf of Tonkin.

Public opinion, not surprisingly, rallied around the president. A Harris poll showed Johnson's ratings shooting up by 30 percent overnight. After the gulf incident and the U.S. retaliation, another Harris poll indicated that public opinion on the U.S. role in Vietnam had reversed. Before the incident, 58 percent of those polled had a negative view of the Johnson administration's handling of Vietnam policy; afterward, 72 percent approved.[201] These numbers would continue to demonstrate hawkishness on the part of the majority of the public through 1965 and 1966.[202]

For a brief, shining moment, Lyndon Johnson's greatest ambitions appeared within reach. He was on his way to his own landslide presidential election, winning over Kennedy's people, and taking on the slain president's mantle. Because the Republicans were on the path to nominating an unelectable right-wing radical to be their standard-bearer in 1964, Johnson could afford to reject Robert Kennedy's campaign to be his vice president, further humiliating his enemy. And Johnson's hopes to uplift the poor and the downtrodden never looked more promising than they did during the election season of 1964. In what may be the purest expression of hubris ever uttered by a president, Johnson would tell his aides, "Those Negroes go off the ground. They cling to my hands like I was Jesus Christ walking in their midst."[203]

Indeed, the 1964 election would prove Lyndon Johnson even more popular than his hero, Franklin Roosevelt, at his height. During the 1936 election barely 36 percent of the nation's newspapers had endorsed FDR's reelection, while 57 percent preferred his opponent, Alf Landon. Twenty-eight years later, according to *Editor and Publisher,* Johnson bested Barry Goldwater in this contest by 42 percent to 35 percent. If one includes only big city newspapers, Goldwater had only three supporters. Johnson also won a larger percentage of the popular vote than Roosevelt ever did and became the first Democrat to carry Vermont since James Monroe in 1820.[204] The president won forty-four of fifty states and saw a substantial increase in his party's already overwhelming majorities in both houses of Congress.[205] In his *Making of the President* series, Theodore H. White called Johnson's victory "the greatest electoral victory that any man ever won in an election of free people."[206] *Time*'s editors hardly went out on a limb in naming the president 1964's "Man of the Year." The magazine printed a cartoon with the tall Texan standing by a White House window early in the morning and shouting, "I am the world—ready or not."[207] At Christmastime Johnson proclaimed that Americans were living in "the most hopeful times since Christ was born in Bethlehem." A *Newsweek* reporter chided the president for his tendency toward exaggeration, but could not help concluding that Johnson was indeed the leader of "the most powerful, most prosperous and most lavishly endowed nation not only of these times but of any times."[208]

The Tonkin incidents had conveniently taken place during the run-up to the mid-August Democratic national convention, when Johnson would seek to portray himself as a tough-minded leader, and his opponent, Barry Goldwater, as an untrustworthy bomb-thrower. And while the president deliberately played down the importance of the Tonkin Gulf Resolution during the election period—in order to better portray himself as the more pacific alternative to Goldwater—he did so only in the service of beginning a war he did not wish to defend in open debate. On the very day Americans were going to the polls to give Johnson his mandate for maintaining the peace, Johnson appointed William Bundy to chair an interdepartmental study group to come up with ways to expand the war. The appointment had actually been made earlier, but its political sensitivity made it impossible to admit during the pre-election period. Despite the reassuring rhetoric of Johnson's presidential campaign, the president, Bundy later recalled, was thinking "in terms of maximum use of the Gulf of Tonkin rationale."[209]

A Provocation?

One question that has never been satisfactorily answered about the Gulf of Tonkin incident is whether the United States had secretly been intending to provoke an attack on August 4, which would explain why U.S. officials were so quick to behave as if one had occurred before they could confirm the precise details. (The famously paranoid film director, Oliver Stone, suggests just such a scenario, which he links to JFK's murder, in his 1991 film *JFK*) In fact, creating such provocations has been a time-honored tradition of U.S. policy ever since the *Maine* was exploded in a Cuban harbor in 1898, leading to an irresistible popular demand for war there. Indeed, Robert Kennedy mused aloud at an ExComm meeting on October 16, 1962, that a trumped-up *Maine*-like incident might be just what the government needed to solve the Cuban Missile Crisis—at least in its earliest stages. And the U.S. Joint Chiefs of Staff were deeply involved in attempting to plan a series of provocations against Cuba in the period before the missile crisis for the explicit purpose of provoking a war.[210]

Despite his knowledge of these proposals, Robert McNamara continued to insist that it was "inconceivable that anyone even remotely familiar with our society and system of government could suspect the existence of a conspiracy" to provoke a war.[211] William Bundy added that a provocation was not planned because "it didn't fit in with our plans at all, to be perfectly blunt about it. We didn't think the situation had deteriorated to the point where we had to consider stronger action on the way things lay in South Vietnam."[212]

The facts appear to tell another story. George Ball has insisted that the *Maddox* was sent up the Tonkin Gulf "primarily for provocation." While Ball also allowed that "there was some intelligence objective" in the mission, he nevertheless believed, "there was a feeling that if the destroyer got into some trouble, that would provide the provocation we needed."[213] Michael Forrestal cabled Rusk on August 3, "You probably know that the action against the MADDOX took place within the same 60-hour period as an OPLAN 34A harassing action by SV forces against two islands of DRV coast . . . It seems likely that the North Vietnamese and perhaps Chicoms have assumed that the destroyer was part of the operation." Another Forrestal cable to Rusk demonstrates that "the White House," meaning McGeorge Bundy for certain and probably Johnson as well, specifically approved the August 4 raids after they had been made aware of what had taken place on August 2. Johnson and Bundy had concluded that the July 30–31 series of attacks were probably responsible for the August 2 incident, and yet they went ahead and ordered more such attacks for August 3, planning in advance what U.S. retaliation would be if these resulted in a similar North Vietnamese response. Similarly, on August 3, Ambassador Maxwell Taylor in Saigon proposed to Washington that if in the near future, North Vietnamese forces were to acquire Soviet MIG jets, the United States should deliberately invite them to attack U.S. reconnaissance aircraft there.

In early September, Daniel Ellsberg's boss, John McNaughton, wrote a draft "Plan of Action for South Vietnam," in which he suggested that the United States "provoke a military DRV response and to be in a good position to seize on that response . . . to commence a crescendo of GVN-US military actions against the DRV." The plan recommended resuming the DeSoto patrols off the coast of North Vietnam along with 34A actions, both of which had been suspended, and added: "The main further question is the extent to which we should add elements to the above actions that would tend deliberately to provoke a DRV reaction, and consequent retaliation by us. Examples of actions to be considered would be running U.S. naval patrols increasingly close to the North Vietnamese coast and/or associating them with 34A operations."[214] Days later, Taylor, Rusk, Wheeler, and McNamara approved a paper suggesting that the United States might wish to deliberately invite an attack on a U.S. naval patrol in order to create an excuse for retaliation. And another memo circulated by William Bundy openly discussed the possibility that the United States might want to boost U.S. naval patrols in the Gulf of Tonkin "increasingly close to the NV coast." These actions "would tend to provoke a DRV reaction and consequent retaliation by us."[215] Ellsberg says this notion was shelved as being too risky to undertake before an election. But the planning continued.[216] Moreover, the administration already had its Bill Bundy–authored congressional resolution ready to go, and was waiting only, as McNamara put it, should "the enemy act suddenly"—something he deemed to be unlikely back in June.[217]

Given all these factors, coupled with its unnecessarily hasty response, the evidence for a deliberate provocation by the United States in the Gulf of Tonkin is powerful. It was the unvarnished opinion of Kenneth Blackwell, the head of the British Consul-General in Hanoi, at the time that "the only plausible explanation of the incident seems to be that it was a deliberate attempt by the Americans to provoke the North Vietnamese into hostile reaction."[218]

In fact, the political groundwork for the manipulation of such an incident was being prepared just moments before it took place. At a White House dinner on July 26, Johnson reportedly told Fulbright that the South Vietnamese regime was in danger of collapse and a resolution in support of the war effort might be necessary to shore it up. This occurred a few days after an initial approach to Fulbright on the same topic by George Ball. Both men were quite explicit about the resolution's value in depriving Goldwater of the "soft on Communism" issue in the coming election. The day after the Johnson-Fulbright tête-à-tête at the White House, Ambassador Taylor, acting on the explicit instructions of Secretary of State Rusk, promised General Khanh that he might expect U.S. air attacks on North Vietnam in the very near future.[219] It is also quite possible that, well below this level in Saigon, U.S. officials in South Vietnam who were eager to expand the conflict were attempting to provoke an attack without the explicit knowledge of their superiors. Edwin Moïse notes that the officials "who were making requests and recommendations to the Navy about what the DeSoto patrols should do, and then scheduling OPLAN 34A raids in the light of the schedule of the DeSoto patrol, could have decided to maximize the chances that the North Vietnamese would think that the destroyer was somehow involved in the raids, and attack it."[220] Indeed, the raids were suspended immediately after the August 4 incident.[221]

Finally, four years later, when the administration was forced to testify on the issue before the Fulbright-led hearings, Johnson admitted to McNamara that the administration had a "better case" on the fact that an attack of some kind occurred than "on the charge that we did provoke the attack."[222] None of this evidence proves conclusively that the U.S. military had been ordered to create a provocation and hence acted overly eagerly to start a war when it thought it had one. But it does give lie to McNamara's insistence that the idea of a deliberate U.S. provocation at Tonkin is not as "inconceivable" as he would have led his country to believe.

"Tonkin" in Vietnam

As we have seen, the official U.S. portrayal of the events of August 4, 1964, was an uneasy mixture of self-deception and deliberate dishonesty. What was honest confusion in the beginning became outright lying once the truth of the event emerged, and the president was forced to cover up the less than honest manner in which he had taken the country to war.

In the first place, the administration may have caused exactly the situation it was seeking to avoid in North Vietnam. The incident inspired a kind of cottage industry among the uninformed on Rusk's staff (and elsewhere) to explain North Vietnam's motivation for its dastardly and apparently irrational deed.[223] As these analyses were based on false information, the paths they plotted for the U.S. government were naturally corrupted by a false understanding of events.

While the American public may have been ignorant of its government's actions, in North Vietnam, where the attacks were taking place, the government was fully aware of the concerted covert action campaign through which the United States and its ARVN allies had been bombing its country and sabotaging its industrial infrastructure. The nationality of the pilot or the leader of the sabotage squad was immaterial to them, as they were well aware of how ineffective the South Vietnamese forces were without direction from their American masters.

According to the Hanoi-based research of Edwin Moïse, it was the distorted U.S. portrayal of the Tonkin Gulf incident and the ensuing attack that led the North Vietnamese to conclude that it would be hopeless to try to work out any kind of modus vivendi with the Americans. From their perspective there was no point in seeking to placate the United States by moderating their behavior toward South Vietnam or in seeking to avoid direct combat with the United States. An article in the November 1964 issue of the DRV Navy journal *Hai Quan* (Navy) reported, "After fabricating the 'second Tonkin Gulf incident,' the Americans used it as a pretext to retaliate. But actually, all their plots were arranged beforehand."[224] Premier Pham Van Dong insisted that the "criminal action was prepared in a planned fashion: it was the first step in carrying out the plot of 'carrying the war to the North.'" General Hoang Van Trai argued that the United States had staged the incident in order to set a precedent for extensive bombing of North Vietnam in the near future.[225]

The Vietnam scholar Gareth Porter has described an extraordinary session of the ruling party's Central Committee that was convened a week after the Tonkin Gulf incident. "Party leaders concluded that direct U.S. military intervention in the South and the bombing of the North were probable and that the party and government had to prepare for a major war in the South. In September the first combat units of the Vietnam People's Army began to move down the Ho Chi Minh Trail." William Duiker, a Vietnamese-speaking former U.S. foreign service officer, notes an official Vietnamese history published shortly after the war that describes a Politburo meeting that considered the worrisome military prospect of a U.S. intervention and decided upon the need to "achieve a military victory in the next one to two years." The Politburo then called for more aggressive plans to destroy strategic hamlets, expand liberated base areas, and obliterate DRV forces. Porter, who inspected the Vietnamese archives on this matter, concurs. "Up to this point," he notes, "party strategists in Hanoi had consistently hoped to avoid actions that might incite the United States to escalate its role in the conflict in South Vietnam." But after the Tonkin Gulf events, "clearly party leaders had concluded that the United States was preparing to intervene directly in the conflict in South Vietnam and that the best way to avoid such a contingency was to achieve a decisive victory before Washington could gear itself up to move from the stage of 'special war' to limited war." Hanoi appointed one of its two top military officers to head up the effort.[226] Indeed, U.S. intelligence officers confirm that units of regimental size did not begin entering the South until late in 1964. The North Vietnamese also undertook a major upgrading of the Ho Chi Minh Trail itself, to allow arms and armies to travel from north to south with greater ease, as well as upgrading the quality of their anti-aircraft defenses.[227] *The Official History of the People's Army of Vietnam,* speaking the lumbering language of Marxist/Leninism, tells the story of the United States "fabricating the Gulf of Tonkin incident to deceive both the people of the world and U.S. domestic public opinion," so that "the American imperialists openly used their air forces to attack North Vietnam." The result was an "incredibly savage war of destruction against an independent, sovereign nation" that began with "major defeat" for the "imperialists," which "completely surprised and stunned them" with the shooting down of aircraft and the "courageously striking back against the enemy's attack waves."[228] In Vietnam as everywhere else, history is indeed written by the winners.

Military operations within the South also became increasingly aggressive during this period, while Viet Cong commandos began, for the first time, to launch direct attacks on U.S. personnel and installations inside South Vietnam. The Chinese reacted similarly. On August 5, the day after the U.S. air strikes, Zhou Enlai cabled Ho Chi Minh and asked him to "investigate the situation, work out countermeasures and be prepared to fight." By August 7, according to historian David Kaiser, thirty-nine MIG 15/17 jet fighters had flown from Chinese bases to Phuc Yen airfield north of Hanoi. Le Duan, whom Kaiser calls "the most militant leader of the North Vietnamese politburo," visited Mao Zedong and came home with assurances of assistance.[229]

At home, the Chinese responded by beginning an enormously expensive project of moving what industry existed in the country's coastal regions into western mountain areas in order to make it more difficult for the United States to bomb them. More importantly, they also undertook a massive expansion of the network of railroads just north of the Vietnamese border, including the Ningming field, an area that served no purpose within China save that of resupplying North Vietnam. Edwin Moïse concludes that "the overall result was that by the time the U.S. began major escalations of the American role in the war, in February and March of 1965, the Communist forces with which the U.S. had to deal were stronger, better prepared, and better supplied" than if the U.S. government had behaved with greater prudence the previous August.[230] While the Soviets reacted with considerably more composure to the bombing, the war it inspired eventually doomed the extremely promising (though informal) agreement between Dean Rusk and Soviet foreign minister Andrei Gromyko to mutually hold down defense expenditures, thereby improving each side's economy and reducing the risk of both nuclear and conventional war for all concerned.[231]

The raids also had unforeseen effects on U.S. efforts to stabilize the politics of South Vietnam. On August 7, General Nguyen Khanh took advantage of the confusion surrounding the crisis to declare a state of emergency. He then decided to promulgate a new constitution and to have himself declared president. Within ten days, Buddhist and student opposition had spread across the nation, causing civil disturbances in most of the nation's population centers. Soon the unrest overflowed into rural areas, as well, where the continuing influence of the ruling Catholic elite minority fueled more angry protests. Violent rioting ensued, and Khanh was forced, under pressure, to annul his constitution and resign his presidency within fewer than twenty-one days of his original declaration. On August 26 he apparently suffered a breakdown and retired to the resort town of Da Lat, north of Saigon. When no new leader emerged, fighting broke out between Buddhists and Catholics in Saigon, and Ambassador Taylor and General Westmoreland prevailed upon Khanh to return as premier. This, in turn, led to a coup attempt by dissident generals that was aborted at the last minute. The net result was that the raids that American officials in Washington so confidently believed would stiffen the backbone of the South Vietnamese leadership led, instead, to a further weakening of its tenuous hold on power, splitting the country between warring minorities, and creating the conditions for endless chaos at the top of the flailing South Vietnamese state.[232]

Perhaps an equally significant aspect of the impact of Johnson's lies on the war was their effect on the home front. His fabrications about Tonkin ultimately corrupted the quality of the support the president was able to generate for the war effort as well as the democratic underpinnings it required to be successfully prosecuted. As Hannah Arendt would later observe while reading *The Pentagon Papers,* the administration's "policy of lying was hardly ever aimed at the enemy (this is one of the reasons why the papers do not reveal any military secrets that could fall under the Espionage Act), but was destined chiefly, if not exclusively, for domestic consumption, for propaganda at home, and especially for the purpose of deceiving Congress."[233]

Business as Usual

The cover-up began immediately, as discussed earlier, when McNamara and others falsely testified before Congress and gave misleading accounts to the news media, long after the initial explanations should have been called into question in their own minds. The obvious holes in the testimony—such as McNamara's odd argument that Commander Herrick was not part of the U.S. Navy—demonstrate an attitude toward truth as a kind of practical inconvenience to be ignored or wished away when convenient. Indeed, when, in 1966, nineteen members of the North Vietnamese PT boat that had been on duty in the gulf on August 4 were captured, U.S. Pacific Headquarters sent an urgent message with the orders to cease and desist their interrogation immediately. Absolutely no questions about the Tonkin Gulf incident were asked of these prisoners, as interrogators were told to "stay away" from that subject. Those sailors who had been present on August 4 were kept separate from the other Communist prisoners, and were quickly sent back to North Vietnam.[234]

Johnson had learned from the success of the Tonkin experience that he could treat the Senate—and the nation—as dismissively as he pleased. Following his success in misleading both the Congress and his country about the war's origins, Johnson proceeded to operate on the same model with regard to its escalation. On February 13, 1965, the president authorized Operation Rolling Thunder, a systematic and expanding bombing campaign against North Vietnamese targets.[235] The initial decision received extraordinarily favorable public response and was also praised on Capitol Hill. Within two weeks of the Marines' arrival at Da Nang, however, U.S. Army chief of staff Harold K. Johnson requested an additional deployment of three divisions to Vietnam. But Johnson continued to stonewall questions about the change in policy. At a March 13 press conference, he told the country, "Our policy there is the policy that was established by President Eisenhower, as I have stated since I have been President, 46 different times, the policy carried on by President Kennedy and the policy that we are now carrying on."[236]

The subterfuge soon metastasized. At a press conference a week later, Johnson continued to insist, "Our policy in Viet-Nam is the same as it was one year ago, and to those of you who have inquiries on the subject, it is the same as it was 10 years ago."[237] As he was speaking these words, the president had on his desk General Westmoreland's request for ten thousand additional troops to defend South Vietnamese airfields. The same day, March 20, the Joint Chiefs of Staff submitted a plan to Robert McNamara, asking for another two divisions to be deployed to South Vietnam's northern and central provinces.[238] Within two weeks, LBJ added another two divisions—along with twenty thousand support troops—and extended their function beyond mere base security, moving the American role from Rolling Thunder air strikes to aggressive base defense. Not long afterward, Westmoreland gave the president the news that South Vietnam would fall unless he agreed to commit as many as forty-four battalions.[239] (At the time of Westmoreland's warning, the United States had roughly seventy-five thousand troops in Vietnam.) Hearkening back to his conversations with Richard Russell a year earlier, the president listened to General Wallace M. Greene warn him that accomplishing U.S. objectives would require, at minimum, "five years plus 500,000 troops." There was no sugar-coating this discussion. Johnson asked his military advisers, "Do all of you think the Congress and the people will go along with 600,000 people and billions of dollars being spent 10,000 miles away . . . If you make a commitment to jump off a building and you find out how high it is, you may want to withdraw that commitment." The president's trusted friend and close adviser Clark Clifford warned him, "This could be a quagmire. It could turn into an open-ended commitment on our part that would take more and more ground troops, without a realistic hope of ultimate victory." But the Joint Chiefs suggested instead that Johnson call up the Reserves and the National Guard and ask the public to support a larger war effort.[240]

Johnson, however, took none of these steps. Instead he continued to involve the United States more deeply in the war via the resolution he had finagled out of Congress. Ambassador Maxwell Taylor told the president that Senator Fulbright had questioned whether the Tonkin Gulf Resolution covered the impending decision to send new combat divisions to Vietnam. Johnson replied that he did not think any more congressional involvement would be necessary. Later, when reporters asked the same question, the president insisted, "The evidence there is very clear for anybody that has read the [Tonkin Gulf] resolution. That language, just as a reminder to you, said the Congress approves and supports the determination of the President as commander-in-chief to take all—all—all necessary measures to repel any—any—any armed attack against the forces of the United States and to prevent further aggression."[241] Johnson's statement was clearly at odds with an NSC analysis of the Tonkin Gulf Resolution that he had read a week earlier, which concluded that the resolution "was passed on the understanding that there would be consultation with the Congress 'in case a major change in present policy becomes necessary.' "[242]

The president was unwilling even to admit that the United States was making a significant change in its war policy. Rejecting the advice of McNamara, Bundy, and Moyers, among many others, Johnson worried far more about trying to control leaks than about giving the nation an accurate account of the war he was undertaking.[243] When he did acknowledge the buildup, it was simply mentioned at a midafternoon press conference devoted to the Supreme Court that U.S. troop strength would increase in size from 75,000 to 125,000. He added, "Additional forces will be needed later, and they will be sent as requested."[244] After the conference, JCS chairman Wheeler cabled General Westmoreland and advised him, "Do not be surprised or disappointed if the public announcement does not set forth the full details of the program, but instead reflects an incremental approach. This tactic will probably be adopted in order to hold down [the] international noise level."[245] Dean Rusk cabled Alexis Johnson, Taylor's number two in Saigon, and instructed him to take the public position that Washington was "continuing on [the] course previously set. In keeping [to] this policy, the deployment will be spaced over [a] period [of] time with publicity re all deployments kept at [the] lowest key possible." [246] Mac Bundy cautioned everyone in the administration to hew to the president's line. "Under no circumstances," he warned, "should there be any reference to the movement of U.S. forces or other future courses of action."[247] Following a meeting with Walter Lippmann, he advised the president, "the one issue on which Walter has been critical is on what he thinks is your effort to smother debate in a general consensus."[248] Interestingly, the relentlessly hawkish Joe Alsop, who expressed "terror" at the thought that Johnson would adopt his rival Lippmann's view of the war, also warned, through aide Douglass Cater at a July 1965 luncheon, of the danger that the president had "closed down the open dialogue of government in a way that will harm government and harm" Johnson himself.[249]

In fact, Johnson had understated the troop increase he had approved, which would bring the number of U.S. military in Vietnam to 200,000. America was on its way to full-scale war, but nobody was willing to acknowledge the fact. Finally, on June 8, a State Department public information officer named Robert McCloskey confirmed to a *New York Times* reporter that a decision to use U.S. combat troops in Vietnam had "developed over the past several weeks."[250] The following day, *Times* editors took note of the amazing fact that "the American people were told by a minor State Department official yesterday that, in effect, they were in a land war on the continent of Asia. This is only one of the extraordinary aspects of the first formal announcement that a decision has been made to commit American ground forces to open combat in South Vietnam: the nation is informed about it not by the President, nor by a cabinet member, not even by a sub-cabinet official, but by a public relations officer." Remarkably, the article continued, "There was still no official explanation for a move that fundamentally alters the character of the American involvement in Vietnam" into "an American war against the Asians."[251]

Many of the people close to the president urged him to go before Congress and the country and admit the truth of the situation. Henry Cabot Lodge, whom Taylor replaced as ambassador to South Vietnam, asked Johnson, "How do you send young men there in great numbers without telling why?"[252] But Johnson insisted on continuing the charade, concerned that any open talk of war would ruin his chances to pass his domestic legislative agenda. The president explained, "I can get the Great Society through right now—this is a golden time. We've got a good Congress, and I'm the right President and I can do it. But if I talk about the cost of war, the Great Society won't go through. Old Wilbur Mills will sit down there and he'll thank me kindly and send me back my Great Society, and then he'll tell me that they'll be glad to spend whatever we need for the war."[253] Later, he described his plan to downplay the decision in more colorful, Johnsonian, language: "If you have a mother-in-law with only one eye and she has it in the center of her forehead, you don't keep her in the living room."[254]

Meanwhile, behind a facade of optimistic official reports and Pollyannaish patriotism on the part of most of the media, the war was going badly, a fact Johnson seemed to understand better than anyone. He repeatedly complained to his aides, as he did to Robert McNamara on June 21, 1965, that he was

> very depressed about it because I see no program from either Defense or State that gives me much hope of doing anything, except just praying and gasping to hold on . . . and hope they'll quit. I don't believe they're ever going to quit. And I don't see . . . any . . . plan for victory, militarily or diplomatically.[255]

The president had been traveling around the nation, promising voters, as he did in March, "America wins the wars that she undertakes. Make no mistake about it!"[256] Later he exhorted soldiers to "nail the coonskin to the wall" and told them, "We know you're going to get the job done."[257] Jack Valenti, a former top aide and one of Johnson's most tireless defenders in the media for decades after his death, would later attempt to argue that Johnson had always sought a negotiated settlement. "I cannot recall any time when LBJ thought there would be 'victory' in the traditional definition of that word," Valenti wrote.[258] But as Michael Beschloss replied, "The problem is that if this was his intention, he did not confide it to the Americans he was sending into harm's way in Vietnam."[259]

Privately, Johnson confided to his wife in March, according to her diary, "I can't get out and I can't finish it with what I have got. And I don't know what the hell to do."[260] He also told her, regarding Vietnam, that he felt as if he were in a crashing airplane and "I do not have a parachute."[261]

Contrary to popular memory, the media were rarely disapproving of the war, at least until its very latest stages. While reporters did occasionally report critically on many individual military operations, virtually never did any of them call into question the war's essential nobility. In *The Uncensored War* Daniel Hallin identifies a number of "unspoken propositions" that set the tone—and the boundaries—of television reporting on Vietnam. First, news writers cast Vietnam as "our war," a military endeavor that had been taken up on behalf of and with the support of the entire nation. Second, there was a concerted effort to contextualize the fighting in Vietnam as a logical next step in America's military history through comparisons to the two world wars. Typical of the approach was a 1966 NBC report that closed by signing off from "the First Infantry Division, the Big Red One of North Africa, Omaha Beach, Normandy, Germany, and now the Cambodia border." Taking this tactic one step further, many reporters borrowed the soldiers' phrase "Indian Country" to describe Vietcong-controlled territory, invoking the American frontier and its highly romanticized "Wild West" connotations in order to provide a palatable narrative to explain the chaos of Vietnam. A third trope, Hallin notes, is the use of Vietnam as a proving ground for the masculine fortitude of America's young men. In February of 1966, NBC News concluded the following in regard to American forces in Vietnam: "They are the greatest soldiers in the world. In fact, they are the greatest men in the world."[262]

With the military consistently exaggerating its progress against the enemy and the civilians in the Pentagon exaggerating these claims even further, the country was given no reliable information—either from the government, the military, or the media—that might have prepared it for the possibility that the United States could actually lose the Vietnam War. When the truth of the situation eventually became inescapable, therefore, it was all the more shocking. Not only had the administration deceived the nation in order to enter the war in Vietnam; it presented for public consumption a fictional version of the war it eventually fought there as well. Speaking for many of his colleagues, *Washington Post* columnist Richard Cohen would later explain, "All during Vietnam, the government lied to me." As a result, "I'm cynical. I'm the credibility gap version of the Depression baby. I've been shaped, formed by lies."[263] A 1966 article on Tonkin and the war in the countercultural magazine *Ramparts* caught the flavor of the times with its title, "The Whole Damn Thing Was a Lie."[264] A generation later, its impact was undiminished. Citing "Tonkin Bay—the attack-that-wasn't," novelist Clancy Sigal addressed historian Joseph Ellis's fictional portrayal of his own alleged history as a Vietnam War veteran. "Why not lie about Vietnam?" Sigal wrote in the summer of 2001. "Everybody does it. The war in Southeast Asia was born in a lie and conducted in lies by mendacious politicians and spin artists who, to this day, have not been called to account for their falsifications."[265]

William Fulbright began to realize almost immediately that he had been duped by his old friend. Although he had not been taken into the administration's confidence, he had heard reports of the escalation plans that began immediately after the election. When Ambassador Maxwell Taylor came to testify before his committee in early December, he attempted to grill him on those plans. Taylor allowed that a consensus was developing in favor of a larger-scale military commitment to save the South Vietnamese government. But what was the point of going to war, Fulbright inquired, to save a country that had no real government and did not, in important respects, exist as a nation.[266]

In fact, Fulbright's estimate was low. But it hardly mattered. He had already given his permission and convinced his colleagues to give the administration statutory authority to deploy a million troops if it saw fit—at least that was how Johnson and his advisers interpreted it. And nothing would so embitter William Fulbright for the rest of his life than the knowledge that he had been played for a fool.

Fulbright's relationship with Johnson soon began to deteriorate. In February 1965, when informed by an aide that Fulbright was "hurt" regarding the level of consultation he was receiving, Johnson replied that the senator "was a cry baby" and Johnson could not "continue to kiss him every morning before breakfast."[267] "Tell the son-of-a-bitch I'm playing golf," Fulbright screamed when the president did phone him at home.[268] Fulbright issued a blistering denunciation of Johnson's intervention in the Dominican Republic in the spring of 1965, and most bitingly the "lack of candor" that, according to Fulbright's analysis, characterized "the whole affair." He had sent the president a copy of the speech he intended to give twenty-four hours in advance, insisting that he sought only to help correct the "faulty advice" the president had been receiving. Johnson did not reply to the note or the speech, but simply cut Fulbright off as a friend and political ally and let it be known that he was "hurt" and "indignant" by this public display of disloyalty.[269]

Fulbright's Revenge

Sometime in the autumn of 1965 Fulbright became convinced that Johnson was regularly lying to him. Having by now little common feeling for the president, personally or politically, and genuinely anguished about the direction of the war, he decided in early 1966 to convene the Foreign Relations Committee in a set of high-profile hearings on its progress. Fulbright had grown increasingly embittered over the role Johnson had asked him to play two years earlier in shepherding the Gulf of Tonkin Resolution through the Senate. Johnson and company had deliberately kept him in the dark during the passage of the Resolution about Commodore Herrick's cables that called the attack into question, to say nothing of all of the later evidence that would have demonstrated that no attack had taken place. Fulbright said that if he had been aware of the cables and the competing evidence back in August 1964, "I certainly don't believe I would have rushed into action" and introduced the Gulf of Tonkin Resolution for the Johnson administration. "I think I did a great disservice to the Senate," Fulbright admitted. "The least I can do . . . is to alert . . . future Senates that these matters are not to be dealt with in this casual manner."[270] In January of 1966 *The New York Times* reported that the chairman of the Senate Foreign Relations Committee had informed the secretary of state that "there was no legal basis for what the Government was doing in Viet-Nam."[271] The stage was set.

The hearings, which began during the second week of February 1966, were carried live on network television, and provided the most dramatically uncomfortable moments yet for the Johnson administration. Now, the very factors that had worked in favor of the official version of events were used to subvert it. As author Michael X. Delli Carpini writes, "The confrontations were highly newsworthy, given the legitimate nature of the opposition (a respected senator), the stature of the forum (the Capitol building), and the confrontational nature of the issue (Congress vs. the president; a heated challenge to the president's Vietnam policy by a member of his own party and a former supporter)."[272] NBC and CBS covered most of the hearings live—at considerable cost to each one in lost advertising—and millions of Americans tuned in to watch administration officials be grilled by Fulbright. Most were made to look foolish, duplicitous, or both, as they repeatedly tried to put a favorable spin on what was becoming an obviously calamitous situation. The hearings would mark the beginning of what would become a critical mass of respectable Establishment dissent, transforming the face of public opposition to the war from unruly, unkempt, and occasionally violent demonstrators to respected military men, diplomats, and scholars.

Fulbright's own history as a southern segregationist and critic of liberal internationalism gave him a peculiar political authority as a critic of the war, since he could not easily be pigeonholed as a typical liberal. Moreover, the hearing witness list featured such admired figures as General James Gavin, who served as assistant chief of staff of the Army at the time of the fall of Dien Bien Phu, and the much admired diplomat George Kennan, known throughout the Establishment as the "Father of Containment." Like Gavin, he called for an end to America's commitment to the war as soon as possible and a negotiated truce with North Vietnam.[273] Korean War hero General Matthew Ridgway also sent a letter to the committee endorsing this view.[274] *The New York Times* soon started publishing long editorials in support of Fulbright, demanding answers to his questions of the officials and even using the duplicity they demonstrated as a way of raising the question of how to end American involvement in the war. "The United States will never extricate itself with honor from its Vietnam involvement," the editors wrote, "unless it achieves a better comprehension of how it became entrapped."[275] Walter Lippmann chimed in that the hearings had now "broke through the official screen and made visible the nature of the war and whence our present policy is leading us."[276]

The hearings received widespread coverage abroad and the endorsement of many members of the ruling Labour Party in England, supposedly America's staunchest ally. Robert Kennedy also added his voice, taking pains to associate himself with the committee's tough questioning of Johnson's policies, and driving Johnson to distraction with what the president considered his naked duplicity. On March 2, Kennedy called for an indefinite halt to the bombing and the beginning of unconditional peace talks. By now even supporters of the war and of Johnson, like Jacob Javits (R-NY) and Jennings Randolph (D-WV), wanted to rein in what they believed to be the president's usurpation of Congress's war-making powers. Random House rushed out a transcript of the hearings in book form. In the country at large, prominent businessmen began to question the wisdom of the war in public for the first time, leading eventually to the creation of an organization called Negotiations Now, whose membership featured more than six hundred business executives.[277] Quite appropriately, the executives were concerned that Johnson and McNamara had misled the country in estimating the financial burden of the war, which was now wreaking havoc on the nation's balance of payments, and threatening both growth and interest rates. Politically, Johnson's approval rating for his handling of the war dropped during this period—between January 26 and February 26, it declined from 63 percent to below 49 percent. "Never have I known Washington," wrote Bill Moyers to Theodore White, "to be so full of dissonant voices as it is today."[278]

McGeorge Bundy called the hearings "a declaration of war" against the administration and noted that they "were so taken by the White House."[279] President Johnson, livid with fury at Fulbright's success in giving the dissenters their day in court, telephoned network heads and demanded they discontinue coverage immediately. He then prevailed upon J. Edgar Hoover to instigate an FBI investigation to determine whether Fulbright and the committee were receiving information from Communists. Fulbright was put under strict surveillance, and the Bureau, operating on the logic of McCarthyism, discovered many "parallels" between statements made by committee witnesses and "documented Communist Party publications or statements of communist leaders." On Johnson's explicit orders, Hoover's men also attempted to provide Everett Dirksen and Bourke Hickenlooper with "evidence that Fulbright was either a communist agent or a dupe of the communist powers." According to agent C. D. DeLoach, the two men believed that Fulbright was "deeply involved and very much obligated to communist interests," owing, all suspected, to his bitterness at Johnson's refusal to name him secretary of state.[280]

This misguided action only hints at the degree to which Johnson's paranoia would overtake his political judgment during the Vietnam period, and at his willingness to use the instruments of state to attempt to quash virtually all legitimate dissent and criticism by attributing them to Communist conspiracy. The same reasoning would soon be employed to explain why millions of Americans, including millions of middle-class citizens and many loyal Democrats, had joined the peace movement. Another explanation Johnson was willing to consider was George Reedy's theory that, in essence, the administration had overestimated the intelligence of normal Americans, whose growing antipathy to the war was not the result of a developing understanding that escalation had been achieved through deception, but evidence of a more generalized ignorance. "We have been assuming that the American people know a lot of things that they simply don't know and have presented some arguments which are really too sophisticated for the audience," he wrote to Johnson.[281]

The net result of Johnson's subterfuge on Tonkin was Fulbright's transformation into the nation's most influential peacenik. In April he went before the Newspaper Publishers Association and announced his fear of America's "arrogance of power," comparing the nation's "overextension of power and mission to [that] which brought ruin to ancient Greece, Napoleonic France, and to Nazi Germany." (This prompted Senator Goldwater to call for the Arkansan's resignation, over his deliberately having given "aid and comfort to the enemy.")[282] Meanwhile, Fulbright started focusing in more and more on Tonkin. The committee chair remembered that Wayne Morse had received a call from inside the Pentagon during the original incidents suggesting that he ask McNamara for the *Turner Joy* and *Maddox* logbooks. McNamara had said they were unavailable at the time, and Morse did not possess the power to force him to hand them over. When, in 1966, Fulbright asked George Ball if he had thought the attack had really occurred, Ball repeated to him his recollection of LBJ's flying fish comment.

Soon, owing to the publicity the initial hearings received, more and more informants sought to get their stories on the record. An Associated Press article that ran in the *Arkansas Gazette* in July 1967 contained interviews with members of the crew of both destroyers. It raised significant questions about the official account, noting the doubts of some crew members that they had encountered any ships at all. The story also cited the planning efforts for a resolution that the administration had made well before the incident took place.[283] (This piece, the product of a ten-reporter investigative team, went ignored in such AP subscribers as *The New York Times, The Washington Post, The Washington Star,* and *The Baltimore Sun*.)

Fulbright's aides also started receiving mysterious reports from someone who had read of Fulbright's regrets about the Resolution in an article in *Newsweek*. The anonymous writer explained, in a letter, "I have known that the second North Vietnamese PT boat attack almost certainly did not actually occur. In all that time I have never been able to find a way to disclose this information to a responsible person or organization who could and would use it constructively rather than destructively to the embarrassment of the U.S. government." He continued further that the "U.S. Navy patrols in the Gulf of Tonkin were undertaken apparently to bait the North Vietnamese." The author, who later revealed himself to be Commander Jack Cowles, who had been forty-six years old and stationed in Flag Plot, the Navy's "war room," on August 4, 1964, offered his hypothesis that McNamara had become convinced that the attacks were genuine when Lyndon Johnson ordered the retaliation, but that others who had evaluated the Navy's combat action reports had decided they were fictional. Commander Cowles's own suspicions were confirmed when he heard of the interrogation of the crews and commanders of two captured North Vietnamese PT boats months later. They were the same vessels that had been identified as having attacked the *Maddox* and the *Turner Joy,* but no one on the boats had information on any such attacks, either planned or carried out.

Cowles eventually agreed to a meeting with Fulbright, who questioned him at length and came away impressed by his bona fides. The commander was rewarded for his stepping forward with a forced psychiatric examination by his naval superiors, along with the suggestion that he retire on "physical disability" for his own good. He refused and ended up with a pointless job until he reached mandatory retirement age in 1969, following a full decade without promotion.[284]

Another clue appeared when a letter was published in the *New Haven Register,* subsequently picked up by an Associated Press wire report. Its author, a Connecticut high school teacher named John White, noted that he had served in August 1964 as a commissioned naval officer aboard the USS *Pine Island* in the Pacific. He recalled the "confusing radio messages" sent back and forth at that time between the U.S. destroyers—"confusing because the destroyers themselves were not certain they were being attacked." White said he had spoken to the chief sonarman of the *Maddox,* who had informed him of a negative reading on the sonar scope picture, "meaning no torpedoes were fired through the water at the ship or otherwise. . . . Yet the Pentagon reported to the President that North Vietnam had attacked us and the President reported it to Congress. Why? . . . in a moment of panic, based on false information, the President was given unprecedented powers, which today enable him to conduct an undeclared war involving over a half million men and costing billions of dollars."[285] White also sent a copy of his letter to Fulbright, who was now more eager than ever to go forward with a second set of hearings, these focusing on the events of Tonkin itself.[286]

Johnson sent longtime naval aide, now Deputy Secretary of Defense Paul Nitze, to see Fulbright in the hopes of getting the hearings killed. The meeting took place on December 14, 1967, with Richard Russell and Navy Secretary Paul R. Ignatius present. Nitze admitted that there had been some initial confusion about the attacks, but insisted that looking any further into the matter would be a "bad show" for the United States, as it would "give one hell of a lot of credence" to Communist propagandists. For what he hoped to be his trump card, Nitze brought the alleged intercepts from the August 4 incident and insisted they constituted "conclusive" evidence of a genuine attack, although he refused to allow either senator to take notes and pledged them to total secrecy.[287] But Fulbright proved decidedly unimpressed and

Russell, perhaps no less eager to try to reassert the institutional prerogatives of his own committee, supported his colleague. Russell insisted that the Senate was entitled to all the relevant documents, and not merely the ones Nitze insisted proved his case.[288] An anonymous patriot inside the Pentagon, who possessed extremely detailed knowledge of what had taken place in the gulf that night and subsequent efforts to bury it, began sending Fulbright letters that guided his requests for information from the administration. The author explained that he did so not because he thought the incident had been a "put-up job," but rather "a confused bungle which was used by the President to justify a general course of action and policy that he had been advised by the military to follow." However, once Fulbright and his committee started asking for exactly the right documents—particularly the navy logbooks, the record of communications passing through the National Military Command center for the night in question, and McNamara's own still top-secret study by the Weapons System Evaluation Group—the letters stopped arriving.[289]

When, in early 1968, as the national tide had already begun to turn against the war, Fulbright made a public announcement of his intentions to hold hearings on Tonkin, Johnson grew apoplectic. In a memo he dictated to be sent to Fulbright—and for which he instructed his secretary, "Don't file. Tear up. Flush away. We didn't send it. I don't want a record of it"—the president instructed the Arkansan that "The men in Hanoi [are] . . . taking comfort, as their newspapers and radio indicate every day, from every sign of confusion and division and doubt in the United States. On the other hand, the government in Saigon, as it meets this stern test, is shaken by symptoms of confusion, bitterness, political moves and division in the United States." He was, to be blunt, getting ready to accuse the chairman of the Senate Foreign Relations Committee of giving aid and comfort to the enemy if he continued with his inquiry over what happened at Tonkin. Johnson did not send the letter, but his aides spared no efforts in trying to derail the hearings. Fulbright, however, would not budge.

Against the backdrop of the siege of Khe Sahn and just preceding the Tet Offensive, the hearings took on an added drama, owing to the seizure on the morning of January 23, 1968, by North Korea of the U.S. intelligence ship, the *Pueblo.* Three American sailors were wounded and one killed. Johnson immediately ordered a nuclear carrier to the scene, and a second war scare ensued. Fulbright may well have prevented another military response when he told a Pine Bluff audience, "I can tell you now that I don't think there will be any 24-hour resolution on this incident." The *Pueblo* affair, Fulbright's biographer Randall Woods points out, encouraged people to seek a fuller explanation of what really happened at Tonkin. Even *The Washington Post*'s editorial page, directed by the staunchly devoted pro-Johnson editor Russell Wiggins, opined that it was time the country had "all the facts on what happened in the Gulf of Tonkin in August 1964."[290] Though he had grown to despise Fulbright and had little but contempt for the rest of the members of the Foreign Relations Committee, Robert McNamara agreed to testify before the committee in the hopes, perhaps, of rescuing his now sullied reputation before he departed the administration to become head of the World Bank.

The examination, which took place on February 20, 1968, in executive session in Room S-116 of the Capitol building, lasted seven and a half hours. McNamara stuck, essentially, to the same story he had told nearly four years earlier, explaining that "even with the advantage of hindsight, I find that the essential facts of the two attacks appear today as they did then." He maintained the falsehood of repeated visual sightings of signs of an attack, including "gunfire against the patrol." He termed the accusation that the United States might have provoked the attack intentionally both "inconceivable" and "monstrous." When the committee raised the issue of the captured North Vietnamese PT boat commanders who had insisted that no attack took place, McNamara responded with the alleged testimony of a "senior officer of the North Vietnamese Navy" that had just "come to light within the past few days," and that corroborated the administration's version, though he produced no evidence of such an officer nor his account. (In fact, the man's name appeared in a naval interrogation report dated July 1966.)[291] More significantly, McNamara produced a document from what he called an "unimpeachable" North Vietnamese source with details about the attack. When Fulbright asked to examine the document himself, the secretary immediately reclassified it but did read portions of it aloud, insisting upon completion, "I submit that any reasonable explanation of these messages leads one to the conclusion that the attack was under way." It is highly probable that McNamara was reading the NSA intercepts upon which McNamara and Sharp had placed so much emphasis four years earlier, not realizing they were confusing the dates of the first and second attacks. McNamara also stonewalled when Fulbright produced Herrick's confusing cables, in which the commodore began to wonder if any attack had occurred at all. McNamara continued to insist on the validity of the intercepts, which he finally agreed to show the committee only on the condition that the room be cleared of the committee's staff. The senators, with limited knowledge of intelligence documents, had to rely solely on McNamara's descriptions of what the intercepts contained.[292]

The secretary also continued to insist that the now publicly known OPLAN 34A raids had no connection to the destroyer patrols. He did so despite the fact that, on the morning of August 3, after the first attack, he had advised the president to leak the fact that these patrols might have inspired the first incident, in order to calm down congressional outrage and Republican demands for full-scale war.[293] (Richard Russell was the designated leaker, and dutifully passed the message to reporters.) Indeed, Dean Rusk had cabled Ambassador Taylor after that day's attack, saying, "We believe that present OPLAN 34A activities are beginning to rattle Hanoi and *Maddox* incident is directly related to their effort to resist these activities. We have no intention [of] yielding to this pressure."[294] When Fulbright produced cables indicating that Commodore Herrick did not agree with this assessment, and hence had cabled his superiors on August 3 to cancel the patrol, McNamara gave no ground: "Even with the advantage of hindsight I find the essential facts of the two attacks appear today as they did then, when they were fully explored with Congress."[295] Congress had done anything but "fully explore" the fact of the attack, having simply accepted the word of Johnson and McNamara about it.

Despite an agreement between the committee chair and the defense secretary that neither one would make any substantive remarks to the media regarding the session, McNamara immediately issued a twenty-one-page document allegedly "proving" his case for the attack. In it, he blasted Fulbright and the committee for impugning his integrity and that of the president. But the following day Fulbright pulled out his "ace in the hole": not only had the administration gone to considerable lengths to conceal the evidence of its mistake in the first place, it had locked up an officer who had tried to tell the truth, Commander Cowles, in a mental ward. With extreme disingenuousness, McNamara testified, "I believe that the truth will support itself, and I am perfectly prepared to have . . . anybody . . . come in and examine the raw material available in the Department."[296]

When *The New York Times* reported that the president was now considering General Westmoreland's request for an additional 206,000 troops in March 1968, together with the news that the president believed he did not require any congressional sanction to do so, beyond the Gulf of Tonkin Resolution, events finally came to a head. Fulbright declared the resolution to be "null and void," like "any contract based on misrepresentation." He apologized to the nation for having guided the measure through the Senate, admitting, "I regret it more than anything I have ever done in my life."[297] On the Senate floor a dozen of his colleagues rose to applaud the Arkansan's speech and to call for a full-scale debate on the war. Gaylord Nelson commented, "If the Senator from Arkansas had stood on the floor of the Senate, in the middle of that debate in 1964 and had said that the resolution authorizes a ground commitment or an unlimited number of troops . . . he would have been soundly defeated."[298]

With both Vietnam and U.S. foreign policy in shambles, McNamara finally left the Pentagon to become president of the World Bank at the end of February 1968. He later testified in a court case involving General Westmoreland and CBS News that virtually all of the public optimism he displayed about the war had been deceptive. As early as November 3, 1965, or "mid-1966 or sooner," depending on different parts of his deposition, McNamara had decided that the war was "unwinnable militarily." On the witness stand, he would attempt to justify his deception with a semantic sleight of hand. "I said it cannot be won by military action. We had a two-track approach, one political and the other military."[299]

The Nightmare Arrives

Meanwhile, as 1968 wore on, Johnson's political prospects continued to deteriorate. Robert Kennedy announced his price for his staying out of the race against the president: he wanted a committee to be appointed, whose members Kennedy himself would stipulate, to find an honorable solution to the war. He also intimated that it might be necessary for Lyndon Johnson to confess the error of his ways. Meanwhile, Senator Eugene McCarthy (D-MN) had stalked out of the committee room when he heard Nicholas Katzenbach claim virtually unlimited authority for the administration to prosecute the war solely on the basis of the Gulf of Tonkin Resolution. Exasperated by what he termed the administration's "doctrine of Papal infallibility," McCarthy announced to his staff, "somebody's going to have to take these guys on, and I'm getting ready to do it even if I have to run for President."[300] He did, and received 42.2 percent of the vote in the March 12 New Hampshire primary, deeply embarrassing the president and inspiring Robert Kennedy to abandon his ultimatum and enter the race himself two days later.

Johnson and Kennedy shared a passionate mutual hatred for many good reasons, both personal and political. Their history was filled with venomous, underhanded attempts to destroy each other's careers. But because they also practiced completely opposite forms of politics, each man's attempt to apply his personal vision to the Vietnam War drew a dividing line across the American political process that was in effect unbridgeable. "The biggest danger to American stability is the politics of principle," Johnson once told Doris Kearns, "which brings out the masses in irrational flights for unlimited goals, for once the masses begin to move, then the whole thing begins to explode."[301] No politician practiced this form of principled populism in the Johnson era with more verve and enthusiasm than the dreaded Robert Kennedy.

And now, Bobby Kennedy was returning, not only to defeat Johnson, but to grind him into political dust. Moreover, he was bringing along as many of his brothers' old advisers—the men whose approval had meant so much to the insecure Texan—as he could. That Johnson, with considerable justice, had sincerely believed that he was fighting the war in Vietnam because he had been urged to do so by these same Kennedy intellectuals, in order to honor the slain president's own commitment, made the wound Bobby inflicted all the more painful to bear. The younger brother now threw off his sulking depression of recent years and in his quest to snatch back his brother's holy mantle, the junior senator from New York appeared to blame virtually all the country's ills on the mendacious warmonger in the White House. Who was responsible not just for the war, but for the riots, the dropouts, the drugs? Kennedy asked. It was not "those who were calling for change," like Kennedy and his antiwar minions, he cried to full-throated applause, his fists in the air. "They are the ones, the President of this United States, President Johnson, they are the ones who divide us!"[302]

The country was falling apart and all of the dreams Lyndon Johnson had had to help the poor and people of color were collapsing into a political horror story. At the height of his popularity, Johnson had begun to build a domestic legacy that might even have surpassed that of FDR. Beginning in 1964 Johnson engineered the passage of the Economic Opportunity Act, the creation of Medicare, the Head Start Program, the Motor Vehicle Safety Act, and the Voting Rights bill, among others. Many of these proved to be remarkable successes. Medicare made medical services available to virtually all of the elderly in America. Head Start provided 500,000 children with healthy meals and improved education in the summer of 1965 alone.[303]

But ballooning war appropriations soon destroyed the nation's balance of payments and reduced both available funds and political will to fund any of Johnson's ambitions. He soon found himself forced to scale back his plans. In 1968, the president rejected Hubert Humphrey's pleas for the kinds of domestic programs that he, himself, had championed in prewar years, and he could not bring himself to endorse the conclusions of the Kerner Commission on race, because he could not find the money to fund its recommendations.[304] While many have been quick to criticize Johnson's Great Society for its failure to end poverty, discrimination, and other urban ills, the truth is we will never know how well these efforts might have succeeded had Vietnam not swallowed most of them up. In April 1970, with the State Department officially neutral, the Senate Foreign Relations Committee finally voted to repeal the Gulf of Tonkin Resolution by a vote of 13 to 1.[305] But the lawful repeal of the resolution ended up frustrated by the Nixon administration and its Senate allies, most notably Robert Dole of Kansas, who attached it to a military sales bill before it could come to a vote. The repeal passed the Senate twice by votes of 81 to 10 and 57 to 5, respectively, but was never voted on in the House.[306] In January 1971, however, President Nixon did sign a bill authorizing credit terms for the sale of U.S. goods to other nations, with a hastily tacked-on provision repealing the Gulf of Tonkin Resolution attached. The repeal merited four wire service paragraphs buried inside *The New York Times.*[307] Perhaps this was a fitting legacy for a resolution conceived and executed in so much confusion, deception, and political manipulation.

The war had created its own fault lines in American society as it deepened, and exacerbated those that arrived of their own accord. The military nearly destroyed itself under the strain of the enormous weight of deception it was forced to carry, as both officers and enlisted soldiers came to despise what they viewed as a deeply dishonest and untrustworthy civilian leadership. "The war was not lost in the field," wrote Major H. R. McMaster. "It was lost in Washington, D.C.," owing to the "arrogance, weakness, lying in the pursuit of self-interest, and, above all, the abdication of responsibility to the American people" by Lyndon Johnson and his top advisers.[308] The fact of fighting for lies no doubt contributed to the sense of hopelessness and alienation that led to so much drug addiction and mental and emotional dysfunction among those who had served in the war. Recovery, both for the individuals and the institution, would take decades. At home, as Thomas Powers has observed, "The violence in Vietnam seemed to elicit a similar air of violence in the United States; an appetite for extremes; people felt that history was accelerating, time was running out, great issues were reaching a point of final decision."[309] People drew political lines, class lines, age lines, and racial lines, among others, and came to view anyone on the other side of them with hatred, suspicion, fear, or all three. Johnson was unleashing J. Edgar Hoover and the FBI on lawful American citizens, violating civil liberties, and ignoring the Constitution. Student groups were being secretly funded and infiltrated by the FBI. Government agents posing as demonstrators were inciting others to violence for the purpose of entrapment and political gain. Civil war or violent repression sometimes seemed a genuine possibility. The antiwar movement provided the fuel for the explosion of a youthful New Left whose leaders had little but contempt for the older liberal leaders whose wisdom had led to this disastrous war. They spoke casually of revolution and devoted themselves to acts of increasingly confrontational protest. The war and the forced integration of the public schools tore asunder FDR's old coalition, which had served as the Democratic Party's base and provided Johnson with the commanding majority he had earned just four years earlier—shortly after Tonkin. Now Jews resented blacks, young people hated workers, southern conservatives detested northern liberals, and, in every case, the reverse was also true. The war not only ended Lyndon Johnson's presidency, it destroyed the Democratic Party's dominance of presidential politics and dealt Roosevelt's liberal coalition a blow from which it has still not recovered.

Speaking on April 4, 1967, from the pulpit of the Riverside Baptist Church in New York City, exactly one year before his assassination, Dr. Martin Luther King Jr. defied the heavy pressure of the Johnson administration to draw, publicly, the "very obvious and almost facile connection" between the war "and the struggle for a just society at home." The war, King argued, had left America's commitment to civil rights and social justice "broken and eviscerated as if it were some idle political thing of a society gone mad on war." Johnson's war policies were "taking the black young men who had been crippled by our society" and sending them "eight thousand miles away to guarantee liberties in Southeast Asia which they had not found in Southwest Georgia or East Harlem." The United States, he concluded, had become "the greatest purveyor of violence in the world today."[310] Here was the leader of the people whom Johnson was trying to help, denouncing him for fighting a war he thought necessary to protect the social programs he offered them. A war designed to keep internal peace was now turning the entire nation into a continuous political battlefield, with citizens forming movements and challenging politicians' right to speak and act on their behalf. "We are at the moment when our lives must be placed on the line if our nation is to survive its own folly," King demanded. "Every man of humane convictions must decide on the protest that best suits his convictions, but we all must protest."[311]

The president could find no solace anywhere. Student demonstrators burned him in effigy and routinely chanted, "Hey, hey, LBJ. How many kids did you kill today?" At one meeting with his advisers, just a day before his resignation speech, Johnson left scrawled messages on a piece of paper that read:

> MURDERER-HITLER
> STOP THE WAR.
> ESCALATE THE PEACE[312]

Johnson appeared to become convinced that the students were being manipulated by foreign, enemy powers, though he did not specify which ones. When he received a secret report from CIA director Richard Helms that argued to the contrary, that the rebellion was home-grown and "The communists can take little comfort from any of this," Johnson noted that "the Federal Bureau of Investigation operates at present on a restricted basis in collecting information on United States radicals." He therefore asked Helms to "consider having the Bureau authorized to use more advanced investigative techniques" to find evidence for his convictions.[313] From the seeds of such suspicions grow police-state tactics.

Even among his enemy's enemies, Johnson received no quarter. For American conservatives, including those who had once formed the northern ethnic and southern bases of the Democratic Party, the looting, rioting, and violent antiwar demonstrations raised the same fundamental question as the failing war in Vietnam. As one presidential aide put it, "How can this great country allow itself to be pushed around and humiliated by a violent minority?"[314]

It was a unique situation in American history, with the nation's leadership unable to appear in public without inciting some violent episode or being attacked in vicious verbal terms as liars and "war criminals." This was true regardless of whether they were appearing to make a speech or to buy some groceries. Not only was Robert McNamara manhandled by an unruly group of a thousand Harvard students in Cambridge, but he could not find a tennis partner—save McGeorge Bundy—on Martha's Vineyard. One protester went so far as to deliberately immolate himself in plain view of McNamara's Pentagon office window.[315] The strain that Vietnam engendered finally appeared to be too much for McNamara. His responsibility for the war and all its attendant catastrophes brought him to the brink of a breakdown, in the opinions of many around him. Looking haggard and short of sleep, he would rage and scream to the point of disorientation at meetings, breaking off on occasion to cry in the curtains. Johnson feared he would "pull a Forrestal"—that is, commit suicide.[316] McNamara later insisted that he had not been "near emotional and physical collapse" at the time.

Indeed, McNamara's disquiet would have been understandable for any public servant who believed himself to be an honorable man. But even when he was truthful—or he tried to be—it was on the basis of self-deception constructed out of a willful ignorance of uncomfortable facts, as in the case of the Tonkin Gulf. It was not until 1995, when he traveled to Vietnam and met with his former adversaries, that the supremely self-confident McNamara would willingly admit his error. There had been no attack on any American ships on August 4, 1964. Much of what the United States had tried to do in Vietnam, he said, was "wrong, terribly wrong."[317] But while McNamara did question his own judgment and that of his colleagues, he never addressed the role he played in deliberately misleading Congress and the nation about what he knew and when he knew it. The lies, he felt, were not a sufficiently significant aspect of his failure even to mention in the two book-length studies of the war and its lessons eventually issued under his name.

Undoubtedly it was worse for Lyndon Johnson. Through his lies and deceptions about Vietnam, from the moment he began the misadventure on

August 4, 1964, the master politician and inveterate dealmaker had set the stage for his own political suicide. For politically speaking, long before he announced his surprise decision on March 31, 1968, to withdraw from the presidential contest, the coalition builder had become a man without a country. Harry McPherson, the president's trusted adviser, wrote to him, "I think the course we seem to be taking now will lead either to Kennedy's nomination or Nixon's election, or both."[318] But for the horrible historic contingency of a madman, Sirhan Sirhan, he may well have been right. Instead it was Humphrey who would be the beneficiary of Johnson's lies. Thus did Johnson's political paranoia ultimately give life to his deepest psychological fears.

By the end Johnson felt so drained and exhausted from the continuous battle that he did not believe he could survive another four years in office. He was terrified he would end up like Woodrow Wilson, incapacitated by a stroke or worse, "stretched out upstairs in the White House, powerless to move, with the machinery of the American government in disarray around him." He later told Doris Kearns of a dream of "being chased on all sides by a giant stampede. . . . I was being forced over the edge by rioting blacks, demonstrating students, marching welfare mothers, squawking professors and hysterical reporters. And then the final straw. The thing I feared from the first day of my presidency was actually coming true. Robert Kennedy had openly announced his intention to reclaim the throne in the memory of his bother. And the American people, swayed by the magic of his name, were dancing in the streets."[319]

Johnson was ending his presidency a broken man, a political victim of his falsehoods about the war in Vietnam. He had wanted to build a Tennessee Valley Authority in Southeast Asia and help the black and poor raise themselves into the great American middle class. All this would happen once he just won the war. But the war could not be won, and his failure to admit this had brought nothing but senseless destruction.

Johnson finally came to face reality. In late March he accepted the recommendations of a group of "Wise Men" assembled by McGeorge Bundy. The hawkish former secretary of state, Dean Acheson, who had fought for war with Cuba in the ExComm, now argued that the time had come to find a way to wind down American efforts and search for an honorable path to withdrawal.[320] On March 31, 1968, Johnson announced a unilateral halt of the bombing of North Vietnam along with his own decision not to run for a second full presidential term. He would, "as he had feared," be dead within five years. The first substantive sentence in his *New York Times* obituary would note that the president's "vision of a Great Society dissolved in the morass of war in Vietnam. . . ."[321]

The resignation announcement may have ended Johnson's nightmare but it did little to rescue the nation from the destructive course down which his dishonesty had set it. Robert Kennedy was assassinated on June 6, 1968, paving the way for the election of Richard Nixon, who, like Johnson, campaigned on a peace platform but ended up expanding the war and lying about it to his fellow citizens. It is hardly a coincidence that the two great civic crises of the Nixon administration—its attempt to forestall the publication of the *Pentagon Papers* and the series of scandals collectively known under the rubric of Watergate—both derived initially from his desire to prevent the public from knowing the truth about the war in Vietnam. In the former case, Nixon was actually protecting the lies of the Johnson administration, including those relating to Tonkin, OPLAN-34A, and the DeSoto patrols. In the latter, he was exhibiting exactly the same kind of arrogance and unwillingness to play by the rules of democratic government that had caused Johnson to destroy himself and his party and help lead the country into what appeared at the time to be unending chaos.

The violation of public trust and the corruption of public leadership that Tonkin inspired continued to haunt U.S. politics for decades. Convicted of lying to Congress about his knowledge during the Iran-Contra scandal, State Department official Elliott Abrams took refuge in the tradition of presidential lying. In seeking to avoid jail, he and his lawyers specifically cited the example of Robert McNamara's deliberate misleading of Congress in the aftermath of the Gulf of Tonkin episode. "If they could lie to dupe the nation into war without sanction," Abrams was saying in effect, "why can't I do it, too?" (Abrams also cited the decision of Kennedy and his advisers to mislead both Congress and the nation about its willingness to withdraw the missiles from Turkey during the Cuban Missile Crisis as a precedent for his actions.)[322] This was the same lesson that Reagan's national security adviser, Robert McFarlane, drew from its history. As he explained to interviewer Charlie Rose, "President Johnson distorts the events of the Gulf of Tonkin. We get into a war. We lose a lot of lives. Nobody charges him and nobody really vilifies him for lying or distorting. Well, George [H.W.] Bush today can look back on that experience and say, 'Wait a minute. This Iran-contra thing was peanuts. Nobody got killed. Nobody got hurt. Consequently, for me to be held account when President Johnson isn't, isn't fair.'"[323]

Shortly after the Tonkin incidents, James Stockdale, soon to be shot down over North Vietnam and spend seven and a half years in a Vietnamese prison camp, was visited on the flight deck by Alvin Friedman, from DOD, and Jack Stempler, special assistant to McNamara. "We were sent out here just to find out one thing," Stempler told him. "Were there any fuckin' boats out there the other night or not?" Stockdale told himself that that question had "said it all." He could "stand right there in the cabin and write the script of what was to come: Washington's second thoughts; the guilt, the remorse, the tentativeness, the changes of heart, the back-out. And a generation of young Americans would get left holding the bag."[324] That Vietnam had begun with a lie was not the only objection most Americans felt by the time it had thoroughly infected the country's politics. The conflict was by its very nature futile and hopeless and morally questionable, as well. A policy asking that young men be sent into battle to become killers, and even die for reasons no one can sensibly explain, is hardly tenable for long in a political democracy. But the fact that it was revealed to have been undertaken under the dark of night—through lies, misinformation, and deliberate subterfuge over the Gulf of Tonkin incident—gave the anger it inspired a far uglier, more vicious tinge. Tragically, but perhaps appropriately for a politician so steeped in scripture, Lyndon Johnson had reaped what he had sown.

V. RONALD W. REAGAN, CENTRAL AMERICA, AND THE IRAN-CONTRA SCANDAL

I hope I never see the day when any of us stand up and say we cannot accept the word of the president of the United States, no matter what party we belong to. —Senator David Boren (D-OK)[1]

On a crisp May afternoon in 1996, a small group of mourners quietly gathered for a memorial service at the national cemetery in Arlington, Virginia. Comprised of widows, children, friends, and bereaved parents of soldiers who had been killed in a secret war the United States had fought in the tiny Latin American nation of El Salvador about a decade and half earlier, the service was the first glimmer of official recognition of the truth regarding their losses. Twenty-one Americans had been killed in action fighting in El Salvador, but because neither the Pentagon nor the Reagan White House had ever acknowledged this fact, the fallen soldiers had never received their due honors.

El Salvador was a kind of orphaned war in the Washington of the late 1970s and early 1980s. Ruled by a military junta with a terrible human rights record even for Latin America, and facing a Marxist-led guerrilla insurgence, the Salvadorans could not or would not curb their murderous ways sufficiently to earn an open embrace either from Jimmy Carter's White House or from the Democratic-controlled Congress. But at the same time, neither was either one willing to let the regime collapse entirely and thus open themselves to the charge of having "lost" not one but two nations to Communism. (Neighboring Nicaragua's Somoza dictatorship had been allowed to fall in 1979. That made El Salvador's potential collapse intolerable.) The Carter administration temporarily cut off economic and military aid to the Salvadoran regime in December 1980, but fully restored it in January 1981 when it appeared that collapse might be on the horizon. When the Reagan administration came into office in January 1981, one of its first priorities was providing enough military firepower to the Salvadorans to win their war against the guerrillas irrespective of any human rights offenses they might commit on their way to victory.

With Vietnam still fresh in everyone's memory, Congress had, in 1981, placed a firm limit of fifty-five U.S. military advisers, and strict rules of engagement prohibited them from participating in combat operations. U.S. forces inside El Salvador, however, quickly dispensed with such niceties. The Reagan administration suppressed reports of American soldiers' involvement in the fighting and instructed U.S. field commanders not to issue any requests for combat commendations. The military advisers there did receive combat pay, however, and in the field, they carried their own weapons, inspiring the Marxist FMLN guerrillas to target them as they would any enemy fighter. So critical to the Reagan administration's public relations efforts was the appearance of adherence to congressional stipulations, however, that when a U.S. news crew videotaped an American colonel carrying an M-16 rifle in El Salvador in 1982, he was immediately flown out of the country. Another particularly gruesome example of official obfuscation was revealed by a Knight-Ridder report about an elite Army helicopter unit, the 160th Task Force of the 101st Airborne Division. It ended with a chilling quote from a former covert military specialist, who explained the practice of "bodywashing." "If a guy is killed on a mission," the former officer said, "and if it was sensitive politically, we'd ship the body back home and have a jeep roll over on him at Fort Huachuca [a remote Army intelligence base in Arizona] or we'd arrange a chopper crash, or wait until one happened and insert a body or two into the wreckage later. It's not that difficult."[2]

In February 1983, Staff Sergeant Jay T. Stanley was wounded by ground fire in a U.S. helicopter and became the first U.S. military casualty of the Salvadoran civil war. The U.S. embassy originally tried to provide a cover story, telling reporters that the helicopter had been ferrying Stanley and other advisers to repair a radio relay station. Eventually the Americans were forced to admit that it and another chopper were carrying U.S. advisers who had been directing Salvadoran combat operations from the air. Once again, the three men involved in the incident were ordered out of the country.

Tiny El Salvador was, of course, just one small corner of an entire regime aflame with civil war and counterinsurgency during this period. Nicaragua, Guatemala, and, to a lesser extent, Honduras were all caught up in a decade-long reign of terror and destruction that proved far stronger than any commitment to regional democracy or even civil society. By the time the Salvadorans finally ended their twelve-year civil war in December 1992, roughly 75,000 people had been killed out of a population of just over 5.5 million in a country the size of Massachusetts. In neighboring Nicaragua, a U.S.-supported civil war resulted in the deaths of about 40,000 people out of a population of about 3.6 million. In Guatemala, with a population around 9.3 million, somewhere between 150,000 and 200,000 people were murdered or "disappeared" by the government over the course of three decades—a third of these during the 1980s. In each of these conflicts, the number of people killed proved greater, proportionate to their respective populations, than the number of American soldiers killed in the American Civil War, World War I, World War II, and Korean and Vietnamese wars combined. Even after the various combatants had laid down their arms, however, the physical devastation continued to stymie development. But having lost interest in its proxy wars, the United States all but abandoned the region to its fate, relegating its bloody role in the region's history to a minor incident in the larger Cold War drama. Aside from the several dozen military advisers caught in the occasional firefight in Salvador or Nicaragua, few Americans suffered any significant consequences from U.S. involvement in these wars. What did suffer grievously, however, was the quality of America's democracy, together with the Reagan administration's own standing both at home and abroad.

"He Makes Things Up . . ."

Ronald Reagan's relationship to the truth has always been a problematic issue for historians, just as it had been for journalists; this is particularly true for people who wish to maintain a dutiful respect for the office he occupied for eight years, and for the voters who put him there. His own official biographer Edmund Morris called him "an apparent airhead."[3] The late Clark Clifford stirred up a minor hornets' nest in the early years of Reagan's presidency by applying the term "amiable dunce."[4] The editors of news magazines appeared to prefer the term "disengaged." All of these constructions, however, are prevarications that sidestep the fact that Reagan, as president, repeatedly and deliberately misled the American people. The most common defense offered by his supporters—if it can be called a defense—is that Reagan successfully misled himself no less energetically. In retrospect, it is quite remarkable that the American political system managed to function so effortlessly with so mercurial a figure seated in its most august office. It is almost as if the entire political system agreed to pretend that Reagan was a far more stable and engaged leader than he gave any indication of being because the truth was somehow too frightening to contemplate. Whether it was all part of a brilliant act, or evidence of the then yet-to-be-diagnosed onset of Alzheimer's, will likely never be known.

The anecdotal evidence of what was politely termed Reagan's "disengagement" remains startling, even today. He frequently convinced himself of historical truths on the basis of old movies he half-recalled.[5] He pretended to one White House visitor to have participated in the liberation of German concentration camps at the end of World War II though he had never even gone overseas as a soldier. He entertained a strange fascination with the End of Days, and was even known to speculate that they might take place during his presidency. He invented what he called "a verbal message" from the Pope in support of his Central American policies, which was news to everyone at the Vatican.[6] He announced one day in 1985 that South Africa—though still ruled by the vicious apartheid regime of P. W. Botha—had somehow "eliminated the segregation that we once had in our own country."[7] Such strange pronouncements by the president of the United States eventually grew to be considered so routine that rarely did anyone in the White House ever bother to correct them. The president simply had a penchant, one former senior adviser admitted, to "build these little worlds and live in them." One of his children added, "He makes things up and believes them."[8] What is more astounding is the fact that he convinced other people to believe them too.

Reagan may very well have believed his own inventions, but his advisers—men such as Caspar Weinberger, William Casey, Alexander Haig, George Shultz, Robert McFarlane, Thomas Enders, Elliott Abrams, and Oliver North—enjoyed no such excuses for following suit. Their deceptions were largely a matter of short-term political self-interest. Perhaps each believed himself to have done so in the service of a higher calling—a deeper patriotism—as many of them later testified. If so, it was patriotism of a particularly self-serving variety, as it apparently justified in their calculations decisions that put their own judgment above the U.S. court system and the Constitution it sought to enforce. These bureaucrats lied because they felt that Congress and the country were not to be trusted with the truth. They lied because the truth did not serve their larger purposes and because (they thought) lying carried no sanction in the system. The truth, for many of these individuals, carried with it no intrinsic value in public life. Moreover, much of the Congress—Republicans politically aligned with the president as well as many Democrats who were not—unquestioningly accepted these lies and made them the basis of legislation throughout the decade. Political expediency demanded that they not devote too much time and energy to distinguishing the truth in the administration's pronouncements, lest the ideological and political winds swirling around the conflict pick them up and sweep them away. Those few legislators who would not play along found themselves subjected to a vociferous torrent of political and ideological abuse as their political reward.

The motivation for the many untruths the administration told about its policies in Central America was partially political and partially ideological. The Reagan administration came to power with any number of plans designed to reverse what it believed to be the dangerous decline in America's global standing and the respect it commanded from allies and enemies alike. It wanted to revive both the military and the CIA and put the Communist side on notice that the United States would no longer be a patsy in the grand game of proxy warfare. "Let us tell those who fought in that war that we will never again ask young men to fight and possibly die in a war our government is afraid to win," Reagan promised during the 1980 presidential campaign.[9] It was one promise he intended to keep.

The documentary history of the Reagan presidency remains under lock and key at the Ronald Reagan Presidential Library in Simi Valley, California, due, in large measure, to a presidential order signed by President George H. W. Bush overturning previous law, by executive fiat. But thanks to the careful reconstruction of these events of the period by historians including Walter LaFeber, Cynthia Arnson, and William LeoGrande, coupled with the tireless declassification efforts by the invaluable National Security Archive in Washington, we now have a portrait of how the media eagerly helped the Reagan administration create its fictional Central America. While many journalists did distinguish themselves by investigating the details of the many false assertions made by Reagan administration officials during the course of the decade, these same reporters stopped short of accusing the administration of deliberate dishonesty. The explanation for this timidity was partially psychological and partially political. The election of Ronald Reagan had been a shock to most members of the elite media. As William Greider, then a top editor at *The Washington Post,* noted, Reagan's electoral success had been "quite traumatic for the press, editors, and reporters. Not on a partisan level, as conservatives imagine, but because it seemed to confirm the message of the critics that the press was out of touch with the rest of the country. The general aura and dimension of Reagan's victory were far beyond what the press imagined might happen. It was a sense of 'My God, they've elected this guy who nine months ago we thought was a hopeless clown. . . . [T]here's something going on here and we don't understand and we don't want to get in the way.'"[10] Greider's boss, the legendary Ben Bradlee, concurred, observing a "return to deference" in his own paper and those of his colleagues. Bradlee attributed the media's generosity to Reagan as "part of a subconscious feeling . . . that we were dealing with someone this time who really, really, really disapproved of us, disliked us, distrusted us, and that we ought not give him any opportunities to see he was right."[11] Bradlee believed that after Watergate, much of the public implicitly warned the media, "'Okay, guys, now that's enough, that's enough.' The criticism was that we were going on too much, and trying to make a Watergate out of everything. And I think we were sensitive to that criticism much more than we should have been, and that we did ease off."[12]

The media's new deference was widely noticed and much appreciated at 1600 Pennsylvania Avenue. As James Baker, Reagan's media-savvy adviser and later cabinet officer would later admit, "I don't think we had anything to complain about."[13] And White House director of communications David Gergen said he found a much greater "willingness to give Reagan the benefit of the doubt than there was [for] Carter or Ford."[14] After the deranged John Hinckley shot the president in March 1981, reporters were particularly eager to cover the president with a degree of sympathy that bordered on hero worship. As Gergen recalled, "The March shooting . . . transformed the whole thing. We had new capital . . . a second honeymoon."[15]

With an acquiescent news media and a paralyzed Democratic Party, the Reagan administration was given a virtual free hand to construct its Central American policies on the basis of a wholly self-constructed version of reality—one that adhered to the ideological and political contours of debate inside Washington, but otherwise floated untethered to reality. Washington's Central American discourse sometimes sounded as if its participants had stepped through the looking glass. The leader of the most powerful nation in the world deemed tiny, pathetically poor Nicaragua to be a threat to the security of Texas. He declared an official "State of Emergency," suspending significant constitutional strictures owing to alleged events in equally unthreatening El Salvador. When these efforts failed to excite any alarm in the system, the Reagan team went one incredible step further: it set up a shadow, secret government apparatus designed to carry out its own foreign and military policy, shielded from the inconvenient constitutional barriers of laws, debate, and sometimes even reason.

Rewind: Guatemala, 1954

Central America has historically functioned as a "backyard" to American politicians and a backwater in American politics, a situation that has invited a great deal of under-the-radar adventurism. Excluding the occasional crisis—the most prominent of these being Teddy Roosevelt's decision to foment a revolution in Panama in order to build a canal there—the region was largely ignored by the media, by most politicians, and undoubtedly by most Americans. But the alleged threat of Communism was more than enough in the

1950s to make any U.S. politician stand up and take notice, and President Eisenhower—a strong believer in the value of a covert foreign policy—was no exception. It was in that administration's 1954 decision to overthrow the democratically elected government of Guatemala's Jacobo Arbenz and then lie about it, where the Reagan administration found its clearest precedent for its own approach to the region.

The CIA undertook to overthrow Arbenz at least in part because of pressure from United Fruit Company, which feared the expropriation of its massive agricultural holdings. U.S. authorities explicitly denied any involvement. UN ambassador Henry Cabot Lodge, for example, called the coup "a revolt of Guatemalans against Guatemalans."[16] Secretary of State John Foster Dulles rejoiced that "disputes between the Guatemalan government and the United Fruit Company . . . [had been] cured by the Guatemalans themselves."[17] And as President Eisenhower was privately congratulating CIA director Allen Dulles (John Foster's brother) and a contingent of agents—saying, "Thanks to all of you. You've averted a Soviet beachhead in our hemisphere"—the U.S. Department of State was readying a formal statement that would read, "The department has no evidence that indicates that this is anything other than a revolt of Guatemalans against the government."[18]

The media, meanwhile, played along with the charade. Newspapers and newsmagazines printed entirely fictional accounts of the crisis according to official scripts. Following a secret governmental request to its publisher, *The New York Times* even went so far as to remove from Guatemala its correspondent, Sidney Gruson, whose aggressive precoup reporting had alarmed Allen Dulles.[19] The Guatemalans knew, though. Unlike their gullible American counterparts, they did not accept unquestioningly the veracity of Secretary of State John Foster Dulles's melodramatic claim that "Official documents now in the possession of the U.S. Government provide proof of the evil purpose of the Kremlin to destroy the inter-American system."[20] What they saw instead was the United States overthrowing a democratically elected government in the name of "democracy." Providence placed a young, recently graduated Argentinean physician named Ernesto "Che" Guevara in Guatemala during these events. The coup taught him a lesson about the United States that he would never forget. Guevara soon traveled to Cuba, where he helped Fidel Castro mount his anti-imperialist revolution, and later to other nations, including, eventually, Bolivia, where he would be assassinated with the help of the U.S. Central Intelligence Agency—his death converting him into perhaps the world's first global symbol of anti-American revolution and the personification of heroic resistance to perceived U.S. imperialism anywhere in the world, including within the United States itself.

The CIA's overthrow of the Arbenz government resulted in nearly forty years of unbroken military dictatorship in Guatemala, coupled with the brutal suppression of nearly all forms of human rights and civil liberties. The agency's hand-picked replacement regime, headed by coup leader Colonel Castillo Armas, immediately declared a new law establishing the death penalty for a series of political "crimes" alleged to be associated with Communism. These included many traditional labor union activities. Armas also disenfranchised three-quarters of Guatemala's voting population by banning illiterates from the electoral rolls. He outlawed all political parties, labor confederations, and peasant organizations and he postponed indefinitely all presidential elections. Over time, Guatemala developed into a country led by military-backed terrorists. The military became a caste unto itself, boasting its own bank, investment funds, and industrial projects. Its top leadership enjoyed vast ranches in an area called "Zone of the Generals" and regularly sold Mafia-style protection to the country's large landowners. Semiofficial death squads attacked virtually every sector of civil society, murdering lawyers, schoolteachers, journalists, peasant leaders, priests and religious workers, politicians, trade union organizers, students, and professors with de facto impunity. The brunt of the regime's brutality, however, was borne by the nation's indigenous Mayan Indians. Committing what in 1999 the UN-sponsored Historical Clarification Commission termed "genocide," the government exterminated more than 200,000 people, mostly Mayans, during its dictatorial reign of terror.

What was America's response to the genocide of the regime it placed in power? U.S. government agencies remain mum on the question, and their records are sealed. The nine-volume official report of Guatemala's Historical Clarification Commission accuses the American government of aiding what it names as its nation's official "criminal counterinsurgency."[21] It cites declassified U.S. documents, for example, that place a CIA officer in the room where Guatemalan intelligence officers—men responsible for death squad killings—planned their covert operations in 1965. These documents demonstrate that the CIA and other U.S. officials played a key role in the latter half of the 1960s in centralizing command structures and communications of agencies that would direct the official violence for decades. The Historical Clarification Commission also found that until the mid-1980s, U.S. government officials "exercised pressure to maintain the country's archaic and unjust socioeconomic structure" in addition to its lethal counterinsurgency operations.[22]

The total level of U.S. cooperation with the Guatemalan regime beyond CIA assistance is difficult to gauge. As Walter LaFeber notes, "Washington officials were not pleased with their own creation in Guatemala but—much as one hesitates to stop feeding a pet boa constrictor—they were reluctant to cut off aid and face the consequences."[23] U.S. leaders from Eisenhower and Dulles through Nixon, Ford, and Kissinger ignored the regime's brutality in deference to its anti-Communism. But the Carter administration complicated its position by denouncing the regime's human rights record, ultimately leading Guatemala to reject U.S. aid as inexcusable interference in its internal affairs. By 1982, during the Reagan administration, the killing appeared to be reaching a kind of gruesome climax. Under the dictatorship of General Efrain Rios Montt, a born-again evangelical Christian, the army massacred as many as fifteen thousand Indians on the suspicion that they had cooperated with, or might offer aid to, antigovernment guerrillas. Entire villages were leveled and countless peasants were forcibly relocated to aid the counterinsurgency. At one point, when as many as forty thousand survivors tried to find refuge in Mexico, army helicopters strafed the camps.[24] It was at this propitious moment that President Reagan took the opportunity to congratulate Rios Montt for his dedication to democracy, adding that he had been getting "a bum rap" from U.S. liberals in Congress and the media.[25] Moreover, in the midst of this killing rampage, U.S. ambassador to Guatemala Frederick Chapin announced, "The killings have stopped. . . . The Guatemalan government has come out of the darkness and into the light." In fact, the number of civilians killed by death squads doubled to roughly 220 a month by late 1983.[26] In a secret report to his superiors, Chapin decried the "horrible human rights realities in Guatemala," and argued that a consistent policy demanded that the United States "overlook the record and emphasize the strategic concept or we can pursue a higher moral path."[27] The Reagan administration ignored his advice. Though Congress would not authorize additional aid, U.S. funds still reached Rios Montt through Israel and Taiwan, in addition to the still-secret amounts available via the CIA.[28] Following an election in 1985, the U.S. embassy publicly declared that the "final step in the reestablishment of democracy in Guatemala" had taken place and accordingly restored all of its aid moneys. President Bush was forced to cut it off once more in 1990, following the murder of a U.S. citizen by Guatemalan soldiers, but covert CIA aid continued uninterrupted.[29]

Few if any of the horrific events in Guatemala ever made the front pages of America's newspapers during this period, much less the network evening newscasts. In truth, Guatemala was considered to be an insignificant sideshow for U.S. foreign policy and caused little controversy in Congress or the media. Because U.S. politicians never saw any real danger of "losing" Guatemala to Communism after 1954, they also saw little reason to get involved much in the issues raised by the genocide there. For the same reason, no U.S. administration felt much pressure to acknowledge the truth about the degree of its involvement with the regime in power. The policy could largely be conducted in secrecy, with only the occasional false homily about Guatemalan democracy and not much in the way of congressional response or media investigation. The lying, therefore, was minimal. The same, unfortunately, cannot be said of tiny, tortured El Salvador.

"Spanish for 'Vietnam'?"

It is fair to say that when Ronald Reagan and the members of his administration came to office in January 1981, human rights violations committed by anti-Communist governments were not a big concern. The intellectual underpinnings of the new administration's foreign policy were provided by Reagan's choice for UN representative, a previously unknown academic named Jeane Kirkpatrick. Reagan decided to pluck the Georgetown professor from professional obscurity after being given an article she wrote in the neoconservative journal *Commentary,* published by the American Jewish Committee, in which she mocked Jimmy Carter for his distaste for anti-Communist dictatorships. Kirkpatrick argued that such *authoritarian* regimes should be supported, since they were vastly preferable to the *totalitarian* dictatorhips that sought to control the inner lives of their citizens and that tended to ally themselves with the Soviet Union or Cuba. Not only were these anti-Communist countries amenable to American interests, Kirkpatrick believed that they could become true democracies if given the time. "Decades, if not centuries, are normally required for people to acquire the necessary disciplines and habits."[30]

The Reagan team came to office planning to "draw a line" against the advance of Communism and chose El Salvador as its proving ground. Its members did not intend to allow any concerns about the niceties of human rights, religious rights, or any other kinds of rights to interfere with its victory on the existential battlefield. With El Salvador in mind, Reagan's newly confirmed secretary of state, General Alexander Haig, announced, "International terrorism will take the place of human rights" as the foundation of U.S. foreign policy, "because it is the ultimate of abuse of human rights."[31] By "terrorism" he meant not attacks against the civilian populations for the purpose of political intimidation, as we commonly understand the term, but guerrilla resistance to U.S.-supported authoritarian regimes—a definition that was later extended, in the case of Nicaragua, to include governmental resistance to U.S.-supported guerrillas.

If a majority of Congress had shared these biases, the lies that soon characterized virtually every aspect of U.S. policy in El Salvador would not have been necessary. But El Salvador had already become the subject of considerable contention under the Carter administration. Ever since Harry Truman watched helplessly as Mao's Marxist revolution seized power in China in 1949, and thereby helped unleash the monster of McCarthyism, no president—particularly no Democratic president—wished to face the accusation of any nation going Communist on his "watch." As we have seen in the previous chapter, this fear was among the primary motivations for Lyndon Johnson's disastrous decision to bet his presidency on Vietnam. But the members of the Carter administration who had witnessed Vietnam (and many of whom had served at the highest levels of the Johnson administration) actually feared "another Vietnam" as much as they feared "another China." They were well aware of the dangers of the United States allowing itself to become tethered, politically, to an unpalatable and unsustainable ally in an unwinnable war. Although the Carter team tried repeatedly to help the Salvadoran junta stave off the Marxist rebels, it consistently found itself forced to cut off its aid owing to the Salvadorans' inability to control the murderous rampages of their security forces. According to Robert White, Carter's ambassador to El Salvador, these security forces were "responsible for the deaths of thousands and thousands of young people, and they have executed them on the mere suspicion that they are leftists or sympathize with leftists." To its credit, the Carter administration tried to confront this conundrum of how, as White put it, to "supply military assistance to a force that is going to use that military assistance to assassinate, to kill, in a totally uncontrolled way?"[32] But it never solved the problem.

The Salvadoran elite was led by a group of men who murdered not only opposition politicians, labor leaders, peasants, and workers, but also their nation's most beloved member of the Catholic Church. In March 1980, Archbishop Oscar Arnulfo Romero was assassinated in a hospital chapel while delivering a funeral mass shortly after he read a letter during a Sunday homily in San Salvador's Metropolitan Cathedral opposing further U.S. military aid.[33] The meeting at which the assassination was planned, according to a secret December 1981 cable from Ambassador Deane Hinton, had been chaired by ex-major Roberto D'Aubuisson, former intelligence officer for the National Guard and the primary political figure among the rightist parties of both the military and political establishments. D'Aubuisson was never prosecuted for his role in the killing, and neither the Carter administration (which did not have definite information) nor the Reagan administration (which did) was willing to punish the government for its inability to rein in this notorious assassin. Between 1980 and 1986, Senator Patrick Leahy (D-VT), a member of the Committee on Intelligence, repeatedly asked the administration officials for information regarding Romero's killing. According to Leahy, "They said they didn't know anything about it. It was obvious that D'Aubuisson was intimately involved in the Archbishop's murder and it was obvious that the US Government did not want to acknowledge that, because it would destroy their policy. Lies were built on lies."[34]

In December 1980, however, following the vicious paramilitary murder of four American churchwomen, the Carter administration did briefly suspend all military aid. But it quickly reinstated the funding just a week before it left office. Three days later, it actually increased the amount of aid and added a pledge to "support the Salvadoran Government in its struggle against left-wing terrorism supported covertly . . . by Cuba and other Communist nations."[35] For the first time since 1977, the United States included weapons in its aid to the Salvadoran government as Carter deployed a special discretionary fund allowing him to reprogram funds absent congressional oversight or interference. Carter justified his decision with the charge that the Nicaraguan Sandinistas were supplying weapons to the Salvadoran guerrillas. In addition, he suspended outstanding portions of the controversial $75 million U.S. aid package to Nicaragua's revolutionary leaders.[36]

Of Death Squads and Certification Hearings

The Reagan administration was considerably less conflicted about the Salvadoran civil war than its predecessor. Although the murder of innocents by U.S.-supplied forces was, for Reagan and his advisers, a nonissue, the killings, particularly when they involved church leaders, nuns, and U.S. citizens, did create problems of public perception. A church-based protest movement arose across the United States and increasing numbers of legislators grew more uncomfortable about voting for aid to the junta. This, in turn, necessitated the inconvenience of lobbying legislators and spinning journalists. The White House had to deal with the special problem it faced in House Speaker Tip O'Neill (D-MA). Haunted by his regret at having voted in favor of the Gulf of Tonkin Resolution as a young congressman, O'Neill saw Central America as a means of atonement. Moreover, a group of Maryknoll nuns in his district, including his nonagenarian aunt, Sister Eunice "Annie" Tolan, lobbied him continuously to restrict any aid to the killers. "I have a lot of friends in the Maryknoll Order, and they keep me highly informed," O'Neill explained at the time. "They look at it . . . like Vietnam."[37] As a result, the old-time "all politics are local" throwback to the days of the *The Last Hurrah* devoted himself to doing everything possible to shut down aid to the junta in El Salvador. O'Neill rarely carried half of the House of Representatives with him, and almost never more than a third of the Senate. But he did ensure a pitched battle—and hence a fresh harvest of Reagan administration lies—every time the issue came up.

The Reagan administration, meanwhile, hit the ground running, so to speak, in its propaganda offensive on behalf of Salvador's killer elite. Its first problem was the political fallout from the assassination of the American churchwomen. Many members of Congress were furious about the Carter administration's decision to resume military aid to the regime following the killings, but lacked a forum to voice their anger until the Reagan administration unpacked its bags a week later. The first reaction of the new team was to try to blame the nuns for their own murders. Jeane Kirkpatrick, for instance, insisted, "The nuns were not just nuns. The nuns were also political activists . . . on behalf of the [opposition] Frente and somebody who is using violence to oppose the Frente killed these nuns."[38] Secretary of State Alexander Haig even speculated that the nuns fired back at their assassins, as he told the House Foreign Affairs Committee: "The vehicle that the nuns were riding in may have tried to run a roadblock or may have accidentally been perceived to have been doing so, and there may have been an exchange of fire."[39] In fact, the United States had done virtually nothing to discover the identities of the women's murderers or to attempt to bring them to justice. Robert White, while still the holdover ambassador in El Salvador, sent a confidential cable to Secretary Haig that read, "It is amazing to me that the department can state publicly that the investigation of the nuns' deaths is proceeding satisfactorily. This is not backed up by any reporting from this embassy. I reiterate for the record that in my judgment there is no sign of any sincere attempt to locate and punish those responsible for this atrocity."[40] He was immediately fired. Undersecretary of State Walter Stoessel later admitted that the department had "no evidence that the four American missionaries were engaged in political activity as we define it."[41]

Nevertheless, the department continued to try to exonerate the still-unknown killers. In 1983, an internal State Department investigation again concluded that "The evidence of lack of higher involvement is persuasive." As late as July 1993, an official State Department postmortem on El Salvador policy repeated the conventional wisdom that it was "more likely that the chaotic and permissive atmosphere at the time, not high-level military involvement, was behind the crime." In fact, seventeen years after the killings, all four of the former national guardsmen convicted of the crime have admitted that they were acting on "orders from above."[42] A United Nations–sponsored investigation, also published in 1993, helped to substantiate their confessions, reporting that Colonel Oscar Edgardo Casanova Vejar (the provincial National Guard commander) and his cousin, Colonel Carlos Eugenio Vides

Casanova (the commander of the National Guard and later the minister of defense), at the very least, "knew that members of the National Guard had committed the murders under orders."[43] But Ambassador Robert White went further, charging that the murders were almost certainly ordered by the two men and that his embassy possessed compelling evidence of a cover-up. (In July 2002, a West Palm Beach jury ordered General Vides Casanova and General José Guillermo García to pay $54.6 million to three torturing-and-kidnapping victims, setting a key precedent in the prosecution of human rights law.)[44]

At the time, however, the administration managed to effectively disarm its critics on the issue of the nuns simply by promising to conduct an investigation and ensure that the guilty would be punished. Democrats felt powerless to oppose this charade. The party remained in a state of shock regarding the extent of public repudiation in the 1980 election. Not only had the incumbent Democrat Jimmy Carter lost in a landslide, but the Republicans had just enjoyed their most successful congressional election result in thirty-four years. The media, too, were in the most fervent stages of the traditional presidential "honeymoon," during which they celebrated the administration's most visible members and paid tribute to their moral bravery and intellectual acumen. Aside from Reagan himself, the most celebrated of these media heroes was General Haig. As he was attempting to deceive Congress about the identity of the churchwomen's murderers, the new secretary of state found himself celebrated in a *Time* cover story as the new "vicar" of foreign policy—a soldier/statesman who, in his wife's words, resembled "a Greek God."[45]

The administration used this period of goodwill to paint a picture of consistent progress in its alleged struggle for human rights. Although the killings continued at an alarming rate, they were almost always blamed on the guerrillas. "I think it is safe to say," Acting Assistant Secretary of State John Bushnell told the Senate Foreign Relations Committee in early 1981, "that the number [of civilians] who are killed by unauthorized activities of the security forces . . . are certainly not as great as the number that are killed by the forces of the left."[46] Bushnell's unsupported assertion was contradicted at the time by the reporting of at least three human rights organizations operating inside El Salvador. When asked to account for this discrepancy, Bushnell attacked their findings and went so far as accusing the Archdiocese of the Salvadoran Catholic Church of having been infiltrated by Communists.[47]

President Reagan would eventually offer up his own theories. He mused in December 1983, "I'm going to voice a suspicion I've never said aloud before . . . I wonder if all this is rightwing, or if those guerilla forces have not realized that . . . they can get away with these violent acts, helping to try to bring down the government and the rightwing will be blamed for it."[48] In fact the military's own assessment contradicted Reagan's unsupported hypothesis. As early as November 1981, a Pentagon assessment team found that the Salvadoran military "generally dismissed" the issues of "institutional violence" and "extreme rightist terrorism" as inaccurate or insignificant. Moreover, the team could find no ballast within the armed forces "to oppose the propensity of the more conservative officers to tolerate the use of excessive force and violence."[49] The classified report, signed by Brigadier General Fred E. Woerner, warned, "Unabated terror from the right and continued tolerance of institutional violence could dangerously erode popular support to the point where the armed forces would be viewed not as the protector of society, but as an army of occupation."[50] Similarly, in April 1982, a Salvadoran captain named Ricardo Alejandro Fiallos explained to a congressional inquiry that the Salvadoran death squads were "made up of members of the security forces. And acts of terrorism credited to these squads, such as political assassinations, kidnappings, and indiscriminate murder, are, in fact, planned by high-ranking military officers, and carried out by members of the security forces."[51] Again, a year later, the Republican-controlled Senate Intelligence Committee found it to be "undeniable . . . that significant political violence—including death squad activity—has been associated with elements of the Salvadoran security establishment, especially its security service. . . . Numerous Salvadoran officials in the military and security forces as well as other organizations have been involved in encouraging or conducting death squad activities or other violent human rights abuses."[52] When the war ended and the Catholic archdiocese in San Salvador assembled the numbers, the result was as follows: for the period between 1980 and 1989, government-sponsored or assisted death was found to account for 41,048 murders; left-wing-guerrilla-assisted deaths, just 776.[53] Every one of the administration's reports to Congress and the country was wrong, therefore, by a factor of nearly 5,500 percent. It would stretch credulity to attribute consistent miscalculations of this magnitude to simple incompetence.

No one in Washington seemed to care about these discrepancies; nor were they willing to hold Reagan responsible for knowing much of anything, which may have been the true basis of his political genius. Reagan, who died at age ninety-three in June 2004, was not then, and is not today, accused of having willfully lied. He believed what he wanted to believe and did not let facts interfere with his quasi-religious convictions. His underlings cannot take refuge in this infantilizing excuse. Each was fully aware that America's Salvadoran allies were massacring innocents at a prodigious pace and, with few exceptions, they lied in order that the United States might continue to be able to supply these killers with better and more lethal weaponry.

Congressional opponents nevertheless scrambled to find a basis to challenge the administration, and eventually came up with an unwieldy combination of two separate amendments to the Foreign Assistance Act of 1961. Section 116 of the act, passed in 1975, outlawed economic aid to nations engaged in "gross violations" of human rights unless the aid would directly benefit needy people. Section 502(b) precluded U.S. military assistance to governments guilty of a "consistent pattern of gross violations" of human rights unless the president deemed the aid in question was vital to U.S. national security.[54]

The strategy took shape under a new law authored by Congressmen Stephen Solarz (D-NY) and Jonathan Bingham (D-NY) and Senator Christopher Dodd (D-CT). The legislation would have the Reagan administration cut off all aid to the Salvadoran government and to remove its fifty-five military advisers if the president could not "certify" that improvements had occurred in six separate areas of conduct: human rights, control of the security forces, economic reforms, fair elections, peaceful negotiations with the guerrillas, and the ongoing investigation of the murders of six U.S. citizens—including the four churchwomen.[55]

These were decidedly imperfect tools to demand veracity from an administration committed to deception. Moreover, Congress was hardly pure in its own truth-seeking efforts. While its members wanted a forum to complain about human rights violations, they were unwilling to accept responsibility for a policy that could lead to the fall of the Salvadoran government to the Marxist rebels. The new process enabled them to issue statements for the benefit of peace, labor, or church groups, which would make the local newspapers and television broadcasts in their communities—where opposition to the administration's policies rarely wavered. They could embarrass their opponents to score political points, but what they could not do was force the Reagan administration to tell the truth. And if the latter were willing to lie to Congress—to certify progress where in fact there was none—well, then, the entire process would become a sham.

Not surprisingly, the administration viewed the entire congressional effort with undisguised contempt. Deane Hinton, Reagan's ambassador to El Salvador, dismissed it as a way for Congress "to be for and against something at the same time." The legislators, he insisted, "didn't want to take the responsibility to deny resources to the government of El Salvador and on the other hand they didn't want to endorse it. So they created a certification procedure and made the rest of us jump through the hoop, and the President had to certify it."[56] Assistant secretary of state for human rights and humanitarian affairs Elliott Abrams, who would soon become assistant secretary of state for inter-American affairs, termed the certification process a way for Congress "to fund the war" because "It didn't want to risk being blamed, if the guerrillas won . . . while reserving the right to call us Fascists."[57]

Decidedly minimal success in controlling the Salvadoran military's campaign of abduction, murder, and torture during the certification period forced administration members, including President Reagan, to lie to Congress repeatedly. Beginning on January 28, 1982, Reagan certified to Congress that "The Government of El Salvador is making a concerted and significant effort to comply with internationally recognized human rights." He noted, "Statistics compiled by our embassy in San Salvador indicate a declining level of violence over the past year and a decrease in alleged abuses by security forces."[58] While the administration could not account for all the killings that took place, it did offer its own theory about them: "Guerrilla bands routinely operate accompanied by family members and other non-combatants . . . making it difficult to avoid non-combatant casualties when these groups are found and engaged by the military."[59]

Then-assistant secretary of inter-American affairs Thomas Enders conceded, in his testimony, "The results are slow in coming. I would agree with you on that. But they are coming. . . . The figures show it."[60] That very same week, however, two human rights organizations, the American Civil Liberties Union and the Americas Watch, jointly released a lengthy, heavily footnoted report detailing charges that the Salvadoran government was committing "some 200 politically motivated murders a week," or more than four times the number to which Enders was willing to admit.[61] In addition, it regularly condoned the use of "murders, mutilations, tortures and rapes" by its semiofficial paramilitary forces, according to Contra leader Edgar Chamorro in a letter to *The New York Times*.[62] Enders and his staff did their best to discredit reports of civilian deaths reported by these human rights organizations, but they did not bother to undertake any efforts to arrive at accurate numbers for themselves. Rather, they relied on the flawed methods that understated the violence. In seeking to assess the administration's accuracy, members of the House Intelligence Committe's Subcommittee on Oversight and Evaluation soon discovered that Enders and others often "supported policy claims with assertions based on little more than official statements of the Salvadoran military."[63] In other words, the U.S. government was taking the word of the killers themselves for how many people they had killed.

When the embassy did attempt its own assessment, moreover, the primary source it chose upon which to base its calculations was the casualty listings in Salvadoran newspaper reports. But these publications, embassy officials admitted, "only report deaths in areas where they momentarily have correspondents."[64] As these areas rarely included the rural battlegrounds where most of the killings took place, the number of actual murders was profoundly underreported. For instance, in 1981, Salvadoran newspapers reported 1,449 people killed in the relatively peaceful department of Santa Ana, but only 247 and 47, respectively, killed in the "battleground departments" of Morazan and Chalatenango.[65] Even if the Salvadoran newspapers had been able to obtain accurate counts, they almost certainly depressed the numbers as a matter of editorial policy. Recall that El Salvador in the early 1980s was a society under siege by right-wing terrorists protected by the military. Virtually all left-of-center and many centrist journalists in El Salvador had been either murdered or forced into exile. The rightist ideological bent of all the remaining Salvadoran newspapers led them to ignore right-wing terrorist attacks whenever feasible. Only thirteen such attacks were cited in 1981, and only one outside the capital.[66] Lastly, though they may not have been aware of it themselves, embassy officials were likely being deceived by the CIA. One element of the agency's covert operations, approved by Ronald Reagan in a March 9, 1981, intelligence "finding," was a press project in El Salvador designed to promote unfavorable representations of the rebels and favorable representations of the government. A public relations campaign with this agenda could hardly be expected to be too scrupulous about the truth. It seems likely that the embassy's reporting would have been corrupted by the fictions that the CIA was helping the killers in Salvador to spread about themselves and their opponents.

It was precisely at this moment, however, on the eve of the first certification hearings, that the administration found itself faced with reports of a grisly massacre in the tiny village of El Mozote, in the guerrilla-friendly canton of Morazan. On the day before the first hearing, January 26, 1982, Raymond Bonner of *The New York Times* and Alma Guillermoprieto of *The Washington Post* simultaneously reported on an incident in which each believed that many hundreds of unarmed civilians had been summarily murdered by "uniformed soldiers." (Bonner put the number of victims between 722 and 926.) Neither reporter had seen the massacre take place, and both noted that their guides to the site had been associated with the Salvadoran guerrillas. Yet the journalists saw the corpses firsthand, and photographer Susan Meiselas documented many of them as well.[67]

When these stories ran on the front pages of America's two leading newspapers, the administration knew that it had an enormous problem. It would be extremely embarrassing for the president to put his name on a statement certifying that the Salvadoran military was making genuine progress in meeting human rights goals set by the United States just one day after a report of a massacre by those very troops. The fact that both reports implicated an elite U.S.-trained and -equipped battalion only compounded the problem. Over $100 million of military and economic aid was at stake, and Secretary Enders said he later remembered thinking that "Coming on top of everything else, El Mozote, if true, might have destroyed the entire effort. . . . I certainly thought so when I first heard about it." The war, he feared, would become "unfundable."[68]

The embassy accordingly sent two young officers to investigate the matter. (Reports of the massacre were first made available to U.S. officials on January 6, but in the absence of news coverage, they had not inspired any investigation.) Although the investigators never reached El Mozote for fear of their own safety, they did come away from their interviews with refugees from the town believing that something akin to a massacre had taken place. The entire investigation took less than a day. The Americans refused a guerrilla offer of a guided tour of the site. Instead, they conducted their interviews of "intimidated, scared" refugees in the presence of soldiers wearing the very uniforms as the men who had conducted the massacre. "It was probably the worst thing you could do," one of those sent to check it out, Defense attaché Major John McKay, later admitted. Nevertheless, McKay noted that in speaking to these villagers, "You could observe and feel this tremendous fear. . . . I was in Vietnam, and I recognized the ambience. The fear was overriding, and we sensed it and could tell that the fear was not instilled by the guerrillas."[69] One elderly couple even described seeing "dozens of bodies," as the men reported in their cable to Washington, but grew fearful of discussing it in the presence of the soldiers. "This is something one should talk about in another time in another country," one villager explained.[70] Years later, each of the investigators admitted to reporter Mark Danner that what they had seen and heard that day deeply troubled them. As McKay said, "In the end, we went up there and we didn't want to find that anything horrible had happened . . . and the fact that we didn't get to the site turned out to be very detrimental to our reporting—the Salvadorans, you know, were never very good about cleaning up their shell casings."[71] His colleague in the investigation, Todd Greentree, concluded that the interviews he conducted "convinced me that there had probably been a massacre, that they had lined people up and shot them."[72] Yet both men understood the political context of their investigation. They were charged with writing a report that would "have credibility among people who were far away and whose priorities were—you know, we're talking about people like Tom Enders—whose priorities were definitely not necessarily about getting at exactly what happened."[73]

By the time their report reached Enders, the young men's tentative observations about what had so concerned them about the villagers' stories had already been recast to the contours of the Reagan party line. "We sent two Embassy officers down to investigate the reports . . . of the massacre in Mozote," Enders explained to Congress. "It is clear from the report that they gave that there has been a confrontation between the guerrillas occupying Mozote and attacking government forces last December." But Enders insisted that there was "no evidence to confirm that government forces systematically massacred civilians in the operations zone, or that the number of civilians remotely approached the seven hundred and thirty-three or nine hundred and twenty-six victims cited in the press." Enders also noted that the embassy officials were told that "probably not more than three hundred" people lived in the entire canton, "and there are many survivors including refugees, now." So he therefore found it difficult to believe, he said, that many people had actually been killed. Enders also attacked by name reports of the Human Rights Commission and Amnesty International, both of which charged that a massacre had taken place and offered testimony to support this claim.[74]

Without any independent confirmation, then-assistant secretary of state for human rights and humanitarian affairs Elliott Abrams sought to cast further aspersions on the reporters' stories as well as on their characters. The El Mozote case "is a very interesting one in a sense," he remarked to the Senate Committee on Foreign Relations, "because we found, for example, that the numbers, first of all, were not credible, because as Secretary Enders notes, our information was that there were only three hundred people in the canton."[75] Abrams's argument was deliberately misleading, as Danner would later point out, because both news reports had been absolutely clear that the mass killing had taken place in several hamlets. This particular argument was of a piece with the rest of the administration strategy to discredit the massacre reports by whatever means necessary. "We find . . . that it is an event that happened in mid-December [but it] is then publicized when the certification comes forward to the committee," Abrams continued. "So, it appears to be an incident which is at least being significantly misused, at the very best, by the guerrillas."[76]

Joining in this campaign of vilification of the *Times* and *Post* reporters was the Reagan administration's reliable ally in ideological warfare, *The Wall Street Journal*'s editorial page. On February 10, the *Journal*'s editors published a lengthy editorial entitled "The Media's War," in which it blamed what it termed the public's "badly confused" perceptions about the war on the "way the struggle is being covered by the U.S. press." As its central argument, the page simply parroted the administration line. ("Extremists of the right and left do most of their murder in the dark of the night. Some of both factions are soldiers, but both have also learned long ago the trick of dressing in military uniforms to confuse their victims.") But the piece also accused Bonner and Guillermoprieto of being "overly credulous" of the peasants' accounts of the Mozote massacre and dismissed their eyewitness reporting and interviewing as little more than a "propaganda exercise." (No mention was made of Meiselas's photographs.) Moreover, the editorial equated the embassy investigation of the matter—one in which representatives involved never made it to the village in question and then saw their conclusions softened and their concerns minimized virtually to nothing—with those of the reporters who had filed directly from the site.[77]

The campaign continued as *Journal* editor George Melloan took the extraordinary step of appearing on television to insinuate a secret agenda on the journalists' part. He told his interviewer that "obviously" *Times* reporter Raymond "Bonner has a political orientation," and compared his reporting to that of Herbert Matthews's "glorification of Fidel Castro in the 1950s" that "became a permanent embarrassment to *The New York Times*."[78] (Matthews, who covered Castro during the Cuban revolution, was removed from the Cuban story once Castro came to power, and left the *Times* shortly thereafter.) Accuracy in Media, then an influential conservative pressure group, took up this charge and treated numerous television talk shows to accusations that Bonner and Guillermoprieto were engaging in a deliberate hoax no less serious than that undertaken in the 1930s by Walter Durranty, the infamous *Times* correspondent who sought to whitewash Joseph Stalin's mass murders. In its newsletter, the group charged Bonner with conducting "a propaganda war favoring the Marxist guerrillas in El Salvador."[79]

It is a mark of just how surreal the debate had become in the United States in the early 1980s that two journalists who had uncovered evidence of a massacre could find themselves compared to a reporter who had failed to detect massacres taking place on his watch. But the tactic worked. In August 1982, the *Times* recalled Bonner to New York and assigned him to the Metro desk. Executive editor A. M. Rosenthal had let it be known that he was extremely uncomfortable with Bonner's reporting of the conflict. Offering the official explanation that Bonner needed more seasoning, he chose as a replacement a reporter named Shirley Christian, whose reporting for *The Miami Herald* had been much more consistent with the Reagan administration's ideological line. Whatever the editor's intent, the effect of Bonner's transfer on those reporters who remained in Central America was deeply chilling.

Because, more than a decade after the fact, journalist Mark Danner decided to devote himself to discovering the truth of what happened in El Mozote, today we have a far clearer picture of what actually took place there, and of what administration members who tried to discredit journalistic reports of the massacre knew at the time. It stands as a devastating rebuke to those inside and outside of power who parroted the administration's line. Shortly after Bonner, Guillermoprieto, and Meiselas returned and presented their evidence to readers, State Department officials received a confidential cable from U.S. ambassador to Honduras John Negroponte reporting on a visit by a U.S. embassy official and a House Foreign Affairs Committee staff member to a Colomoncagua refugee camp, where many of the survivors of Morazan had fled. The cable described the refugees' account of "a military sweep in Morazan December 7 to 17 which they claim resulted in large numbers of civilian casualties and physical destruction, leading to their exodus."[80] Negroponte, who was to become George W. Bush's ambassador to Iraq in 2004, himself noted that the "names of villages cited coincide with *New York Times* article of January 28 same subject." He noted that the refugees' "decision to flee at this time when in the past they had remained during the sweeps . . . lends credibility to reportedly greater magnitude and intensity of . . . military operations in Northern Morazan."[81] The State Department, however, decided to keep this information secret. By the time of the second certification report—which appeared six months later, in July 1982—the massacre reports were ancient history. Enders now bragged of "many fewer allegations of massacres during this reporting than last," a trend he attributed to the fact that "many earlier reports proved to be fabricated or exaggerated."[82] Like its predecessor, the second certification resulted in a noisy hearing, but a solid majority backed the Reagan administration's aid to the regime. This time military aid was more than doubled, from $35 million to $82 million, and economic aid increased to more than twice that amount.[83] In 1993, Enders finally admitted to a reporter, "I now know that the materials that we and the embassy passed on to Congress were wrong."[84]

It took a decade's passing and the Salvadorans themselves to determine, definitively, what took place in El Mozote. In the fall of 1992, investigators for the postwar Salvadoran Truth Commission spent more than thirty-five days digging through the burial sites filled with decomposed bodies, bones, skulls, and bullet cartridges. They identified more than five hundred human remains in El Mozote and its surrounding villages.[85] Of the 143 human remains discovered in the sacristy of the Mozote church, 136 were judged to be children or adolescents, of whom the average age was six. Of the remaining seven adults, six were women, one in the third trimester of pregnancy.[86] When all the forensics had been uncovered, the commission revealed at least twenty-four people had participated in the shooting and that every cartridge but one had come from a U.S.-manufactured and -supplied M-16 rifle. Of these, "184 had discernible head-stamps, identifying the ammunition as having been manufactured for the United States Government at Lake City, Missouri."[87] No one has ever been officially charged or tried for any crimes associated with the actions taken in El Mozote, which were deemed by Danner to be "the largest massacre in modern Latin American history." For this bit of good fortune, the murderers may be grateful for the lies of the Reagan administration and the men and women who willingly told them.

By the time of its second certification battle in July 1982, whatever appetite congressional opponents to Reagan's policies had for battle had disappeared. "We've won," an administration official bragged at the time. "We've succeeded in making the issue of human rights in El Salvador boring."[88] The certification process continued, but by now everyone merely went on playing their assigned role, with little doubt about the outcome of any given vote. The Salvadorans, meanwhile, held a series of national elections that further bolstered the administration's political case in the media and in Congress. With its opposition successfully under control, the Reagan administration apparently felt that it enjoyed the luxury of providing statements that accorded more closely with reality. These pronouncements had the ironic effect of demonstrating how dishonest their earlier representations had been. In contrast to the first two certifications, the third one admitted that "human rights abuses continue and . . . the further development of democracy and the protection of human rights are not to be taken for granted" in El Salvador. The administration also lamented the "systematic ineffectiveness" of the Salvadoran judicial system and acknowledged a need for "further improvement in military discipline."[89] But deputy assistant secretary of defense for inter-American affairs Nestor Sanchez noted optimistically that "the Salvadorans are at least now taking prisoners," an observation that might be taken as an admission that summary executions had previously been the normal modus operandi.[90] Even with the Reagan team's newfound confidence, however, Secretary of State George Shultz still felt a need to continue to castigate those in the United States who wished to focus on human rights abuses, particularly those "churchmen who want to see Soviet influence in El Salvador improved." (Shultz's remark was deleted from the published record of the hearing.)[91]

But death squad murders, which were never as low in number as the administration claimed, began to trend upward again in midautumn 1983. Moreover, the killers had by then turned their attention to the very centrist forces upon whom the United States was hoping to base its political strategy. Leaders of moderate peasant unions, church workers, members of the Christian Democratic Party leadership, and even the number-three official in the Salvadoran Foreign Ministry were taken out of their homes, tortured, and shot. U.S. ambassador Thomas Pickering admitted that "We know by their selection of victims and other information" that two key death squads "are not guerrilla organizations."[92] Not coincidentally, the U.S. embassy around this time began to leak the names of those military and government officials it knew to be involved in death squad killings—this despite Secretary Enders's previous insistence to Congress that the death squads were a "phenomenon which is without a center" and, hence, were uncontrollable by any Salvadoran authority with which the United States had any dealings.[93]

As we have seen, the true extent of the death count was so much worse than what was reported that the Reagan administration apparently felt compelled to try to limit Americans' access to information about El Salvador. While it could not directly control or censor the Salvadoran-based reporters of U.S. media outlets, it did have considerable success in intimidating them, particularly after Raymond Bonner lost his job. As one reporter told Michael Massing, who investigated the question for the *Columbia Journalism Review,* the Bonner case "left us all aware that the embassy is quite capable of playing hardball. . . . If they can kick out the *Times* correspondent, you've got to be careful."[94] Most of the media lost their taste for covering Salvador at all, once it ceased to be the scene of pitched battles in Congress. The killings continued, but the coverage did not. Meanwhile, the administration did everything it could to keep the victims of their allies from telling their stories. In April 1984, the State Department barred Guillermo Ungo, a Salvadoran Social Democrat allied with the FMLN, from entering the United States. A few months later, it did the same to four Salvadoran women from CO-MADRES (Committee of Mothers and Relatives of Political Prisoners Disappeared and Murdered in El Salvador). The mothers had been invited to receive the first Robert F. Kennedy Human Rights Award by Georgetown University, but were refused entry because the State Department insisted that they advocated violence. When questioned exactly how they advocated violence, a State Department spokesperson replied, "I can't be forthcoming with the information."[95] At the same time Roberto D'Aubuisson—identified by the U.S. embassy itself as the leader of a large network of right-wing assassins, and the killer of Archbishop Romero—was welcomed to the United States, in the hopes of creating a better working relationship with him. It was also around this period that the FBI undertook an undercover investigation of the antiwar organization CISPES (Committee in Solidarity with the People of El Salvador) that featured illegal office break-ins, surveillance, and the like. No illegal activity, except that of the U.S. government, was uncovered.[96]

What informed the administration's continuing paranoia on this topic? After all, it had already won the public opinion battle within Washington policy and media circles on El Salvador, and had prevailed in every certification contest, facing down both congressional and journalistic critics. Politically speaking, though, the administration did have rational reasons for feeling itself to be under siege. Despite its many political victories, administration members remained frustrated by continuing poll numbers that demonstrated that even though the aid policy could continue unimpeded, Americans would not approve a U.S. military intervention in Central America under virtually any imaginable circumstances.[97] Given the rampant corruption and general ineffectiveness of the Salvadoran fighting forces—which were analogous in many ways to those of America's South Vietnamese allies two decades earlier—the direct military option often seemed inevitable if a Communist victory was to be avoided. Many in the administration felt themselves forced to plan for this contingency, in both Salvador and neighboring Nicaragua. On April 17, 1985, *The New York Times* published portions of a leaked copy of a secret document in which the White House asserted that "direct application of US military force . . . must realistically be recognized as an eventual option, given our stakes in the region, if other policy alternatives fail."[98] But such a course would be impossible so long as the public remained adamantly opposed to any aspect of U.S. military involvement in Central America.

Perhaps also the administration's attitude grew out of the knowledge that its lies about El Salvador constituted only a small part of its many misrepresentations regarding Central America. Next door in Nicaragua, an entire secret foreign policy was underway, featuring a covert war, shady payments to drug and arms dealers, a massive propaganda operation, and, eventually, sophisticated arms sales, Bibles, and birthday cakes for America's sworn terrorist enemies in Iran. At any moment this edifice could come crashing down, bringing with it a possibility of criminal charges and the potential ruination of Reagan's presidency. The Reagan people consequently sought to contain all discussion of Central America within the parameters of debate that they themselves defined, with no unauthorized disclosures that might invite their opponents to uncover the truth about the enormity of the subversion of democracy they had undertaken.

"One Day's Drive from Texas"

While Ronald Reagan cared deeply about stopping the spread of Marxism everywhere, particularly in Central America, his deepest sympathies lay not with the Salvadoran government, but with the Nicaraguan rebels. Fighting to overthrow the revolutionary Sandinista regime—which had been briefly and quite gingerly tolerated by the Carter administration when it first came to power in 1979 and its ideology appeared unclear and perhaps unformed—the

Contras were initially the creation of the remnants of the Somoza dictatorship. They received small amounts of training from the semifascist Argentinean junta, until the CIA and various members of the Reagan administration took up their cause. During his first administration, Reagan's handlers would not let him give voice to his deep passion for their cause, fearing that too much attention to war in Central America would worry voters and undermine Reagan's mandate to cut taxes on the rich and cut government services for the poor. After Reagan won reelection in 1984, however, his advisers decided to loosen the reins a bit. Reagan's first speech following his second inaugural ceremony was devoted to the topic. "The Sandinistas have been attacking their neighbors through armed subversion," the president informed the nation, and they had even established relations with Ayatollah Khomeini's Iran. Both statements were untrue.[99] Ironically, they were true about Reagan and the United States, as Americans would soon learn to their considerable shock and chagrin. To understand how this situation developed, and the lies that made it possible, we must return to the earliest days of the first Reagan administration.

On February 6, 1981, a front-page *New York Times* article informed readers that "The Soviet Union and Cuba agreed last year to deliver tons of weapons to Marxist-led guerrillas in El Salvador." The report based these charges on "secret documents reportedly captured from the insurgents by Salvadoran security forces," which were leaked to the paper by members of the Reagan administration.[100] The *Times*'s scoop unleashed a flurry of similar stories and follow-ups also orchestrated by Reagan officials. These culminated in late February with the release of a State Department White Paper, "Communist Interference in El Salvador," that described the Salvadoran civil war as "a textbook case of indirect armed aggression by Communist powers through Cuba," and mirrored, in several instances, the language of a similarly misleading White Paper issued by the State Department on South Vietnam in February 1965.[101] Many reporters accepted these conclusions without question. For instance, ABC correspondent Barrie Dunsmore reported from the State Department that the report "firmly establishes the links between leftist insurgents in El Salvador and Communist governments worldwide."[102] It was "Communist interference in El Salvador" that set the stage for U.S. intervention in Nicaragua.

Secretary of State Haig had originally sought to generate support for military action against Cuba, which he called "the source" of unrest in Central America. He even promised the president, that, if given "the word," he would "turn that fucking island into a parking lot."[103] Michael Deaver later recalled that Haig's offer "scared the shit" out of him, and Reagan's closest advisers quickly ensured that the secretary would not be allowed to see Reagan alone, lest the overly impressionable president be persuaded by one of his plans.[104] Haig also leaked a proposal for a U.S. blockade of Cuba, which would have committed the nation to an act of war. But the popular reaction was so extreme—so deep was the fear of the United States tying itself down in "another Vietnam"—that he was immediately forced to retreat. Deaver and James Baker instructed Haig to tone down his rhetoric, as it was diverting attention from the administration's economic program.

His Cuba crusade rejected, Haig turned his attention to Nicaragua. The secretary claimed to have "unchallengeable" proof of a "massive" arms flow from the Nicaraguans to the Salvadoran rebels. Unveiled in closed congressional intelligence briefings, this "proof" consisted of photographs of extended Nicaraguan runways, burned Miskito villages, and a few military bases, but no actual arms traffic. Moreover, U.S. intelligence reports had concluded that what had once been a significant arms flow between the two nations had slowed to a trickle or stopped completely by 1981. This was likely an effort to stave off exactly the kind of military efforts the Reagan administration was threatening, as is confirmed by Haig's memoir.[105] But Haig and the rest of the administration refused to take "yes" for an answer. They continued to lie about the arms flow as a pretext for their much larger military plans for the region.

The House Intelligence Subcommittee on Oversight and Evaluation eventually concluded that most of what the administration had claimed about the arms shipments was "flawed by several instances of overstatement and overinterpretation."[106] As former Senate Intelligence Committee vice chairman Daniel Patrick Moynihan noted at the end of 1983 after he had done his utmost to clarify the issue of smuggled arms, "Show us one . . . one shotgun." But, according to Moynihan, when they "couldn't produce a shotgun shell . . . it became clear that the administration was lying."[107] Six weeks after Haig's testimony, even the State Department was forced to admit that it could locate no contemporaneous evidence of ongoing Nicaraguan arms shipments to Salvadoran rebels. The department even acknowledged that the United States had "no hard evidence of arms movements through Nicaragua."[108]

Although the administration never did offer any convincing evidence for its position, it did manage to convince Congress to fund a low-level war to implement it. Its soldiers were the "Contras" and were drawn initially from the ranks of Anastasio Somoza's hated National Guard, and trained by the neofascist Argentineans, before being supplied with weapons and training by the CIA, and public relations advice from the State Department. Authorization for the covert war came in the form of a secret "finding" signed by the president on March 9, 1981.[109]

The Contra aid program was clothed in falsehoods from its inception. CIA director William Casey believed in lying to Congress as a matter of principle and genially referred to its denizens as "those assholes on the Hill."[110] Whenever he had planned covert operations involving sensitive information in the past, his instincts were to dissemble, deny, and disappear. Nicaragua was no exception. Even when he did speak in public or to Congress about such matters, Casey seemed to have what Caspar Weinberger termed a "built-in scrambler" that made his responses to questions unintelligible. (He could not even pronounce the word "Nicaragua" properly, saying it "Nicawawa," and leading one Democrat on the committee to joke that no one should be allowed to overthrow the government of a country he could not pronounce.) As Norm Mineta (D-CA), a member of the House Committe on Intelligence charged with keeping the CIA accountable, complained, "We are like mushrooms. They keep us in the dark and feed us manure."[111]

When the congressional intelligence committees initially voted funds to enable Casey to equip the Contras to interdict the arms he said were being smuggled into El Salvador, he promised a fighting force of approximately five hundred men.[112] By the time Casey briefed the committee on its progress in February 1982, that number had already been doubled, and it was just the beginning.[113] Although committee Democrats failed to shut down the operation, they did succeed in attaching conditions to the funds, insisting that "The program was to be directed only at the interdiction of arms to the insurgents of El Salvador."[114] The CIA was specifically enjoined from using any money "for the purpose of overthrowing the government of Nicaragua or provoking a military exchange between Nicaragua and Honduras."[115] (Many congressional critics of the administration worried that it would attempt to trump up one of the many border skirmishes between the Sandinistas and the Honduran-based Contras into a Gulf of Tonkin–style excuse for war.)

It's difficult to imagine that the representatives really believed their laws could be enforced in these circumstances. First, what Nicaraguan exile was going to risk his life for the cause of interdicting the arms flow into El Salvador? The Contras were fighting to win, as their commander, Enrique Bermudez, made abundantly clear to reporters. "We are Nicaraguans and our objective is to overthrow the Communists and install a democratic government in our country," he announced.[116] To do so, they attacked not military targets, as the CIA had promised, but undefended civilian targets, such as farms, granaries, and small villages, in the manner of terrorists, rather than guerrillas seeking to win popularity among the population. Second, even if scrupulously observed, congressional conditions were unlikely to make any material difference in the manner in which the program was administered. When *Newsweek* revealed the growing size and audacity of the operation, Casey put the number of contras at fifteen hundred, but the magazine's estimate was closer to four thousand.[117]

Numerous congressmen vented their outrage over the lies they discovered, and a few tried to shut down the Contra program entirely. But the dissenters never had a chance of passing their bills through both houses of Congress, much less getting them signed into law by the president. The best they could do was to introduce a series of bills designed to limit U.S. involvement. Once again, in December 1982, the entire Congress voted, and the president signed into law, a bill prohibiting the use of funds "for the purpose of overthrowing the government of Nicaragua."[118] And once again, the CIA simply ignored it, conducting Nicaraguan affairs as Casey saw fit.

Despite congressional prohibition, Casey and his deputies continued to urge the Contras to do everything they could to try to overthrow the Sandinistas. Leaders were coached about how to state their case in public but, former Contra front man Edgar Chamorro admitted, "In private, they always said, 'The president wants you to go to Managua.'"[119] Reagan kept himself to his script, as when he was asked by a reporter whether his plan aimed for a Contra military victory. "No," he replied, straight-faced, "because that would be violating the law." He made the same claim in a televised address to the nation in April 1983.[120] In private, officials were not so cautious. When a U.S. ambassador abroad asked William Casey, "What's the real goal, Bill? What are you trying to do?" the director of central intelligence answered unhesitatingly, "Get rid of the Sandinistas."[121]

Impatient to get to Managua and frustrated by both congressional limitations and the fighting abilities of its ragtag allies, the CIA often took matters into its own hands, committing secret acts of war against the Nicaraguan government and its citizens and then disguising its operational role. The most blatant of these acts was revealed on January 3, 1984, by the Nicaraguans themselves, when they announced that the CIA was mining its harbors.[122] This information had escaped the attention of the U.S. media—whose members tended to dismiss the Sandinista government's claims out of hand—until March 21, when a Soviet oil tanker sustained serious damage from a mine while entering Managua's Puerto Sandino. The Soviets, condemning the explosion as a "grave crime" and "an act of banditry and piracy," delivered a furious protest to the U.S. ambassador in Moscow, who, under orders from his superiors in Washington, refused to accept it, insisting that the U.S. bore no responsibility for the mining.[123] Meanwhile Contra front man Adolfo Calero joyously attempted to take credit once the news of the mining finally appeared in the U.S. media. In the ensuing weeks, ships from Japan, Panama,

Liberia, the Netherlands, and the USSR suffered mining damage at Nicaragua's three main ports, injuring fifteen sailors and killing two fishermen.[124]

The entire episode unfolded like an eerie television rerun of the Gulf of Tonkin incident, transported in time and space. Just as the United States had refused to accept responsibility for the OPLAN 34-A raids it had planned, equipped, and guided against North Vietnam's coastline in 1964, so too the CIA conceived of the plan, hired the agents to conduct it, and provided them with both the mines and the technical expertise necessary to lay them. All operations were overseen by CIA "mother ships" operating out of a secret base on Tiger Island, Honduras. The agents were ferried from the CIA ships—positioned just beyond the twelve-mile coastal limits of Nicaragua—to the ports by CIA helicopters. When on occasion an operation would prove too difficult for the CIA contract workers to carry out, it would be turned over to U.S. Navy SEALs.[125] Yet Secretary of Defense Caspar Weinberger, recalling his predecessor Robert McNamara, declared outright, "The United States is not mining the harbors of Nicaragua."[126]

The decision to proceed with the mining had been vociferously opposed by Secretary of State George Shultz, who termed the scheme "dangerous" and "outrageous," before Reagan overruled him.[127] The members of the congressional oversight committees were uniformly furious over what they considered not only the foolishness of the decision itself, but also the administration's failure to inform Congress that it was planning to undertake it. In fact, it was later discovered that William Casey had informed the Senate Intelligence Committee of the mining, but in a single sentence that every member of the committee later admitted to have found unintelligible. Casey repeated this same sentence to the committee members five days later in order to secure the $21 million in funding the agency required, which the members appropriated, apparently, without knowing where the funds were going. When Barry Goldwater, the famed conservative Republican chair of the committee, finally figured out what had happened, he grew so enraged that he began to read the CIA's classified report of the entire affair in open session on the floor of the Senate. Although the Committee on Intelligence staff quickly stopped him, and the report was expunged from the *Congressional Record,* the CIA's secret war was secret no more. The next day's *Wall Street Journal* reported that despite repeated official denials, the U.S. government was indeed mining Nicaragua's harbors and lying about it.[128] This revelation came more than four months after Managua initially tried to bring it to the world's attention.

Once again the deceived congressmen went through the motions of expressing their indignation, with a few new voices added to the chorus. Goldwater released a remarkable letter he wrote to William Casey, complaining, "I am pissed off."[129] Daniel Patrick Moynihan, the committee's vice chairman, resigned over the incident, accusing Casey of "running a disinformation operation against the committee." But he rescinded his resignation once Casey offered him a pro-forma apology.[130] (Casey told his deputy John McMahon, "I sure as hell didn't want to do it. . . . I only apologized to save the Contras.")[131] Casey was also forced to recall his division chief for operations in Latin America, Duane "Dewey" Clarridge, from South Africa, where he was in the process of negotiating aid to the Contras from the apartheid regime there. Despite considerable documentary evidence attesting to the trip, Clarridge later denied having made it to congressional investigating committees; he was eventually indicted on seven counts of perjury, before being pardoned by President George H. W. Bush. At the time, however, no one took any action on the matter. On April 26, the Senate Intelligence Committee issued a press release noting that Casey and its members had "agreed on the need for more thorough and effective oversight procedures" and that the CIA had "pledged its full cooperation in this effort."[132] At the same time, however, Casey was secretly working with Oliver North to solicit funds in Saudi Arabia for the Contras in order to circumvent these same congressional restrictions.

The World Court condemned the mining in a unanimous 15–0 decision. (Refusing to defend its actions, the United States withdrew from the court.) Publicly, U.S. officials defended themselves by claiming the right of "collective self-defense" against Nicaragua because of Sandinista aid to the Salvadoran guerrillas. This was a stretch by almost anyone's imagination. Furthermore, the United States was not party to any treaty with El Salvador through which this aid could be invoked had El Salvador requested it—which, by no means irrelevantly, it had not. The very idea of the United States having to "defend" itself against Nicaragua, moreover, was insulting to common sense. As one administration official admitted of the defense at the time, "Unfortunately, it's bullshit."[133] The Senate concurred, and voted 84–12 to condemn the mining.

The next sequence of deliberate deceptions came in October of the same year, when news reports revealed that the CIA had published and distributed what later became known as a "murder manual," recommending the "selective use of violence" for the purpose of "neutralizing" Sandinista government officials. As the story broke just days before a planned presidential debate between Reagan and the 1984 Democratic presidential nominee, Walter Mondale, the president was forced to speak to the issue. Reagan explained that the manual "was turned over to the agency head of the CIA in

Nicaragua, to be printed, and a number of pages were excised. . . . And he sent it on up here to CIA where more pages were excised before it was printed. But some way or other, there were twelve of the original copies that got out down there and were not submitted for this printing process by the CIA."[134] Once again, this account was false from start to finish. The manual had actually been authored by a CIA contract employee. Nothing was excised at CIA headquarters except one line about hiring criminals.[135] Three thousand copies were distributed by the agency—not twelve, as the president had claimed—and the Contras printed up to two thousand more.[136]

In March 1986, the administration decided to create yet another Contra crisis—indeed one that appears to have been anticipated by congressional legislation. Here, the Reagan administration announced that between fifteen hundred and two thousand Nicaraguan troops had invaded Honduras. Unfortunately, the Hondurans themselves professed to be unaware of any invasion of their country and refused to ask for help. This recalcitrance infuriated Department of State official William Walker, who screamed at his embassy personnel in Honduras, "You have got to tell them to declare there was an incursion!"[137] "You don't have a choice in this one," U.S. ambassador John Ferch subsequently informed the president of Honduras. "You've got to get a letter up there right now. . . . They are going bonkers up there. This is absurd, but you've got to do it." Ferch was forced out soon afterward.[138]

Lying about Nicaragua became such a prominent part of the Reagan administration Central American policy that a special office almost exclusively for this purpose, called the Office of Public Diplomacy (OPD), was set up by a presidential directive. Its separation from the CIA itself was necessary because the 1947 National Security Act specifically enjoins the spy agency from engaging in domestic activities, as did President Reagan's Executive Order 12333, which prohibits the agency from participating in any actions "intended to influence United States political processes, public opinion . . . or media."[139] These strictures proved a mere inconvenience, however, as Director Casey transferred CIA propaganda specialist Walter Raymond Jr. to the National Security Council for exactly these purposes. (Raymond had retired from the CIA but continued to meet regularly with Casey in his new capacity.) OPD was housed in the State Department but reported directly to Adviser for National Security William Clark. Under the direction of Cuban émigré Otto J. Reich, the office worked closely with Raymond, Elliott Abrams, Oliver North, and CIA Task Force chief Alan Fiers. Its mandate, according to Raymond, was to "concentrate on gluing black hats on the Sandinistas and white hats on the UNO [the Contras]."[140]

OPD undertook this task on several fronts including offering privileges to favored journalists, placing ghostwritten articles over the signatures of Contra leaders in the nation's leading opinion magazines and op-ed pages, and generally publicizing negative stories about the Sandinistas, whether true or not.[141] OPD enjoyed a $935,000 annual budget plus eight professional staffers on loan from State, Defense, U.S. Information Agency, and Agency for International Development.[142] In the first year of its operation alone, it sent attacks on the Sandinistas to 1,600 college libraries, 520 political science faculties, 122 editorial writers, 107 religious organizations, and countless reporters, right-wing lobbyists, and members of Congress, according to its own records. It booked advocates for 1,570 lecture and talk-show engagements; in a single week during March 1985, the OPD officers bragged in a memo of having fooled the editors of *The Wall Street Journal* into publishing an op-ed allegedly penned by an unknown professor, guided an NBC news story on the Contras, written and edited op-ed articles to be signed by Contra spokesmen, and planted lies in the home media about the experiences of a congressman who visited Nicaragua. Otto Reich boasted of his ability to convince editors and executives to replace reporters he did not like with those he did and warned those reporters who did not cooperate that he would be watching them in the future, a threat that proved effective against National Public Radio, which Reich termed "Moscow on the Potomac." (One reporter there recalls an editor asking him, "What would Otto Reich think?" with regard to one of his stories.)[143] Among the lies peddled by OPD agents and employees were stories that portrayed the Sandinistas as virulent anti-Semites, that reported a Soviet shipment of MIG jets to Managua, and that revealed U.S. reporters in Nicaragua to be receiving sexual favors—both heterosexual and homosexual—from Sandinista agents in exchange for favorable coverage. The latter accusation, published in the July 29, 1985, issue of *New York,* came directly from Reich, who denied responsibility. Accuracy in Media, secretly under contract to OPD, soon began naming these journalists, despite the fact that the charges were entirely fictional.[144] Following the Iran–Contra revelations, a 1987 report by the U.S. comptroller general would later find that Reich's office had "engaged in prohibited, covert propaganda activities," and the office was soon shut down.[145]

Nicaragua's "Founding Fathers"

Before its various functions were revealed, however, one of the most significant of OPD's efforts was to convince Congress and the media of the democratic credentials of the civilian leaders that Oliver North and his associates selected to represent the Contras abroad. Named the "United Nicaraguan Opposition" or "UNO" by their American sponsors when the organization was created in San José, Costa Rica, in June 1985, these individuals were instructed on how to handle journalists' questions and never to admit that they received payment or instructions from anyone in the administration. They were also told not to give voice to any desire to overthrow the Sandinistas, but to insist, instead, that they were fighting to "create conditions for democracy."[146] (In fact, in July 1985, Oliver North would author a three-phase plan whose explicit purpose was the overthrow of the Sandinista regime.)[147] Together with top officials of the State Department, the CIA, and the National Security Council, OPD went to enormous effort and considerable expense to paint its three chosen Nicaraguan civilians as the true leaders of the Contras. The UNO was the brainchild of North. Its leaders—Edgar Chamorro, an ex-Jesuit seminarian turned advertising man, Arturo Cruz, the disaffected former Sandinista ambassador to the United States, and Adolfo Calero, the former manager of Managua's Coca-Cola bottling plant—were handpicked by the administration in order to manufacture the facade of a democratic Contra leadership. Its "San José Declaration" was written by Calero, Cruz, and North in a Miami hotel room. North admitted at the time that the declaration was almost meaningless and noted in a memo, "The only reason Calero agreed to sign was because the criteria established for the Sandinistas were, he knew, impossible for them to meet." Its point, they all agreed, was to "convince the U.S. Congress that the opposition was led by reasonable men," and nothing more.[148] In reality, true power rested alone with the generals, particularly a former Somocista colonel, Enrique Bermudez, who considered the directorate to be nothing more than his army's "political branch" and a facade at that.[149] Although both Calero and Bermudez had worked with the Agency for years, the CIA preferred Bermudez because he stuck to the business at hand without getting any fancy airs about it. When Chamorro once attempted to urge his fellow "leaders" on the "facade" directorate to replace the antidemocratic Bermudez, he found himself berated by John Mallet, the former deputy CIA station chief, as a "stupid . . . imbecile" for believing that anyone in the civilian directorate could remove a Contra general.[150]

The administration introduced the Contra directorate to the news media at an event at the Carnegie Endowment for International Peace in Washington, attracting dozens of television cameras and hundreds of reporters. The men were repeatedly asked whether they were being paid by any arm of the U.S. government to represent the Contras. Repeatedly, they insisted they were not, taking great offense at the implication that their motives were monetary, rather than patriotic. (Arturo Cruz, who was being paid $7,000 per month by North, after being transferred from the CIA payroll, was particularly adamant on this point.)[151] In fact, all of them had many other money-making opportunities available to them through the various branches of the CIA's covert aid program, in which corruption was rampant and tens of millions of dollars never accounted for. According to a private 1985 memo by Robert Owen, North's liaison to the Contras, to his boss, the UNO was entirely "a creation of the USG[overnment] to garner support from Congress. . . . In fact, almost anything it has accomplished is because the hand of the USG has been there directing and manipulating." Its leaders, moreover, according to Owen's memo, were "liars and greed and power motivated."[152]

While Ronald Reagan was famous for delegating away much of his presidency, when it came to misleading the nation about Nicaragua, he shouldered more than his fair share of the burden. On March 16, 1986, in a televised address from the Oval Office, he made one unsupported assertion after another, most of them demonstrably untrue. "Ask yourselves," cried the president, "what in the world are the Soviets, North Koreans, Cubans, and terrorists from the PLO and the Red Brigades doing in our hemisphere, camped on our doorstep"; "The Catholic Church has been singled out—priests have been expelled from the country, Catholics beaten in the streets after attending mass"; "The entire Jewish community [has been] forced to flee Nicaragua"; "The Sandinistas have made clear [that] the road to victory . . . goes through Mexico." Reagan vastly exaggerated the military capabilities of the Sandinistas, even when judged by the inflated statistics offered by his own State and Defense departments. Finally, he accused "top Nicaraguan government officials" of being "deeply involved in drug trafficking." He even displayed a grainy photo that he described as portraying a Sandinista official loading cocaine onto a plane heading for the United States. "There seems to be no crime to which the Sandinistas will not stoop," the president declared. "This is an outlaw regime."[153]

Once again, credible evidence for the U.S. government's contention of terrorist cells located in Nicaragua was simply unavailable. While the Sandinistas did harass priests who opposed their leadership, they rarely jailed them and never tortured or killed them, as was done so frequently in neighboring El Salvador. Moreover, the members of Nicaragua's tiny Jewish community who fled their country did not claim religious persecution; they were economic refugees, not political ones. Nicaragua, it need hardly be added, was an extremely unhappy place to live under the twin burden of blatant Sandinista misrule—under its confused and combative Marxist leadership—and the American-imposed war. The country's leaders never mentioned extending their revolution to Mexico, at least not in any serious fashion for which administration members could produce evidence. Finally, the infamous drug-smuggling photo displayed by the president proved to be that of a convicted criminal now working as a U.S. government informer to try to get his sentence reduced. He turned out to be the only person U.S. drug enforcement agents were ever able to identify as having tried to smuggle drugs from Nicaragua to the United States.[154]

By mid-1986, it should have been obvious to anyone paying attention that almost everything the administration maintained about its policies in Central America was based on deliberate deception. How then did official Washington manage to miss this pattern of deceit? Part of the answer lay in the laws pertaining to intelligence information and oversight. Representative Lee Hamilton (D-IL), a member of the House Foreign Affairs Committee and former chairman of the Select Committee on Intelligence, later complained, "Several members of Congress, including myself, knew that U.S. intelligence did not support President Reagan's claim that Nicaragua's Sandinista government was shipping 'a flood of arms' to communist guerrillas in El Salvador, but we were unable to respond to the president's assertions because the information was classified."[155] But the problem had much deeper roots. Most senators and congressmen, even the Democrats, simply could not bring themselves to believe that their president, secretary of state, secretary of defense, national security adviser, and director of central intelligence, as well as their deputies, were lying. Led by Representative Edward Boland (D-MA), Congress had begun, in 1982, to pass annual "Boland Amendments" designed to prevent the CIA or any other official arm of the U.S. government from participating in the Contras. They regularly rewrote the legislation adapting the law to try to deal with any wily alternative the administration might invent to evade its strictures. These tasks were undertaken with all appropriate seriousness. Before one of the votes, in fact, Boland looked to history as he enjoined his colleagues to join him in shutting down the administration's war. "When we adopted the Gulf of Tonkin resolution" in 1964, he warned, "we did not have all the facts. We could not—many of us could not—see where it would take us. Today the House does not suffer from that disadvantage. You have heard in secret session the numbers of fighters armed, the cost of the program, the plans for expansion. At the same time, you know the Sandinistas are not wearing white hats."[156] What Boland and company failed to anticipate was the administration's capacity for deception. Senator David Boren (D-OK) gave voice to the prevailing prejudice in Washington during the 1980s when he announced from the Senate floor: "I hope I never see the day when any of us stand up and say we cannot accept the word of the president of the United States, no matter what party we belong to."[157]

A second problem was related to the strange brand of ideological warfare the administration initiated in 1980, and the cowering effect it had on both

Congress and the news media. While not everyone believed the official lies, few were willing to say so publicly, lest they invite a storm of rhetorical abuse upon themselves. The election of Ronald Reagan signaled the ascent of a "New Right" in the United States, built on the foundation of a series of grievances that had been growing among many Americans since the late 1960s. Reaction to the excesses of the antiwar movement and the collapse of the civil had, by the late seventies, bred anxieties in many middle-class Americans that proved a fertile breeding ground for an angry backlash against the Left. Together with ever-present class-based and racial resentments, the stagflationary macroeconomic impact of Vietnam, followed by the oil shocks of the 1970s, put further stress on Americans' willingness to accept progressive tax rates and generous welfare policies. Meanwhile, conservative organizers exploited widespread distaste with unpopular Supreme Court decisions relating to abortion, school prayer, and racial integration. Finally, many Americans found themselves feeling helpless and angry in the face of Soviet military adventurism coupled with a veritable explosion of anti-American nationalism throughout the Third World. Together with the humiliation and denial that comes with losing a war, and the collapse of the authority of the traditional foreign policy Establishment that planned and executed it, these forces helped legitimize ideas that just a decade earlier would have been considered beyond the political pale.

In the worldview of the New Right, all the uncomfortable changes the country was undergoing were welded together into a single critique of "liberal elite culture." Like the doctrinaire Marxists a number of them had once been, the conservative ideologues professed to discover a secret conspiracy ruling American political and cultural life. The media came to stand for what neoconservative "godfather" Irving Kristol named the "New Class," made up of "scientists, teachers, and educational administrators," whom they accused of looking down with contempt at ordinary Americans. The members of the New Class had somehow manipulated Americans to believe that they were an evil people who rained death and destruction on Vietnam; as for Watergate, the liberal press had carried out a successful "coup d'état" (in *Commentary* editor Norman Podhoretz's judgment) merely to satisfy their own collective vanity. In the aftermath of Vietnam and the Establishment's failure of will, the New Class radicals, according to the New Right's interpretation, had seized control of the entire Establishment, including the Council on Foreign Relations, the Trilateral Commission, and the Ivy League.

The ranks of the first-generation neoconservatives were largely composed of former leftists of primarily—but not exclusively—Jewish academic origin, who transferred their intellectual allegiance to capitalism and American military power but retained their obsession with theological disputation and political purity. The job of the neoconservative intellectual, Kristol once remarked, was "to explain to the American people why they are right and to the intellectuals why they are wrong." His most influential ally in this effort was the late Robert Bartley, then editorial-page editor of *The Wall Street Journal.* Both men were already fierce Cold Warriors, but Bartley, tutored by Kristol, soon enlisted in the New Class war as well. The *Journal* editorial pages soon became the tribal drum for counterrevolution, and businesspeople across the nation were alerted to the dangers of the New Class.

As conservative individuals and corporate funders proved eager to underwrite the neoconservatives' ideological assault on the old liberal establishment, the terms of Washington's insider debate began to change. A new conservative counterestablishment arose, and it did a masterful job of duplicating Establishment institutions in the service of eventually displacing them. The American Enterprise Institute (AEI), the Center for Strategic and International Studies (CSIS), the Heritage Foundation, and literally hundreds of smaller ideological organizations soon supplanted those providing homes to liberals and moderates. Sun Myung Moon's Unification Church committed more than a billion dollars to publishing the *Washington Times,* a daily alternative to *The Washington Post.* Having made insufficient progress in discreetly colonizing the Council on Foreign Relations, the conservatives founded the Committee on the Present Danger (CPD), a Cold War–obsessed cadre of disaffected hawkish "wise men" and neoconservative intellectuals that would furnish fifty-nine members of the Reagan national security team including the president himself. CPD was dedicated to propagating its belief that "the principal threat to our nation, to world peace, and to the cause of human freedom is the Soviet drive for dominance" and its "long-held goal of a world dominated from a single center—Moscow."[158]

In combination these ideologically focused forces were able to create a context for the Reagan administration in the Washington of the 1980s in which its lies were treated as truth. The once discredited tactic of McCarthyism reappeared in a new, more sophisticated form. Podhoretz wrote, "In a conflict where the only choice is between Communists and anti-Communists, anyone who refuses to help the anti-Communists is helping the Communists."[159] UN ambassador Jeane Kirkpatrick lashed out at House Democrats whose opposition to policy made "the United States the enforcer of Brezhnev's doctrine of irreversible communist revolution" and later claimed that "there are people in the US Congress . . . who would actually like to see the Marxist forces take power" in Central America.[160] And writing in *The Washington Post,* Reagan's director of communications Pat Buchanan charged that by blocking Contra aid, the Democrats had become "with Moscow, co-guarantor of the Brezhnev doctrine in Central America."[161]

While Democrats did not wish to be seen to be responding to threats quite this outrageous, neither were they eager to accept the political risks likely to be associated with "losing" Central America, however fanciful the charge. The editors of the once-liberal *New Republic* played a key role in ensuring the triumph of the administration's policies with this key constituency. The magazine's attacks were more sophisticated than those of Buchanan or Podhoretz, but were no less pointed in intent or effect. "There are Democrats," its editors complained, "including some in Congress, who positively identify with the Sandinistas, their social designs, their political ends, and even their hostility to the United States." House Speaker Tip O'Neill did not genuinely care about the welfare of Central America; rather, he wanted "so badly to wound his nemesis Ronald Reagan that the real issues at stake count for very little."[162] Human rights groups who reported on the Contras' lax standards toward the murder, rape, and torture of innocents were slandered in the magazine's pages as "Sandinista sympathizers."[163] Those in Congress who focused on such abuses—which, after all, were being conducted courtesy of U.S. taxpayer dollars—found themselves slurred as a "Sandinista Chorus" which "cares genuinely neither for liberties nor for law, but for the dictatorships and their causes."[164]

The support that President Reagan's Central American policies received in what had once been the liberal flagship publication in America was indicative of the gentle media treatment he enjoyed throughout his presidency. Early in Reagan's term, news outlets would frequently point out what they termed to be "mistakes" in the president's understanding of reality. The president's supporters frequently complained about this practice and soon reporters relented. Reagan the symbol had grown into something far larger than Reagan the politician. When the president appeared at the privately financed ceremony to celebrate the refurbishing of the Statue of Liberty on July 4, 1986, the editors of *Time* opined that Reagan was "a sort of masterpiece of American magic—apparently one of the simplest, most uncomplicated creatures alive, and yet a character of rich meanings, of complexities that connect him with the myths and powers of his country in an unprecedented way."[165] Pundit Morton Kondracke, then Washington bureau chief of *Newsweek,* suggested that the president had become "a kind of magic totem against the cold future."[166] As a result of this kind of fawning toward the president from the very people charged with the professional responsibility of balanced criticism, the two-party system and the watchdog role of the media all but attenuated considerably. Democratic political consultant Robert Squier advised his clients that there was little point in mounting an opposition to the president. "We've given up running against Ronald Reagan—there's no advantage to it."[167]

Some journalists were well aware of the deception being perpetrated vis-à-vis Central America, but were unable to break through the thicket of lies that surrounded any given subject. In a few cases Oliver North intervened with editors to kill stories that he insisted would reveal secret operations and potentially endanger the lives of U.S. hostages. *Washington Post* reporter Joanne Omang grew so frustrated at being fed a consistent diet of what she knew to be lies about Central America by Elliott Abrams and Robert McFarlane that she quit her job to try out a career as a novelist. "They said that black was white," and Omang, given the constrictions of objective journalism, had no choice but to agree. "Although I had used all my professional resources I had misled my readers."[168]

A "Neat Idea"

James Madison wrote in 1788 that the U.S. Constitution gives Congress the "power over the purse" as a means of reducing the "overgrown prerogatives" of the government's other branches. This power, Madison wrote, is "the most complete and effectual weapon with which any constitution can arm the immediate representatives of the people."[169] Without such restraint, as one congressional committee would report, the nation could be placed on "the path to dictatorship." When the president and his men embarked on what would be their most daring set of deceptions—the complicated set of activities collectively known as the "Iran-Contra affair"—George Shultz tried to make exactly this point to his colleagues in a meeting of the National Security Council. "You cannot spend funds Congress doesn't either authorize you to obtain or appropriate. That is what the Constitution says, and we have to stick to it."[170] Instead, Reagan's men chose to ignore this fundamental Constitutional tenet through a program of private fund raising. As North later put it, "It was . . . almost drawn up by Director Casey, how these would be outside the US government. . . . The two criteria that Director Casey and I talked about [were] that these had to be stand-alone, offshore commercial ventures—[and] that they ought to be, ultimately, revenue producers: that they would generate their own revenue and be self-sustaining."[171]

North and Casey, together with their allies in the bureaucracy—primarily Robert McFarlane and later John Poindexter at the National Security Council, Elliott Abrams at the State Department, and Alan Fiers and Clair George at the CIA—constructed their "stand-alone" foreign policy apparatus to prosecute their secret war in Central America. Eventually they expanded it, almost by happenstance, to cover U.S. Middle East policy as well. At the same time as President Reagan was promising the nation that "America will never make concessions to terrorists—to do so would only invite more terrorism,"[172] his underlings were engaging in a secret foreign policy in which they supplied sophisticated weapons to Iran—deemed a "terrorist" nation by the State Department—as ransom for American hostages being held in Lebanon. A few members of the administration, most notably Secretary of State George Shultz and Secretary of Defense Caspar Weinberger, grew alarmed and sought to distance themselves from it when they found that they could not stop it. Shultz, in particular, argued that Reagan was committing "impeachable offenses" and repeatedly threatened to resign. But he lacked the nerve to carry through his threat and, hence, allowed himelf to be used as the front man for a phony foreign policy.[173]

Most of the lies that Reagan administration members told about Central America might well have remained secret if Oliver North and his minions had not insisted on mixing them up with the lies they told about the Middle East. When North and Poindexter decided it would be a "neat idea" to use the excess profits from the Iranian arms sales to fund weapons for the Contras, the illegal aid to the Contras and the illegal shipment of weapons to Iran became entwined in a single scandal. Poindexter later claimed under oath that he approved this politically perilous program without even so much as mentioning it to President Reagan. "I made a very deliberate decision not to ask the president, so that I could insulate him from the decision and provide some future deniability for the president if it ever leaked out," he testified.[174] But Poindexter could not produce a single document to support this alarming contention, though he did admit to discussing the implementation of a "fall-guy" plan should the program ever become public.[175] Coincidentally, the same "fall-guy" plan also called for North to take the "fall" for the diversion itself, and for Poindexter and everyone else connected to the policies to insist that Reagan possessed no knowledge of any illegal activities conducted in his name. It was the ability of these men to focus public attention almost exclusively on the diversion—one for which investigators could locate no evidence that would either convict or exonerate the president—that likely spared Reagan the ordeal of an impeachment trial. Whether both Poindexter and Reagan were lying about the degree of the latter's involvement in the scheme—as they lied about so much else relating to the multifaceted plot—is information that both men likely will take to the grave.

The tally of Iran-Contra–related official lies is remarkable both for its breadth and the sheer audacity of invention. That the officials in question truly appeared to believe that the entire undertaking could be kept secret simply by insisting that it did not exist reveals an almost childlike faith in the power of words to make and remake the world. The fact that it worked as long as it did is testament to the gullibility of Congress and the Washington media, as well as to the power of the presidency to control the political discourse. A secret foreign policy of this scope proved to be an enormous undertaking, requiring a large corporate infrastructure and the cooperation of hundreds of people—and thousands of soldiers—across several continents simultaneously. As Congress limited military aid to the Contras in 1985 and 1986, the administration secretly culled $34 million from third-party nations for the Nicaraguan rebels and an additional $2.7 million from private American benefactors. North and company organized a group of civilian businessmen and retired U.S. officials to privately maintain the Contra assistance program, called "the enterprise." They provided their own pilots, airplanes, and operatives, financed through Swiss bank accounts. All the while, the administration denied to members of Congress and oversight committees that they knew anything about these activities whenever reports of one would turn up in the media.[176] It was not until November 1986 that Iran-Contra finally came to light—not because of any Washington-based investigative journalists, but owing to a report in an obscure Lebanese weekly newspaper, *al-Shiraa*.

Thanks to the enormous amount of testimony taken by the Tower Commission, the joint congressional investigating committee, and independent counsel Lawrence Walsh's team of lawyers, we have a remarkably detailed historical record of the Iran-Contra scandal and its ensuing cover-up. Rather than revisit that extremely complicated and tendentious story in full, for purposes of this discussion we can consider simply the lies that sustained it and their consequences, both for the administration and for the nation.

1. SEPTEMBER 1985–AUGUST 1986: MCFARLANE, POINDEXTER, AND NORTH REPEATEDLY LIE TO CONGRESS ABOUT NSC/CIA EFFORTS IN SUPPORT OF THE CONTRAS AND IN VIOLATION OF THE BOLAND AMENDMENT. In the spring of 1985, as House and Senate Democrats grew concerned that laws were being flouted, thirty-seven members of the House wrote President Reagan that support for anti-Sandinista elements in Honduras was a violation of the Boland amendment and urged him to act in "strict compliance" with the law. McFarlane, who then was national security adviser, replied to House Foreign Affairs Committee chair Lee Hamilton (D-IL) that he could state "with deep personal conviction" that these concerns were unfounded. "I want to assure you that my actions, and those of my staff, have been in compliance with both the spirit and the letter of the law," McFarlane wrote. "There have not been, nor will there be, any expenditures of NSC funds which would have the effect of supporting directly or indirectly military or paramilitary operations in

Nicaragua." In follow-up correspondence, he added, "It is equally important to stress what we did not do. We did not solicit funds or other support for military or paramilitary activities either from Americans or third parties."[177] McFarlane sent similar letters to the chiefs of the Senate Intelligence Committee, Patrick Leahy (D-VT) and David Durenberger (R-MN). North, who drafted the letters for McFarlane, later admitted that they were "false, erroneous, misleading, evasive and wrong."[178] But they achieved their desired effect: shutting down further congressional inquiry. In fact, McFarlane had already successfully solicited a $32 million donation for the Contras from the Saudis; a contribution was hardly "volunteered" as McFarlane insisted. Moreover, he was well aware of solicitations made to Israel, Taiwan, and South Korea for money, weapons, or both. McFarlane directed North to alter the content of the relevant memos dealing with his knowledge of these activities, but North, through either malice or negligence, failed to do so. All of these lies formed the basis of McFarlane's decision to plead guilty to four counts of withholding information from Congress, for which he was sentenced to two years' probation, a $20,000 fine, and two hundred hours of community service.

John Poindexter, who replaced McFarlane at the National Security Council following McFarlane's resignation on December 4, 1985, repeated the same lies in seeking to convince Congress that the earlier guarantees remained valid. Poindexter claimed never to have looked at North's letters before offering this assurance. If he had done so, however, as he later explained, his objective "would have been to withhold information."[179] While being questioned during the Iran-Contra hearings, Poindexter helpfully explained, "I didn't want Congress to know the details of how we were implementing the president's policy." To prevent this, he was willing to substitute what he termed an "untruth."[180] Like McFarlane, Poindexter also relied on Oliver North to a considerable degree as his proxy. At a meeting in the White House Situation Room, according to the committee notes of the occasion, North told congressional leaders that he had merely given the Contras advice on human rights and on their need for an improved civic image. He had given them no military advice and knew of no specific military operations. As Lee Hamilton later testified, North also stated that he had not assisted the Contras with money or military advice, and had not violated the Boland Amendment in any way. He blamed a "Soviet disinformation campaign" for any information that contradicted his story.[181] Congressman Dave McCurdy (D-OK) was so impressed that he expressed the hope that North's answers would end all further inquiry. Chair Lee Hamilton was also more than satisfied. He instructed members to table resolutions of inquiry directing the president to provide documentation relating to all NSC contacts and support for the

Contras. "Based on our discussions and review of the evidence provided, it is my belief that the published press allegations [regarding North] cannot be proven."[182]

When questioned about this meeting during his testimony in 1987, North explained, "I will tell you right now, counsel, and all of the members here gathered, that I misled the Congress. . . . I participated in preparation of documents for the Congress that were erroneous, misleading, evasive, and wrong, and I did it again here when I appeared before the committee convened in the White House Situation Room and I make no excuses for what I did."[183] North simply stated that he "didn't want to show Congress a single word on this whole thing." Both North and Poindexter were convicted of lying to and obstructing Congress, but their convictions were reversed by the Court of Appeals on the grounds that the trials had been tainted by immunized testimony before Congress.[184]

2. OCTOBER 1986: REAGAN, SHULTZ, ABRAMS, GEORGE, AND FIERS LIE TO AND MISLEAD CONGRESS AND THE MEDIA ABOUT U.S. INVOLVEMENT IN THE CONTRA WAR FOLLOWING THE DOWNING OF A U.S. PLANE IN NICARAGUA. A second sequence of lies was spawned on October 5, 1986, when Sandinista soldiers shot down a small plane carrying three Americans ferrying weapons to the Contras in southern Nicaragua from the CIA-controlled Illopango air base in El Salvador. The plane's two American pilots were killed in the crash, but its cargo kicker, Eugene Hasenfus, survived. Captured by the Sandinistas, he quickly admitted his role in the operation and stated that he believed the entire effort was controlled by the CIA and sanctioned by the U.S. government. The discovery of the flight sent U.S. officials into a panic, for it held the potential to reveal to the world that the United States was in fact guilty of exactly the crime for which it had so thunderously denounced Nicaragua—that of using the territory of one nation to aid rebels in another for the purposes of government subversion. The plane was one of several operated by Project Democracy, the named coined by North for the effort to secretly deliver aid to the Contras. Once the operation was shut down, CIA operatives were ordered to fly the remaining planes in Project Democracy's "little air force," as North called it, to a remote airfield, where bulldozers had dug a large pit. As North wrote in his 1991 memoir, "The planes were pushed into the pit, covered with explosives, and blown up. The remaining wreckage was saturated with fuel and then cremated. The fire burned for days. When the smoke finally cleared, the charred remains were buried. . . . One might call it the ultimate cover-up."[185]

Asked about an American government connection by a reporter, President Reagan responded that there was "absolutely none," adding, "There is no government connection with that plane at all. . . . We've been aware that there are private groups and private citizens that have been trying to help the contras—to that extent—but we did not know the particulars of what they're doing." Secretary Shultz explained that the flight had been undertaken by "private people" who "had no connection to the U.S. Government at all." He based this assertion, he later said, on assurances from U.S. assistant secretary of state Elliott Abrams, who would soon emerge as the most forceful and energetic perpetrator of this particular falsehood. Immediately after the first news reports began to appear, Abrams showed up on CNN and told reporters Rowland Evans and Robert Novak that no one connected to the U.S. government had been associated with the flights because "That would be illegal. We are barred from doing that and we are not doing it. This was not in any sense a U.S. government operation. None." He then went on to blame the U.S. Congress for the men's deaths and Hasenfus's capture. "The reason this is going on, the reason that there are Americans who were killed and shot down is that Congress won't act" to fund the Contras, Abrams said.[186]

Abrams then appeared before the House Subcommittee on Western Hemisphere Affairs and insisted that "The flight in which Mr. Hasenfus took part was a private initiative. It was not organized, directed, or financed by the U.S. Government." Abrams repeated his assurances to the Senate Foreign Relations Committee and the Senate Intelligence Committee in ensuing days. On the latter two occasions, he was accompanied by CIA deputy director of operations Clair George and CIA Central America task force chief Alan Fiers. Both men, according to Fiers, were "taken aback" by the sweeping nature of Abrams's denials. Because the various committees had by this time learned that they could scarcely trust the administration members to tell the truth where Central America was concerned, they posed the same questions repeatedly. Each time, however, Abrams offered the same response, speaking, he said, for "the government as a whole." While George and Fiers both responded with much greater circumspection, they did not challenge Abrams when he made statements they knew to be false, and they maintained against all evidence that the CIA was not involved "indirectly in arranging, directing, or facilitating resupply missions conducted by private individuals in support of the Nicaraguan democratic resistance." This was obviously a lie, and one Abrams would later defend on the basis of its having been no worse than anything Kennedy's aides said after the Cuban Missile Crisis, or Johnson's during the Tonkin incidents. In attempting to defend his dishonesty, Abrams would testify to the Tower board of inquiry that he had been "careful" to avoid knowledge of the flight by refusing to ask North any questions that might have shed light on the activities. But because his statements to Congress had been based on what he termed "complete knowledge," such qualifications convinced no one. As a result of this testimony, Abrams was forced to plead guilty to charges that he had unlawfully withheld material information from Congress about the Hasenfus affair. He was also expelled from the D.C. Bar. Alan Fiers accepted a plea bargain in which he pled guilty to withholding information from Congress, while George went to trial and was convicted of two counts of perjury. All three were set free, however, by presidential pardons from George H. W. Bush following the 1992 election.[187]

3. OCTOBER 1986: ABRAMS LIES TO THE SENATE INTELLIGENCE COMMITTEE ABOUT HIS ROLE IN RAISING FUNDS FOR CONTRAS FROM THE SULTAN OF BRUNEI. Yet another Elliott Abrams tale of fiction involved his hapless attempt to secure funds for the Contras from the sultan of Brunei. Abrams himself had arranged the donation, traveling to London under an alias to meet with Brunei's foreign minister. The money was mislaid, however, when North's secretary, Fawn Hall, transposed the numbers of the account number for the wire transfer. When Abrams was asked directly about this by Senator Bill Bradley during a hearing before the Senate Select Committee on Intelligence on November 25, 1986, he responded angrily, "We're not, you know, we're not in the fund-raising business. We don't engage, I mean, the State Department's function in this has not been to raise money, other than to raise it from Congress."[188] This lie also formed part of Abrams's eventual plea bargain as well as having been a basis for his extremely reluctant apology to the committee for "testimony that was 'misleading.'" It led one Intelligence Committee member, Senator Thomas Eagleton (D-MO), to note for the record that Abrams's testimony made him "want to puke."[189]

4. NOVEMBER 1986: REAGAN LIES ABOUT HIS KNOWLEDGE OF IRAN INITIATIVE; CASEY, POINDEXTER, GATES, AND NORTH CONSTRUCT A DELIBERATELY FALSE CHRONOLOGY OF THEIR ACTIONS. CASEY AND POINDEXTER TESTIFY FALSELY TO CONGRESS ABOUT THEIR RESPECTIVE ROLES. One of the great misconceptions of the Iran-Contra scandal is the widely held belief that when then-attorney general Meese called a press conference on November 25, 1986, to announce his discovery of the famous "diversion" of funds from the weapons sales to Iran to pay for weapons for the Contras, he was finally revealing the truth of what took place. As Oliver North pointed out in his memoir, the administration had much to gain by focusing on the diversion. This particular detail was so dramatic, so sexy, that it

> might actually—well, divert public attention from other, even more important aspects of the story, such as what else the President and his top advisers had known about and approved. And if it could be insinuated that this supposedly terrible deed was the exclusive responsibility of one mid-level staff assistant at the National Security Council (and perhaps his immediate superior, the national security adviser), and that this staffer had acted on his own (however unlikely that might be), and that, now that you mention it, his activities might even be criminal—if the public and the press focused on that, then maybe you didn't have another Watergate on your hands after all.[190]

The story of the arms sales broke, originally, in *al-Shiraa* on November 3, 1986. The Iranian Speaker of the Parliament, Ali Akbar Hashemi Rafsanjani, confirmed it in a speech to the Iranian Parliament the following day, adding the details about McFarlane's delivery of a Bible and a chocolate cake as thank-you gifts for the meeting. At this point, chief of staff Donald Regan told the president that the time had come to finally "go public" about the effort. But Poindexter disagreed and carried the day. The president went forth to assure reporters it was a story that "came out of the Middle East and that, to us, has no foundation."[191] Presidential press secretary Larry Speakes later admitted that Reagan "knew [this remark] was wrong at the time."[192] Six days later, the president changed his story in a televised address to the nation when he admitted to shipping some missiles to Iran, but he lied once again when he insisted that "Taken together, [the missiles] could easily have fit into a single cargo plane." The crisis continuing to build, Reagan went before the press eight days later, on November 19, and continued to stick to his incredible story. He perpetuated the falsehood that the United States "had nothing to do with other countries or their shipments of arms to Iran, including Israel."[193] By this time, however, Poindexter had already briefed the press about the U.S. negotiations with Israel to provide the weapons, and so the falsity of Reagan's account was transparent to everyone but the president himself.

The pressure for a credible explanation of the affair continued to increase. Congress demanded testimony from Casey and Poindexter. It was at this point that the two men joined with North and CIA deputy director Robert Gates to construct a false chronology of the "enterprise" in order to cover up their illegal deeds and protect their president. In this document they perpetuated Reagan's earlier set of lies by arguing that no one in the CIA knew that anything but oil-drilling equipment had been delivered to Iran. North further tailored the chronology to suggest that no one in the entire U.S. government had been aware of the truth of the matter, when, in fact, George Shultz had contemporaneous notes proving that he, McFarlane, and Reagan were all fully briefed about the true nature of the shipments. Shultz then queried State Department legal adviser Abraham Sofaer regarding the extent of his legal responsibility to tell the truth about this, and Sofaer told him that, yes, he was legally bound to do so. So informed, Shultz threatened to resign if the chronology was not corrected. Casey died of a brain hemorrhage before he could be asked about the false chronology, but both North and Poindexter later testified that he was aware that the chronologies were deliberately "inaccurate."[194]

5. NOVEMBER 1986: THE "DIVERSION" IS DISCOVERED. NORTH LIES TO MEESE ABOUT HIS INVOLVEMENT WITH CONTRAS. MEESE HOLDS A PRESS CONFERENCE AND LIES ABOUT THE EXTENT OF HIS KNOWLEDGE AND OF REAGAN'S; MEESE ALSO LIES ABOUT NORTH AND POINDEXTER'S INVOLVEMENT IN CONTRA OPERATION; MEESE INSTRUCTS MEMBERS OF NATIONAL SECURITY TEAM TO PASS ALONG FALSE INFORMATION ABOUT THEIR KNOWLEDGE OF REAGAN'S ACTIONS. Following the discovery of the famous "diversion" memo in North's office by U.S. Department of Justice officials, Attorney General Meese attended a November 24 meeting with Reagan, Bush, Weinberger, Shultz, Poindexter, Regan, and Casey. There, America's top law enforcement officer instructed the other men in the room that while the weapons deliveries to Iran may have been illegal, Reagan knew nothing about them. Meese then inquired as to whether anyone felt any differently. Special counsel Lawrence Walsh said Meese "appeared to have spearheaded an effort among top officials to falsely deny presidential awareness of the HAWK transaction [shipments to Iran]."[195] In fact, Shultz, Meese, Regan, Weinberger, and Poindexter were well aware that the statement was false. Weinberger's contemporaneous notes of the December 7, 1985, meeting demonstrate that the shipment was discussed in considerable detail in the presence of the president. (Weinberger would also deny any knowledge of the deed to the congressional committees, though his notes later indicated that it had been he who had approved the transfer of the HAWK missiles from DOD stocks in November 1985.)[196] Early the next morning, just hours before he would reveal the story of the diversion to the public, Meese met privately with Casey, but Meese insisted that he did not attempt to secure any information from him and kept no record of the conversation.[197]

When Meese and the president finally did go public with the story on November 25, they did so with yet another flurry of falsehoods. Meese, who did most of the talking, told reporters that Israeli shipments of U.S. weapons to Iran in 1985 had not been authorized by, and were unknown to, President Reagan, and, furthermore, they "did not involve at that time, the United States." All the United States did, Meese claimed, was send "small amounts of defensive weapons and spare parts to Iran," not as ransom, but to improve relations. Meese argued that "the operations were legal because the president had signed a Finding authorizing the necessary covert operations." The original cover story had been that the shipments did not need a Finding because they had been conducted by Israel without the knowledge or approval of the president. The Finding was signed retroactively. Meese further claimed that "No American person actually handled any of the funds that went to the forces in Central America." In fact, North, Abrams, and Casey, among others, were directing these efforts personally.[198]

Later, during North's trial, under questioning by North's lawyer, Brendan Sullivan, Meese concurred with Sullivan's statement that Meese had not been "conducting a criminal investigation or formal investigation of any kind" when he sought out North, Poindexter, and company to inquire about what was going on behind the curtain. Rather, the U.S. attorney general, Sullivan said, was merely engaging in "more or less a chat among colleagues . . . almost like coworkers in the administration . . . trying to understand . . . the basic facts." Meese's focus, Sullivan said, "was not really the focus of an attorney general wearing the attorney general's hat, but it was basically to try to gather information to protect the president as best you could and deal with this enormous political problem brewing in Congress." Thus North, Meese explained, "had no obligation" to answer his questions truthfully.[199]

6. JANUARY 1987: WEINBERGER LIES TO THE TOWER COMMISSION AND TO THE PUBLIC ABOUT HIS ROLE. According to independent counsel Lawrence Walsh, Secretary of Defense Caspar Weinberger "deliberately lied" to the Tower Commission, to Congress, and to Walsh's investigators "regarding the president's knowledge of the Iran initiative."[200]

7. DECEMBER 1986–NOVEMBER 1992: VICE PRESIDENT BUSH CONSISTENTLY LIED ABOUT HIS KNOWLEDGE OF THE AFFAIR DURING HIS DECEMBER 12 INTERVIEW WITH THE TOWER COMMISSION AND DURING THE 1988 AND 1992 PRESIDENTIAL CAMPAIGNS. On December 3, 1986, then–vice president George H.W. Bush told an audience at the American Enterprise Institute in Washington, "I am not aware of, and I oppose . . . any ransom payments or any circumvention of the will of Congress and the law of the United States."[201] The vice president claimed not to know anything about the hostage trading issue until late 1986, when Senator David Durenberger (R-MN) briefed him on the Senate Intelligence Committee's hearing. Bush repeatedly told members of the media that the proposals of which he had been informed had never been "presented as an arms-for-hostages swap," and he wrote in his 1988 campaign

autobiography that if he had known about the "serious doubts" that both Shultz and Weinberger harbored about the proposed trade, "we might have seen the project in a different light, as a gamble doomed to fail."[202] Bush further explained to David Broder of *The Washington Post* that "Maybe I would have had a stronger view. But when you don't know something, it's hard to react. . . . We were not in the loop."[203] In response to at least three separate questions from Broder, Bush insisted that he had not been made aware of the two cabinet officers' strenuous objections to the deal. Records clearly show, however, that the vice president had missed only one meeting where objections were raised. He had been present at the January 7, 1986, meeting at which George Shultz insisted that he "expressed myself as forcefully as I could." Contemporaneous notes made by both Weinberger and Shultz also recall Bush's forceful advocacy of the mission.

Bush was able to finesse questions about these contradictions during the 1988 presidential campaign, and he easily defeated the Democratic nominee, Massachusetts governor Michael Dukakis. But in June 1992, the issue of Bush's deceptions arose again when Walsh made public his discovery of Weinberger's seventeen hundred pages of notes. In late September, a former member of Reagan's NSC staff named Howard Teicher said in interviews with Ted Koppel of ABC's *Nightline* and later with David Johnston of *The New York Times* that, together with Oliver North, he had fully briefed Bush on all activities relating to McFarlane's mission to Iran.[204] On October 13, Bush further confused the issue when he told NBC's Katie Couric that he "knew about the arms for hostages." Asked whether indeed he had known about the swap, Bush responded, "Yes, and I've said so all along, given speeches on it." The White House explained that Bush had misunderstood the question and, furthermore, that Bush knew of both the arms shipments and the hostages being released, but didn't know that they were part of the same deal until it became public in late 1986.[205] But Bush's continual revisions about his involvement made it impossible to know what he wanted people to believe about the issue, except, perhaps, that he wanted it to go away.

8. 1988–1992: SHULTZ AND WEINBERGER CONSISTENTLY MISLEAD SPECIAL COUNSEL LAWRENCE WALSH REGARDING THE EXTENT OF THEIR KNOWLEDGE OF IRAN-CONTRA–RELATED ACTIONS. According to Walsh's report, his investigation discovered numerous notes and memoranda prepared for Secretary Shultz that demonstrated that he had been kept far better informed about the activities of Messrs. North, Poindexter, and McFarlane than he had been willing to admit when questioned under oath. Shultz eventually conceded that his

testimony had been "incorrect," but Walsh declined to pursue the matter because he was unwilling to prosecute the only top official who had consistently attempted to put the brakes on the operation. According to Walsh's final report, Weinberger "deliberately lied to the Tower Commission, to Congress and to us." His notes confirmed that he knew in advance that the president had authorized the 1985 HAWK shipment, after Weinberger had warned Reagan that the proposed shipment was illegal. The president, according to Weinberger, replied that he "could answer charges of illegality but he couldn't answer charges that 'big strong President Ronald Reagan passed up a chance to free the hostages.'" When the president joked about going to jail, Weinberger told him he "would not be alone."[206]

9. 1987–1990: PRESIDENT REAGAN AGAIN OFFERS NUMEROUS STATEMENTS AT VARIANCE WITH THE DOCUMENTED HISTORY OF THE AFFAIR. In May 1987, while still president, Reagan claimed before a group of newspaper editors, "As a matter of fact, I was very definitely involved in the decisions about support to the freedom fighters. It was my idea to begin with."[207] But in August of the same year, he insisted, "In capital letters, I did not know about the diversion."[208] In 1990, speaking of both the weapons sales and the diversion during John Poindexter's trial, Reagan insisted, "It was a covert action that was taken at my behest," though he still claimed not to know any of the details of what had actually taken place.[209] The president continued to insist that he understood what he called "the Iran-Contra so-called affair" while the rest of the world did not. The Iranians to whom he and North had provided weapons were "individuals not in the government, not government forces of Iran."[210] Reagan, who would later be diagnosed with Alzheimer's, said in testimony for Poindexter's trial, "To this day, I don't have any information or knowledge that . . . there was a diversion . . . to this day, do not recall ever hearing that there was a diversion. . . . No one has proven to me that there was a diversion."[211]

The Final Escape

In the midst of the scandal and the extreme reactions its initial revelation inspired, partisans drew battle lines according to political interest. Former Republican Armed Services chair, Senator John Tower (R-TX)—who had been Ronald Reagan's initial choice to direct the CIA, before seeing his nomination derailed owing to charges of a reputation for excessive fondness for liquor and women—was picked to direct it. Tower was joined by former senator and secretary of state Edmund Muskie and former (and future) adviser for national security affairs Brent Scowcroft. The commission took testimony from many—but not all—of the leading players in the scandal but had no power to compel it from those exposed to criminal risk. Its extremely generous conclusions hewed closely to the administration's script as laid out in the original "fall guy" plan. The president was found guilty only of an overly indulgent "management style" that allowed his aides to conduct a foreign policy without his knowledge. But he was specifically exonerated on having been aware of the diversion, which was deemed by all to be the key determinant of Reagan's level of guilt as well as his political future.

When Congress stepped into the investigation many months later, it did so in the context of a viciously partisan debate between Republicans and Democrats as to just how much truth was good for the country. The principle of covert action itself was never seriously questioned. The only issue that concerned the committee, therefore, was whether this particular covert action might have gone a bit too far, and who might be held responsible for it.

In the case of Oliver North, congressional investigators faced a unique problem. North was not merely an admitted liar, but an unrepentant one. He was proud of his lies to Congress, the media, and the American people. He would follow the same course if given the chance, he proudly stated, leaving Congress helpless in the face of such brazenness. With his rows of service medals, his telegenic smile, and his patriotic homilies, North cut a swashbuckling figure with which few members wished to tangle. He was playing the "fall guy" role to the hilt, but with a wink. He was taking the fall, yes, but only because the cowardice of others had driven him to it. He let it be known that he had not acted alone. But now, here he was before Congress, ready to withstand (and return) enemy fire as long as it took.

The strategy worked flawlessly. Through the concerted efforts of the right-wing organizations who viewed North as a hero, Congress found itself inundated with tens of thousands of telegrams and phone calls demanding that North be given a medal for courage and bravery, rather than be compelled to testify, much less prosecuted. In his immunized testimony, his lies were greeted with cheers from his supporters and fearful appeasement by the lawmakers. When it was over, Congress was hardly any closer to the truth than when it had begun. But the entire investigation had been crippled by the favoritism shown to North and the cowardice displayed by so many of the investigators.

The irony of this situation is that the reported reaction of the country to North's testimony was actually at odds with most Americans' profound disapproval of both his methods and his aims.[212] The committee's unwillingness to prosecute North proved less a reaction to the genuine beliefs of the American people than to a phony "Potemkin" pretense of a public reaction created by administration supporters and other conservative movement figures. Most of the media fell for it as well. *Time,* for instance, reported that "the Boy

Scout and the patriot had the nation rooting for him," while *Newsweek* subtitled its cover story "The 'Fall Guy' Becomes a Folk Hero." Its attendant coverage argued that North "somehow embodied Jimmy Stewart, Gary Cooper and John Wayne in one bemedaled uniform."[213] The coverage in both newsweeklies was directly contradicted by published polls at the time, including their own. *Time*'s own poll showed that 61 percent believed that the term "national hero" did not describe North. According to *Newsweek*'s polls, 45 percent of respondents believed that North was a patriot and a hero, while 48 percent did not. On July 9, 1987, *The CBS Evening News with Dan Rather* reported, without evidence, "96 percent of you back North up, saying you approve of his actions." The broadcast went on to compare North to Rambo and Dirty Harry.[214] Overall, in four separate polls taken in June and July of 1987, between 68 and 81 percent of Americans questioned disagreed with the appellation "hero" when applied to Oliver North. The labels "villain," "victim," "dangerous," "fanatic," and "can be bought" proved considerably more popular.[215]

Just as they had managed to close their eyes to the story as it unfolded, many reporters proved eager to minimize its significance once it was finally uncovered. Journalists appeared to reserve their greatest measure of contempt for the one man who had been charged to discover the truth, once Congress botched the opportunity: the Republican jurist, Lawrence W. Walsh of Oklahoma. Armed with the power to compel witnesses, as well as a cadre of investigators, Walsh was able to demonstrate that many of the top officials in the administration—including Secretary of Defense Caspar Weinberger, Secretary of State George Shultz, and even Vice President George Bush—had lied about their involvement throughout the investigation. This news was met with a collective yawn among Washington journalists. Writing in *The Washington Post Magazine,* Marjorie Williams described Walsh's sense of duty as "anachronistic," mocking the notion that Walsh believed it "a serious matter—a serious crime—for members of the executive branch to lie to Congress and other investigators."[216] David E. Rosenbaum of *The New York Times* observed on the paper's front page that the issues of Iran-Contra had been "basically lost on the American public." Administration members on trial for lying to Congress and the country were transformed from "miscreants" to "martyrs." "As for Mr. Walsh," Rosenbaum wrote, "he himself may turn out to be the most widely scorned figure in the whole affair."[217]

Whatever Walsh might have hoped to achieve, however, was almost immediately undone by the December 24, 1992, decision of then–lame duck president George H. W. Bush—himself vulnerable to postpresidential prosecution—to issue pardons to anyone and everyone involved with the scandal. The pardons preempted the scheduled trials of Duane "Dewey" Clarridge and Secretary of Defense Weinberger. "The Iran-contra cover-up has now been completed," Walsh told *Newsweek,* adding, "It's hard to find an adjective strong enough to characterize a president who has such contempt for honesty." Walsh said the pardon "shows a disdainful disregard for the rule of law. It gives the impression that people in high office with strong political connections can get favored treatment. And I think that is a terrible impression for the president of the United States to give."[218]

But while justice may not have been served to the individual criminals who participated in the various lies and machinations that constituted the Reagan administration's secret foreign policy, these lies could hardly be said to have gone entirely unpunished. Most significantly, the revelations all but put an end to official government support for the Contra war. "It's going to be a cold day in Washington before any more money goes to Nicaragua," Senator David Durenberger noted on the day the story broke. "Ollie may have killed off his Nicaraguan program."[219] This prediction proved prescient. Aid was discontinued in February 1988 as Congress and the Bush administration pressured Contra leaders to lay down their arms and agree to a peace plan—one that the Reagan administration had resisted with all of its resources for the previous eight years.

The Reagan presidency also suffered, as the president was revealed to be, at best, a leader who had no idea what was happening in his own administration. Reagan himself appeared increasingly confused. When testifying before the Tower Commission, he read aloud the stage directions his staff had given him as part of his testimony.[220] Politically, he never recovered. "Reagan's not just a lame duck," the right-wing organizer Howard Phillips announced, "he's a capon." Indeed, the Republicans were trounced in the 1986 election, and as a result, Robert Bork's nomination to the Supreme Court was rejected, a major embarrassment to the president and setback to the conservative movement. At the end of 1987, *Congressional Quarterly* calculated that the president's success rate in Congress had fallen to the lowest level since it began keeping records in 1953.

Then there is the matter of George Bush's 1992 presidential election campaign. Bush managed to skirt the scandal in his successful 1988 campaign, while many of the details of his involvement remained secret. But owing to the doggedness of Lawrence Walsh's investigation, the affair came back to haunt him four years later, as just before Election Day, 1992, Walsh released evidence demonstrating that Bush, by then the incumbent, had been lying all along. Walsh had only paraphrased Weinberger's extensive notes in June 1992, when the former defense secretary was indicted on new charges. But four days before the election, Walsh released excerpts of the notes, including one made during the January 7, 1986, meeting. The note details the decision to send four thousand TOW (antitank) missiles to Iran in exchange for five hostages. "George Shultz and I opposed—Bill Casey, Ed Meese and VP favored," Weinberger wrote.

Bush partisans, reportedly including the president himself, blamed Walsh's release of the incriminating contemporaneous notes by Caspar Weinberger as the primary cause of his reelection loss. *New York Times* reporter David Johnston noted four days after the election, "In the finger-pointing ambiance of the post-election White House, the Walsh-as-saboteur theory has already risen to the status of received wisdom. Some Bush loyalists suggested that Mr. Walsh had finally achieved by negative publicity what he failed to accomplish in the courts: driving a Reagan administration official from office over the affair."[221]

Clearly there is a great deal of blame to go around in this tawdry episode. Not only the media but also Congress chose to overlook the steady stream of lies the administration issued on a regular basis. As then–deputy director and later director of Central Intelligence Robert Gates pointed out, "The first ingredient in the Contra time bomb was an administration unwilling to make a major national political issue of Nicaragua and live with the results, yet so committed to the Contra cause that it would thwart the obvious will of Congress and, unprecedentedly, run a foreign covert action out of the White House funded by foreign governments and private citizens."[222] Gates also noted, "In October 1986, the Senate rejected by a vote of 50–47 an amendment that would have required the administration to report to Congress on official involvement with the Contras' private benefactors. What kind of message did that send CIA people in the field?" Congress, obviously, could have acted much more strenuously to ensure that it received truthful briefings from the administration. But it made attempts to do so only fitfully and without any commitment to seeing them through.

To the degree that Reagan, Bush, and company were forced to suffer the consequences for Iran-Contra, they had only themselves to blame. The success of their campaign of disinformation about El Salvador had convinced them that they could lie about foreign affairs with near total impunity. Congress and the media offered no effective challenge. They committed acts of war, incited the murder of Sandinista sympathizers, and offered false evidence in support of their policies, and yet Congress refused to call them to account. Coupled with the decimation of a significant proportion of Central America, the murder of tens of thousands of innocents, the worldwide humiliation of the government of the United States, the subversion of our own system of laws, and the further undermining of trust in our own democratic processes on the part of our citizenry, the political penalty paid by the perpetrators of these falsehoods turned out to be trivial at best. Indeed, many of those successfully prosecuted by Judge Walsh, including Elliott Abrams and John Poindexter, not only received full postelection pardons from President George H. W. Bush, but were also showered with top jobs and prestigious appointments in the administration of his son. So, too, did others implicated in the conflict, such as John Negroponte and Otto Reich. Others, such as Oliver North, found themselves celebrated in the conservative media universe of cable news and talk radio. The nation may have suffered for the lies of the Reagan administration in Central America; so, too, undoubtedly did the victims of the repressive regimes and guerrilla armies the United States secretly supported. The policy eventually collapsed on itself, and the perpetrators' dishonesty was unmasked. But the nation never faced up to the consequences of what it meant to be led by dishonest officials. Those who had done the lying were not personally discredited, merely temporarily inconvenienced. In the long run, President Reagan's reputation returned to its prescandal levels and the entire episode came to be viewed by many as just a bump on the road to Cold War victory. With many of the same figures again in power, voicing no regret or repentance with regard to the consequences of their deception, the United States seemed poised to repeat its unhappy history of attempting to subjugate historically grounded reality to ideologically based fiction. President George W. Bush would emulate not so much his father—who was but a bit player in this story, and wound down the efforts that led to the scandal—but Ronald Reagan, who inspired his underlings to acts dishonest and illegal by virtue of his unyielding ideological convictions coupled with an unwillingness to adjust them in the face of reality. Eighteen years after the revelation of the Iran-Contra affair to the American people, the second Bush administration found itself embroiled in a similar conflict over whether it had taken the nation to war in Iraq on the basis of arguments and evidence it knew—or easily could have known—to be false. With many of the same people and their supporters in similar jobs as the first time around, it appeared as if the second Bush administration was almost self-consciously refusing to learn the obvious lessons of the recent past. Just as George Santayana had predicted, by ignoring history, Americans had condemned themselves to repeat it.

VI. CONCLUSION: GEORGE W. BUSH AND THE POST-TRUTH PRESIDENCY

> Men do not flee from being deceived as much as from being damaged by the deception: what they hate at this stage is basically not the deception but the bad, hostile consequences of certain kinds of deceptions.
>
> —Friedrich Nietzsche[1]

It hardly needs to be said that presidential dishonesty—like so many things in life—is not what it used to be. Before the 1960s, few could even imagine that a president would deliberately mislead them on matters so fundamental as war and peace. When presidential lying was finally proven to be a fact, its revelation helped force both Lyndon Johnson and his successor, Richard Nixon, out of the office. LBJ's false assurances regarding the second Tonkin Gulf incident along with their later exposure would prove to be a significant factor in his own political demise, the destruction and repudiation of his party, and the ambitious Texan's personal humiliation and disgrace. Much the same can be said about his successor, the no-less ambitious or dishonest Nixon. He, too, paid for his deceptions with his presidency, his reputation, and a degrading defeat for his party in the following presidential election.

But by the time of the Iran-Contra scandal in the mid-eighties—little more than a decade after Nixon's public disgrace—lying to the public had become an entirely mundane matter, one that could be easily justified on behalf of a larger cause. During the planning of the secret weapons sales to Iran, Reagan cabinet officials, as well as the president himself, warned of the direst conceivable consequences in the event of its revelation. George Shultz, in particular, argued during the crucial meetings that President Reagan was committing "impeachable offenses." But when cautioned again by Caspar Weinberger, Reagan replied, "[T]hey can impeach me if they want; visiting days are Wednesday." At another critical Iran-Contra planning meeting, Reagan predicted to his assembled advisers that in the event of a leak to the media, "We'll all be hanging by our thumbs in front of the White House."[2]

While the revelation did convulse the nation's political system for a year or so, the president and his men seem to have overestimated the cost of being proven liars as well as suppliers of weapons to terrorists. Presidents Reagan and Bush remained nationally admired and, to many people, beloved figures, subject to nary a mention of the lies and crimes described in detail in the previous pages of this work. The events of Iran-Contra barely rated a mention in the media during the weeklong celebration of Reagan's life following his June 2004 death at age ninety-three.

Perhaps we ought not be surprised. After all, former secretary of state Henry A. Kissinger—who is described even by his close friends and admirers as a near-pathological liar—continues his decades-long reign as perhaps the prince of media foreign policy analysts and celebrated society dinner guests; this is not in spite of his reputation but—at least in part—because of it. For instance, writing in 2001, David Halberstam wrote of Kissinger's "singular strength" in being able to "dissemble when necessary" and to remember all of the various lies he had told to each individual.[3] Halberstam intended no irony, apparently considering the ability to lie convincingly to be a necessary quality for statesmanship. Note that ex-president Jimmy Carter, who earned a reputation for being painfully honest in public life, enjoys no such cachet in the media or insider political Establishment.[4] While one cannot identify the willingness to purposely mislead as the foundation for either man's popularity—or lack thereof—one suspects the existence of an unspoken bias that too much truth telling is not considered an entirely admirable quality in a politician by many Americans.

From the standpoint of personal political consequences, the act of purposeful deception by an American president depends almost entirely on the context in which it occurs. Just about the only safe prediction a politician can make before telling a lie or authorizing one to be told in his name is that he or she will not be able to predict its ultimate consequences. Bill Clinton was impeached for his decision to "lie" under oath about adultery—a choice that, fortunately for many of his predecessors in office, no previous president had ever faced. In Clinton's case, his most vociferous critics succeeded largely in galvanizing the country on the president's behalf and in making themselves appear ridiculous. At the moment the conservative quest to remove Clinton from office reached its zenith—the day of his impeachment—the president's personal approval rating rose to an astronomical 68 percent.[5] Still, lying about his affair with Monica Lewinsky, both to the nation and to the grand jury, was the most costly mistake Clinton ever made, including having the affair itself. The act was a product of a combination of weakness and arrogance that resulted in the betrayal of both his closest supporters and many of his own most deeply held presidential ambitions. Despite the egregious invasion of Clinton's privacy by self-appointed virtue police in both the Republican Party and the Washington media, he should have found a way to protect his privacy without resorting to deliberate deception while under oath.

To the relief of many made uncomfortable by the complicated moral questions raised by a president who lied about what most people consider to be a private, moral sphere, Clinton's successor, George W. Bush, returned the presidency to the tradition of presidential deception relating to key matters of state, particularly those of war and peace. Bush may have claimed as a candidate that he would "tell the American people the truth," but as president, he effectively declared his right to mislead whenever it suited his purpose. The Bush Department of Justice argued before the U.S. Supreme Court that his administration required the right "to give out false information . . . incomplete information and even misinformation" whenever it deemed necessary.[6] This claim went beyond even then Department of Defense official Arthur Sylvester's famous formulation offered on behalf of President Kennedy during the Cuban Missile Crisis, when he claimed, "It's inherent in [the] government's right, if necessary, to lie to save itself."[7]

Misled into War . . . Again

As president, George W. Bush has appeared remarkably unconcerned with the question of whether he even appeared to be speaking truthfully. As the liberal commentator Michael Kinsley would observe early in the administration's tenure, "Bush II administration lies are often so laughably obvious that you wonder why they bother. Until you realize: They haven't bothered. If telling the truth was less bother, they'd try that, too. The characteristic Bush II form of dishonesty is to construct an alternative reality on some topic and to regard anyone who objects to it as a sniveling dweeb obsessed with 'nuance,' which the president of this class, I mean of the United States, has more important things to do than worry about."[8] In another famous explanation, this one offered by a Bush press aide in response to a string of revelations of Bush falsehoods relating to the reasons offered by the president for invading Iraq, "The President of the United States is not a fact-checker."[9]

The almost ostentatious lack of concern for veracity has been most prominent in the administration's foreign policy pronouncements, but it is evident in almost every area of governance. For instance, when he began presenting budgets that were radically out of balance despite his having campaigned as a fiscal conservative, Bush excused himself with the explanation, "As I said in Chicago during the campaign, when asked about should the government ever deficit spend, I said only under these circumstances should government deficit spend: if there is a national emergency, if there is a recession, or if there's a war." In fact, it was his opponent, Al Gore, not Governor Bush, who offered these exceptions during the 2000 campaign.[10] When Bush's Office of Management and Budget was fingered by a *New York Times* columnist, the economist Paul Krugman, for having released figures that greatly understated the size of the likely budget deficit to be caused by his extravagant tax cuts aimed primarly at the wealthy, the OMB offered up a revised press release on the Internet in place of the earlier one, without acknowledging any changes had been made.[11] Three years later, in February 2004, a front-page *Washington Post* report reviewed the history of the administration's statistical offerings on the economy and noted that they "significantly overstated the government's fiscal health and the number of jobs the economy would create." Another story in the same paper, on the very same day, proclaimed as its headline, "Bush Assertion on Tax Cuts Is at Odds with IRS Data." (And to the job of "fact-checker" was added that of "statistician" by White House press secretary Scott McLellan in his ever-growing list of things that the president of the United States officially was not.)[12]

As soon became clear in the apparently endless surprises about the true nature of the Iraqi threat in the aftermath of the ground war of spring 2003, a cavalier attitude toward veracity represented the administration's modus operandi. The case Bush made to convince the nation to embark on its first-ever "preventative" war was riddled with deception from start to finish. The examples of purposeful fraud in the Bush White House's portrayal of the level of alleged threat to Americans' safety and security posed by Iraq's Saddam Hussein are so extensive that only a few examples can be offered here.[13] In September 2002, with British prime minister Tony Blair, Bush claimed, "I would remind you that when the inspectors first went into Iraq and were denied—finally denied access, a report came out of the Atomic—the IAEA [International Atomic Energy Agency]—that they were six months away from developing a [nuclear] weapon. I don't know what more evidence we need." In fact, the estimate to which Bush was referring was more than a decade old and was made before Iraq's military capabilities were decimated in the Gulf War. His press secretary, Ari Fleischer, tried to claim in *The Washington Post* that "It was in fact the International Institute for Strategic Studies that issued the report concluding that Iraq could develop nuclear weapons in as few as six months." But that report, which was unavailable at the time Bush originally made his claim, did not support Bush's statement, either.

In a speech to the nation, Bush also added, "Iraq could decide on any given day to provide a biological or chemical weapon to a terrorist group or individual terrorists," an alliance that "could allow the Iraqi regime to attack America without leaving any fingerprints." But this claim, too, was wholly unsupported and contradicted by CIA intelligence. The testimony, declassified after Bush's speech, rated the possibility as "low" that Hussein would initiate a chemical or biological weapons attack against the United States but might take the "extreme step" of assisting terrorists if provoked by a U.S. attack. In the same speech, Bush warned the nation that Iraq possessed a growing fleet of unmanned aircraft that could be used "for missions targeting the United States." But a CIA report suggested that the fleet was more of an "experiment" and "attempt" and labeled it a "serious threat to Iraq's neighbors and to international military forces in the region"—but said nothing about its having sufficient range to threaten the United States.[14]

Bush's repeated dishonesty did not become widely known to the public until the famous controversy regarding "sixteen words" in his 2003 State of the Union address, referring to the story he told about Iraq's alleged purchase of "yellow-cake" uranium from the African nation of Niger.[15] But the focus on the mere "sixteen words" by the media was most notable for the successful spin that the White House managed to put on the story. For it wasn't that these sixteen words alone in the president's State of the Union message were false. Much of what was presented as evidence for the American attack on Iraq dissipated upon receiving postwar scrutiny. Some of these examples derived, no doubt, from honest errors, relating to the difficulty of accurately assessing decidedly murky intelligence. But Bush and his staff could easily have communicated the complexity of this judgment to the country had honesty been among their primary concerns. In fact, they purposely insisted on exactly the opposite: certainty of knowledge where none was possible. The president and his advisers were virtually unanimous in their insistence that the threat facing the United States from Saddam Hussein and his alleged weapons of mass destruction was all but inarguable. Let just a few examples suffice:

- "Intelligence gathered by this and other governments leaves no doubt that the Iraq regime continues to possess and conceal some of the most lethal weapons ever devised." George W. Bush, address to the nation, March 17, 2003.[16]
- "Simply stated, there is no doubt that Saddam Hussein now has weapons of mass destruction." Dick Cheney, speech to Veterans of Foreign Wars National Convention, August 26, 2002.[17]

- "We know they have weapons of mass destruction. . . . There isn't any debate about it. [It is] beyond anyone's imagination" that UN inspectors would fail to find such weapons if they were given the opportunity. Donald Rumsfeld, September 2002.[18]
- "I'm absolutely sure that there are weapons of mass destruction there, and the evidence will be forthcoming." Colin Powell, remarks to reporters, May 4, 2003.[19]
- "We do know, with absolute certainty, that he is using his procurement system to acquire the equipment he needs in order to enrich uranium to build a nuclear weapon." Dick Cheney, NBC's *Meet the Press,* September 6, 2002.

In fact, every one of the above statements was later judged to be false by the president's own weapons inspections team.[20] While many in and out of government shared the misperception that Iraq might be in possession of such weaponry, only the Bush administration—supported by the Blair administration in Britain—insisted that there could be no possible room for disagreement in assessing the conflicting shards of evidence. In fact, a number of experts within the U.S. government itself were fully aware of how sketchy and incomplete were its sources about Iraq's WMD program, but these people were either ignored or purposely discredited. For instance, a secret September 2002 report of the Pentagon's Defense Intelligence Agency informed Secretary Rumsfeld, "There is no reliable information on whether Iraq is producing and stockpiling chemical weapons, or whether Iraq has—or will—establish its chemical warfare agent production facilities," according to U.S. officials interviewed by the *Los Angeles Times.*[21] When Bruce Hardcastle, a defense intelligence officer for the Middle East, South Asia, and counterterrorism, explained to Bush officials that they were misreading the evidence, according to Patrick Lang, former head of Human Intelligence at CIA, the Bush administration not only removed Hardcastle from his post. "They did away with his job. They wanted just liaison officers who were junior. They didn't want a senior intelligence person who argued with them. Hardcastle said, 'I couldn't deal with these people.' They are such ideologues that they knew what the outcome should be and when they didn't get it from intelligence people they thought they were stupid. They start with an almost pseudo-religious faith. They wanted the intelligence agencies to produce material to show a threat, particularly an imminent threat. Then they worked back to prove their case. It was the opposite of what the process should have been like, that the evidence should prove the case." Greg Thielman, the former head of the Department of State's Bureau of Intelligence and Research, likewise observed, "What everyone in the intelligence community knew was that the White House couldn't care less about any kind of information that there were no WMD or that the U.N. inspectors were very effective. Everyone knew the White House was deaf to that input. It was worse than pressure; they didn't care."[22]

In early October 2003, David Kay, head of the Bush administration's Iraq Survey Group (ISG) charged with finding weapons in postwar Iraq, formally told Congress that after searching for nearly six months, and spending more than $300 million, he and his team could find no evidence of chemical or biological weapons in Iraq, and discovered that the nation's nuclear program was in only "the very most rudimentary" state.[23] This was consistent with claims made previously by administration officials in unguarded moments—claims that went ignored in the near-hysterical atmosphere that the administration stoked during its buildup to war. Two years earlier, for instance, in a February 2001 meeting with Egypt's foreign minister in Cairo, Secretary of State Powell defended the UN economic sanctions then in force against Hussein's Iraq with the explanation, "Frankly, they have worked. He has not developed any significant capability with respect to weapons of mass destruction. He is unable to project conventional power against his neighbors."[24] And, yet, President Bush's commitment to his own fictional version of an alleged Iraqi threat was so strong that he continued to insist on veracity even after his own weapons inspector dismissed it. "Iraq's WMD program spanned more than two decades, involved thousands of people, billions of dollars, and was elaborately shielded by security and deception operations that continued even beyond the end of Operation Iraqi Freedom," Bush argued, adding, entirely falsely, "That is what the report said."[25]

Despite being disproven by its own experts, the administration attempted to maintain the fiction that his prewar arguments and warnings had been borne out with false claims of imaginary discoveries. Asked in the summer of 2003, "Where are the weapons of mass destruction?" Bush replied, "We found them." Vice President Cheney, too, claimed, months later, that "Conclusive evidence now demonstrates that Saddam Hussein did in fact have weapons of mass destruction."[26] Finally, when pressed by ABC News's Diane Sawyer to address the disjunction between his prewar claims and his postwar discoveries, Bush laughed off the reporter's distinction between desire and capability. "What's the difference?" Bush asked.[27] Later, in his third State of the Union address, instead of acknowledging to the nation the misguided nature of his previous warnings following these revelations, Bush attempted a rhetorical sleight of hand, speaking not of Hussein's actual weaponry but of something he termed "weapons-of-mass-destruction-related-program-activity."[28]

A similar pattern emerges when one examines President Bush's repeated attempts to tie Saddam Hussein to Osama bin Laden, a connection that most Americans came to take for granted even though no credible evidence was ever put forth to support it. In an October 7, 2002, speech given in Cincinnati, Bush claimed that high-level contacts between Hussein and al Qaeda "go back a decade." While Bush's statement may be technically accurate, it is also grossly misleading. The contacts in question took place in the early 1990s, when the al Qaeda organization was in its infancy, and the two men were largely allied against the Saudi monarchy. Bush informed his audience that leaders of al Qaeda left Afghanistan for Baghdad, and spoke of a "very senior al Qaeda leader who received medical treatment in Baghdad this year." But, in fact, the Jordanian in question, Abu Mussab Zarqawi, was not, according to U.S. intelligence, actually a member of the bin Laden organization but was the head of a different, unaffiliated group. He traveled under many aliases and spent more time in Iran and Lebanon than in Iraq.[29] Bush and company also repeatedly made the case for war by publicizing the claims of an Iraqi defector named Ihsan Saeed al-Haideri, who maintained that he had been employed at illegal chemical, biological, and nuclear facilities around Baghdad long after the man was revealed to have repeatedly failed polygraph examinations and been rejected as unreliable by U.S. intelligence agencies.[30] The defector's discredited testimony forms a key portion of Secretary of State Powell's argument for war before the United Nations Security Council in February 2003, and he admitted, more than a year later, that his "sourcing was inaccurate and wrong and in some cases, deliberately misleading." And yet even after Powell's admission, in May 2004, a lengthy document in support of the war that relied in part on these same charges remained on the White House's official website.[31]

Vice President Cheney made constant reference to an alleged meeting between lead September 11 hijacker Mohamed Atta and an Iraqi intelligence official, Ahmed Khalil Ibrahim Samir al-Ani, which was said to have occurred in Prague in April 2001. The claim, which was based on the report of a single uncorroborated informant to Czech intelligence, was bandied about repeatedly by pundits sympathetic to the administration's war plans. *The New York Times*'s William Safire even termed it to be an "undisputed fact." Cheney, meanwhile, continued to describe the meeting as "pretty well confirmed," even after Czech president Havel informed President Bush that it had almost certainly not taken place. Moreover, when the high-level al Qaeda leader, Abu Zubaydah, was finally captured in March 2002 in Pakistan, he informed his captors that bin Laden had personally rejected the idea of any kind of alliance with Hussein.[32] Zubaydah's explanation was soon corroborated by testimony from top al Qaeda agents captured later in the spring, including one of the key planners of the September 11 attacks, Khalid Shaikh Mohammed.[33] In July 2003, U.S. military forces finally captured Samir al-Ani, who also denied that any such meeting took place.[34]

When it came to politically or ideologically convenient assertions, the Bush administration proved remarkably unimpressed by the claims of evidence. When, after a careful examination of all the relevant data, including classified data, the official 9/11 Commission staff announced it could find "no credible evidence that Iraq and Al Qaeda cooperated on attacks against the United States," or of any "collaborative relationship" at all between the two, both Bush and Cheney remained unmoved. Asked about the discrepancies between its repeated assertions of an intimate connection and evidence-based conclusion of the Commission staff, Bush replied, "The reason I keep insisting that there was a relationship between Iraq and Saddam and al Qaeda, because there was a relationship between Iraq and al Qaeda." Vice President Cheney, who, only a day before the report was released, had continued to claim that Saddam Hussein had enjoyed "long-established ties with al Qaeda," proved even more combative in the face of contrary evidence. Cheney told a CNBC interviewer "on the question of whether or not there was any kind of a relationship, there clearly was a relationship. It's been testified to. The evidence is overwhelming." He then went on to list what he termed "a whole series of contacts" that he said contradicted the Commission's findings, and even refused to give up his belief that the famous Prague meeting—for which the Commission also could find no evidence—may have taken place. In his repeated references to a "report from the Czechs," about the alleged Prague meeting, Cheney never once noted that President Vaclav Havel himself had withdrawn the contention and blamed the confusion on a single intelligence officer with a drinking problem. Asked by the show's host whether he had claimed that the meeting had been "pretty-well confirmed," Cheney replied, "No, I never said that." In fact, appearing on NBC's *Meet the Press,* on December 9, 2001, Cheney had used these exact words before its many millions of viewers.[35] If any top members of the Bush administration, including the president and vice president, feel any remorse for the falsehoods, either deliberate or unintentional, with which they deceived the nation to make their misleading case for war, the evidence to demonstrate as much is remarkably thin.

In many respects, the atmosphere created by the Bush team was similar to that fostered by President Johnson during the period when Congress passed the Gulf of Tonkin Resolution in August 1964. The Bush deception employed the same manufactured atmosphere of crisis—with analogous exaggeration of the enemy's abilities and similar sorts of pressure placed on investigators and analysts to justify a political course upon which the leadership had already decided to embark. Major General Anthony Zinni, who headed the U.S. Central Command from 1997 to 2000 and was later George W. Bush's special envoy to the Israeli-Palestinian negotiations, observed after the war, "Here we have some strategic thinkers who have long wanted to invade Iraq. They saw an opportunity, and they used the imminence of the threat and the association with terrorism and the 9/11 emotions as a catalyst and justification. It's another Gulf of Tonkin." (After making this statement, Zinni was informed by Bush administration officials that he "will never be used by the White House again.")[36]

The president was aided in his effort to deceive the nation, it must be added, by many in the media. America's most influential interlocutor of foreign affairs, *The New York Times*'s Thomas Friedman, wrote, "As far as I'm concerned, we do not need to find any weapons of mass destruction to justify this war. . . . Mr. Bush doesn't owe the world any explanation for missing chemical weapons (even if it turns out that the White House hyped this issue). It is clear that in ending Saddam's tyranny, a huge human engine for mass destruction has been broken."[37] The editors of *The Washington Post* in large measure concurred. "While the Bush administration may have publicly exaggerated or distorted parts of its case," they wrote, dismissing the inherent value of truth in presidential claims relating to war and peace, "much of what it said reflected a broad international consensus."[38] This too was false, as no nation's population supported the Bush war in Iraq, save Israel's, and Tony Blair's Britain was the only one to contribute to it in significant measure.

The media's delicate treatment of Bush continued even as his justifications for the war were revealed to be fictional. When Bush falsely claimed, following the war, "Did Saddam Hussein have a weapons program? And the answer is: absolutely. And we gave him a chance to allow the inspectors in, and he wouldn't let them in," even a sympathetic reporter like CNN's Howard Kurtz was forced to admit that this assertion had "no relation to reality," as the inspectors had been in Iraq for months before the invasion, making what they insisted was considerable progress in mapping out the weapons Hussein did or did not have. But when Kurtz asked *Washington Post* White House reporter Dana Milbank about Bush's false proclamation on his CNN media program, *Reliable Sources,* the reporter, who had established a deserved reputation as the toughest of all the regular White House correspondents, responded, "I think what people basically decided was this is just the president being the president. Occasionally he plays the wrong track and something comes out quite wrong. He is under a great deal of pressure."[39] No less incredibly, Bush made the same blatantly false assertion months later, at a January 2004 press conference with the Polish president. And for a second time, the mainstream media almost uniformly ignored it. Speaking of Hussein and the inspectors, who were in Iraq at the time Bush announced his decision to go to war, the president's exact words were, "It was his choice to make, and he did not let us in."[40] After witnessing President Bush's tolerant treatment with respect to this uncontestable untruth Secretary of Defense Donald Rumsfeld made a similarly indefensible claim two months later. Responding to CNN's Wolf Blitzer's question about whether, in retrospect, it had been a "mistake to go to war at that time instead of giving the UN more time to continue their own inspections," the defense secretary replied, "Well, the UN inspectors were not in there. The UN inspectors were out." When Blitzer noted that the inspectors had departed only because the United States had made it clear that the war was about to begin, Rumsfeld quickly changed the subject, demanding, "How many resolutions do you want to have?" and charging, again falsely, that Iraq was shooting at U.S. planes "every other day."[41]

If George W. Bush's penchant for deliberate deception was hardly a secret within insider circles, it was ultimately considered to be rather insignificant. In September 2002, ABC's nonpartisan guide to inside politics, *The Note,* noted that the Bush team has always had a credibility problem with some reporters because of its insistence that "up is down" and "black is white."[42] When Dana Milbank bravely collected a number of Bush's falsehoods in a front-page *Washington Post* story in late October 2002, he (or his editors) deliberately avoided using the verb "lie." Instead, readers were treated to complicated linguistic circumlocutions such as the following: Bush's statements represented an "embroidering of key assertions." Presidential assertions were clearly "dubious, if not wrong." The president's "rhetoric has taken some flights of fancy . . . taken some liberties . . . omitted qualifiers," and "simply outpace[d] the facts."[43] Indeed, the words "President Bush lied" have not, to my knowledge, appeared in any major American newspaper during the president's term. Legendary *Washington Post* editor Ben Bradlee observes, "Even the very best newspapers have never learned how to handle public figures who lie with a straight face. No editor would dare print this version of Nixon's first comments on Watergate, for instance: '"The Watergate break-in involved matters of national security," President Nixon told a national TV audience last night and for that reason he would be unable to comment on the bizarre burglary. That is a lie.'" Part of the explanation for this is deference to the office and the belief that the American public will not accept a mere reporter's calling the president a liar. Another factor is the insular nature of Washington's insider culture—a society in which it is considered a graver matter to label another person a "liar" than it is to actually be one. And, finally, together with the rise of Reaganism and the ascension of the Republican Far Right, many ideologically driven reporters view their allegiance to the cause of their allies as trumping that of their journalistic responsibilities. The journalist Robert Novak—who played so significant a role in attempting to destroy the credibility of State Department official Joseph Wilson by announcing the identity of his CIA-agent spouse when Wilson was revealing Bush's deception regarding the phony Niger uranium sale—admitted during the Iran-Contra crisis that he did not mind at all being the conduit of official lies so long as they served the ideological causes in which he believed. In that particular case, Novak was explaining that he "admired" Reagan official Elliott Abrams for lying to him on his television program in order to hide the U.S. government role in support of the Contras.[44] Novak's admission that the truth took a backseat to his own ideological loyalties—as was the case with his role in the Wilson-Plame affair—did nothing to diminish his standing among the top coterie of journalists in Washington, nor endanger his status as a columnist for *The Washington Post* and a regular commentator on CNN.

Such deference—to say nothing of the ideological self-censorship—is not only not in the interest of the nation, it is a disservice to the president as well. As the cases studied in this book have demonstrated, presidents do themselves no favors when they tell significant lies to the nation, and journalists do no favors to either party when they let those lies pass without comment. As Ben Bradlee observes in his ruminations on the topic, "Just think for a minute how history might have changed if Americans had known then that their leaders felt the [Vietnam] war was going to hell in a handbasket? In the next seven years, thousands of American lives and more thousands of Asian lives would have been saved. The country might never have lost faith in its leaders."[45]

The virtue of truth in the American presidency had, for all practical purposes, become entirely operational. Whether its citizens were aware of it or not, the presidency now operated in a "post-truth" political environment. American presidents could no longer depend on the press—its powers and responsibilities enshrined in the First Amendment—to keep them honest. And the resulting death, destruction, and general chaos that seemed ready to explode on a daily basis in Iraq following the U.S. invasion seemed to be just one price that "reality" was demanding in return.

In George W. Bush's case, the cost of lying was also partially personal, as his popularity ratings fell significantly in February 2004 in the wake of David Kay's revelations about the true state of Iraq's weapons program.[46] A *Time*/CNN poll found that only 44 percent of Americans now considered Bush to be "a leader you can trust."[47] But more critically for the nation, and the future security of the planet, according to a range of foreign policy experts surveyed by *The Washington Post*—including die-hard Bush supporters—Bush's untrustworthiness profoundly undermined the credibility of the administration abroad, its ability to do business in the world on the basis of its good word, and the value of U.S. intelligence. The consequences were hardly academic. "The foreign policy blowback is pretty serious," admitted Kenneth Adelman, a member of the Pentagon's Defense Advisory Board and an extremely hawkish supporter of the war. Richard Haas, the (Republican) former head of the Department of State Policy Planning office under President Bush, admitted that the result was to "make it more difficult on some future occasion if the United States argues the intelligence warrants something controversial, like a preventive attack." Indeed, following the revelations about Bush's misleading of the nation, China rejected U.S. intelligence that North Korea has a secret program to enrich uranium for use in weapons, thereby considerably complicating American efforts to reduce the likelihood of a nuclear standoff in that region.[48]

"To Begin the World All Over Again"

Why do American presidents feel compelled to deceive Congress, the media, and their country about their most significant decisions? Perhaps the most elegant defense for such behavior can be found in the arguments of a mentor of a number of the planners of President Bush's war in Iraq. Abram M. Shulsky, who headed the Pentagon's Office of Special Forces, whose work was used to override professional CIA analyses in favor of war, was, like the war's primary intellectual inspiration, Undersecretary of Defense Paul Wolfowitz, as well as many other neoconservatives, an admirer of the late political philosopher and refugee from Nazi Germany, Leo Strauss, who died in 1973. Together with Gary Schmitt, who heads the Project for a New American Century—the Washington think tank where the war strategy was originally conceived—Shulsky authored an essay published in 1999 entitled "Leo Strauss and the World of Intelligence (by Which We Do Not Mean *Nous*)." In it, the authors argue that Strauss's idea of hidden meaning "alerts one to the possibility that political life may be closely linked to deception. Indeed, it suggests that deception is the norm in political life, and the hope, to say nothing of the expectation, of establishing a politics that can dispense with it is the exception."[49]

Robert Pippin, the chairman of the Committee on Social Thought at the University of Chicago and a critic of Strauss, explains, "Strauss believed that good statesmen have powers of judgment and must rely on an inner circle. The person who whispers in the ear of the King is more important than the King. If you have that talent, what you do or say in public cannot be held accountable in the same way." NYU philosopher Stephen Holmes concurs, "They believe that your enemy is deceiving you, and you have to pretend to agree, but secretly you follow your own views." He continued, "The whole story is complicated by Strauss's idea—actually Plato's—that philosophers need to tell noble lies not only to the people at large but also to powerful politicians." Even Strauss's admirers concede this point. Joseph Cropsey, Strauss's close friend and colleague at the University of Chicago, as well as the editor of his work, explains that in Straussian thought, a degree of public deception is considered absolutely necessary. "That people in government have to be discreet in what they say publicly is so obvious—'If I tell you the truth I can't but help the enemy.'"[50]

However high-minded, the argument does not really convince. In the examples examined here—including those involving George W. Bush—we find that presidents lie largely for reasons of political convenience. The decisions to lie—if these can even be considered "decisions," as there is no evidence that any of the presidents discussed here even considered the ramifications of telling the truth—were bred of a fundamental contradiction at the heart of the practice of American democracy. American presidents have no choice but to practice the diplomacy of great power politics, but American citizens have rarely if ever been asked to understand the world in these terms. As the dissident Kennedy-Johnson aide George Ball observed, in 1967, "We have used the vocabulary and syntax of Wilsonian Universalism while actively practicing the politics of alliances and spheres of influence and it is now time that we stopped confusing ourselves with our political hyperbole."[51] The result, more often than not, is that when deals must be struck and compromises made on behalf of large purposes, presidents tend to prefer deception over education. This choice is one with deep roots in American history, politics, and culture, dating back to the founding of the nation itself.

At the time of their revolution, Americans believed they were opening what Thomas Jefferson termed a new "chapter in the history of man."[52] The two enormous oceans that separated them from the rest of the world's great powers, along with the magnificent physical bounty provided by their lands, constituted, in their eyes, a sign of divine providence. As a consequence, Americans considered themselves to be outside of, and unbounded by, the system of great power politics that had historically guided relations between nations. "We have it in our power," cried Thomas Paine, in a phrase frequently borrowed by Ronald Reagan, "to begin the world all over again."[53] Even the profoundly unsentimental Alexander Hamilton was imbued with this intoxicating vision. "It seems to have been reserved," he wrote in *Federalist 1,* "to the people of this country, by their conduct and example, to decide the important question, whether societies of men are really capable or not, of establishing good government from reflection and choice, or whether they are forever destined to depend, for their political constitutions, on accident and force . . . a wrong election of the part we shall act, may, in this view, deserve to be considered as the general misfortune of mankind."[54] In his choice of words, Hamilton was echoing his contemporary Benjamin Franklin, who wrote from Paris to a friend in 1777, "It is a common observation here that our cause is the cause of all mankind, and that we are fighting for their liberty in defending our own. It is a glorious task assigned to us by Providence, which has, I trust, given us spirit and virtue equal to it."[55]

The founders blamed the European system of politics between nation-states for the breeding of war and poverty. Their natural inclination was to attempt to withdraw themselves entirely from the world of diplomats and armies.[56] Albert Gallatin, then a Republican leader in Congress, tried to limit the number of American ministers accredited to European capitals. He argued that as the primary purpose of American foreign policy was commercial, consuls could handle all the necessary diplomacy. Americans even refused to appoint diplomats with the rank of ambassador until 1893, believing that the title smacked of royalism. Gallatin and his Jeffersonian allies also sharply opposed Federalist plans to expand the Navy, which they insisted would threaten the survival of republican institutions at home.[57] Americans sought to enjoy the material benefits of liberal trade, while simultaneously protecting their fragile republican institutions from the degenerative moral viruses running rampant in the Old World. No matter how just the cause of a foreign power might be, the founders counseled abstention.

In what would become the sacred tablets of U.S. foreign policy for the nation's first century, President Washington's Farewell Address counseled future generations to protect their noble experiment by remaining above the petty animosities of European politics, and to value peace above almost any other goal. While he recommended "harmony" and "liberal intercourse" with all nations, Americans were never to "seek nor grant exclusive favors or preferences." "There can be no greater error," Washington insisted, "than to expect or calculate upon real favors from nation to nation."[58] John Quincy Adams, perhaps the nation's most successful diplomat, drew on these same ideas and achieved even greater heights of eloquence, when, in 1821, he issued a blistering warning for the ages:

> Wherever the standard of freedom and independence has been or shall be unfurled, there will her [America's] heart, her benedictions and her prayers be. But she goes not abroad, in search of monsters to destroy. She is the well-

> wisher to the freedom and independence of all. She is the champion and vindicator only of her own. . . . She well knows that by once enlisting under other banners than her own, were they even the banners of foreign independence, she would involve herself, beyond the power of extrication, in all the wars of interest and intrigue, of individual avarice, envy, and ambition, which assume the colors and usurp the standard of freedom. . . . She might become the dictatress of the world; she would no longer be the ruler of her own spirit.[59]

However dramatically the world has changed since the days of Washington and Quincy Adams, the American attitude toward the typical give-and-take of relations between nations has scarcely matured.[60] Between its founding in the late eighteenth century and its ascension to world power status in the early twentieth, the United States underwent periods of withdrawal and expansion, of missionary fervor and commercial imperialism, of attempted "isolation" and gunboat diplomacy. But rarely if ever did America's leaders attempt to explain the need for patient compromise and strategic trade-offs in diplomatic exchange between nations. Whether looking inward or outward, whether seeking to buy and sell merchandise or seeking to save souls, whether providing an example to the world or forcibly reordering its societies, Americans continued to view themselves very much as innocents in a corrupt world, who descend into that corruption at the expense of their national identity.

In the late nineteenth and early twentieth centuries, this desire to disengage from foreign influences transformed itself into a zealous missionary impulse to remake the world in our own image—a desire that perhaps reached its rhetorical zenith under President Wilson. To Wilson, nothing that concerned humanity could be "foreign or indifferent to" the interests of the United States.[61] We were the planet's "only idealistic nation," charged with "redeem[ing] the world by giving it peace and justice."[62] In 1915 Wilson announced that America could "not confine our enthusiasm for individual liberty and free national development to the incidents and movements of affairs which affect only ourselves. We feel it wherever there is a people that tries to walk in these difficult paths of independence and right."[63] While Wilson's missionary impulse may have directly contradicted the belief by Washington and Adams et al. that the United States should steer clear of foreign entanglements, it was nevertheless inspired by the same conviction that America was different—better than other nations, and charged with a divine duty not to allow itself to be dragged into their petty, self-interested manipulations. The Wilsonian tradition remained strong in the presidencies of both FDR and

JFK, and indeed their speeches are imbued with its characteristic rhetorical flourishes and global ambitions.

This tendency is hardly surprising as both are carrying out a tradition with the deepest roots imaginable on American soil. In his landmark 1952 essay, *Errand in the Wilderness,* Perry Miller suggested that the Puritan crossing of the Atlantic had been "an essential maneuver in the drama of Christendom." The Puritans left England not as indigent refugees, but as "an organized task force of Christians" bent on creating a model of a reformed society that their fellow Englishman at home could emulate."[64] They came to create, in the words of their leader John Winthrop, "a City upon a Hill, [for] the eyes of all people are upon us." It was Winthrop whom Ronald Reagan quoted in a nationally televised presidential debate in 1980.[65]

"Public Opinion and Its Problems"

American political rhetoric tends to accept, a priori, claims like Reagan's divine provenance, moral superiority vis-à-vis the rest of the world, and an allegedly unyielding commitment to democracy at home and abroad. The truth, however, as most of us recognize, is that our history opens up each one of these claims to rather considerable challenge. It is important that we likewise understand that, even with the best of intentions, the exercise of political democracy is inherently problematic and only partially practicable. In a series of visionary works on its inner workings published in the early 1920s, Walter Lippmann examined what he believed to be the necessary preconditions for the operation of a successful democratic republic—a competent, civic-minded citizenry with access to relevant details of public policy. He found that the entire notion is dangerously utopian and ought to be shelved. At the heart of republican theory, in Lippmann's view, stood the "omnicompetent" citizen. "It was believed that if only he could be taught more facts, if only he would take more interest, if only he would listen to more lectures and read more reports, he would gradually be trained to direct public affairs." Unfortunately, Lippmann concluded, "The whole assumption is false."[66]

In truth, Lippmann argued, "public opinion" is shaped in response to people's "maps" or "images" of the world, and not to the world itself.[67] Mass political consciousness does not pertain to the actual environment, but to an intermediary "pseudo-environment." To complicate matters, this pseudo-environment is further corrupted by the manner in which it is perceived. Citizens have only limited time and attention to devote to issues of public concern. News is designed for mass consumption, and, hence, the media must employ a relatively simple vocabulary and linear story line to discuss highly complex and decidedly nonlinear situations. The competition for readership (and advertising dollars) drives the press to present news reports in ways that sensationalize and oversimplify, while more significant information goes unreported and unremarked upon. Given both the economic and professional limitations of the practice of journalism, Lippmann argued, news "comes [to us] helter-skelter." This is fine for a baseball box score, a transatlantic flight, or the death of a monarch. But where the picture is more nuanced, "as for example, in the matter of a success of a policy or the social conditions among a foreign people—where the real answer is neither yes or no, but subtle and a matter of balanced evidence," then journalism "causes no end of derangement, misunderstanding and even misinterpretation."[68] And here, it must be added, Lippmann was identifying a problem that has since increased in both time and scope, as media sensationalism and public apathy have increased manyfold since the publication of his prophetic work.

Lippmann's pseudo-environment is not composed only of the information we receive; it consists, in equal measure, of what Lippmann terms "the pictures in our heads." Voters react to the news through the lens of a personal history containing certain stereotypes, predispositions, and emotional associations that determine their interpretations. We emphasize that which confirms our original beliefs and disregard or denigrate what might contradict them. Lippmann compares the average citizen to a blind spectator sitting in the back row of a sporting event. "He does not know what is happening, why it is happening, what ought to happen; he lives in a world which he cannot see, does not understand and is unable to direct."[69] As a result, Lippmann lamented, democracy, in modern society, operates for only "a very small percentage of those who are theoretically supposed to govern."[70] No one expects a steelworker, musician, or banker to understand physics, Lippmann believed, so why should they be expected to understand politics?

John Dewey replied to Lippmann in the May 3, 1922, *New Republic* and later in an important, though tendentiously written work, *The Public and Its Problems,* published in 1927.[71] Dewey conceded that voters were not "omnicompetent"—that is, "competent to frame policies, to judge their results, competent to know . . . what is for his own good" and passionately shared his republican hope that government could be formed to inspire generosity and civic-mindedness in the citizenry.[72] But he disagreed with Lippmann's sanguine trust in the beneficence of elites. "A class of experts," he argued, "is inevitably so removed from common interests as to become a class with private interests and private knowledge, which in social matters is not knowledge at all."[73] An expert shoemaker may know best how to fix a shoe, but only its wearer knows where it hurts. "Democracy must begin at home . . . and its home is in the neighborly community."[74] Unfortunately, Dewey noted, "Indifference is the evidence of current apathy, and apathy is testimony to the fact the public is so bewildered that it cannot find itself."[75]

Taken together, the traditions described above provide at least a partial explanation for the constancy of presidential deception in American political life. On the one hand, Americans carry an unrealistic picture of the world "in their heads"—one based on their faith in their own divine direction, disinterested altruism, and democratic bona fides, rather than the realities of politics, force, and diplomacy. But they remain immune to education regarding these realities, in part because of the power these myths continue to enjoy in our education system, media, and larger social discourse, as well as the failures inherent in the practice of democracy. These failures, moreover, are exaggerated in the American case by a particular distaste for the practice of power politics and a media that has insufficient commercial incentive to provide the basics of civic literacy to its audience. Even those presidents with the best of intentions come to view deception as an unavoidable consequence of a system that simply cannot integrate the unpleasant realities of international diplomacy. However preferable it might be to tell the truth, the short-term costs of lying, given that the culture seems to expect them, are negligible. And as Friedrich Nietzsche instructed, these temptations are virtually impossible to resist. While people may desire "the agreeable life-preserving consequences of truth, [they are] indifferent to pure knowledge, which has no consequences, [and are] even hostile to possibly damaging and destructive truths." The long-term costs of lying—at least at the moment the lie is being told—are almost always invisible.[76] The ultimate costs for this easy calculation, however, are considerable, not only to the nation, and to the cause of democracy, but also to the aspirations and legacies of the presidents themselves.

Whether this situation is remediable depends on one of two possibilities: either future presidents become convinced that the long-term cost of deception outweighs its short-term benefits, or the public matures to the point of seeking to educate itself about the need for complicated arrangements in international politics that do not comport with the nation's caricatured notion of itself as a force for innocence and benevolence the world over. The obvious solution would be to convince U.S. presidents of the value of substituting a long-term strategic vision in place of their present-minded, short-term tactical views. But "Nothing in politics is more difficult than taking the long view," notes the reporter Ronald Brownstein. "For politicians, distant gain is rarely a persuasive reason to endure immediate pain. Political scientists would say the system has a bias toward the present over the future. Parents might say politicians behave like perpetual teenagers. The problem, for politicians as much as teenagers, is that the future has a pesky habit of arriving."[77]

Political courage in truth telling is not entirely without recent precedent. Harry Truman apparently considered offering Americans a morsel of the kind of straight talk for which he is often perhaps overly generously credited upon his return from Potsdam. Speechwriter Samuel Rosenman authored a draft of a radio speech that bravely admitted, "I must in all candor say that I did not like this provision of the Berlin agreement. I still do not like it. Until almost the end of the Conference, I declined to agree to it. However, every international agreement has in it the element of compromise. This one is no exception. No one nation can expect to get everything it wants. It is a question of give and take—of being willing to meet your neighbor half-way. In this instance there is much to justify the action taken. Most of it had already been agreed on at Crimea."[78] When it came time for Truman to speak these words to the country, however, he dropped the section regarding the provisions of the agreement he did not favor and spoke only in the abstract of the worthiness of compromising with a neighbor.[79] (He was almost certainly referring to the drawing of the Oder–Neisse line and the expulsion of the Germans.) Even so banal and imprecise an admission was apparently judged too risky for the president to say aloud. While Truman gave Americans more of the story than most presidents would have, he spoke of concession and compromise in such general terms that they were unlikely to inspire any genuine debate about the merits in this particular case. When it came to specifics, he spoke only of the aspects of the agreement likely to be popular with Americans.

To find an example of a modern statesman offering the kind of truth-telling proposed here, we must turn to France's President Charles de Gaulle in the midst of that nation's disengagement with its longtime colony, Algeria, during the late 1950s and early 1960s. When the painful moment of separation arrived, de Gaulle did not seek to deceive his nation. Rather, he treated his compatriots like adults, advising them to swallow the bitter pill and find a way to achieve France's aims of national greatness by alternative means. It was no mean feat. De Gaulle's concessions to achieve Algerian independence had inspired an attempted coup d'état at home and many feared the possibility of civil war—dangers no American president has been asked to face for over a century and a half.[80]

In addition to these challenges, de Gaulle even had the same Cold War excuse that American leaders have found so compelling a justification for their lies, for he was well aware of the potential for Soviet mischief in Algeria and that he faced a danger in that regard either way. He told a Tunisian visitor that he was concerned that the FLN could fall into "Khrushchev's clutches" and that it was more important to him than the fact that they represented "nine-tenths" of the Algerian population, in sentiment, at least. He also noted that the Soviet ambassador in Paris left him with the "clear impression that his country intended to intervene more and more in Algeria."[81] And yet de Gaulle took none of the dishonest shortcuts that are second nature to U.S. presidents today. He allowed himself to be denounced by right-wing members of the Assembly for "capitulation," but became a hero to the country at large.[82] As Tony Smith notes in his history of the incident, "That Algeria is such a relatively minor issue comes in large measure from the way de Gaulle isolated and discredited his opponents while at the same time rallying the mass of his countrymen to a new vision of themselves in the world. With bold policy initiatives on matters relating to the Atlantic Alliance, European unity, and Eastern Europe, the General restored a sense of his country's international importance. As for Algeria, he achieved what the 4th Republic had lost all hope of doing by 1957: by granting independence he maintained (and indeed even increased) the self-respect of his people."[83]

If the accounts told in this book teach us anything, it is that presidents cannot lie about major political events that have potentially serious ramifications—particularly those relating to war and peace—with impunity. These lies inevitably turn into monsters that strangle their creators. Had FDR told the truth about Yalta to the country, it is far more likely that the United States would have participated in the creation of the kind of world community he envisioned when he made his ultimately counterproductive secret agreements. John Kennedy's deception about the nature of the deal to which he agreed to ensure the removal of Soviet missiles from Cuba also proved enormously detrimental to his hope to create a lasting, stable peace in the context of Cold War competition. Lyndon Johnson destroyed not only his ambitious hopes to create a "Great Society," but also his own presidency and most of his political reason for being. And Ronald Reagan, through his lies about Central America, created a dynamic through which his advisers believed they had a right to initiate a secret, illegal foreign and military policy whose aims were almost perfectly contradictory to the president's stated aims in such crucial areas as dealing with governments deemed to be terrorist. When it was finally revealed, this disjunction paralyzed U.S. diplomacy and nearly caused the downfall of the Reagan administration as well. In 1992, it had the effect of undermining George Bush's second presidential candidacy.

In a better world, future U.S. presidents would learn the obvious lessons from the experiences of their predecessors: Protect genuine secrets by refusing to answer certain questions, certainly. Put the best face on your own actions and those of the politicians you support, of course. Create a zone of privacy for yourself and your family that is declared off-limits to all public inquiry. But do not, under any circumstances, lie.

NOTES

I. Introduction: On Lies, Personal and Presidential

1. Maureen Dowd, "Liberties: Xiao Bushi on the Tiger," *New York Times,* April 8, 2001.
2. When I raised the question to Ms. Dowd in a phone call, she said she thought the point was better made in William Safire's Sunday "On Language" column in *The New York Times Magazine.*
3. See "Report: Presidents Washington Through Bush May Have Lied About Key Matters," *The Onion,* December 4, 2002.
4. Michael Getler, "Wanted: More Woodwards (and Bernsteins)," *The Washington Post,* May 2, 2004.
5. The Jayson Blair episode received 1,428 mentions in U.S. newspapers in the two weeks after *The New York Times* detailed his fabrications, in addition to a single *Times* article of more than fourteen thousand words, one of the longest it has ever published. For a discussion of the treatment of Bush's deceptions, see Susan D. Moeller, "Media Coverage of Weapons of Mass Destruction," May 5–26, 1998; October 11–31, 2002; May 1–21, 2003, Center for International and Security Studies, University of Maryland (College Park, MD, 2004), *http://www.cissm.umd.edu/documents/WMDstudy_full.pdf.* See also Eric Alterman, *What Liberal Media? The Truth About Bias and the News,* paperback ed. (New York: Basic Books, 2004), 268–92.
6. Oddly, however, the impeachment articles voted by the House of Representatives failed to specify exactly what Bill Clinton had done to deserve it. Yes, we were told that he had lied and allegedly conspired to obstruct justice, but many presidents had done the same thing. Why Clinton? Which lie, exactly, was the one that sent him into the history books with this symbol of ignominy forever beside his name? Fortunately, for history's sake, while the articles themselves remained wholly vague on this point, House impeachment manager Bill McCollum (R-FL) was willing to offer an explanation. It is the only one, insofar as I could discover, that explains the mystery at the center of the drama. Speaking to the nation during the dramatic hearings, McCollum read from page 547 of what he called "the big document that we have published here." The page, taken from Clinton's deposition, read as follows:

   Clinton: "You are free to infer that my testimony is that I did not have sexual relations as I understood the term to be used."

   Question: "Including touching her breasts, kissing her breasts, or touching her genitalia?"

   Clinton: "That's correct."

   "That is specifically, if anybody wants to know, where the president committed perjury," McCollum instructed the nation. "If you remember, that it was a very specific definition and it included in it touching of breasts and genitalia." See Jeffrey Toobin, *A Vast Conspiracy* (New York: Random House, 2000), 360.

7. Quote in Eric Boehlert, "The Press vs. Al Gore," *Rolling Stone,* December 6–13, 2000.
8. For a lengthy discussion of the role of lies in the 2000 campaign, see Alterman, *What Liberal Media? The Truth About Bias and the News* (New York: Basic Books, 2003), 148–75.
9. Michel de Montaigne, *Essays,* J. M. Cohen, trans. and intro. (New York: Penguin Books, 1978), 31.
10. In her extremely useful study of the various implications of lies and lying, Evelin Sullivan lists the number of forms deception takes according to just the Freudian model, as developed by Anna Freud. She lists them as follows:

- *Denial* is the ego's way to protect the self from unpleasant reality by making it refuse to perceive it.
- *Repression* prevents painful or dangerous thoughts from entering consciousness.
- *Displacement* discharges pent-up feelings, usually of hostility, on objects less dangerous than those that actually aroused the emotion.
- *Isolation* cuts off emotional charge from hurtful situations or separates incompatible attitudes by compartments impervious to logic; it does so by never allowing connected thoughts about conflicting attitudes or about their relation to each other.
- *Rationalization* is the attempt to prove to oneself that one's behavior is rational and justifiable and thus worthy of the approval of oneself and others.
- *Projection* places blame for one's difficulties on others or attributes one's own desires to others.
- *Sublimation* gratifies or works off frustrated sexual desires by substituting them for nonsexual desires socially accepted by one's culture.
- *Fantasy* gratifies frustrated desires in imaginary achievements, most commonly through daydreaming.
- *Reaction formation* prevents dangerous desires from being expressed by exaggerating opposing attitudes and types of behavior and using them as barriers.
- *Introjection* incorporates external values and standards into the ego structure so the self is not at the mercy of them as external threats.

Additional ego-defense mechanisms Sullivan lists as being suggested by later researchers include:

- *Distortion,* which grossly reshapes external reality to meet the inner needs of the one doing the distorting.
- *Hypochondriasis,* which transforms anger toward another person into anger toward oneself and then into the perception of pain and other physical symptoms.
- Passive-aggressive behavior, which involves hurting or defeating oneself in order to make others feel guilty or thwart their wishes.
- *Disassociation,* which moves ideas, memories, or experiences that may elicit intolerable feelings out of conscious awareness.
- *Suppression,* which excludes thought or feelings from the conscious but differs from repression in allowing retrieval of memories at a more appropriate time.

See Evelin Sullivan, *The Concise Book of Lying* (New York: Farrar, Straus & Giroux, 2001), 175–76. See also, for example, Ludwig Wittgenstein, *Philosophical Investigations,* 2nd ed., G. E. M. Anscombe, trans. (Oxford: Basil Blackwell, 1958); Michel Foucault,

The Archeology of Knowledge, A. M. Sheridan, trans. (New York: Pantheon, 1972); Jacques Derrida, *Of Grammatology,* Gayatri Chakravoty Spivak, trans. (Baltimore: Johns Hopkins University Press, 1976); William James, *Essays in Pragmatism,* Albury Castell, ed. and intro. (New York: Hafner, 1948); Richard Rorty, *Philosophy and the Mirror of Nature* (Princeton, NJ: Princeton University Press, 1979); John Dewey, *The Public and Its Problems* (New York: H. Holt and Co., 1927), which should be read in concert with Walter Lippmann, *Public Opinion* (New York: Penguin Books, 1946, © 1922). For useful discussions of some of these authors and the issues they raise for the study of history, see Peter Novick, *That Noble Dream: The Objectivity Question and the American Historical Profession* (New York: Cambridge University Press, 1988); Terry Eagleton, *Literary Theory: An Introduction* (Cambridge, MA: Blackwell, 1996, © 1983); Robert B. Westbrook, *John Dewey and American Democracy* (Ithaca, NY: Cornell University Press, 1991); Alan Ryan, *John Dewey and the High Tide of American Liberalism* (New York: W. W. Norton, 1995); Todd Gitlin, *The Twilight of Common Dreams: Why America Is Wracked by Culture Wars* (New York: Metropolitan Books, 1995); Richard Rorty, *Achieving Our Country: Leftist Thought in Twentieth-Century America* (Cambridge, MA: Harvard University Press, 1998) and *Philosophy and Social Hope* (New York: Penguin Books, 1999); Robert F. Berkhofer, *Beyond the Great Story: History as Text and Discourse* (Cambridge, MA: Harvard University Press, 1995); Louis Menand, ed., *Pragmatism: A Reader* (New York: Vintage, 1997); Louis Menand, *The Metaphysical Club: A Story of Ideas in America* (New York: Farrar, Straus & Giroux, 2001); Mark Lilla, *New French Thought: Political Philosophy* (Princeton, NJ: Princeton University Press, 1994) and *The Reckless Mind: Intellectuals in Politics* (New York: New York Review of Books, 2001); James T. Kloppenberg, "Pragmatism: An Old Name for Some New Ways of Thinking?" *Journal of American History* 83 (June 1996): 136–37; Frank Ninkovich, "No Post-Mortems for Postmodernism, Please," *Diplomatic History* 22 (Summer 1998); Todd Gitlin, "Postmodernism: Roots and Politics—What Are They Talking About?" *Dissent* (Winter 1989); Perez Zagorin, "History, the Referent, and Narrative: Reflections on Postmodernism Now," *History & Theory* 38 (February 1999).

11. Friedrich Nietzsche, "On Truth and Lie in an Extra Moral Sense" (a fragment published posthumously) in *The Portable Nietzsche,* Walter Kaufmann, ed., intro., trans. (New York: Penguin Books, 1954), 42–47.
12. Ibid. I share with Friedrich Nietzsche the view "What is a word? The image of a nerve stimulus in sounds. But to infer from the nerve stimulus, a cause outside us, that is already the result of a false and unjustified application of the principle of reason . . . The different languages, set side by side, show that what matters with words is never the truth, never an adequate expression; else there would not be so many languages. The 'thing in itself' (for that is what pure truth, without consequences, would be) is quite incomprehensible to the creations of language and not at all worth aiming for."
13. Theodore Sorensen, *Kennedy* (New York: Harper and Row, 1965), 509.
14. Seymour Hersh, "A New National Bargain," *OLAM* 5761 (Summer 2000): 15.
15. Ibid.
16. All citations are to the King James version.
17. Sullivan, *The Concise Book of Lying,* 25.
18. St. Augustine, "Against Lying," *Treatises on Various Subjects,* Roy J. Defarrari, ed., *The Fathers of the Church,* vol. 16 (Washington: Catholic University of America Press, 1952), ch. 18, par. 37.
19. See Thomas Aquinas, *Summa Theologica,* The Fathers of the English Dominican Province, trans. (London: Burns, Oates & Washbourne, 1922), 2:2 ques. 100, art. 4; and "The Evil of Lying," in *Summa of Theology: The Pocket Aquinas,* Vernon J. Bourke, ed. (New York: Washington Square Press, 1968), 218.

20. The social philosopher known as "Miss Manners" appears on point to this author in this regard when she explains, "The moral superiority of substituting 'You look awful' and 'I find your parties such a drag that I'd rather stay home and do nothing' for such sinful untruths as 'How nice to see you' and 'Oh, I'm sorry, I'm busy then' is not apparent to Miss Manners." See Judith Martin, *Miss Manners Rescues Civilization* (New York: Crown, 1996), 96.
21. See Immanuel Kant, "On the Supposed Right to Lie from Altruistic Motives," in *The Critique of Practical Reason and Other Writings,* Lewis White Beck, ed. and trans. (Chicago: University of Chicago Press, 1949), 346–50. Benjamin Constant from France, 1797, part VI, no. 1, 121–24, is quoted in Kant's essay. See also Benjamin Constant, *Political Writings,* Biancamaria Fontana and Raymone Guess, eds. (New York: Cambridge University Press, 1988).
22. Hannah Arendt, "Lying in Politics: Reflections on the Pentagon Papers," in *Crises of the Republic* (New York: Harcourt Brace Jovanovich, 1972), 4.
23. See Deborah A. Kashy and Bella M. DePaulo, "Who Lies," *Journal of Personality and Social Psychology* 70(5) (1998): 1037.
24. Bella M. DePaulo, Deborah A. Kashy, Susan E. Kirkendol, Melissa M. Wyer, and Jennifer A. Epstein, "Lying in Everyday Life," *Journal of Personality and Social Psychology* 70(5) (1998): 991, 993.
25. David Shaw, "Tinseltown Spins Yarns—Media Take Bait," *Los Angeles Times,* February 12, 2001.
26. John Horn, "The Reviewer Who Wasn't There," *Newsweek,* June 11, 2001.
27. Liza Featherstone, "Faking It: Sex, Lies, and Women's Magazines," *Columbia Journalism Review,* March 2002, *http://www.alternet.org/story.html?StoryID=12543.*
28. *Wall Street Journal,* June 20, 2002; *New York Times,* June 22, 2002 (for Rite Aid); *New York Times,* June 26, 2002 (for Wal-Mart); *Washington Post,* June 26, 2002, and *Wall Street Journal,* September 19, 2002 (*http://online.wsj.com/home/us*) (for WorldCom); *Wall Street Journal,* June 28, 2002 (for Xerox); *Wall Street Journal,* August 7, 2002 (for Tyco International).
29. James Lardner, "Why Should Anyone Believe You?" *Business 2.0,* March 2002, 42.
30. Tim Rutten, "Digging for the Truth in Colson's Column," *Los Angeles Times,* March 29, 2002, *http://www.imglmb1.com/tribune/0207/tld_att_latimes.html.*
31. Louis Menand, "False Fronts," *New Yorker,* July 23, 3001.
32. Sally Quinn, "Not in Their Backyard: In Washington, That Letdown Feeling," *Washington Post,* November 2, 1998.
33. Ibid.
34. George F. Will, *Washington Post,* December 20, 1998.
35. Thomas Nagel, "The Shredding of Public Privacy," *Times Literary Supplement,* January 24, 1999.
36. See Sissela Bok, *Lying: Moral Choices in Public and Private Life* (New York: Vintage, 1978), 139.
37. See Walter Lippmann, *The Phantom Public* (New York: Macmillan and Co., 1924), 13–14.
38. Dean Acheson, *Present at the Creation: My Years in the State Department* (New York: W. W. Norton, 1969), 375.
39. Robert Entman notes that the most detailed data on the public's use of the news media come from the 1974 national survey by the University of Michigan Center for Political Studies (CPS), which portrays a public that fails to meet these expectations. Respondents who said they read two or three newspapers and all four types of news coverage "frequently" represent only 5.6 percent of the sample. Those who read the four categories frequently but only in one paper represent 6.5 percent of the sample, for a total of no more than 12 percent who are frequent readers. To take another angle,

slightly under one in seven Americans (13.7 percent) report reading two or more papers and watching the national evening news frequently. All of these data are based on self-reports and imprecise categories like "frequently"; they almost certainly overestimate media use. Most people believe it desirable to show interest, and many inflate their claims of good citizenship. The number who attend carefully and habitually to a variety of media is probably lower than the data suggest.

Similar results emerge from less detailed questions on the 1984 Michigan CPS survey. For example, those who report watching the national news on TV five, six, or seven days during the previous week and regularly reading two or three newspapers total 15.5 percent of the sample, close to the 1974 result. In the past decade, newspaper circulation per household and the ratings of national news shows have both decreased markedly. These data suggest that no more than 15 percent of the public fulfills the standard of extensive and intensive use of a variety of media to monitor news of public affairs. The 1984 survey also asked respondents which party had majorities in the House and Senate before and after the 1984 election. The election did not alter party dominance; the Democrats had controlled the House for thirty years, the Republicans had run the Senate for four. With four chances to give a correct answer (House and Senate preelection, House and Senate postelection), only 19.7 percent got four correct and 6.0 percent got three. About half the sample knew one or two answers, and a quarter, none. Or consider this: the percentage of the public unable to name any congressional candidate in their district was 45 percent in 1956. In 1984, 68 percent failed. If there are any trends in the data, they are not toward more knowledge or voting, despite rising education and the growing number of media outlets. Reflecting this decline, Kiky Adato adds, between 1968 and 1988, the average sound bite or block of uninterrupted speech fell from 42.3 seconds for presidential candidates in 1968 to only 9.8 seconds in 1988. In 1968 almost half of all sound bites were 40 seconds or more, compared to less than 1 percent in 1988. In 1968, candidates' sound bites frequently lasted for over a minute on the evening news. Twenty years later, such moments had disappeared entirely. See Robert N. Entman, *Democracy Without Citizens: Media and the Decay of American Politics* (New York: Oxford University Press, 1989), 23–26; Kiky Adato, "The Incredible Shrinking Sound Bite" (Cambridge, MA: Joan Shorenstein Barone Center, June 1990), 4; and James S. Fishkin, *Democracy and Deliberation: New Directions for Democratic Reform* (New Haven: Yale University Press, 1991), 52.

40. Estimated Size of the Attentive Public (percent of the population):

Author	*Date*	*Type of Indicator*	*Size*
Free and Cantril	1967	Knowledge	26
Kriesberg	1949	Knowledge	25
Devine	1970	Behavior, interest, media exposure	25
Genco	1984	Interest, media exposure	22
NSB NSF	1983	Interest, knowledge, media exposure	20
Cohen	1966	Knowledge	19
Marttila & Kiley	1985	Knowledge	18
Levering	1978	Knowledge	15
V.O. Key	1961	Interest	15
Rosi	1965	Behavior, knowledge	13
Rosenau	1961	Behavior, interest	10
Cohen	1966	Behavior, interest	9
SSRC	1947	Knowledge	8

See Thomas W. Graham, "Public Opinion and U.S. Foreign Policy Making Decision Making," in David A. Deese, *The New Politics of American Foreign Policy* (New York: St. Martin's Press, 1994).

41. See John Stuart Mill, *Considerations on Representative Government* (South Bend, IN: Gateway Editions, 1962), 34.
42. Quoted in Edward Walsh, "Harbury Loses Bid to Sue U.S. Officials," *Washington Post,* June 21, 2002. See also Wendy Kaminer, "Lies and Consequences," *American Prospect* 13(9), May 20, 2002.
43. Sissela Bok, *Secrets: On the Ethics of Concealment and Revelation* (New York: Vintage Books, 1983), 177.
44. John M. Orman, *Presidential Secrecy and Deception* (Westport, CT: Greenwood Press, 1980), 4.
45. See William Earl Weeks, *John Quincy Adams and American Global Empire* (Lexington: University Press of Kentucky, 1992), 99, 144, 145.
46. *http://www.sewanee.edu/faculty/Willis/Civil_War/documents/Lincoln5por.html.*
47. See Walter LaFeber, *The American Age: United States Foreign Policy at Home and Abroad Since 1750* (New York: W. W. Norton, 1989), 382. See also Richard J. Barnet, *The Rocket's Red Glare: When America Goes to War—The President and the People* (New York: Simon & Schuster, 1990), 214; Robert Dallek, *Franklin D. Roosevelt and American Foreign Policy: 1932–1945* (New York: Oxford University Press, 1979); and Warren F. Kimball, *The Juggler: Franklin Roosevelt as Wartime Statesman* (Princeton, NJ: Princeton University Press, 1991).
48. John A. Thompson, "The Exaggeration of American Vulnerability: The Anatomy of a Tradition," *Diplomatic History* 16(1) (1992): 28.
49. See Barnet, *The Rocket's Red Glare,* 211.
50. See LaFeber, *The American Age,* 382; Barnet, *The Rocket's Red Glare,* 207, 214; Dallek, *Franklin D. Roosevelt and American Foreign Policy,* 312–13; Eric Alterman, *Who Speaks for America? Why Democracy Matters in Foreign Policy* (Ithaca, NY: Cornell University Press, 1998), 72–74; and Kimball, *The Juggler,* introduction. See also Thompson "The Exaggeration of American Vulnerability"; and Richard W. Steele, "The Great Debate: Roosevelt, the Media, and the Coming of the War, 1940–1941," *Journal of American History* 71, no. 1 (1984): 71–75. The circumstances leading up to the involvement of the United States in the Second World War, especially questions surrounding Roosevelt and any previous knowledge he might have had regarding the attack at Pearl Harbor, have been the subject of considerable controversy for nearly fifty years. Investigations by Secretary of the Navy Frank Knox immediately after that attack and by a distinguished panel of military experts, led by Supreme Court Justice Owen Roberts, in the months that followed both concluded that the Pacific command was to blame, not a conspiracy within the American government. The Pacific command was already on its highest alert by the end of November, and Pearl Harbor was only one of a number of potential targets for the Japanese. Moreover, careful study by scholars such as Roberta Wohlstetter and David M. Kennedy have concluded, in Kennedy's words, that the conspiracy notion is "a thesis that simply will not bear close examination in light of the president's unwavering insistence on the priority of the Atlantic and European theaters and the unambiguous conviction of the naval and military advisers that not Japan but Germany was the truly dangerous adversary." (Kennedy does, however, fault FDR for failing to pursue a diplomatic solution.) Yet, theories of Roosevelt's complicity have endured, stoked repeatedly by his Republican opponents and the far-right isolationist press. There is no evidence, either available at the time or unearthed

since, that demonstrates Roosevelt acted negligently with regard to the Japanese threat. For two recent examples of the genre, see Howard W. French, "Pearl Harbor Truly a Sneak Attack, Papers Show," *New York Times,* December 9, 1999; and Thomas Fleming, *The New Dealers' War: FDR and the War Within World War II* (New York: Basic Books, 2001), 45–48. See also David M. Kennedy, *Freedom from Fear: The American People in Depression and War, 1929–1945* (New York: Oxford University Press, 1999), 524–25; and Roberta Wholstetter, *Pearl Harbor: Warning and Decision* (Stanford, CA: Stanford University Press, 1962), 44–47. For past discussions among those who argue that Pearl Harbor might have been a "back door" for FDR: Charles A. Beard, *President Roosevelt and the Coming of the War, 1941: A Study in Appearances and Realities* (1948; reprinted, Hamden, CT: Shoe String Press, 1968); and Charles Tansill, *Back Door to War: The Roosevelt Foreign Policy, 1933–1941* (Chicago: Regnery, 1952). This view was disputed by James B. Crowley, "A New Deal for Japan and Asia: One Road to Pearl Harbor," in *Modern East Asia: Essays in Interpretation,* Crowley, ed. (New York: Harcourt, Brace, 1970), 235–63; and Herbert Feis, "War Came at Pearl Harbor: Suspicions Considered," *Yale Review* (1951). For an early ad hominem overview, see Samuel E. Morrison, "Did Roosevelt Start the War? History Through a Beard," *Atlantic Monthly* (August 1948): 91–97.

51. See Thomas A. Bailey, *Man in the Street: The Impact of American Public Opinion on Foreign Policy* (New York: Macmillan, 1948), 13.
52. Orman, *Presidential Secrecy and Deception,* 46.
53. See "United States Objectives and Programs for National Security," April 14, 1950, *Foreign Relations of the United States, 1950,* vol. I (Washington, D.C.: GPO, 1977), 244, 234–92. See also Ernest May, ed., *American Cold War Strategy: Interpreting NSC 68* (Boston: St. Martin's Press, 1993). For the long telegram, see George F. Kennan, *Memoirs: 1925–1950* (Boston: Little Brown, 1967), 271–97. See also his elaboration of its central points in X, "The Sources of Soviet Conduct," *Foreign Affairs,* July 1946. See also Michael J. Hogan, *A Cross of Iron: Harry S. Truman and the Origins of the National Security States, 1945–1954* (New York: Cambridge University Press, 1998), 10, 12.
54. See James Bamford, *Body of Secrets: Anatomy of the Ultra-Secret National Security Agency from the Cold War Through the Dawn of a New Century* (New York: Doubleday, 2001), 53. See also Michael R. Beschloss, *Mayday: Eisenhower, Khrushchev and the U-2 Affair* (New York: Harper & Row, 1986), 51–52; and David Wise and Thomas B. Ross, *The U-2 Affair* (New York: Random House, 1962), 83. For an accusation of *The New York Times's* willing participation in Eisenhower's deceit, see Ted G. Carpenter, *The Captive Press: Foreign Policy Crises and the First Amendment* (Washington, D.C.: Cato Institute, 1995), 56.
55. See Bamford, *Body of Secrets,* 54.
56. Ibid., 59–60.
57. Ibid., 60–62. For Richard Helms, see Thomas Powers, *The Man Who Kept the Secrets: Richard Helms and the CIA* (New York: Alfred A. Knopf, 1979), 304–5.
58. The quote ends, "And if I had to do it all over again, we would have kept our mouths shut." See David Wise, *The Politics of Lying: Government Deception, Secrecy and Power* (New York: Random House, 1973), 35.
59. Richard Morin and Dan Balz, "Americans Losing Trust in Each Other and Institutions; Suspicion of Strangers Breeds Widespread Cynicism," *Washington Post,* January 28, 1996.
60. Richard Morin and Dana Milbank, "Most Think Truth Was Stretched to Justify Iraq War," *Washington Post,* February 13, 2004.
61. Albert Hirschman, *The Rhetoric of Reaction* (Cambridge: Harvard University Press, 1991), 36–37. See also Robert Merton's classic, "The Unanticipated Consequences of Purposive Social Action," *American Sociological Review* 1 (December 1936): 894–904;

and Garrett Hardin, "The Cybernetics of Competition," *Perspectives in Biology and Medicine* (Autumn 1963): 77.

62. Robert Jervis, *System Effects: Complexity in Political and Social Life* (Princeton, NJ: Princeton University Press, 1998), 10–11. See also J. R. McNeill, *Something New Under the Sun: An Environmental History of the Twentieth-Century World* (New York: Norton, 2000).
63. Jervis, *System Effects,* 56.
64. For a discussion of "causal mechanisms," see Larry Griffin and Charles C. Ragin, "Some Observations of Formal Methods of Qualitative Analysis," *Sociological Methods and Research* 23 (1994): 13. For a discussion of the "inherent logic of events," see Andrew Abbott, "From Causes to Events: Notes on Narrative Positivism," *Sociological Methods and Research* 20 (1992): 445. For the "impact of decisions," see Terry Lynn Karl, *The Paradox of Plenty: Oil Booms and Petro-States* (Berkeley: University of California Press, 1991), 11. For useful discussions of the notion of "path dependency," see James Mahoney, "Path Dependence in Historical Sociology," *Theory and Society* 29 (2000); and Paul Pierson, "Increasing Returns, Path Dependence, and the Study of Politics," *American Political Science Review* 94 (June 2000).
65. See Chalmers Johnson, *Blowback: The Costs and Consequences of American Empire* (New York: Metropolitan Books, 2000), 8–10.

II. Franklin D. Roosevelt, Harry S. Truman, and the Yalta Conference

1. William Safire, "Putin's China Card," *New York Times,* June 18, 2001.
2. Jim Hoagland, "Bush with the Vision Thing," *Washington Post,* June 21, 2001.
3. Diane Shaver Clemens, *Yalta* (New York: Oxford University Press, 1970), 103–4.
4. See Russell D. Buhite, *Decisions at Yalta: An Appraisal of Summit Diplomacy* (Wilmington, DE: Scholarly Resources Inc, 1986), 1. According to a report prepared by the Medical Department of the U.S. Navy in advance of Roosevelt's arrival, Churchill had good reason to worry about lice. One section of the report advises a course of D.D.T. in kerosene to treat the provided accommodations' "bed bug infestation." "Report of Medical Department Activities at Crimean Conference," Ross T. McIntire Papers, box 4, Franklin D. Roosevelt Library, Hyde Park, NY (hereafter FDRL).
5. For Roosevelt, see U.S. Department of State, Foreign Relations of the United States (hereafter FRUS), Diplomatic Papers: *The Conferences at Malta and Yalta, 1945* (Washington, D.C.: GPO, 1955), 4–5. For Churchill, see Winston Churchill, *The Second World War,* Vol. 6: *Triumph and Tragedy* (London: Cassell, 1954), 341. See also W. Averell Harriman, with Elie Abel, *Special Envoy to Churchill and Stalin, 1941–1946* (New York: Random House, 1975), 390.
6. The American delegation's briefing materials read as follows: "Politically, while this Government probably would not oppose predominant Soviet influence in the area [Poland and the Balkans] neither would it desire to see American influence to be completely nullified." See "Reconstruction of Poland and the Balkans: American Interests and Soviet Attitude," Harry L. Hopkins Papers, container 170, folder 2, FDRL.
7. See *Appendix to the U.S. Congressional Record,* 81st Cong., 2nd sess., 1950, XCVI, A541. See also David Fromkin, *In the Time of the Americans* (New York: Alfred A. Knopf, 1995), 479; Alger Hiss, "Yalta: Modern American Myth," *Pocket Book Magazine,* no. 3, September 1955, 14.
8. Leahy repeatedly wrote that this was a project in which he had "no confidence." See William D. Leahy Diary, September 19, October 2, December 15, 1944, reel 3, William D. Leahy Papers, Manuscript Division, Library of Congress, Washington,

D.C.; Leahy Diary, February 11, May 20, 1945, reel 4, Leahy Papers. See also Eben A. Ayers Diary, August 8, 1945, Eben A. Ayers Papers, Harry S. Truman Library, Independence, MO (hereafter HSTL); and Daniel Yergin, *Shattered Peace: The Origins of the Cold War and the National Security State* (Boston: Houghton Mifflin, 1977), 73.

9. See Henry L. Stimson Diary, July 15–24, 1945, Henry L. Stimson Diaries, Manuscript Division, Library of Congress, Washington, D.C.
10. For Catledge, see Richard Reeves, "Why Presidents Lie," *George,* May 2000, 54.
11. Geoffrey Ward, *A First-Class Temperament* (New York: Book-of-the-Month Club, 1989), xiii.
12. Ibid., 5.
13. Franklin D. Roosevelt, Public Papers, 1944–45, vol. 13, 405.
14. See, for instance, Louis Halle, *The Cold War as History* (New York: Chatto and Windus, 1967); Dexter Perkins, *The Diplomacy of a New Age: Major Issues in U.S. Policy Since 1945* (Bloomington: Indiana University Press, 1967); Robert Divine, *Roosevelt and World War II* (Baltimore: Johns Hopkins Press, 1969); Arthur M. Schlesinger Jr., *The Vital Center* (Boston: Houghton Mifflin, 1949); Arthur M. Schlesinger Jr., "The Origins of the Cold War," *Foreign Affairs* 46 (October 1967); Arthur M. Schlesinger Jr., *The Crisis of Confidence* (New York: Houghton Mifflin, 1969); Herbert Feis, *From Trust to Terror: The Onset of the Cold War, 1945–1950* (New York: W. W. Norton, 1970); Herbert Feis, *The War They Waged and the Peace They Sought* (Princeton, NJ: Princeton University Press, 1957); Herbert Feis, *Between War and Peace: The Potsdam Conference* (Princeton, NJ: Princeton University Press, 1960); Robert Maddox, The *New Left and the Origins of the Cold War* (Princeton, NJ. Princeton University Press, 1973); Robert W. Tucker, *The Radical Left and American Foreign Policy* (Baltimore: Johns Hopkins Press, 1971); John Lewis Gaddis, *The United States and the Origins of the Cold War, 1941–1947* (New York: Columbia University Press, 1972); William Henry Chamberlin, *America's Second Crusade* (Washington, D.C.: Regnery, 1950); Lisle Rose, *After Yalta: America and the Origins of the Cold War* (New York: Scribner, 1973); Adam B. Ulam, *Expansion and Co-Existence: The History of Soviet Foreign Policy* (New York: Praeger, 1968); William Taubman, *Stalin's American Policy: From Entente to Détente to Cold War* (New York: W. W. Norton, 1982); Charles S. Maier, "Revisionism and the Interpretation of Cold War Origins," *Perspectives in American History* 4 (1970): 313–47; Hugh Thomas, *Armed Truce: The Beginnings of the Cold War,* 1945–46 (New York: Atheneum, 1987); Norman A. Grabner, "Cold War Origins and the Contemporary Debate: A Review of Recent Literature," *Journal of Conflict Resolution* 13 (March 1969): 123-32; Henry A. Kissinger, *Diplomacy* (New York: Simon & Schuster, 1994). See also Churchill, *The Second World War.*
15. See, for instance, William Appleman Williams, *The Tragedy of American Diplomacy* (New York: Dell Publishing Company, 1959 and 1972); William Appleman Williams, *American-Russian Relations, 1781–1947* (New York: Octagon Books, 1952); Denna Frank Flemming, *The Cold War and Its Origins, 1917–1960* (Garden City, NY: Doubleday, 1961); Gar Alperovitz, *Atomic Diplomacy: Hiroshima and Potsdam—The Use of the Atomic Bomb and the American Confrontation with Soviet Power* (New York: Simon & Schuster, 1965); Barton J. Bernstein, ed., *Towards a New Past: Dissenting Essays in American History* (New York: Pantheon Books, 1968); Barton J. Bernstein, ed., *Politics and Policies of the Truman Administration* (Chicago: Quadrangle Books, 1970); Gabriel Kolko, *The Politics of War: The World and United States Foreign Policy, 1943–1945* (New York: Random House, 1968); Bruce Kulick, *American Policy and the Division of Germany: The Clash with Russia over Reparations* (Ithaca, NY: Cornell University Press, 1972); Lloyd C. Gardner, *Architects of Illusion: Men and Ideas in American Foreign Policy, 1941–1949* (Chicago: Quad-

rangle Books, 1970); Athan Theoharis, *The Yalta Myths: An Issue in U.S. Politics, 1945–1955* (New York: Oxford University Press, 1970); Martin Sherwin, *A World Destroyed: The Atomic Bomb and the Grand Alliance* (New York: Knopf, 1975); Yergin, *Shattered Peace;* Thomas J. McCormick, *America's Half-Century* (Baltimore: Johns Hopkins University Press, 1989); Deborah Welch Larson, *Origins of Containment: A Psychological Explanation* (Princeton, NJ: Princeton University Press, 1985); Fred Inglis, *The Cruel Peace: Everyday Life in the Cold War* (New York: Basic Books, 1991); Carolyn Eisenberg, *Drawing the Line: The American Decision to Divide Germany, 1944–1949* (New York: Cambridge University Press, 1996); Christopher Lasch, "The Cold War: Revisited and Revisioned," *New York Times Magazine,* January 14, 1968; Edward Pessen, *Losing Our Souls: the American Experience in the Cold War* (Chicago: I. R. Dee, 1993).

16. See, for instance, John Lewis Gaddis, "The Emerging Post-Revisionist Synthesis on the Origins of the Cold War," *Diplomatic History* 7 (Summer 1983): 171–90. (See also the responses by Lloyd C. Gardner, Lawrence S. Kaplan, Warren F. Kimball, and Bruce Kuniholm.); John Lewis Gaddis, *We Now Know: Rethinking Cold War History* (New York: Oxford University Press, 1997); Geir Lundested, *The American Non-Policy Toward Eastern Europe* (New York: Humanities Press, 1975); Melvyn Leffler, *A Preponderance of Power: National Security, the Truman Administration and the Cold War* (Stanford, CA: Stanford University Press, 1992); Fromkin, *In the Time of the Americans;* Vladislav Zubok and Constantine Pleshakov, *Inside the Kremlin's Cold War: From Stalin to Khrushchev* (Cambridge, MA: Harvard University Press, 1996); Michael J. Hogan, *A Cross of Iron;* Marc Trachtenburg, *A Constructed Peace: The Making of the European Settlement, 1945–1963* (Princeton, NJ: Princeton University Press, 1999).
17. Gaddis, *We Now Know,* 25. Many historians, however, challenge Gaddis's view. Vojtech Mastny, for instance, writes, "Despite Stalin's ideological dedication, revolution was for him a means to power rather than a goal in itself." Similarly Zubok and Pleshakov point out that Stalin promoted world revolution, not as a goal in and of itself, but rather that it provided the rationale for building a strong Soviet Union. See Vojtech Mastny, *Cold War and Soviet Insecurity: The Stalin Years* (New York: Oxford University Press, 1996), 3–5; Zubok and Pleshakov, *Inside the Kremlin's Cold War,* 15.
18. Melvyn Leffler, "The Cold War: What Do 'We Now Know'?" *American Historical Review* (April 1999): 523.
19. Colonel Jim Atwood, quoting General Lucius Clay, CNN, *The Cold War,* episode 9, "The Wall," broadcast November 22, 1998.
20. Robert E. Sherwood, *Roosevelt and Hopkins: An Intimate History* (New York: Harper Brothers, 1948), 869.
21. Ibid, 870.
22. "Big 3 Agreement Lauded by Hoover," *New York Times,* February 13, 1945.
23. "Congress Leaders Praise Big Three," *New York Times,* February 13, 1945. See also Sherwood, *Roosevelt and Hopkins,* 870.
24. "History at Yalta," *New York Times,* February 14, 1945, in which the *Times* celebrated the results of the talks, as "justifying and surpassing most of the hopes placed on this fateful meeting." *The Washington Post* suggested that the conference report would "remove a lot of bogeys . . . about the relations of the allied powers." *The Christian Science Monitor* found itself "grateful for the clear evidence of progress both in the spirit and the practice of cooperation." The Republican *New York Herald Tribune* added that "the whole which emerges is self-consistent, is rational, and affords a firm foundation upon which all together can advance to the next stages of the immense task before us." It also added that "the overriding fact" is that the conference "has produced another great proof of Allied unity, strength, and power of decision." The *Philadelphia Record* called

the conference "the greatest United Nations victory of the war." See "Pro and Con of National Issues: Crimea Meeting Press Appraisal of the Results," *U.S. News & World Report,* February 23, 1945. See also Hiss, "Yalta: Modern American Myth," 7; James F. Byrnes, *Speaking Frankly* (New York: Harper Brothers, 1947), 45.

25. "After Yalta: So the Big Three Didn't Break Up After All, Now What?" *Life,* February 26, 1945.
26. *Time,* February 19, 1945.
27. Walter Lippmann, "Today and Tomorrow," *New York Herald Tribune,* February 15, 1945.
28. On Katyn and the timing of FDR's information, see Benjamin B. Fischer, "Stalin's Killing Field," *Studies in Intelligence* (Winter 1999–2000): 63,64.
29. By 1944, close to half the population believed Russia could be trusted. On the question of pro-Soviet propaganda, both official and unofficial, see Melvin Small, "How We Learned to Love the Russians: American Media and the Soviet Union During World War II," *Historian* 36(3) (1974): 475.
30. U.S. Department of State, *The Fort-nightly Survey of American Opinion on International Affairs,* no. 19, March 7, 1945, 2–3.
31. "After Yalta: So the Big Three Didn't Break Up After All, Now What?" *Life,* February 26, 1945.
32. Historian Athan Theoharis identifies twenty-eight congressional districts where Polish Americans composed a significant portion of the voting population at the time of the accord and whose representatives, therefore, could be expected to be most critical of the accord. They fall primarily in New York City, Chicago, Cleveland, Detroit, Milwaukee, Gary, Buffalo, upstate Wisconsin, and the industrial areas of Connecticut, New Jersey, and Pennsylvania. See Theoharis, *The Yalta Myths,* appendix Q, 238.
33. See for instance, The Honorable John Lesinski to Franklin D. Roosevelt, February 24, 1945, Papers of Harry S. Truman, President's Secretary's Files, box 186, Misc. Correspondence file, HSTL. For the Polish American Congress, see its "Memorandum to the Senate of the United States on the Crimea Decisions Concerning Poland," March 1945, Papers of Harry S. Truman, SMOF: Naval Aide to the President Files, 1945–53, box 7, Communications file, "Churchill to Truman, April 1945," HSTL.
34. See Hiss, "Yalta: Modern American Myth," 8.
35. *Time,* February 26, 1945. See also Robert L. Messer, *The End of an Alliance: James F. Byrnes, Roosevelt, Truman, and the Origins of the Cold War* (Chapel Hill: University of North Carolina Press, 1980), 54–70; and Townsend Hoopes and Douglas Brinkley, *Driven Patriot: The Life and Times of James Forrestal* (New York: Vintage Books, 1993 [also 1992]), 247.
36. Press and Radio Conference #9 Held by War Mobilization Director James F. Byrnes on Tuesday, February 13, 1945, at 4:05 M.E.W.T., in the Conference Room, East Wing of the White House, James F. Byrnes Papers, folder 637(3), Clemson University Library, Clemson, South Carolina; and Yalta Minutes, February 5–9, 1945, Byrnes Papers, folder 622.
37. Press and Radio Conference #9; and Yalta Minutes, February 6, 1945.
38. *New York Times,* February 11, 1945; and "Yalta Legman," *Newsweek,* February 9, 1945. For other interpretations of Byrnes's motivations, see Trachtenburg, *A Constructed Peace* 11–12; and Fraser Harbutt, *The Iron Curtain: Churchill, America and the Origins of the Cold War* (New York: Oxford University Press, 1986), 86–92.
39. Strangely, and somewhat tragically for his own political future, Byrnes never gave up his illusions about Yalta. After sowing confusion about the agreement—as the master manipulator FDR had undoubtedly intended—Byrnes would ultimately see his hopes ruined and his career terminated over his inability to coerce the reality of the accords

into the shape of the false impressions he created with his bombastic press briefings and congressional testimony.

In an April 7, 1945, diary entry, Harold Ickes suggests that the specter of Yalta was one of several factors that had created tension between the new president and his secretary of state. Harold Ickes Diary, April 7, 1945, Harold Ickes Papers, Manuscript Division, Library of Congress, Washington, D.C.

40. James B. Reston, "Light on Foreign Policy Awaited," *New York Times,* February 11, 1945.
41. See *New York Times,* February 4, 1945; and Arthur H. Vandenberg, "The Need for Honest Candor: Clarification of Our Foreign Policy," *Vital Speeches of the Day,* February 1, 1945, 226–30. See also Bernard K. Duffy, "James F. Byrnes's Yalta Rhetoric," *Journal of Political Science* 10(2) (1983): 61–69.
42. Reston later credited his reporting talents to the "compulsory plagiarism" of the ideas of "well-informed officials" in high-level quarters. See Eric Alterman, "The Ultimate Insider," *Columbia Journalism Review* (September–October 1991): 49.
43. James B. Reston, "Pacific War Role for Soviets Hinted," *New York Times,* February 13, 1945.
44. Walter Lippmann, "Today and Tomorrow," March 3, 1945.
45. Reporting from London, *New York Times* reporter Raymond Daniell, for instance, practically winked at his readers when, in explaining Roosevelt's failure to secure the disputed city of Lwow for a reconstituted Poland, he noted, "it seems likely that the Crimea Conference agreed on some secret protocols, that, to avoid the sinister connotations of that phrase, should perhaps be called gentleman's agreements." Giving the Soviet position on Poland its sunniest conceivable spin, Daniell implied that Stalin had retained Lwow specifically for the purpose of returning it to the Poles in a statesmanlike fashion. Daniell noted that Stalin "made it clear that he had no intention of interfering in the domestic affairs of the new Polish state." Later in the week, however, he added a note of caution. "For much depends," he wrote, "on the interpretations that are placed in practice upon some of the generalities and ambiguities in the 2,500 word communiqué. . . ." He concluded, however, on an extremely optimistic tone, observing, "the pledge to tell the peoples that they will be assisted by the three powers in choosing their own form of government may be considered a victory for Mr. Roosevelt and American idealism." Raymond Daniell, "Crimea Parley Provides Pattern for Europe," *New York Times,* February 18, 1945.
46. "After Yalta: So the Big Three Didn't Break Up After All, Now What?" *Life,* February 26, 1945.
47. See Ross T. McIntire, *White House Physician* (New York: G. P. Putnum's Sons, 1946), 204–5.
48. For FDR's overall condition, see Robert H. Ferrell, *The Dying President: Franklin D. Roosevelt, 1944–1945* (Columbia: University of Missouri Press, 1998), 105–9. Stettinius's diary observations continue: "The President seemed rested and calm and said that he had gotten plenty of sleep on the way here. He said he had been resting ten hours every night since leaving Washington but still couldn't understand why he was not slept out." But he also added, "I wish to emphasize that at all times from Malta through the Crimean Conference and the Alexandria meeting, I always found him to be mentally alert and fully capable of dealing with each situation as it developed. The stories that his health took a turn for the worse either on the way to Yalta or at the Conference are, to the best of my knowledge, without foundation." According to Churchill's personal physician, Lord Moran, "To a doctor's eye, the President appears a very sick man. He has all the symptoms of hardening of the arteries of the brain in an advanced stage, so that I give him only a few months to live." The day before he and Churchill left England for

the conference, Moran had received a disturbing letter from Dr. Roger Lee, the president of the American Medical Association and former president of the American College of Physicians. Dr. Lee reported that Roosevelt had suffered an attack of heart failure eight months before, and described his temperament: "He was irascible and became very irritable if he had to concentrate his mind for long." Anthony Eden, however, noted that "I do not believe that the President's declining health altered his judgment, though his handling of the Conference was less sure than it might have been." During his return trip, the pool reporter for the International News Service, Bob Nixon, came aboard ship in Algiers and remembered how "thin, haggard, and gray" the president looked, although he seemed in good voice, good spirits, and appeared lucid." See Diane Shaver Clemens, *Yalta,* 102–4; see also Edward R. Stettinius Jr., *Roosevelt and the Russians: The Yalta Conference* (Garden City, NY: Doubleday and Co., 1949), 72; Thomas M. Campbell and George C. Herring, eds., *Diaries of Edward R. Stettinius Jr., 1943–1946* (New York: New Viewpoints, 1975), 235; Lord Charles Moran, *Churchill: Taken from the Diaries of Lord Moran* (Boston: Houghton Mifflin, 1966), 234, 239, 242–43, 247; Anthony Eden, *The Reckoning* (Boston: Houghton Mifflin, 1965), 593. See also a letter from V. Bereshkev to Arthur Schlesinger Jr. regarding Roosevelt's health. In his estimation, Roosevelt was alert with a firm grasp of the discussions and agreements at Yalta. Franklin D. Roosevelt Library, Miscellaneous Documents, box 2, FDRL.

49. See Jan Kenneth Herman, "The President's Cardiologist," *Navy Medicine* 81(2) (March–April 1990), 13.
50. Indeed, while James Byrnes noted in a conversation that Roosevelt "at Yalta was clearly not himself," he did not indicate that his infirmity compromised his negotiating position. He even suggested that Stalin may have deferred to Roosevelt on several points due to the president's condition. See Davies Diary, June 6, 1945, box 17, Davies Papers.
51. See Samuel I. Rosenman, *Working with Roosevelt* (New York: Harper and Co., 1952), 527–28. Rosenman also commented, "I was dismayed at the halting, ineffective manner of delivery. He ad-libbed a great deal—as frequently as I had ever heard him. Some of his extemporaneous remarks were wholly irrelevant, and some of them almost bordered on the ridiculous." The latter comments appear in "Oral History Interview with Judge Samuel I. Rosenman," New York, New York, October 15, 1968, and April 23, 1969, interview by Jerry N. Hess, courtesy of the Harry S. Truman Presidential Library, *http://www.trumanlibrary.org/oralhist/rosenmn.htm.*
52. See Knud Krakau, "American Foreign Relations: A National Style?" *Diplomatic History* 8(3) (1984): 265.
53. Harriman to Roosevelt, October 10, 1944; Roosevelt to Harriman, October 11, 1944, FRUS, 1944, IV, 1006, 1009; W. Averell Harriman memo of conversations with FDR, October 21–November 19, 1944, Harriman Papers. See also Rudy Abramson, *Spanning the Century: The Life of W. Averell Harriman, 1891–1986* (New York: William Morrow, 1992), 387; Warren F. Kimball, *Forged in War: Roosevelt, Churchill and the Second World War* (New York: William Morrow, 1997), 289.
54. When the London Poles read the final declarations of the Yalta Conference, they immediately convened to issue this statement: "The method adopted in the case of Poland is a contradiction to the elementary principles binding the Allies, and constitutes a violation of the letter and spirit of the Atlantic Charter and the right of every nation to defend its own interests." They had only themselves to blame, however, if this result surprised them. President Roosevelt had long ago lost patience with their demands. He complained to British Lieutenant Miles, "I am sick and tired of these people. . . . Do [they] expect us and Great Britain to declare war on Joe Stalin if they cross your previous frontier? Even if we wanted to, Russia can still field an army twice

our combined strength, and we would just have no say in the matter at all." Anthony Eden observed in June 1944 that "the poor Poles are sadly deluding themselves if they place any faith in these vague and generous promises. The President will not be embarrassed by them hereafter." While Churchill was generally more concerned with Poland at Yalta than was Roosevelt, he too had long ago lost patience with what he believed to be the romantic and unpractical nature of the London government-in-exile. In the Autumn of 1944, he finally exploded, "You are no government if you are incapable of taking any decision. You are a callous people who want to wreck Europe. I shall leave you to your own troubles." See Edward Raczynski, *In Allied London* (London: Weidenfeld and Nicolson, 1962), 266. See also Lloyd C. Gardner, *Spheres of Influence: The Great Powers Partition Europe from Munich to Yalta* (Chicago: I. R. Dee, 1993); Larson, *Origins of Containment,* 22–24, 78–82.

55. The full text of the accord can be found, among other places, in the report of the Senate Foreign Relations Committee, *World War II International Agreements and Understandings,* 83rd Congress, 1st sess., 1953, GPO. All quotations are derived from the official text.
56. See Messer, *The End of an Alliance,* 51. Note that the authors of the original text were James Byrnes and Alger Hiss.
57. Page minutes of meeting of foreign ministers, February 10, 1945. U.S. Department of State, *FRUS, The Conferences at Malta and Yalta, 1945,* 872–3. See also Mastny, *Cold War and Soviet Insecurity,* 251.
58. See the discussion in Barton J. Bernstein, "American Foreign Policy and the Origins of the Cold War," in Bernstein, *Politics and Policies of the Truman Administration,* 21.
59. Woodford McClellan, "Molotov Remembers: Review of 'Sto sorok besed s Molotvym: Izdnevnika F Chuyeva,'" *Cold War International History Project Bulletin* 1 (Spring 1992): 17–20. See also Felix Chuev, ed., *Molotov Remembers: Inside Kremlin Politics: Conversations with Felix Chuev* (Chicago: I. R. Dee, 1993), 76.
60. See William D. Leahy, *I Was There: The Personal Story of the Chief of Staff to Presidents Roosevelt and Truman, Based on His Notes and Diaries Made at the Time* (New York: Whittlesey House, 1950), 315–16. See also Gardner, *Spheres of Influence,* 237; Melvin Leffler, "Adherence to Agreements: Yalta and the Experiences of the Early Cold War," *International Security* 11:1 (Summer 1986).
61. This estimate appears in Dimitri Volkogonov, *Stalin: Triumph and Tragedy,* Harold Timken, ed. and trans. (New York: Grove Weidenfeld, 1991), 505.
62. Stalin's story comes to us from Akai Mgeladze, *Stalin, kakim ya ego znal* (Tibilisi, 2001), 137, and is cited in Simon Sebag Montefiore, *Stalin: The Court of the Red Tsar* (New York: Knopf, 2004), 484.
63. See Fromkin, *In the Time of the Americans,* 482.
64. A State Department report written in advance of the conference concluded that any proposal for effective three-power control of Poland was "unrealistic." Secretary of War Henry Stimson informed Secretary of State Stettinius that vis-à-vis Poland, "The Russians with their possession have 99 and 44/100 percent of the law." On Churchill, see Sir John Colville, *The Fringes of Power: Downing Street Diaries* (London: Norton, 1985), entry for January 23, 1945. See also Messer, *The End of an Alliance,* 50, for the State Department and Stimson's observations.
65. See Edgar Snow, *Journey to the Beginning* (London: Random House, 1959), 357.
66. See Churchill, *The Second World War,* vol. 6, 198. For a more accurate view than that presented by Churchill, see Albert Resis, "The Churchill-Stalin Secret 'Percentages' Agreement on the Balkans, Moscow, October 1944," *American Historical Review* 83(2) (April 1978): 368–78, whose discussion is based on a reading of "Anglo-Russian Political Conversations at Moscow, October 9–October 17, 1944," PREM, 9/434/4 9565.

See also "The Meaning of TOLSTOY: Churchill, Stalin and the Balkans, Moscow, October 1944," Joseph M. Siracusa, ed. *Diplomatic History* 3 (Fall 1979): 443–63; Charles Gati, "Hegemony and Repression in the Eastern Alliance," in *Origins of the Cold War: An International History,* Melvyn Leffler and David S. Painter, eds. (London: Routledge, 1994), 175–98; Marc Trachtenberg, *A Constructed Peace,* 4–8; E. L. Woodward, *British Foreign Policy in the Second World War* (London: H. M. O. Stationary Office, 1970–76), 150; F. W. D. Deakin, "European Resistance Movements, 1939–1945," in *British Policy Towards Wartime Resistance in Yugoslavia and Greece,* Phyllis Auty and Richard Clogg, eds. (London: Macmillan, 1975), 244–47; Geoffrey Roberts, "Ideology, Calculation and Improvisation: Spheres of Influence and Soviet Foreign Policy, 1939–1945," *Review of International Studies* (October 1999): 655–73; and Norman Davies, *Europe: A History* (New York: Oxford University Press, 1996), 1037. The relevant portion of the discussion with FDR can be found in *FRUS, 1944, IV,* 1006, and Churchill to Roosevelt, October 18, 1944, and Roosevelt to Churchill, October 22. For the truncated Soviet record, see Oleg A. Rzheshevsky, "Soviet Policy in Eastern Europe, 1944–45: Liberation or Occupation?" in *End of the War in Europe, 1945,* Gill Bennett, ed., (London: HMSO, 1996), 161–72. Churchill's alleged memo is reproduced, at least according to the claim of the author, in C. L. Sulzberger's *A Long Row of Candles: Memoirs and Diaries, 1939–1954* (New York: Macmillan and Co., 1969), photograph following 525.

67. See Churchill, *The Second World War,* vol. 6, 201; and Harriman, *Special Envoy,* 358. Despite Harriman's advice, the U.S. government was aware of these discussions at least by the late spring of 1944, according to Hopkins's memorandum. Harry Hopkins, "American Policy Toward Spheres of Influence," Harry L. Hopkins Papers, group 24, container 170, folder 1.
68. See *Churchill and Roosevelt: The Complete Correspondence,* vol. 3, C-678/1 (May 21, 1944), edited with commentary by Warren F. Kimball (Princeton, NJ: Princeton University Press, 1984). See also Kimball, *Forged in War,* 252–53; and Kimball, *The Juggler,* 98–99.
69. See Fromkin, *In the Time of the Americans,* 483–84; and C. L. Sulzberger, *Such a Peace: The Roots and Ashes of Yalta* (New York: Continuum, 1982), 88, 95.
70. See Briefing Book Paper for the Yalta Conference in U.S. Department of State, *FRUS, The Conferences at Malta and Yalta, 1945,* 234.
71. Throughout the war, and during the Yalta negotiations, Averell Harriman observed, Roosevelt "consistently show[ed] very little interest in Eastern European matters except as they affect sentiment in America." In his personal papers, Harriman even quotes Roosevelt, explaining in May of 1944, that he did not care "whether the countries bordering Russia became communized." See Harriman, *Special Envoy,* 366; "Secret and Personal Memorandum of Conversations with the President During Trip to Washington, D.C., October 21–November 19, 1944," container 175, Papers of W. Averell Harriman, Manuscript Division, Library of Congress, Washington, D.C., 9; and William Larsh, "W. Averell Harriman and the Polish Question, December 1943–August 1945," *East European Politics and Societies* 7(3) (1993): 545. For a different interpretation of Roosevelt and the Polish question, see Trachtenburg, *A Constructed Peace,* 8–10.
72. See U.S. Department of State, *FRUS, The Conferences at Cairo and Tehran, 1943,* 511–512.
73. Zbigniew Brzezinski, "The Future of Yalta," *Foreign Affairs* 63 (Winter 1984–85): 279; Harriman, *Special Envoy,* 366; Larsh, *W. Averell Harriman and the Polish Question,* 545; and Larson, *Origins of Containment,* 11.
74. All quotations from Roosevelt's address to Congress are taken directly from the text of the speech, widely reprinted in the *Congressional Record,* March 1, 1945, and elsewhere.
75. Interestingly, this language seems to be taken, nearly verbatim, from a memorandum

written for Rosenman by Bohlen outlining successes to be heralded in the speech. Bohlen is more forthright about the terms of the agreement on Poland, but is able to portray it as the best solution for the Polish people. Charles Bohlen, "Memorandum for Judge Rosenman," February 18, 1945, Samuel I. Rosenman Papers, container 27, folder 7, FDRL.

76. See "Far East: Russian Desires," Harry L. Hopkins Papers, Sherwood Collection, Book 10: Yalta Conference, group 24, container 337, folder 6, FDRL.
77. See Stettinius Jr., *Roosevelt and the Russians,* 98; and Byrnes, *Speaking Frankly,* 42–4.
78. *Congressional Record,* 84th Congress, 1st sess., 1955, CI, Part 3, 3383.
79. According to a secret memo sent from Yalta by an aide to Harry Hopkins to James F. Byrnes, "The President has received completely satisfactory replies from the Prime Minister and Marshall Stalin on additional votes to achieve parity for the United States, if necessary. In view of the fact that nothing on the subject appears in the communiqué, the President is extremely anxious that no aspect of this question be discussed even privately." The memo is signed by Ogden Kniffin, Major, C. E., Kniffin to Byrnes, February 13, 1945, Byrnes Papers, folder 622.
80. Truman is quoted in Arnold A. Offner, *Another Such Victory: President Truman and the Cold War, 1945–1953* (Stanford, CA: Stanford University Press, 2002), 19–20.
81. "For us to have four or five members, six if India is included, when Russia has only one is asking a great deal of an Assembly of this kind. In view of other important concessions by them which are achieved or pending I should like to be able to make a friendly gesture to Russia in this matter. That they should have two besides their chief is not much to ask, and we will be in a strong position, in my judgment, because we shall not be the only multiple voter in the field." See Churchill, *The Second World War,* vol. 6, 359–60.
82. See Doris Kearns Goodwin, *No Ordinary Time: Franklin and Eleanor Roosevelt: The Home Front in World War II* (New York: Simon & Schuster, 1994), 586.
83. See Beatrice Berle and Travis Jacobs, *Navigating the Rapids, 1918–1971: From the Papers of Adolf A. Berle* (New York: Harcourt Brace Jovanovich, 1973), 477.
84. "Roosevelt and Churchill: United but Divided," *New York Times,* June 11, 1972.
85. See Conrad Black, *Roosevelt: Champion of Freedom* (New York: Public Affairs, 2003), 1106.
86. Winston Churchill to Franklin D. Roosevelt, February 28, 1945, Map Room Files, container 7; Churchill to Roosevelt, March 8, 1945, Map Room Files, container 7; Churchill to Roosevelt, March 13, 1945, Map Room Files, container 7; "MR-OUT-94," February 3, 1945, Map Room Files, container 21; Churchill to Roosevelt, March 10, 1945, Map Room Files, container 7; and Churchill to Roosevelt, March 27, 1945, Map Room Files, container 7, FDRL.
87. Interestingly, Churchill uses the term "our interpretation," urging Roosevelt that the only alternative to imposing a "Russian version of democracy" is to "stand by our interpretation of the Yalta declaration." Churchill to Roosevelt, March 27, 1945, Map Room Files, container 7, FDRL.
88. In the draft, intended to convey a united American-British position, Churchill wrote to Stalin that they did not consider the Moscow discussions to be in "the spirit of Yalta nor indeed, at points, the letter." He expresses specific concern with the veto of the Moscow Commission of any Pole of whom the Soviet government or the Lublin Poles disapprove, thus hindering the inclusion of any London Poles. Similarly, he conveys his dismay of Molotov's withdrawal of an offer for outside observers to enter Poland. Churchill to Roosevelt, March 31, 1945, Map Room Files, container 7. In a telegram of the same day, Roosevelt responded favorably to Churchill's message and sent his own message to Stalin as well. Interestingly, in addition to expressing his own concern over

the state of the Polish negotiations, Roosevelt makes several references to the potential disappointment of the American public on these issues as well: "You are, I am sure, aware that genuine popular support in the United States is required to carry out any Government policy foreign or domestic. The American people make up their own mind and no Governmental action can change it. I mention this fact because the last sentence of your message about Mr. Molotov's attendance at San Francisco made me wonder whether you give full weight to this factor," Roosevelt to Churchill, March 31, 1945, Map Room Files, container 7; and Roosevelt to Stalin, March 31, 1945, Map Room Files, container 7.

89. Churchill's language often conveyed a great sense of urgency. In a telegram to Roosevelt on March 13, 1945, Churchill wrote, "We can, of course, make no progress at Moscow without your aid, and if we get out of step the doom of Poland is sealed." Churchill to Roosevelt, March 13, 1945, Map Room Files, container 7.

90. Roosevelt did not want to confront Stalin directly, but to achieve a compromise "under the guise of a general political truce." In Roosevelt's words their joint objective is "a cessation on the part of the Lublin Poles of the measures directed against their political opponents in Poland." Roosevelt to Churchill, March 11, 1945, Map Room Files, container 7. In a telegram of March 15, 1945, Roosevelt still sought to assure Churchill that there was no divergence between the American and British interpretations of the Yalta agreement. Roosevelt to Churchill, March 15, 1945, Map Room Files, container 7. (In this exchange, Roosevelt and Churchill discuss the situation in Romania at length as well. I have chosen, however, to focus on the divergences over Poland, as they have elicited the bulk of historical commentary.) Yet, despite these claims, Roosevelt repeatedly urges restraint. He cautions Churchill that they must take into account Stalin's view that the London Poles engaged in "terrorist" activities against the Red Army. Similarly, he points out that the United States and Great Britain need to be mindful of the propaganda implications of their actions. He writes, "We must be careful not to give the impression that we are proposing a halt in the land reforms. This would furnish the Lublin Poles with an opportunity to charge that they and they alone defend the interests of the peasants against the land lords." Roosevelt to Churchill, March 11, 1945, Map Room Files, container 7.

91. This occurred as American and British negotiators tried to force the Soviets to accept a larger role for the London-based Poles than they had agreed to at Yalta. FDR admitted in the letter to Churchill that "if we attempt to evade the fact that we placed, as clearly shown in the agreement, somewhat more emphasis on the Lublin Poles than on the other two groups from which the new government is to be drawn I feel we will expose ourselves to the charge that we are attempting to go back on the Crimea decision." See Roosevelt to Churchill, March 29, 1945, Map Room Files, container 7. Stalin's response to Churchill's and Roosevelt's telegrams on March 31 echo Roosevelt's message. Stalin to Roosevelt, April 7, 1945, Map Room Files, container 9, folder 3. See also Leffler, "Adherence to Agreements," 95; and Kimball, ed., *Churchill and Roosevelt,* vol. 3, 593. See also Harriman, *Special Envoy,* 406–14, 439–40; Charles E. Bohlen, *Witness to History, 1929–1960* (New York: W. W. Norton, 1973), 188–92; and Clemens, *Yalta,* 306.

92. *The Diaries of Sir Alexander Cadogan, O.M., 1938–1945,* David Dilks, ed. (New York: G. P. Putnam's Sons, 1972), 716. See also Jon Meacham, *Franklin and Winston: An Intimate Portrait of an Epic Friendship* (New York: Random House, 2003), 324.

93. Kimball, *Forged in War,* 322.

94. Bradley F. Smith and Elena Agarossi, *Operation Sunrise: The Secret Surrender* (New York: Basic Books, 1979), 72–104.

95. According to Harriman, Roosevelt told this to Anna Rosenberg at a luncheon. Harriman was told this by Anne O'Hare McCormick, who had seen the president on the day he left Washington for Warm Springs; she later shared with him her recollection of that final talk. The president told her that while he "fully believed what he has said in his report to Congress on the Yalta Conference decisions," he had nevertheless concluded, "Averell is right; we can't do business with Stalin. He has broken every one of the promises he made at Yalta." Harriman continues, "But he had found Stalin was not a man of his word; either that or Stalin was not in control of the Soviet government." This information is contained in a January 25, 1954, memorandum written by Harriman and cited in his memoirs: Harriman, *Special Envoy,* 44. Those who see the cold war as inevitable irrespective of the actions taken by any American leader tend to point to this quotation frequently. Harriman and Admiral Leahy also recount a sharp disagreement between Roosevelt and Stalin immediately following the conference over the terms of Germany's surrender, in which the president noted his "bitter resentment of [Stalin's] informers, whoever they are for such vile misrepresentations of my actions or those of my trusted subordinates." Stalin, however, soon apologized, and FDR termed the matter a "minor" disagreement, in the final cable he sent before his death, much to Harriman's chagrin. President Truman's biographical sympathizers also tend to take this view. Lloyd Gardner, a historian less sympathetic to the president, also notes, "Even in the last two weeks of his life, however, when some observers saw Roosevelt 'toughening up' his attitude toward the Russians, he [i.e., Truman] wrote banker Thomas Lamont to thank him for a note praising the Yalta compromises on Poland's frontiers. 'It is unfortunate, as you so wisely observe, that in the field of international politics so many Americans are still living in the age of innocence.'" See Leahy, *I Was There,* 334; Harriman, *Special Envoy,* 436–440; and Gardner, *Spheres of Influence,* 238.
96. The argument is almost perfectly analogous to that over whether John F. Kennedy would have continued and expanded U.S. participation in the Vietnam War.
97. The language of the accord directed U.S. Ambassador Harriman, Soviet Foreign Minister Molotov, and British Ambassador Archibald Clark-Kerr "to consult in the first instance in Moscow with members of the present Provisional Government and with other Polish democratic leaders from within Poland and from abroad, with a view to the reorganization of the present Government along the above lines [that is, on a broader democratic basis]." Churchill, however, instructed Clark-Kerr "to promote the formation of a new reorganized Polish government sufficiently representative of all Poland for us to recognize it." This clearly contradicted the language of the accord, which spoke only of a "reorganized" version of the Polish Provisional Government, "which is now functioning in Poland." Harriman, meanwhile, insisted that exiled leaders be consulted on the formation of the new government and that the Lublin government be accorded no special powers in determining the invitation list. See James Forrestal, *The Forrestal Diaries,* Walter Millis, ed., (New York: Viking, 1951), 48–51; Harry S. Truman, *Memoirs of Harry S. Truman: Year of Decisions,* vol. I (Garden City, NY: Doubleday and Co., 1955), 81; Leffler, "Adherence to Agreements," 95; Clemens, *Yalta,* 173–215; Martin F. Herz, *Beginnings of the Cold War* (New York: McGraw-Hill, 1966), 38–92; and Richard C. Lukas, *The Strange Allies: The United States and Poland, 1941–5* (Knoxville: University of Tennessee Press, 1978), 128–42.
98. Leffler, "Adherence to Agreements," 96.
99. Woodward, *British Foreign Policy in the Second World War,* 501.
100. See Isaac Deutscher, "Myths of the Cold War," in David Horowitz, ed., *Containment and Revolution* (London: Blond, 1967), 17.

101. Offner, *Another Such Victory,* 456.
102. Ibid. For a clear statement of Offner's thesis on this part, and Truman's failures, see chapter 16, 456–70.
103. Kimball, *Forged in War,* 242.
104. For Eleanor Roosevelt's comment, see "Unfinished Notes" (August 1941), Belle Willard Roosevelt Papers, Manuscript Division, Library of Congress, Washington, D.C.
105. Zubok and Pleshakov, *Inside the Kremlin's Cold War,* 69.
106. Ibid., 275–76.
107. Ibid., 277.
108. Norman M. Naimark, *The Russians in Germany: A History of the Soviet Zone of Occupation, 1945–1949* (Cambridge: Harvard University Press, 1995), 467.
109. "Anglo-Russian Political Conversations at Moscow, October 9–October 17, 1944," 7, 40–42. See also Resis, "The Churchill-Stalin Secret 'Percentages' Agreement," 8–9.
110. See Vladimir O. Pechatnov, "The Big Three After World War II: New Documents on Soviet Thinking About Postwar Relations with the United States and Great Britain," Cold War International History Project, working paper no. 13, Woodrow Wilson Center for Scholars, 22.
111. Ibid. See also Zubok and Pleshakov, *Inside the Kremlin's Cold War,* chapter 1; and William C. Wohlforth, "New Evidence on Moscow's Cold War," *Diplomatic History* 211 (Spring 1997): 234–35. Pechatnov's conclusions are drawn from several analytical reports from the records of the Archive of the Foreign Policy of the Russian Federation, written by three prominent Soviet diplomats—Ivan M. Maisky, Maxim M. Litvinov, and Andrei A. Gromyko—between January 1944 and the summer of 1945. These men, he notes, were "the most experienced Soviet experts on the West and all active participants in the forging of the Grand Alliance, [and] were by then at the forefront of Soviet post-war planning: Litvinov as Foreign Minister V. M. Molotov's deputy and chairman of the Ministry's special Commission on post-war order and preparation of peace treaties; Maisky, another Assistant People's Commissar for Foreign Affairs, in charge of the reparation program; and Gromyko as an Ambassador to the USA leading the Soviet team at the United Nations preparatory talks."
112. Norman Naimark, "The Soviets and the Christian Democrats: The Challenge of a 'Bourgeois Party in Eastern Germany,' 1945–1949," *East European Politics and Societies* 9 (Fall 1995): 3.
113. David Holloway, *Stalin and the Bomb: The Soviet Union and Atomic Energy, 1939–1954* (New Haven, CT: Yale University Press, 1994), 168.
114. Sergei N. Goncharov, John W. Lewis, and Xue Litai, *Uncertain Partners: Stalin, Mao and the Korean War* (Stanford, CA: Stanford University Press, 1993), 3. According to NSA intercepts, in a Yenan-to-Moscow message on September 27, 1945, the Chinese Communist Party (CCP) requested a Soviet airlift of its troops to Manchuria so that they could arrive ahead of Chiang Kai-shek's (Jiang Jieshi's) and U.S. troop movements to the area, even though the Soviets had promised not to help the CCP in a treaty with Chiang (signed August 14, 1945). How exactly Stalin responded is unknown. The CCP promised the Soviets safe and secret landing areas and "a great quantity" of gasoline that had been captured from the Japanese, as incentives for the airlift. The Soviets were already supplying the CCP with captured Japanese weapons. The document in question, entitled "COMINT and the PRC Intervention in the Korean War" (labeled "TOP SECRET UMBRA"), is undated and its author unidentified. It can be found on the National Security Agency Web site, at *http://www.nsa.gov/korea/papers/prc_intervention_korean_war.pdf.* The information in question appears on pp. 5–7. For further background, see Goncharov, Gaddis, and Xue, *Uncertain Partners,* 8, 14; Chen Jian, *Mao's China and the Cold War* (Chapel Hill: University of

North Carolina Press, 2001), 34–38; and Michael Sheng, *Battling Western Imperialism* (Princeton, NJ: Princeton University Press, 1997), 98–118.

115. See Kathryn Weathersby, "Soviet Aims in Korea and the Origins of the Korean War, 1945–50: New Evidence from the Russian Archives," Cold War International History Project, working paper no. 8, Woodrow Wilson Center (November 1993): 5–19; Kathryn Weathersby, "To Attack or Not to Attack," *Cold War International History Project Bulletin* 5 (Spring 1995): 1–9; and Kathryn Weathersby, "New Russian Documents on the Korean War," *Cold War International History Project Bulletin* 6–7 (Winter 1995/1996): 30–35. See also Wohlforth, "New Evidence on Moscow's Cold War," 236–37.
116. Joseph E. Davies Journal, April 23, 1945, box 16, Joseph E. Davies Papers, Manuscript Division, Library of Congress, Washington, D.C.; and Joseph E. Davies Diary, April 23, 1945, box 16, Davies Papers. See also Larson, *Origins of Containment,* 158.
117. See Zubok and Pleshakov, *Inside the Kremlin's Cold War,* 69; and Wohlforth, "New Evidence on Moscow's Cold War," 236–37.
118. Papers of Harry S. Truman, Post Presidential Files, box 643, Memoirs files, "Discussion, January 23, 1954."
119. Lloyd Gardner seems to suggest such a possibility in Gardner, *Spheres of Influence.*
120. I am no less troubled by FDR's inexcusably callous treatment of German and East European Jewish refugees during the war, but that is hardly germane to this argument.
121. Quoted in Gardner, *Architects of Illusion,* 76.
122. See Davies Diary, May 21, 1945, box 17, Davies Papers; and Joseph C. Grew, *Turbulent Era: A Record of Forty Years in the U.S. Diplomatic Service,* Vol. 2, Walter Johnson, ed., Nancy Harvison Hooker, asst. (Boston: Houghton Mifflin, 1952), 1485n. At the time, Grew was soon to become acting secretary of state, a position in which he served from June 28, 1945, to July 3, 1945; this was the period between the effective resignation of Secretary of State Edward Stettinius Jr. and the effective appointment of James F. Byrnes as secretary of state. See also Sherwin, *A World Destroyed,* 176; and Robert Scialiano, "Politics, the Constitution, and the President's War Power," in Deese, *The New Politics of American Foreign Policy,* 153–58.
123. Davies, a consistent proponent of patience and improved relations with Moscow, grew disappointed with Truman's approach. He laid out a different approach, one that was closer in his view to that pursued by FDR, in a long memorandum entitled "Deterioration in Relations Between the Soviets and Britain and the United States and Its Serious Threat to Peace," September 29, 1945, Papers of Harry S. Truman, President's Secretary's Files, box 117, Potsdam file, HSTL.
124. See Peter Grosse, *Operation Rollback: America's Secret War Behind the Iron Curtain* (Boston: Houghton Mifflin, 2000), 70; and Taubman, *Stalin's American Policy,* 259.
125. See Jonathan Daniels, *The Man of Independence* (Philadelphia: Lippincott, 1950), 285.
126. See John Lewis Gaddis, "The Insecurities of Victory," in *The Long Peace: Inquiring into the History of the Cold War* (New York: Oxford University Press, 1987).
127. See Daniels, *The Man of Independence,* 278.
128. For more on Truman, see Messer, *The End of an Alliance,* 134; and Fromkin, *In the Time of the Americans,* 489.
129. David McCullough, *Truman* (New York: Simon & Schuster, 1992), 382.
130. Morgenthau's diary is quoted in Messer, *The End of an Alliance,* 70. See also Offner, *Another Such Victory,* 23.
131. U.S. Department of State, *FRUS, 1945, V,* 1075. See also Averell Harriman, *Peace with Russia?* (New York: Simon & Schuster, 1959), 3–4. For a more thorough explanation of the background of this argument, see Diane S. Clemens, "Averell Harriman, John

Deane, the Joint Chiefs of Staff, and the 'Reversal of Co-operation' with the Soviet Union in April 1945," *International History Review* 14 (1992): 227–306.

132. See Kai Bird, *The Chairman: John J. McCloy: The Making of the American Establishment* (New York: Simon & Schuster, 1992), 69
133. See Harriman, *Special Envoy,* 291. For the January 19, 1944, press conference, which Harriman insisted be treated "on background," see Larsh, "W. Averell Harriman and the Polish Question," 528.
134. Larsh, "W. Averell Harriman and the Polish Question," 531–34.
135. Molotov "deeply regretted" Harriman's departure from Moscow, because he did so much for the "cause of Soviet-American relations." Khrushchev, in his memoirs, said Harriman had "conducted policies that were very much to our liking." See Nikita Khrushchev, *Khrushchev Remembers,* Vol. 2 (London, 1972), 414; and U.S. Department of State, *FRUS, 1945, VI,* 782–85; Harriman, *Special Envoy,* 531. See also 711-61/10-2645, Record Group 59, U.S. Department of State Central Decimal Files, National Archives, Washington, D.C.; and Thomas, *Armed Truce,* 143.
136. Harriman, *Special Envoy,* 514–15.
137. See Walter LaFeber, *The New Empire: An Interpretation of American Expansion, 1860–1898* (Ithaca, NY: Cornell University Press, 1963); *The Panama Canal: The Crisis in Historical Perspective* (New York: Oxford University Press, 1978); and *Inevitable Revolutions: The United States in Central America,* 2nd ed., (New York: W. W. Norton, 1993).
138. See Winston Churchill to Anthony Eden, January 8, 1942, in Churchill, *The Second World War,* vol. 3, 696; and Gardner, *Architects of Illusion,* 59.
139. Clemens, "The 'Reversal of Co-operation,'" 282.
140. Papers of Harry S. Truman, Post-Presidential Files, box 643, Memoir file, "Cabinet," HSTL.
141. See Henry L. Stimson Diary, April 23 and 26, May 10, 1945, reel 9; and Charles E. Bohlen, "Memorandum of Meeting at the White House, 2:00 P.M., April 23," Papers of Harry S. Truman, President's Secretary's File, "Russia," box 187, file "Russia Molotov," HSTL.
142. Henry L. Stimson and McGeorge Bundy, *On Active Service in Peace and War* (New York: Harper, 1948), 609–11. See also Yergin, *Shattered Peace,* 82–83; Stimson Diary, April 23, 1945; and Forrestal, *The Forrestal Diaries,* 49.
143. Stimson Diary, April 23, 1945.
144. Leahy, *I Was There,* 351; and Leahy Diary, April 23, 1945, reel 4, Leahy Papers. See also Stimson Diary, April 23, 1945; and Forrestal, *The Forrestal Diaries,* 49.
145. Leahy Diary, April 23, 1945; and Leahy, *I Was There,* 352. See also Sherwin, *A World Destroyed,* 158; Bohlen Memo, April 23, 1945.
146. "Interview with W. Averell Harriman," Papers of Harry S. Truman, Post-Presidential Files, box 641, Memoir file "Harriman," HSTL. See also Harriman, *Special Envoy,* 140, Stimson Diary; April 23, 1945; Forrestal, *The Forrestal Diaries,* 49; and Bohlen Memo, April 23, 1945.
147. The telegram traffic, collected for Truman in order by date, can be found in Papers of George Elsey, "Historical Reports and Research Notes," box 1, folder 2. The "minimize" telegram is numbered 742 and dated April 11, Papers of George Elsey, "Historical Reports and Research Notes," box 1, folder 2.
148. "The Polish Problem," May 30, 1945.
149. See Bohlen Memo, April 23, 1945; Fromkin, *In the Time of the Americans,* 488–89; and McCullough, *Truman,* 374–75.
150. Martin J. Sherwin suggests that while Truman wished to dramatize this meeting in his

memoirs, others present at the meeting believed that the president "was already convinced of the need for 'rather brutal frankness,'" particularly on Poland, before the meeting began. See Sherwin, *A World Destroyed,* 157. This interpretation is augmented by entries in the Stimson Diary, April 23, 1945; Leahy Diary, April 23, 1945; Bohlen Memo, April 23, 1945; Leahy, *I Was There,* 352; and Forrestal, *The Forrestal Diaries,* 48–51.

151. The latter called only for a "reorganized" version of the Polish Provisional Government, "which is now functioning in Poland." See Forrestal, *The Forrestal Diaries,* 50–51; and Truman, *Year of Decisions,* 80–81.

152. Truman, *Year of Decisions,* 82.

153. For other memoirs and critical accounts of this meeting, see Bohlen, *Witness to History,* 213; R. J. Donovan, *Conflict and Crisis: The Presidency of Harry S. Truman, 1945–49* (New York: W. W. Norton, 1977), 37–39; William E. Pemberton, *Harry S. Truman: Fair Dealer and Cold Warrior* (Boston: Little, Brown, 1989), 47; Clemens, "The 'Reversal of Co-operation,'" 305; and Andrei Gromyko, *Memories,* Harold Shukman, trans. (London: Hutchinson, 1989), 96.

154. Davies Journal, April 30, 1945, box 16, Davies Papers.

155. See McCullough, *Truman,* 374–75; Gardner, *Spheres of Influence,* 255; Larson, *Origins of Containment,* 152–8; and Leffler, "Adherence to Agreements," 88. An interesting character, Stimson was intensely proud of his service in the field artillery in the First World War and still preferred to be called "Colonel Stimson." McCullough, *Truman,* 377.

156. Note that according to the official "Cold War Recognition" certificates issued by the Department of Defense, the U.S. government put the beginning of the cold war on September 2, 1945, the day that the Japanese formally surrendered aboard the USS *Missouri.* I see little historical justification for that choice, however, and no attempt by Congress or DOD to defend it on historical grounds.

157. See Abramson, *Spanning the Century,* 396.

158. Charles E. Bohlen, "Memorandum of Conversation," April 20, 1945, Papers of Harry S. Truman, President's Secretary's File, "Russia," box 187, file "Russia Molotov," HSTL.

159. Zubok and Pleshakov, *Inside the Kremlin's Cold War,* 95, n304. See also Gromyko, *Memories,* 258–59.

160. See Alonzo L. Hamby, *Man of the People: A Life of Harry S. Truman* (New York: Random House, 1995), 317–18. Strangely, Hamby footnotes not only Harriman, Special Envoy, but also Bohlen.

161. See Truman, *Year of Decisions,* 81–82, 99; Harriman, Special Envoy, 452–54; William Leahy Diary, April 23, 1945; and *FRUS, 1945, V,* 256–59. See also Abramson, *Spanning the Century,* 396; John Lewis Gaddis, "The Insecurities of Victory," in *The Long Peace,* 31; Yergin, *Shattered Peace,* 83; and Adam Ulam, *The Rivals* (New York: Viking Press, 1971), 64.

162. See Lloyd C. Gardner, *Architects of Illusion,* 61–62.

163. I. F. Stone, "Trieste and San Francisco," *Nation,* May 26, 1945.

164. See Ernest K. Lindley, "How Good Is Russia's Word?" *Newsweek,* April 30, 1945; and *Newsweek,* May 21, 1945. See also Harriman, *Special Envoy,* 456.

165. Charles L. Mee Jr., *Meeting at Potsdam* (New York: Evans, 1975), 4–5.

166. Longtime Truman aide Matthew J. Connelly suggests that the president "had a great deal of confidence in Mr. Byrnes because of their association in the Senate. Mr. Byrnes came from South Carolina, and talked to Mr. Truman and immediately decided that he would take over. Mr. Truman to Mr. Byrnes, I'm afraid, was a nonentity, as Mr. Byrnes thought he had superior intelligence." See Oral History Interview with Matthew J. Connelly, New York, New York, August 21, 1968, interview by Jerry N. Hess, available courtesy of the Harry S. Truman Library, *http://www.trumanlibrary.org/oralhist/connly3.htm.*

167. Messer, *The End of an Alliance,* 70.

168. Ibid., 56. Byrnes had insisted that the talks resulted in concrete decisions, "not merely declarations," regarding "free and unfettered elections" in Poland.
169. James F. Byrnes to Truman, April 25, 1945, Byrnes Papers. A second copy of this document, along with Byrnes's bound notes, can be found in "Crimean Conference" folder, Papers of Harry S. Truman, SMOF: Naval Aide to the President Files, 1945–53, box 11. For more on Byrnes's note, see Gar Alperovitz, with the assistance of Sanho Tree et al., *The Decision to Use the Atomic Bomb and the Architecture of an American Myth* (New York: Knopf, 1995), 217.
170. The agreements stated: "I. WORLD ORGANIZATION It was decided: 1. That a United Nations conference on the proposed world organization should be summoned for Wednesday, 25 April, 1945, and should be held in the United States of America. The nations to be invited to this conference should be: (a) the United Nations as they existed on 8 Feb., 1945; and (b) Such of the Associated Nations as have declared war on the common enemy by 1 March, 1945." Here are Hiss's notes on the subject.:

> "Pres. [FDR]: We have phrase Associated N[ation]s meaning nations which have broken rel[ation]s but haven't declared war [on Germany.]
>
> The list of nations which Mr Stett[inius] gave to Mr Molotov at lunch today.
>
> St[alin] asked about Argentina.
>
> Pres.: *Not an assoc. nation.* [emphasis added]
>
> St[alin]: If "associates" come in that would include Argentina. Would include Turkey.
>
> Pres.: My idea and it would save my life would be to invite those who [the word "have" scratched out here] are on the list who have helped us *on condition* [emphasis in original] that they declare war.
>
> St[alin]: Before or after they declare war?
>
> Pres.: Before, put a time limit, say 1st of March.
>
> St.: agreed."

Hiss's notes are confirmed by minutes of the meeting taken by James F. Byrnes. These read:

> The President . . . In addition to those nations that have signed, there are a small number called associate nations which have worked with us. They broke diplomatic relations but did not declare war.
>
> The Marshall: What about Argentina?
>
> The President: The Argentines are not in at all.
>
> The Marshall: But the Argentines broke relations with Germany.
>
> The President: But have not been accepted as an associated nation.
>
> The Marshall: I am not for the Argentines . . .
>
> The President: My idea would be to invite those states which are associate nations that have helped us. We could invite them on the condition that they would declare war.

> The Marshall: Why should they not?
>
> The President: Right away. Put a time limit on them.
>
> The Marshall: Say by the first of March.
>
> The President: All right the first of March.
>
> The Prime Minister: I was glad to hear the President say these nations would be required to declare war before they would be invited to the conference. I feel like the Marshall. . . .

See *FRUS, The Conferences at Malta and Yalta, 1945,* 783, and Yalta Minutes, February 8, 1945, Byrnes Papers, folder 622. See also "Nations to be Invited to the United Nations Conference," and "Policy Toward Argentina," Harry L. Hopkins Papers, container 170, folder 2; and "Protocol of the Proceeding of the Crimea Conference," Harry L. Hopkins Papers, Sherwood Collection, book 10: Yalta Conference, group 24, container 337, folder 7.

The decision, while tied up in the larger, complicated question of U.S. relations with the rest of Latin America, where support for Argentina was strong, as well as in the still-heated Polish dispute, proved largely to be the brainchild of the wily assistant secretary of state for inter-American affairs—and future Republican vice president—Nelson A. Rockefeller, who had placed a memorandum on the matter before FDR and gotten his signature, though it is far from clear that the president understood what he was signing. Argentina had not only maintained its diplomatic relations with the Nazis for two full years after the United States entered the war, it also served as a base for Axis espionage and subversion around the hemisphere. One *Washington Post* writer criticized the U.S. delegation's eagerness to forgive and forget as making sense in a context "more for the next war than the upcoming peace." Similar complaints were lodged by the editors of *The New Republic* and by columnist Walter Lippmann. Following the decision of the U.S. delegation to publicize its dispute with the USSR over Poland, Molotov decided to hold his own press conference regarding Argentina, where he mockingly read a series of damning quotations from Cordell Hull and FDR regarding that Fascist regime. "Why should not Poland be represented if Argentina is?" Molotov demanded. Certainly Stalin must have been impressed as well. In a truly slippery interpretation offered up four decades later, for instance, Henry Kissinger argued that, "when it decided to organize resistance to Soviet expansionism, America did so on the basis of Stalin's failure to keep his word as given at Yalta and as the American leaders and public had understood it." Kissinger does not mention that this understanding was itself the result of lying, secrecy, willful manipulation, and selective memory on the part of America's leaders.

On Rockefeller's subterfuge, see Bohlen, *Witness to History,* 206–7. See also Ferrell, *The Dying President,* 112. Harriman later said he demanded of Rockefeller, "Nelson, are you the ambassador to the Argentines or for the Argentines?" Harriman, *Special Envoy,* 455–56. See Herbert Elliston, "Argentina Action: More Fear Than Strength," in *Report on San Francisco* (Washington, D.C.: Washington Post, 1945) 314–15; "Pandora's Box at the U.N.C.I.O," in ibid., 10–11; "Spain and Argentina," *New Republic,* April 30, 1945, 573; and *Congressional Record,* 79th Congress, 1st sess., May 3, 1945, A2046. See also the excellent discussion of this topic in Randall B. Woods, "Conflict or Community: The United States and Argentina's Admission to the United Nations," *Pacific Historical Review* (August 1977): 361–86. For more on the entire issue of Latin America at the conference, see Albert Vannucci, "The Influence of Latin American Governments on the Shaping of United States Foreign Policy: The Case of U.S.-Argentina Relations, 1943–1948," *Journal of Latin American Studies* (November 1986): 355–82. For a discussion of the Soviet role in the Argentina matter, see Mario Rapoport, "Argentina and the Soviet Union: History of Political and Commercial Relations (1917-1955)," *Hispanic American Historical Review* (1986): 252. Molotov is quoted in the *New York Herald Tribune,* May 1, 1945, and cited in Gardner, *Architects of Illusion,* 61–64; Kissinger, *Diplomacy,* 415.

Some contend that Stalin surreptitiously violated the "letter and spirit" of the Yalta accords in September 1945 by aiding the Chinese Communists rather than Chiang's government. The relevant portion of the Yalta Accords reads: "For its part, the Soviet Union expresses it readiness to conclude with the National Government of China a pact of friendship and alliance between the U.S.S.R. and China in order to render assistance to China with its armed forces for the purpose of liberating China from the Japanese yoke." I disagree that such aid, if in fact it occurred, constitutes a violation of the above. Stalin also signed an accord with Chiang in August 1945, after negotiations during which Stalin promised to refrain from aiding the Chinese Communists. Again, whatever aid took place here strikes me as outside the purview of the accords themselves. The NS document, "COMINT and the PRC Intervention in the Korean War," is available at *http://www.nsa.gov/korea/papers/prc_intervention_ korean_war.pdf.* In any case, if the violations did occur, they occurred long after the Argentina incident at the United Nations.

171. On the very day that Truman lectured Molotov on Soviet compliance, Admiral Leahy wrote in his diary, "The consensus of opinion . . . that the time has arrived to take a strong American attitude toward the Soviet Union, and that no particular harm could be done to our war prospects if Russia should slow down or even stop its war effort in Europe and in Asia." See Leahy, *I Was There,* 351; and Leahy Diary, April 23, 1945.
172. In fact, the president later insisted that he had not intended to reverse Soviet lend-lease aid, only to review it in light of the changed circumstances, but his desires were overcome by overzealous enforcement of his initial orders at the level of individual naval officers. This appears highly unlikely, however. The president had four days to modify the order after signing it. Joseph Grew, the lend-lease administrator, insured that the order would come as a shock when he denied to the Soviets that it would take place, one day before it went into effect. Harriman, according to Grew's report to the secretary of state, "said that we would be getting 'a good tough slashback from the Russians but that we would have to face it." See Herbert Feis, *Between War and Peace,* 28–30, 101. See also Bernstein, "American Foreign Policy and the Origins of the Cold War," in *Twentieth-Century America: Recent Interpretations,* 2nd ed., Barton J. Bernstein and Allen J. Matusow, eds. (New York: Harcourt Brace Jovanovich, 1972), 28. For Stalin's reaction, which was made to Harry Hopkins, see "How the Cold War Started," *U.S. News & World Report,* March 3, 1950, 14.
173. Harriman, *Special Envoy,* 455–56, 457, 461.
174. Truman apparently told Joseph Davies, charging him with "the utmost secrecy," that he had scheduled the Potsdam meeting to coincide with the Nevada atomic bomb test. Davies Diary, May 21, 1945, box, 17, Davies Papers. This entry, written in 1954, was based on notes of his conversation with Truman that Davies had kept locked in his safe.
175. In Truman's words, Stalin was quite accommodating to American concerns at Potsdam. His agreement, however, was short-lived. In an oral history, several years after the end of his presidency, Truman said, "No, I got a very favorable impression of [the Soviets]. There was no difficulty in getting Stalin to agree to those things we wanted done. But [after Potsdam] he went back to Moscow and broke everything. . . ." Harry S. Truman Oral History Interview, Post Presidential Files, HSTL.

176. Memo for the President by Stimson, September 11, 1945, U.S. Department of State, *FRUS, The Conference of Berlin (The Potsdam Conference), 1945,* vol. 2, 40–45. Harriman spoke for many when he asked, "How urgent or important was it that Russia should join the war against Japan?" Truman and Byrnes both decided that Soviet participation was no longer desirable upon hearing of the bomb, and Stimson advised the same. From his post at the Moscow embassy, Harriman helped prod the Chinese leaders to construct more and more delaying tactics to obstruct the Sino-Soviet negotiations over Russian entry into the war. See Leffler, *A Preponderance of Power,* 83. See also Harriman, *Special Envoy,* 455–57, 461. The decision to withhold the information regarding the bomb also put a further strain on U.S.-Soviet relations, quite understandably. *The New York Times* reported that "The insistence by the inventors of mankind's most horrible weapon on withholding the secret from their ally has produced a most evident reaction in Moscow." See C. L. Sulzberger, "Big Three Try Again to Ease World Strains," *New York Times,* December 16, 1945. See also Bernstein, "American Foreign Policy and the Origins of the Cold War," 47.
177. Harriman, *Special Envoy,* 455–57, 461.
178. See Messer, *The End of an Alliance,* 105. Truman shared Byrnes's sentiments. See Entry for July 25, 1945, Truman Diary.
179. Stimson Diary, September 4, 1945.
180. This advice appeared in a memo authored by Joseph Grew, and can be found, along with Stimson's comments on it, in Stimson Diary, May 13, 1945, reel 9, Library of Congress. See also Grew, *Turbulent Era,* II, 1455–56; and Messer, *The End of an Alliance,* 100.
181. Truman quoted in Gardner, *Architects of Illusion,* 58.
182. James Byrnes explained to Soviet Foreign Minister Molotov that battlefield destruction had transformed the situation in Germany and now prevented the granting of reparations on the order of those discussed at Yalta. The Soviets reluctantly accepted this argument and agreed to reduce their demands, which the United States then promptly ignored as well. See Eisenberg, *Drawing the Line,* 103. At Yalta, according to James F. Byrnes's minutes, FDR explained to Churchill and Stalin, "The time has come to set up some kind of reparations commission which will do the best it can for every country in accordance with its needs and in accordance with the ability of the Germans to supply those needs." See Yalta Minutes, February 5, 1945, Byrnes Papers, folder 622. For Stalin's offer on Poland, see Barton J. Bernstein, "American Foreign Policy and the Origins of the Cold War," 358. (Bernstein's essay is reprinted from *Politics and Policies of the Truman Administration.*) Bernstein goes on to add, "In Budapest [in 1945] free elections were held and the Communist party was routed; and early in November, just two days after the United States recognized Hungary, the Communists lost in the national elections there. In Bulgaria elections took place in 'complete order and without disturbance,' and, despite American protests, a Communist-dominated single ticket (representing most of the political parties) triumphed." He concludes, "while the Soviet Union would not generally permit in Eastern Europe conditions that conformed to Western ideals, Stalin was pursuing a cautious policy and seeking accommodation with the West." This view, however, is disputed in a paper published in 2001 by Eduard Mark in which he argues, "In recent years, materials on this subject have become available in Russia and Eastern Europe. The British government, moreover, has only recently revealed that it intercepted Moscow's instructions to the European communist parties from mid-1943 through 1945." According to Mark's research, "In Eastern Europe, where the strategy became known after the war as Narodniya demokratiya (Popular Democracy), the intent was to leverage the power of the small communist parties through the creation of broad communist-dominated coalitions that outwardly ob-

served the conventions of 'bourgeois democracy.' The purposes of this tactic were (a) to divide or otherwise render ineffective local opposition; (b) to create centers of political attraction which would consolidate popular support through programs of reform and recovery; and (c) to minimize Western objections to the creeping establishment of regimes dominated by communists and directly subject to Moscow lest the USSR be drawn into dangerously premature conflict with its allies and forfeit the substantial advantages to be gained from continued association with them." He concludes: "The value of a socialized Eastern Europe for Stalin was, by contrast, absolute in two ways. It was explicitly, the ultimate aim of his policies in Eastern Europe, an aim deeply rooted in his regime's ideology and his personal beliefs. From his Marxist-Leninist perspective, moreover, it was obviously more prudent that the military security of the USSR should ultimately be entrusted to a glacis of socialized states in Eastern Europe than to agreements with capitalist states that he viewed as intrinsically predatory potential enemies. They, not the shattered Germany, were the chief source of his fears for the future." See Eduard Mark, "Revolution by Degrees: Stalin' s National-Front Strategy for Europe, 1941–1947," Cold War International History Project, working paper no. 31 (*http://cwih si.edu/working%20papers-pdf.htm*), 6–7. Mark's view is consistent with that put forth in a variety of essays by Geoffrey Roberts, including those argued in "Stalin and the Cold War," *Europe-Asia Studies,* December 1997, and "Ideology, Calculation and Improvisation."

183. Averell Harriman, quoted in "Off the Record Discussion of the Origins of the Cold War," May 31, 1967. In the possession of the author.
184. See *Chicago Tribune,* March 24, 1947; Grosse, *Operation Rollback,* 199; and Theoharis, *The Yalta Myths,* 52–53.
185. These elections took place in Chicago, Milwaukee, and Detroit. See Robert D. Ubriaco Jr., "Bread and Butter Politics or Foreign Policy Concerns: Class Versus Ethnicity in the Midwestern Polish Community During the 1946 Congressional Elections," *Polish American Studies* 51(2) (1994): 5–32.
186. Joseph E. Grew, "Political Situation in Poland," May 6, 1945, Papers of Harry S. Truman, President's Secretary's Files, box 186, Misc. Correspondence file, HSTL.
187. Yergin, *Shattered Peace,* 171.
188. Hopkins told Stalin that "in a country like ours public opinion is affected by specific incidents and in this case the deterioration in public opinion in regard to our relations with the Soviet Union was centered in our inability to carry into effect the Yalta agreement on Poland." Top Secret Harriman memo, dated 8:00 P.M., May 28, 1945, W. Averell Harriman Private Papers.
189. Taubman, *Stalin's American Policy,* 104.
190. According to Gaddis's 1972 interpretation, "The Russian dictator was immune from pressures of Congress, public opinion or the press." Stalin's absolute powers offered him "more chances to surmount the international restraints on his policy than were available to his democratic counterparts in the West." See John Lewis Gaddis, *The United States and the Origins of the Cold War,* 360–61.
191. See Thomas G. Paterson, "Presidential Foreign Policy: Public Opinion and Congress: The Truman Years," *Diplomatic History* 3(1) (1979): 10–11.
192. Davies notes that his talk with Lippmann was strictly "off-the-record." Franklin D. Roosevelt to Winston Churchill, March 29, 1945, in U.S. Department of State, *FRUS, Diplomatic Papers: 1945, V,* 189; Davies Diary, June 5, 6, 9, 1945, box 17, Davies Papers; Memorandum of Conversation, May 23, 1945, Davies Papers; and 711.61/5–2345, records group 59, National Archives, College Park, MD. See also Larson, *Origins of Containment,* 118.

193. See Davies Diary, June 6, 1945. Based on his interpretation of the Yalta agreement, Byrnes said, "There was no question as to what the spirit of the agreement was. There was no intent that a new government was to be created independent of the Lublin Government." See also Leffler, "Adherence to Agreements," 97.
194. See Fromkin, *In the Time of the Americans,* 492; Yergin, *Shattered Peace,* 127–29; and Taubman, *Stalin's American Policy,* 120.
195. McCormick, *American's Half-Century,* 65.
196. Fromkin, *In the Time of the Americans,* 491.
197. Gardner, *Architects of Illusion,* 60.
198. See "Neighboring Nations in One World," Department of State Bulletin 13 (4 November 1945): 709–11.
199. McCullough, *Truman,* 490.
200. See Hugh DeSantis, *Diplomacy of Silence: The American Foreign Service, The Soviet Union and the Cold War, 1933-1947* (Chicago: University of Chicago Press, 1980), 147–52. See also Harriman, *Special Envoy,* 515; and Leffler, *A Preponderance of Power,* 40, 47.
201. "Unless Russia is faced with an iron fist and strong language," Truman wrote to Byrnes in an unsent January 5, 1948, letter, "another war is in the making." Harry S. Truman, *Off the Record: The Private Papers of Harry S. Truman,* Robert H. Ferrell, ed. (New York, Harper & Row, 1980), 80.
202. The number of people dissatisfied with the level of Allied cooperation fell from 46 percent just before the conference to just 15 percent immediately afterward. The number of Americans who saw the conference as a success numbered more than five times the number that dissented. See Memorandum for the President from Secretary of State Edward Stettinius, "Reaction to the Crimean Conference," March 13, 1945, President's Secretary's Files, container 129, Crimean Conference, FDRL; "Public Reaction to the Crimean Conference," March 27, 1945, Official File 200, container 67, Crimean Conference, FDRL; and Messer, *The End of an Alliance,* 61.
203. The number of people imploring the U.S. government to trust the Soviet Union, according to pollsters, dropped from an all-time high of 55 percent in March 1945 to just 35 percent a year later. See *Public Opinion Quarterly* 10 (Spring 1946): 115.
204. This was particularly true in 1945 and 1946, when the number of Americans telling pollsters that foreign affairs problems were of vital importance fell to 7 percent in October, 1945, rose to only 23 percent in February 1946, and then fell back down to 11 percent the following June. These numbers are in contrast to an all-time high of 81 percent in November 1941. See Gabriel Almond, *The American People and Foreign Policy* (New Haven, CT: Yale University Press, 1960), 73.
205. A. J. Taylor, writing in *New Statesman* and *Nation* in April 19, 1953, first used the term to apply to "the Establishment," which "talks with its own branded accent, eats different meals at different times from the rest of the populace, has its privileged system of education, its own religion, its powerful offices both visible and invisible." Henry Fairlie, writing of the same group in *The Spectator,* termed them, "A group of powerful men, who know each other, or at least know someone who knows anyone they may need to know; who share assumptions so deep that they do not need to be articulated; and who contrive to wield power outside the constitutional or political forms: the power to put a stop to things they disapprove of, to promote the men they regard as reliable; and to clock the unreliable; the power, in a word, to preserve the status quo." Geoffrey Hodgson defined the U.S. version, in 1970, as "a self-recruited group of men, virtually no women, who have shared a bipartisan philosophy towards, and have exercised practical influence on, the course of American defense and foreign policy . . . To qualify a man must have a reputation for ability in this field that is accepted by at least

two of three worlds; int'l business, banking and the law in New York; the world of government in Washington; and the academic world, especially in Cambridge . . ." From WWII until the late 1960s at least, by a history of common action, they shared policy of "liberal internationalism," an instinct for the center, and a habit of working privately throughout the power of the newly bureaucratized presidency. See Leonard Silk and Mark Silk, *The American Establishment* (New York: Basic Books, 1980), 8; and Geoffrey Hodgson, "The Establishment," *Foreign Policy* (3), 3,13.

206. David Lawrence, "The Tragedy of Yalta," *U.S. News & World Report,* March 2, 1945.
207. "Funeral March," *Time,* February 26, 1945.
208. This characterization does not entirely do justice to the case of "The Ghosts on the Roof," authored by *Time's* foreign editor Whittaker Chambers and published on March 3, 1945. The essay will be discussed in the context of the Hiss-Chambers case later in this chapter.
209. "Vote Secret, Soviet Pole Demand Casts Shadows for San Francisco," *Newsweek,* April 9, 1945.
210. "The Nations," *Time,* April 9, 1945.
211. Ibid.
212. *Time,* June 11, 1945.
213. Hanson Baldwin, "America at War: Victory in the Pacific," *Foreign Affairs* 24(1) (October 1945): 35.
214. Henry Luce, "Dumbarton Oaks and San Francisco," *Fortune* supplement, May 1945.
215. U.S. Department of State, *The Department of State Bulletin* 12:302 (April 8, 1945): 600.
216. See Leffler, *A Preponderance of Power,* 28. See also Messer, *The End of an Alliance,* 64–70, 77; and Rose, *After Yalta,* 244–62.
217. Memorandum of the Press and Radio News Conference, Tuesday, September 4, 1945 (Not for the Press) (For Departmental Use Only), Byrnes Papers, folder 598.
218. U.S. Senate, Committee on Foreign Relations, *Hearings on the Investigation of Far Eastern Policy,* 79th Congress, 1st sess., 1945, 233.
219. Memorandum of the Press and Radio News Conference, Tuesday, January 29, 1946 (Not for the Press) (For Department Use Only), Byrnes Papers, folder 556. See also "Secret of the Kuriles," *Time,* February 11, 1946.
220. In his memoirs, Byrnes explains, "I did not know of this agreement, but the reason is understandable. At the time, I was not Secretary of State. Mr. Stettinius was Secretary. [Though he says he had hardly anything to do with it either.] . . . The agreement as to the Kurile Islands was reached in private conversations among the Big Three instead of at the conference table, and the protocols, including this one, were signed on February 11. Had I been in Yalta [he left a day early] that day it is probable that I would have learned of it. When the President returned, he did not mention it to me and the protocol was kept locked in his safe at the White House. In the early summer I learned that President Roosevelt had undertaken to induce China to make the concessions affecting Port Arthur, Dairen, and the railroad, but it was not until some time after I became Secretary of State that a news story from Moscow caused me to inquire and learn of the full agreement. I presented the matter to President Truman and he requested Admiral Leahy to transfer to the State Department those documents at the White House containing agreements with foreign government. I wanted to know how many IOUs were outstanding." See Byrnes, *Speaking Frankly,* 43. Stettinius skirts the issue of his own knowledge in his defense of the Far Eastern accord in Stettinius Jr., *Roosevelt and the Russians,* 303–6. For a more accurate version, see Messer, *The End of an Alliance,* 170.
221. See U.S. Senate, Committee on Foreign Relations, *Hearings on the Investigation of Far Eastern Policy,* 79th Congress, 1st sess., 1945, 233; and Theoharis, *The Yalta Myths,* 37.

222. Charles E. Bohlen, "Memorandum of Conversation," April 22, 1945, Papers of Harry S. Truman, President's Secretary's File, "Russia," box 187, file "Russia Molotov," HSTL.
223. The memo appears to have been prepared by Elsey with Captain James K. Vardaman Jr., before being shown to the president. See James K. Vardaman Jr., "Memorandum for the President," June 12, 1945, Papers of George Elsey, box 3, "Historical Reports and Research Notes, Yalta Conference Briefings" file, HSTL.
224. See Leffler, *A Preponderance of Power,* 84.
225. Harriman, *Special Envoy,* 494–98.
226. *Chicago Tribune,* September 6, 1945.
227. See Harold B. Hinton, "Stalin's Price to Fight Japan Bared by Accord on Japan," *New York Times,* February 12, 1945. FDR's secret deal on the Far East turned out to be quite popular, particularly once China and Russia worked out their own accord based on the initial Stalin-Roosevelt negotiations. The August 28, 1945, *New York Times* called the agreement "a victory for peace as great as any scored on the battlefield . . . they fulfill all the requirements of both the UN Charter and of the Cairo Declaration. . . ." "The Chinese-Russian treaty must be a great disappointment to the prophets of doom. . . . The prestige of Chunking is greatly enhanced by this treaty." Their benefits, it said, had been obtained "at what seems to be a very reasonable price." And *Life,* which later turn vehemently anti-Yalta, noted on September 10, 1945, that the Chinese Russian negotiations had brought "an agreement which was as great a victory for common sense as the defeat of Japan was for armed might. The Soong-Stalin treaties contain less ammunition for pessimists than any diplomatic event of the last 20 years . . . the present prospects of China are a vindication of American policy in Asia for almost 50 years." See "The Russo-Chinese Pact," *New York Times,* August 28, 1945, 18. See also Hiss, "Yalta: Modern American Myth."
228. Not even the *Chicago Tribune* called for repudiation of the accords. *Chicago Tribune,* February 1, 1946. See also Republican Senate Policy Committee, "Chronology of Secret Agreements at Yalta," *Republican News,* March 1946.
229. Arthur Krock, "In the Nation," *New York Times,* February 12, 1945.
230. This was true of *The New York Times, Newsweek, U.S. News & World Report, Time, The Saturday Evening Post,* the *Chicago Herald American,* among many others. See Theoharis, *The Yalta Myths,* 46–7.
231. "The Skeletons in the Closet" (editorial), *New York Times,* March 26, 1947.
232. See Theoharis, *The Yalta Myths,* 45.
233. *U.S. News & World Report,* May 17, 1946.
234. "From Stettin in the Baltic to Trieste in the Adriatic, an iron curtain has descended across the Continent," Winston Churchill, Fulton, Missouri, March 5, 1946.
235. George Kennan, Telegram dated March 20, 1946, Harry S. Truman Administration "Newsclippings" file, box 64, Papers of George Elsey, HSTL.
236. For more on the *Times,* see Harbutt, *The Iron Curtain,* 172. For Vandenberg, see Gaddis, *The United States and the Origins of the Cold War.* For the long telegram, see Kennan, *Memoirs: 1925–1950,* 271–97. See also his elaboration of its central points in "The Sources of Soviet Conduct," *Foreign Affairs,* July 1946, reprinted in Hamilton Fish Armstrong, ed., *The Foreign Affairs Reader* (New York: Harper & Brothers, 1947), 464–83. See also Hogan, *A Cross of Iron,* 10.
237. Leahy Diary, November 28 and December 11, 1945, reel 4, Leahy Papers. See also Yergin, *Shattered Press,* 155.
238. Truman privately expressed his "sharp disapproval of the recent attitude of appeasement toward the Soviet government," and feared "it will be difficult to induce the Secretary of State to tacitly admit fault in our present appeasement attitude." Meanwhile,

criticism in the liberal press called Soviet promises there as "a mess of pottage" and admonished Truman to "take a lesson" from the "tragedy" of Yalta. According to the medical examiner's April 1946 report, Byrnes's health was essentially unchanged since before his trip to Yalta. He was pronounced to be "in very good condition." See *New York Times,* February 5, 1946; and *Washington Post,* February 1, 1946. For Truman's comments, see Cabell Phillips, "'Inner Circle' at the White House," *New York Times Magazine,* February 24, 1946; Leahy Diary, February 20, 1946, and February 21, 1946, reel 4, Leahy Papers; and Messer, *The End of an Alliance,* 177–79.

239. See Grosse, *Operation Rollback,* 89.
240. Drafts of this letter, done for Clifford by Elsey, Harry S. Truman Administration, box 63, folder 2, Papers of George Elsey, HSTL.
241. The report, entitled "American Relations with the Soviet Union: A Report to the President by the Special Council to the President, September—, 1946," can be found in Arthur Krock, *Sixty Years on the Firing Line* (New York: Funk and Wagnalls, 1968), appendix A, 421–82. The original draft, entitled "Comments on Soviet Compliance with International Agreements Undertaken Since January 1941," "Russia," file 4 of 8, box 15, Clark Clifford Papers, HSTL.
242. Offner, *Another Such Victory,* 180–81.
243. Dean Acheson, *Present at the Creation,* 220–25. See also Dean Acheson, *Sketches from Life of Men I Have Known* (New York: Harper & Row, 1961), 108; Hoopes and Brinkley, *Driven Patriot,* 278; and Harry S. Truman, *Memoirs: 1946, Year of Trial and Hope* (New York: Signet, 1956), 128. For more on Vandenberg's influence on Truman, the media, and the foreign policy process, see James Reston, *Deadline: A Memoir* (New York: Random House, 1991), 168. See also Patrick Lloyd Hatcher, *The Suicide of An Elite: American Internationalists and Vietnam* (Stanford, CA: Stanford University Press, 1990) 206; and Eric Alterman, *Sound & Fury: The Making of the Punditocracy,* 2nd ed. (Ithaca, NY: Cornell University Press, 2000), 42.
244. *Congressional Record,* 79th Congress, 2nd sess., 1946, XCII, Part 4, 6216–17.
245. Harry S. Truman, speech, April 17, 1948, Washington, D.C., and press conference, April 23, 1948.
246. Harry S. Truman to Eleanor Roosevelt, March 16, 1948. See also Eleanor Roosevelt to Harry S. Truman, March 13, 1948, President's Secretary's File, box 322, Potsdam file, HSTL.
247. Mrs. Robert Taft, urged on by her husband to try to "butter Van up" at a dinner party, complained that "he buttered himself so thoroughly that I really couldn't find a single ungreased spot." See Yergin, *Shattered Peace,* 47.
248. *Congressional Record,* 79th Congress, 2nd sess., 1946, XCII, Parts 3, 7, 8, and 9, 3841, 9060–63. See also Reston, *Deadline,* 159.
249. Harold B. Hinton, "U.S. Review on Orient Gets Spur in Visit by Quirino; Vandenburg Urges Clarity," *New York Times,* August 7, 1949.
250. William C. Bullitt, "How We Won the War and Lost the Peace," Part One, *Life,* August 30, 1948.
251. William C. Bullitt, "How We Won the War and Lost the Peace," Part Two, *Life,* August 30, 1948. The manner in which President Roosevelt's Far East concessions led to the victory of Mao's forces is explained by California Republican William F. Knowland. He explained, on the floor of the Senate on August 8, 1949, that "the Yalta agreement, in trading off something which did not belong to us, but belonged to China, without the knowledge or consent of the Chinese Government, was an indefensible act, both in international law and in good morals. I believe that by that action we made certain that the Communist forces would not only control Manchuria, because the Russians

were given actual control of the Manchurian Railroad as well as the port of Dairen; but in addition it made almost inevitable the Communist domination of north China. [Yalta] pulled the rug out from under the legal government of China, embargoed the shipment of arms to them at the time the Soviet Government was supplying to the Chinese Communists arms captured from the Kwantung Japanese Government, which were estimated by our military authorities to be sufficient to quip 1,000,000 men for 10 years. At the very same time, we were levying an embargo upon the legal government of China which was an ally of ours, a historic friend since the Hay doctrine of 1899, a fellow member of the United Nations and one of the Big Five. While we were pulling the rug out from under them, the Soviet Union was taking care of its friends." *Congressional Record,* 81st Congress, 1st sess., 1949, XCV, Part 3, 1949. Note that Churchill also found it useful in later years to blame FDR's ill health for the failures of Yalta. "We can now see the deadly hiatus which existed between the fading of President Roosevelt's strength and the growth of the President's grip of the vast world problem. In this melancholy void one President could not act and the other could not know." See Kimball, *Forged in War,* 324.

252. For Clark Clifford, see Barnet, *The Rocket's Red Glare,* 280–81. See also Robert A. Divine, *Foreign Policy and U.S. Presidential Elections, 1940–1948* (New York: New Viewpoints, 1974), 172.
253. "Summary of Remarks of Charles E. Bohlen at the Fourth Meeting of the Working Group Participating in the Washington Exploratory Talks on Security, July 20, 1948," reproduced in Frank Kofsky, *Harry Truman and the War Scare of 1948* (New York: St. Martin's Press, 1995), appendix A, 287. Kofsky's entire book makes the larger case for the artificial nature of the war scare quite convincingly, although his attribution of the need to save America's aviation industry as its motivation is insufficiently complex.
254. Ibid., 135.
255. See Athan Theoharis, "The Escalation of the Loyalty Program," in Bernstein, *Politics and the Policies of the Truman Administration,* 243. See also Sam Tanenhaus, *Whittaker Chambers: A Biography* (New York: Random House, 1996), 206.
256. The exact figure is 3,154, drawn from Ellen Schrecker, *Many Are the Crimes: McCarthyism in America* (Boston: Little, Brown, 1998), 298.
257. *Congressional Record,* 81st Congress, 1st sess., 1949, XCV, Part 3, A1343–44.
258. Raymond Swing, "What Really Happened at Yalta," *New York Times Magazine,* February 20, 1949.
259. For a complete report on the Ladd-Hiss interview, see Ladd's memorandum to J. Edgar Hoover, March 25, 1946, Federal Bureau of Investigation Files. See also Allen Weinstein, *Perjury: The Hiss-Chambers Case,* 2nd ed. (New York: Random House, 1997), 318.
260. See Roger Morris, *Richard Milhous Nixon: The Rise of an American Politician* (New York: Henry Holt, 1990), 391.
261. Here is Whittaker Chambers's description of his decision to become a Communist: "One day early in 1925, I sat down on a concrete bench on the Columbia campus, facing a little Greek shrine and the statue of my old political hero, Alexander Hamilton. The sun was shining, but it was chilly, and I sat huddled in my overcoat. I was there to answer once and for all two questions. Can a man go on living in a world that is dying? If he can, what should he do in the crisis of the twentieth century?" Whittaker Chambers, *Witness* (New York: Random House, 1952), 195.
262. Ibid., 331.
263. Weinstein, *Perjury,* 313. See also Alger Hiss, "Memorandum of Duties in the Department of States, 1944 Until January 15, 1947," September 1948, Hiss Defense Files.
264. Unaware that Roosevelt had decided to give the Soviets three votes, "one of the Pres-

ident's experts [presumably Hiss], unaware of Roosevelt's reaction, drafted for Stettinius a list of arguments against including any of the individual Soviet Republics among the initial members of the peace organization." When the Russians made counter arguments, a subcommittee consisting of Hiss, Gromyko, and Gladwyn Jebb, the British representative, agreed to have it typed. When Hiss at the plenary session first looked at the newly typed copy of the report, he protested to Eden that it contained a statement of American support for the Russian proposal, and that this had not been agreed. Eden replied, "You don't know what has taken place." FDR had not mentioned to Stettinius any discussions he had had with British and he had just heard about it. It did reflect on Hiss's lack of influence over the proceedings at Yalta. See Stettinius, *Roosevelt and the Russians,* 195–197. See also Forest C. Pogue, "The Big Three and the United Nations," in John Snell et al., *The Meaning of Yalta* (Baton Rouge: Louisiana State University, 1956), 182; and Weinstein, *Perjury,* 312–13.

265. Hiss's superiors at the State Department, fervent anti-Communists all, found no evidence of disloyalty in any of his actions at Yalta or elsewhere. One of his colleagues, however, Frederick B. Lyons, did muse aloud in a memo written in 1948 that if Hiss had conveyed the recommendations of the Far Eastern committee to the Russians, it would have allowed the Soviets to "know what we hoped to do and make their plans accordingly. Hence perhaps their insistence upon their claims as their price upon entry into the war against Japan." See Weinstein, *Perjury,* 320.
266. See David Remnick, "Unforgiven," in *The Devil Problem & Other True Stories,* rev. ed. (New York: Picador, 1997), 113–32.
267. "Testimony of David Whittaker Chambers," August 3, 1948, open session before the U.S. House Committee on Internal Security. See *Congressional Record,* 81st Congress, 1st sess., 1949, XCV, Part 3, 3767–71. See also Chambers, *Witness,* 689; and Alger Hiss, *In the Court of Public Opinion* (New York: Alfred A. Knopf, 1957), 147.
268. W. H. Lawrence, "Communists Solid for Dewey to Win, Truman Declares," *New York Times,* September 29, 1948.
269. See *Time,* May 28, 1945.
270. See Yergin, *Shattered Peace,* 406.
271. *Washington Post,* December 10, 1948.
272. Robert Bendiner, "The Trials of Alger Hiss," *Nation,* June 11, 1949. See also Ralph de Toledano, *Seeds of Treason: The Story of the Chambers-Hiss Tragedy* (New York: Funk and Wagnalls Co., 1950), chap. 13; and Alistair Cooke, *A Generation on Trial: USA vs. Alger Hiss* (New York: Alfred A. Knopf, 1950).
273. See Hiss, *In the Court of Public Opinion,* 212.
274. *New York Herald Tribune,* July 10, 1949. See also Tanenhaus, *Whittaker Chambers,* 412.
275. See *Congressional Record,* 81st Congress, 2nd sess., 1950, XCV, Part 3, 900–4. Mundt also reprinted thousands of copies of his Senate speech and distributed them across the nation. In it the subtitles of his speech claimed "Hiss's Job Was to Pervert Policy," "The White House Obstructed Investigation," and "Why Today's Political Plotters Must Be Stopped." See Weinstein, *Perjury,* 453.
276. For the entire conversation, see Theoharis, *The Yalta Myths,* 93.
277. See *Congressional Record,* 81st Congress, 2nd sess., 1950, XCV, Part 3, 756
278. See *Congressional Record,* 81st Congress, 1st sess., 1949, XCV, Part 1, A1047–48.
279. Weinstein, *Perjury,* 451.
280. See Jim Bishop, *FDR's Last Year* (New York: William Morrow, 1974).
281. See *Congressional Record,* 81st Congress, 2nd sess., 1950, XCV, Part 3, 1046. See also Theoharis, *The Yalta Myths,* 128; and Fred J. Cook, "Hiss the Prothonatary Warbler," *Nation,* September 21, 1957, 142–80.

282. "Gen. Hurley on Yalta: FDR Tried to Back Out," *U.S. News & World Report,* June 9, 1951.
283. Hurley is quoted in U.S. Senate Committee on Foreign Relations and Committee on Armed Services, *Military Situation in the Far East, Hearing to Conduct an Inquiry into the Military Situation in the Far East and the Facts Surrounding the Relief of General Douglas MacArthur from His Assignments in That Area,* 82nd Congress, 1st sess., 1951, Part 4, 2837–39. See also Russell D. Buhite, "Patrick J. Hurley and the Yalta Far Eastern Agreement," *Pacific Historical Review* 37:3 (1968): 343–53. The "blueprint" quote appears on page 349.
284. Weinstein, *Perjury,* 453–54.
285. "Had our Government listened to those of us who really knew the Far East, we should not today be fighting the armies of Soviet China and Korea and perhaps soon enough in French Indochina and India," explained George Sokolsky over the American Broadcasting Co. radio stations on November 5, 1950.
286. Harold B. Hinton, "Marshall U.S. Foe, M'Carthy Charges," *New York Times,* June 15, 1951.
287. In February, the Republican members of the House and Senate adopted a statement, together with the Republican National Committee, denouncing "the secret agreements of Yalta." Styles Bridges asked, "How long must we go on attempting to justify Mr. Roosevelt's mistake at Yalta?" Karl Mundt wondered why FDR thought it "necessary" to keep "someone who thought communism a noble thing" on his advisory staff. "Perhaps a more alert and critical attitude by the Republican Party would have compelled [Roosevelt and Truman] to clean house more thoroughly . . . Perhaps if we Republicans had insisted sooner and more ardently on a disclosure of the secret agreements made at Yalta we would have discovered much sooner that there must have been influence at work at that unfortunate conference which had other causes to serve and other motives to fulfill than a consideration of American interests and world security and integrity." *Congressional Record,* 81st Congress, 2nd sess., 1950, XCVI, Part 2, 1541. On Bridges and Mundt, see Theoharis, *The Yalta Myths,* 91–92.
288. See Robert A. Taft, *A Foreign Policy for Americans* (Garden City, NY: Doubleday and Co., 1951), 50–51.
289. On Taft, see Theoharis, *The Yalta Myths,* 102.
290. "V.F.W. Condemns Yalta 'Sell-Out,' " *New York Times,* September 2, 1950.
291. On *The New Leader,* see Kenneth O'Reilly, "Liberal Values, Cold War, and American Intellectuals: The Trauma of the Alger Hiss Case," in Athan Theoharis, ed., *Beyond the Hiss Case: The FBI, Congress and the Cold War* (Philadelphia: Temple University, 1982), 313.
292. See Arthur Schlesinger, "A Shameful Story," *New York Times Book Review,* March 19, 1978; and O'Reilly, "Liberal Values, Cold War, and American Intellectuals," 316.
293. Ibid., 315.
294. *Witness* was the ninth best-selling book of 1952. *New York Times Book Review,* June 8, 1952; and *Time,* May 26, 1952. See Tanenhaus, *Whittaker Chambers,* 463; and Stephen J. Whitfield, *The Culture of the Cold War* (Baltimore: Johns Hopkins University Press, 1991), 18.
295. Sidney Hook, *New York Times Book Review,* May 23, 1953. Reviewing the book in *Partisan Review* in 1952, Rahv wrote, "Chambers may be exaggerating in saying that in those years it was the Popular Front mind that dominated American life, but he is hardly exaggerating when he specifies that it was that mind which then dominated most avenues of communication between the intellectuals and the nation. It told the nation what it should believe it made up the nation's mind for it. The Popular Fronters had made themselves the 'experts.' They controlled the narrows of news and opinion . . . the nation . . . could not grasp or believe that a conspiracy on the scale of communism was possible or that it had already made so deep a penetration." And the fierce

resistance which Chambers encountered when he finally broke through with his testimony to the nation at large was essentially a symptom of the anguish of the Popular Front mind and its unreasoning anger at being made to confront the facts of political life. The importance of the Hiss case was precisely that it dramatized that mind's struggle for survival and all its vindictiveness under attack. That mind is above all terrified of the disorder and evil of history, and it flees the harsh choices which history so often imposes. It fought to save Hiss in order to safeguard its own illusions and to escape the knowledge of its gullibility and chronic refusal of reality. See Philip Rahv, "The Sense and Nonsense of Whittaker Chambers," in Arabel J. Porter and Andrew J. Dvosin, eds., *Essays on Literature and Politics, 1932–1972* (Boston: Houghton Mifflin, 1978), 322–23.

296. "It was the opinion of some of the State Department group who were on President Roosevelt's staff at the conference that Marshal Stalin had difficulties with the Politburo, when he returned to Moscow, for having been too friendly and for having made too many concessions to the two capitalist nations which could, in dogmatic Marxist eyes, never be really trusted by Communist Russia. Certain members of the Politburo may well have taken the line that the Soviet Union had been virtually sold out at Yalta." See Stettinius Jr., *Roosevelt and the Russians,* 309–10. See also Edward R. Stettinius Jr., "After Yalta: Why the FDR-Stalin Pact Broke Down," *Look,* July 5, 1949.
297. *Time*'s anonymous reviewer, for instance mocks the "always, easily infected handsome 'Big Ed' Stettinius [who] earnestly told Uncle Joe that if they all worked together after the war, every house in Russia could have plumbing and electricity." The book, the reviewer sneers, "applauds the bankruptcy of statesmanship" in offering the "excuse for FDR's tragic weakness on the Polish issue is that the Russians were already in Poland." *Time,* November 7, 1949.
298. *FRUS, The Conference of Berlin,* I, 13. See also *Ulam, Expansion and Co-Existence,* 314–77.
299. Appendix to the *Congressional Record,* 81st Congress, 2nd sess., 1950, XCVI, A5410, A5416.
300. On the "might have been" issue, I recommend chapter 10 of Schrecker, *Many Are the Crimes.*
301. Schrecker, *Many Are the Crimes,* 400.
302. *Congressional Record,* 81st Congress, 2nd sess., 1950, XCVI, Part 2, A4752.
303. Acheson's opponents, especially Senator McCarthy, vigorously denounced his January 12 "Press Club" speech in which he explicitly excluded Korea from the U.S. defense umbrella. For details, see Bruce Cumings, *The Origins of the Korean War,* Vol. 2: *The Roaring of the Cataract, 1947–1950* (Princeton, NJ: Princeton University Press, 1991), 416–19, 436–39. For the *Chicago Tribune* and Republican congressional charges regarding the alleged sellout of Korea at Yalta, see *Congressional Record,* 81st Congress, 2nd sess., 1950, XCVI, Part 1, 572, 635; and Theoharis, *The Yalta Myths,* 98.
304. For Acheson and Truman, see Walter LaFeber, "NATO and the Korean War," *Diplomatic History* 13:4 (Fall 1989): 473; Krock, *Sixty Years on the Firing Line,* 260; and Steven L. Rearden, *The Evolution of American Strategic Doctrine: Paul H. Nitze and the Soviet Challenge* (Boulder, CO: Westview Press, 1984), 30.
305. *The New York Times* is quoted in Theoharis, *The Yalta Myths,* 96.
306. Herbert Hoover, speaking in Des Moines, Iowa, August 30, 1951, reprinted in *The New York Times,* August 31, 1951.
307. U.S. Senate, Committee on Foreign Relations, *Hearings on the Japanese Peace Treaty and Other Treaties Relating to Security in the Pacific,* 82nd Congress, 2nd sess., 1952, 4.
308. *New York Times,* February 7, 1952.
309. *Chicago Herald Tribune,* April 13, 1952.
310. For Krock and Moley, see Theoharis, *The Yalta Myths,* passim.

311. See "New Evidence," *Time,* June 25, 1951.
312. *Congressional Record,* 82nd Congress, 2nd sess., 1952, XCVIII, Part 10, A274–41.
313. See Theoharis, *The Yalta Myths,* 137–38. Roosevelt's daughter, Anna Roosevelt Halsted, who had traveled with him to Yalta, took issue with Senator Taft's characterization of her father's actions at Yalta. After listening to a radio address by Taft to the Republican Club of the District of Columbia, Roosevelt wrote to Taft to request a transcript of his remarks so that, in her words, she could "study some of the statements you made for, to be quite frank, I was so stunned by the inaccuracies, innuendoes, and half truths concerning the Yalta Conference that I should like to go over them carefully." Anna Roosevelt to Robert A. Taft, January 29, 1951, Anna Roosevelt Halsted Papers, box 85, folder 3, FDRL. Roosevelt received the requested transcript along with a short note from Taft offering to answer any of her criticisms. Taft to Roosevelt, February 9, 1951, Anna Roosevelt Halsted Papers, box 85, folder 3. The statements in Taft's speech that elicited the most criticism from Roosevelt about the portrayal of the negotiations at Yalta is evidenced by the sentences that she underlined in his speech and the rebutted in a subsequent letter of March 8, 1951. She took greatest issue with Taft's charges that her father had allowed Harriman and Hopkins to dominate the policy at Yalta and that the United States had naively believed that "Soviet Russia was a peace-loving democracy." Roosevelt to Taft, March 8, 1951, and "Radio Address of Robert A. Taft to the Republican Club of the District of Columbia," January 29, 1951, Anna Roosevelt Halsted Papers, box 85, folder 3. Anna was not the only Roosevelt child to be dogged by the specter of Yalta. James Roosevelt, Franklin's son and by the mid-1950s a congressman from California, received letters regarding what was perceived as unfair criticism of Yalta and the former president in the press, in particular the *Los Angeles Times.* One newspaper clipping sent to him, a column by Westbrook Pegler that appeared in the *Los Angeles Examiner,* aired the claims of a naval interpreter that Yalta was "one of the biggest drunken brawls [he] ever saw." Nan Blair to James Roosevelt, April 13, 1955, and "One Colossal Brawl," James Roosevelt Papers, container 405, folder 6, FDRL.
314. See Theoharis, *The Yalta Myths,* 137–38.
315. For Eisenhower's deferral to McCarthy on the matter of George Marshall, see Anthony Leviero, "Truman Declares General Betrays Moral Principles," *New York Times,* October 10, 1952; James Reston, "Stevenson Scores Rival on M'Carthy in Wisconsin Talks," *New York Times,* October 9, 1952.
316. "The 1952 Republican Platform," *Congressional Quarterly Almanac* (Washington, DC: Congressional Quarterly, 1952), 491.
317. "Eisenhower Frees Chiang to Raid Mainland; Bids Congress Void All 'Secret' Pacts Abroad; Would End Controls; Opposes Tax Cuts Now," *New York Times,* July 11, 1952. *The Saturday Evening Post* had been conducting a long campaign on the issue. See for instance, Ann Sue Cardwell, "Why Not Repudiate Yalta's Betrayal of Poland and Weaken Soviet Grip?" *The Saturday Evening Post,* May 12, 13, 1950.
318. "The 1952 Democrat Platform," *Congressional Quarterly Almanac* (Washington, DC: Congressional Quarterly, 1952), 496.
319. Eisenhower urged "the repudiation of the Yalta agreement, which through the violation of the principles of the Atlantic Charter and through its unilateral violation by the Soviet government, has resulted in the enslavement of Poland. Thus we will have to give hope to the people of Poland and to all the American friends of Poland. . . ." See *Time,* September 20, 1952; and Richard Nixon, *New York Times,* October 6, 1953.
320. In his first State of the Union Address, Eisenhower promised that he would "recognize no kind of commitment contained in secret understandings of the past with foreign governments which permit this kind of enslavement." See "Eisenhower Urges Con-

gress to Accuse Russia of Pacts," *New York Times,* February 3, 1953. See also Senate Foreign Relations Committee, *World War II International Agreements and Understandings,* 83rd Congress, 1st sess., 1953, 1.

321. *New York Times,* February 21, 1953.
322. See *Congressional Record,* 84th Congress, 1st sess., 1955, CI, Part 3, 2031; *Chicago Tribune,* February 12, 1955; and Theoharis, *The Yalta Myths,* 199. See also "Secret Agreements," *Congressional Quarterly Almanac,* 1953 (Washington, DC: Congressional Quarterly, 1953), 224–25.
323. "Yalta—Eight Years Later," *New York Times,* February 4, 1953.
324. Samuel L. Sharp, "Yalta Repudiated," *New Republic,* February 18, 1953.
325. Robert A. Caro, *The Years of Lyndon Johnson: Master of the Senate* (New York: Alfred A. Knopf, 2002), 493–4, 524–5.
326. Samuel Shaffer, *On and Off the Floor: Thirty Years as a Correspondent on Capitol Hill* (New York: Newsweek Books, 1980), 63.
327. *New York Times,* February 24, 1953, in Caro, *The Years of Lyndon Johnson,* 525.
328. Neil MacNeil, *Dirksen: Portrait of a Public Man* (New York: World Publishing Company, 1970), 114.
329. On Eisenhower, see Theoharis, *The Yalta Myths,* 173.
330. For Senator H. Alexander Smith (R-NJ), see Duane A. Tanenbaum, "The Bricker Amendment Controversy: Its Origins and Eisenhower's Role," *Diplomatic History* 9(1) (1985): 79. See also Walter LaFeber, *America, Russia, and the Cold War, 1945–1966* (New York: Wiley, 1967), 178–79. For a useful discussion of the Bricker Amendment, see Richard A. Melanson, "Domestic Politics and American Foreign Policy, 1947–1994: A Conceptual Framework," National War College, National Defense University, prepared for delivery at the annual meeting of the Society for Historians of American Foreign Relations, Bentley College, Waltham, MA, June 1994. For a fruitful account of the legislative means through which the measure was finally defeated, see Caro, *The Years of Lyndon Johnson,* 527–41.
331. For Eisenhower, see *New York Times,* March 4, 1955.
332. Foster Dulles told an executive session of the Senate Foreign Relations Committee that the agreements could be a useful way to "hold the Soviet Union to certain things that they promised . . . [while] we do not feel that we ourselves are necessarily bound in the light of their own defaults." Senate Foreign Relations Committee, *Executive Sessions of the Senate Foreign Relations Committee* (Historical Series), 84th Congress, 1st sess., 1955 (made public in April, 1978), 455.
333. For more on this episode, see John F. Stacks, *Scotty: James B. Reston and the Rise and Fall of American Journalism* (New York: Little, Brown, 2003), 143–46.
334. See Kimball, *Forged in War,* 287–88; Martin Gilbert, *Winston S. Churchill,* Vol. 7: *Road to Victory* (Boston: Houghton Mifflin, 1986), 1038–39.
335. Elie Abel, "Poles' Fate Fixed," *The New York Times,* March 17, 1955. Churchill had particular justification for his anger; the State Department, in an incompetent attempt to erase his anti-French and Polish asides, merely had the effect of highlighting them for lazy reporters. Churchill was heard to say, "I do not care much about the Poles, myself," and agreeing with FDR that they were indeed "a quarrelsome people, not only at home but also abroad."
336. See James B. Reston, "Tragedy of Yalta Laid to Disunity," *New York Times,* March 18, 1955; Peter D. Whitney, "Churchill Finds Mistakes in U.S. Version of Yalta; Envoys Score Disclosure," *New York Times,* March 18, 1955; "Republicans Weigh Action Denouncing Wartime Talks," *New York Times,* March 18, 1955; and "Yalta in French Eyes," *New York Times,* March 18, 1955. See also the account in Reston, *Deadline,* 236–45.

337. This particular accusation was made in the Senate by Lyndon Johnson. *Congressional Record,* 84th Congress, 1st sess., 1955, CI, Part 3, 3336.
338. *Congressional Record,* 84th Congress, 1st sess., 1955, CI, Part 3, 3351.
339. Ibid., 3138.
340. "Hiss Identifies Yalta Notation," *New York Times,* March 17, 1955.
341. *Congressional Record,* 84th Congress, 1st sess., 1955, CI, Part 3, 3031.
342. "Nixon Sees No Attempt to Sell Out at Yalta," *Los Angeles Times,* March 18, 1955.
343. See for instance "War Documents Gratify Lehman," *New York Times,* October 21, 1955.
344. See Fromkin, *In the Time of the Americans,* 479.
345. See Walter Lippmann, *Washington Post,* April 13, 1955, op-ed page.
346. A related version of the far-right's argument made in support of the dissident general would be resuscitated a decade later by Leftist historian Gar Alperovitz, using much of the same evidence, to argue that Truman's decision to drop the bomb was motivated not by a desire to win the Pacific war but to intimidate the Soviet Union. See Alperovitz, *Atomic Diplomacy;* Alperovitz, *The Decision to Use the Bomb.*
347. See "Top State Rivals Cross Paths Here," *New York Times,* October 6, 1958; "Harriman Called Yalta 'Architect,'" *New York Times,* April 29, 1955; and "Eisenhower Won't Join in Attack on Harriman," *New York Times,* May 5, 1955.
348. For further discussion of both reports, see Theoharis, *The Yalta Myths,* 207.
349. Raymond J. Sontag, "Reflections on the Yalta Papers," *Foreign Affairs* 33(4) (July 1955): 622.
350. *Congressional Record,* 84th Congress, 1st sess., 1955, CI, Part 4, 5157; and U.S. Senate, Committee on Foreign Relations, *Hearings on Senate Resolution Favoring the Discussion at the Coming Geneva Conference of the Status of Nations Under Communist Control,* 84th Congress, 1st sess., 1955.
351. *Congressional Record,* 84th Congress, 1st sess., 1955, March 24, 1955, 3627–35.
352. U.S. Senate Committee on Armed Services and Committee on Foreign Relations, *Military Situation in the Far East,* 82nd Congress, 1st sess., 1951, 2839.
353. Its author, John Campbell, found it ominous that Soviet spokespeople were "so insistent on proclaiming the end of the Cold War," and warned, "We can expect periodic shifts in the Soviet line as they seek to win advantage by one means or another." John C. Campbell, "Negotiation with the Soviets: Some Lessons of the War Period," *Foreign Affairs* 34(2) (January 1956): 319.
354. *The Times*'s editors added, however, that negotiations "may be worth-while when the West can lead from strength instead of weakness, and can negotiate without the necessity of agreement at any cost." *New York Times,* January 27, 1955.
355. The skeptics need not have worried themselves. The Eisenhower-Dulles proposals put forth at Geneva for "Open Skies" between the United States and the USSR made any negotiations with the secretive Soviet state impossible. For a helpful discussion, see McGeorge Bundy, *Danger and Survival: Choices About the Bomb in the First Fifty Years* (New York: Random House, 1987), 295–305.
356. See Henry Kissinger, *Nuclear Weapons and Foreign Policy* (New York: W. W. Norton, 1969), 57.
357. This was due in part to Hiss's own dogged efforts to clear his name after he was released from prison in 1955, but it also related to the intimate association that the case had with Yalta. When President Eisenhower nominated Charles Bohlen, FDR's Yalta interpreter, to be ambassador to the USSR in 1953, his confirmation hearings became yet another occasion to revisit the damage that the spy, Hiss, had allegedly caused at Yalta. Senator Homer Ferguson demanded to know of Bohlen whether Hiss had "prepared any data

or obtained any information upon which the agreements were had." He asked what parts of the discussions Hiss had taken part in. He was particularly insistent on knowing whether Hiss played a significant role in the secret Far Eastern accord, because "as it turned out now, it [Yalta] had a great influence on what has happened in China." Bohlen begged to differ, but Ferguson was far from mollified. And while the case was continually fought and refought on the most minute of details, the Yalta issue never faded far into the background. Hiss's first publication upon leaving prison was a 4,700-word article defending Yalta. It was published by Pocket Books alongside another book by ex-Communist Max Eastman, who called Yalta "acquiescence under insult." *The New York Times* considered the appearance of the article worthy of an article itself. Even today, the issue continues to excite passions on both sides. When in 1996 the National Security Agency released a series of Communist intercepts sent to Moscow during the 1940s called the "Venona" documents, right-wing polemicist Eric Breindel insisted that they demonstrated that Hiss "was still a Soviet agent in 1945" when he went to Yalta. "No wonder," Breindel continues, "Soviet diplomat Andrei Gromyko—in a rare manifestation of post-war Soviet-American cooperation—told his U.S. counterparts in the summer of 1945 that Moscow wouldn't object to the appointment of Mr. Hiss as secretary-general of the U.N.'s founding conference." In 2001, Basic Books published a history of the war entitled *The New Dealers' War* by Thomas Fleming, who notes the presence of "one of Russia's secret agents at the heart of the conference." See Charles E. Bohlen Nomination, Committee on Foreign Relations, U.S. Senate, 83rd Congress, 1st sess., 1953, 123–25. See also Peter Hiss, "Hiss Pens Defense of Yalta Meeting," *New York Times,* October 12, 1955; Hiss, "Yalta: Modern American Myth"; Eric Breindel, "Hiss's Guilt," *New Republic,* April 15, 1996; Eric Breindel, "New Evidence in the Hiss Case," *Wall Street Journal,* March 14, 1996; Eric Breindel, "Alger Hiss: A Glimpse Behind the Mask," *Commentary,* November 1988; and Thomas Fleming, *The New Dealers' War,* 484. Other recent arguments based in part on the Venona document and touching on the Hiss case in large part or tangentially can be found in Tanenhaus, *Whittaker Chambers;* Weinstein, *Perjury;* Allen Weinstein and Alexander Vassilliev, *The Haunted Wood: Soviet Espionage in America—The Stalin Era* (New York: Random House, 1999); Harvey Klehr and John Earl Haynes, *Venona: Decoding Soviet Espionage in America* (New Haven, CT: Yale University Press, 1999); Tony Hiss, *The View from Alger's Window: A Son's Memoir* (New York: Alfred A. Knopf, 1999); Schrecker, *Many Are the Crimes;* Nigel West, *Venona: The Greatest Secret of the Cold War* (London: HarperCollins, 1999); John Lowenthal, "Venona and Alger Hiss," *Intelligence and Security* 15(3) (Autumn 2000); John Erman, "The Alger Hiss Case: A Half-Century of Controversy," *Studies in Intelligence,* Fall 2000–2001, 1–14; Jacob Weisberg, "Cold War Without End," *New York Times Magazine,* November 28, 1999, *http://www.nytimes.com;* Joshua Micah Marshall, "Exhuming McCarthy," *American Prospect,* no. 43 (March–April 1999), *http://www.prospect.org;* and Victor Navasky, "Cold War Ghosts: The Case of the Missing Red Menace," *Nation,* July 16, 2001. For arguments infused with some of the hysteria and bad faith of the McCarthy period itself, see Herbert Romerstein and Eric Breindel, *The Venona Secrets: Exposing Soviet Espionage and America's Traitors* (Washington, D.C.: Regnery, 2000); and Arthur Herman, *Joseph McCarthy: Re-examining the Life and Legacy of America's Most Hated Senator* (New York: Free Press, 2000). For my own short critique, see Eric Alterman, "I Spy with One Little Eye," *Nation,* April 29, 1996. The actual documents in question can be found in Robert L. Benson and Michael Warner, eds., *Venona: Soviet Espionage and American Response, 1939–1957* (Washington, D.C.: National Security Agency and Central Intelligence Agency, 1996). The key document relating to Hiss is No. 1822 and is dated March 30, 1945, with a much-disputed footnote dated August 8, 1969.

On the fortieth anniversary of his death, Mr. Chambers was lionized "as a compassionate conservative and loyal Republican" at private event for a hundred people in the Old Executive Office Building organized by a White House aide and prominent Republicans, including William F. Buckley Jr. See Elaine Sciolino, "G.O.P. Devotees Pay Honor to Whittaker Chambers," *New York Times,* July 10, 2001; and Ralph Z. Hallow, "White House Honors Memory of Whittaker Chambers," *Washington Times,* July 10, 2001, *http://www.washtimes.com.* For the case of Anthony Lake, see NBC's *Meet the Press,* November 24, 1996, transcript. See also Jacob Heilbrunn, "The Great Equivocator: Dr. Maybe Heads for the CIA," *New Republic,* March 24, 1997. In the summer of 2002, a new charge surfaced in a book by Jerrold and Leona Schecter, in which the authors allege that Soviet Military Intelligence claim that in the midst of the Yalta talks, Hiss offered up regular briefings to the Soviet General Mikhail Milshtein, deputy director of the GRU, in which he exposed U.S. negotiating plans and shared his thoughts about the views of the various American negotiators. But the accusation, which is unsupported by any documentary evidence, is also contradicted by a previous book coauthored by the Schechters together with Pavel Sudoplatov, the former Soviet intelligence agent who also accused Robert Oppenheimer of acting as a spy. Sudoplatov said that Hiss had spied for the Soviets during the 1930s, but seemed innocent of any knowledge of Hiss's alleged and—it must be added—still unproved role as a mole at Yalta. For the accusation, see Jerrold Schecter and Leona Schecter, *Sacred Secrets: How Soviet Intelligence Operations Changed American History* (New York: Brasseys, 2002), 130–33. Harvey Klehr notes of the book, "Some of the secret material in *Sacred Secrets* sounds plausible and appears to fit with what we already know about Soviet espionage. But, since no sources and no archives are identified, and there are so many small errors, even those of us disposed to believe many of the Schecters' claims will remain unsatisfied." See Harvey Klehr, "Spies Like Us: The Schecters Get the History of Soviet Espionage Not Quite Right," *Weekly Standard,* July 1, 2002.

Following the Schecters, yet another wave of books and articles arrived with further arguments and counterarguments, none of which did much to change the minds of those on the other side of the case. See, for instance, Eduard Mark, "Who Was 'Venona's Ales'? Cryptanalysis and the Hiss Case," *Intelligence and National Security* 18, no. 3 (Autumn 2003); John Earl Haynes and Harvey Klehr, *In Denial: Historians, Communism, and Espionage* (San Francisco: Encounter Books, 2003). For the Elizabeth Bentley–related aspects of the case, see Kathryn S. Olmsted, *Red Spy Queen: A Biography of Elizabeth Bentley* (Durham: University of North Carolina Press, 2002); and Lauren Kessler, *Clever Girl: Elizabeth Bentley's Life In and Out of Espionage* (New York: HarperCollins, 2003). For documentary evidence on the entire period, see Katherine L. Herbig and Martin F. Wiskoff, "Espionage Against the United States by American Citizens, 1947–2001," PERSEREC Technical Report 02–5 (Monterey, CA: Defense Personnel Security Research Center, 2002), *http://www.fas.org/sgp/library/spies.pdf.* Finally, in *Alger Hiss's Looking-Glass Wars: The Covert Life of a Soviet Spy* (New York: Oxford University Press, 2004), G. Edward White attempts to cover the waterfront of the case, though it adds little that was not to be found in Tanenhaus, *Whittaker Chambers,* supplemented by some of the sources named above.

III. John F. Kennedy and the Cuban Missile Crisis

1. Richard Rovere, "Letter from Washington," *New Yorker,* November 3, 1962.
2. Arthur Schlesinger Jr., *A Thousand Days: John F. Kennedy in the White House* (Boston: Houghton Mifflin, 1965), 841.
3. Roger Hilsman, Letter to the Editor, *New York Review of Books,* May 8, 1969.

4. Robert F. Kennedy, *Thirteen Days: A Memoir of the Cuban Missile Crisis* (New York: New American Library, 1969), 56.
5. *Time,* November 8, 1982.
6. Richard Strout, "TRB from Washington," *New Republic,* December 11, 1962.
7. McGeorge Bundy, "The Presidency and the Peace," *Foreign Affairs,* April 1964.
8. Ibid.
9. Transcript of Sylvester speech as published in *Congressional Record, Senate,* 88th Cong., 1st sess., June 24, 1963, 859.
10. *Hearings,* House Foreign Operations and Government Information Subcommittee, 88th Cong., 1st sess., 19 March 1963, 15. See also Wise, *The Politics of Lying,* 39. Elie Abel, who had been asked by the administration to replace Sylvester, attributed the secretary's decision to make this statement to the fact that "Arthur is rather excitable. He tends very frequently when he's excited to overstate the proposition. Now if he had said that there are situations in which a government sometimes has to tell less than the whole truth nobody would have argued with him. But he overstated it and tried to make it appear that it somehow was the sacred duty of governments to lie. . . . That, of course, gets everybody's back up." Elie Abel Oral History, 12, John F. Kennedy Library, Boston, MA (hereafter JFKL).
11. William Manchester, *One Brief Shining Moment: Remembering Kennedy* (Boston: Little, Brown, 1983), 215.
12. Walter Trohan, *Chicago Tribune,* October 27, 1962.
13. Zbigniew Brzezinski, "The Implications of Change for United States Foreign Policy," *Department of State Bulletin,* 52 (July 1967), 19–23.
14. *Newsweek,* November 5, 1962.
15. *Time,* November 2, 1962.
16. *New York Times,* November 4, 1962.
17. James Reston, "The President's View," *New York Times,* October 29, 1962.
18. When Stewart Alsop proposed writing the article to the editor of *The Saturday Evening Post,* the journalist was quite confident that John Kennedy would see him and provide inside access. See Stewart Alsop to Benn Hibbs, October 26, 1962, Joseph and Stewart Alsop Papers, Special Correspondence-Saturday Evening Post, October–December 1962, box 31, Library of Congress, Washington, D.C. (hereafter LC).
19. Stewart Alsop and Charles Bartlett, "In Time of Crisis," *Saturday Evening Post* CCXXXXV (December 8, 1962), 15–21.
20. Ibid., 16, 20.
21. McNamara and Bundy made these comments at an October 16 meeting with the president among others. See Timothy Naftali and Philip Zelikow, eds., *The Presidental Recordings: John F. Kennedy: The Great Crises II* (New York: W. W. Norton), 440. These conversations were originally published in an earlier edition of the transcripts, Ernest R. May and Philip Zelikow, eds., *The Kennedy Tapes: Inside the White House During the Cuban Missile Crisis* (Cambridge, MA: The Belknap Press of Harvard University Press, 1997). Questions about the accuracy of their transcription were raised, however. See Sheldon M. Stern, "What JFK Really Said," *Atlantic Monthly* 285, no. 5 (May 2000); and Sheldon M. Stern, "The 1997 Published Transcripts of the JFK Cuban Missile Crisis Tapes: Too Good to Be True?," *Presidential Studies Quarterly* 30 (September 2000). The editors then made every effort to address these concerns in the more complete version. The references here are all to the second, more accurate version.
22. See "Transcript of 2nd ExComm Meeting, October 16, 1962, 6:30–7:35," in Laurence Chang and Peter Kornbluh, eds., *The Cuban Missile Crisis, 1962: An NSA Reader* (New York: New Press, 1992), 97–114. See also Kai Bird, *The Color of Truth: McGeorge and*

William Bundy, Brothers in Arms: A Biography (New York: Simon & Schuster, 1998) 226; Sheldon M. Stern, *Averting "The Final Failure": John F. Kennedy and the Secret Cuban Missile Crisis Meetings* (Stanford, CA: Stanford University Press, 2003), 91; and Elie Abel, *The Missile Crisis* (Philadelphia: Lippincott, 1966), 51.

23. For a breakdown of U.S. and Soviet nuclear capabilities at the time, see especially Raymond L. Garthoff, *Reflections on the Cuban Missile Crisis* (Washington, D.C.: The Brookings Institution, 1987), 142. For further discussion on this point, see also Barton J. Bernstein, "Reconsidering the Missile Crisis: Dealing with the Problems of the American Jupiters in Turkey," in James A. Nathan, ed., *The Cuban Missile Crisis Revisited* (New York: St. Martins Press, 1992), 65; and Kai Bird, *The Chairman: John J. McCloy, The Making of the American Establishment* (New York: Simon & Schuster, 1992), 524.
24. Alsop and Bartlett, "In Time of Crisis," 16.
25. Ibid., 18. Kennedy, according to Joseph Alsop, was "openly contemptuous of Stevenson. Always. He loved to hear jokes about him, and I was only too eager to make them. He saw him as a self-regarding, posturing fellow. He came under the—he came more than well within the category that the President disliked: the sort of attitudinizing liberal. [After the missile crisis] Kennedy evinced a marked lack of admiration for his judgment and degree of resolution." See Joseph Alsop Oral History, interviewed by Elspeth Rostow, June 23, 1964, Washington, D.C., 73–74, JFKL.
26. Alsop and Bartlett, "In Time of Crisis," 18. The official who made the comment was later identified as NSC staffer Michael Forrestal, who had been instructed by the Kennedys to offer up their version of the story to Bartlett and others. Joseph Alsop, Stewart's brother, attempted to use the article as evidence, in a column, that the president was looking to fire Stevenson until he was talked out of it in advance by McGeorge Bundy, who had been alerted to the article—before it was published—by the president himself. Upon completion of the article, Alsop anticipated that it would generate "much talk" and urged that the Post prepare a reply to the expected negative reaction of Stevenson. See Stewart Alsop to Hibbs, November 19 and November 29, 1962, Joseph and Stewart Alsop Papers, Special Correspondence-Saturday Evening Post, October–December 1962, box 31, LC.
27. "U.S. Bases Abroad," *Time,* November 9, 1963.
28. Schlesinger Jr., *A Thousand Days,* 827.
29. Sorensen, *Kennedy,* 714.
30. Bundy, *Danger and Survival,* 435. See also Philip Nash, *The Other Missiles of October: Eisenhower, Kennedy and the Jupiters, 1957–1963* (Chapel Hill: University of North Carolina Press, 1997), 3.
31. See, for example, Graham T. Allison, *Essence of Decision: Explaining the Cuban Missile Crisis* (Boston: Little, Brown, 1971).
32. Sorensen, *Kennedy,* 714. This general narrative framework can be found in a number of early accounts, including, for example: Alsop and Bartlett, "In Time of Crisis"; Abel, *The Missile Crisis*; Schlesinger Jr., *A Thousand Days;* Hugh Sidey, *John F. Kennedy, President* (New York: Atheneum, 1964); Richard E. Neustadt, "Afterword: JFK (1968)," in *Presidential Power: The Politics of Leadership* (New York: John Wiley, 1960, 1968); Henry M. Pachter, *Collision Course: The Cuban Missile Crisis and Coexistence* (New York: Frederick A. Praeger, 1963); Edward Weintal and Charles Bartlett, *Facing the Brink: An Intimate Study of Crisis Diplomacy* (New York: Charles Scribner's Sons, 1967); Richard E. Neustadt and Graham T. Allison, "Afterword" to Kennedy, *Thirteen Days;* and Alexander L. George, "The Cuban Missile Crisis, 1962," in Alexander L. George, David K. Hall, and William E. Simons, eds., *The Limits of Coercive Diplomacy: Laos, Cuba, Vietnam* (Boston: Little, Brown, 1971), 86–143.

33. Walter Lippmann, *Washington Post,* November 13, 1962. The T&T column "Blockade Proclaimed" appeared in *The Washington Post* on October 25, 1962, see *http://www.mtholyoke.edu/acad/intrel/cuba/lippmann.htm.* For mention of Stevenson and of the inaugural address, see Walter Lippmann Oral History, Interview by "Mrs. Farmer," 1964, 3–6, JFKL.
34. "Turkey Relieved at U.S. Firmness: Gratified That Bases Were Not Bargained Away," *New York Times,* October 29, 1962.
35. *U.S. News & World Report,* November 12, 1962, 43.
36. See summary of a November 2, 1962, article from *Akis* sent to the State Department by the U.S. embassy in Turkey, National Security File, box 226, NATO-Weapons, Cables, Turkey, JFKL.
37. "Their Bases and Ours," *Time,* November 2, 1962.
38. For this proposed interpretation, see Nash, *Other Missiles,* 153.
39. For example, on the floor of the Senate, Senator Barry Goldwater (R-Arizona) asked, "Mr. President, what goes on?" He demanded to know if the removals, and other things, were "some kind of deal involving Cuba and disarmament plans?" *Congressional Record,* 88th Cong., 1st sess., February 19, 1963, 2534–35. See also Nash, *Other Missiles,* 167.
40. See C. L. Sulzberger, *The Last of the Giants* (New York: Macmillan, 1970), 928.
41. Rusk testimony, January 25, 1963, and McNamara testimony, February 21, 1963, *Executive Sessions of the Senate Foreign Relations Committee* (Historical Series), vol. 15: 105–6, 111.
42. See, for example, Transcript of Press and Radio News Briefing, November 27, 1962, and January 23, 1963, Transcripts of Daily News Conferences of the Department of State, vols. 27 and 28: October–December 1962 and January–March 1963, RG 59, General Records of the Department of State, Records of the Office of News and Its Predecessors, National Archives, College Park, MD.
43. *Meet the Press,* Non-classified, Interview, December 16, 1962, item no. CC02755, in National Security Archive Microfiche Collection, *Cuban Missile Crisis, 1962* (Washington, D.C.: National Security Archive, 1990). (Available online at Digital National Security Archive: *www.nsarchive.chadwyck.com*). Hereafter NSA.
44. NATO Missiles in Turkey, Confidential, Cable State, December 6, 1962, Rusk to U.S. Embassy, Turkey, item no. CC02690; and [Summary of Dean Rusk's October 28, 5:00 P.M. Briefing of Latin American and OAS Ambassadors] Confidential, Cable State, October 28, 1962, item no. CC01509, NSA. In his meeting with the Latin American and OAS ambassadors, Rusk claimed, "In these negotiations U.S. has made no deals, no unknown transactions, no understandings behind scenes."
45. NBC *White Paper,* "Cuba: The Missile Crisis," February 9, 1964. See also Nash, *Other Missiles,* 158.
46. Pachter, *Collision Course,* 52–53.
47. Roger Hilsman, "The Cuban Crisis: How Close We Were to War," *Look,* August 25, 1964. In this article, Hilsman also repeats Rusk's "eyeball to eyeball" comment, reporting that the secretary said it not to Bundy, but to John Scali of ABC News. This implies either that the author is adding a bit more melodrama to his story, or that Rusk loved his bon mot so much he repeated it over and over. The latter seems more likely, as Hilsman quotes Rusk telling Scali to "be sure to report" his comment when the time comes. See also Hilsman, *To Move a Nation,* 219.
48. Memorandum from ABC Correspondent John Scali to the Director of the Bureau of Intelligence and Research (Hilsman), undated, in *FRUS, 1961–1963, Vol. XI: Cuban Missile Crisis and Aftermath,* 227.

49. Hilsman, *To Move a Nation,* 222.
50. Abel, *The Missile Crisis.*
51. Abel notes that Paul Nitze also read from his contemporaneous notes to Abel, but did not let him see them. He discusses his sources in his oral history, 25, JFKL.
52. Ibid., 95–96. Elie Abel Oral History, Interviewed by Dennis J. O'Brien, March 18, 1970, New York City, 12. See also Roswell L. Gilpatric Oral History, Interviewed by Dennis J. O'Brien, May 5, 1970, 113, JFKL.
53. Ibid., 95.
54. Ibid., 193–94.
55. Ibid., 96. Abel later said, "I haven't always agreed with Adlai on everything, but it seems to me his role here was really quite an honorable one, and maybe even a brave one." Elie Abel Oral History, 24, JFKL.
56. See Roger Hagan, "Cuba: Triumph or Tragedy," *Dissent* 10 (Winter 1963): 13–26; Roger Hagan and Barton J. Bernstein, "The Military Value of Missiles in Cuba," *Bulletin of the Atomic Scientists* (February 1963); Leslie Dewart, "The Cuban Crisis Revisited," *Studies on the Left* 5 (Spring, 1965): 15–40; Ronald Steel, "Endgame," *New York Review of Books,* March 13, 1969, reprinted in Ronald Steel, *Imperialists and Other Heroes: A Chronicle of the American Empire* (New York: Random House, 1971); Roger Hilsman and Ronald Steel, "An Exchange on the Missile Crisis," *New York Review of Books,* May 8, 1969, 36–38; and Sidney Lens, *The Military-Industrial Complex* (Kansas City: Pilgrim Press, 1970), 91.
57. See James Daniel and John G. Hubbell, *Strike in the West: The Complete Story of the Cuban Crisis* (New York: Holt, Reinhart and Winston, 1963); Thomas Lane, *The Leadership of President Kennedy* (Caldwell, Idaho: The Caxton Printers, 1964); Mario Lazo, *Dagger in the Heart: American Policy Failures in Cuba* (New York: Funk and Wagnalls, 1968); Paul D. Bethel, *The Losers: The Definitive Report, by an Eyewitness of the Communist Conquest of Cuba and the Soviet Penetration in Latin America* (New Rochelle, NY: Arlington House, 1969); Malcolm E. Smith Jr., *Kennedy's Thirteen Greatest Mistakes in the White House* (New York: The National Forum of America, 1968); and Dean Acheson, "Dean Acheson's Version of Robert Kennedy's Version of the Cuban Missile Affair: Homage to Plain Dumb Luck," *Esquire,* February 1969, 76–77.
58. Kennedy, *Thirteen Days,* 108–9.
59. A multitude of influential books, articles, and other works base much of their analyses of the Turkish Jupiter issue on the information given by Robert Kennedy in *Thirteen Days.* See, for example, Neustadt, "Afterword: JFK (1968)," in *Presidential Power;* Neustadt and Allison, "Afterword" to Kennedy, *Thirteen Days*; Lens, *The Military-Industrial Complex*; Graham T. Allison, "Conceptual Models and the Cuban Missile Crisis," *American Political Science Review* 63(3) (September 1969): 689–718; Allison, *Essence of Decision;* George, "The Cuban Missile Crisis, 1962"; James A. Nathan, "The Missile Crisis: His Finest Hour Now," *World Politics* 27 (January 1975): 269–88; Henry Fairlie, *The Kennedy Promise: The Politics of Expectation* (Garden City, NY: Doubleday, 1973); Barton J. Bernstein, "Courage and Commitment: The Missiles of October," *Foreign Service Journal* (December 1975): 9–11, 24–27; Barton J. Bernstein, "The Cuban Missile Crisis," in Lynn H. Miller and Ronald W. Pruessen, eds., *Reflections on the Cold War: A Quarter-Century of American Foreign Policy* (Philadelphia: Temple University Press, 1974), 108–42; Bruce Miroff, *Pragmatic Illusions: The Presidential Politics of John F. Kennedy* (New York: David McKay, 1976); Thomas G. Paterson, "Bearing the Burden: A Critical Look at JFK's Foreign Policy," *Virginia Quarterly Review* 54 (Spring 1978): 193–212; Herbert Dinnerstein, *The Making of a Missile Crisis, October 1962* (Baltimore: Johns Hopkins University Press, 1976); Jerome H. Kahan and Anne K. Long, "The

Cuban Missile Crisis: A Study of Its Strategic Context," *Political Science Quarterly* 87 (December 1972): 564–94; Robert Beggs, ed., *The Cuban Missile Crisis* (London: Longman Group Ltd., 1971); and Richard J. Walton, *Cold War and Counterrevolution: The Foreign Policy of John F. Kennedy* (New York: Viking Press, 1972).

60. Although Robert Kennedy did, apparently, send a copy to his brother. As Ernest May and Philip Zelikow note, "the original is in the President's Office Files of JFK, not in the Robert Kennedy Papers. Nor does it appear in Rusk's papers. This indicates that it may have been drafted for Rusk but never shown to him." See May and Zelikow, *The Kennedy Tapes,* 608. Another possibility is that Kennedy drafted it expressly for the historical record but never intended to send or act upon it.

61. Memorandum from Attorney General Kennedy to Secretary of State Rusk, 30 October 1962, in *FRUS, 1961–1963, vol. XI,* 270–71. See also Arthur Schlesinger Jr., *Robert Kennedy and His Times* (Boston: Houghton Mifflin, 1978), 545.

62. Schlesinger Jr., *Robert Kennedy,* 545.

63. *FRUS, 1961–1963, vol. XI,* 271, *n*2.

64. Schlesinger Jr., *Robert Kennedy,* 545–46. The letter from Khrushchev to President Kennedy, dated October 28, 1962, that Robert Kennedy handed back to Dobrynin was first published in *Problems of Communism* (Spring 1992): 60–62, and also appears in *FRUS, 1961–1963, Vol. VI: Kennedy-Khrushchev Exchanges,* 189–90.

65. "The Lessons of the Cuban Missile Crisis," *Time,* September 27, 1982.

66. Bundy, *Danger and Survival,* 432–34.

67. This new material has inspired an avalanche of scholarly reexamination of the crisis, much of which I have relied upon for my own analysis. See, for example, James G. Blight and David A. Welch, *On the Brink: Americans and Soviets Reexamine the Cuban Missile Crisis,* 2d ed. (New York: Noonday, 1990); James G. Blight, Bruce J. Allyn, and David A. Welch, *Cuba on the Brink: Castro, the Missile Crisis, and the Soviet Collapse* (New York: Pantheon, 1993); Nathan, *The Cuban Missile Crisis Revisited;* Robert Smith Thompson, *The Missiles of October: The Declassified Story of John F. Kennedy and the Cuban Missile Crisis* (New York: Simon & Schuster, 1992); Mary S. McAuliffe, ed., *CIA Documents on the Cuban Missile Crisis* (Washington, D.C.: CIA History Staff, October 1992); Gen. Anatoly I. Gribkov and Gen. William Y. Smith, *Operation ANADYR: U.S. and Soviet Generals Recount the Cuban Missile Crisis* (Chicago: Edition Q, 1994); Dino A. Brugioni, *Eyeball to Eyeball: The Inside Story of the Cuban Missile Crisis,* rev. ed. (New York: Random House, 1990, 1991); and Chang and Kornbluh, *The Cuban Missile Crisis, 1962.* For Dobrynin's own recollections of the crisis, see Anatoly Dobrynin, *In Confidence: Moscow's Ambassador to America's Six Cold War Presidents (1962–1986)* (New York: Times Books, 1995). From the Cold War International History Project (CWIHP), see Raymond L. Garthoff, "The Havana Conference on the Cuban Missile Crisis," *CWIHP Bulletin* 1 (Spring 1992): 2–4; Mark Kramer, "Tactical Nuclear Weapons, Soviet Command Authority, and the Cuban Missile Crisis," *CWIHP Bulletin* 3 (Fall 1993): 40, 42–46; James G. Blight, Bruce J. Allyn, and David A. Welch, "Kramer vs. Kramer, Or, How Can You Have Revisionism in the Absence of Orthodoxy?" ibid., 41, 47–50; Philip Brenner and James G. Blight, "Cuba, 1962: The Crisis and Cuban-Soviet Relations: Fidel Castro's Secret 1968 Speech," *CWIHP Bulletin* 5 (Spring 1995): 1, 81–85; Alexandr Fursenko and Timothy Naftali, "Using KGB Documents: The Scali-Feklisov Channel in the Cuban Missile Crisis," *CWIHP Bulletin* 10 (March 1998): 58, 60–62; "Russian Foreign Ministry Documents on the Cuban Missile Crisis," introduction by Raymond L. Garthoff, *CWIHP Bulletin* 5 (Spring 1995): 58, 63–77; Vladislav M. Zubok, "'Dismayed by the Actions of the Soviet Union': Mikoyan's Talks with Fidel Castro and the Cuban Leadership, November 1962," *CWIHP Bulletin* 5

(Spring 1995): 59, 89–92, 93–109, 159; Mark Kramer, "The 'Lessons' of the Cuban Missile Crisis for Warsaw Pact Nuclear Operations," ibid., 59, 110, 112–115, 160; and James G. Hershberg, "Anatomy of a Controversy: Anatoly F. Dobrynin's Meeting with Robert F. Kennedy, Saturday, 27 October 1962," ibid., 75, 77–80.

68. See Bruce J. Allyn, James G. Blight, and David A. Welch, eds., *Back to the Brink: Proceedings of the Moscow Conference on the Cuban Missile Crisis, January 27–28, 1989* (Lanham, MD: University Press of America, 1992), 92–93.

69. See Blight and Welch, *On the Brink,* 82–83; and Rusk, *As I Saw It,* 240–41. See also Thomas J. Schoenbaum, *Waging Peace and War, Dean Rusk in the Truman, Kennedy and Johnson Years* (New York: Simon & Schuster, 1988).

70. Mark Kramer contends that Dobrynin has retracted this claim. See Kramer, "Tactical Nuclear Weapons," 40, 42–46; and Blight, Allyn, and Welch, "Kramer vs. Kramer," 41, 47–50. Barton J. Bernstein adds the following perspective, explaining why he doubts that the Friday, October 26, meeting took place. "In January 1989, Dobrynin claimed that the issue of a Turkey-Cuba missile trade first came up in his conversation with Robert Kennedy on Friday, October 26, and that the attorney general, after making a quick phone call to the president that evening, said that it was a subject that the American government would consider. Dobrynin's recent claim of such a conversation on the 26th seems very dubious. If it had occurred, why did both Kennedy brothers at the ExComm sessions on Saturday seem surprised and dismayed by Khrushchev's public demand for such a trade? Both brothers would have been far better prepared on the 27th for this Soviet demand even though it was public, and they could have moved the ExComm rather speedily to endorse it. Or the brothers could have easily held an earlier meeting on Saturday with a small group, rather than the special evening meeting to arrange for secret acceptance of a deal on the Jupiters." Bernstein, "Reconsidering the Missile Crisis," 125–26, *n*183. For the White House logs, see President's Telephone Memorandum, October 26, 1962, POF, JFKL; see also Stern, *Averting "The Final Failure,"* 289–90. Stern notes that Sergei Khrushchev believes the phone logs support the belief in the veracity of the encounter and has said so in a correspondence with the author.

71. Dobrynin, *In Confidence,* 94.

72. Dobrynin's cable to the Soviet Foreign Ministry:

> 27 October 1962:
> TOP SECRET
> Making Copies Prohibited
> Copy No. *1*CIPHERED TELEGRAM
>
> "And what about Turkey?" I asked R. Kennedy.
>
> "If that is the only obstacle to achieving the regulation I mentioned earlier, then the president doesn't see any unsurmountable difficulties in resolving this issue," replied R. Kennedy. "The greatest difficulty for the president is the public discussion of the issue of Turkey. Formally the deployment of missile bases in Turkey was done by a special decision of the NATO Council. To announce now a unilateral decision by the president of the USA to withdraw missile bases from Turkey—this would damage the entire structure of NATO and the U.S. position as the leader of NATO, where, as the Soviet government knows very well, there are many arguments. In short, if such a decision were announced now it would seriously tear apart NATO."

> "However, President Kennedy is ready to come to agree on that question with N. S. Khrushchev, too. I think that in order to withdraw these bases from Turkey," R. Kennedy said, "we need 4–5 months. This is the minimal amount of time necessary for the U.S. government to do this, taking into account the procedures that exist within the NATO framework. On the whole Turkey issue," R. Kennedy added, "if Premier N. S. Khrushchev agrees with what I've said, we can continue to exchange opinions between him and the president, using him, R. Kennedy and the Soviet ambassador. However, the president can't say anything public in this regard about Turkey," R. Kennedy said again. R. Kennedy then warned that his comments about Turkey are extremely confidential; besides him and his brother, only 2–3 people know about it in Washington.

Russian Foreign Ministry Archives, Moscow, cited in Richard Ned Lebow and Janice Gross Stein, *We All Lost the Cold War* (Princeton, NJ: Princeton University Press, 1994), appendix, 523–26.

73. Nikita S. Khrushchev, *Khrushchev Remembers: The Last Testament,* trans. and ed. Strobe Talbott (Boston: Little, Brown, 1970), 497; and Dobrynin, *In Confidence,* 88–9. Fyodor Burlatsky, one of Nikita Khrushchev's speechwriters, has maintained that the Jupiter promise was very important and that this was the most important message that convinced Khrushchev to change his course. But Sergo Mikoyan, the son of Khrushchev adviser A. Mikoyan, insists that this is not the case. "The major reason why Khrushchev gave in was the ultimatum and the threat of imminent escalation," he argues. "The Jupiter thing was not a definite promise by Robert Kennedy, nothing official. And it was not the main part of this message. The Jupiters definitely were a side issue. The statement said: You take out the missiles or it will be done by us. That's what counted . . . the thing that made Khrushchev give in was the ultimatum, the threat of an air strike and an invasion and the inevitable escalation." Since both men, however, are relying on secondary evidence and hearsay, neither is in a position to shed direct light on Khrushchev's decision-making process. For their opinions, see Bernard Grenier, "The Cuban Missile Crisis Reconsidered: The Soviet View: An Interview with Sergo Mikoyan," *Diplomatic History* 14 (Spring 1990): 220.
74. Dobrynin's report on this meeting:

> Telegram from Soviet Ambassador to the USA Dobrynin to USSR MFA:
> 28 October 1962
> TOP SECRET
> Making Copies Prohibited
> Copy No. *1*CIPHERED TELEGRAM
>
> According to everything it was evident that R. Kennedy with satisfaction, it is necessary to say, really with great relief met the report about N. S. Khrushchev's response.
>
> In parting, R. Kennedy once again requested that strict secrecy be maintained about the agreement with Turkey. "Especially so that the correspondents don't find out. At our place for the time being even Salinger does not know about it." (It was not entirely clear why he considered it necessary to mention his name, but he did it.)

> I responded that in the Embassy no one besides me knows about the conversation with him yesterday. R. Kennedy said that in addition to the current correspondence and future exchange of opinions via diplomatic channels, on important questions he will maintain contact with me directly, avoiding any intermediaries.
>
> Before departing, R. Kennedy once again gave thanks for N. S. Khrushchev's quick and effective response.

Archive of Foreign Policy of the Russian Federation, Moscow, cited in "Russian Foreign Ministry Documents on the Cuban Missile Crisis," introduction by Raymond Garthoff, 76. See also Dobrynin, *In Confidence,* 89.

75. See Alexandr Fursenko and Timothy Naftali, *One Hell of a Gamble: Khrushchev, Castro and Kennedy, 1958–1964* (New York: W. W. Norton, 1997), 284–85.
76. CNN's *The Cold War,* "Cuba," episode 10, November 29, 1998.
77. Letter from Chairman Khrushchev to President Kennedy, October 28, 1962, in *FRUS, 1961–1963, vol. VI,* 189.
78. Dobrynin, *In Confidence,* 90. See also Dobrynin's contemporaneous memorandum on the meeting, Telegram from Soviet Ambassador to the USA A. F. Dobrynin to the USSR Foreign Ministry, October 30, 1962, in *CWIHP Bulletin* 8–9 (Winter 1995–96), 303–4.
79. Sergei N. Khrushchev, 641.
80. Indeed, Lippmann had visited with George Ball a day before publishing the column and Ball had not sought to dissuade him. See Ronald Steel, *Walter Lippmann and the American Century* (Boston: Little, Brown, 1980), 535. For Lippmann's article, see Walter Lippmann, "Blockade Proclaimed," *Washington Post,* October 25, 1962, *http://www.mtholyoke.edu/acad/intrel/cuba/lippmann.htm.*
81. See Fursenko and Naftali, *One Hell of a Gamble,* 275, 393–94. See also Nash, *Other Missiles,* 132–37.
82. *New York Times,* October 24 and October 25, 1962; see also Nash, *Other Missiles,* 133.
83. See Bernstein,"Reconsidering the Missile Crisis," 125–26, *n*183.
84. Blight and Welch, *On the Brink,* 256–57.
85. See Fursenko and Naftali, *One Hell of a Gamble,* 249–50. Fursenko and Naftali note, however, that no confirmation of this has yet been found in U.S. archives. Ibid., 389, *n*20.
86. See Sergei N. Khrushchev, *Nikita Khrushchev and the Creation of a Superpower* (University Park: Pennsylvania State Press, 2000), 594–95.
87. See, for instance, Garthoff, *Reflections on the Cuban Missile Crisis,* 86–88; and Michael Beschloss, *The Crisis Years: Kennedy and Khrushchev, 1960–63* (New York: Harper Collins, 1991), 536.
88. Kennedy, *Thirteen Days,* 108–9.
89. Blight, Allyn, and Welch, *Cuba on the Brink,* 224.
90. Nikita Khrushchev, *Khrushchev Remembers: The Glasnost Tapes,* trans. and ed. Jerrod L. Schecter with Vyacheslav Luchkov (Boston: Little, Brown, 1990), 182.
91. "I suggested, and was supported by Ted Sorensen and others, that we ignore the latest Khrushchev letter and respond to his earlier letter's proposal, as refined in the offer made to John Scali." Kennedy, *Thirteen Days,* 101–2.
92. See, for example, Cuban Missile Crisis Meetings, October 27, 1962, *Transcript-Presidential Recordings,* JFKL, 2, 3, 8. See also Mark. J. White, *Missiles in Cuba: Kennedy, Khrushchev, Castro and the 1962 Crisis* (Chicago: Ivan R. Dee, 1997), 214–19; and Beschloss, *Crisis Years,* 528.

93. White, *Missiles in Cuba,* 130–31. In his oral history, Scali also related a conversation that he estimates to have taken place in 1972 with a Soviet official who informed him "those proposals were never relayed to Moscow" because "they were never considered important." He could not, however, identify the official in question, as the conversation occurred a decade previous to the oral history interview. See John Scali Oral History, interviewed by Sheldon Stern, November 17, 1982, 10, JFKL.
94. Cuban Missile Crisis Meetings, October 16, 1962, 6:30–7:55, *Transcript-Presidential Recordings,* JFKL. See also Blight and Welch, *On the Brink,* 307; and May and Zelikow, *The Kennedy Tapes,* 100–101.
95. Stern, *Averting "The Final Failure,"* 254.
96. See Fred Kaplan, "The War Room: What Robert Dallek's New Biography Doesn't Tell You About JFK and Vietnam," *Slate,* May 19, 2003, *http://slate.msn.com/id/2083136;* and Fred Kaplan, "The Evasions of Robert McNamara," *Slate,* December 19, 2003, *http://slate.msn.com/id/2092916.* See also Fred Kaplan, "Kennedy and Cuba at 35," *Boston Sunday Globe,* October 12, 1997; and Stern, *Averting "The Final Failure,"* 98f, 269f, 281f, 299f. In addition, see Eric Alterman, "The Century of the 'Son of a Bitch,'" *Nation,* December 12, 2000 (posted November 26, 2003).
97. Hans Morgenthau, *Truth and Power: Essays of a Decade, 1960–1970* (New York: Praeger, 1970), 158.
98. Thomas Halper, *Foreign Policy Crisis* (Columbus, OH: Charles E. Merrill, 1971), 189–93.
99. Alsop and Bartlett, "In Time of Crisis," 16–20. Ironically, an article like the Alsop-Bartlett piece actually undermined policy makers' confidence in their ability to speak openly and frankly in such forums because it made clear that ExComm conversations were quickly leaked to the press in politically damaging ways. Adlai Stevenson certainly believed that this would lead to self-censorship that might endanger national security. See [Statement by Adlai Stevenson on His Role in the Cuban Crisis] Non-Classified, Statement, December 3, 1962, item no. CC02670, NSA. See also the *U.S. News & World Report* article that analyzed the impact of the Alsop-Bartlett piece and concluded, "The cover of secrecy has been ripped from what should be [the Kennedy administration's] most secret policy deliberations. Highest officials of the Government faced the prospect that any out-of-step opinion—at the most confidential level—could result in public exposure. It had happened once. It could happen again." "After Cuba: Who Stood for What," *U.S. News & World Report,* December 17, 1962.
100. Nathan, "The Heyday of the New Strategy," in Nathan, *The Cuban Missile Crisis Revisited,* 21.
101. Ibid.
102. See George Ball, *The Past Has Another Pattern* (New York: W. W. Norton and Co., 1982), 295, 309. See also Thomas G. Paterson, "Fixation with Cuba: The Bay of Pigs, Missile Crisis, and Covert War Against Castro," in *Kennedy's Quest for Victory: American Foreign Policy, 1961–63* (New York: Oxford, 1989), 149.
103. See John Barlow Martin, *Adlai Stevenson and the World* (Garden City, NY: Doubleday and Co., 1977), 634.
104. Bernstein, "Reconsidering the Missile Crisis," in Nathan, *The Cuban Missile Crisis Revisited,* 104, 125–26, *n*183.
105. Quoted in Stern, *Averting "The Final Failure,"* 100. (Note that Stern's rendering has, in this instance, cleaned up Kennedy's diction a bit, leaving out repeated and partial words.)
106. See White, *Missiles in Cuba,* 98.
107. Garry Wills, *The Kennedy Imprisonment* (Boston: Little, Brown, 1980), 166.
108. Barton J. Bernstein, "Understanding Decisionmaking, U.S. Foreign Policy, and the

Cuban Missile Crisis: A Review Essay," *International Security* 25 (1) (Summer 2000): 134–64, especially 161. No archival records of this meeting are as yet available.

109. This statement is not meant to imply a final judgment as to exactly why the Soviets decided to place the missiles in Cuba and, indeed, I do not think that question is terribly relevant to my inquiry here. I do think it certain, however, that the perceived threat to Cuba would have played a considerable role in such a decision, as may have other problems, including the overall politico/military balance between the superpowers, the continuing Berlin crisis, Khrushchev's internal considerations, etc. Khrushchev certainly chose to emphasize the threat to Cuba post-facto, when he allegedly argued, "Our goal was . . . to keep the Americans from invading Cuba, and to that end, we wanted to make them think twice by confronting them with our Missiles." See Nikita Khrushchev, *Khrushchev Remembers: The Last Testament,* 496. For an early, extended discussion that offers conclusions that I do not share, see Arnold J. Horelick, "The Cuban Missile Crisis," *World Politics* 16 (April 1964): 378–83. For the most recent evidence on the question, see Fursenko and Naftali, *One Hell of a Gamble,* 181–82.
110. Donald F. Chamberlain, CIA Inspector General, to Walt Elder, June 5, 1975, Rockefeller Commission Papers, Gerald R. Ford Library Materials, JFK Assassination Materials Project, National Archives, College Park, MD. Chamberlain's letter quotes from Operation Mongoose documents including Robert Kennedy's January 19, 1962, memo to McCone. See also Fursenko and Naftali, *One Hell of a Gamble,* 150.
111. Barton J. Bernstein, "Commentary: Reconsidering Khrushchev's Gambit—Defending the Soviet Union and Cuba," *Diplomatic History* 14(2) (Spring 1990): 234.
112. James G. Hershberg, "Before 'The Missiles of October': Did Kennedy Plan a Military Strike Against Cuba?" in Nathan, *The Cuban Missile Crisis Revisited,* 237.
113. The proposals, which were passed along to Secretary McNamara but never acted upon, are in Joint Chiefs of Staff, Top Secret/Special Handling/Noforn Report, "Report by the Department of Defense and Joint Chiefs of Staff Representative on the Caribbean Survey Group to the Joint Chiefs of Staff on Cuba Project," March 9, 1962, in the papers of the Assassinations Records Review Board (ARRB). See especially, Annex to Appendix to Enclosure A, "Pretexts to Justify U.S. Military Intervention in Cuba," 8–11. See also Bamford, *Body of Secrets,* 84–85.
114. Memorandum of Mongoose Meeting Held on Thursday, October 4, 1962, item no. CC00520, NSA. On October 11, Edward Landsdale reported back to the group that proposals for stepping up Operation Mongoose were being prepared. Action Proposals, Mongoose, Top Secret, Memorandum, October 11, 1962, item no. CC02244, NSA.
115. May and Zelikow, *The Kennedy Tapes,* 46.
116. Memorandum for the Record, October 16, 1962, in *FRUS, 1961–1963, vol. XI,* 43–45.
117. For examples of Soviet awareness about U.S. actions relating to Cuba, see M. Zakharov and S. Ivanov to N. S. Khrushchev, September 14, 1962; and Cable from USSR Ambassador to the USA A. F. Dobrynin to Soviet Foreign Ministry, October 15, 1962, in *CWIHP Bulletin* 8–9 (Winter 1996–97): 278. See also James Hershberg, "More Evidence on the Cuban Missile Crisis: More Documents from the Russian Archives," ibid., 270–77.
118. Bruce J. Allyn, James G. Blight, and David A. Welch, "Essence of Revision: Moscow, Havana, and the Cuban Missile Crisis," *International Security* 14 (3) (Winter 1989–1990): 145. See also Laurence Chang, "The View from Washington and the Views from Nowhere: Cuban Missile Crisis Historiography and the Epistemology of Decision Making," in Nathan, *The Cuban Missile Crisis Revisited,* 141–42.
119. Central Intelligence Agency, "The Military Build-up in Cuba," no. 85-3-62, CIA Records; Thomas L. Hughes to acting secretary of state, "Daniel's Conversation with Castro," December 13, 1963, box 23-F-1-2F, Hubert H. Humphrey Papers, Minnesota

Historical Society, cited in Thomas G. Paterson, "Commentary: The Defense-of-Cuba Theme and the Missile Crisis," *Diplomatic History* 14(2) (Spring 1990): 255.

120. U.S. officials certainly understood the problematic aspects of the Jupiters' presence in Turkey. Before going on his honeymoon in late August 1962, John McCone took Robert Kennedy aside and suggested that the United States pull its Jupiters out of Turkey so that they would not pose such an inviting target for Soviet vengeance. Tommy Thompson predicted on October 17 that Khrushchev would "justify his actions because of missiles in Italy and Turkey." McCone, "Memorandum of Meetings with the President," August 23, 1962, doc. 8, in McAuliffe, ed., *CIA Documents on the Cuban Missile Crisis*; and "MemCon, October 17, 1962, 8:30 A.M.," ibid., 160. See also Fursenko and Naftali, *One Hell of a Gamble,* 204; and Nash, *Other Missiles,* 120.
121. Philip Zelikow, Timothy Naftali, and Ernest May, eds., *The Presidential Recordings: John F. Kennedy:* Volumes 1–3, *The Great Crises* (New York: W. W. Norton, 2001), 451.
122. Bernstein, "Commentary," 233.
123. Abel, *The Missile Crisis,* 193.
124. Kennedy, *Thirteen Days,* 94–95.
125. For example, Schlesinger Jr., in *Robert Kennedy* (542), implies that the president had long been trying to remove them. Kenneth O'Donnell and David Powers, moreover, state that JFK had given the order five times. O'Donnell and Powers, with Joe McCarthy, *"Johnny, We Hardly Knew Ye": Memories of John Fitzgerald Kennedy* (Boston: Little, Brown, 1972), 337. See also Roger Hilsman, *The Cuban Missile Crisis: The Struggle Over Policy* (Westport, CT: Praeger, 1996), 202–3; Abel, *The Missile Crisis,* 168–71; Allison, *Essence of Decision,* 44, 101, 142, 226; Morton H. Halperin and Arnold Kanter, "The Bureaucratic Perspective: A Preliminary Framework," in Halperin and Kanter, *Readings in American Foreign Policy: A Bureaucratic Perspective* (Boston: Little Brown, 1973), 35; and I. M. Destler, *Presidents, Bureaucrats, and Foreign Policy: The Politics of Organization Reform* (Princeton, NJ: Princeton University Press, 1974), 3.
126. "It would have been better to dump them in the ocean instead of trying to dump them on our allies," Eisenhower later admitted. See Nash, *Other Missiles,* 3.
127. Ibid., 100–112.
128. "Recollection by Dean Rusk of Negotiating Channel through Andrew Cordier and Details of Negotiations to Remove Jupiters Prior to Crisis, 2/ 25/87," The Cuban Missile Crisis, 1962: The Making of U.S. Policy, NSA microfiche collection, available at *http: / /www.cwi org.*
129. Barton J. Bernstein, "Trading the Jupiters in Turkey, *Political Science Quarterly* 95, no. 1 (Spring 1987): 97–125.
130. National Security Action Memorandum No. 181, Top Secret, August 23, 1962, item no. CC00295, NSA.
131. *TASS* published its complaint on September 11, and *The New York Times* reprinted it the next day. For a transcript of Kennedy's September 13 press conference, see *New York Times,* September 14, 1962. See also Donald L. Hafner, "Bureaucratic Politics and 'Those Frigging Missiles,' JFK, Cuba and the U.S. Missiles in Turkey," *Orbis,* Summer 1977, 318.
132. Attempts to Equate Soviet Missile Bases in Cuba with NATO Jupiter Bases in Italy and Turkey, Unclassified, Internal Paper, October 10, 1962, item no. CC00570, NSA. In this case, the administration was concerned with the secret Soviet installation of surface-to-air missiles in Cuba. The memo argued that the Jupiter deployment had taken place with fully public notification, in accordance with United Nations standards for collective self-defense.

133. Zelikow et al., eds., *The Presidential Recordings,* 611. As early as October 19, Kennedy's speechwriter Ted Sorensen produced a draft statement announcing the imposition of a blockade that also stated U.S. willingness to negotiate the elimination of NATO bases in Turkey and Italy. Draft of Speech, October 19, 1962, Theodore Sorensen Papers, box 49, Classified Subjects Files 1961–1964, Cuba Subjects, JFKL. A summary of another draft speech, this one intended in the event of a U.S. air strike on the Cuban missile bases, further indicates that Kennedy considered the withdrawal of the Turkish missiles as a potentially useful way to resolve the crisis. Synopsis of President's Speech, Summary, Theodore Sorensen Papers, box 48, Cuba General, JFKL.
134. Ibid., 361–62. The request for this assessment, issued on October 24, was also cabled to Ambassador Thomas Finletter in Paris in reference to the potential NATO reaction. Cable State, October 24, 1962, National Security File, box 226, NATO-Weapons, Cables, Turkey, JFKL. Both Hare and Finletter responded that Turkey valued its Jupiter missiles and would be resistant to their removal, although replacement with submarine-based Polaris missiles could smooth the process. For Hare, see [Assessment of Consequences for the NATO Alliance if the Jupiters Are Traded for the Cuban Missiles—In Three Sections] Secret, Cable Ankara, October 26, 1962, item no. CC01470, NSA. For Finletter, see [Turkish Position with regard to Trading Jupiters for Soviet Missiles in Cuba] Secret, Cable Paris, October 25, 1962, item no. CC01328, NSA.
135. Ormsby-Gore to Foreign Office, October 27, 1962, cited in White, *The Cuban Missile Crisis* (London: Macmillan and Co., 1996), 222.
136. Cuban Missile Crisis Meetings, October 27, 1962, *Presidential Recordings-Transcripts,* JFKL, 32–38.
137. Zelikow et al., eds., *The Presidential Recordings,* 364.
138. Kaplan, "War Room."
139. Stevenson to JFK, October 17, 1962, Sorensen Papers, box 49, JFKL, emphasis in original. See also White, *The Cuban Missile Crisis,* 172.
140. Martin, *Adlai Stevenson and the World,* 724. George Ball explains, "in urging that we offer such a trade, Stevenson was not putting forth an idea not already discussed. The reason for the excessive expression of outrage was that he proposed it late in the day, after the President and the ExComm had already settled on another course. Not having been present during the week-long argument, Stevenson appeared to the weary members of the ExComm as ignoring all the anguished hours of discussion that had already taken place." Ball, *The Past Has Another Pattern,* 295. See also White, *The Cuban Missile Crisis,* 171.
141. This statement had previously been credited to John McCone rather than McCloy. See May and Zelikow, eds., *The Kennedy Tapes,* 464; and Beschloss, *Crisis Years,* 508. But Sheldon Stern listened carefully to the ExComm tape and concluded this was in error. See Stern, *Averting "The Final Failure,"* 273, *n* 231.
142. Harriman wrote, "There has undoubtedly been great pressure on Khrushchev for a considerable time to do something about our ring of bases, aggravated by our placing Jupiter missiles in Turkey." Harriman suggested that Khrushchev had been pushed to take bold action by a tough group in the Kremlin, and such a trade might ease the pressure that the premier was feeling from this faction. W. Averell Harriman, Memorandum on Kremlin Reactions, October 22, 1962, Averell Harriman Papers, Special File, Public Service, Kennedy/Johnson Administrations, Cuba, box 452, LC. On October 25, the Brazilian government offered a proposal calling for the denuclearization of Latin America, coupled with guarantees of the territorial integrity of all countries in the area. At a minimum, this plan would have required the withdrawal of all Soviet nuclear systems from Cuba and American ones from Guantanamo Bay and Puerto Rico. In exchange for this, all involved countries would have renewed their commitments not to

invade Cuba and Cuba would have promised not to invade any country in the region. See Garthoff, *Reflections on the Cuban Missile Crisis,* 74, 116. Furthermore, on October 26, Harriman expressed his support for the Brazilian proposal and offered suggestions for additional diplomatic maneuvers in case that proved insufficient to resolve the crisis. First among these was to offer an agreement on removal of all nuclear weapons from the territory of non-nuclear powers. For the U.S., Harriman specifically stated, "This would mean the removal of our missiles from Turkey and Italy. . . ." W. Averell Harriman, Memorandum, October 26, 1962, Harriman Papers, Special File, Public Service, Kennedy/Johnson Administrations, Cuba, box 452, LC.

143. Schlesinger Jr., *Robert Kennedy,* 556.
144. Fursenko and Naftali, *One Hell of a Gamble,* 321.
145. Stewart Alsop, *The Center: The Anatomy of Power in Washington* (London: Hodder and Stoughton, 1968), 192. See also, White, *The Cuban Missile Crisis,* 167.
146. Bartlett is quoted in Sally Bedell Smith, *Grace and Power: The Private World of the Kennedy White House* (New York: Random House, 2004), 324.
147. Alsop and Bartlett, "In Time of Crisis."
148. Kenneth O'Donnell Oral History, cited in Thomas, *Robert Kennedy: His Life,* 232. Meanwhile, Kennedy cynically sent his press secretary, Pierre Salinger, out to publicly deny the *Post*'s report that Stevenson had supported a missile trade and to commend him on his performance during the crisis. News Conference at the White House, Unclassified, Press Briefing, December 3, 1962, item no. CC02669, NSA. Kennedy even sent Stevenson a letter of support, expressing his regret over the "unfortunate fuss" that had arisen over the *Post* article. In it, Kennedy stated, "The fact that Charles Bartlett was a co-author of this piece has made this particularly difficult for me—perhaps you have had the same problem with personal friends in the newspaper profession. In this particular case, I did not discuss the Cuban crisis or any of the events surrounding it with any newspapermen—and I am certain that the quotations in the *Saturday Evening Post* article did not come from the White House." Kennedy to Stevenson, December 4, 1962, Theodore Sorenson Papers, box 48, Cuba-General, JFKL.
149. Walter Johnson, ed., *The Papers of Adlai E. Stevenson, VIII* (Boston: Little, Brown, 1972–79), 351–52. See also White, *The Cuban Missile Crisis,* 167.
150. Ball, *The Past Has Another Pattern,* 158. See also White, *The Cuban Missile Crisis,* 177; and Beschloss, *Crisis Years,* 467.
151. Gilbert Harrison, "Why Stevenson," *The New Republic,* December 15, 1962, 6.
152. Robert F. Kennedy Oral History, 322, JFKL. See also Jeff Sheshol, *Mutual Contempt: Lyndon Johnson, Robert Kennedy, and the Feud that Defined a Decade* (New York: W. W. Norton, 1997), 98–99.
153. W. W. Rostow to Lyndon B. Johnson, October 5, 1968; and Lyndon B. Johnson Daily Diary, October 24, 1962, to October 30, 1962, Lyndon B. Johnson Library, Austin, TX (hereafter LBJL). See also Beschloss, *Crisis Years,* 509.
154. Kennedy, *Thirteen Days,* 46; and RFK Oral History Interview, February 1965, JFKL. See also Paterson, "Fixation with Cuba," 149.
155. Fursenko and Naftali, *One Hell of a Gamble,* 323.
156. Joe Alsop, "The Soviet Plan for Deception," *Washington Post,* November 5, 1962.
157. See Telegram from Soviet Ambassador to the USA Dobrynin to USSR Foreign Ministry, November 5, 1962, in *CWIHP Bulletin* 8–9 (Winter 1996–97), 325–26.
158. "Khrushchev's Oral Communication of December 10, 1962," *Problems of Communism* 41, special edit. (Spring 1992).
159. "Kennedy Letter of December 14, 1962," ibid. See also Fursenko and Naftali, *One Hell of a Gamble,* 323.

160. Bundy, *Danger and Survival,* 432–36.
161. Theodore Sorensen, letter to the author, June 12, 1998. Note that the version Sorensen offers up in his oral history on the presidency contains the same falsehoods he previously perpetuated. This is hardly unusual, however, given the agreements of the men involved to maintain their secrecy. See Theodore C. Sorensen Oral History, interviewed by Carl Kaysen, March 26, 1964, 66–67. For similarly flawed, privately offered accounts see Robert F. Kennedy Oral History, interviewed by John Barlow Martin, May 14 1964, 322; and Llewellyn Thompson Oral History, interviewed by Elizabeth Donahue, March 25, 1964, 23–26, JFKL.
162. Schlesinger, Jr., *Robert Kennedy,* 547.
163. Pierre Salinger, *With Kennedy* (Garden City, NY: Doubleday, 1966), 299.
164. Benjamin C. Bradlee, *Conversations with Kennedy* (New York: W. W. Norton, 1975), 131–33.
165. See Hilsman, *To Move a Nation,* 196. See also Richard Ned Lebow, "The Traditional and Revisionist Interpretation Reevaluated: Why Was Cuba a Crisis?" in Nathan, *The Cuban Missile Crisis Revisited,* 164.
166. Galbraith is quoted in Ronald Steel, "Endgame," *New York Review of Books,* March 13, 1969, 15–22.
167. See Kennedy, *Thirteen Days,* 67. Based upon their interpretation of the tape-recorded conversation, Ernest May and Philip Zelikow instead place this exchange at around 7:30 P.M. on Tuesday, October 23. See May and Zelikow, *The Kennedy Tapes,* 342, especially *n*18.
168. Thomas G. Paterson and William J. Brophy, "October Missiles and November Elections: The Cuban Crisis and American Politics, 1962," *Journal of American History* 73 (1) (June 1986): 95–96.
169 See Brugioni, *Eyeball to Eyeball,* 151–53. See also Stern, *Averting "The Final Failure,"* 162
170. "The Ugly Choice," *Time,* September 14, 1962.
171. "The Monroe Doctrine and Communist Cuba," *Time,* September 21, 1962.
172. Paterson and Brophy, "October Missiles and November Elections," 96.
173. See McAuliffe, *CIA Documents on the Cuban Missile Crisis.*
174. Theodore C. Sorensen, Memo for the Files, September 6, 1962, Cuba Collection, State/FOIA, Theodore C. Sorensen Papers, Classified Subject Files, 1961–64, General, 1962, JFKL. See also Fursenko and Naftali, *One Hell of a Gamble,* 197.
175. Kennedy apparently realized this on October 16 when he said, "Last month I should have said that we don't care." Cuban Missile Crisis Meetings, October 16, 1962, *Presidential Recordings-Transcripts,* JFKL, 15. See also Bundy, *Danger and Survival,* 413.
176. "Kennedy's Patience," *Chicago Tribune,* September 15, 1962. On September 14, *The New York Times* ("Kennedy Hints at War Talk"), *The Washington Post* ("President Urges U.S. to 'Keep Head' on Cuba"), and the *Chicago Tribune* ("No Cuba Threat: Kennedy") carried detailed reports about the Cuba situation on their respective front pages. The next day's *Times* and *Post* each sounded a much more restrained tone than the *Tribune.* The *Times*'s editors opined: "The Cuba question today is complex, delicate dangerous—but not dangerous enough to justify rash action. President Kennedy has been firm and frank. If Premiers Khrushchev and Castro were issuing a challenge, it has been answered. This can go so far—and not further." The *Post* editors concurred : "Rash and impulsive military adventures, much as they may be clamored for, are to be resisted as long as direct military safety permits and so far as the integrity of the other American countries allows." "Kennedy, Cuba, and the USSR," *New York Times,* September 14, 1962; and "Soviet-Cuban Crisis," *Washington Post,* September 14, 1962.
177. William L. Ryan, "Writer Tells How Russians Control Cuba," *Chicago Tribune,* Sep-

tember 14, 1962; Anthony Burton, "Close-up of Russia in Cuba," *Chicago Tribune,* September 17, 1962; and Jules Dubois, "Report Russia Shear Power from Castro," *Chicago Tribune,* September 25, 1962.

178. Paterson and Brophy, "October Missiles and November Elections," 96–97.
179. See Max Holland, "A Luce Connection: Senator Keating, William Pawley, and the Cuban Missile Crisis," *Journal of Cold War Studies* I (Fall 1999): 139–67; and Brigitte Nacos, "Press, Presidents, and Crises," (PhD diss., Columbia University, 1987), 51.
180. See Lawrence Freedman, *Kennedy's Wars: Berlin, Cuba, Laos, and Vietnam* (New York: Oxford University Press, 2000), 161.
181. Ted Sorensen's brother wrote the policy guidance. Thomas Sorensen, "Information Policy Guidance on Cuba," October 21, 1962, Cuba-Subjects, General and Historical Information, box 48, Classified Subjects File, Theodore C. Sorensen Papers, JFKL, 3. See also Nash, *Other Missiles,* 119.
182. Quoted in Graham Allison, "Cuban Missiles and Kennedy Macho," *Washington Monthly,* October 1972.
183. "Why Cuba Isn't Like Turkey," *Chicago Tribune,* October 24, 1962.
184. [Guidance for U.S. Officials at Home and Abroad in Explaining U.S. Actions Against Soviet Bases in Cuba] Confidential, Cable State, October 24, 1962, item no. CC01150, NSA.
185. Conservative attacks, made in ignorance of the missile trade, that accused President Kennedy of allegedly being too soft on the Soviets and the Cubans include: Daniel and Hubbell, *Strike in the West;* Lane, *The Leadership of President Kennedy;* Lazo, *Dagger in the Heart;* Bethel, *The Losers;* Smith Jr., *Kennedy's Thirteen Greatest Mistakes;* and Acheson, "Dean Acheson's Version of Robert Kennedy's Version of the Cuban Missile Affair."
186. See Steel, "Endgame."
187. Paul H. Nitze, *From Hiroshima to Glasnost: At the Center of Decision: A Memoir* (New York: Grove Weidenfeld, 1989), 237.
188. Spruille Braden, *Diplomats and Demagogues* (New Rochelle, NY: Arlingotn House, 1971), 430–31. See also Gaddis Smith, *The Last Years of the Monroe Doctrine* (New York: Hill and Wang, 1994), 110.
189. Robert D. Crane, "The Cuban Crisis: A Strategic Analysis of American and Soviet Policy," *Orbis,* Winter 1963, 549, 562.
190. David Lowenthal, "U.S. Cuban Policy: Illusion and Reality," *National Review,* January 9, 1963, 16.
191. Richard M. Nixon, "Cuba, Castro and John F. Kennedy," *Reader's Digest,* November 1964.
192. See Paterson and Brophy, "October Missiles and November Elections," 108.
193. Nacos, "Press, Presidents, and Crises," 80.
194. Brugioni, *Eyeball to Eyeball,* 468–69.
195. Blight and Welch, *On the Brink,* 81–82.
196. JCS to President Kennedy, "Recommendation for Execution of CINCLANT OPLANS 312 and 316," JCSM-844-62, October 28, 1962, OSD Records, 71-A-2896, National Records Center, Suitland, MD.
197. Senator Richard Russell (D-GA), chairman of the Armed Services Committee, Senator James William Fulbright (D-AK), chairman of the Foreign Relations Committee, and Senator Bourke Hickenlooper (R-IA) each expressly advocated a strike on Cuba instead of a blockade. See John McCone's notes on the leadership meeting on October 22, Memorandum for the File, October 24, 1962, in *FRUS, 1961–1963, vol. XI,* 158–61. See also Paterson and Brophy, "October Missiles and November Elections," 104.
198. For example, in 1987, McGeorge Bundy explained, "I've listened to the tapes of the

October 27th meetings, and I can say with a high degree of confidence that I don't think there was any worry of that kind whatsoever. I have no recollection of anyone voicing any fear of being lynched over the affair in Cuba." *Proceedings of the Hawk's Cay Conference on the Cuban Missile Crisis,* Marathon, FL, March 5–8, 1987, Final Version (Center for Science and International Affairs, Harvard University, April, 1988), 115. Ted Sorensen went a step further and argued that Kennedy opted for the blockade in full knowledge that it would adversely affect his political standing. Sorensen contended, "JFK was convinced that his course of action would hurt his party in the elections," and Kennedy recognized that the air strike would "be a swifter and more popular means of removing the missiles before Election Day." Theodore C. Sorensen, *The Kennedy Legacy* (New York, Macmillan and Co., 1969), 190. See also Lebow, "The Traditional and Revisionist Interpretation Reevaluated," 163.

199. See Paterson and Brophy, "October Missiles and November Elections," 102.
200. I. F. Stone, "The Brink," *New York Review of Books,* April 14, 1966, reprinted as "What Price Prestige?" in Robert A. Divine, ed., *Cuban Missile Crisis,* 2nd. ed. (NY: Marcus Weisner Publishing, 1988), 159–62. Stone was basing his assessment on Elie Abel's account. Ronald Steel made similar charges at the time. See Steel, "Endgame," reprinted in Steel, *Imperialists and Other Heroes.*
201. Gribkov and Smith, *Operation ANADYR,* 166–77. Gribkov originally offered a figure of 98 tactical warheads, but later amended this to 158. See Bird, *The Color of Truth,* 245. See also Stuart H. Newberger, "Secrets of October 1962: Opening Cuban Missile Crisis Files Under FOIA," *American Bar Association Journal,* October 1992; and Robert A. Divine, "Alive and Well: The Continuing Cuban Missile Crisis Controversy," *Diplomatic History* 18 (4) (1994): 551–61.
202. Scholars continue to debate the issue. Alekandr Fursenko and Timothy Naftali argue that in a memorandum to the Soviet commander in Cuba, dated September 8, 1962, Khrushchev made clear "that the use of nuclear weapons can only be authorized by a direct order from Moscow" and that this documentary evidence "should dispel any remaining doubt that the Soviet commander in Cuba, General Pliev, was not given oral authorization to use the tactical nuclear missiles." Working with the same Soviet document, however, Raymond Garthoff contends that Fursenko and Naftali overlook important passages that evoke a more ambiguous interpretation of where this order placed fire control authority. He concludes that "the instructions on employment in combat of the air defense forces assigned responsibility to the Commander of the Group of Soviet Forces in Cuba, in contrast to the guidance on employment of the nuclear MRBM and IRBM missile forces . . . which was specifically reserved for a signal from Moscow. The employment of Army (Luna) and Air Force (cruise missile FKR-1 and IL-28) tactical nuclear forces was not specifically limited to advance approval from Moscow, with one interesting exception: the employment of nuclear cruise missiles against the U.S. base at Guantanamo was reserved for a 'signal from the General Staff.'" Each scholar, nonetheless, agrees that once the crisis became a public affair, Khrushchev clearly affirmed that the use of any nuclear weapon required advance approval by Moscow. Alekandr Fursenko and Timothy Naftali, "The Pitsunda Decision: Khrushchev and Nuclear Weapons," *CWIHP Bulletin* 10 (March 1998): 223–27; and Raymond Garthoff, "New Evidence on the Cuban Missile Crisis: Khrushchev, Nuclear Weapons, and the Cuban Missile Crisis," *CWIHP Bulletin* 11 (Winter 1998): 251–62.
203. Alexander M. Haig Jr., with Charles McCarry, *Inner Circles: How America Changed the World: A Memoir* (New York: Warner Books, 1992), 102–3.
204. Henry Kissinger, "Strains on the Alliance," *Foreign Affairs* 41(2) (January 1964): 262.
205. Indeed, the U.S. Embassy in Italy contended that Italian government and public opin-

ion would probably have minimal objection to a U.S. missile withdrawal. [Assessment of Possibility of Withdrawing Jupiter Missiles from Italy—In Two Section], Secret, Cable Rome, October 26, 1962, item no. CC01463, NSA.

206. Barton Bernstein offers some vivid examples of these dire worries:

> McCone said, according to the minutes, "the Soviet weapons in Cuba were pointed at our heart and put us under great handicap to carry out our commitment to the free world.". . . Assistant Secretary of Defense Paul Nitze, an ardent cold warrior since the Truman years, opposed the Soviet proposal at the beginning of the meeting: "It would be anathema to the Turks to pull the missiles out . . . the next Soviet step would be denuclearization of the entire NATO area." His unstated implications were familiar: Concessions would only beget Soviet demands for more concessions. Where would America draw the line? Why should allies trust America's promise? . . . "This could create one hell of a mess," concluded Robert Komer, a Bundy aide, in early November. "Early removal of JUPITERS would revive all [our allies'] latent fears [even though] our Cuban performance has greatly bucked [them] up," Komer told Bundy. In early January 1963, Komer, still ignorant of the deal, tried to persuade the President not to remove the weapons. "Turkish political outlook is quite uncertain and we see trouble ahead," Komer reported.

Bernstein, "Reconsidering the Missile Crisis," in Nathan, *The Cuban Missile Crisis Revisited,* 78, 84, 99. For an example of Komer's warnings about creating a "crisis of confidence" about U.S. commitments to allies, see Komer to Bundy, November 12, 1962, National Security File, box 226, NATO-Weapons, Turkey, JFKL. Steward Alsop, in attacking Stevenson, insisted that Kennedy "sincerely believed that such concessions as Stevenson proposed . . . would encourage the Soviets, as Hitler was encouraged in the time of Munich, to further adventures in the expectation of further concessions." Robert W. Merry, *Taking on the World: Joseph and Stewart Alsop—Guardians of the American Century* (New York: W. W. Norton, 1996), 394. For examples of these views in the official and semiofficial histories see, for instance, Abel, *The Missile Crisis,* 95; Pachter, *Collision Course,* 66; Schlesinger Jr., *A Thousand Days,* 829–30; and Sorensen, *Kennedy,* 752–54.

207. Bundy, *Danger and Survival,* 436–37.
208. Bernstein, "Trading the Jupiters in Turkey," 113–14.
209. Quoted in I. F. Stone, "The Brink," in Divine, ed., *Cuban Missile Crisis,* 160.
210. Bernstein, "Trading the Jupiters in Turkey," 113–16.
211. Kennedy to the secretary of state, August 21, 1961, box 82–98, National Security File, JFKL. See also Frank Costigliola, "Kennedy, the European Allies and the Failure to Consult," *Political Science Quarterly* 110 (1) (1995): 105–23.
212. Theodore Sorensen Oral History Interview, JFKL.
213. Memorandum of Conversation, October 28, 1962, in *FRUS, 1961–1963, vol. XI,* 288.
214. Harold Macmillan, *At the End of the Day, 1961–1963* (New York: Harper & Row, 1973), 212–13.
215. Sergei N. Khrushchev *Nikita Khrushchev,* 636–37. For insight into Soviet efforts to avoid a major break with their Cuban allies over the resolution of the crisis, see Hershberg, "More Evidence on the Cuban Missile Crisis: More Documents from the Russian Archives," and related Soviet documents in *CWIHP Bulletin* 8–9 (Winter 1996–97): 270–77, 278–347.

216. "Prime Minister Castro's Letter to Premier Khrushchev, October 31, 1962," document 59, in Chang and Kornbluh, *The Cuban Missile Crisis, 1962,* 254.
217. Blight, Allyn, and Welch, *Cuba on the Brink,* 215.
218. Mikoyan went on to further explain his indignation over Castro's reaction to the resolution of the crisis: "You know that fellow Castro is crazy. He kept me, Mikoyan, waiting for ten days without seeing me. I finally told him that I was going to go home and he would be sorry. He finally saw me. That Castro is crazy." Rusk, *As I Saw It,* 245.
219. See the transcript of Khrushchev's Speech to the Supreme Soviet, December 12, 1962, in the State Department Bureau of Intelligence and Research's compilation of Soviet post-crisis statements provided to Averell Harriman. Memorandum, Undated, Harriman Papers, Special File, Public Service, Kennedy/Johnson Administrations, Cuba, box 452, LC. See also the discussion of this point in Fursenko and Naftali, *One Hell of a Gamble,* 324.
220. See Dobrynin, *In Confidence,* 98; and CNN's *The Cold War,* episode 10, "Cuba," November 29, 1998.
221. Fursenko and Naftali, *One Hell of a Gamble,* 353–54. See also William Taubman, *Khruschchev: The Man and His Era* (New York: W. W. Norton, 2002), 575–77.
222. See Bird, *The Color of Truth,* 249.
223. *Public Papers of the Presidents: John F. Kennedy, 1961–1963,* 3 vols. (Washington, D.C.: GPO, 1962–64), December 30, 1962. See also Richard Reeves, *President Kennedy* (New York: Simon & Schuster, 1993), 445.
224. See Peter Kornbluh, "Kennedy and Castro: The Secret Quest for Accomodation," National Security Archive Electronic Briefing Book No. 17, August 16, 1999; and Philip Brenner, "Thirteen Months: Cuba's Perspective on the Missile Crisis," in Nathan, *The Cuban Missile Crisis Revisited,* 187–219.
225. Writing on October 30 to the Foreign Ministry in Moscow, Soviet negotiators confirmed that "taking into account President Kennedy's desire, communicated through Robert Kennedy in his conversation with Comrade Dobrynin on 27 October, we will not raise the issue of American bases in Turkey in our negotiations . . . in New York." Telegram from Soviet Deputy Foreign Minister Kuznetsov and Ambassador to the UN Zorin to USSR Foreign Ministry, October 30, 1962, in *CWIHP Bulletin* 8–9 (Winter 1996–97): 302–3. Replying to this telegram, the Soviet Foreign Minister reiterated, "you should not in any circumstance touch on this issue in your negotiations with U Thant and the USA representatives in New York, since it is the subject of direct negotiations between Moscow and Washington." Telegram from USSR Foreign Minister A. A. Gromyko to the Soviet Mission in New York, November 1, 1962, in ibid., 309–10.
226. See Bernstein, "Reconsidering the Missile Crisis," 99.
227. May and Zelikow, *The Kennedy Tapes,* 691–92.
228. *Congressional Record,* 88th Congress, 1st sess., February 25, 1963.
229. *Congressional Record,* 88th Congress, 1st sess., February 19, 1963, 2534–35.
230. *Congressional Record,* 88th Congress, 1st sess., August 15, 1963, appendix, A4936.
231. Lens, *The Military-Industrial Complex,* 91.
232. Paterson, "Bearing the Burden," 106.
233. Martin Amis, *Experience* (New York: Talk Miramax Books, 2000), 137.
234. One of the earliest attempts to extract lessons from the crisis specifically lauded the administration's success in keeping information and deliberations secret during the crisis. Moreover, it emphasized the importance of such secrecy for the quick and satisfactory resolution of these types of situations. See "Some Lessons from the First Two Weeks of the Cuban Crisis," Top Secret, Memorandum, November 1, 1962, item no. CC01806, NSA.

235. Procedures for Handling Media Representatives, Non-Classified, Memorandum, October 27, 1962, item no. CC01493, NSA.
236. McGeorge Bundy to Joseph Alsop, November 27, 1962, Joseph and Stewart Alsop Papers, General Correspondence, November–December 1962, box 18, LC. Bundy was responding to Alsop's direct appeal to the president on the matter. Interestingly, Alsop stated that he did not think the directive would cause much harm during the Kennedy administration, but feared the precedent that it set for future administrations that would use such policies to limit the media's ability to gather information and report on government actions. See Alsop to the President, November 24, 1962, and Alsop to Bundy, November 26, 1962, Joseph and Stewart Alsop Papers, General Correspondence, November–December 1962, box 18, LC.
237. Memorandum from Robert Manning, Assistant Secretary for Public Affairs to all Assistant Secretaries of State, Procedures Relating to Contacts with News Media Representatives, November 27, 1962, Transcripts of Daily News Conferences of the Department of State, Vol. 27: October–December 1962, RG 59, General Records of the Department of State—Records of the Office of News and Its Predecessors, National Archives, College Park, MD. This memorandum was presented to members of the media by Manning at a press conference immediately after its distribution to the assistant secretaries. The State Department did suspend the reporting procedures; however, it did not eliminate the directive and reserved the right to reinstate them at any time.
238. Quoted in Nacos, "Press, Presidents, and Crises," 39.
239. Ibid., 63.
240. "Strange Aftermath of the Cuban Deal," *U.S. News & World Report,* November 12, 1963.
241. "News as a Weapon," *Chicago Tribune,* November 2, 1962, editorial.
242. *U.S. News & World Report,* November 5, 1962.
243. "The Crisis," *Newsweek,* November 12, 1962.
244. Quoted in Nacos, "Press, Presidents, and Crises," 63.
245. Allison, *Essence of Decision.* All subsequent references to *Essence of Decision* refer to the original text published in 1971. In 1999, together with Philip Zelikow, Allison published an updated edition in which most if not all of its errors of fact were corrected. See Graham T. Allison and Philip Zelikow, *Essence of Decision: Explaining the Cuban Missile Crisis,* 2d ed. (New York: Longman, 1999). The later book was the subject of a long and detailed examination by Barton J. Bernstein, who notes that while the authors corrected most of the factual mistakes in the original edition, "the revised book almost never states what major interpretations have been changed, or why. The new edition usually avoids an explicit dialogue with the earlier edition, or its critics, and an explicit acknowledgement of mistakes in the 1971 edition." A second important review appeared in *Diplomatic History* in the summer of 2001 by Bruce Kuklick. The reviewer faults the original edition for missing the relationship of Berlin and Germany to Soviet thinking, but also for an overall intellectual and epistemological confusion about just what kinds of lessons it seeks to impart. See Bernstein, "Understanding Decisionmaking," 134–64, especially 164; and Bruce Kuklick, "Reconsidering the Missile Crisis and Its Interpretation," *Diplomatic History* 25(1) (Summer, 2001): 517–23. For more detail on the role of Germany in Soviet thinking, see Trachtenberg, *A Constructed Peace,* part 3.
246. Colin Gray, *The Soviet-American Arms Race* (Farnborough: Saxon House, 1976), 28.
247. See David A. Welch, "The Organizational Process and Bureaucratic Politics Paradigms: Retrospect and Prospect," *International Security* 17 (2) (Fall 1992): 112. See also Steve Smith, "Allison and the Cuban Missile Crisis: A Review of the Bureaucratic Politics Model of Foreign Policy Decision-Making," in *Millennium: Journal of International Stud-*

ies 9 (1); Hafner, "Bureaucratic Politics and 'Those Frigging Missiles,'"; Robert J. Art, "Bureaucratic Politics and American Foreign Policy: A Critique," *Policy Sciences* 4 (December 1973): 467–90; and Stephen D. Krassner, "Are Bureaucracies Important (Or Allison Wonderland)," *Foreign Policy* 7 (Summer 1972): 159–79.

248. Allison, *Essence of Decision,* ix. See also Welch, "The Organizational Process," 112.
249. Neustadt, Hilsman, and Schilling have been colleagues at Columbia. Halperin was Schilling's student at Columbia and a colleague of I. M. Destler's at Brookings. Neustadt was a presidential transition adviser to Kennedy. Hilsman was in the Department of State's Bureau of Intelligence and Research and assistant secretary of state for Far Eastern Affairs. Halperin served as deputy assistant secretary of defense and staff member of the NSC under Johnson and Nixon. Halperin's book was written with the assistance of a Brookings study group of which Neustadt, Schilling, Allison, and Destler were members. See Hafner, "Bureaucratic Politics and 'Those Frigging Missiles,'" 308.
250. Allison, "Conceptual Models and the Cuban Missile Crisis," 689–718.
251. See Graham T. Allison, "Cuban Missiles and Kennedy Macho," *Washington Monthly,* October 1972, 15–19.
252. Allison, *Essence of Decision,* 129–30, 309, *n*123.
253. Dan Caldwell later demonstrated that Allison had also been misinformed with regard to the movement of the blockade. See D. Caldwell, "A Research Note on the Quarantine of Cuba," *International Studies Quarterly* 22 (1978): 625–33.
254. Allison, *Essence of Decision,* 229.
255. Ibid., 228.
256. Ibid., 230.
257. J. Garry Clifford, "Bureaucratic Politics" *Journal of American History* (June 1990): 162. See also Graham T. Allison and Morton H. Halperin, "Bureaucratic Politics: A Paradigm and Some Policy Implications," *World Politics* 25 (Spring 1972): 40–80; Morton H. Halperin, "The Decision to Deploy the ABM: Bureaucratic and Domestic Politics in the Johnson Administration," ibid., 62–96; Morton Halperin, with the assistance of Priscilla Clapp and Arnold Kanter, *Bureaucratic Politics and Foreign Policy* (Washington, D.C.: The Brookings Institution, 1974); Destler, *Presidents, Bureaucrats, and Foreign Policy;* David J. Alvarez, *Bureaucracy and Cold War Diplomacy: The United States and Turkey, 1943–1946* (Thessaloníki: Institute for Balkan Studies, 1980); Stephen D. Cohen, *The Making of United States International Economic Policy: Principles, Problems, and Proposals for Reform* (New York: Praeger, 1977); Jerel A. Rosati, "Developing a Systematic Decision-Making Framework: Bureaucratic Politics in Perspective," *World Politics* 33 (January 1981); Leslie Gelb with Richard K. Betts, *The Irony of Vietnam: The System Worked* (Washington, D.C.: The Brookings Institution, 1979); James C. Thomson, "On the Making of U.S. China Policy, 1961–1969," *China Quarterly* 50 (April–June 1973): 220–43; and Robert P. Haffa Jr., "Allison's Models: An Analytic Approach to Bureaucratic Politics," in John E. Endicott and Roy W. Stafford Jr., eds., *American Defense Policy* (Baltimore, MD: Johns Hopkins University Press, 1977), 224.
258. Krassner, "Are Bureauracies Important," 160–61.
259. Allison, *Essence of Decision,* 181. Barton Bernstein addresses this point in "Understanding Decisionmaking," 134-64.
260. Krassner, "Are Bureaucracies Important," 162. Schlesinger Jr. is quoted in Daniel Elsberg, "The Quagmire Myth and the Stalemate Machine," *Public Policy* (Spring 1971), 218.
261. See Clifford, "Bureaucratic Politics," 163. See also Theodore Draper, "Reagan's Junta: The Institutional Sources of the Iran–Contra Affair," in Charles W. Kegley and Eugene Wittkopf, eds., *The Domestic Sources of American Foreign Policy: Insight and Evidence* (New York, 1988), 131–41.

262. Krassner, "Are Bureaucracies Important," 168.
263. Blight and Welch, *On the Brink,* 104–5.
264. Garthoff, *Reflections of the Cuban Missile Crisis,* 87; and Sorensen, *The Kennedy Legacy,* 192.
265. See Martin Walker, *The Cold War: A History* (New York: Henry Holt, 1994), 181.
266. See Jack Snyder, *Myths of Empire: Domestic Politics and International Ambition* (Ithaca, NY: Cornell University Press, 1991), 41–42. See also Francis Rourke, *Bureaucracy, Politics, and Foreign Policy* (Boston: Little, Brown, 1969).
267. FDR ensured the creation of the United Nations and acquired an ally in the war with Japan; Kennedy secured the removal of all "offensive" Soviet weaponry from Cuba.
268. See Schlesinger Jr., *A Thousand Days,* 840–41.
269. Address to the Democratic National Convention, Robert F. Kennedy, Atlantic City, NJ, August 27, 1964, at JFKL Web site: *http://www.cs.umb.edu/jfklibrary/r082764.htm.* See also Inglis, *The Cruel Peace,* 165.
270. Hilsman, *To Move a Nation,* 227.
271. Blight and Welch, *On the Brink,* 147–48.
272. Henry A. Kissinger, "Reflections on Cuba," *Reporter,* November 22, 1962, 21–24.
273. See Bundy, *Danger and Survival,* 445–47. See also Rusk et al., "The Lessons of the Cuban Missile Crisis," *Time,* September 27, 1982.
274. See Schlesinger Jr., *A Thousand Days,* 831.
275. George, "The Cuban Missile Crisis, 1962," x.
276. Bernstein, "Reconsidering the Missile Crisis," 106.
277. Ibid.
278. George, "The Cuban Missile Crisis, 1962," xi.
279. Nathan, "The Heyday of the New Strategy," 1.
280. Ibid., 5.
281. See, for example, the letter from White House aide Bill Moyers that stated "I am impressed by the report in the Cuban crisis, the idea of a blockade did not emerge almost until the last minute—and not until a working group such as [the ExComm] . . . provided the combustion in which new ideas are born." Letter to the President, Unsigned, from the files of Bill Moyers, February 1965, in David M. Barrett, *Lyndon B. Johnson's Vietnam Papers: A Documentary Collection* (College Station, TX: Texas A&M University Press, 1997), 103.
282. Brian VanDeMark, *Into the Quagmire: Lyndon Johnson and the Escalation of the Vietnam War* (New York: Oxford, 1991), 48.
283. Telegram from the Department of State to the Embassy in Vietnam, December 29, 1965, in *FRUS, 1964–1968,* vol. III: *Vietnam, July–December 1965,* 741.
284. Cyrus Vance Oral History Interview, March 9, 1970, Interview no. 3, 11, LBJL.
285. Memorandum from Secretary of Defense McNamara to President Johnson, July 20, 1965, in *FRUS, 1964–1968,* vol. III, 171, 176.
286. Blight and Welch, *On the Brink,* 155–56.
287. W. W. Rostow to Harriman, January 28, 1966, box 499, Harriman Papers, LC. See also Randall B. Woods, *Fulbright: A Biography* (New York: Cambridge University Press, 1995), 408.
288. Russell to Louis Wolfson, January 4, 1966, in Barrett, *Lyndon B. Johnson's Vietnam Papers,* 302–3.
289. David Kaiser, *American Tragedy: Kennedy, Johnson and the Origins of the Vietnam War* (Cambridge, MA.: Harvard University Press, 2000), 370.
290. See Dewart, "The Cuban Crisis Revisited," 40. When confronted with this criticism, McNamara concurred that the Cuban experience was hardly irrelevant to U.S. strategy in Vietnam. But it was not the neat "lessons learned" paradigm that he was endorsing.

Rather, in his view, it was simple common sense in both instances. The "rationale" in Vietnam, he explains, "was exactly the same rationale for preferring the quarantine during the Cuban missile crisis. I mean, if you just say the hell with it, let's go all out, bomb them—Cubans, or Vietnamese—into oblivion, look what you are doing. You are practically requiring the Soviets, or in certain circumstances, the Chinese, to retaliate militarily. And then what happens. I'll tell you what: we're in a major war between nuclear powers." See Blight and Welch, *On the Brink,* 194.

291. Doris Kearns, *Lyndon Johnson and the American Dream* (New York: Harper & Row, 1976), 177–78. Kearns points out that her source materials are her personal notes taken "verbatim" during her time with Johnson. See ibid., 401.
292. Robert Dallek, *Flawed Giant: Lyndon Johnson and His Times, 1961–1973* (New York: Oxford University Press, 1998), 100.
293. Notes of Meeting, July 26, 1965, in *FRUS, 1964–1968, vol. III,* 255.
294. Wills, *The Kennedy Imprisonment,* 189.
295. Michael R. Beschloss, *Taking Charge: The Johnson White House Tapes, 1963–1964* (New York: Simon & Schuster, 1997), 238.
296. Kearns, *Lyndon Johnson,* 253–54.
297. Ibid.
298. VanDeMark, *Into the Quagmire,* 50.
299. Beschloss, *Taking Charge,* 357.
300. Notes of the Leadership Meeting, White House, Washington, August 4, 1964, in *FRUS, 1964–1968, Vol. I: Vietnam, 1964,* 616.
301. Ibid., 619. See also H. W. Brands, *The Wages of Globalism: Lyndon Johnson and the Limits of American Power* (New York: Oxford University Press, 1995), 228.
302. Theodore H. White, *The Making of the President, 1964* (New York: Atheneum, 1965), 373–74. See also Beschloss, *Crisis Years,* 509.
303. Stone, "The Brink," 160.
304. When I raised this issue in a letter to Theodore Sorensen, he replied: "There is merit in your suggestion that earlier full disclosure of JFK's position in resolving the Cuban Missile Crisis might have helped sober those would-be imitators who argued that his posture consisted only of threats of force against the Soviet Union." (He notes that he was the most junior of the people who knew about "RFK's oral message on JFK's behalf regarding the assured ultimate dismantling of the Jupiters in Turkey." He was also, he says, the "least 'officially' connected to national security matters and . . . felt I had not authority to reveal this information on my own." It was McGeorge Bundy who proposed the *Time* article in 1982, and therefore the 1989 Moscow conference, he says, revealed nothing new. Sorensen added that "several passages in *The Kennedy Legacy* as well as Kennedy made clear, it was always public knowledge that JFK relied substantially on communications, negotiations, and diplomacy to help end the crisis. . . . [But] Very possibly, as your letter suggests, an earlier disclosure of JFK's assurance to Khrushchev regarding the missiles in Turkey would have slowed down LBJ's and Nixon's plunge into Viet Nam, but I doubt it." Theodore Sorensen to the author, June 12, 1998.
305. Sorensen, *The Kennedy Legacy,* 208.
306. Robert McNamara, *In Retrospect: The Tragedy and Lessons of Vietnam* (New York: Times Books, 1995), 96–97.
307. Mark Falcoff, "Learning to Love the Missile Crisis," *National Interest,* Summer 1989, 63–64.
308. Ibid., 69–70.

309. National Security Planning Group Meeting, Top Secret, Minutes, November 11, 1984, item no. C03316, NSA. See also Chang, "The View from Washington and the Views from Nowhere," 132.
310. Les Aspin, *Washington Post,* January 8, 1991.
311. David E. Sanger, "Bush Sees 'Urgent Duty' to Pre-empt Attack by Iraq," *New York Times,* October 8, 2002.
312. Ibid.
313. Christopher Maquis, "Missile Crisis Cited to Make Opposite Points," *New York Times,* October 8, 2002, *http://www.nytimes.com/2002/10/09/international/09GLOB.html*; and Alison Mitchell, "Lawmakers Make Their Cases as Votes on Use of Force Draw Near," *New York Times,* October 9, 2002.
314. Fred Kaplan, "Bush's Cuban Missile Fantasy, 2002 and 1962: No Comparison," *Slate,* October 9, 2002, *http://www.slate.com/?id=2072167.* A similar argument can be found in Jefferson Morley, "A Precedent That Proves Neither Side's Point," *Washington Post,* October 13, 2002, *http://www.washingtonpost.com/wp-dyn/articles/A15080-2002Oct11.html.* For analogy arguments on both sides, see Todd S. Purdum, "The Missiles of 1962 Haunt the Iraq Debate," *New York Times Week in Review,* October 13, 2002, *http://www.nytimes.com/2002/10/13/weekinreview/13PURD.html?ex=1035602226&ei=1&en=4a5bfa9a808c33d4*; and Kevin Sullivan, *Washington Post,* October 11, 2002.
315. Michael Dobbs, "Listen to Kennedy on Cuba for Clues About Bush on Iraq," *Washington Post,* January 19, 2003.
316. Fred Kaplan, "Bush's Cuban Missile Fantasy 2002 and 1962," *Slate,* October 9, 2002, *http://www.slate.com/?id=2072167.*
317. Reeves, *President Kennedy,* 420–21. Barton J. Bernstein wrote of Reeves, "He seems not to understand, and perhaps not to know, of the recent evidence that Kennedy made a *secret* offer [on October 27] to trade American missiles in Turkey for Soviet missiles in Cuba." See Bernstein, "A Thousand Days in the White House," *Washington Post Book World,* October 31, 1993, 5.
318. Richard Reeves, "Thirteen Days in October," *New York Times,* October 8, 1997.
319. Roger Hilsman, *The Cuban Missile Crisis: The Struggle over Policy,* preface.
320. Ibid., 124.
321. Ibid., 134.
322. Bruce Handy, "Blast from the Past," *Vanity Fair,* February 2001, 271.
323. See "Ads for Missile-Crisis Movie Are Pulled Because of Errors," *New York Times,* January 13, 2001.
324. See "Senator Kennedy Praises Movie About His Brothers," *Associated Press,* February 2, 2001. See also, for instance, Jay Carr, "To the Brink and Back," *Boston Globe,* January 12, 2001; Roger Ebert, "Thirteen Days," *Chicago-SunTimes,* January 12, 2001; and Desson Howe, "A Thrilling 'Thirteen Days,'" *Washington Post,* January 12, 2001. For two exceptions to this praise, along with a discussion of why it took place, see Eric Alterman, "Thirteen Days of Our Lives," *Nation,* January 29, 2001; and Michael Nelson, "Thirteen Days Doesn't Add Up," *Chronicle of Higher Education,* February 2, 2001. The film did, however, generate the following:

> In a PBS-sponsored online discussion devoted to the film, Robert McNamara was asked, "Wasn't . . . the U.S. agreement to take missiles out of Turkey the quid pro quo that brought the Cuban missile crisis to an end?" He responded, "There was no U.S. agreement to take missiles out of Turkey. As a matter of fact, the movie, contrary to some history books, correctly por-

trays what I heard the president tell Bobby to convey to Ambassador Dobrynin, the Soviet ambassador in Washington. What Bobby said to Dobrynin was: 'The agreement is if you will take the missiles out of Cuba under UN supervision'—which they did not do—but they took them out—but not under the UN supervision—'if you will agree to take the missiles out of Cuba under UN supervision, we, the U.S., will agree not to invade Cuba.' Now, that was not a difficult agreement to agree to because we had no intention of invading, although neither Castro nor Khrushchev were certain of that before the crisis came up. And I think the fear of invasion may have motivated each of them to the movement of the missiles into Cuba.

"But, in any event, we then had discussed in the president's office before Bobby went to see Dobrynin, the status of the Jupiter missiles in Cuba. They were militarily obsolete. In a sense, they were a pile of junk from a military point of view. But they were of very critical political importance to Turkey and to NATO. And during the crisis, during the 13 days, we had considered making the removal of the missiles from Cuba a part of a deal with Khrushchev. And we had discussed that with both the Turks and with NATO, and both the Turks and NATO vehemently opposed any such deal.

"They said it will be taken by our peoples in Turkey and in Europe as a sign of U.S. weakness; it will put in doubt the credibility of the U.S. security guarantee to defend Turkey and to defend NATO if you yield under pressure from the Soviets to take those weapons out. And, therefore, the Turks and we at NATO are strongly opposed to that. And for that reason the advisers to the president had advised him not to make it part of the deal, and he himself was opposed to making it part of the deal. However, before the Cuban Missile Crisis arose, before the start of the 13 days, he had said to the State Department, 'We've got to get those missiles out of there; they are worthless and they will attract Soviet fire in the event of Soviet attack, in the event of crisis, so let's get them out of there.'

"So with the reasons I mentioned, neither the Turks nor NATO wanted them out, so action had not been taken to get them out. But in this critical meeting in the president's office when that small group of six or seven of us were present—we all agreed that they were a pile of junk militarily and we should get them out of there, but because of the way in which action to remove them under the threat of Soviet pressure—the way in which that would be interpreted as weakness by the Turks and by NATO, we could not make it part of the agreement.

"So the president agreed, and he told Bobby to tell Dobrynin that we agreed to pledge we would not invade Cuba in return for Khrushchev taking Soviet missiles out of Cuba. And, in addition, Dobrynin could tell Khrushchev that unilaterally—not part of an agreement, but unilaterally—we were going to take the Jupiter missiles out of Turkey and replace them, in effect, by Polaris submarines off the coast of Turkey. So that was the deal. It was not an agreement; it was a statement of unilateral action."

See *http://www.newshour.com,* February 22, 2001.

325. White, *The Cuban Missile Crisis,* 220.
326. McNamara, *In Retrospect,* 97.

327. Blight and Welch, *On the Brink,* 174.
328. Ibid., 162.
329. Roger Hilsman and Ronald Steel, "An Exchange of Views," *New York Review of Books,* May 8, 1969, 36–38.
330. Truman is quoted in Gardner, *Architects of Illusion,* 56. See also Truman, *Memoirs: Year of Decisions,* 444–45. Truman was echoing a view expressed by General Lucius Clay in Berlin: "The Russians understand only one thing, that's force." Colonel Jim Atwood, quoting Clay on CNN's *The Cold War,* episode 9, "'The Wall," broadcast November 22, 1998.
331. See Harris Wofford, *Of Kennedys and Kings* (New York: Farrar, Straus & Giroux, 1980), 426.

IV. Lyndon B. Johnson and the Gulf of Tonkin Incidents

1. Tim Weiner, "Once Commandos for U.S., Vietnamese Are Now Barred," *New York Times,* April 14, 1995.
2. McNamara, *In Retrospect,* 120.
3. Fredrik Logevall, *Choosing War: The Lost Chance for Peace and the Escalation of War in Vietnam* (Berkely: University of California Press, 1999), 204.
4. Edwin E. Moïse, *Tonkin Gulf and the Escalation of the Vietnam War* (Chapel Hill: University of North Carolina Press, 1996), 226
5. "Letter to the Department of State from the International Security Agency, April 22, 1955," excerpted in Len Ackland, ed., *Credibility Gap: A Digest of the Pentagon Papers* (Philadelphia: American Friends Service Committee, 1972), 35.
6. Dwight D. Eisenhower, *Mandate for Change, 1953–1956: The White House Years* (Garden City, NY: Doubleday, 1963), 372. See also Theodore Draper, "The American Crisis: Vietnam, Cuba and the Dominican Republic," *Commentary* (January 1967): 29.
7. "Memorandum from Secretary of Defense Robert McNamara to President Johnson, March 13, 1964," quoted in George Mct. Kahin, *Intervention: How America Became Involved in Vietnam* (New York: Alfred A. Knopf, 1986), 91.
8. *The Pentagon Papers: The Defense Department History of Decisionmaking on Vietnam.* The Senator Gravel edition, vol. 2 (Boston: Beacon, 1971–1972), 22.
9. Kaiser, *American Tragedy,* 277.
10. Figures appear in "America in Vietnam," *New York Times,* April 30, 1985.
11. D. Michael Shafer, "The Vietnam Combat Experience: The Human Legacy," in D. Michael Shafer, ed., *The Legacy: The Vietnam War in the American Imagination* (Boston: Beacon Press, 1990), 93.
12. David Brown, "Children's Leukemia Risk Tied to Agent Orange," *Washington Post,* April 20, 2001.
13. Robert Buzzanco, *Vietnam and the Transformation of American Life* (Malden, MA: Blackwell, 1999), 115.
14. Ibid.
15. Thomas G. Paterson, "Historical Memory and Illusive Victories: Vietnam and Central America." *Diplomatic History* 12, no. 1 (1988): 10.
16. Buzzanco, *Vietnam and the Transformation,* 114.
17. See John Mueller, *War, Presidents and Public Opinion* (New York: John Wiley & Sons, 1973), 113.
18. Figure cited in David Halberstam, *The Best and the Brightest* (New York: Random House, 1969). See also Bird, *The Color of Truth,* 297.
19. See Robert A. Caro, "Lyndon B. Johnson," in Robert A. Wilson, ed., *Power and the*

Presidency (New York: PublicAffairs, 1999), 80; and Robert A. Caro, *The Path to Power: The Years of Lyndon Johnson* (New York: Alfred A. Knopf, 1982), xviii.

20. Caro, "Lyndon B. Johnson," 81.
21. Lloyd Gardner, *Pay Any Price: Lyndon Johnson and the Wars for Vietnam* (Chicago: Ivan R. Dee, 1995), 9.
22. Caro, "Lyndon B. Johnson," 74.
23. Acheson cited in George C. Herring, *LBJ and Vietnam: A Different Kind of War* (Austin: University of Texas Press, 1994), 16.
24. Joseph Califano, *The Triumph and Tragedy of Lyndon Johnson: The White House Years* (New York: Simon & Schuster, 1991), 10.
25. Caro, *The Path to Power,* xix.
26. Ibid.
27. Clark Clifford with Richard Holbrooke, *Counsel to the President* (New York: Random House, 1991), 386.
28. Robert Kennedy Oral History, 322, JFKL. RFK apparently repeated this story to journalist Rowland Evans, who related it using the description of "congenital liar" by the president. See Rowland Evans Oral History, Interview by Roberta F. Greene, July 30, 1970, Washington, D.C., 18, JFKL.
29. Kearns, *Lyndon Johnson,* 253.
30. LaFeber excerpts and "frontier" quotations from Walter LaFeber, "The Rise and Fall of American Power, 1963–1975," in William Appleman Williams et al., eds., *America in Vietnam: A Documentary History* (New York: Anchor, 1985), 216.
31. See Blema S. Steinberg, *Shame and Humiliation: Presidential Decision Making on Vietnam* (Pittsburgh: University of Pittsburgh Press, 1996), 8–13.
32. Kearns, *Lyndon Johnson,* 251–52.
33. David Halberstam, "LBJ and Presidential Machismo," in Jeffrey Kimball, *To Reason Why: The Debate About the Causes of U.S. Involvement in the Vietnam War* (Philadelphia: Temple University Press, 1990), 201.
34. Beschloss, *Taking Charge,* 370–72.
35. Ibid., 363–70 and 400–404.
36. See Brugioni, *Eyeball to Eyeball,* 152–53
37. Logevall, *Choosing War,* 282.
38. *New York Times,* October 4, 1964. See also Logevall, *Choosing War,* 242.
39. Logevall, *Choosing War,* 148. See also *The Pentagon Papers,* Gravel Edition, 3:174.
40. Manning to LBJ, June 15, 1964, box 54, NSF VN, LBJL. See also Logevall, *Choosing War,* 149.
41. Beschloss, *Taking Charge,* 398. See also "Mansfield memo to the President, December 7, 1963," Files of McGeorge Bundy, NSF, Country File, Vietnam, box 1, LBJL; and his memo to the President of February 1, 1964, Files of McGeorge Bundy, NSF, Memos to President, box 1, LBJL.
42. See, for instance, telephone conversation between the President and Senator Fulbright (to Senator Fulbright), December 2, 1963, JFK Assas. Related Conversations, LBJL.
43. Logevall, *Choosing War,* 168.
44. Though Morgenthau's views, extremely abbreviated, were at least brought to the president's attention by his aide, Harry McPherson, in March 1965 following a dinner hosted by Senator Frank Church. See McPherson's memo to the president, March 5, 1965, Harry McPherson Office Files, White House Aides, LBJL.
45. Ronald Steel, *Walter Lippmann and the American Century* (Boston: Little, Brown, 1980), 550. See also Logevall, *Choosing War,* 143.

46. Michael R. Beschloss, ed. *Reaching for Glory: Lyndon Johnson's Secret White House Tapes, 1964–65* (New York: Simon & Schuster, 2001), 168.
47. Ibid., 166.
48. Logevall, *Choosing War,* 283.
49. *New York Times,* March 19, 1964. See also Thomas Powers, *The War at Home: Vietnam and the American People, 1964–1968* (New York: Grossman, 1973), 3–4. See also Logevall, *Choosing War,* 195.
50. Walter Isaacson and Evan Thomas, *The Wise Men: Six Friends and the World They Made* (New York: Simon & Schuster, 1986), 650.
51. *Washington Post,* November 30, 1964. See also Logevall, *Choosing War,* 288
52. Hubert H. Humphrey, *Education of a Public Man: My Life and Politics* (Garden City, NY: Doubleday, 1976), 320–24. See also Logevall, *Choosing War,* 347.
53. Logevall, *Choosing War,* 391.
54. Michael Barone, *Our Country: The Shaping of America from Roosevelt to Reagan* (New York: Free Press, 1990), 399. See also Logevall, *Choosing War,* 288.
55. This point is noted in Andrew L. Johns, "Opening Pandora's Box: The Genesis and Evolution of the 1964 Congressional Resolution on Vietnam," *Journal of American-East Asian Relations* 6, nos. 2–3 (Summer–Fall, 1997): 178. For a discussion of Kennedy's nervousness about raising this point in debate, see Schlesinger Jr., *A Thousand Days,* 71–72.
56. Telephone conversation transcript, Johnson to Russell, May 27, 1964, LBJL.
57. Robert D. Schulzinger, *A Time for War: The United States and Vietnam, 1941–1975* (New York: Oxford University Press, 1997), 145.
58. Beschloss, *Reaching for Glory,* 402.
59. Kearns, *Lyndon Johnson,* 252–53.
60. Quoted in Clifford, *Counsel to the President,* 417.
61. Quoted in David M. Barrett, *Uncertain Warriors: Lyndon Johnson and His Vietnam Advisers* (Lawrence: University of Kansas, 1993), 15.
62. Tom Wicker, *JFK and LBJ: The Influence of Personality upon Politics* (New York: Penguin, 1968), 205.
63. For more evidence on this point, see James K. Galbraith, "Exit Strategy," *Boston Review,* October–November 2003, *http://www.bostonreview.net/BR28.5/galbraith.html;* and Kaiser, *American Tragedy,* 213–84.
64. See Frederick Nolting, *From Trust to Tragedy* (New York: Praeger, 1988), 21; and Stanley Karnow, *Vietnam: A History* (New York: Viking, 1983), 214.
65. See Steinberg, *Shame and Humiliation,* 83.
66. Caro, *Path to Power,* 141–42.
67. Bird, *The Color of Truth,* 272.
68. Kaiser, *American Tragedy,* 475.
69. Logevall, *Choosing War,* 133.
70. Ibid., 34.
71. Robert McNamara, *Argument Without End: In Search of Answers to the Vietnam Tragedy* (New York: PublicAffairs, 1999), 215–17. As Robert Jervis noted in the online discussion group, H-Diplo (February 1, 1999), the book's argument provides "a fascinating but fundamentally misleading account that reveals that McNamara still has as much trouble understanding opposing viewpoints as he did when he was Secretary of Defense. The book seems to accept a great deal of blame while really being, at a deeper level, self-exculpatory."
72. Deborah Shapley, *Promise and Power: The Life and Times of Robert McNamara* (Boston: Little, Brown, 1993), 277.

73. Johnson quote is from a letter to Mansfield from July 28, 1965, in Steinberg, *Shame and Humiliation,* 81.
74. David Halberstam, "LBJ and Presidential Machismo," in Kimball, *To Reason Why,* 201.
75. See Beschloss, *Taking Charge,* 411.
76. Snyder, *Myths of Empire,* 300.
77. Robert Scheer, "The Hoax of Tonkin," in *Thinking Tuna Fish, Talking Death: Essays on the Pornography of Power* (New York: Hill and Wang, 1988), 157.
78. David Halberstam, *The Best and the Brightest,* 434.
79. Kaiser, *American Tragedy,* 407.
80. McNamara proudly reproduced the text of this letter in *In Retrospect,* 315.
81. I do think Robert Caro has forever settled this argument regarding Johnson's character, which is amply on display in volume 3 of *The Years of Lyndon Johnson: Master of the Senate.* The evidence is scattered throughout but collected in an excerpt that appeared in *The New Yorker,* March 4, 2002, *http://www.newyorker.com.* To give just a small flavor of literally dozens of examples, Caro quotes Johnson telling his chauffeur that Johnson once yelled at his substitute limousine driver, "Let me tell you one thing, nigger. As long as you are black, and you're gonna be black till the day you die, no one's gonna call you by your goddamn name. So no matter what you are called, nigger, you just let it roll off your back like water, and you'll make it. Just pretend you're a goddamn piece of furniture."
82. Logevall, *Choosing War,* 145.
83. Halberstam, *The Best and the Brightest,* 532.
84. Ibid., 414.
85. Dallek, *Flawed Giant,* 491.
86. David Halberstam, "LBJ and Presidential Machismo," 201.
87. Moïse, *Tonkin Gulf,* 33.
88. Diary Backup, January 15, 1966, LBJL.
89. Isaiah Berlin Oral History, JFKL. See also Kaiser, *American Tragedy,* 41.
90. *New York Times,* October 29, 1962.
91. Beschloss, *Taking Charge,* 390.
92. Ibid., 258.
93. "I know of no plans that have been made to that effect," Johnson replied. Public Papers of the President, Lyndon B. Johnson, 1963–1964. I, 377–79, LBJL. See also Kaiser, *American Tragedy,* 322.
94. "President Lyndon B. Johnson, Statements on Vietnam, Campaign Period 1964," NSC Histories, NSF, Gulf of Tonkin Attack, August 1964, box 38, "Presidential Decisions—Gulf of Tonkin Attacks of Aug. 1964," tab 10, LBJL. See also Richard E. Neustadt and Ernest R. May, *Thinking in Time: The Uses of History for Decision-Makers* (New York: Free Press, 1986), 77.
95. Moïse, *Tonkin Gulf,* 50–68. See also J. J. Herrick memo entitled "Chronology of Events; gulf of Tonkin 4 August 1964," dated "13 July 1964 [13 August 1964]." For more on OPLAN, see "Annex D to Appendix C, Maritime Operations," Papers of Edwin E. Moïse, box 1, AC 91-18/2, LBJL.
96. According to the official version of this conflict published by the U.S. Naval Historical Center, "The MADDOX opened fire on the enemy, then 9,000 yards from the ship, with her 5-inch and 3-inch guns. Unobserved by MADDOX, the first [PT] boat in the enemy formation, T-336, launched one of her two torpedoes at a range of between 9,000 and 5,000 yards . . . the second and third vessels, T-339 and T-333, pressed the attack. Within 3,000 yards of MADDOX, T-339 launched two torpedoes . . ." Edward Marolda and Oscar Fitzgerald, *The United States Navy and the Vietnam Conflict,* Vol. 2:

From Military Assistance to Combat, 1959–1965 (Washington, D.C.: Naval Historical Center, 1986), 416–17. Note that even if, as this account claims, the North Vietnamese did fire on the *Maddox,* they were well beyond the range of being able to hit it.

97. Moïse, *Tonkin Gulf,* 52–55, Herrick memo; and Bamford, *Body of Secrets,* 296–97. See also Marshall Wright and Sven F. Kraemer, Vietnam Information Group, "Presidential Decisions: The Gulf of Tonkin Attacks of August 1964," (Draft) November 1, 1968, 10–11. NSC Histories, NSF, Gulf of Tonkin Attack, August 1964, box 38, "Presidential Decisions–Gulf of Tonkin Attacks of Aug. 1964," tabs 1–8, LBJL.
98. Department of State, Top Secret memorandum, Forrestal to Secretary of State, August 3, 1964, Department of State, *FRUS 1964–1968,* vol.1, 599. See also Richard H. Schultz Jr., *The Secret War Against Hanoi: Kennedy's and Johnson's Use of Spies, Saboteurs and Covert Warriors in North Vietnam* (New York: HarperCollins, 1999), 191; and Bamford, *Body of Secrets,* 297.
99. Bird, *The Color of Truth* 286.
100. Moïse notes that the recall message was mentioned in two contemporary Vietnamese documents: an article on the August 2 incident in the August 1964 issue of the DRV Navy journal *HAI QUAN,* and a report on the various events from August 2 through August 5, by General Hoang Van Thai, unintended for publication. See Moïse, *Tonkin Gulf,* 88–92.
101. Rusk is quoted in Joseph C. Goulden, *Truth Is the First Casualty: The Gulf of Tonkin Affair—Illusion and Reality* (New York: James B. Adler and Co., 1969), 24.
102. Beschloss, *Taking Charge,* 495.
103. See Moïse, *Tonkin Gulf,* 60.
104. See Frank E. Vandiver, *Shadows of Vietnam: Lyndon Johnson's Wars* (College Station, TX: Texas A&M University Press, 1977), 21.
105. Bamford, *Body of Secrets,* 298.
106. Beschloss, *Taking Charge,* 495–97.
107. Quoted in Tom Wells, *The War Within: America's Battles over Vietnam* (Berkeley: University of California, 1994), 11.
108. Scheer, *Thinking Tuna Fish,* 154.
109. Moïse, *Tonkin Gulf,* 211.
110. McGeorge Bundy memo for Mr. George Reedy, August 7, 1965, "A brief chronology of events, August 3–7," August 7, 1964, NSF, NSC History, Gulf of Tonkin Attack, August 1964, box 38, "Presidential Decisions—Gulf of Tonkin Attacks of Aug. 1964," tab 12, LBJL.
111. O'Donnell is quoted in Anthony Austin, *The President's War* (New York: Lippincott, 1971), 30.
112. "Notes Taken at Leadership Meeting by Walter Jenkins," August 4, 1964, Johnson Papers, Meeting Notes File, box 2, LBJL. See also Wright and Kraemer, 27, LBJL; and Gardner, *Pay Any Price,* 138.
113. See telegram in "Presidential Decisions—Gulf of Tonkin Attacks, Vol.1," box 38, NSC History, NSF, tab 13, LBJL.
114. Ibid. See particularly the section labeled "Proof of Attack Messages," which rely quite heavily on alleged visual sightings by a single member of the *Maddox* crew. See also Herrick memo, and Maddox Combat Information Center Log from 0145 August 4 to 0050 August 5, 1964, Maddox Quartermaster Log, from 0934 August 4 to 0644 August 5, 1964, Maddox Deck Log, July 31 through August 5, 1964, Turner Joy Combat Information Center Log, from 0517 to 2357 August 4, 1964, Turner Joy Quartermaster Log, from 0805 to 0310, August 5, 1964, and Turner Joy Deck Log, August 3 through August 5, 1964, Papers of Edwin E. Moïse, "Maddox and Turner Joy Logs" file, LBJL.

115. See Stockdale, *In Love & War,* 19–25. See also Marilyn B. Young, *The Vietnam Wars: 1945–1990* (New York: HarperCollins, 1991), 118.
116. Telephone conversation between Secretary McNamara and Admiral Sharp, August 4, 1964, Reference File, Vietnam, box 2, LBJL. See also Scheer, *Thinking Tuna Fish,* 158; and Gardner, *Pay Any Price,* 137.
117. Schulzinger, *A Time for War,* 144.
118. See Taylor Branch, *Pillar of Fire: America in the King Years, 1963–65* (New York: Simon & Schuster, 1998), 431.
119. *Pentagon Papers* (GPO) 3, IV, C:1, 84.
120. See Robert McNamara, "Memorandum for the President; Subject: South Vietnam," March 16, 1964, The Papers of Lyndon Baines Johnson, President 1963–1969, NSF, National Security Council Histories, Gulf of Tonkin Attack, August 1964, box 38, "Presidential Decisions—Gulf of Tonkin Attacks of Aug. 1964," tab 1, LBJL.
121. An extensive discussion of the genesis of the Gulf of Tonkin Resolution can be found in Johns, "Opening Pandora's Box," 175–206. See also William C. Gibbons, *The U.S. Government and the Vietnam War,* 4 vols. (Princeton, NJ: Princeton University Press, 1986–1996), 2:231–75; Karnow, *Vietnam: A History,* 357–62; and Schulzinger, *A Time for War,* 145–50. Another extremely valuable source on the topic is an unpublished manuscript by William Bundy outlining his view of the development of the war. See Unpublished Manuscript, Papers of William Bundy, box 1, LBJL, especially chapter 13; hereafter "Bundy manuscript."
122. Telephone conversation transcript, Johnson to McGeorge Bundy, March 4, 1964, LBJL.
123. See Minutes, Summary Record of Meeting on Southeast Asia, by Bromley Smith, May 24, 1964, "Presidential Decisions—Gulf of Tonkin Attacks, Vol.1," box 38, NSC History, NSF, LBJL; Agenda, Executive Committee Meeting, May 24, 1964, "Meetings on Southeast Asia, Vol. 1," box 18–19, Files of McGeorge Bundy, NSF, LBJL; "Draft Resolution on Southeast Asia," "Meetings on Southeast Asia, Vol. 1," box 18–19, Files of McGeorge Bundy, NSF, LBJL; *FRUS, 1964–1968,* 1:356–68; and *FRUS, 1964–1968,* 1:369, 371. "Draft Memorandum for Discussion: Alternative public positions for the U.S. on Southeast Asia for the period, July 1–November 15, by McGeorge Bundy," June 10, 1964, Files of McGeorge Bundy, NSF, Memos to President, box 2, LBJL; and "Summary Record of the Meeting on Southeast Asia," Cabinet Room, June 10, 1964, NSF, NS History, Tonkin, box 38, LBJL.
124. See William Bundy, "Memorandum on the Southeast Asia Situation: Probable Developments and the Case for a Congressional Resolution," June 12, 1964; and William Bundy, "Basic Themes in Presenting the Resolution," NSC Histories, NSF, Gulf of Tonkin Attack, August 1964, box 39, "Presidential Decisions—Gulf of Tonkin Attacks of Aug. 1964," tab 25; along with drafts found in NSF, Vietnam Country Files, box 76, "Gulf of Tonkin, 8," LBJL. Compare with text of "Southeast Asia Resolution." [HJ Res. 1145] Text of Public Law, 88–408 78 Stat, 384, approved August 10, 1964, reprinted in *Joint Hearing Before the Committee on Foreign Relations and the Committee on Armed Services,* Senate, 88th Congress, 2nd sess., August 6, 1964 (Washington, D.C.: GPO, 1966), 2.
125. Telephone conversation transcripts, Johnson to Kennedy, June 9, 1964, and May 28, 1964, LBJL.
126. Bundy manuscript, chapters 13, 23, and 30–32. See also *FRUS, 1964–1968,* 1:516–18.
127. Taylor to Department of State, July 27, 1964. *FRUS,* 576–79. See also Gardner, *Pay Any Price,* 134.
128. Moïse, *Tonkin Gulf,* 26–27. See also Austin, *The President's War,* 235.
129. Bundy manuscript, chapters 13, 19, 21, 28. See also Moïse, *Tonkin Gulf,* 28.

130. *FRUS, 1964–1968,* 1:493–96.
131. Haig, *Inner Circles,* 124. To see the telegram traffic between Washington, Honolulu, and the Gulf during both the August 2 and August 4 incidents, see "Presidential Decisions– Gulf of Tonkin Attacks, Vol.1," box 38, NSC History, tabs 9–13, NSF, LBJL.
132. Summary Notes of 537th NSC Meeting, August 4, 1964, 12:35. See Moya Ann Ball, "Revisiting the Gulf of Tonkin Crisis: An Analysis of the Private Communication of President Johnson and his Advisers," *Discourse and Society* 2, no. 3 (1991): 287.
133. Lunch notes, August 4, 164, Bundy Papers, box 1, cited in Gardner, *Pay Any Price,* 560.
134. Wright and Kraemer, 27, LBJL. See also Ball, "Revisiting the Gulf of Tonkin Crisis," 288.
135. "Summary of Leadership Meeting, August 4, 1964," by Walter Jenkins, August 4, 1964, Johnson Papers, Meeting Notes File, box 2, LBJL. See also a slightly different set of notes of the same meeting in NSF, NS History, Tonkin, box 38, tab 21, LBJL.
136. See Scheer, *Thinking Tuna Fish,* 159.
137. See Moïse, *Tonkin Gulf,* 215.
138. LBJ Library Tape, August 4, 1964, 9:15 P.M. See also A. J. Langguth, *Our Vietnam: The War, 1954–1975* (New York: Simon & Schuster, 2000), 304. Note that Saigon time is twelve hours ahead of Eastern Daylight Time, and that Gulf of Tonkin time is eleven hours ahead of EDT. In the Gulf, the destroyers used Saigon time but the carriers used Gulf of Tonkin time. CINPAC in Honolulu is six hours later than EDT. Wright and Kraemer, 15, LBJL.
139. For a chronology, see Moïse *Tonkin Gulf.* For a sanitized version, see also Wright and Kraemer, iii–v, 15–38, LBJL. Moore quoted in *Washington Post,* August 11, 1964.
140. M. Bundy memo for Mr. George Reedy, August 7, 1965, LBJL.
141. H. R. McMaster, *Dereliction of Duty: Lyndon Johnson, Robert McNamara, the Joint Chiefs of Staff and the Lies That Led to Vietnam* (New York: HarperCollins, 1997), 133.
142. Haig, *Inner Circles,* 122.
143. In this memo, Bundy recounts how the administration "narrowly escaped a dangerously early announcement," and explains why, basically explaining that everything took longer than everybody thought it would. McGeorge Bundy, "Memorandum for the President: Chronology of the Gulf of Tonkin," September 4, 1964, NSF, Vietnam Country Files, box 76, "Gulf of Tonkin," LBJL.
144. Beschloss, *Taking Charge,* 390.
145. Ibid., 390.
146. Draft Congressional Resolution, May 24, 1964; Record of NSC Executive Committee Meeting, May 24, 1964; and Bundy to Johnson, June 10, 1964, LBJL.
147. Scheer, *Thinking Tuna Fish,* 156.
148. Ibid., 157.
149. Quoted in Halberstam, *The Best and the Brightest,* 414. See also Kaiser, *American Tragedy,* 336, who says Bundy "jokingly told [Cater] perhaps the matter should not be thought through so far." Kaiser cites *FRUS, 1964–68,* 1:290, and adds, "Apparently relying on anecdotal evidence, Halberstam severely distorted the tone of this exchange in *The Best and the Brightest.*"
150. Lloyd Gardner, "America's War in Vietnam: The End of Exceptionalism?" in Shafer, *The Legacy,* 20.
151. Young, *The Vietnam Wars,* 120–22.
152. Schlesinger Jr., *A Thousand Days,* 252.
153. Beschloss, *Reaching for Glory,* 300.
154. *Congressional Record,* 88th Congress, 1st sess., August 7, 1964, 18399–410.
155. *Congressional Record,* 88th Congress, 1st sess., August 6, 1964, 18402–403. See also Woods, *Fulbright: A Biography,* 354; and Kaiser, *American Tragedy,* 337.

156. *Congressional Record,* 88th Congress, 1st sess., August 7, 1964, 18446–47.
157. *Congressional Record,* 88th Congress, 1st sess., August 7, 1964, 18410–11.
158. See Wells, *The War Within,* 12.
159. Paul Kattenberg, *The Vietnam Trauma in American Foreign Policy* (New Brunswick, NJ: Transaction Books, 1980), 234.
160. McNamara, *In Retrospect,* 128, 142.
161. *New York Times,* August 8, 1962.
162. Moïse, *Tonkin Gulf,* 204–5.
163. Ibid., 198–99.
164. Memorandum for the Record, September 20, 1964, *FRUS, 1964–1968,* 1:778–81. See also Gardner, *Pay Any Price,* 142–43.
165. Ball, *The Past Has Another Pattern,* 379.
166. William Bundy, letter to author, May 13, 1993. (Note: Bundy wrote an unsolicited response to an op-ed article I published in *The New York Times.* It preceded my decision to write this book, though it may have helped inspire it.)
167. It is worth noting, in addition, that McNamara concedes the smaller point, about evidence, to Johnson without the larger point, that the two of them had been misled and hence misled the country themselves about the second incident. The conversation ends with McNamara telling the president, "We shot a warning shot across their bows, so the messages say, and instead of turning around, they kept coming toward the destroyers. And they split up and passed on either side of them, which is what you would do if you were closing for an attack instead of breaking off. But in any case . . . the question you raise is the basic question, and this is what we have been trying to develop evidence on." See Beschloss, *Reaching for Glory,* 38–39
168. Quoted in Wells, *The War Within,* 9.
169. Scheer, *Thinking Tuna Fish,* 153.
170. Michael Forrestal, Oral History Interview, November 3, 1969.
171. Bundy's comments were made on PBS's *McNeil-Lehrer Newshour,* April 17, 1995. See also Logevall, *Choosing War,* 199.
172. "News Conference of Honorable Robert S. McNamara, Secretary of Defense, The Pentagon, Wednesday, August 5, 1964, 12:02 A.M.," NSC Histories, NSF, Gulf of Tonkin Attack, August 1964, box 38, "Presidential Decisions—Gulf of Tonkin Attacks of Aug. 1964," tab 22, LBJL.
173. Regarding the 1.5 inch guns, see Moïse, *Tonkin Gulf,* 183; for the location of the depot, ibid., 220.
174. President Lyndon B. Johnson, "Official Statements on the Gulf of Tonkin Attacks and on U.S. Policy in Vietnam," "Presidential Decisions—Gulf of Tonkin Attacks, Vol.1" box 38, NSC History, NSF, tab 10, LBJL.
175. "Security Council Hears U.S. Charge of North Vietnamese Attacks: Statement by Adlai E. Stevenson, U.S. Representative in the Security Council, August 5, 1964," *Department of State Bulletin,* August 24, 1964, 272–74.
176. Outgoing telegram, Department of State, Action Circular 248, August 7, 1964, NSF, NSC History, Gulf of Tonkin Attack, August 1964, box 38, "Presidential Decisions—Gulf of Tonkin Attacks of Aug. 1964," tab 14, LBJL.
177. U.S. Senate, Foreign Relations Committee, Executive Sessions (Historical Series), XVI, 1064, 88th Congress, 2d sess. (Washington, D.C.: GPO, 1988), 293. See also "Excerpts from the Executive Session, Transcript of the Rusk-McNamara Appearance Before the Joint Committee's Session, August 6, 1964," NSC Histories, NSF, Gulf of Tonkin Attack, August 1964, box 39, "Presidential Decisions—Gulf of Tonkin Attacks of Aug. 1964," tab 27, LBJL. See also Gardner, *Pay Any Price,* 136.

178. Daniel Ellsberg, from *Secrets: A Memoir of Vietnam and the Pentagon Papers* (New York: Viking, 2002), *http://www.ellsberg.net/writing/chapter1.htm*. (The footnote from which this information is drawn appears only in the Web version of the chapter, and not in the print version.)
179. See *Hearings Before the Committee on Foreign Relations,* Senate, 90th Congress, 2nd sess. (The Gulf of Tonkin, The 1964 Incidents), February 20, 1968 (Washington, D.C.: GPO, 1968), 95–96. See also "Questions Raised by Secretary McNamara's Testimony on the Second Tonkin Gulf Incident, Monday, March 11, 1968." See also documents collected under the title "De Soto Patrols, August 3 and August 4," NSC Histories, NSF, Gulf of Tonkin Attack, August 1964, box 39, "Presidential Decisions—Gulf of Tonkin Attacks of Aug. 1964," tab 29, LBJL.
180. "Excerpts from the Executive Session of the Rusk-McNamara Appearance Before the Joint Committee's Session, August 6, 1964," NSF, NS History, Tonkin, box 38, LBJL.
181. Ellsberg, *Secrets.* Ellsberg reprints one such description that he personally circulated in September of 1964. It reads in part: "Two junk capture missions; remove captives for 36–48 hours interrogation; booby trap junk with antidisturbance devices and release; captives returned after interrogation; timing depends upon sea conditions and current intelligence; . . . Demolition of Route 1 bridge by infiltrated team accompanied by fire support teams, place short-delay charges against spans and caissons, place antipersonnel mines on road approaches; . . . Bombard Cape Mui Dao observation post with 81 MM mortars and 40 MM guns from two PTFs; . . . Destruction of section of Hanoi-Vinh railroad by infiltrated demolition team supported by two VN marine squads, by rubber boats from PTFs, place short-delay charges and anti personnel mines around area."
182. See Michael Forrestal memo to Secretary Rusk, August 8, 1964, Gibbons Papers, box 1, LBJL.
183. In 1986 the Naval Historical Center released the second volume of the official history of the Vietnam War, in which some seventy pages were devoted to the Tonkin Gulf incidents and the retaliatory airstrikes. See Edward Marolda and Oscar Fitzgerald, *The United States Navy and the Vietnam Conflict,* Vol. 2: *From Military Assistance to Combat, 1959–1965* (Washington, D.C.: Naval Historical Center, 1986), 393–462. They write:

> The night action of 4 August 1964 in the Gulf of Tonkin dramatically influenced the American approach to the conflict in Southeast Asia. Based upon actual sightings, sonar and radar reports, intelligence on enemy activities, and other pertinent information, indicating that the North Vietnamese fast craft attacked *Maddox* and *Turner Joy* on the night of 4 August, U.S. Leaders initiated a prompt and forceful response (Marolda and Fitzgerald, 461).

184. This was true at least on the day of the author's most recent visit in early 2002; LBJL.
185. Rusk, *As I Saw It,* 444.
186. One honorable exception to this media celebration can be found in Daniel Ford's report in the August 24, 1964, issue of *The Nation.* In that article he concluded, "we are fighting a war and losing a revolution in South Vietnam." The magazine's editors also complained that "the excessive retaliatory action the president saw fit to order brings us closer to World War III."
187. *Time,* August 14, 1964. See also Moïse, *Tonkin Gulf,* 230.
188. "Sea Action: This is No Drill," *Newsweek,* August 17, 1964.
189. See Michael X. Delli Carpini, "Vietnam and the Press," in Shafer, *The Legacy,* 136–37.

190. "The President Acts," *New York Times,* August 5, 1964.
191. James Reston, "North Vietnam's Motives," *New York Times,* August 6, 1964.
192. Hanson W. Baldwin, "Sea Clashes in Asia," *New York Times,* August 5, 1965.
193. Delli Carpini, "Vietnam and the Press," 137.
194. John A. Bovey, telegram, from U.S. Embassy, Paris to Department of State, "Press Story on U.S. Support for SVN Guerilla [sic] Operations in North, August 8, 1964," "Presidential Decisions—Gulf of Tonkin Attacks, Vol.1," box 38, NSC History, NSF, tab 8, LBJL.
195. *New York Times,* August 5, 1964.
196. *New York Daily News,* editorial, August 6, 1964.
197. "Vietnam: We Seek No Wider War," *Newsweek,* August 17, 1964.
198. See Kathleen J. Turner, *Lyndon Johnson's Dual War: Vietnam and the Press* (Chicago: University of Chicago Press, 1985), 85.
199. "The Tonkin Gulf Mystery," *New York Times,* September 23, 1964.
200. Johnson quoted in Beschloss, *Reaching for Glory,* 32.
201. John M. Blum, *Years of Discord: American Politics and Society, 1961–1974* (New York: W. W. Norton, 1991), 232. See also Moïse, *Tonkin Gulf,* 225–26.
202. Benjamin Page and Robert I. Schapiro, *The Rational Public: Fifty Years of Trends in American Policy Preferences* (Chicago: University of Chicago Press, 1992), 227–31.
203. Hugh Sidey, *A Very Personal Presidency* (New York: Atheneum, 1968), 122.
204. James L. Baughman, "The Self-Publicist from Pedernales: Lyndon Johnson and the Press," *Diplomatic History* 12 (1988): 104. See also David T. Bazelon, "Big Business and the Democrats," *Commentary* 39 (May 1965): 39–46.
205. In the 1964 election, the Democrats won two senate seats, raising their majority to 68 to 37 in that body, and thirty-seven additional House seats, giving them an advantage of 295 to 140 in the House.
206. Theodore H. White, *The Making of the President, 1968* (New York: Atheneum, 1969), 22.
207. See Logevall, *Choosing War,* 281.
208. Kenneth Crawford, "Most Hopeful Times," *Newsweek,* January 4, 1965. See also Maurice Isserman and Michael Kazin, *America Divided: The Civil Wars of the Sixties* (New York: Oxford University Press, 1999), 127.
209. Young, *The Vietnam Wars,* 127. See also Gardner, *Pay Any Price,* 149.
210. Among the amazing proposals on the Chiefs' wish list—code-named "Operation Northwoods"—contained in a section of a report titled, in part, "Pretexts to Justify U.S. Military Intervention in Cuba," which was delivered to Robert McNamara in March 1962, but never acted upon, were:

- to blow up the NASA spacecraft in which John Glenn orbited the earth and then "provide irrevocable proof that . . . the fault lies with the Communists et al. Cuba." This would be accomplished by "manufacturing various pieces of evidence which would prove electronic interference on the part of the Cubans."
- "a series of well coordinated incidences to take place in and around" the U.S. Navy base at Guantánamo Bay, Cuba, including dressing "friendly" Cubans in Cuban military uniforms and have them "start riots near the main gate of the base. Others would pretend to be saboteurs inside the base. Ammunition would be blown up, fires started, aircraft sabotaged, mortars fired at the base with damage to its installations."
- to "blow up a U.S. ship ["Remember the Maine!"] in Guantanamo Bay and blame Cuba" as "casualty lists in U.S. newspapers would cause a helpful wave of indignation."
- to "develop a Communist Cuban terror campaign in the Miami area, in other Florida cities and even in Washington." This terror campaign against American citizens and Cubans living in the U.S., the Joint Chiefs suggested, might include "exploding a few

plastic bombs in carefully chosen spots, the arrest of Cuban agents and the release of prepared documents substantiating Cuban involvement . . . Hijacking attempts against civil air and surface craft" designed to appear "as harassing measures condoned by the Cuban government."

- The creation of "an incident which will demonstrate convincingly that a Cuban aircraft has attacked and shot down a chartered civil airliner en route from the United States to Jamaica, Guatemala, Panama or Venezuela. The destination would be chosen only to cause the flight plan route to cross Cuba. The passengers could be a group of college students on a holiday or any grouping of persons with a common interest to support chartering a non-scheduled flight."

The proposals are contained in "Joint Chiefs of Staff, Top Secret/Special Handling/Noforn Report, Report by the Department of Defense and Joint Chiefs of Staff Representative on the Caribbean Survey Group to the Joint Chiefs of Staff on Cuba Project," March 9, 1962, in the papers of the Assassinations Records Review Board (ARRB). See particularly, Annex to Appendix to Enclosure A, "Pretexts to Justify U.S. Military Intervention in Cuba," 8–11. This existence of this report first came to the attention of the author in Bamford, *Body of Secrets,* 84–85.

211. More than three years later, the Joint Chiefs would promote yet another "pretext plan" for war, this one involving the United States and North Korea, during the Pueblo crisis. This one involved a proposal by the Joint Chiefs to send the Sigint ship *Banner,* almost unmanned, off North Korea's shores to act as a potential target for the purpose of providing an excuse for war. See Bamford, *Body of Secrets,* 270–72.
212. Michael Charlton and Anthony Moncrieff, *Many Reasons Why: The American Involvement in Vietnam* (New York: Hill and Wang, 1978), 117. See also McNamara, *In Retrospect,* 140.
213. Charlton, *Many Reasons Why,* 108. See also Moïse, *Tonkin Gulf,* 100.
214. Moïse, *Tonkin Gulf,* 100–101. See also Ellsberg, *Secrets.*
215. *Pentagon Papers* (Gravel), 3:193, 3:110.
216. Daniel Ellsberg conversation, November 3, 1994.
217. McNamara quoted in Robert Mann, *A Grand Delusion: America's Descent into Vietnam* (New York: Basic Books, 2001), 346.
218. See Logevall, *Choosing War,* 202.
219. Saigon to State, July 27, 1964, box 6, NSF VN, LBJL. See also Logevall, *Choosing War,* 201.
220. Moïse, *Tonkin Gulf,* 101.
221. See State Department memo dated August 7, Dean Rusk to U.S. Embassy, Saigon, advising suspension of the raids, confirmed two days later, "Presidential Decisions—Gulf of Tonkin Attacks, Vol. 1," box 38, NSC History, NSF, tab 8, LBJL.
222. "Notes of the President's Luncheon Meeting with Foreign Policy Advisers," by Tom Johnson, February 20, 1968, Tom Johnson Notes, box 2, LBJL.
223. See for instance, Memo to Secretary Rusk from W. W. Rostow, "Speculation on the Background and Possible Implications of the Tonkin Gulf Incident," August 5, 1964; and Memo to Secretary Rusk, from Thomas L. Hughes, [Bureau of Intelligence and Research], "Peiping and Hanoi: Motivations and Probable Reactions to Gulf of Tonkin Crisis," both memos located in NSC Histories, NSF, Gulf of Tonkin Attack, August 1964, box 38, "Presidential Decisions—Gulf of Tonkin Attacks of Aug. 1964," tab18, LBJL.
224. Moïse, *Tonkin Gulf,* xv.
225. Ibid., 250–51.
226. See William J. Duiker, *Ho Chi Minh: A Life* (New York: Hyperion, 2000) 540–41, 17; and Gareth Porter, "Coercive Diplomacy in Vietnam: The Tonkin Gulf Policy Re-

considered?" Jayne Werner and David Hunt, eds., *The American War in Vietnam* (Ithaca, NY: Cornell University Southeast Asia Program #13, 1993), 18–21.

227. Moïse, *Tonkin Gulf,* 251–52.
228. Military History Institute of Vietnam, *Victory in Vietnam: Official History of the People's Army of Vietnam,* Merle L. Pribbenow trans., foreword by William J. Duiker (Lawrence: University of Kansas Press, 2002), 132.
229. Kaiser, *American Tragedy,* 339.
230. Moïse, *Tonkin Gulf,* 253.
231. Kaiser, *American Tragedy,* 493.
232. A thorough account of these crises can be found in Logevall, *Choosing War,* 218–21.
233. Arendt, "Lying in Politics," 14.
234. Author's phone interview with Edwin Moïse, June 9, 1994.
235. VanDeMark, *Into the Quagmire,* 72.
236. President's News Conference, March 13, 1965. Public Papers: Lyndon B. Johnson, 1965, book I, 274–81.
237. President's News Conference, March 20,1965, Public Papers: Lyndon B. Johnson, 1965, book I, 299–307. See also *Pentagon Papers,* vol. 3, 324.
238. See CINCPAC 192207Z and JCS Memorandum 204–65, cited in VanDeMark, *Into the Quagmire,* 102.
239. Neustadt, "Afterword: JFK (1968)," 78.
240. Larry Berman, *Planning a Tragedy* (New York: W. W. Norton, 1982), 112–21.
241. VanDeMark, *Into the Quagmire,* 164.
242. McGeorge Bundy to Johnson, June 11, 1965, "Vol. 4," CNF, VN, box 54, NSF, LBJL. See also VanDeMark, *Into the Quagmire,* 257*n*.
243. President's News Conference, April 1, 1965. Public Papers: Lyndon B. Johnson, 1965, book I, 364–72. On one of many occasions, Moyers recommended that the president issue a kind of "white paper" speech in which he detailed "the history of our commitment." Moyers Memo to the President, February 9, 1965, Reference File, Vietnam, box 1, LBJL. For Bundy, citing McNamara, see the former's memo to the president, February 16, 1965, Reference File, Vietnam, box 2, LBJL. For one of Johnson's many angry attempts to plug a leak about the truth of his policies and the options he was considering, see "Notes on telephone conversation between the president and Under Sec. Ball, 10:00," February 15, 1965, NSF, Ball Papers, box 7, LBJL.
244. President's News Conference, July 28, 1965. Public Papers: Lyndon B. Johnson, 1965, book II, 795.
245. Quoted in Larry Berman, "Coming to Grips with Lyndon Johnson's War," *Diplomatic History* 17 (Fall 1993): 530.
246. Quoted VanDeMark, *Into the Quagmire,* 110.
247. Ibid., 111.
248. Memo to the president, March 15, 1965, Files of McGeorge Bundy, NSF, Memos to the President, box 3, LBJL.
249. Cater memo to the president, July 26, 1965, Reference File, Vietnam, box 1, LBJL.
250. Halberstam, *LBJ and Presidential Machismo,* 586.
251. "Ground War in Asia," *New York Times,* June 9, 1965.
252. See Valenti notes, "July 21–27, 1965, Meetings on Vietnam," MNF, box 1, LBJL. See also VanDeMark, *Into the Quagmire,* 207.
253. William Manchester, *The Glory and the Dream: A Narrative History of America, 1932–1972* (Boston: Little, Brown, 1974; reprint edition, New York: Bantam, 1975), 1053.
254. Robert Dalleck, *Flawed Giant: Lyndon Johnson and His Times, 1961–1973* (New York: Oxford University Press, 1998), 277.

255. Beschloss, *Reaching for Glory,* 343.
256. Johnson's quote, borrowed from Beschloss, appears in Cal Thomas's syndicated column of November 15, 1991, entitled "George McGovern Was Right," *http://www.townhall.com,* and in Michael Beschloss, "LBJ's Unwinnable War," *Washington Post,* December 1, 2001.
257. Beschloss, "LBJ's Unwinnable War," *Washington Post,* December 1, 2001.
258. Jack Valenti, "LBJ's Unwinnable War," *Washington Post,* November 28, 2001.
259. Beschloss, "LBJ's Unwinnable War."
260. Beschloss, *Reaching for Glory,* 217.
261. Beschloss, "LBJ's Unwinnable War."
262. See Daniel Hallin, *The Uncensored War* (New York: Oxford University Press, 1986),142–47.
263. Richard Cohen, *Washington Post,* January 31, 1980.
264. Donald Duncan, "The Whole Damn Thing Was a Lie," *Ramparts,* February 1966, 27–31.
265. Clancy Sigal, "Caught in a Fantasy Amid Subterfuge," *Los Angeles Times,* June 29, 2001.
266. See Randall Woods, *Fulbright: A Biography,* 406
267. The "cry baby" reference is handwritten by the president on a memo dated February 8, 1965, to Johnson from Douglass Cater, Reference File, Vietnam, box 1, LBJL.
268. Cited in Randall B. Woods, "The Anatomy of Dissent: J. William Fulbright and the Vietnam War," unpublished manuscript, 1994, 4.
269. See Rowland Evans and Robert Novak, *Lyndon B. Johnson: The Exercise of Power* (New York: New American Library, 1966), 529.
270. Cited in Scheer, *Thinking Tuna Fish,* 158–59.
271. Reported in *The New York Times* on January 29, 1965, and cited in "Statements Bearing on the Powers of the President Under the Gulf of Tonkin Resolution," NSC Histories, NSF, Gulf of Tonkin Attack, August 1964, box 39, "Presidential Decisions—Gulf of Tonkin Attacks of Aug. 1964," tab 33, LBJL.
272. Delli Carpini, "Vietnam and the Press," 140.
273. Wells, *The War Within,* 68.
274. Woods, *Fulbright: A Biography,* 405.
275. "Investigating Tonkin Gulf," *New York Times,* January 26, 1968.
276. Lippmann is quoted in Goulden, *Truth Is the First Casualty,* 179.
277. Wells, *The War Within,* 137.
278. Woods, *Fulbright: A Biography,* 410.
279. Ibid., 411.
280. Woods, 407–8. See also *William C. Berman, William Fulbright and the Vietnam War: The Dissent of a Political Realist* (Kent, OH: Kent State University Press, 1988), 68.
281. Reedy's memo to Johnson quoted in Turner, *Lyndon Johnson's Dual War,* 157.
282. Goulden, *Truth Is the First Casualty,* 179.
283. *Arkansas Gazette,* July 16, 1967.
284. Austin, *The President's War,* 165.
285. "Letters to the Editor," *New Haven Register,* December 6, 1967.
286. Austin, *The President's War,* 165.
287. Goulden, *Truth Is the First Casualty,* 207–8.
288. Austin, *The President's War,* 171–72.
289. Ibid., 177. The secretary's report, according to Fulbright's informant, was entitled "Command and Control of the Tonkin Gulf Incident, August 4–5, 1964." It is dated February 26, 1965, and was declassified on May 11, 1992. It can be found in Papers of Edwin E. Moïse, box 1, AC 91–18/1, LBJL.
290. "Midwife to History," *Washington Post,* January 27, 1968.
291. Goulden, *Truth Is the First Casualty,* 214.

292. *Hearings Before the Committee on Foreign Relations,* 16. See also Shapley, *Promise and Power,* 454–55; "Notes of the President's Luncheon Meeting with Foreign Policy Advisers," by Tom Johnson, February 20, 1968, Tom Johnson Notes, box 2, LBJL.

Years later, when Fulbright was finally able to secure permission for Foreign Relations Committee staff to examine the intercepts, they discovered that all but one of them did in fact refer to August 2. The August 4 intercept, according to J. Norville Jones, one of the staffers who read it, also appeared to be "A boastful summary of the attack of August 2 [and] even the NSA officials could not say that it definitely related to the August 4 action. In addition, the time sequence of the intercept and the reported action from the U.S. Navy destroyers did not jibe." Perhaps not so surprisingly, Jones, who served on the committee staff from 1954 to 1979 and chaired it for his final three years, notes, the "NSA could not find the original of the August 4 intercept, although it did have originals of the others." Jones revealed this information in a letter to the editor of *The Washington Post* entitled "Robert McNamara's Bad Information," November 23, 1995.

293. See Gardner, *Pay Any Price,* 135.
294. Rusk to Taylor, August 3, 1964, *FRUS, 1964–1968,* 1:603–4. See also Gardner, *Pay Any Price,* 136.
295. *Hearings Before the Committee on Foreign Relations,* 107. See also Shapley, *Promise and Power,* 454.
296. *Hearings Before the Committee on Foreign Relations,* 107.
297. Woods, *Fulbright,* 472. See also Gardner, *Pay Any Price,* 442.
298. Woods, *Fulbright,* 472.
299. Shapley, *Promise and Power,* 601.
300. Woods, *Fulbright,* 482.
301. Kearns, *Lyndon Johnson,* 332–33.
302. Shesol, *Mutual Contempt,* 425.
303. Buzzanco, *Vietnam and the Transformation of American Life,* 158.
304. Shesol, *Mutual Contempt,* 415.
305. John W. Finney, "Fulbright Panel Votes to Repeal Tonkin Measure; Acts to End a Basis for War Involvement as Well as '57 Mideast Declaration," *New York Times,* April 11, 1970. The text of the new resolution read: "Resolved by the Senate (the House of Representatives concurring), That under the authority of section 3 of the joint resolution commonly known as the Gulf of Tonkin Resolution and entitled 'Joint Resolution to Promote the Maintenance of International Peace and Security in Southeast Asia,' approved August 10, 1965 (78 Stat.384: Public Law 88–4–8), such joint resolution is terminated effective upon the day that the second session of the Ninety-first Congress is Adjourned." Note that the State Department, which had vigorously opposed this action under Johnson, switched to a neutral position. See "State Department Now Neutral on Repeal of Tonkin Resolution," *New York Times,* March 13, 1970.
306. John W. Finney, "GOP Acts to End Cambodia Debate/In Shift, Nixon Backers in Senate Press for Votes," *New York Times,* June 24, 1970; John W. Finney, "Senate, 79–5, Reaffirms War Powers of President," *New York Times,* June 23, 1970; "Gulf of Tonkin Measure Voted in Haste and Confusion in 1964," *New York Times,* June 25, 1970; John W. Finney, "Senators 81–10, Vote for Repeal of Tonkin Action/G.O.P. Seizes Initiative on Resolution Johnson Used as Basis for Wider War/House Backing Needed/Doves Accuse Republicans of Indulging in Crude and Cynical Partisanship," *New York Times,* June 25 1970; John W. Finney, "Senate Votes Again for Tonkin Repeal," *New York Times,* July 11, 1970.
307. "Gulf of Tonkin Resolution Is Repealed Without Furor," *New York Times,* January 14, 1971.
308. McMaster, *Dereliction of Duty,* 333–34.

309. Quoted in Isserman, *America Divided,* 181.
310. Buzzanco, *Vietnam and the Transformation of American Life,* 2.
311. Ibid., 3.
312. Lloyd C. Gardner, *Pay Any Price: Lyndon Johnson and the Wars for Vietnam* (Chicago: Ivan R. Dee, 1995), 457.
313. Johnson memo to Richard Helms, September 4, 1968, NSF, Intelligence File, box 2-II, LBJL.
314. Gardner, *Pay Any Price,* 462.
315. See Shapley, *Promise and Power,* 353–54, 377, 426–27, 444, 463, 496, 513.
316. Dallek, *Flawed Giant,* 495.
317. McNamara, *In Retrospect,* xvi.
318. McPherson to LBJ, March 18, 1968, Office Files of Harry McPherson, box 53, LBJL. See also Gardner, *Pay Any Price,* 448; and Robert Mann, *A Grand Delusion: America's Descent Into Vietnam* (New York: Basic Books, 2001), 595–96.
319. Kearns, *Lyndon Johnson,* 342–43.
320. See "Notes of the President's Meeting with His Foreign Policy Advisers, March 26, 1968," by Tom Johnson, Tom Johnson Notes, box 2, LBJL; "Summary of Notes" Meeting Notes File, Special Advisory Group, box 2, LBJL; and [Additional unsigned notes, March 26, 1968], Meeting Notes File, box 2, LBJL.
321. "Lyndon Johnson, 36th President, Is Dead," *New York Times,* January 23, 1973.
322. See, for instance, Elliott Abrams, *Undue Process: A Story of How Political Differences Are Turned into Crimes* (New York: Free Press, 1993), 221–222.
323. Robert McFarlane on *The Charlie Rose Show,* WNET, November 1, 1994.
324. Stockdale, *In Love & War,* 35–36.

V: Ronald W. Reagan, Central America, and the Iran–Contra Scandal

1. See Cynthia J. Arnson, *Crossroads: Congress, the President, and Central America, 1976–1993,* 2nd ed. (University Park, PA: Pennsylvania State University Press; 1993), 197.
2. The Knight Ridder story, authored by Frank Greve and Ellen Warren, appeared in that chain's national newspapers on December 16, 1984, and can be found in any number of its newspapers. For a larger discussion of the issues it raised, see Robert Parry, "Lost History: Death, Lies, and Bodywashing: The USA's Secret War in El Salvador, 1981–1992," *http://www.consortiumnews.com/archive/lost.html,* originally posted on May 27, 1996.
3. Edmund Morris, *Dutch: A Memoir of Ronald Reagan* (New York: Modern Library, 1999), 579.
4. James M. Perry, "For the Democrats, Pam's Is the Place for the Elite to Meet," *Wall Street Journal,* October 8, 1981. See also Lou Cannon, *President Reagan: The Role of a Lifetime,* 2nd ed. (New York: Public Affairs, 2000), 105.
5. Reagan also once offered up a history of the Spanish–American War that was completely at odds with the recorded history of that conflict but hewed almost exactly to a fictional version put forth in an old Henry Fonda movie, *Blockade.* See Jane Mayer and Doyle McManus, *Landslide: The Unmaking of the President, 1984–1988* (Boston: Houghton Mifflin, 1988), 92–93.
6. "Remarks at a Conference on Religious Liberty, April 16, 1985," *Reagan Papers,* 1985, book 1, 437–40; Joanne Omang, "Democrats Draft Latin Aid Options," *Washington Post,* April 18, 1985; Sara Gilbert, "Vatican Disputes Reagan Statements," *Washington Post,* April 19, 1985. See also William M. LeoGrande, *Our Own Backyard: The United States in Central America, 1977–1992* (Chapel Hill: University of North Carolina Press; 1998), 419.

7. Mayer and McManus, *Landslide,* 131.
8. Eric Alterman, "Where's the Rest of Him?" *The Nation,* March 27, 2000.
9. "Vietnam: A Television History: Roots of War (1945–1953)," *The American Experience* (Boston: WGBH, 1983), transcript available at *http://www.pbs.org/wgbh/amex/vietnam/101ts.html.*
10. Mark Hertsgaard, *On Bended Knee: The Press and the Reagan Presidency* (New York: Farrar, Straus & Giroux, 1988), 99–100.
11. Ibid., 101.
12. Ibid.
13. Ibid., 3–4.
14. Ibid., 101.
15. Ibid.,116.
16. Anthony Marro, "When the Government Tells Lies," *Columbia Journalism Review,* supplement, Special 40th Anniversary edit., November/December 2001, 98.
17. Stephen Schlesinger and Stephen Kinzer, *Bitter Fruit,* expanded ed. (Cambridge, MA: Harvard University Press, 1999), 216–17.
18. Ibid., 218.
19. Tim Weiner, "Role of CIA in Guatemala Told in Files of Publisher," *New York Times,* June 7, 1997.
20. Radio and television address, June 30, 1954, U.S. Department of State, American Foreign Policy, 1950-1955. Basic Documents, 2 vols. (Washington, D.C.: GPO, 1957), 1: 1311–15. See also Walter LaFeber, *Inevitable Revolutions: The United States in Central America,* 2nd ed. (New York: W. W. Norton, 1993), 126.
21. Kate Doyle, "Death Squad Diary," *Harper's Magazine,* June 1, 1999.
22. Glenn Garvin and Edward Hegstrom, "Racism Cited in Guatemala War: Truth Commission Blames US, Cuba," *Miami Herald,* February 26, 1999.
23. LaFeber, *Inevitable Revolutions,* 260.
24. Ibid., 321.
25. Ibid., 322.
26. Ibid.
27. Quoted in Kate Doyle, "Death Squad Diary." See also Kate Doyle, Director, Document 18, February 1983, "Ríos Montt Gives Carte Blanche to Archivos to Deal with Insurgency," CIA, secret cable, *National Security Archive Electronic Briefing Book No. 11, U.S. Policy in Guatemala, 1966–96, http://www.gwu.edu/~nsarchiv/NSAEBB/NSAEBB11/docs/.*
28. LaFeber, *Inevitable Revolutions,* 322.
29. Ibid., 360–61.
30. Jeane Kirkpatrick, "Dictatorships and Double Standards," *Commentary,* November 1979, 34–45.
31. Secretary Haig, news conference, January 28, 1981, U.S. Department of State, Bureau of Public Affairs, *Current Policy* 258, 5. See also Arnson, *Crossroads,* 55.
32. Testimony of Robert White, U.S. Congress, House Committee on Appropriations Subcommittee of Foreign Operations, *Foreign Assistance and Related Programs Appropriations for 1982,* Hearings, Part 1, 97th Congress, 1st sess. (Washington, D.C.: GPO, 1981), 3, 17. See also Arnson, *Crossroads,* 58.
33. Arnson, *Crossroads,* 41.
34. Clifford Krauss, "How U.S. Actions Helped Hide Salvador Human Rights Abuses," *New York Times,* May 21, 1993.
35. U.S. Department of State, Press Statement, January 17, 1981, 1. See also Arnson, *Crossroads,* 51.

36. Arnson, *Crossroads,* 51.
37. Tip O'Neill press conference, February 23, 1982. See John A. Farrell, *Tip O'Neill and the Democratic Century* (New York: Little, Brown, 2001), 612.
38. Lawyers Committee for International Human Rights, *A Report on the Investigation into the Killings of Four American Churchwomen in El Salvador,* New York, September 1981, Appendix 1-4. See also Arnson, *Crossroads,* 62–3.
39. U.S. Congress, House Committee on Foreign Affairs, *Foreign Assistance Legislation for Fiscal Year 1982,* Part 1, Hearings, March 13, 18, 19, and 23, 97th Congress, 1st sess. (Washington, D.C.: GPO, 1981), 163. See also, Arnson, *Crossroads,* 63.
40. Quoted in Krauss, "How U.S. Actions Helped Hide."
41. David E. Anderson, *Washington News,* United Press International, April 22, 1981.
42. Larry Rohter, "Salvadorans Who Slew American Nuns Now Say They Had Orders," *New York Times,* April 3, 1998.
43. Quoted in Krauss, "How U.S. Actions Helped Hide."
44. Stephen Kinzer, "U.S. and Central America: Too Close for Comfort," *New York Times,* July 28, 2002.
45. George J. Church, Dean Brelis, and Gregory H. Wierzynski, "The Vicar Takes Charge," *Time,* March 16, 1981.
46. *Hearings Before the Committee on Foreign Relations*, 97th Congress, 1st sess., March 18 and April 9, 1981 (Washington, D.C.: GPO, 1981), 57. See also LeoGrande, *Our Own Backyard,* 93.
47. U.S. Congress, House Committee on Appropriations, Subcommittee on Foreign Operations, *Foreign Assistance and Related Programs Appropriations for Fiscal Year 1982,* Part 1, Hearings, February 25, March 24, and April 29, 1981, 97th Congress, 1st sess. (Washington, D.C.: GPO, 1981), 276. See also, LeoGrande, *Our Own Backyard,* 93.
48. "Question and Answer Session with High School Students on Domestic and Foreign Policy Issues, December 2, 1983," *Reagan Papers,* 1983, book 2, 1642–47. See also LeoGrande, *Our Own Backyard,* 230.
49. Brigadier General Fred E. Woerner, "Report of the El Salvador Military Strategy Assistance Team," San Salvador, November 1981, 1, 17, 24, 45, 47. See also Arnson, *Crossroads,* 84.
50. See Krauss, "How U.S. Actions Helped Hide."
51. U.S. Congress, House Committee on Appropriations Subcommittee on Foreign Operations, *Foreign Assistance and Related Programs Appropriations for Fiscal Year 1982,* Part 1, Hearings, 36. See also, Arnson, *Crossroads,* 60*n*.
52. Robert Parry, "Senate Panel Ties Salvadoran Officers to 'Terrorist Underground,'" Associated Press, October 11, 1984; "Senate Report Finds No Americans Aided Salvadoran Killings," Reuters, October 11, 1984.
53. These figures are cited in Charles William Maynes, "Dateline Washington: A Necessary War?" *Foreign Policy,* Spring 1991, 162.
54. Arnson, *Crossroads,* 12.
55. Arnson, *Crossroads,* 69.
56. Mark Danner, *The Massacre at El Mozote* (New York: Vintage, 1994), 91.
57. Ibid., 90–1.
58. Arnson, *Crossroads,* 86.
59. The White House, Presidential Determination No. 82–4, "Memorandum for the Secretary of State, Subject: Determination to Authorize Continued Assistance for El Salvador," January 28, 1982, 1–2, and accompanying Justification, 1–6. See also Arnson, *Crossroads,* 86.

60. Danner, *Massacre,* 137.
61. Americas Watch Committee and American Civil Liberties Union, "Human Rights in El Salvador," press release, January 26, 1982, subsequently published as *Report on Human Rights in El Salvador* (New York: Vintage Books, 1982). See also Arnson, *Crossroads,* 85.
62. See Anthony Lewis, "Abroad at Home; Rights and Wrongs," *New York Times,* January 20, 1986.
63. U.S. Congress, House, Permanent Select Committee on Intelligence Subcommittee on Oversight and Evaluation, *U.S. Intelligence Performance on Central America: Achievements and Selected Instances of Concern,* Staff Report, September 22, 1982, 97th Congress, 2nd sess. (Washington D.C.: GPO, 1982), 17. See also Arnson, *Crossroads,* 89.
64. LeoGrande, *Our Own Backyard,* 153.
65. Ibid.
66. Ibid.
67. Alma Guillermoprieto, "Salvadoran Peasants Describe Mass Killing," *Washington Post,* January 27, 1982; Raymond Bonner, "Massacre of Hundreds Is Reported in Salvador Village," *New York Times,* January 28, 1982.
68. Danner, *Massacre,* 92–5.
69. Ibid., 108.
70. Ibid., 112.
71. Ibid., 124.
72. Ibid., 108.
73. Ibid., 116.
74. Ibid., 126.
75. Ibid., 127.
76. Ibid.
77. "The Media's War," *Wall Street Journal,* editorial, February 10, 1982. See also Danner, *Massacre,* 133–36.
78. Danner, 137.
79. Ibid.
80. Ibid., 136.
81. Ibid., 136–7.
82. Cited in Joan Didion, "'Something Horrible' in El Salvador," *New York Review of Books,* July 14, 1994.
83. Danner, *Massacre,* 142.
84. Clifford Krauss, "How U.S. Actions Helped Hide."
85. The Salvadoran Truth Commission identified more than five hundred corpses and conceded that many more were not identified. The exact number of victims may never be known. In 1992, Tutela Legal, a Salvadoran human rights group, published a list of 794 casualties of the El Mozote massacre. In *The Massacre at El Mozote* (1994), Mark Danner updates that list to 767, a figure that proved to be within the range reported by Raymond Bonner almost a decade earlier. Danner, *Massacre,* 157–58, 264, 280–304.
86. Danner, *Massacre,* 254.
87. Ibid., 159. In reaction to the news that they slandered the reporters who told the truth about the massacre and generally misinformed their readers about the size and scope of the human rights abuses committed both by the army it favored and the rebels it opposed, the *Journal* editors said they found the Truth Commission to be "on the tendentious side." Accepting the fact that their side had committed many of the killings of which it had been accused, they still felt that the greater responsibility lay with the guerrillas who "started the war." The editors also noted, "If we're going to revisit the atrocities of war, we ought to remember what the war was about, and take some note

of history's verdict on the moral claims of the contending sides." See "Salvador and Nicaragua," *Wall Street Journal,* March 19, 1993.

88. Suzanne Garment, "The El Salvador Rights Campaign Begins to Fade," *Wall Street Journal,* August 6, 1982. See also LeoGrande, *Our Own Backyard,* 172.
89. U.S. Department of State, "Report on the Situation in El Salvador with Respect to the Subjects Covered in Section 728(d) of the International Security and Development Cooperation Act of 1981," January 21, 1983, 1–67. See also Arnson, *Crossroads,* 119.
90. U.S. Congress, Senate Committee on Foreign Relations, *Presidential Certification on Progress in El Salvador,* Hearings, February 2, 1983, 98th Congress, 1st sess. (Washington D.C.: GPO, 1983), 20, 93, 545–46. See also Arnson, *Crossroads,* 119
91. Arnson, *Crossroads,* 120.
92. Text, U.S. Ambassador to El Salvador Thomas R. Pickering's address before the American Chamber of Commerce in San Salvador, November 25, 1983, 10. See also Arnson, *Crossroads,* 142.
93. Joanne Omang, "U.S. Seeks to Oust Salvador Officials Tied to Death Squads," *Washington Post,* November 5, 1983; Lydia Chavez, "U.S. Presses Salvador to Act on Men Tied to Death Squads," *New York Times,* November 5, 1983; U.S. Congress, House Committee on Foreign Affairs, Subcommittees on Human Rights and International Organizations and Western Hemisphere Affairs, U.S. Policy on El Salvador, Hearings, February 4 and 28 and March 7 and 17, 1983, 98th Congress, 1st sess. (Washington, D.C.: GPO, 1983), 16. See also Arnson, *Crossroads,* 141.
94. Hertsgaard, *On Bended Knee,* 197.
95. LaFeber, *Inevitable Revolutions,* 295.
96. Ibid., 295–6.
97. For instance, during this period, any hint of using U.S. forces encountered heavy public opposition: "In March 1982, ABC/Washington Post found that 82% opposed sending U.S. troops; in May 1983, this figure stood at 85%, and 79% wanted the U.S. to 'stay out' of El Salvador. There was also substantial opposition to military and economic aid: an NBC poll early in 1984 indicated that 71% opposed military aid, while 64% opposed economic aid to El Salvador." Moreover, "Even if it was the 'only way' to prevent the government from 'being overthrown by the leftist guerrillas,' at the peak of support in February 1984 no more than 35% of the public favored sending U.S. troops." The same was true of the administration's policies toward Nicaragua. Public support for the Contras never edged much beyond 33 percent, according to Benjamin I. Page and Robert Y. Schapiro, *The Rational Public: Fifty Years of Trends in American Policy Preferences* (Chicago: University of Chicago Press, 1992), 275–76.
98. Hedrick Smith, "A Larger Force of Latin Rebels Sought by U.S.," *New York Times,* April 17, 1985. See also Arnson, *Crossroads,* 195.
99. Mayer and McManus, *Landslide,* 48.
100. Juan de Onis, "Soviet-Bloc Nations Said to Pledge Arms to Salvador Rebels," *New York Times,* February 6, 1981.
101. Juan de Onis, "U.S. Officials Concede Flaws in Salvador White Paper but Defend Its Conclusion," *New York Times,* June 10, 1981. Regarding the South Vietnam White Paper: "The hard core of the communist forces attacking South Vietnam are men trained in North Vietnam. They are ordered into the South and remain under the military discipline of the military high command in Hanoi. . . . Increasingly the forces sent into the South are native North Vietnamese who have never seen the South." See Marvin E. Gettleman, Jane Franklin, Marilyn B. Young, H. Bruce Franklin, eds., *Vietnam and America: A Documented History* (New York: Grove Press, 1995), 287.
102. Hertsgaard, *On Bended Knee,* 111.

103. LeoGrande, *Our Own Backyard,* 82.
104. Ibid.
105. Haig explains, "The flow of arms into Nicaragua and thence into El Salvador slackened, a signal from Havana and Moscow that they had received and understood the American message." Alexander M. Haig Jr., *Caveat: Realism, Reagan and Foreign Policy* (New York: Macmillan, 1984), 131. See also Arnson, *Crossroads,* 76.
106. David Hoffman and George Lardner Jr., "Hill Panel to Disclose Criticism of Intelligence on Central America," *Washington Post,* September 22, 1982.
107. Daniel Patrick Moynihan, "System of Secrecy Has Served Liars Well," *Albany Times Union,* May 3, 1992. See also Arnson, *Crossroads,* 275.
108. U.S. Department of State, press release, April 1, 1981, 1–2. See also Arnson, *Crossroads,* 75–76.
109. LeoGrande, *Our Own Backyard,* 115.
110. Ibid., 300.
111. Ibid.
112. Alfonso Chardy and Juan Tamayo, "CIA Deepens U.S. Involvement," *Miami Herald,* June 5, 1983. See also LeoGrande, *Our Own Backyard,* 299–300.
113. Don Oberdorfer and Patrick E. Tyler, "U.S. Backed Nicaraguan Rebel Army Swells to 7,000 Men," *Washington Post,* May 8, 1983. See also LeoGrande, *Our Own Backyard,* 299–300.
114. LeoGrande, *Our Own Backyard,* 301.
115. Bernard Weinraub, "Congress Renews Curbs on Actions Against Nicaragua," *New York Times,* December 23, 1982.
116. Philip Taubman, "Nicaraguan Exile Limits Role of U.S.," *New York Times,* December 9, 1982.
117. John Brecher, John Walcott, David Martin, and Beth Nissen, "A Secret War for Nicaragua," *Newsweek,* November 8, 1982. See also LeoGrande, *Our Own Backyard,* 302.
118. LeoGrande, *Our Own Backyard,* 304.
119. Ibid., 307.
120. "Let us be clear as to the American attitude toward the Government of Nicaragua. We do not seek its overthrow." Quoted in *New York Times,* April 28, 1983.
121. Mayer and McManus, *Landslide,* 72.
122. Stephen Kinzer, "Nicaraguan Port Thought to be Mined," *New York Times,* March 14, 1984. See also LeoGrande, *Our Own Backyard,* 330.
123. Dusko Doder, "Soviets Blame U.S. in Tanker Blast," *Washington Post,* March 22, 1984; "U.S. Denies Responsibility," *New York Times,* March 22, 1984. See also LeoGrande, *Our Own Backyard,* 330.
124. LeoGrande, *Our Own Backyard,* 330.
125. Andres Oppenheimer, "Poor Islanders Fear a Role in Contra War Despite Chance of Jobs," *Miami Herald,* November 1, 1986; Mark Fazlollah, "NSC Bypassed Military with Covert Operations," *Miami Herald,* July 26, 1987; "CIA Employees Fought Nicaraguans," *Washington Post,* December 20, 1984. See also LeoGrande, *Our Own Backyard,* 331.
126. Doyle McManus, "U.S. Didn't Mine Ports: Weinberger," *Los Angeles Times,* April 9, 1984. See also LeoGrande, *Our Own Backyard,* 330.
127. George P. Shultz, *Turmoil and Triumph: My Years as Secretary of State* (New York: Charles Scribner's Sons, 1993), 308. See also LeoGrande, *Our Own Backyard,* 330–31.
128. David Rogers, "U.S. Role in Mining Nicaraguan Harbors Is Larger Than First Thought," *Wall Street Journal,* April 6, 1984.
129. "Goldwater Writes CIA Director Scorching Letter," *Washington Post,* April 11, 1984. See also LeoGrande, *Our Own Backyard,* 334.

130. "Moynihan's Statement on Quitting Panel Job," *New York Times,* April 16, 1984. See also LeoGrande, *Our Own Backyard,* 335.
131. LeoGrande, *Our Own Backyard,* 335–36.
132. See Peter Kornbluh, "The Iran-Contra Scandal: A Postmortem," *World Policy Journal* 5, no.1 (Winter 1987–88): 137.
133. LeoGrande, *Our Own Backyard,* 339.
134. "Text of the Second Reagan-Mondale Debate," *Washington Post,* October 22, 1984. See also LeoGrande, *Our Own Backyard,* 365.
135. Joel Brinkley, "CIA Chief Defends Manual for Nicaraguan Rebels," *New York Times,* November 2, 1984. See also LeoGrande, *Our Own Backyard,* 365.
136. Joel Brinkley, "CIA Disputes Reagan on Primer," *New York Times,* October 23, 1984. See also LeoGrande, *Our Own Backyard,* 366.
137. Roy Gutman, "Competing in Blunders: Washington vs. Managua," *Washington Post,* March 20, 1988. See also LeoGrande, *Our Own Backyard,* 458.
138. LeoGrande, *Our Own Backyard,* 458–59.
139. Cited in Peter Kornbluh and Malcolm Byrne, eds., *The Iran-Contra Scandal: The Declassified History* (New York: The New Press, 1993), 4.
140. Robert Parry and Peter Kornbluh, "Reagan's Pro-Contra Propaganda Machine," *Washington Post,* September 4, 1988.
141. William Finnegan, "Castro's Shadow: America's Man in Latin America, and His Obsession," *New Yorker,* October 14, 2002.
142. Joanne Omang, "The People Who Sell Foreign Policies," *Washington Post,* October 15, 1985.
143. See Finnegan, "Castro's Shadow."
144. See Robert Parry and Peter Kornbluh, "Iran-Contra's Untold Story," *Foreign Policy* (Fall 1988): 3–30. For Reich's denial, see Finnegan, "Castro's Shadow."
145. Quoted in Finnegan, "Castro's Shadow."
146. LeoGrande, *Our Own Backyard,* 306–7.
147. Cited in Kornbluh and Byrne, eds., *The Iran-Contra Scandal,* 391.
148. Rita Beamish, "Contra Leaders Joined Umbrella Group Only to Impress Congress," Associated Press, July 13, 1987.
149. "The Contras: How U.S. Got Entangled," *Los Angeles Times,* March 4, 1985. See also LeoGrande, *Our Own Backyard,* 307.
150. Arturo Cruz Jr., *Memoirs of a Counter-Revolutionary* (New York: Doubleday, 1989), 254–55; Sam Dillon, "CIA Joins in Contra Feuding," *Miami Herald,* May 18, 1988. See also LeoGrande, *Our Own Backyard,* 540.
151. LeoGrande, 489.
152. Cited in Kornbluh and Byrne, eds., *The Iran-Contra Scandal,* 53–54.
153. Eldon Kenworthy, "Where Pennsylvania Avenue Meets Madison Avenue: The Selling of Foreign Policy," *World Policy Journal* 5, no.1 (Winter 1987–88): 114–15. See also Joanne Omang, "Where Is the Evidence That Nicaragua Is a Center Of?" *Washington Post,* national weekly edit., August 5, 1985.
154. Mayer and McManus, *Landslide,* 211.
155. Arnson, *Crossroads,* 275.
156. *Congressional Record,* July 27, 1983, H 5722. See also Arnson, *Crossroads,* 134.
157. Arnson, *Crossroads,* 197.
158. Anne H. Cahn, "Perspectives on Arms Control: How We Got Oversold on Overkill," *Los Angeles Times,* July 23, 1993.
159. Eric Alterman, *Sound & Fury: The Washington Punditocracy and the Collapse of American Politics* (New York: HarperCollins, 1992), 194.

160. Arnson, *Crossroads,* 123.
161. David S. Broder, "Buchanan's Scorn," *Washington Post,* March 16, 1986.
162. "Democrats and Commandantes," *New Republic,* July 28, 1986.
163. Fred Barnes, "The Sandinista Lobby," *New Republic,* January 20, 1986.
164. "The Sandinista Chorus," *New Republic,* August 25, 1986.
165. Lance Morrow, Laurence I. Barrett, and Barrett Seaman, "Yankee Doodle Magic: What Makes Reagan So Remarkably Popular a President," *Time,* July 7, 1986. See also Mayer and McManus, *Landslide,* 248.
166. Morton Kondracke, "The Myth and the Man," *Newsweek,* July 29, 1985.
167. Mayer and McManus, *Landslide,* 248.
168. Malcolm Byrne and Peter Kornbluh, "Iran-Contra: The Press Indicts the Prosecutor," *Columbia Journalism Review* (March/April 1994): 44.
169. James Madison, *The Federalist Papers,* No. 58.
170. Cited in Mayer and McManus, *Landslide,* 191.
171. Ibid., 149.
172. President's news conference of June 18, 1985, available online at the Reagan Library's Web site, *http://www.reagan.utexas.edu/resource/speeches/1985/61885c.htm.*
173. Theodore Draper, *A Very Thin Line: The Iran Contra Affairs* (New York: Hill and Wang, 1991), 59.
174. Mayer and McManus, *Landslide,* 192.
175. Ibid., 193.
176. Arnson, *Crossroads,* 183.
177. Lawrence E. Walsh, *Firewall: The Iran-Contra Conspiracy and Cover-Up* (New York: W. W. Norton, 1997), 190; Draper, *A Very Thin Line,* 117–19.
178. See Robert C. McFarlane, Testimony at Joint Hearings Before the House Select Committee to Investigate Covert Arms Transactions with Iran and the Senate Select Committee on Secret Military Assistance to Iran and the Nicaraguan Opposition (Washington, D.C.: GPO, 1987), 100-2, 170.
179. See John M. Poindexter, ibid., 100-8, 82.
180. Cited in Kornbluh and Byrne, eds., *The Iran-Contra Scandal,* 118.
181. Draper, *A Very Thin Line,* 345.
182. See Peter Kornbluh, "The Iran-Contra Scandal: A Postmortem," *World Policy Journal* 5, no.1 (Winter 1987–88): 135.
183. North's testimony at joint hearings before the House and Senate select committees, 100-7, Part I, pp. 179–80.
184. Draper, *A Very Thin Line,* 346.
185. Oliver North with William Novak, *Under Fire: An American Story* (New York: HarperCollins, 1991), 272.
186. *Evans & Novak,* transcript, CNN, October 11, 1986.
187. Draper, *A Very Thin Line,* 355–61.
188. Ibid., 366–70.
189. Ibid., 371–72; Mayer and McManus, *Landslide,* 352, 407.
190. North, *Under Fire,* 7–8.
191. Kornbluh and Byrne, eds., *The Iran-Contra Scandal,* 305.
192. Mayer and McManus, *Landslide,* 295
193. Cited in Kornbluh and Byrne, eds., *The Iran-Contra Scandal,* 304–6.
194. Draper, *A Very Thin Line,* 490.
195. Lawrence E. Walsh, *Iran-Contra: The Final Report,* Vol. I (New York: Times Books, 1994), 505. See also Theodore Draper, "Walsh's Last Stand," *New York Review of Books,* March 3, 1994.

196. Walsh, *Iran-Contra: The Final Report,* 408–12.
197. Draper, *A Very Thin Line,* 537.
198. *National Security Archives Reader,* 310.
199. Walsh, *Firewall,* 189–90.
200. Ibid., 338–43.
201. Ibid., 452.
202. Ibid., 453.
203. David S. Broder, "Bush Asserts Vindication in Iran Affair, Says Key Facts Were Denied Him," *Washington Post,* August 6, 1987.
204. Walsh, *Firewall,* 456.
205. Ibid., 457–58.
206. Ibid., 343–45.
207. Draper, *A Very Thin Line,* 570.
208. Ibid., 570.
209. Ibid., 570–71.
210. Mayer and McManus, *Landslide,* 389.
211. Cited in Kornbluh and Byrne, eds., *The Iran-Contra Scandal,* 336.
212. See Amy Fried, *Muffled Voices: Oliver North and the Politics of Public Opinion* (New York: Columbia University Press, 1997), 113.
213. See Lance Morrow, "Charging up Capitol Hill: How Oliver North Captured the Imagination of America," *Time,* July 20, 1987; "Ollie North Takes the Hill," *Newsweek,* July 20, 1987.
214. Cited in Fried, *Muffled Voices,* 117.
215. While North's popularity did jump during the days of his testimony in July 1987, this never translated into support for what he had done, or for President Reagan's policies in either Iran or Nicaragua. The percentage of Americans questioned who considered North to be a hero ranged from 4 percent in a *Los Angeles Times* poll taken July 10, 1987, which was far lower than the percentage who believed that North "could be bought," to 19 percent in an ABC News poll taken the next day. See Fried, *Muffled Voices,* 84–88, 112–13, and 222–27.
216. *Washington Post Magazine,* April 11, 1993.
217. David E. Rosenbaum, "The Inquiry That Couldn't," *New York Times Week in Review,* January 19, 1994.
218. Lawrence E. Walsh, *Firewall,* 506.
219. Mayer and McManus, *Landslide,* 350.
220. Ibid., 378.
221. Walsh, *Firewall,* 467–68.
222. See Robert M. Gates, *From the Shadows: The Ultimate Insider's Story of Five Presidents and How They Won the Cold War* (New York: Simon & Schuster, 1996), 393.

VI: Conclusion: George W. Bush and Our Post-Truth Presidency

1. Friedrich Nietzsche, "On Truth and Lie in an Extra Moral Sense," a fragment published posthumously in *The Portable Nietzsche,* Walter Kaufmann, ed., intro., trans. (New York: Penguin Books, 1954), 42–47.
2. Draper, *A Very Thin Line,* 59.
3. For instance, the celebrated author and journaiist David Halberstam writes, "The singular strength of Kissinger was not just his skill at dissembling when necessary, his unusual ability to tell ten different people ten completely different stories about what he was doing on a given issue and remember what version of the story he had told to

which person." See David Halberstam, *War in a Time of Peace: Bush, Clinton and the Generals* (New York: Scribners, 2001), 286–87.

4. In his 1999 book, *Shadow: Five Presidents and the Legacy of Watergate,* author/journalist Bob Woodward, an insider's insider, excoriates Carter for his pledge and then goes on to attack the president for, in his view, mischaracterizing a meeting that Carter had held with Woodward and his boss, *Washington Post* Executive Editor Ben Bradlee, to a group of congressmen. To Woodward and much of the Washington establishment, this mischaracterization—if indeed it was one, rather than a simple misunderstanding—brought Carter down to the same level as politicians such as Richard Nixon and Lyndon Johnson. Woodward writes that after the meeting, he was "left with a feeling of distaste. I had a sickening sense of foreboding, of here-we-go-again with another president." Woodward did not wish to endure "strife with the new president" and so he decided to switch to covering the Supreme Court. This was as close as anyone has come to pinning a lie on President Carter and it is not all that close. Interestingly, much of insider Washington grew to loathe Carter much as it would later loathe Clinton. Oddly, the reasons were exactly the opposite. Carter was viewed as pathologically honest, to the point where he refused to engage in even the typically unquestioned lying—white and otherwise—necessary to grease the skids of the machinery of insider politics. Bob Woodward, *Shadow: Five Presidents and the Legacy of Watergate* (New York: Simon & Schuster, 1999), 42, 52.
5. See Eric Alterman, *What Liberal Media? The Truth About Bias and the News* (New York: Basic Books, 2003), 146.
6. Edward Walsh, "Harbury Loses Bid to Sue U.S. Officials: Rebel's Widow Alleged Deception," *Washington Post,* June 21, 2002.
7. John M. Orman, *Presidential Secrecy and Deception: Beyond the Power to Persuade* (Westport, CT: Greenwood Press, 1980), 46.
8. Michael Kinsley, "Lying in Style," *http://www.slate.com,* April 18, 2002.
9. Dana Milbank and Dana Priest, "Warning in Iraq Report Unread," *Washington Post,* July 19, 2003.
10. See "President Works on Economic Recovery During NY Trip," October 2001, *http://www.whitehouse.gov/news/releases/2001/10/20011003-4.html;* Jonathan Chait, "Red Handed," *The New Republic,* May 13, 2002, *http://www.tnr.com/doc.mhtml?i=20020513&s=chait051302;* Dana Milbank, "A Sound Bite So Good, the President Wishes He Had Said It," *Washington Post,* July 2, 1992; Dana Milbank, "Karl Rove, Adding to His To-Do List," *Washington Post,* June 25, 2002.
11. See Paul Krugman, "The Memory Hole," *New York Times,* August 6, 2002.
12. See Dana Milbank, "White House Forecasts Often Miss the Mark," *Washington Post,* February 24, 2004; and Jonathan Weisman, "Bush Assertion on Tax Cuts Is at Odds with IRS Data," *Washington Post,* February 24, 2004. For the "not a statistician" quotation, see "Bush Aides Back Off Jobs Numbers," CBS News, February 18, 2004, *http://www.cbsnews.com/stories/2004/02/18/national/main600945.shtml.*
13. See Eric Alterman and Mark Green, *The Book on Bush: How George W. (Mis)leads America* (New York: Viking, 2004), 266–322. Note: portions of this section have been drawn from that work.
14. For the lies about Iraqi military capabilities, see "President Bush, Prime Minister Blair Discuss Keeping the Peace," September 7, 2002," *http://www.whitehouse.gov/news/releases/2002/09/20020907-2.html;* Joseph Curl, "Agency Disavows Report on Iraq Arms," *Washington Times,* September 27, 2002, *http://www.washtimes.com/printarticle.asp?action=print&ArticleID=20020927-500715;* Dana Milbank, "For Bush, Facts Are Malleable," *Washington Post,* October 22, 2002, *http://www.washingtonpost.com/ac2/wp-dyn?pagename=*

article&node=&contentId=A61903-2002Oct21¬Found=true; Barton Gelman and Walter Pincus, "Depiction of Threat Outgrew Supporting Evidence," *Washington Post,* August 10, 2003; Eric Alterman, "Bush Lies, Media Swallows," *Nation,* November 7, 2002, *http://www.thenation.com/doc.mhtml?i=20021125&s=alterman;* and International Institute for Strategic Study, "Iraq WMD Dossier Statement: Iraq's Weapons of Mass Destruction: A Net Assessment, An IISS Strategic Dossier," September 9, 2002, *http://www.iiss.org/news-more.php?itemID=88.* See also Brendan Nyhan, "Making Bush Tell the Truth," *http://www.salon.com,* November 5, 2002.

15. See Joseph Wilson, *The Politics of Truth: Inside the Lies That Led to War and Betrayed My Wife's CIA Identity* (New York: Carroll and Graf, 2004), 325–65.
16. George W. Bush, "Address to the Nation," March 17, 2003, *http://www.whitehouse.gov/news/releases/2003/03/20030317-7.html.*
17. Vice President Dick Cheney, "Vice President Speaks at VFW 103rd National Convention; Remarks by the Vice President to the Veterans of Foreign Wars 103rd National Convention," August 26, 2002, *http://www.whitehouse.gov/news/releases/2002/08/20020826.html.*
18. Mitchell Landsberg, "Ample Evidence of Abuses, Little of Illegal Weapons," *Los Angeles Times,* June 15, 2003.
19. Colin Powell, Remarks after NBC's *Meet the Press,* Washington, D.C., May 4, 2003, *http://www.state.gov/secretary/rm/2003/20166.html.*
20. On this point, see Thomas Powers, "The Vanishing Case for War," *New York Review of Books,* December 4, 2003.
21. Robert Scheer, "Bad Iraq Data from Start to Finish," *Nation,* June 11, 2003.
22. See Sidney Blumenthal, "There Was No Failure of Intelligence," *Guardian,* February 5, 2004, *http://www.guardian.co.uk/comment/story/0,3604,1141116,00.html.*
23. Dana Priest and Walter Pincus, "Search in Iraq Finds No Banned Weapons," *Washington Post,* October 3, 2003.
24. A videotape of Powell's remarks was shown on MSNBC's *Countdown with Keith Olberman,* September 24, 2003, and a transcript can be found at *http://www.msnbc.com/news/971717.asp.*
25. Dana Priest and Dana Milbank, "Iraq Sought Missile Parts, President Says," *Washington Post,* October 4, 2003.
26. Greg Miller, "Cheney Is Adamant on Iraq 'Evidence': Vice President Revives Assertions on Banned Weaponry and Links to Al Qaeda That Other Administration Officials Have Backed Away From," *Los Angeles Times,* January 23, 2004.
27. Richard W. Stevenson, "White House Memo: Remember 'Weapons of Mass Destruction'? For Bush, They Are a Nonissue," *New York Times,* December 18, 2003, *http://www.nytimes.com/2003/12/18/politics/18PREX.html.*
28. *http://www.whitehouse.gov/stateoftheunion/2004/.*
29. Priest and Milbank, "Iraq Sought Missile Parts."
30. Jonathan S. Landay, "White House Released Claims of Defector Deemed Unreliable by CIA," Knight Ridder Newspapers, May 17, 2004, *http://www.myrtlebeachonline.com/mld/myrtlebeachonlline/news/special_packages/iraq/8690113.html.*
31. See The White House, "A Decade of Deception and Defiance: Saddam Hussein's Defiance of the United Nations," September 12, 2002, *http://www.whitehouse.gov/news/releases/2002/09/iraqdecade.pdf*
32. John B. Judis and Spencer Ackerman, "The First Casualty," *New Republic,* June 30, 2003.
33. Bill Keller, "The Boys Who Cried Wolfowitz," *New York Times,* June 14, 2003.
34. Reuters, "Iraqi, Possibly Tied to 9/11, Is Captured," *New York Times,* July 9, 2003.

35. Bush's comments can be found in FDCH E-media, "Transcript: President Bush Speaks About 9/11 Commission," June 17, 2004, available on *http://www.nytimes.com*. Cheney's quotes are taken from CNBC's "Capital Report," June 17, 2004, available on *http://www.msnbc.com*. For Cheney's "pretty well confirmed" remarks see NBC's "Meet the Press," Transcript, December 9, 2001, available on *http://www.msnbc.com,* and Greg Miller, "No Proof Connects Iraq to 9/11, Bush Says," *Los Angeles Times,* September 18, 2003. The Commission staff report can be found in "Staff Statement Number 15," *New York Times,* June 17, 2004, *http://www.nytimes.com*. For more, see also Walter Pincus and Dana Milbank, "Al Qaeda–Hussein Link Is Dismissed," *Washington Post,* June 17, 2004, and Philip Shenon and Richard W. Stevenson, "Leaders of 9/11 Panel Ask Cheney for Reports That Would Support Iraq-Qaeda Ties," *New York Times,* June 19, 2004.
36. See Eric Alterman, "Why Chickenhawks Matter," *Nation,* December 1, 2003.
37. Thomas L. Friedman, "The Meaning of a Skull," *New York Times,* April 27, 2003.
38. "Keep Looking," *Washington Post,* June 25, 2003.
39. CNN's *Reliable Sources,* July 20, 2003, transcript, *http://www.cnn.com/TRANSCRIPTS/0307/20/rs.00.html*.
40. The White House, "President Bush Welcomes President Kwasniewski to White House," January 27, 2004, *http://www.whitehouse.gov/news/releases/2004/01/20040127-3.html*. See also Joe Conason, "Mr. Bush's Fantasy Planet," *http://www.salon.com,* January 27, 2004.
41. CNN, *Late Edition with Wolf Blitzer,* March 14, 2004, *www.cnn.com/TRANSCRIPTS/2004.03.14.html*.
42. ABC's *The Note,* September 3, 2002, *http://www.abcnews.go.com/sections/politics/DailyNews/TheNote.html*.
43. Dana Milbank, "For Bush, Facts Are Malleable: Presidential Tradition of Embroidering Key Assertions Continues," *Washington Post,* October 22, 2002.
44. See Eric Alterman, "Democracy's Lies," *New York Times,* November 4, 1991.
45. Benjamin C. Bradlee, "Reflections on Lying," The Press-Enterprise Lecture Series, No. 32, University of California, Riverside, January 7, 1977.
46. Richard Morin and Dana Milbank, "Most Think Truth Was Stretched to Justify Iraq War," *Washington Post,* February 13, 2004.
47. See Nancy Gibbs, "When Credibility Becomes an Issue," Time, February 16, 2004, *http://www.time.com*.
48. Glenn Kessler, "Arms Issue Seen as Hurting U.S. Credibility Abroad," *Washington Post,* January 19, 2004.
49. Gary J. Schmitt and Abram N. Shulsky, "Leo Strauss and the World of Intelligence (By Which We Do Not Mean *Nous*)," in Kenneth L. Deutsch and John Murley, eds., *Leo Strauss, the Straussians and the American Regime* (New York: Rowan and Littlefield, 1999), 407–21.
50. Seymour M. Hersh, "Selective Intelligence," *New Yorker,* May 12, 2003. See also Leo Strauss, *An Introduction to Political Philosophy,* Hilail Gildin, ed. (Detroit: Wayne State University Press, 1990); and Deutsch and Murley, eds., *Leo Strauss.*
51. Lloyd Gardner, "America's War in Vietnam: The End of Exceptionalism?" in *The Legacy: The Vietnam War in the American Imagination,* D. Michael Shafer, ed. (Boston: Beacon Press, 1990), 20.
52. Jefferson to Joseph Priestley, March 21, 1801, *The Works of Thomas Jefferson,* Paul L. Ford, ed. (New York: G. Putnam's Sons, 1905), 9:218.
53. Paine and Reagan are quoted in Arthur Schlesinger Jr., "Foreign Policy and the American Character: The Cyril Foster Lecture" (Oxford, England: Oxford University Press, 1983), 8.

54. See Alexander Hamilton, John Jay, and James Madison, *The Federalist,* Jacob E. Cooke, ed. (Middletown, CT: Wesleyan University Press, 1961), 3. See also Michael Howard, *War and the Liberal Conscience* (New Brunswick, NJ: Transaction Publishers, 1977); and Felix Gilbert, *To the Farewell Address: Ideas of Early American Foreign Policy* (Princeton, NJ: Princeton University Press, 1961).
55. See Benjamin Franklin to Samuel Cooper, Paris, May 1, 1777, *The Works of Benjamin Franklin,* 12 vols., John Bigelow, ed. (New York: G. Putnam's Sons, 1904), 7:215–16.
56. "I can see no necessity but great inconveniences in sending Ministers abroad and receiving them at home," Elbridge Gerry explained to John Adams in 1783. "The inconveniences of being entangled with European politics, of being the puppets of European statesmen, of being gradually divested of our virtues and republican principles, of being a divided, influenced and dissipated people; of being induced to prefer the splendor of a court to the happiness of our citizens; and finally of changing our form of government from vile Aristocracy or an arbitrary Monarchy." See James H. Huston, "Intellectual Foundations of Early American Diplomacy," *Diplomatic History* 1, no. 1 (1977): 8.
57. *Annals of Congress 1798,* 5th Cong., 1119–32; Gerry quoted in Huston, "Intellectual Foundations of Early America Diplomacy," 8. See also Robert David Johnson, *The Peace Progressives and American Foreign Relations* (Cambridge, MA: Harvard University Press, 1995), 15.
58. George Washington, Farewell Address, September 17, 1796, *http://www.yale.edu/lawweb/avalon/washing.htm.*
59. Adams quoted in William Appleman Williams, "The Age of Mercantilism, 1740–1828," in *William Appleman Williams Reader,* Henry W. Berger, ed. (Chicago: Ivan R. Dee, 1992), 216.
60. See, for instance, Ivo H. Daaldier and James M. Lindsey, *America Unbound: The Bush Revolution in Foreign Policy* (Washington, D.C.: Brookings Institution Press, 2003); John Newhouse, *Imperial America: The Bush Assault on the World Order* (New York: Alfred A. Knopf, 2003); Michael Hirsh, *At War with Ourselves: Why America is Squandering Its Chance to Build a Better World* (New York: Oxford University Press, 2003); and Clyde Prestowitz, *Rogue Nation: American Unilateralism and the Failure of Good Intentions* (New York: Basic Books, 2003). See also Alterman and Green, *The Book on Bush.*
61. Woodrow Wilson, "An Address in the Princess Theater, Cheyenne, Wyoming," September 24, 1919; Woodrow Wilson, *The Public Papers of Woodrow Wilson,* vol. 63, Arthur S. Link et al., eds. (Princeton, NJ: Princeton University Press, 1966), 474.
62. Arthur Schlesinger Jr., "Foreign Policy and the American Character," in *The Cycles of American History* (Boston: Houghton Mifflin, 1986), 54. See also Lawrence E. Gelfand, "Where Ideals Confront Self-Interest: Wilsonian Foreign Policy" *Diplomatic History* 18, no. 1 (1994).
63. See Henry A. Kissinger, *Diplomacy* (New York: Simon & Schuster, 1994), 45.
64. Perry Miller, *Errand in the Wilderness* (Cambridge, MA: The Belknap Press of Harvard University Press, 1956).
65. For Ronald Reagan, see Alterman, *Who Speaks for America?,* 53.
66. See Walter Lippmann, *A Preface to Morals* (New York: Macmillan, 1929), 278–79.
67. Ibid.; Robert B. Westbrook, *John Dewey and American Democracy* (Ithaca, NY: Cornell University Press, 1991), 55
68. See Walter Lippmann, *Liberty and the News* (New York: Harcourt, Brace and Howe, 1920), 38–41.
69. See Walter Lippmann, *The Phantom Public* (New York: Macmillan and Co., 1924), 13–14.
70. See Walter Lippmann, *Public Opinion* (New York: Penguin Books, 1946), 164.

71. John Dewey, *The Public and Its Problems* (New York: H. Holt, 1927).
72. See William A. Galston, "Salvation through Participation: John Dewey and the Religion of Democracy," *Raritan* 12 (1993): 158. See also Westbrook, *John Dewey and American Democracy,* 310.
73. John Dewey cited in Hilary Putnam,"A Reconsideration of Deweyan Democracy," in *Renewing Philosophy,* Hillary Putnam, ed. (Cambridge, MA: Harvard University Press, 1992), 188–89.
74. See Dewey, *The Public and Its Problems,* 368.
75. Ibid., 122–23.
76. Friedrich Nietzsche, "On Truth and Lie in an Extra Moral Sense" (a fragment published posthumously) in *The Portable Nietzsche,* Walter Kaufmann, ed., intro., trans. (New York: Penguin Books, 1954), 42–47.
77. Ronald Brownstein, "Knowing Hard Choices Can Be Painful, Bush Dodges Them," *Los Angeles Times,* June 10, 2002, *http://www.latimes.com/news/printedition/asection/la-000040776jun10.column?coll=la%2Dnews%2Da%5Fsection.*
78. "Draft of a Speech by President Truman on Berlin Conference," Papers of Samuel I. Rosenman, President's Secretary's Files, box 322, Potsdam file, HSTL.
79. See Harry S. Truman, "Report to the American People on the Potsdam Conference," August 9, 1945, in Dennis Merrill, ed., *Documentary History of the Truman Presidency,* vol. 2, 412, also at *http://www.presidency.ucsb.edu/site/docs/pppus.php?admin=033&year= 1945&id=97.*
80. Tony Smith, *The French Stake in Algeria, 1945–1962* (Ithaca, NY: Cornell University Press, 1978), 178–80.
81. Jean Lacouture, *DeGaulle, The Ruler, 1945–1970,* Alan Sheridan, trans. (New York: W. W. Norton, 1992) 312.
82. Ibid., 312.
83. Smith, *French Stake in Algeria,* 178–80.

WORKS CITED

PRIMARY SOURCES

Contemporary Newspapers and Periodicals

American Prospect
The Atlantic Monthly
The Boston Globe
Boston Review
Chicago Herald American
Chicago Sun-Times
Chicago Tribune
The Christian Science Monitor
Chronicle of Higher Education
CNN Cold War Series
Columbia Journalism Review
Commentary
Dissent
Esquire
Foreign Affairs, 1945, 1946, 1955, 1956, 1967, 1984–85
Foreign Policy
Fortune
George
Harper's Magazine
Journal of Cold War Studies
Life
LOOK
Los Angeles Examiner
Los Angeles Times
National Review
New York Daily News
New York Herald Tribune
The New York Times
The New York Times Magazine
The New York Times Review of Books
Newsweek
Partisan Review
Philadelphia Record
Reader's Digest
Rolling Stone
The Saturday Evening Post

The Nation
The New Republic
The New Yorker
Time
U.S. News & World Report
Vanity Fair
The Wall Street Journal
Washington Monthly
The Washington Post
The Washington Post National Weekly Edition
The Washington Times
World Policy Journal

Unpublished Primary Sources

Elie Abel Oral History, John F. Kennedy Library, Boston, MA.
Joseph Alsop Oral History, John F. Kennedy Library, Boston, MA.
Joseph and Stewart Alsop Papers, Manuscript Division, Library of Congress, Washington, D.C.
Eben A. Ayers Papers, Harry S. Truman Library, Independence, MO.
George Ball Papers, Lyndon B. Johnson Library, Austin, TX.
Charles Bartlett Oral History, John F. Kennedy Library, Boston, MA.
Isaiah Berlin Oral History, John F. Kennedy Library, Boston, MA.
William Bundy, Letter to Author, May 13, 1993.
William F. Bundy Papers, Lyndon B. Johnson Library, Austin, TX.
James F. Byrnes Papers, Clemson University Library, Clemson, SC.
Clark Clifford Oral History, Harry S. Truman Library, Independence, MO.
Joseph E. Davies Papers, Manuscript Division, Library of Congress, Washington, D.C.
Elsey Papers, Harry S. Truman Library, Independence, MO.
Rowland Evans Oral History, John F. Kennedy Library, Boston, MA.
Federal Bureau of Investigation Files, J. Edgar Hoover Building, Washington, D.C.
Michael Forrestal Oral History Interview, John F. Kennedy Library, Boston, MA.
Gibbons Papers, Lyndon B. Johnson Library, Austin, TX.
Roswell L. Gilpatric Oral History, John F. Kennedy Library, Boston, MA.
Anna Roosevelt Halsted Papers, Franklin D. Roosevelt Library, Hyde Park, NY.
W. Averell Harriman Oral History, John F. Kennedy Library, Boston, MA.
W. Averell Harriman Papers, Manuscript Division, Library of Congress, Washington, D.C.
Alger Hiss Defense Files, Alger Hiss Papers, Harvard Law School Library, Harvard University, Cambridge, MA.
Harry L. Hopkins Papers, Franklin D. Roosevelt Library, Hyde Park, NY.
Harold Ickes Papers, Manuscript Division, Library of Congress, Washington, D.C.
Lyndon B. Johnson Papers, Lyndon B. Johnson Library, Austin, TX.
Tom Johnson Notes, Lyndon B. Johnson Library, Austin, TX.
John F. Kennedy Assassination Related Conversations, Lyndon B. Johnson Library, Austin, TX.
John F. Kennedy Papers, John F. Kennedy Library, Boston, MA.
Robert F. Kennedy Oral History Interviews, John F. Kennedy Library, Boston, MA.
William D. Leahy Diary, William D. Leahy Papers, Manuscript Division, Library of Congress, Washington, D.C.
Walter Lippmann Oral History, John F. Kennedy Library, Boston, MA.
Isador Lubin Papers, Franklin D. Roosevelt Library, Hyde Park, NY.

Ross T. McIntire Papers, Franklin D. Roosevelt Library, Hyde Park, NY.
Harry McPherson Office Files, White House Aides, Lyndon B. Johnson Library, Austin, TX.
Map Room Files, Franklin D. Roosevelt Library, Hyde Park, NY.
Meeting Notes File, Special Advisory Group, Lyndon B. Johnson Library, Austin, TX.
Edwin Moïse Interview with Author, June 9, 1994.
Edwin Moïse Papers, Lyndon B. Johnson Library, Austin, TX.
National Archives of the United States, College Park, MD.
Record Group 59, General Records of the Department of State.
Rockefeller Commission Papers, Gerald R. Ford Library Materials, J.F.K. Assassination Materials Project.
National Security Files, Lyndon B. Johnson Library, Austin, TX.
Kenneth O'Donnell Oral History, John F. Kennedy Library, Boston, MA.
Official File, Franklin D. Roosevelt Library, Hyde Park, NY.
OSD Records, National Records Center, Suitland, MD.
President's Personal File, Franklin D. Roosevelt Library, Hyde Park, NY.
President's Secretary's Files, Franklin D. Roosevelt Library, Hyde Park, NY.
Belle Willard Roosevelt Papers, Manuscript Division, Library of Congress, Washington, D.C.
James Roosevelt Papers, Franklin D. Roosevelt Library, Hyde Park, NY.
Samuel I. Rosenman Papers, Franklin D. Roosevelt Library, Hyde Park, NY.
John Scali Oral History, John F. Kenny Library, Boston, MA.
Theodore C. Sorenson Papers and Oral History, John F. Kennedy Library, Boston, MA.
Henry L. Stimson Diaries, Manuscript Division, Library of Congress, Washington, D.C.
Llewellyn Thompson Oral History, John F. Kennedy Library, Boston MA.
Harry S. Truman Oral History Interview, 1955, Post Presidential Files, Harry S. Truman Library, Independence, MO.
Cyrus Vance Oral History Interview, March 9, 1970, Interview No. 3, Lyndon B. Johnson Library, Austin, TX.
Vietnam Reference File, Lyndon B. Johnson Library, Austin, TX.

Published Primary Sources

Address to the Democratic National Convention, Robert F. Kennedy, Atlantic City, NJ, August 27, 1964, at JFKL website: *http://www.cs.umb.edu/jfklibrary/r082764.htm*.
Annals of Congress 1798, 5th Congress.
Barrett, David M., ed. *Lyndon B. Johnson's Vietnam Papers: A Documentary Collection*. College Station, TX: Texas A&M University Press, 1997.
Berle, Beatrice, and Travis Jacob. *Navigating the Rapids, 1918–1971: From the Papers of Adolf A. Berle.* New York: Harcourt Brace Jovanovich, 1973.
Bradlee, Benjamin C. "Reflections on Lying." The Press-Enterprise Lecture Series. Number 32, University of California, Riverside, January 7, 1977.
Chang, Laurence, and Peter Kornbluh, eds. *The Cuban Missile Crisis, 1962: An NSA Reader.* New York: New Press, 1992.
Congressional Quarterly Almanac, 1952, 1953.
Johnson, Walter, ed. *The Papers of Adlai E. Stevenson,* VIII. Boston: Little, Brown, 1972–79.
"Khrushchev's Oral Communication of December 10, 1962." *Problems of Communism* 41, special edit. (Spring 1992).
McAuliffe, Mary S., ed. *CIA Documents on the Cuban Missile Crisis.* Washington, D.C.: CIA History Staff, October 1992.
Military History Institute of Vietnam. *Victory in Vietnam: Official History of the People's Army of*

Vietnam. Merle L. Pribbenow, trans. Foreword by William J. Duiker. Lawrence: University of Kansas Press, 2002.

National Security Archive Microfiche Collection. *Cuban Missile Crisis, 1962.* Washington, D.C.: National Security Archive, 1990. Available online at *Digital National Security Archive: http://www.nsarchive.chadwyck.com.*

The Pentagon Papers: The Defense Department History of Decisionmaking on Vietnam. The Senator Gravel Edition, Vol 2. Boston: Beacon, 1971–72.

Public Papers of the Presidents: John F. Kennedy, 1961–1963, 3 vols. Washington, D.C.: Government Printing Office, 1962–4.

Public Papers of the Presidents: Lyndon B. Johnson, 1963–1964, Vol 1. Washington, D.C.: Government Printing Office, 1964–6.

"Record of Conversation Between Comrade I. V. Stalin and Chairman of the Central People's Government of the People's Republic of China, Mao Zedong, 22 January 1950." *Cold War International History Project Bulletin* 6–7 (Winter 1995–96).

"Russian Documents on the Cuban Missile Crisis." *Cold War International History Project Bulletin* 8–9 (Winter 1996–97).

"Russian Foreign Ministry Documents on the Cuban Missile Crisis." *Cold War International History Project Bulletin* 5 (Spring 1995).

"Translated Russian and Chinese Documents on Mao Zedong's Visit to Moscow, December 1949–February 1950, Document 1: Telegram, Mao Zedong to Liu Shaoqi, 18 December 1949." *Cold War International History Project Bulletin* 8–9 (Winter 1996–1997).

U.S. Congress. *Congressional Record,* 1945–1946, 1949–1950, 1952, 1955, 1962, 1963.

———. House of Representatives. Foreign Operations and Government Information Subcommittee. *Hearings Before the House Foreign Operations and Government Information Subcommittee.* 88th Congress, 1st sess., 1963. Washington, D.C.: Government Printing Office.

———.———. Committee on Appropriations, Subcommittee on Foreign Operations. *Foreign Assistance and Related Programs Appropriations for Fiscal Year 1982, Hearings,* Part 1. 97th Congress, 1st sess. Washington, D.C.: Government Printing Office.

———.———. Committee on Government Reform, Minority Staff, Special Investigations Division. *Iraq on the Record: The Bush Administration Public Statements on Iraq.* Prepared for Rep. Henry A. Waxman. Washington, D.C.: Government Printing Office, 2004.

———. Senate. Committee on Foreign Relations. *Executive Sessions of the Senate Foreign Relations Committee* (Historical Series), Vol. 15, 1963. Washington, D.C.: Government Printing Office.

———.———.———. *Executive Sessions of the Senate Foreign Relations Committee* (Historical Series), Vol. 16, 1988. Washington, D.C.: Government Printing Office.

———.———.———. *Hearings Before the Committee on Foreign Relations, The Gulf of Tonkin, The 1964 Incidents.* 90th Congress, 2nd sess., 1968. Washington, D.C.: Government Printing Office.

———.———.———. *Hearings on the Investigation of Far Eastern Policy.* 79th Congress, 1st sess., 1945. Washington, D.C.: Government Printing Office.

———.———.———. *World War II International Agreements and Understandings.* 83rd Congress, 1st sess., 1953. Washington, D.C.: Government Printing Office.

U.S. Department of State. *Bulletin,* 1945.

———. *Foreign Relations of the United States (FRUS), 1944, Vol. IV: Europe.* Washington, D.C.: Government Printing Office, 1966.

———. *FRUS, 1945, Vol. V: Europe.* Washington, D.C.: Government Printing Office, 1967.

———. *FRUS, 1945, Vol. VI: The British Commonwealth, The Far East.* Washington, D.C.: Government Printing Office, 1969.

———. *FRUS, 1950, Vol. I: National Security Affairs, Foreign Economic Policy.* Washington, D.C.: Government Printing Office, 1977.

———. *FRUS, 1961–1963, Vol. VI: Kennedy-Khrushchev Exchanges.* Washington, D.C.: Government Printing Office, 1996.

———. *FRUS, 1961–1963, Vol. XI: Cuban Missile Crisis and Aftermath.* Washington, D.C.: Government Printing Office, 1997.

———. *FRUS, 1964–1968, Vol. I: Vietnam, 1964.* Washington, D.C.: Government Printing Office, 1992.

———. *FRUS, 1964–1968, Vol. III: Vietnam, July–December 1965.* Washington, D.C.: Government Printing Office, 1996.

———. *FRUS, The Conference of Berlin (The Potsdam Conference), 1945, Vol. 2.* Washington, D.C.: Government Printing Office, 1960.

———. *FRUS, The Conferences at Cairo and Tehran, 1943.* Washington, D.C.: Government Printing Office, 1961.

———. *FRUS, The Conferences at Malta and Yalta, 1945.* Washington, D.C.: Government Printing Office, 1955.

———. *The Fort-nightly Survey of American Opinion on International Affairs,* No. 19, March 7, 1945.

Washington, George. "Farewell Address," September 17, 1796. *http://www.yale.edu/lawweb/avalon/washing.htm.*

The White House. "A Decade of Deception and Defiance: Saddam Hussein's Defiance of the United Nations," September 12, 2002. *http://www.whitehouse.gov/news/releases/2002/09/iraqdecade.pdf.*

Wilson, Woodrow. "An Address in the Princess Theater, Cheyenne Wyoming," September 24, 1919. *The Public Papers of Woodrow Wilson,* ed. Arthur S. Link et al. Princeton, NJ: Princeton University Press, 1966–.

SECONDARY SOURCES

Books and Articles

Abbott, Andrew. "From Causes to Events: Notes on Narrative Positivism." *Sociological Methods and Research* 20 (1992).

Abel, Elie. *The Missile Crisis.* Philadelphia: Lippincott, 1966.

Abrams, Elliott. *Undue Process: A Story of How Political Differences Are Turned into Crimes.* New York: Free Press, 1993.

Abramson, Rudy. *Spanning the Century: The Life of W. Averell Harriman, 1891–1986.* New York: William Morrow, 1992.

Acheson, Dean. "Dean Acheson's Version of Robert Kennedy's Version of the Cuban Missile Affair: Homage to Plain Dumb Luck." *Esquire,* February 1969.

———. *Present at the Creation: My Years in the State Department.* New York: W. W. Norton, 1969.

———. *Sketches from Life of Men I Have Known.* New York: Harper & Row, 1961.

Ackland, Len, ed. *Credibility Gap: A Digest of the Pentagon Papers.* Philadelphia: American Friends Service Commitee, 1972.

Allison, Graham T. "Conceptual Models and the Cuban Missile Crisis." *American Political Science Review* 63(3) (September 1969).

———. "Cuban Missiles and Kennedy Macho." *Washington Monthly,* October 1972.

———. *Essence of Decision: Explaining the Cuban Missile Crisis.* Boston: Little, Brown, 1971.

———, and Morton H. Halperin. "Bureaucratic Politics: A Paradigm and Some Policy Implications." *World Politics* 25 (Spring 1972).

———, and Philip Zelikow. *Essence of Decision: Explaining the Cuban Missile Crisis.* 2nd ed. New York: Longman, 1999.

Allyn, Bruce J., James G. Blight, and David A. Welch, eds. *Back to the Brink: Proceedings of the Moscow Conference on the Cuban Missile Crisis, January 27–28, 1989.* Lanham, MD: University Press of America, 1992.

———. "Essence of Revision: Moscow, Havana, and the Cuban Missile Crisis." *International Security* 14 (3) (Winter 1989–1990).

Almond, Gabriel. *The American People and Foreign Policy.* New Haven, CT: Yale University Press, 1960.

Alperovitz, Gar. *Atomic Diplomacy: Hiroshima and Potsdam—The Use of the Atomic Bomb and the American Confrontation with Soviet Power.* New York: Simon & Schuster, 1965.

———. *Cold War Essays.* Garden City, NY: Anchor Books, 1970.

———, with the assistance of Sanho Tree et al. *The Decision to Use the Atomic Bomb and the Architecture of an American Myth.* New York: Knopf, 1995.

Alsop, Stewart. *The Center: The Anatomy of Power in Washington.* London: Hodder and Stoughton, 1968.

———, and Charles Bartlett. "In Time of Crisis." *Saturday Evening Post* CCXXXXV (December 8, 1962).

Alterman, Eric. *Sound & Fury: The Making of the Punditocracy.* 2nd ed. Ithaca, NY: Cornell University Press, 2000.

———. *What Liberal Media? The Truth About Bias and the News.* New York: Basic Books, 2003, 2004.

———. *Who Speaks for America? Why Democracy Matters in Foreign Policy.* Ithaca, NY: Cornell University Press, 1998.

———, and Mark Green, *The Book on Bush: How George W. (Mis)leads America.* New York: Viking, 2004.

Alvarez, David J. *Bureaucracy and Cold War Diplomacy: The United States and Turkey, 1943–1946.* Thessaloníki: Institute for Balkan Studies, 1980.

Amis, Martin. *Experience.* New York: Talk Miramax Books, 2000.

Aquinas, Thomas. "The Evil of Lying." In Vernon J. Bourke, ed. *Summa of Theology: The Pocket Aquinas.* New York: Washington Square Press, 1968.

———. *Summa Theologica.* The Fathers of the English Dominican Province, trans. London: Burns, Oates & Washbourne, 1922.

Arendt, Hannah. "Lying in Politics: Reflections on the Pentagon Papers," in *Crises of the Republic.* New York, Harcourt Brace Jovanovich, 1972.

Armstrong, Hamilton Fish, ed. *The Foreign Affairs Reader.* New York: Harper & Brothers, 1947.

Arnson, Cynthia J. *Crossroads: Congress, the President, and Central America, 1976–1993,* 2nd ed. State College, PA: Pennsylvania State University Press, 1993.

Art, Robert J. "Bureaucratic Politics and American Foreign Policy: A Critique." *Policy Sciences* 4 (December 1973).

Austin, Anthony. *The President's War.* New York: Lippincott, 1971.

Auty, Phyllis, and Richard Clogg, eds. *British Policy Towards Wartime Resistance in Yugoslavia and Greece.* London: Macmillan, 1975.

Bailey, Thomas A. *Man in the Street: The Impact of American Public Opinion on Foreign Policy.* New York: Macmillan, 1948.

Ball, George. *The Past Has Another Pattern.* New York: W. W. Norton, 1982.

Ball, Moya Ann. "Revisiting the Gulf of Tonkin Crisis: An Analysis of the Private Communication of President Johnson and His Advisers." *Discourse and Society* 2 (3) (1991).

Bamford, James. *Body of Secrets: Anatomy of the Ultra-Secret National Security Agency from the Cold War Through the Dawn of a New Century.* New York: Doubleday, 2001.

Barnet, Richard J. *Intervention and Revolution: The United States and the Third World.* New York: World Publishing Co., 1968.

———. *The Rocket's Red Glare: When America Goes to War—The Presidents and The People.* New York: Simon & Schuster, 1990.

———, and Marcus Raskin. *After 20 Years: Alternatives to Cold War in Europe.* New York: Random House, 1965.

Barone, Michael. *Our Country: The Shaping of America from Roosevelt to Reagan.* New York: Free Press, 1990.

Barrett, David M. *Lyndon B. Johnson's Vietnam Papers: A Documentary Collection.* College Station, TX: Texas A & M University Press, 1997.

———. *Uncertain Warriors: Lyndon Johnson and His Vietnam Advisors.* Lawrence: University of Kansas Press, 1993.

Baughman, James L. "The Self-Publicist from Pedernales: Lyndon Johnson and the Press." *Diplomatic History* 12 (1988).

Bazelon, David T. "Big Business and the Democrats." *Commentary* 39 (May 1965).

Beard, Charles A. *President Roosevelt and the Coming of the War, 1941: A Study in Appearances and Realities.* 1948; reprinted, Hamden, CT: Shoe String Press,1968.

Beggs, Robert, ed. *The Cuban Missile Crisis.* London: Longman Group Ltd., 1971.

Bennett, Gill, ed. *End of the War in Europe, 1945.* London: HMSO, 1996.

Benson, Robert L., and Michael Warner, eds. *Venona: Soviet Espionage and American Response, 1939–1957.* Washington, D.C.: National Security Agency and Central Intelligence Agency, 1996.

Berkhofer, Robert F. *Beyond the Great Story: History as Text and Discourse.* Cambridge, MA: Harvard University Press, 1995.

Berman, Larry. "Coming to Grips with Lyndon Johnson's War." *Diplomatic History* 17 (Fall 1993).

———. *Planning a Tragedy.* New York: W. W. Norton, 1982.

Berman, William C. *William Fulbright and the Vietnam War: The Dissent of a Political Realist.* Kent, OH: Kent State University Press, 1988.

Bernstein, Barton J. "Commentary: Reconsidering Khrushchev's Gambit—Defending the Soviet Union and Cuba." *Diplomatic History* 14(2) (Spring 1990).

———. "Courage and Commitment: The Missiles of October." *Foreign Service Journal* (December 1975).

———. "The Cuban Missile Crisis." In Lynn H. Miller and Ronald W. Pruessen, eds. *Reflections on the Cold War: A Quarter-Century of American Foreign Policy.* Philadelphia: Temple University Press, 1974.

———. *Politics and Policies of the Truman Administration.* Chicago: Quadrangle Books, 1970.

———. "Reconsidering the Missile Crisis: Dealing with the Problems of the American Jupiters in Turkey." In James A. Nathan, ed. *The Cuban Missile Crisis Revisited.* New York: St. Martin's Press, 1992.

———. "Trading the Jupiters in Turkey." *Political Science Quarterly* 95 (1) (Spring 1980).

———. "Understanding Decisionmaking, U.S. Foreign Policy, and the Cuban Missile Crisis: A Review Essay." *International Security* 25 (1) (Summer 2000).

———, ed. *Towards a New Past: Dissenting Essays in American History.* New York: Pantheon Books, 1968.

———, and Allen J. Matusow, ed. *Twentieth-Century America: Recent Interpretations.* 2nd ed. New York: Harcourt Brace Jovanovich, 1972.

Beschloss, Michael R. *Mayday: Eisenhower, Khrushchev and the U-2 Affair.* New York: Harper & Row, 1986.

———. *Taking Charge: The Johnson White House Tapes, 1963–1964.* New York: Simon & Schuster, 1997.

———, ed. *Reaching for Glory: Lyndon Johnson's Secret White House Tapes, 1964–65.* New York: Simon & Schuster, 2001.

Bethel, Paul D. *The Losers; The Definitive Report, by an Eyewitness of the Communist Conquest of Cuba and the Soviet Penetration in Latin America.* New Rochelle, NY: Arlington House, 1969.

Bird, Kai. *The Chairman: John J. McCloy: The Making of the American Establishment.* New York: Simon & Schuster, 1992.

———. *The Color of Truth: McGeorge and William Bundy, Brothers in Arms: A Biography.* New York: Simon & Schuster, 1998.

Bishop, Jim. *FDR's Last Year.* New York: William Morrow, 1974.

Black, Conrad. *Roosevelt: Champion of Freedom.* New York: Public Affairs, 2003.

Blight, James G., and David A. Welch. *On the Brink: Americans and Soviets Reexamine the Cuban Missile Crisis.* 2d ed. New York: Noonday, 1990.

———. "Kramer vs. Kramer, Or, How Can You Have Revisionism in the Absence of Orthodoxy?" *Cold War International History Project Electronic Bulletin* (Fall 1993).

———, and Bruce J. Allyn. *Cuba on the Brink: Castro, the Missile Crisis, and the Soviet Collapse.* New York: Pantheon, 1993.

Blum, John M. *Years of Discord: American Politics and Society, 1961–1974.* New York: W. W. Norton, 1991.

Bohlen, Charles E. *Witness to History, 1929–1960.* New York: W. W. Norton, 1973.

Bok, Sissela. *Lying: Moral Choices in Public and Private Life.* New York: Vintage, 1978.

———. *Secrets: On the Ethics of Concealment and Revelation.* New York: Vintage, 1983.

Bornet, Vaughan Davis. *The Presidency of Lyndon B. Johnson.* Lawrence: University of Kansas Press, 1983.

Braden, Spruille. *Diplomats and Demagogues.* New Rochelle, NY: Arlington House, 1971.

Bradlee, Benjamin C. *Conversations with Kennedy.* New York: W. W. Norton, 1975.

Branch, Taylor. *Pillar of Fire: America in the King Years, 1963–65.* New York: Simon & Schuster, 1998.

Brands, H. W. *The Wages of Globalism: Lyndon Johnson and the Limits of American Power.* New York: Oxford University Press, 1995.

Brenner, Philip. "Thirteen Months: Cuba's Perspective on the Missile Crisis." In Nathan, ed. *The Cuban Missile Crisis Revisited.*

Brenner, Philip, and James G. Blight. "Cuba, 1962: The Crisis and Cuban-Soviet Relations: Fidel Castro's Secret 1968 Speech." *Cold War International History Project Bulletin* 5 (Spring 1995).

Broder, David. *Beyond the Front Page.* New York: Simon & Schuster, 1987.

Brugioni, Dino A. *Eyeball to Eyeball: The Inside Story of the Cuban Missile Crisis.* Rev. ed. New York: Random House, 1990, 1991.

Brzezinski, Zbigniew. "The Implications of Change for United States Foreign Policy." *Department of State Bulletin* 52 (July 1967).

Buhite, Russell D. *Decisions at Yalta: An Appraisal of Summit Diplomacy.* Wilmington, DE: Scholarly Resources, Inc., 1986.

———. "Patrick J. Hurley and the Yalta Far Eastern Agreement. *Pacific Historical Review* 37 (3) (1968).

Bundy, McGeorge. *Danger and Survival: Choices About the Bomb in the First Fifty Years.* New York: Random House, 1987.

———. "The Presidency and the Peace." *Foreign Affairs* 42 (April 1964).

Buzzanco, Robert. *Vietnam and the Transformation of American Life.* Malden, MA: Blackwell, 1999.

Byrnes, James F. *Speaking Frankly.* New York: Harper Brothers, 1947.

Cadogan Alexander. *The Diaries of Sir O. M., 1938–1945.* David Dilks, ed. New York: G. P. Putnam's Sons, 1972.

Caldwell, D. "A Research Note on the Quarantine of Cuba." *International Studies Quarterly* 22 (1978).

Califano, Joseph. *The Triumph and Tragedy of Lyndon Johnson: The White House Years.* New York: Simon & Schuster, 1991.

Campbell, Thomas M., and George C. Herring, eds. *Diaries of Edward R. Stettinius Jr., 1943–1946.* New York: New Viewpoints, 1975.

Cannon, Lou. *President Reagan: The Role of a Lifetime.* New York: Simon & Schuster, 1991.

———. *President Reagan: The Role of a Lifetime.* 2nd ed. New York Public Affairs, 2000.

Caro, Robert A. *The Path to Power: The Years of Lyndon Johnson.* New York: Alfred A. Knopf, 1982.

———. *The Years of Lyndon Johnson: Master of the Senate.* New York: Alfred A. Knopf, 2002.

Carpenter, Ted G. *The Captive Press: Foreign Policy Crises and the First Amendment.* Washington, D.C.: Cato Institute, 1995.

Chamberlin, William Henry. *America's Second Crusade.* Washington, D.C.: Regnery, 1950.

Chambers, Whittaker. *Witness.* New York: Random House, 1952.

Chang, Laurence. "The View from Washington and the Views from Nowhere: Cuban Missile Crisis Historiography and the Epistemology of Decision Making." In Nathan, ed. *The Cuban Missile Crisis Revisited.*

Charlton, Michael, and Anthony Moncrieff. *Many Reasons Why: The American Involvement in Vietnam.* New York: Hill and Wang, 1978.

Chuev, Felix, ed. *Molotov Remembers: Inside Kremlin Politics: Conversations with Felix Chuev* Chicago: I. R. Dee, 1993.

Churchill, Winston. *The Second World War.* Vol. 3: *The Grand Alliance*; Vol. 6: *Triumph and Tragedy*. London: Cassell, 1951, 1954.

Clemens, Diane S. "Averell Harriman, John Deane, the Joint Chiefs of Staff, and the 'Reversal of Co operation' with the Soviet Union in April 1945." *The International History Review* 14 (1992).

———. *Yalta.* New York: Oxford University Press, 1970.

Clifford, Clark, with Richard Holbrooke. *Counsel to the President.* New York: Random House, 1991.

Clifford, J. Garry. "Bureaucratic Politics." *Journal of American History* (June 1990).

———. "President Truman and Peter the Great's Will," *Diplomatic History* 4 (Fall 1980).

Cohen, Stephen D. *The Making of United States International Economic Policy: Principles, Problems, and Proposals for Reform.* New York: Praeger, 1977.

Colville, Sir John. *The Fringes of Power: Downing Street Diaries.* London: W. W. Norton, 1985.

Constant, Benjamin. *Political Writings.* Biancamaria Fontana and Raymone Guess, eds. New York: Cambridge University Press, 1988.

Cooke, Alistair. *A Generation on Trial: USA vs. Alger Hiss.* New York: Alfred A. Knopf, 1950.

Costigliola, Frank. "Kennedy, the European Allies and the Failure to Consult." *Political Science Quarterly* 110 (1) (1995).

Crane, Robert D. "The Cuban Crisis: A Strategic Analysis of American and Soviet Policy." *Orbis* (Winter 1963).

Crowley, James B. "A New Deal for Japan and Asia: One Road to Pearl Harbor." In *Modern East Asia: Essays in Interpretation,* Crowley, ed. New York: Harcourt, Brace, 1970.

Cumings, Bruce. *The Origins of the Korean War.* Vol. 1, *Liberation and the Emergence of Separate Regimes, 1945–1947.* Princeton, NJ: Princeton University Press, 1981.

———. *The Origins of the Korean War.* Vol. 2, *The Roaring of the Cataract, 1947–1950.* Princeton, NJ: Princeton University Press, 1991.

Daaldier, Ivo H., and Lindsey, James. M. *America Unbound: The Bush Revolution in Foreign Policy.* Washington, D.C.: Brookings Institution Press, 2003.

Dallek, Robert. *Flawed Giant: Lyndon Johnson and His Times, 1961–1963.* New York: Oxford University Press, 1998.

———. *Franklin D. Roosevelt and American Foreign Policy: 1932–1945.* New York: Oxford University Press, 1979.

Daniel, James, and John G. Hubbell. *Strike in the West: The Complete Story of the Cuban Crisis.* New York: Holt, Reinhart and Winston, 1963.

Daniels, Jonathan. *The Man of Independence.* Philadelphia: Lippincott, 1950.

Danner, Mark. *The Massacre at El Mozote.* New York: Vintage, 1994.

Davies, Norman, *Europe: A History.* New York: Oxford University Press, 1996.

de Toledano, Ralph. *Seeds of Treason: The Story of the Chambers-Hiss Tragedy.* New York: Funk and Wagnalls Co., 1950.

Deese, David A., ed. *The New Politics of American Foreign Policy.* New York: St. Martin's Press, 1994.

Defarrari, Roy J. ed., *The Fathers of the Church.* Washington, D.C.: Catholic University of America Press, 1952.

DePaulo, Bella M., Deborah A. Kashy, Susan E. Kirkendol, Melissa M. Wyer, and Jennifer A. Epstein. "Lying in Everyday Life." *Journal of Personality and Social Psychology* 70(5) (1998).

Derrida, Jacques. *Of Grammatology.* Gayatri Chakravoty Spivak, trans. Baltimore, MD: Johns Hopkins University Press, 1976.

DeSantis, Hugh. *Diplomacy of Silence: the American Foreign Service, the Soviet Union and the Cold War, 1933–1947.* Chicago: University of Chicago Press, 1980.

Destler, I. M. *Presidents, Bureaucrats, and Foreign Policy: The Politics of Organization Reform.* Princeton, NJ: Princeton University Press, 1974.

Dewart, Leslie. "The Cuban Crisis Revisited." *Studies on the Left* 5 (Spring 1965).

Dewey, John. *The Public and Its Problems.* New York: H. Holt and Co., 1927.

Dinnerstein, Herbert. *The Making of a Missile Crisis, October 1962.* Baltimore, MD: Johns Hopkins University Press, 1976.

Divine, Robert A. "Alive and Well: The Continuing Cuban Missile Crisis Controversy." *Diplomatic History* 18 (4) (1994).

———. *Foreign Policy and U.S. Presidential Elections, 1940–1948.* New York: New Viewpoints, 1974.

———. *Roosevelt and World War II.* Baltimore, MD: Johns Hopkins University Press, 1969.

Dobrynin, Anatoly. *In Confidence: Moscow's Ambassador to America's Six Cold War Presidents (1962–1986).* New York: Times Books, 1995.

Donovan, R. J. *Conflict and Crisis: The Presidency of Harry S. Truman, 1945–1949.* New York: W. W. Norton, 1977.

Draper, Theodore. "The American Crisis: Vietnam, Cuba and the Dominican Republic." *Commentary* (January 1967).

———. *A Very Thin Line: The Iran Contra Affairs.* New York: Hill and Wang, 1991.

Duffy, Bernard K. "James F. Byrnes' Yalta Rhetoric." *Journal of Political Science* 10(2) (1983).

Duiker, William J. *Ho Chi Minh: A Life.* New York: Hyperion, 2000.

Eagleton, Terry. *Literary Theory: An Introduction.* Cambridge, MA: Blackwell, 1996.

Eden, Anthony. *The Reckoning.* Boston: Houghton Mifflin, 1965.

Eisenberg, Carolyn. *Drawing the Line: The American Decision to Divide Germany, 1944–1949.* New York: Cambridge University Press, 1996.

Eisenhower, Dwight D. *Mandate for Change, 1953-1956: The White House Years.* Garden City, NY: Doubleday, 1963.

Ellsberg, Daniel. *Secrets: A Memoir of Vietnam and the Pentagon Papers.* New York: Viking, 2002.

———. "The Quagmire Myth and the Stalemate Machine." *Public Policy* (Spring 1971).

Entman, Robert N. *Democracy Without Citizens: Media and the Decay of American Politics.* New York: Oxford University Press, 1989.

Fairlie, Henry. *The Kennedy Promise: The Politics of Expectation.* Garden City, NY: Doubleday, 1973.

Farrell, John A. *Tip O'Neill and the Democratic Century.* New York: Little, Brown, 2001.

Feis, Herbert. *Between War and Peace: The Potsdam Conference.* Princeton, NJ: Princeton University Press, 1960.

———. *From Trust to Terror: The Onset of the Cold War, 1945–1950.* New York: W. W. Norton, 1970.

———. "War Came at Pearl Harbor: Suspicions Considered." *Yale Review* (1951).

———. *The War They Waged and the Peace They Sought.* Princeton, NJ: Princeton University Press, 1957.

Ferrell, Robert H. *The Dying President: Franklin D. Roosevelt, 1944–1945.* Columbia: University of Missouri Press, 1998.

Fishkin, James S. *Democracy and Deliberation: New Directions for Democratic Reform.* New Haven, CT: Yale University Press, 1991.

Fleming, Thomas. *The New Dealers' War: FDR and the War Within World War II.* New York: Basic Books, 2001.

Flemming, Denna Frank. *The Cold War and Its Origins, 1917–1960.* Garden City, NY: Doubleday, 1961.

Forrestal, James. *The Forrestal Diaries.* Walter Millis, ed. New York: Viking, 1951.

Foucault, Michel. *The Archeology of Knowledge.* A. M. Sheridan, trans. New York: Pantheon, 1972.

Franklin, Benjamin. *The Works of Benjamin Franklin.* Vol. 7. John Bigelow, ed. New York: G. P. Putnam's Sons, 1904.

Freedman, Lawrence. *Kennedy's Wars: Berlin, Cuba, Laos, and Vietnam.* New York. Oxford University Press, 2000.

Freeland, Richard M. *The Truman Doctrine and the Origins of McCarthyism: Foreign Policy, Domestic Politics, and Internal Security, 1946–48.* New York: Alfred A. Knopf, 1972.

Fried, Amy. *Muffled Voices: Oliver North and the Politics of Public Opinion.* New York: Columbia University Press, 1997.

Fromkin, David. *In the Time of the Americans.* New York: Alfred A. Knopf, 1995.

Fursenko, Alexandr and Timothy Naftali. *One Hell of a Gamble: Khrushchev, Castro and Kennedy, 1958–1964.* New York: W. W. Norton, 1997.

———. "The Pitsunda Decision: Khrushchev and Nuclear Weapons." *CWIHP Bulletin* 10 (March 1998).

———. "Using KGB Documents: The Scali-Feklisov Channel in the Cuban Missile Crisis." *CWIHP Bulletin* 10 (March 1998).

Gaddis, John Lewis. "The Emerging Post-Revisionist Synthesis on the Origins of the Cold War." *Diplomatic History* 7 (Summer 1983).

———. *The Long Peace: Inquiring into the History of the Cold War.* New York: Oxford University Press, 1987.

———. *The United States and the Origins of the Cold War, 1941–1947.* New York: Columbia University Press, 1972.

———. *We Now Know: Rethinking Cold War History.* New York: Oxford University Press, 1997.

Galston, William A. "Salvation Through Participation: John Dewey and the Religion of Democracy." *Raritan* 12 (1993).

Gardner, Lloyd C. "America's War in Vietnam: The End of Exceptionalism?" In D. Michael Shafer, ed. *The Legacy: The Vietnam War in the American Imagination*. Boston: Beacon Press, 1990.

———. *Architects of Illusion: Men and Ideas in American Foreign Policy, 1941–1949*. Chicago: Quadrangle Books, 1970.

———. *Pay Any Price: Lyndon Johnson and the Wars for Vietnam*. Chicago: Ivan R. Dee, 1995.

———. *Spheres of Influence: The Great Powers Partition Europe from Munich to Yalta*. Chicago: Ivan R. Dee, 1993.

Garthoff, Raymond L. "The Havana Conference on the Cuban Missile Crisis." *CWIHP Bulletin* 1 (Spring 1992).

———. "New Evidence on the Cuban Missile Crisis: Khrushchev, Nuclear Weapons, and the Cuban Missile Crisis." *CWIHP* 11 (Winter 1998).

———. "Russian Foreign Ministry Documents on the Cuban Missile Crisis." Introduction. *CWIHP Bulletin* 5 (Spring 1995).

———. *Reflections on the Cuban Missile Crisis.* Washington, D.C.: The Brookings Institution, 1987.

Gates, Robert M. *From the Shadows: The Ultimate Insider's Story of Five Presidents and How They Won the Cold War.* New York: Simon & Schuster, 1996.

Gelb, Leslie, with Richard K. Betts. *The Irony of Vietnam: The System Worked*. Washington, D.C.: The Brookings Institution, 1979.

Gelfand, Lawrence E. "Where Ideals Confront Self-Interest: Wilsonian Foreign Policy." *Diplomatic History* 18(1) (1994).

George, Alexander L. "The Cuban Missile Crisis, 1962." In Alexander L. George, David K. Hall, and William E. Simons, eds. *The Limits of Coercive Diplomacy: Laos, Cuba, Vietnam*. Boston: Little, Brown, 1971.

Gettleman, Mark E., Jane Franklin, Marylin B. Young, and H. Bruce Franklin, eds. *Vietnam and America : A Documented History.* New York: Grove Press, 1995.

Gibbons, William C. *The U.S. Government and the Vietnam War.* 4 vols. Princeton, NJ: Princeton University Press, 1986-1996.

Gilbert, Felix. *To the Farewell Address: Ideas of Early American Foreign Policy.* Princeton, NJ: Princeton University Press, 1961.

Gilbert, Martin. *Winston S. Churchill,* Vol. 7: *Road to Victory.* Boston: Houghton Mifflin, 1986.

Gitlin, Todd. *The Twilight of Common Dreams: Why America Is Wracked by Culture Wars.* New York: Metropolitan Books, 1995.

Goncharov, Sergei N., John W. Lewis, and Xue Litai. *Uncertain Partners: Stalin, Mao and the Korean War.* Stanford, CA: Stanford University Press, 1993.

Goodwin, Doris Kearns. *No Ordinary Time: Franklin and Eleanor Roosevelt: The Home Front in World War II*. New York: Simon & Schuster, 1994.

Goulden, Joseph C. *Truth Is the First Casualty: The Gulf of Tonkin Affair—Illusion and Reality.* New York: James B. Adler and Co., 1969.

Grabner, Norman A. "Cold War Origins and the Contemporary Debate: A Review of Recent Literature." *Journal of Conflict Resolution* 13 (March 1969).

Gray, Colin. *The Soviet-American Arms Race.* Farnborough: Saxon House; Lexington Books, 1976.

Grenier, Bernard. "The Cuban Missile Crisis Reconsidered: The Soviet View: An Interview with Sergo Mikoyan." *Diplomatic History* 14 (Spring 1990).

Grew, Joseph C. *Turbulent Era: A Record of Forty Years in the U.S. Diplomatic Service.* Vol. 2. Walter Johnson, ed. Nancy Harvison Hooker, asst. Boston: Houghton Mifflin, 1952.

Gribkov, Gen. Anatoly I., and Gen. William Y. Smith. *Operation ANADYR: U.S. and Soviet Generals Recount the Cuban Missile Crisis.* Chicago: Edition Q, 1994.

Griffin, Larry J. "Narrative, Event-Structure and Causal Interpretation in Historical Sociology." *American Journal of Sociology* 98 (1993).

———, and Charles C. Ragin. "Some Observations of Formal Methods of Qualitative Analysis." *Sociological Methods and Research* 23 (1994).

Gromyko, Andrei. *Memories.* Harold Shukman, trans. London: Hutchinson, 1989.

Grosse, Peter. *Operation Rollback: America's Secret War Behind the Iron Curtain.* Boston: Houghton Mifflin, 2000.

Haffa Robert P., Jr. "Allison's Models: An Analytic Approach to Bureaucratic Politics." In John E. Endicott and Roy W. Stafford Jr., eds. *American Defense Policy.* Baltimore, MD: Johns Hopkins University Press, 1977.

Hafner, Donald L. "Bureaucratic Politics and 'Those Frigging Missiles,' JFK, Cuba and the U.S. Missiles in Turkey." *Orbis* (Summer 1977).

Hagan, Roger, and Barton J. Bernstein. "The Military Value of Missiles in Cuba." *Bulletin of the Atomic Scientists* (February 1963).

Haig, Alexander M., Jr., with Charles McCarry. *Inner Circles: How America Changed the World: A Memoir.* New York: Warner Books, 1992.

Halberstam, David. *The Best and the Brightest.* New York: Random House, 1969.

———. *The Fifties.* New York: Villard, 1993.

Halle, Louis. *The Cold War as History.* New York: Chatto and Windus, 1967.

Hallin, Daniel. *The Uncensored War.* New York: Oxford University Press, 1986.

Halper, Thomas. *Foreign Policy Crisis: Appearance and Reality in Decision Making.* Columbus, OH: Charles E. Merrill, 1971.

Halperin, Morton H. "The Decision to Deploy the ABM: Bureaucratic and Domestic Politics in the Johnson Administration." In Richard Head and Evan Rokke, *American Defense Policy.* Baltimore: Johns Hopkins University Press, 1973.

———, and Arnold Kanter. "The Bureaucratic Perspective: A Preliminary Framework." In Halperin and Kanter, eds. *Readings in American Foreign Policy: A Bureaucratic Perspective.* Boston: Little Brown, 1973.

———, with the assistance of Priscilla Clapp and Arnold Kanter. *Bureaucratic Politics and Foreign Policy.* Washington, D.C.: The Brookings Institution, 1974.

Hamby, Alonzo L. *Man of the People: A Life of Harry S. Truman.* New York: Random House, 1995.

Hamilton, Alexander, John Jay, and James Madison. *The Federalist.* Jacob E. Cooke, ed. Middletown, CT: Wesleyan University Press, 1961.

Harbutt, Fraser. *The Iron Curtain: Churchill, America and the Origins of the Cold War.* New York: Oxford University Press, 1986.

Hardin, Garrett. "The Cybernetics of Competition." *Perspectives in Biology and Medicine* (Autumn 1963).

Harriman, Averell. *Peace with Russia?* New York: Simon & Schuster, 1959.

———, with Elie Abel, *Special Envoy to Churchill and Stalin, 1941–1946.* New York: Random House, 1975.

Harris, T. George. "A Policy Maker's View: Experience vs. Character." *Psychology Today* (March 1975).

Hatcher, Patrick Lloyd. *The Suicide of an Elite: American Internationalists and Vietnam.* Stanford, CA: Stanford University Press, 1990.

Herbig, Katherine L., and Martin F. Wiskoff. "Espionage Against the United States by American Citizens, 1947–2001." PERSEREC Technical Report 02–5. Monterey, CA: Defense Personnel Security Research Center, 2002.

Herman, Arthur. *Joseph McCarthy: Re-examining the Life and Legacy of America's Most Hated Senator.* New York: Free Press, 2000.

Herman, Jan Kenneth. "The President's Cardiologist." *Navy Medicine* 81(2) (March–April 1990).

Herring, George C. *LBJ and Vietnam: A Different Kind of War.* Austin: University of Texas Press, 1994.

Hersh, Seymour. *The Dark Side of Camelot.* New York: Little, Brown, 1997.

Hershberg, James G. "Anatomy of a Controversy: Anatoly F. Dobrynin's Meeting with Robert F. Kennedy, Saturday, 27 October 1962." *Cold War International History Project Bulletin* 5 (Spring 1995).

———. "Before 'The Missiles of October': Did Kennedy Plan a Military Strike Against Cuba?" In Nathan, ed. *The Cuban Missile Crisis Revisited.*

Herstgaard, Mark. *On Bended Knee: The Press and the Reagan Presidency.* New York: Farrar, Straus & Giroux, 1988.

Herz, Martin F. *Beginnings of the Cold War.* New York: McGraw-Hill, 1966.

Hilsman, Roger. *The Cuban Missile Crisis: The Struggle Over Policy.* Westport, CT: Praeger, 1996.

———. *To Move a Nation.* Garden City, NY: Doubleday, 1967.

Hirschman, Albert. *The Rhetoric of Reaction.* Cambridge: Harvard University Press, 1991.

Hirsh, Michael. *At War with Ourselves: Why America is Squandering Its Chance to Build a Better World.* New York: Oxford University Press, 2003.

Hiss, Alger. *In the Court of Public Opinion.* New York: Alfred A. Knopf, 1957.

———. "Yalta: Modern American Myth." *Pocket Book Magazine* 3 (September 1955).

Hiss, Tony. *The View from Alger's Window: A Son's Memoir.* New York: Alfred A. Knopf, 1999.

Hodgson, Godfrey. *America in Our Time.* New York: Random House, 1978.

Hogan, Michael J. *A Cross of Iron: Harry S. Truman and the Origins of the National Security States, 1945–1954.* New York: Cambridge University Press, 1998.

Holloway, David. *Stalin and the Bomb: The Soviet Union and Atomic Energy, 1939–1954.* New Haven, CT: Yale University Press, 1994.

Hoopes, Townsend, and Douglas Brinkley. *Driven Patriot: The Life and Times of James Forrestal.* New York: Vintage Books, 1993.

Horelick, Arnold J. "The Cuban Missile Crisis." *World Politics* 16 (April 1964).

Horowitz, David, ed. *Containment and Revolution.* London: Blond, 1967.

Howard, Michael. *War and the Liberal Conscience.* New Brunswick, NJ: Transaction Publishers, 1977.

Humphrey, Hubert H. *Education of a Public Man: My Life and Politics.* Garden City, NY: Doubleday, 1976.

Huston, James H. "Intellectual Foundations of Early American Diplomacy." *Diplomatic History* 1(1) (1977).

Inglis, Fred. *The Cruel Peace: Everyday Life in the Cold War.* New York: Basic Books, 1991.

Ingram, Kenneth. *History of the Cold War.* London: Darwen Finlayson. 1955.

Isaacson, Walter, and Evan Thomas. *The Wise Men: Six Friends and the World They Made.* New York: Simon and Schuster, 1986.

Isserman, Maurice, and Michael Kazin. *America Divided: The Civil Wars of the Sixties.* New York: Oxford University Press, 1999.

James, William. *Essays in Pragmatism.* Albury Castell, ed. and intro. New York: Hafner, 1948.

Jefferson, Thomas. *The Works of Thomas Jefferson.* Vol. 9. Paul L. Ford, ed. New York: G. P. Putnam's Sons, 1905.

Jervis, Robert. *System Effects: Complexity in Political and Social Life.* Princeton, NJ: Princeton University Press, 1998.

Jian, Chen. *Mao's China and the Cold War.* Chapel Hill: University of North Carolina Press, 2001.

Johns, Andrew L. "Opening Pandora's Box: The Genesis and Evolution of the 1964 Congressional Resolution on Vietnam." *Journal of American-East Asian Relations* 6 (Summer/Fall 1997).

Johnson, Chalmers. *Blowback: The Costs and Consequences of American Empire.* New York: Metropolitan Books, 2000.

Johnson, Robert David. *The Peace Progressives and American Foreign Relations* Cambridge, MA: Harvard University Press, 1995.

Kagan, Robert. *A Twilight Struggle: American Power and Nicaragua, 1997–1990.* New York: Free Press, 1996.

Kahan, Jerome H., and Anne K. Long, "The Cuban Missile Crisis: A Study of Its Strategic Context." *Political Science Quarterly* 87 (December 1972).

Kahin, George McT. *Intervention: How America Became Involved in Vietnam.* New York: Alfred A. Knopf, 1986.

Kaiser, David. *American Tragedy: Kennedy, Johnson and the Origins of the Vietnam War.* Cambridge, MA: Harvard University Press, 2000.

Kant, Immanuel. "On the Supposed Right to Lie from Altruistic Motives." In *The Critique of Practical Reason and Other Writings.* Lewis White Beck, ed. and trans. Chicago: University of Chicago Press, 1949.

Karl, Terry Lynn. *The Paradox of Plenty: Oil Booms and Petro-States.* Berkeley: University of California Press, 1991.

Karnow, Stanley. *Vietnam: A History.* New York: Viking, 1983.

———. *Vietnam: A History.* 2nd ed. New York: Penguin Books, 1997.

Kashy, Deborah A., and Bella M. DePaulo. "Who Lies." *Journal of Personality and Social Psychology* 70(5) (1998).

Kattenberg, Paul. *The Vietnam Trauma in American Foreign Policy.* New Brunswick, NJ: Transaction Books, 1980.

Kearns, Doris. *Lyndon Johnson and the American Dream.* New York: Harper & Row, 1976.

Kennan, George F. *Memoirs: 1925–1950.* Boston: Little, Brown, 1967.

———, and John Lukacs. *George F. Kennan and the Origins of Containment, 1944-1946: The Kennan-Lukacs Correspondence.* Columbia: University of Missouri Press, 1997.

Kennedy, David M. *Freedom from Fear: The American People in Depression and War, 1929–1945.* New York: Oxford University Press, 1999.

Kennedy, Robert F. *Thirteen Days: A Memoir of the Cuban Missile Crisis.* New York: New American Library, 1969.

Kessler, Lauren. *Clever Girl: Elizabeth Bentley's Life In and Out of Espionage.* New York: HarperCollins, 2003.

Khrushchev, Nikita. *Khrushchev Remembers: The Glasnost Tapes.* Jerrod L. Schecter, trans. and ed., with Vyacheslav Luchkov. Boston: Little, Brown, 1990.

———. *Khrushchev Remembers: The Last Testament.* Strobe Talbott, trans. and ed. Boston: Little, Brown, 1970.

Khrushchev, Sergei N. *Nikita Khrushchev and the Creation of a Superpower.* University Park, PA: Pennsylvania State Press, 2000.

Kimball, Jeffrey. *To Reason Why: The Debate About the Causes of U.S. Involvement.* Philadelphia: Temple University Press, 1990.

Kimball, Warren F. *Churchill and Roosevelt: The Complete Correspondence.* Vol. 3. Princeton, NJ: Princeton University Press, 1984.

———. *Forged in War: Roosevelt, Churchill and the Second World War.* New York: William Morrow, 1997.

———. *The Juggler: Franklin Roosevelt as Wartime Statesman.* Princeton, NJ: Princeton University Press, 1991.

Kissinger, Henry A. *Diplomacy.* New York: Simon & Schuster, 1994.

———. *Nuclear Weapons and Foreign Policy.* New York: W. W. Norton, 1969.

———. "Strains on the Alliance." *Foreign Affairs* 41(2) (January 1964).

Klehr, Harvey, and John Earl Haynes. *In Denial: Historians, Communism, and Espionage.* San Francisco: Encounter Books, 2003.

———. *Venona: Decoding Soviet Espionage in America.* New Haven, CT: Yale University Press, 1999.

Kloppenberg, James T. "Pragmatism: An Old Name for Some New Ways of Thinking?" *Journal of American History* 83 (June 1996).

Kofsky, Frank. *Harry Truman and the War Scare of 1948.* New York: St. Martin's Press, 1995.

Kolko, Gabriel. *Anatomy of a War: Vietnam, the United States, and the Modern Historical Experience.* New York: The New Press, 1994.

———. *The Politics of War: The World and United States Foreign Policy, 1943–1945.* New York: Random House, 1968.

———, and Joyce Kolko. *The Limits of Power: The World and United States Foreign Policy, 1945–1954.* New York: Harper & Row, 1972.

Kornbluh, Peter. "Kennedy and Castro: The Secret Quest for Accommodation." National Security Archive Electronic Briefing Book No. 17, 1999.

———, and Malcolm Byrne, eds. *The Iran-Contra Scandal: The Declassified History.* New York: The New Press, 1993.

Krakau, Knud. "American Foreign Relations: A National Style?" *Diplomatic History* 8 (3) (1984).

Kramer, Mark. "The 'Lessons' of the Cuban Missile Crisis for Warsaw Pact Nuclear Operations." *Cold War International History Project Bulletin* 5 (Spring 1995).

———. "Tactical Nuclear Weapons, Soviet Command Authority, and the Cuban Missile Crisis." *Cold War International History Project Electronic Bulletin* 3 (Fall 1993).

Krassner, Stephen D. "Are Bureaucracies Important (Or Allison Wonderland)." *Foreign Policy* 7 (Summer 1972).

Krock, Arthur. *Sixty Years on the Firing Line.* New York: Funk and Wagnalls, 1968.

Kuclick, Bruce. *American Policy and the Division of Germany: The Clash with Russia over Reparations.* Ithaca, NY: Cornell University Press, 1972.

———. "Reconsidering the Missile Crisis and Its Interpretation." *Diplomatic History* 25(1) Summer 2001.

Lacouture, Jean. *DeGaulle, The Ruler, 1945–1970.* Alan Sheridan, trans. New York: W. W. Norton, 1992.

LaFeber, Walter. *The American Age: United States Foreign Policy at Home and Abroad Since 1750.* New York: W. W. Norton, 1989.

———. *America, Russia, and the Cold War, 1945–1966.* New York: Wiley, 1967.

———. *America, Russia, and the Cold War, 1945–1990.* 7th ed. New York: McGraw-Hill, 1993.

———. *Inevitable Revolutions: The United States in Central America.* 2nd ed. New York: W. W. Norton, 1993.

———. "Jefferson and American Foreign Policy." In Peter S. Onuf, *Jeffersonian Legacies.* Charlottesville: University of Virginia Press, 1993.

———. "NATO and the Korean War." *Diplomatic History* 13(4) (Fall 1989).

———. *The New Empire: An Interpretation of American Expansion, 1860–1898.* Ithaca, NY: Cornell University Press, 1963.

———. *The Panama Canal: The Crisis in Historical Perspective.* New York: Oxford University Press, 1978.

Lane, Thomas. *The Leadership of President Kennedy.* Caldwell, ID: The Caxton Printers, 1964.

Langguth, A. J. *Our Vietnam: The War, 1954–1975.* New York: Simon & Schuster, 2000.

Larsh, William. "W. Averell Harriman and the Polish Question, December 1943–August 1945." *East European Politics and Societies* 7 (3) (1993).

Larson, Deborah Welch. *Origins of Containment: A Psychological Explanation*. Princeton, NJ: Princeton University Press, 1985.

Lazo, Mario. *Dagger in the Heart; American Policy Failures in Cuba*. New York: Funk and Wagnalls, 1968.

Leahy, William D. *I Was There: The Personal Story of the Chief of Staff to Presidents Roosevelt and Truman, Based on His Notes and Diaries Made at the Time*. New York: Whittlesey House, 1950.

Lebow, Richard Ned. "The Traditional and Revisionist Interpretation Reevaluated: Why Was Cuba a Crisis?" In Nathan, ed. *The Cuban Missile Crisis Revisited*.

———, and Janice Gross Stein. *We All Lost the Cold War*. Princeton, NJ: Princeton University Press, 1994.

Leffler, Melvin P. "Adherence to Agreements: Yalta and the Experiences of the Early Cold War." *International Security* 11 (1) (Summer 1986).

———. "The Cold War: What Do 'We Now Know'?" *American Historical Review* (April 1999).

———. *A Preponderance of Power: National Security, the Truman Administration and the Cold War*. Stanford, CA: Stanford University Press, 1992.

———, and David S. Painter, eds. *Origins of the Cold War: An International History*. London: Routledge, 1994.

Lens, Sidney. *The Military-Industrial Complex*. Kansas City, MO: Pilgrim Press, 1970.

LeoGrande, William M. *Our Own Backyard: The United States in Central America, 1977–1992*. Chapel Hill: University of North Carolina Press, 1998.

Lilla, Mark. *New French Thought: Political Philosophy*. Princeton, NJ: Princeton University Press, 1994.

———. *The Reckless Mind: Intellectuals in Politics*. New York: New York Review of Books, 2001.

Lippmann, Walter. *Essays in the Public Philosophy*. Boston: Atlantic, Little, Brown, 1955.

———. *Liberty and the News*. New York: Harcourt, Brace and Howe, 1920.

———. *The Phantom Public*. New York: Macmillan and Co., 1924.

———. *A Preface to Morals*. New York, Macmillan and Co., 1929.

———. *Public Opinion*. New York: Penguin Books, 1946.

Logevall, Fredrik. *Choosing War: The Lost Chance for Peace and the Escalation of War in Vietnam*. Berkeley, CA: University of California Press, 1999.

Lowenthal, John. "Venona and Alger Hiss." *Intelligence and Security* 15 (3) (Autumn 2000).

Lukas, Richard C. *The Strange Allies: The United States and Poland, 1941–45*. Knoxville: University of Tennessee Press, 1978.

Lundested, Geir. *The American Non-Policy Toward Eastern Europe*. New York: Humanities Press, 1975.

McCormick, Thomas J. *America's Half-Century*. Baltimore: Johns Hopkins University Press, 1989.

McCullough, David. *Truman*. New York: Simon & Schuster, 1992.

McIntire, Ross T. *White House Physician*. New York: 1946.

McMaster, H. R. *Dereliction of Duty: Lyndon Johnson, Robert McNamara, the Joint Chiefs of Staff and the Lies That Led to Vietnam*. New York: HarperCollins, 1997.

Macmillan, Harold. *At the End of the Day, 1961–1963*. New York: Harper & Row, 1973.

McNamara, Robert S. *Argument Without End: In Search of Answers to the Vietnam Tragedy*. New York: PublicAffairs, 1999.

———. *In Retrospect: The Tragedy and Lessons of Vietnam*. New York: Times Books, 1995.

MacNeil, Neil. *Dirksen: Portrait of a Public Man*. New York: World Publishing Company, 1970.

McNeill, J. R. *Something New Under the Sun: An Environmental History of the Twentieth-Century World*. New York: W. W. Norton, 2000.

Maddox, Robert. *The New Left and the Origins of the Cold War*. Princeton, NJ: Princeton University Press, 1973.

Mahoney, James. "Path Dependence in Historical Sociology." *Theory and Society* 29 (2000).

Maier, Charles S. "Revisionism and the Interpretation of Cold War Origins." *Perspectives in American History* 4 (1970).

Manchester, William. *The Glory and the Dream: A Narrative History of America, 1932–1972*. Boston: Little, Brown, 1974; reprint edition, New York: Bantam, 1975.

———. *One Brief Shining Moment: Remembering Kennedy*. Boston: Little, Brown, 1983.

Mann, Robert. *A Grand Delusion: America's Descent into Vietnam*. New York: Basic Books, 2001.

Mark, Eduard. "Revolution by Degrees: Stalin's National-Front Strategy for Europe, 1941–1947." Cold War International History Project, working paper no. 31, Woodrow Wilson Center.

———. "Who Was 'Venona's Ales'? Cryptanalysis and the Hiss Case." *Intelligence and National Security* 18 (3) (Autumn 2003).

Marolda, Edward, and Oscar Fitzgerald. *The United States Navy and the Vietnam Conflict,* Vol. 2: *From Military Assistance to Combat, 1959–1965*. Washington, D.C.: Naval Historical Center, 1986.

Martin, John Barlow. *Adlai Stevenson and the World*. Garden City, NY: Doubleday and Co., 1977.

———. *Adlai Stevenson and the World: The Life of Adlai Stevenson*. Garden City, NY: Doubleday, 1987.

Martin, Lisa L. *Positive Feedback in International Coalitions: Explanation and Measurement*. Cambridge, MA: Center for International Affairs, Harvard University, 1994.

Mastny, Vojtech. *Cold War and Soviet Insecurity: The Stalin Years*. New York: Oxford University Press, 1996.

May, Ernest, ed. *American Cold War Strategy: Interpreting NSC 68*. New York: St. Martin's Press, 1993.

———, and Philip Zelikow, eds. *The Kennedy Tapes: Inside the White House During the Cuban Missile Crisis*. Cambridge, MA: The Belknap Press of Harvard University Press, 1997.

Mayer, Jane, and Doyle McManus. *Landslide: The Unmaking of the President, 1984–1988*. Boston: Houghton Mifflin, 1988.

Meacham, Jon. *Franklin and Winston: An Intimate Portrait of an Epic Friendship*. New York: Random House, 2003.

Mee, Charles L., Jr. *Meeting at Potsdam*. New York: Evans, 1975.

Menand, Louis. *The Metaphysical Club: A Story of Ideas in America*. New York: Farrar, Straus & Giroux, 2001.

———, ed. *Pragamatism: A Reader*. New York: Vintage, 1997.

Merry, Robert W. *Taking on the World: Joseph and Stewart Alsop—Guardians of the American Century*. New York: W. W. Norton, 1996.

Merton, Robert. "The Unanticipated Consequences of Purposive Social Action." *American Sociological Review* 1 (December 1936).

Messer, Robert L. *The End of an Alliance: James F. Byrnes, Roosevelt, Truman, and the Origins of the Cold War*. Chapel Hill: University of North Carolina Press, 1980.

Mill, John Stuart. *Considerations on Representative Government*. South Bend, IN: Gateway Editions, 1962.

Miller, Perry. *Errand in the Wilderness*. Cambridge, MA: The Belknap Press of Harvard University Press, 1956.

Miroff, Bruce. *Pragmatic Illusions: The Presidential Politics of John F. Kennedy*. New York: David McKay, 1976.

Moeller, Susan D. "Media Coverage of Weapons of Mass Destruction, May 5–26, 1998; October 11–31, 2002; May 1–21, 2003." Center for International and Security Studies. College Park: University of Maryland, 2004.

Moïse, Edwin E. *Tonkin Gulf and the Escalation of the Vietnam War.* Chapel Hill: University of North Carolina Press, 1996.

Montaigne, Michel de. *Essays.* J. M. Cohen, trans. and intro. New York: Penguin Books, 1978.

Montefiore, Simon Sebag. *Stalin: The Court of the Red Tsar.* New York: Alfred A. Knopf, 2004

Moran, Lord Charles. *Churchill. Taken from the Diaries of Lord Moran.* Boston: Houghton Mifflin, 1966.

Morgenthau, Hans. *Truth and Power: Essays of a Decade, 1960–1970.* New York: Praeger, 1970.

Morolda, Edward, and Oscar Fitzgerald. *The United States Navy and the Vietnam Conflict,* Vol. 2: *From Military Assistance to Combat, 1959–1965.* Washington, D.C.: Naval Historical Center, 1986.

Morray, Joseph P. *From Yalta to Disarmament: Cold War Debate.* New York: Monthly Review Press, 1961.

Morris, Edmund. *Dutch: A Memoir of Ronald Reagan.* New York: Random House, 1999.

Morris, Roger. *Richard Milhous Nixon: The Rise of an American Politician.* New York: Henry Holt, 1990.

Mueller, John. *War, Presidents and Public Opinion.* New York: John Wiley & Sons, Inc., 1973.

Nacos, Brigitte. "Press, Presidents, and Crises." PhD diss., Columbia University, 1987.

Naimark, Norman M. *The Russians in Germany: A History of the Soviet Zone of Occupation, 1945–1949.* Cambridge, MA: Harvard University Press, 1995.

———. "The Soviets and the Christian Democrats: The Challenge of a Bourgeois Party in Eastern Germany, 1945–1949" *East European Politics and Societies* 9 (Fall 1995).

Nash, Philip. *The Other Missiles of October: Eisenhower, Kennedy and the Jupiters, 1957–1963.* Chapel Hill, NC: University of North Carolina Press, 1997.

Nathan, James A., ed. *The Cuban Missile Crisis Revisited.* New York: St. Martin's Press, 1992.

———. "The Heyday of the New Strategy." In Nathan, ed. *The Cuban Missile Crisis Revisited.*

———. "The Missile Crisis: His Finest Hour Now." *World Politics* 27 (January 1975).

Neustadt, Richard E. "Afterword: JFK (1968)," in *Presidential Power: The Politics of Leadership.* New York: John Wiley, 1960, 1968.

———, and Graham T. Allison. "Afterword" to Robert F. Kennedy, *Thirteen Days: A Memoir of the Cuban Missile Crisis.* New York: W. W. Norton, 1971.

———, and Ernest R. May. *Thinking in Time: The Uses of History for Decision-Makers.* New York: Free Press, 1986.

Newberger, Stuart H. "Secrets of October 1962: Opening Cuban Missile Crisis Files Under FOIA." *American Bar Association Journal* (October 1992).

Newhouse, *John.* Imperial America: The Bush Assault on the World Order. New York: Alfred A. Knopf, 2003.

Nietzsche Friedrich. "On Truth and Lie in an Extra Moral Sense." In Walter Kaufmann, ed., intro., trans. *The Portable Nietzsche.* New York: Penguin Books, 1954.

Ninkovich, Frank. "No Post-Mortems for Postmodernism, Please." *Diplomatic History* 22 (Summer 1998).

Nitze, Paul H. *From Hiroshima to Glastnost: At the Center of Decision: A Memoir.* New York: Grove Weidenfeld, 1989.

Nolting, Frederick. *From Trust to Tragedy.* New York: Praeger, 1988.

Nooteboom, Bart. "Path Dependence of Knowledge: Implications for the Theory of the Firm." In Lars Manusson and Jan Ottoson, eds. *Evolutionary Economics and Path Dependence.* Cheltenham: Edward Elgar, 1997.

North, Oliver. *Under Fire: An American Story.* New York: HarperCollins, 1991.

Novick, Peter. *That Noble Dream: The Objectivity Question and the American Historical Profession.* New York: Cambridge University Press, 1988.

O'Donnell, Kenneth, and David Powers, with Joe McCarthy. *"Johnny, We Hardly Knew Ye": Memories of John Fitzgerald Kennedy.* Boston: Little, Brown, 1972.

Offner, Arnold A. *Another Such Victory: President Truman and the Cold War, 1945–1953*. Stanford, CA: Stanford University Press, 2002.

Olmsted, Kathryn S. *Red Spy Queen: A Biography of Elizabeth Bentley*. Durham: University of North Carolina Press, 2002.

Orman, John M. *Presidential Secrecy and Deception*. Westport, CT: Greenwood Press, 1980.

O'Tuathill, G., and S. Dalby eds. *Rethinking Geopolitics*. New York: Routledge, 1999.

Pachter, Henry M. *Collision Course: The Cuban Missile Crisis and Coexistence*. New York: Frederick A. Praeger, 1963.

Page, Benjamin, and Robert I. Schapiro. *The Rational Public: Fifty Years of Trends in American Policy Preferences*. Chicago: University of Chicago Press, 1992.

Parry, Robert. "Lost History: Death, Lies, and Bodywashing: The USA's Secret War in El Salvador, 1981–1992." *http://www.consortiumnews.com/archive/lost.html*, originally posted on May 27, 1996.

Paterson, Thomas G. "Bearing the Burden: A Critical Look at JFK's Foreign Policy." *Virginia Quarterly Review* 54 (Spring 1978).

———. "Commentary: The Defense-of-Cuba Theme and the Missile Crisis." *Diplomatic History* 14(2) (Spring 1990).

———. "Fixation with Cuba: The Bay of Pigs, Missile Crisis, and Covert War Against Castro," in *Kennedy's Quest for Victory, American Foreign Policy, 1961–63*. New York: Oxford University Press, 1989.

———. "Historical Memory and Illusive Victories: Vietnam and Central America." *Diplomatic History* 12 (1) (1988).

———. "Presidential Foreign Policy: Public Opinion and Congress: The Truman Years," *Diplomatic History* 3 (1) (1979).

———, and William J. Brophy. "October Missiles and November Elections: The Cuban Crisis and American Politics, 1962." *Journal of American History* 73 (1) (June 1986).

Pechatnov, Vladimir O. "The Big Three After World War II: New Documents on Soviet Thinking About Post War Relations with the United States and Great Britain." Cold War International History Project, working paper no. 13, Woodrow Wilson Center for Scholars.

Pemberton, William E. *Harry S. Truman: Fair Dealer and Cold Warrior*. Boston: Little, Brown, 1989.

Perkins, Dexter. *The Diplomacy of a New Age: Major Issues in U.S. Policy Since 1945*. Bloomington: Indiana University Press, 1967.

Pessen, Edward. *Losing Our Souls: The American Experience in the Cold War*. Chicago: I. R. Dee, 1993.

Pierson, Paul. "Increasing Returns, Path Dependence, and the Study of Politics." *American Political Science Review* 94 (2) (June 2000).

Porter, Arabel J., and Andrew J. Dvosin, eds. *Essays on Literature and Politics, 1932–1972*. Boston: Houghton Mifflin, 1978.

Porter, Gareth. "Coercive Diplomacy in Vietnam: The Tonkin Crisis Reconsidered." In Jayne Werner and David Hunt, eds. *The American War in Vietnam*. Ithaca, NY: Cornell University of Southeast Asia Program #13, 1993.

Powers, Thomas. *The Man Who Kept the Secrets: Richard Helms and the CIA*. New York: Alfred A. Knopf, 1979.

———. *The War at Home: Vietnam and the American People, 1964–1968*. New York: Grossman, 1973.

Prados, John. *The Hidden History of the Vietnam War*. Chicago: University of Chicago Press, 1995.

Prestowitz, Clyde. *Rogue Nation: American Unilateralism and the Failure of Good Intentions*. New York: Basic Books, 2003.

Prague, Gordon. *Pearl Harbor: The Verdict of History*. New York: McGraw-Hill, 1986.

Putnam, Hillary. "A Reconsideration of Deweyan Democracy." In Hillary Putnam, ed. *Renewing Philosophy.* Cambridge, MA: Harvard University Press, 1992.

Raczynski, Edward. *In Allied London.* London: Weidenfeld and Nicolson, 1962.

Rapoport, Mario. "Argentina and the Soviet Union: History of Political and Commercial Relations (1917–1955)." *Hispanic American Historical Review* (1986).

Rearden, Steven L. *The Evolution of American Strategic Doctrine: Paul H. Nitze and the Soviet Challenge* Boulder: Westview Press, 1984.

Reeves, Richard. *President Kennedy.* New York: Simon & Schuster, 1993.

Remnick, David. *The Devil Problem & Other True Stories.* New York: Picador, 1997.

Resis, Albert. "The Churchill-Stalin Secret 'Percentages' Agreement on the Balkans, Moscow, October 1944." *The American Historical Review* 83 (2) (April 1978).

Reston, James. *Deadline: A Memoir.* New York: Random House, 1991.

Reynolds, D., ed. *The Origins of the Cold War in Europe: International Perspectives.* New Haven, CT: Yale University Press, 1994.

Roberts, Geoffrey. "Ideology, Calculation and Improvisation: Spheres of Influence and Soviet Foreign Policy, 1939–1945." *Review of International Studies* (October 1999).

———. "Stalin and the Cold War." *Europe-Asia Studies* (December 1997).

———. "Stalin and the Grand Alliance: Public Discourse, Private Dialogues and the Direction of Soviet Foreign Policy, 1941–1947." *Slovo* 13 (2001).

Romerstein, Herbert, and Eric Breindel. *The Venona Secrets: Exposing Soviet Espionage and America's Traitors.* Washington, D.C.: Regnery, 2000.

Rorty, Richard. *Achieving Our Country: Leftist Thought in Twentieth-Century America.* Cambridge, MA: Harvard University Press, 1998.

———. *Philosophy and the Mirror of Nature.* Princeton, NJ: Princeton University Press, 1979.

———. *Philosophy and Social Hope.* New York: Penguin Books, 1999.

Rosati, Jerel A. "Developing a Systematic Decision-Making Framework: Bureaucratic Politics in Perspective." *World Politics* 33 (January, 1981).

Rose, Lisle. *After Yalta: America and the Origins of the Cold War.* New York: Charles Scribner's Sons, 1973.

Rosenman, Samuel I. *Working with Roosevelt.* New York: Harper and Co., 1952.

Rourke, Francis. *Bureaucracy, Politics, and Foreign Policy.* Boston: Little, Brown, 1969.

Rusk, Dean as told to Richard Rusk. *As I Saw It.* New York: W. W. Norton, 1990.

Ryan, Alan. *John Dewey and the High Tide of American Liberalism.* New York: W. W. Norton, 1995.

Salinger, Pierre. *With Kennedy.* Garden City, NY: Doubleday, 1966.

Schaller, Michael. *The United States and China in the Twentieth Century.* 2nd ed. New York: Oxford University Press, 1990.

Scheer, Robert. *Thinking Tuna Fish, Talking Death: Essays on the Pornography of Power.* New York: Hill and Wang, 1988

Schlesinger Arthur M., Jr. *The Crisis of Confidence.* Boston: Houghton Mifflin,1969.

———. *The Cycles of American History.* Boston: Houghton Mifflin, 1986.

———. "Foreign Policy and the American Character." The Cyril Foster Lecture. Oxford, England: Oxford University Press, 1983.

———. *Robert Kennedy and His Times.* Boston: Houghton Mifflin, 1978.

———. *A Thousand Days: John F. Kennedy in the White House.* Boston: Houghton Mifflin, 1965.

———. *The Vital Center.* Boston: Houghton Mifflin, 1949.

Schmidt, Gary J., and Abram M. Shulsky. "Leo Strauss and the World of Intelligence (By Which We Do Not Mean *Nous*)." In *Leo Strauss, the Sraussians and the American Regime,* Kenneth L. Deutsch and John Murley, eds. New York: Rowan and Littlefield, 1999.

Schoenbaum, Thomas J. *Waging Peace and War: Dean Rusk in the Truman, Kennedy and Johnson Years.* New York: Simon & Schuster, 1988.

Schrecker, Ellen. *Many Are the Crimes: McCarthyism in America.* Boston: Little, Brown, 1998.

Schultz, Richard H., Jr. *The Secret War Against Hanoi: Kennedy's and Johnson's Use of Spies, Saboteurs and Covert Warriors in North Vietnam.* New York: HarperCollins, 1999.

Schulzinger, Robert D. *A Time for War: The United States and Vietnam, 1941–1975.* New York: Oxford University Press, 1997.

Schwarz, Benjamin C. *American Counterinsurgency Doctrine and El Salvador: The Frustrations of Reform and the Illusions of Nation Building.* Santa Monica, CA: The Rand Corporation, 1991.

Shafer, D. Michael, ed. *The Legacy: The Vietnam War in the American Imagination.* Boston: Beacon Press, 1990.

Shaffer, Samuel. *On and Off the Floor: Thirty Years as a Correspondent on Capitol Hill.* New York: Newsweek Books, 1980.

Shapley, Deborah. *Promise and Power: The Life and Times of Robert McNamara.* Boston: Little, Brown, 1993.

Sharp, U. S. Grant. *Strategy for Defeat: Vietnam in Retrospect.* San Raphael, CA: Presidio Press, 1978.

Sheng, Michael. *Battling Western Imperialism.* Princeton, NJ: Princeton University Press, 1997.

Sherwin, Martin J. *A World Destroyed: The Atomic Bomb and the Grand Alliance.* New York: Vintage Books, 1973, 1975, 1977.

Sherwood, Robert E. *Roosevelt and Hopkins: An Intimate History.* New York: Harper Brothers, 1948.

Sheshol, Jeff. *Mutual Contempt: Lyndon Johnson, Robert Kennedy, and the Feud That Defined a Decade.* New York: W. W. Norton, 1997.

Sidey, Hugh. *John F. Kennedy, President.* New York: Atheneum, 1964.

———. *A Very Personal Presidency.* New York: Atheneum, 1968.

Silk, Leonard, and Mark Silk. *The American Establishment.* New York: Basic Books, 1980.

Siracusa, Joseph M., ed. "The Meaning of TOLSTOY: Churchill, Stalin and the Balkans, Moscow, October 1944." *Diplomatic History* 3 (Fall 1979).

Small, Melvin. "How We Learned to Love the Russians: American Media and the Soviet Union During World War II." *The Historian* 36 (3) (1974).

Smith, Bradley F., and Elena Agarossi. *Operation Sunrise: The Secret Surrender.* New York: Basic Books, 1979.

Smith, Christian. *Resisting Reagan: The U.S. Central America Peace Movement.* Chicago: University of Chicago Press, 1996.

Smith, Gaddis. *The Last Years of the Monroe Doctrine.* New York: Hill and Wang, 1994.

Smith, Malcolm E., Jr. *Kennedy's Thirteen Greatest Mistakes in the White House.* New York: The National Forum of America, 1968.

Smith, Sally Bedell. *Grace and Power: The Private World of the Kennedy White House.* New York: Random House, 2004.

Smith, Steve. "Allison and the Cuban Missile Crisis: A Review of the Bureaucratic Politics Model of Foreign Policy Decision-Making." *Millennium: Journal of International Studies* 9 (1).

Smith, Tony. *America's Mission: The United States and the Worldwide Struggle for Democracy in the Twentieth Century.* Princeton, NJ: Princeton University Press, 1994.

———. *The French Stake in Algeria, 1945–1962.* Ithaca, NY: Cornell University Press, 1978.

Snell, John, Forrest C. Pogue, Charles F. Delzell, and George A. Lensen. *The Meaning of Yalta.* Baton Rouge, LA: Louisiana State University, 1956.

Snow, Edgar. *Journey to the Beginning.* London: Random House, 1959.

Snyder, Jack. *Myths of Empire: Domestic Politics and International Ambition.* Ithaca, NY: Cornell University Press, 1991.

Sorensen, Theodore C. *Kennedy.* New York: Harper & Row, 1965.

———. *The Kennedy Legacy.* New York, Macmillan and Co., 1969.

Stacks, John F. *Scotty: James B. Reston and the Rise and Fall of American Journalism*. New York: Little, Brown, 2003.

Steel, Ronald. *Walter Lippmann and the American Century.* Boston: Little, Brown, 1980.

———. *Imperialists and Other Heroes: A Chronicle of the American Empire.* New York: Random House, 1971.

———. *Pax Americana*. New York: Viking Press, 1967.

Steele, Richard W. "The Great Debate: Roosevelt, the Media, and the Coming of the War, 1940–1941." *Journal of American History* 71 (1) (1984).

Steinberg, Blema S. *Shame and Humiliation: Presidential Decision Making on Vietnam*. Pittsburgh: University of Pittsburgh Press, 1996.

Stern, Sheldon M. *Averting "The Final Failure": John F. Kennedy and the Secret Cuban Missile Crisis Meetings.* Stanford, CA: Stanford University Press, 2003.

———. "The 1997 Published Transcripts of the JFK Cuban Missile Crisis Tapes: Too Good to Be True?" *Presidential Studies Quarterly* 30 (September 2000).

———. "What JFK Really Said." *Atlantic Monthly* 285 (5) (May 2000).

Stettinius, Edward R., Jr. *Roosevelt and the Russians: The Yalta Conference.* Garden City, NY: Doubleday and Co., 1949.

Stimson, Henry L., and McGeorge Bundy. *On Active Service in Peace and War.* New York: Harper, 1948.

Stockdale, Jim, and Sybil Stockdale. *In Love & War: The Story of a Family's Ordeal and Sacrifice During the Vietnam Years.* New York. Harper & Row, 1984.

Stone, I. F. "What Price Prestige?" In Robert A. Divine, ed. *Cuban Missile Crisis.* 2nd. ed. New York: Marcus Weisner Publishing, 1988.

Strauss, Leo. *An Introduction to Political Philosophy.* Hilail Gildin, ed. Detroit: Wayne State University Press, 1990

Sullivan, Evelin. *The Concise Book of Lying.* New York: Farrar, Straus & Giroux, 2001.

Sulzberger, C. L. *The Last of the Giants.* New York: Macmillan and Co., 1970.

———. *A Long Row of Candles: Memoirs and Diaries, 1939–1954*. New York: Macmillan and Co., 1969.

———. *Such a Peace: The Roots and Ashes of Yalta*. New York: Continuum, 1982.

Taft, Robert A. *A Foreign Policy for Americans.* Garden City, NY: Doubleday and Co., 1951.

Tanenbaum, Duane A. "The Bricker Amendment Controversy: Its Origins and Eisenhower's Role." *Diplomatic History* 9 (1) (1985).

Tanenhaus, Sam. *Whittaker Chambers: A Biography.* New York: Random House, 1996.

Tansill, Charles. *Back Door to War: The Roosevelt Foreign Policy, 1933–1941*. Chicago: Regnery, 1952.

Taubman, William. *Khruschchev: The Man and His Era*. New York: W. W. Norton, 2002.

———. *Stalin's American Policy: From Entente to Détente to Cold War.* New York: W. W. Norton, 1982.

Thelen, Kathleen. "Historical Institutionalism in Comparative Politics." *Annual Reviews in Political Science* (1999). *http://annualreviews.iorg/cgi/content/full/2/1/369*.

Theoharis, Athan, ed. *Beyond the Hiss Case: The FBI, Congress and the Cold War.* Philadelphia: Temple University, 1982.

———. *The Yalta Myths: An Issue in U.S. Politics, 1945–1955*. New York: Oxford University Press, 1970.

Thomas, Evan. *Robert Kennedy: His Life.* New York: Simon & Schuster, 2000.

Thomas, Hugh. *Armed Truce: The Beginnings of the Cold War, 1945–46*. New York: Atheneum, 1987.

Thompson, John A. "The Exaggeration of American Vulnerability: The Anatomy of a Tradition." *Diplomatic History* 16 (1) (1992).

Thompson, Robert Smith. *The Missiles of October: The Declassified Story of John F. Kennedy and the Cuban Missile Crisis.* New York: Simon & Schuster, 1992.

Thomson, James C. "On the Making of U.S. China Policy, 1961–1969." *China Quarterly* 50 (April–June 1973).

Timburg, Robert. *The Nightingale's Song.* New York: Simon & Schuster, 1995.

Todd, Frederick J., Kenneth R. Hammond, and Marilyn M. Wilkins. "Differential Effects of Ambiguous and Exact Feedback on Two-Person Conflict and Compromise." *Journal of Conflict Resolution* 10 (1) (March 1966).

Toobin, Jeffrey. *A Vast Conspiracy.* New York: Random House, 2000.

Trachtenburg, Marc. *A Constructed Peace: The Making of the European Settlement, 1945–1963.* Princeton, NJ: Princeton University Press, 1999.

Truman, Harry S. *Memoirs of Harry S. Truman: Year of Decisions.* Vol. I. Garden City, NY: Doubleday and Co., 1955.

———. *Memoirs: 1946, Year of Trial and Hope.* New York: Signet, 1956.

———. *Off the Record: The Private Papers of Harry S. Truman.* Robert H. Ferrell, ed. New York: Harper & Row, 1980.

Tucker, Robert W. *The Radical Left and American Foreign Policy.* Baltimore, MD: Johns Hopkins University Press, 1971.

Turner, Kathleen J. *Lyndon Johnson's Dual War: Vietnam and the Press.* Chicago: University of Chicago Press, 1985.

Ubriaco Jr., Robert D. "Bread and Butter Politics or Foreign Policy Concerns: Class Versus Ethnicity in the Midwestern Polish Community During the 1946 Congressional Elections," *Polish American Studies* 51 (2) (1994).

Ulam, Adam B. *Expansion and Co-Existence: The History of Soviet Foreign Policy.* New York: Praeger, 1968.

———. *The Rivals.* New York: Viking Press, 1971.

VanDeMark, Brian. *Into the Quagmire: Lyndon Johnson and the Escalation of the Vietnam War.* New York: Oxford University Press, 1991.

Vandenberg, Arthur H. "The Need for Honest Candor: Clarification of Our Foreign Policy." *Vital Speeches of the Day,* February 1, 1945.

Vandiver, Frank E. *Shadows of Vietnam: Lyndon Johnson's Wars.* College Station, TX: Texas A&M University Press, 1977.

Vannucci, Albert P. "The Influence of Latin American Governments on the Shaping of United States Foreign Policy: The Case of U.S.-Argentina Relations, 1943–1948." *Journal of Latin American Studies* (November 1986).

Volkogonov, Dimitri. *Stalin: Triumph and Tragedy.* Harold Timken, ed. and trans. New York: Grove Weidenfeld, 1991.

Walker, Martin. *The Cold War: A History.* New York: Henry Holt, 1994.

Walsh, Lawrence E. *Firewall: The Iran-Contra Conspiracy and Cover-Up.* New York: W. W. Norton, 1997.

Walton, Richard J. *Cold War and Counterrevolution: The Foreign Policy of John F. Kennedy.* New York: Viking Press, 1972.

Ward, Geoffrey. *A First Class Temperament.* New York: Book-of-the-Month Club, 1989.

Weathersby, Kathryn. "New Russian Documents on the Korean War." *Cold War International History Project Bulletin* 6–7 (Winter 1995–1996).

———. "Soviet Aims in Korea and the Origins of the Korean War, 1945–50: New Evidence from the Russian Archives." Cold War International History Project, Working Paper No. 8, Woodrow Wilson Center, November 1993.

———. "To Attack or Not to Attack." *Cold War International History Project Bulletin* 5 (Spring 1995)

Weeks, William Earl. *John Quincy Adams and American Global Empire.* Lexington: University Press of Kentucky, 1992.

Weinstein, Allen. *Perjury: The Hiss-Chambers Case.* 2nd ed. New York: Random House, 1997.

———, and Alexander Vassiliev. *The Haunted Wood: Soviet Espionage in America—The Stalin Era.* New York: Random House, 1999.

Weintal, Edward and Charles Bartlett. *Facing the Brink: An Intimate Study of Crisis Diplomacy.* New York: Charles Scribner's Sons, 1967.

Welch, David A. "The Organizational Process and Bureaucratic Politics Paradigms: Retrospect and Prospect." *International Security* 17 (2) (Fall 1992).

Wells, Tom. *The War Within: America's Battles Over Vietnam.* Berkeley: University of California, 1994.

West, Nigel. *Venona: The Greatest Secret of the Cold War.* London: HarperCollins, 1999.

Westad, O. A., ed. *Cold War Problems.* New York: Cambridge Universtiy Press, 1999.

Westbrook, Robert B. *John Dewey and American Democracy.* Ithaca, NY: Cornell University Press, 1991.

White, Donald E. *The American Century: The Rise and Decline of the United States as a World Power.* New Haven, CT: Yale University Press, 1996.

White, G. Edward. *Alger Hiss's Looking-Glass Wars: The Covert Life of a Soviet Spy.* New York: Oxford University Press, 2004.

White, Mark J. *The Cuban Missile Crisis.* London: Macmillan and Co., 1996.

———. *Missiles in Cuba: Kennedy, Khrushchev, Castro and the 1962 Crisis.* Chicago: Ivan R. Dee, 1997.

White, Theodore H. *The Making of the President, 1968.* New York: Atheneum, 1969.

Whitfield, Stephen J. *The Culture of the Cold War.* Baltimore, MD: Johns Hopkins University Press, 1991.

Wholstetter, Roberta. *Pearl Harbor: Warning and Decision.* Stanford, CA: Stanford University Press, 1962.

Wicker, Tom. *JFK and LBJ: The Influence of Personality upon Politics.* New York: Penguin, 1968.

Williams, William Appleman. "The Age of Mercantilism, 1740–1828." In Henry W. Berger, ed. *William Appleman Williams Reader.* Chicago: Ivan R. Dee, 1992.

———. *America Confronts a Revolutionary World, 1776–1976.* New York: Morrow, 1976.

———. *American-Russian Relations, 1781–1947.* New York: Octagon Books, 1952.

———. *The Tragedy of American Diplomacy.* New York: Dell Publishing Company, 1959, 1972.

———, Thomas McCormick, Lloyd Gardner, and Walter LaFeber, eds. *America in Vietnam: A Documentary History.* New York: Anchor, 1985.

Wills, Garry. *The Kennedy Imprisonment.* Boston: Little, Brown, 1980.

Wilson, Joseph. *The Politics of Truth: Inside the Lies That Led to War and Betrayed My Wife's CIA Identity.* New York: Carroll and Graff, 2004.

Wilson, Robert A., ed. *Power and the Presidency.* New York: PublicAffairs, 1999.

Wilson, Woodrow. *The Public Papers of Woodrow Wilson.* Vol. 63. Arthur S. Link et al., eds. Princeton, NJ: Princeton University Press, 1966.

Wise, David. *The Politics of Lying: Government Deception, Secrecy and Power.* New York: Vintage, 1973.

———, with Elie Abel. *Special Envoy to Churchill and Stalin and Churchill, 1941–1946.* New York: Random House, 1975.

Wise, David and Thomas B. Ross. *The U-2 Affair.* New York: Random House, 1962.

Wittgenstein, Ludwig. *Philosophical Investigations.* 2nd ed. G. E. M. Anscombe, trans. Oxford, England: Basil Blackwell, 1958.

Wofford, Harris. *Of Kennedys and Kings.* New York: Farrar, Straus & Giroux, 1980.

Wohlforth, William C. "New Evidence on Moscow's Cold War." *Diplomatic History* 211 (Spring 1997).

Woods, Randall B. "Conflict or Community The United States and Argentina's Admission to the United Nations." *Pacific Historical Review* (August 1977).

———. *Fulbright: A Biography.* New York: Cambridge University Press, 1995.

Woodward, E. L. *British Foreign Policy in the Second World War.* London: H. M. O. Stationary Office, 1970–76.

Woodward, Robert. *Shadow: Five Presidents and the Legacy of Watergate.* New York: Simon & Schuster, 1999.

Yergin, Daniel. *Shattered Peace: The Origins of the Cold War and the National Security State.* Boston: Houghton Mifflin, 1977.

Young, Marilyn B. *The Vietnam Wars: 1945–1990.* New York: HarperCollins, 1991.

Zagorin, Perez. "History, the Referent, and Narrative: Reflections on Postmodernism Now." *History & Theory* 38 (February 1999).

Zelikow, Philip, Timothy Naftali, and Ernest May, eds. *The Presidential Recordings: John F. Kennedy: Volumes 1–3, The Great Crises.* Vol. 3. New York: W. W. Norton, 2001.

Zubok, Vladislav M. "'Dismayed by the Actions of the Soviet Union': Mikoyan's Talks with Fidel Castro and the Cuban Leadership, November 1962." *Cold War International History Project Bulletin* 5 (Spring 1995).

———, and Constantine Pleshakov. *Inside the Kremlin's Cold War: From Stalin to Khrushchev.* Cambridge, MA: Harvard University Press, 1996.

Websites and TV Broadcasts

CNN's *The Cold War,* Episode 9, "The Wall," November 22, 1998.

CNN's *The Cold War,* Episode 10, "Cuba," November 29, 1998.

CNN's "Reliable Sources," July 20, 2003, transcript, *http://www.cnn.com/TRANSCRIPTS/0307/20/rs.00.html.*

http://www.ellsberg.net

H-Diplo Web Discussion Postings, February 1, 1999, *http://www.h-net.org/~diplo/.*

Robert McFarlane on *The Charlie Rose Show,* WNET, November 1, 1994.

McNeil-Lehrer Newshour, April 17, 1995.

NBC *White Paper,* "Cuba: The Missile Crisis," February 9, 1964.

PBS-sponsored online discussion devoted to the film *Thirteen Days, http://www.newshour.com,* February 22, 2001.

INDEX